Aggression

ITS CAUSES, CONSEQUENCES,
AND CONTROL

McGraw-Hill Series in Social Psychology

CONSULTING EDITOR, Philip G. Zimbardo

Aggression

ITS CAUSES, CONSEQUENCES, AND CONTROL

❖

Leonard Berkowitz
University of Wisconsin–Madison

McGraw-Hill, Inc.

New York   St. Louis   San Francisco   Auckland   Bogotá   Caracas
Lisbon   London   Madrid   Mexico   Milan   Montreal   New Delhi   Paris
San Juan   Singapore   Sydney   Tokyo   Toronto

AGGRESSION
Its Causes, Consequences, and Control

2 3 4 5 6 7 8 9 0   DOC   DOC   9 0 9 8 7 6 5 4 3

ISBN 0-07-004874-6

This book was set in Palatino by The Clarinda Company.
The editors were Christopher Rogers and Fred H. Burns;
the production supervisor was Leroy A. Young.
The cover was designed by Carla Bauer.
R. R. Donnelley & Sons Company was printer and binder.

Cover painting: Otto Dix:"Self-portrait as Mars"
Courtesy of Haus der Meimat, Freital.

Library of Congress Cataloging-in-Publication Data

Berkowitz, Leonard, (date).
    Aggression: its causes, consequences, and control / Leonard
Berkowitz.
        p.   cm. — (McGraw-Hill series in social psychology)
    Includes bibliographical references and index.
    ISBN 0-07-004874-6
    1. Aggressiveness (Psychology)   2. Violence.   I. Title.
II. Series.
BF575.A3B43   1993
155.2'32—dc20   92-33589

Permissions Acknowledgments

The passages cited from Kadushin & Martin (1981) are from Kadushin, A. & Martin, J. (1981), *Child Abuse: An Interactional Event.* Columbia University Press, New York. Reprinted by permission from the publisher.

The passage from Bach & Goldberg (1974) is from Bach, G. & Goldberg, H. (1974), *Creative Aggression.* Doubleday, New York. Reprinted by permission.

The passages from the *New York Times* issues of July 18, 1990, Nov. 2, 1990, and Dec. 13, 1990 are copyrighted 1990 by the New York Times Co. and reprinted by permission.

About the Author

❖

Leonard Berkowitz, Vilas Research Professor in Psychology at the University of Wisconsin–Madison, grew up in New York City and attended New York schools. After service in the U.S. Air Force, he received his Ph.D. from the University of Michigan in 1951 and has been on the faculty of the University of Wisconsin—Madison since 1955, although he has also held visiting appointments at Stanford University, the Center for Advanced Study in the Behavioral Sciences, Oxford, Cornell, and Cambridge Universities, and the University of Western Australia, as well as at the University of Mannheim. Professor Berkowitz was one of the pioneers in the experimental study of altruism and helping but, since 1957, has been engaged mostly in studying situational influences on aggressive behavior, using both laboratory experiments and field interviews with violent offenders in the United States and Britain.

The author of about 170 articles and books, mostly concerned with aggression, he was also the editor of the well-known social psychology series *Advances in Experimental Social Psychology* from its inception in 1964 to his retirement from this post in 1989. He has also written a number of textbooks on social psychology, has been on the editorial boards of several social psychological journals, and has served as the chair of the Publication Board of the American Psychological Association. Berkowitz has been president of the American Psychological Association's Division of Personality and Social Psychology and the International Society for Research on Aggression, and was given distinguished scientist awards by the American Psychological Association and the Society for Experimental Social Psychology.

Most relevant for the present text, his scientific career received an early boost from the publication of *Aggression: A Social Psychological Analysis* by McGraw-Hill in 1962, and it is appropriate that McGraw-Hill is also publishing this volume on aggression as his career nears its close.

This book is dedicated to all of the behavioral scientists who have sought, with considerable intelligence, insight, and scientific rigor, to understand what causes aggression and how this destructive behavior might best be controlled, and who have persisted in their research even though so many people in society at large remain unaware of what they have found.

Contents

— ❖ —

ix

Foreword

❖

To discover where the *action* is in psychology, look to social psychology. In recent years, the field of social psychology has emerged as central in psychology's quest to understand human thought, feeling, and behavior. Thus, we see the inclusion-by-hyphenation of social psychology across diverse fields of psychology, such as social-cognitive, social-developmental, social-learning, social-personality, to name but a few recent amalgamations.

Social psychologists have tackled many of society's most intractable problems. In their role as the last generalists in psychology, nothing of individual and societal concern is alien to social psychological investigators—from psychophysiology to peace psychology, from students' attributions for failure to preventive education for AIDS. The new political and economic upheavals taking place throughout Europe and Asia, with the collapse of Soviet-style communism, are spurring social psychologists to develop new ways of introducing democracy and freedom of choice into the social lives of peoples long dominated by authoritarian rule. Indeed, since the days when George Miller, former president of the American Psychological Association, called upon psychologists to "give psychology back to the people," social psychologists have been at the forefront.

The *McGraw-Hill Series in Social Psychology* is a celebration of the contributions made by some of the most distinguished researchers, theorists, and practitioners of our craft. Each author in our series shares the vision of combining rigorous scholarship with the educator's goal of communicating that information to the widest possible audience of teachers, researchers, students and interested laypersons. The series is designed to cover the entire range of social psychology, with titles reflecting both broad and more narrowly focused areas of specialization. Instructors may use any of these books as supplements to a basic text, or use a combination of them to delve into selected topics in greater depth.

Leonard Berkowitz is recognized internationally as a leading contributor to the empirical investigation of the psychology of aggression. His pioneering laboratory studies stand as models of the systematic analysis of situational factors that stimulate aggressive behavior. Now in his most far-ranging contribution, *Aggression: Its Causes, Consequences, and Control,* Berkowitz gives us a scholarly tour de force in which he integrates laboratory, field, and survey research findings into an elegant synthesis of the state of the art on this vital topic. His carefully worded conclusions distinguish the valid from the common-sense, but false, views of aggression. He critically evaluates the host of theories about the whys of aggression, highlighting the values and limitations of each. But this book goes beyond being the soon-to-be-classic resource on human aggression; it offers impressive new insights and the author's own perceptive interpretations on many aspects of the complex processes involved in human aggression.

His colleagues will welcome it as their primary reference on the scientific analysis of aggression. Students will learn much from it because of the accessible style used to convey scientific and popular viewpoints. Yet, it is possible that the major contribution of this book will lie in informing the intelligent layperson, and influencing leaders of our society, as to the state of current, accurate knowledge in the psychology of aggression and violence. There are few topics in social psychology of more pressing concern to societies everywhere than that of discovering effective means of preventing and reducing the destructive impact of the many forms of aggression we face in our everyday lives. Berkowitz's new contribution helps to focus us in directions from which new solutions may emanate for this age-old problem.

Philip G. Zimbardo
Consulting Editor

Preface

———— ❖ ————

This book is written in hope that it will contribute in some small way to the alleviation of one of our most serious social problems: human aggression. Violence clearly tears at the fabric of society. When parents abuse their children they weaken the bonds of regard and affection that will tie their offspring to themselves and the social order. Frequent muggings and other street crimes lessen the citizenry's faith in their government and also seriously diminish the trust in others that is so necessary for social harmony and the effective collaboration with friends and neighbors in solving shared problems. In so many different ways people can make the world around them much more difficult and troublesome, and at times maybe even more dangerous, when they assault someone else or even encourage others to engage in such behavior. I hope, and believe, that society can do a great deal to lessen this all-too-prevalent aggression if it understands better the fundamental causes of this destructive conduct, what conditions increase the chances that any one person will attack someone else, and what steps are generally most effective in reducing the likelihood of aggressive behavior.

While this book may contribute to this understanding, it doesn't cover all of the many factors that play a part in aggression. It is primarily concerned with the psychological processes within the individual that help promote, or restrain, this behavior and the conditions in the person's past and immediate present that make it more or less likely that he or she will attack someone else when aroused. Nothing is said about the neurological and biochemical mechanisms that are involved in this action, and the book also looks only briefly at the role of hormones, even though biological influences obviously are very important. Nor do I review the psychiatric analyses of the more extreme forms of violence such as serial killing, although the chapter on violent personalities does touch on the behavior of diagnosed psychopaths. Attention is given to the effects of a number of factors emphasized by sociologists, such as poverty and cultural beliefs and values, but again, perhaps not as much as some might wish. By and large, the main focus is on the social psychology of aggression and violence.

Following along in the tradition of contemporary social psychology, several of the chapters place special value on the findings obtained from experiments, and I frequently buttress my arguments by referring to the results of laboratory studies. This certainly doesn't mean that I neglect the often important observations gleaned from field studies and everyday experience or that I believe experimental research is always preferable to other modes of investigation in the social sciences. I have pointed out, in this book and in other writings, that laboratory studies are best employed for only certain purposes, the testing of particular causal hypotheses. It's also quite obvious that for ethical as well as practical reasons well-controlled experiments cannot possibly be carried out to investigate many significant questions, such as whether years of economic deprivation tend to breed criminal tendencies, or whether a parent's frequently repeated abuse of her child heightens the probability that the youngster will develop into a violently inclined adult. Only field studies of people in their natural settings can suggest answers to questions such as these, and the book reports a good deal of such "real world" research. Nonetheless, experiments can be carried out to test other ideas highly relevant to human aggression. As I will try to demonstrate, it is important for us to learn, for instance, whether persons exposed to decidedly unpleasant but psychologically nonthreatening atmospheric conditions are more likely to be assaultive than they otherwise would have been in a more comfortable surrounding and whether the sight of others fighting raises the odds that the viewers will be aggressive themselves. In these cases experiments give us the best chance of determining whether the factor of interest (e.g., the physically unpleasant situation), and not other possible influences, can indeed affect the probability of the given outcome (e.g., lead to greater aggression). No one claims that the results of any one study by itself are totally unequivocal. But we can gain greater confidence in the validity of the notion being tested if we have consistent findings over a number of similar experimental investigations, and so I've tried as much as possible to cite experiments whose results are supported by other similar findings.

However, it should be clear from the outset that this book does not attempt to provide a comprehensive survey of the great many investigations that could have been mentioned even in the topic areas I do take up, whether the studies are experiments or naturalistic observations. I regard the present work as a general introduction to the research and theory of human aggression more than a technical and scholarly review of the pertinent literature, and thus have deliberately selected only some of the pertinent investigations for special attention. In my view these studies are among the very best in their particular research area, and illustrate well the issues I discuss. I do not claim in any of these cases that the studies cited are the final word and that the questions they address are answered once and for all. But I do think they furnish generally good support for arguments I offer and the theoretical points I try to make. Readers wanting to learn of other studies on the topics covered in this work will find that the chapter endnotes contain references to other, related investigations as well as the citations to the studies I do discuss in the body of this text. (The endnotes also occasionally report relevant details about these studies.) Yet even with these additional references, those with special interests in this area would do well to build on the discussion offered here by seeking further information from the many journals and texts I could have, but didn't, review in this book.

One final comment is warranted. Many of the matters discussed in this work are highly controversial and a number of them have political and ideological overtones. Readers might thus be tempted to characterize the position I take in these chapters in political terms, saying I'm a liberal—or a conservative—and then dismiss my arguments as politically biased. While I do hold fairly strong social and political opinions and cannot maintain that I'm free of ideological biases, I would like to note that the views expressed and the conclusions I've drawn range widely over the sociopolitical spectrum. With many conservatives, I believe a good deal of criminal violence is facilitated by inadequate personal restraints and that we need adequate social controls if we are to deal effectively with some violent offenders. At the other end of the political dimension, I think that American society gains little long-term benefit from capital punishment in its efforts to reduce homicide rates, and I am also convinced that the stresses and strains produced of poverty contribute to the development and maintenance of aggressive inclinations. The evidence requires such a mixture of positions. My sociopolitical beliefs and values might well have helped shape these particular views to some degree, but the stances I've taken in this book are also a response, to a considerable extent, to the findings obtained by empirical research. Social policies in areas such as the control and reduction of violence should rest as much as possible on good evidence obtained from scientifically sound research, and I've tried to rely on many of the best studies I know on this topic in writing this book.

Having this base in empirical research, this book is therefore in many ways a truly collaborative endeavor. It wouldn't have been at all possible without the dedication, skill and insights of the many investigators (including Al Bandura, Bob Baron, Ed Donnerstein, Len Eron, David Farrington, Sy Feshbach, Russ Geen, and Dolph Zillmann) who have sought to learn the causes and consequences of human aggression, and I'm pleased to acknowledge my indebtedness to them. I also want to thank Robert Arkin, University of Missouri, Columbia; Avshalom Caspi, University of Wisconsin, Madison; Len Eron, University of Illinois at Chicago; Robert Feldman, University of Massachusetts at Amherst; Roger Johnson, Ramapo College; Jacques-Philippe Leyens,University of Louvain, Belgium; Neil Malamuth, University of California, Los Angeles; Colleen Moore, University of Wisconsin, Madison; David Myers,

University of Alabama, Tuscaloosa; Steven Prentice-Dunn, Hope College; David Senn, Clemson University; and Charles Turner, University of Utah, Salt Lake City, who have read and commented on individual chapters; my students and colleagues in experimental social psychology, in Wisconsin and elsewhere, who have taught me much about many different facets of human behavior; and my editors, Christopher Rogers and Phil Zimbardo, who have been so encouraging and thoughtful in their recommendations. And I'm especially grateful to my wife, Norma, for the recommendations she made about some of the chapters, for the support she has given me as I've labored on this project over the years, and for the oh-so-many other reasons that I hope she knows.

Leonard Berkowitz

Aggression

*ITS CAUSES, CONSEQUENCES,
AND CONTROL*

1 *Whole chapter*

The Problem of Aggression

————— ❖ —————

*I*s there anyone who is not aware of the violence in society? News stories tell us, almost every day, about shootings, muggings, knifings, and assaults, about people fighting and killing each other. Not long ago my local newspaper reported that a young woman broke into an elementary school near Chicago and shot six young students, killing one of them; that an irate father in an affluent suburb of New York City had murdered a judge who had ruled against his daughter in a court case; and that a small community outside Milwaukee was shocked by the slaying of two women.

Violence occurs around the world and in all segments of society. We hear and read about gang battles in the poorest sections of Los Angeles, shootings in Detroit and Miami, muggings in New York's Central Park, bombs exploding in Northern Ireland, a prime minister assassinated in Stockholm, Christians and Moslems warring in the devastated streets of Beirut, Jews fighting with Moslems in the Occupied Territories, and civil wars raging in Africa. Seemingly random acts of violence occur almost everywhere. Again and again, week after week.

These stories are only the most extreme examples of the aggression that takes place every day. Are you aware of how many American husbands and wives hit each other, and of how many parents beat their children? About 15 years ago sociologists Murray Straus, Richard Gelles, and Suzanne Steinmetz attempted to estimate the frequency of violence in American homes by interviewing a representative sample of husbands and wives. The researchers asked these men and women, among other things, about the conflicts that occurred in their families

1

and how the conflicts were resolved. The findings may surprise you. In the investigators' words:

> Drive down any street in America. More than one household in six has been the scene of a spouse striking his or her partner last year [1975]. Three American households in five [in which children live at home] have reverberated with the sounds of parents hitting their children. . . . Overall, every other house in America is the scene of family violence at least once a year.[1]

This is no trivial matter, and not only because of the suffering caused by aggression. It is often difficult to keep violence from spreading. Any one act of aggression is all too likely to produce further aggression. Straus, Gelles, and Steinmetz saw this in their research. The more often the parents in their sample fought with each other, the more likely it was that one or both of them would also beat their children. Furthermore, many of the aggressive parents passed on their aggressive dispositions to their children. Surely this isn't surprising. How children are reared and what experiences they have in their families as they grow up clearly have an influence upon their inclinations toward violence.

Not all aggression, however, can be traced to defective child rearing. Violence arises in many ways and can be seen in many different actions. Some social scientists claim that there is a growing readiness to resort to aggression, presumably because increasing numbers of people feel justified in seeking revenge on others who they think have wronged them. Their anger is supposedly revealed in rudeness and muttered insults as well as in the rise of violent crimes and mass murders. Other writers place part of the blame for widespread aggression on the steady diet of violence offered in movies and on television. Indeed, movie and TV screens do offer a plentiful supply of fighting and killings. According to the National Coalition on Television Violence, by the time the average American reaches 18 years of age, she or he will have seen 32,000 murders and 40,000 attempted homicides on television alone. It has also been estimated that (as of the mid-1980s, at least) more than half the major characters depicted on television are shown being menaced by an average of five to six acts of physical violence per hour. Can all this witnessed violence not have an effect on people in the audience? At the very least, some critics argue, television paints an unrealistic portrait of American society. Crime is far more rampant on the TV screen than in the real world, and avid viewers might come to think that life in contemporary society is much more dangerous and brutal than it actually is. If some people do acquire such a misconception from television, couldn't it influence how they deal with others? Television may not be the only villain in this piece. What about poverty and the mounting disparities in lifestyle between the rich and the poor? Not a few persons undoubtedly resent their inability to enjoy the good things in life that others take for granted.

We can continue with this list of possible causes of aggression. Violence can arise in many ways, and many of them will be examined in this book. We will also consider what can be done to reduce the chances that one person will strike another. How can we lessen the likelihood that frustrated people, who have been prevented from reaching their goals, will attack others around them? Can parents and children be taught to resolve their difficulties without resorting to violence? Specialists have offered a variety of procedures for lessening or controlling aggression, and these will be discussed in detail in later chapters. Some proposed solutions have focused on the external determinants of aggression, arguing that society must reduce individuals' frustration and cut down on the amount of violence portrayed in the movies and on television. Others have emphasized the supposed inner sources of aggression, maintaining that a pent-up aggressive drive can be discharged through make-believe attacks or even through athletic contests or other forms of competition. Still others have favored controlling the inner urge to violence by the use of medication, while many psychologists and other mental health professionals have advocated using behavioral training techniques or helping people to become aware of their suppressed resentments. On the other hand, not a few cynics have insisted that we cannot put much hope in remedial programs, since people supposedly are born with an appetite for hatred and violence.

I have written this book in the belief that an increased knowledge of human psychology can contribute to the reduction of human aggression. If we knew more about what spurs people to assault others, what influences make it easier (or more difficult) to deliberately hurt one's fellows, and what are the consequences of aggression for the attacker as well as for the victim, we could do a great deal to lessen our inhumane treatment of each other.

WHAT IS AGGRESSION?

All Too Many Meanings

The first step in gaining an adequate understanding of aggression is to establish a clear and precise definition of this term. Generally speaking, this book, in common with a number of other research-oriented texts, defines *aggression* as *any form of behavior that is intended to injure someone physically or psychologically.* Although more and more researchers are now adopting this definition, it is not universally accepted, and even today the term "aggression" has many different meanings, in scientific communication as well as in everyday speech. As a consequence, we can't always be sure just what is meant when a person is described as "aggressive" or an action is labeled "violence." Dictionaries aren't always helpful. Several that I have consulted say that the word "aggression" refers to the forcible violation of another's rights and an offensive action or procedure, as well as to boldly assertive behavior. These seem to be widely different actions, but all are called "aggression" in the English language. Mental health professionals and students of animal behavior aren't necessarily any more precise than dictionaries; they also have several different meanings in mind when they use the word "aggression."

Following Everyday Meanings

Sometimes the conception of aggression has been fairly broad in scope. As an example, many psychoanalytically oriented writers posit a general aggressive drive that powers a wide spectrum of behaviors, many of which are not obviously aggressive in nature. An unwarranted attack on another person is viewed as aggression, but so is a striving for independence or a forceful assertion of one's own opinion. This broad conception can create problems. Besides its questionable assumption of a wide-ranging drive that can be channeled into all sorts of different actions, its thinking is actually much too influenced by the way words are used in everyday language—a point that is quite important and deserves special comment.

Consider a statement made in a book on aggression that was written for the ordinary public. The author maintained that "there is no clear dividing line between those forms of aggression which we all deplore and those which we must not disown if we are to survive." For this author, aggression was not only a deliberate attempt to hurt someone but also "the basis of intellectual achievement, of the attainment of independence, and even of that proper pride which enables a man to hold his head high amongst his fellows." The writer clearly assumed there was a very general aggressive drive that energized a wide variety of different behaviors besides direct attacks on other persons. More than this, his evidence for the existence of such a general drive was mainly language usage:

> The words we use to describe intellectual effort are aggressive words. We *attack* problems, or *get our teeth into* them. We *master* a subject when we have *struggled with* and *overcome* its difficulties.[2]

This extremely broad view of aggression essentially encompasses everything that is termed "aggression" in our culture at large. Since assertiveness is often called "aggression"—as when we speak of an "aggressive salesperson" who tries very hard to make a sale—the idea of aggression, by this logic, must include assertiveness as well as all other types of forceful conduct. Moreover, this position also basically holds that the same motivation must be involved in all these actions. This is a questionable assumption indeed.

Defining Aggression without Motivational Assumptions

At the opposite extreme are definitions of aggression that are exceedingly narrow in scope and make virtually no motivational assumptions. Arnold Buss has offered perhaps the best-known version of this nonmotivational conception.[3] At the time when he wrote his book (which was the first modern survey of contemporary psychological research on human aggression), Buss was influenced by the behavioristic bias against supposedly "mentalistic" concepts. He therefore wanted to define aggression descriptively, without making use of subjective ideas such as intention. He also pointed out that intentions were difficult to assess in an objective manner; aggressors often misrepresent their true purposes when they attack someone, and even when they want to be truthful, they might not be able to say what they are actually trying to do. From his perspective, aggression was best regarded simply as "the delivery of noxious stimuli to another."

Such a definition quickly runs into an obvious problem: Surely an accidental "delivery of noxious stimuli to another" is not the same thing as a deliberate attempt to harm someone. The pedestrian who inadvertently bumps into someone on a crowded sidewalk clearly has to be viewed differently from, say, a schoolyard bully who purposely mistreats other children. In addition, what about cases in which a person intentionally hurts others in order to help them—for example, a dentist or a surgeon?

Aggression as Wrongful Behavior

Another possible way to define aggression without reference to intentions is to think of this behavior as a violation of social norms. Many ordinary persons and not a few psychologists say that a person is aggressive when she or he acts contrary to accepted rules of conduct. Taking this position, the eminent social and personality psychologist Albert Bandura has noted that many of us label a behavior as "aggression" when it is not carried out as part of a socially approved role.[4] A person who wields a knife in an attempt to rob someone is clearly violating social rules. Most of us would say that such a knife wielder was being aggressive, whereas a surgeon who cuts into a patient is not seen as an aggressor because this action is part of a socially approved job. Clearly, the word "aggression" has negative connotations for most people, and they are often reluctant to say someone is acting aggressively if they approve of his or her conduct. We call people aggressive mainly if we don't like what they are doing. However, the question is, must people who study aggression on a scientific basis accept the vague and varied meanings the general public has given to this word? Must researchers define aggression as rule-violating behavior just because people in general view it this way?

Two issues are involved: first, whether social science concepts must be restricted to the meanings assigned to words in everyday language, and second, whether it is truly helpful to think of aggression as consisting only of actions that violate social rules.

Must researchers be guided by everyday meanings? Let's begin with the first issue. In my opinion, most researchers would say that a rigid adherence to everyday language would impede scientific development. Whereas every science seeks to establish terms that have clear and specific meanings, ordinary speech is often vague and imprecise. "Aggression" has so many different meanings in normal discourse that knowing what is meant is often difficult. Exactly what do laypeople have in mind when they describe someone as "aggressive"? Are they saying that the person frequently violates social rules (and, if so, what kinds of rules?), or do they mean that the individual is often assertive or masterly, or that she or he seems to be nasty to others? The term "aggression" can refer to many things other than wrongful behavior, but we aren't always sure just what someone who uses the term actually means. Researchers have to get away from the imprecision of everyday language so that our scientific colleagues, our students, and the general public—and indeed, we ourselves—can have a clear idea of exactly what we mean.

Is aggression only socially disapproved behavior? The second issue is closely related to the first. Whether we follow everyday meanings or not, must we view aggression as rule-violating behavior? My answer is "no," because we cannot always specify which particular rules and social norms are relevant to the action in question.

Suppose a man has been insulted. In a rage, he punches the person who offended him. Some onlookers would undoubtedly say the man wasn't being aggressive, because he was justified in retaliating. Many people do indeed think it is permissible to try to get even with others who deliberately mistreated them, but many others believe that it is morally better to "turn the other cheek." An act that some people would look upon as normal and justifiable retaliation is considered unjustified aggression by others.

Also consider the violence that takes place in American families. Legal authorities and most health professionals hold that parents are abusive and aggressive when they beat their children. However, if you were to ask the parents what they were doing, a large number of them would probably say they were only inflicting needed discipline upon willfully disobedient youngsters.[5] From their perspective, they aren't being aggressive at all. Much the same answer would be given by husbands who hit their wives. On the basis of their interviews with a representative sample of married men and women, Straus, Gelles, and Steinmetz concluded that not a few husbands regard "the marriage license as a hitting license."[6] These men think they have a right to beat their wives when the women violate their rules. If you saw a mother spanking her child, you would insist that she was aggressive if you disapproved of her behavior but deny that she was aggressive if you sympathized with her. What about terrorists who hijack an airliner and threaten the passengers? Much of the world condemns hijacking and regards the terrorists as engaged in brutal violence. Yet *the terrorists themselves* maintain that they are fighting for a legitimate cause.

If present-day Americans have a problem in deciding whether the actions of our contemporaries are permissible or not, think of the difficulties we might have if we attempted to label the behavior of other cultures and other historical periods. Only a few hundred years ago, in much of western society, a cuckolded husband had the right to kill his unfaithful wife and her lover. What about the protagonist in Shakespeare's *Othello*? Was Othello being aggressive when he took Desdemona's life, believing she had been unfaithful to him? As a matter of fact, although he admitted the killing, he denied that it was murder, saying that he "did proceed upon just grounds."

In all the instances cited above, if we followed the conception of aggression as wrongful behavior, we could call the behavior "aggression" if we were on one side of the altercation and opposed the action, but not if we were on the opposing side and favored it. Such a state of affairs is obviously unsatisfactory. The classification of an action as aggression or as something else becomes arbitrary. This is not to say, of course, that aggression isn't generally disapproved of. It is—fortunately—but we would do well not to make social disapproval a necessary part of the definition of aggression.

The Goals of Aggression

Most investigators insist that a truly adequate definition of aggression must refer to the attacker's purpose. However, although nearly every theorist agrees that aggression is intended, there is no consensus about what ends aggressors are pursuing when they attempt to hurt others. Do the attackers mainly want to harm their victims, or are they trying to do something else? This is one of the major questions in the scientific study of aggression, and the answers of social scientists differ.

Let's say that a man is enraged by a remark his wife makes, and he strikes out at her in fury. Along with some other writers, I would suggest that such an assault is driven to a considerable extent by an internal "push" (an inner agitation or stimulation) and is aimed primarily at injuring the offender. By contrast, other social scientists, and many lay people as well, emphasize certain objectives other than the target's injury that, we might say (metaphorically), "pull" the blow. The man may think that by hitting and hurting the woman he can assert his dominance over her, teach her not to annoy him again, achieve control over a threatening situation, and so on.

I will come back to these two different conceptions of aggression repeatedly throughout this book. I will say again and again that some attacks are carried out more or less impulsively, whereas others are calculated actions that are performed with the expectation of achieving certain benefits.

Aggression's Noninjurious Goals

Quite a number of social scientists believe that most assaults are motivated by more than a desire to injure a victim. Basically assuming that the aggressors are acting rationally, this perspective maintains that the attackers have another objective in mind, a goal that is more important to them than the desire to hurt their targets: the wish to influence or exert power over another person, or to establish a favorable identity. Of course, these objectives sometimes operate together. Aggressors can try to get their way or to assert their power in order to build up their self-worth. Since several theorists have stressed these purposes separately, I will review them separately here.

Coercion. Some psychologists, most notably Gerald Patterson[7] and James Tedeschi,[8] have argued that aggression is often only a crude attempt at coercion. Attackers may hurt their victims, but, according to both Patterson and Tedeschi, their actions are primarily an attempt to influence the other persons' behavior. They are trying to get the individuals to stop doing something that bothers them.

Patterson's ideas were based chiefly on his investigations of interactions within families. In his research, which will be discussed in more detail later in this book, observers went into the homes of cooperative families and recorded in minute detail how the adults and children behaved toward each other. The psychologists then compared the interactions within "normal" families with those within other families that had problem children (youngsters who were having difficulty with others, usually because they were highly aggressive). They found that the problem youngsters tended to act in a wide variety of unpleasant ways, apparently in order to control the behavior of the other members of their families. They were frequently negative and disapproving, refused to do what they were asked to do, and even struck out at their relatives and others occasionally, evidently in an attempt to force these people to do what they wanted.

Power and dominance. Other theorists have gone further, holding that aggression involves more than coercion. As they see it, aggressive behavior is often aimed at preserving or enhancing the attackers' power and dominance. Aggressors may strike at their victims in an effort to get their own way, but, according to these writers, they want to get their way in order to assert their dominant positions in their relationship with their victims. At the very least, they are trying to show that they aren't subordinate to their victims.

This interpretation is especially prominent in the literature on family violence. Studies in this area have repeatedly demonstrated that when one family member assaults another, the strong is usually victimizing the weak. The most powerful members of the family—those who have the greatest physical strength or have been assigned the greatest status and authority by society at large—are much more likely to assault less powerful family members than to be attacked by them. This presumably happens because the powerful persons are attempting to maintain their dominance through force. Finkelhor[9] has made this interpretation of some of the findings of the research on family violence that was conducted by Straus, Gelles, and Steinmetz. Many of the battered wives studied by the Straus team didn't have paid jobs, were not involved in family decision making, and had little education. Finkelhor suggested that these women had little power relative to their husbands. Thus they were easily abused by their psychologically and sociologically more powerful husbands when there was a dispute.

The dominance perspective typically proceeds from this point in one of two directions. One line of thought (favored by Finkelhor and various feminist-oriented writers) holds that the power differential in itself leads to abuse. The strong hit the weak because, as Gelles has put it, "They can. . . . [People] will use violence in the family if the costs of being violent do not outweigh the rewards."[10] Husbands batter their wives because they believe they have the power, authority, and right to do so, especially when the spouse "gets out of line." A somewhat more complicated, but to my mind more adequate, version of this power analysis is that violence stems not from power differentials but from a struggle for power and dominance. When husbands and wives disagree, they compete for control and influence, and aggression can arise from this struggle. You'll see in Chapter 8, in the discussion of domestic violence, that this type of conflict does occur, and not infrequently.

Impression management. According to yet another school of thought, aggressors are mainly interested in what others think of them. Studies of both youth gangs and violent criminals have long noted that many of these people care greatly about their reputations. Hans Toch was impressed by this kind of concern in his well-known interview study of men who were in jail for violent offenses. According to Toch, many of the offenders were "self-image promoters" who evidently worked hard at "manufacturing the impression" of themselves as "formidable and fearless" and whose fights were "demonstration match-es . . . designed to impress the victim and the audience."[11] Sociologist Richard Felson has expanded on this notion in a thoughtful interpreta-tion of aggression as an attempt at impression management. In his analy-sis, most persons, and not only lawbreakers, believe that a personal chal-lenge casts them in a negative light, especially if they have been attacked. They presumably may then resort to a counterattack in an effort to nulli-fy "the imputed negative identity by showing [their] strength, compe-tence, and courage." In striking at the offenders, they are seeking to show that they are "someone whose self must be respected."[12]

Different Kinds of Aggressive Goals

All the formulations reviewed above have some merit. Each has identi-fied a motive behind some instances of aggression. Some assaults are attempts at coercion, and others are assertions of power and dominance. An assault can even be driven by a desire to demonstrate that one is wor-thy of respect. For that matter, aggressive behavior can be impelled by other motives as well, such as the desire for monetary gain or social approval. Aggression can be carried out for any number of purposes. Indeed, I'll argue later in Chapter 12 that analyses positing an instinctive drive to aggression are seriously flawed because (among other reasons) they fail to recognize the great variety of motives that can impel fighting.

Wanting to Hurt

All aggressive acts do have one thing in common. According to most investigators, this sort of behavior is always aimed at *the deliberate injury of another*. These researchers do not phrase their definitions in exactly the same words, but the great majority of them have much the same idea in mind. An excellent example can be found in the definition of "aggres-sion" offered about fifty years ago by a team of social scientists at Yale University, led by John Dollard and Neal Miller. This classic analysis of the effects of frustrations defined *aggression* formally as "an act whose goal-response is injury to an organism (or organism-surrogate)."[13] In other words, the goal of the act is to do harm. The aggressor wants to hurt the target. Robert Baron, another well-known researcher in this area, phrased the same idea more elaborately. For him, *aggression* is "any form of behavior directed toward the goal of harming or injuring another liv-ing being who is motivated to avoid such treatment."[14] This means that the aggressor realizes that she or he is doing something to the victim that the victim doesn't want to happen. The question is not whether society at large regards the behavior as undesirable. This may or may not be the case. What is more important is that the attacker knows that *the target* doesn't like what he or she is doing.

The Present Definition

In this book, then, the term "aggression" always refers to some kind of *behavior*, either physical or symbolic, *that is carried out with the intention to harm someone.* I will not be using "aggression" as a synonym for "assertiveness," "mastery," or "independence." I will use the term "violence" only in referring to an extreme form of aggression, *a deliberate attempt to do serious physical injury.* For my purposes, "aggression" does not mean wronging someone unless the mistreatment was an intentional effort to hurt the other person.

Is Injury Always the Primary Goal?

Instrumental and emotional aggression.

Aggression Can Satisfy Other Purposes. Even though aggression always involves an intention to do harm, injury isn't always the main objective. Aggressors can have other goals in mind when they assault their victims. A soldier may want to kill his enemy, but his wish may stem from a desire to protect his own life, may be a way to show his patriotism, or may be a means of gaining the approval of his officers and friends. A "hit man" hired by a crime ring may try to kill a certain person, but does this in order to get a large sum of money. Similarly, the members of a violent street gang may assault a group of strangers who enter their neighborhood because they want to show the intruders that they are tough and not to be trifled with. An irate husband may beat his wife in order to assert his dominant status in the family. In all these instances, though the aggressors do intend to hurt or even kill their target, this isn't their primary purpose. Rather, the assault is a means to attain some other objective that is more important to them than their victim's injury. The thought of this purpose "pulls out" the attack.

Psychologists refer to an action that is carried out for some extrinsic purpose, rather than simply for the pleasure of doing it, as "instrumental behavior," and so the aggressive behavior that has another objective besides doing harm is commonly termed "instrumental aggression." The formulations holding that human aggression is typically an attempt at coercion or an effort to preserve one's power, dominance, or social status basically view most aggressive actions as instrumental aggression.

Emotional Aggression. Many social psychologists argue that there is also another kind of aggression in which the primary objective is to do harm. This type of aggression is frequently called "hostile aggression," following the terminology of Feshbach.[15] It can also be thought of as "emotional," "affective," or "angry" aggression, since this is the kind of aggression that occurs when people are unpleasantly aroused and try to hurt someone. I will use the term "emotional aggression" in order to highlight the difference between this behavior and more instrumentally oriented assaults.

Much of the aggression that I will discuss in this book is of an emotional nature. I'll argue frequently that many of us have an urge to attack someone when we feel bad. On many of these occasions we don't necessarily believe we'll profit by assaulting the target, and quite often we know that we will not even be able to lessen the unpleasant state of affairs. Still, we have an impulse to strike out at another person or some thing.

Some Find Pleasure in Hurting Others. The notion of emotional aggression tells us that aggression can be pleasurable. Many persons want to hurt others when they're distressed, and they are gratified when they accomplish this goal. They might even find it pleasant and rewarding to injure their victims (as long as they themselves don't suffer negative consequences). Think of what this means. Some people live in relatively hostile environments and are frequently provoked by others around them. Other people, such as many underprivileged youths in the ghettoes of big cities, have been frequently confronted by their failure to attain the goals society has set for them. They are uncertain of their self-worth and see themselves as powerless in a world beyond their control. They may burn with barely submerged resentment. Whatever the source of people's discontent, we should recognize that some of them repeatedly experience an urge to lash out at others. Isn't it possible, then, that if they do hit other people on these occasions, they will have opportunities to learn that aggression can be pleasurable? More than this, suppose that these particular aggressors also find that they can benefit in other ways by assaulting those around them: they can prove their masculinity, demonstrate that they are powerful and important, gain status in their social groups, and so on. By achieving these desirable outcomes, again they find that aggression can be gratifying. As they are repeatedly rewarded for being assaultive, they can come to find aggression pleasurable for its own sake.

Whatever the precise way in which this happens, the result is that some persons come to enjoy hurting others for pleasure as well as to achieve other benefits. They may then attack someone even when they're not emotionally aroused, simply because they have learned it's fun. If they're bored and unhappy, for example, they may go out on an aggressive spree.

My guess is that some of the shocking violent incidents in New York City that attracted nationwide attention a few years ago came about in just this manner. Do you remember the case of the young woman jogger who was brutally assaulted and raped in New York City's Central Park in April 1989? A gang of about a dozen youths stormed through the park one evening, threatening and attacking anyone they saw, and then jumped on a woman who just happened to be running by. She was beaten so badly that she was in a coma for three weeks.

This violence was undoubtedly prompted by a number of motives.

For one thing, the teenagers may have wanted to show the world (and maybe themselves as well) that they were powerful people who had to be given attention. However, if we consider how they themselves described their conduct, we have to suspect that they had another goal as well: They said that they had been engaged in a "wilding." They had "gone wild" and behaved violently "just for the hell of it." Whatever else may have contributed to the assault, they also evidently sought the pleasure of making someone suffer. The unfortunate woman just happened to be available for this hostile purpose.

There have also been seemingly senseless attacks on homeless men; which were described as follows:

> A gang of young men wielding knives and bats went on a Halloween rampage Wednesday night, assaulting several homeless people on the footbridge to Wards Island and leaving one of them dead among the garbage-strewn weeds, his throat slashed. . . .
>
> The group of about 10 young men, some wearing Halloween masks, apparently attacked the homeless men for thrills. . . .
>
> Detectives investigating the attacks theorized today that the violence escalated on Wednesday night as the youths tried to outdo each other. "They were getting their jollies attacking the homeless," said one investigator. . . . "It's like in the jogger case. Sometimes when the blood gets flowing, people go crazy."[16]

How can we explain this? What were the young assailants doing? The victims didn't have any money and weren't "invading their turf." Did the gang members really think they were asserting their masculinity by cruelly beating tired, sick old men who were too weak to defend themselves? Maybe the detective was right. They were "getting their jollies" by inflicting pain. I wonder if this type of aggression isn't more common than many believe. Violent gangs may often attack others "just for the hell of it" and for the pleasure they get from inflicting pain, as well as to achieve a sense of power, control, and mastery.

Evidence of the desire to hurt. Since there is considerable controversy in the social sciences about the existence of this kind of emotional aggression, an experiment reported by Baron may help to convince the doubters.[17] In this study, the subjects, male university students, were first told the ostensible purpose of the study and then were deliberately either angered or treated in a neutral manner by the experimenter's confederate. Each subject then had ten opportunities to give the confederate electric shocks, supposedly as punishment for a mistake that the individual had made on a learning task. In each of these opportunities, the subject was required to deliver a shock but was free to vary the shock's intensity from exceedingly mild to quite severe.[18] Equally important, in half the cases the subject could see a meter on an apparatus in front of him that supposedly indicated how much pain the recipient of the shock felt when each shock was delivered. (Of course, as is standard in this type of research, no one was actually shocked, and the information on the level of "pain" was invented by the experimenter and was the same for all participants.) The question under investigation was how the information about the target's pain would influence the intensity of the punishment given by the participant over the course of the ten trials.

The main findings are summarized in Figure 1-1. As you can see, when the subjects had not been angered by the individual they were punishing, the information about the target's pain lessened the intensity of the shocks they gave. This information reminded them that they were hurting the other person; not wanting to inflict pain, they reduced the painfulness of the shocks. Furthermore, Baron reported, these subjects also tended to feel bad upon seeing the information about the victim's pain.

By contrast, the same information actually heightened the intensity of the punishment delivered by the angry subjects. Having been provoked earlier by the recipient of the shock, they wanted to hurt this individual. The information essentially told them that they were getting close to their goal of inflicting a sufficient amount of pain and thus stimulated them to even stronger aggression. This is analogous to the way the first few bites of a meal stimulate a hungry person to develop an even stronger desire to eat. The angry men apparently enjoyed their "ini-

FIGURE 1-1
Aggression level (transformed shock intensity x duration) as a function of the subjects' emotional state and their information about the victim's pain.
(Adapted from Baron (1977), *Human Aggression*, p. 263. Copyright Plenum Publishing Corp.)

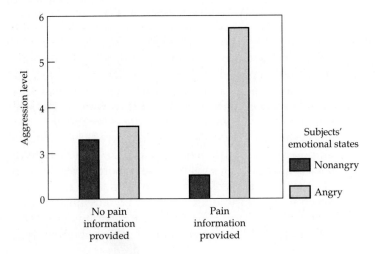

tial bites"; besides inciting them to "bite" harder, the information on pain also tended to improve their mood.

Instigating conditions. Besides "instrumental aggression" and "emotional aggression," other terms can be used to label these two kinds of aggression. No matter what terms we employ, however, it may be helpful to regard instrumental aggression as relatively rational and easily understood behavior (from the attacker's vantage point anyway) and emotional aggression as much less guided by conscious thought.

Other Distinctions

Physical and verbal, direct and indirect forms of aggression. Aggressive actions can also be classified in other ways. They can be differentiated, for example, in terms of their *physical nature*—whether they are *physical actions,* such as punches or kicks, or *verbal statements*, which could be expressed as questionnaire ratings intended to harm the person being evaluated, or as curses or even threats. We may be interested in *how directly the action is an attack on the aggressor's primary target* (the person the aggressor wants to hurt most), rather than being a more roundabout way of doing harm to this person. Let's suppose that a man has been insulted by a colleague at work. He might hit the offending person (direct physical aggression) or insult him in return (direct verbal attack), or he might spread unfavorable stories about this individual in order to damage his reputation (indirect verbal aggression).

Dollard and his associates, the Yale psychologists I mentioned earlier, have given us a good illustration of indirect aggression in symbolic form:

> Subjects were hired for the ostensible purpose of studying the influence of fatigue upon simple physiological functions and were then prevented from sleeping at all during one night. They were habitual smokers but [were] not allowed to smoke. For long periods of time they were required to sit still without being allowed to amuse themselves by reading, talking, or playing games. . . . After being subjected to these and other frustrations, they manifested considerable aggression against the experimenters. But part of this aggression, as was indicated by later reports, was not expressed directly because of the social situation. . . . One of the subjects produced two sheets of drawings in which violent aggression was represented in an unmistakable manner. [See Figure 1-2.] Dismembered and disembowled bodies were shown in various grotesques positions . . . all portraying a shocking injury to the human body. Furthermore, when the creator of these pictures was asked, by another subject, who the people represented in the drawings were, he replied, "Psychologists!" And his fellow sufferers were all obviously amused.[19]

Although it was intended to be humorous, this little anecdote actually makes some serious points. The Dollard group suggested that the strongest aggressive tendencies created by a provocation (or frustration) are directed toward the perceived source of the difficulty. Aroused people would therefore prefer to attack the source of their troubles in as direct a fashion as possible, much as the subjects in the above psychology experiment presumably wanted to lash out directly at the psychologists who were frustrating them. However, just as the Yale subjects only dared to show their antagonism indirectly in cartoon form, provoked persons will express their aggressive inclinations only indirectly (if at all) if they believe that a direct attack will be punished. In much the same way, nasty remarks, hostile jokes, and "catty" gossip are also examples of indirect aggression that probably grow out of inhibited direct aggression.

Consciously controlled versus impulsive (or expressive) aspects of aggression. Aggressive actions can also be described in terms of yet another dimension, a dimension that in my view has not received sufficient attention in research on aggression: the degree to which the behav-

FIGURE 1-2
Spontaneous drawings made by a sleep-deprived subject.
(From Sears et al. (1940), Journal of Psychology, 9: 277–281. Reprinted with permission of the Helen Dwight Reid Educational Foundation, published by Heldref Publications, 1319 18th Street, Washington, D.C. 20036 Copyright 1940.)

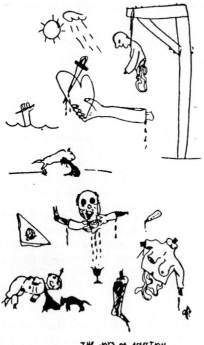

THE JOYS OF AFFECTION

ior is either *consciously controlled* or *impulsive*. Some attacks are carried out calmly, deliberately, and with a clear aim in mind. The aggressors know what goals they want to achieve and believe that their assaults have a good chance of paying off. The "hit man" takes a calculated risk in killing his victim, thinking he is far more likely to benefit than to suffer the consequences. A young girl may slap her little brother in order to gain her mother's attention.

There are also times, however, when attacks are carried out with little thought—with little consciousness of either what might be gained beyond injuring the target or the costs that might be incurred. As several psychologists have put it, there's a short circuiting of the normal evaluation process. Emotionally aroused aggressors usually have an urge to strike out at an available target. Whether because of the intense emotional agitation within them and/or because of the nature of their personalities, some people don't stop to think of what might happen if they do hit their victims (physically or verbally). Their attention is focused primarily upon what they most want to do at that time—their aggressive purpose—and they don't consider alternative courses of action and the possible negative consequences.

Many homicides are actually instances of this type of aggression. Some years ago, a veteran detective in Dallas, Texas, described many of the murders he had encountered in just this way: "Murders," he said, "result from little ol' arguments about nothing at all. . . . Tempers flare. A fight starts, and somebody gets stabbed or shot."[20] What he was saying, of course, was that these killings were spontaneous acts of passion rather than the results of thought-out determinations to destroy the victims.

Such homicides are the extreme instances of relatively impulsive and nonconsciously controlled aggression, but there are less extreme and less dramatic examples that may sound familiar. Haven't you ever acted less friendly to another person than you had wanted to or "told someone off" more harshly than you had consciously intended? Maybe you said things you hadn't consciously meant to say, or perhaps you even made aggressive physical movements that you couldn't entirely control. If you have done any of these things, you're certainly not alone.

Many social scientists and mental health specialists have neglected impulsivity in emotional aggression. They seem to believe that virtually every act of aggression follows a more or less deliberate calculation of the action's possible costs and benefits. I argue that such considerations and evaluations are at times short-circuited, especially under the heat of intense feelings. The failure to recognize this factor, it seems to me, results in a seriously incomplete understanding of human aggression.

External influences on impulsive aggression. Thoughtless acts of impulsive aggression don't just "pop out" all by themselves. Nor are they necessarily motivated by unconscious hostility. In my view, they are emotional reactions that are often "pushed out" by intense stimulation inside the person. While many readers will be able to accept this point readily, many others will probably be surprised to find that the intensity of internal stimulation can be influenced by seemingly innocuous features of the surrounding situation. Something nearby can strengthen the internal "push" to aggression so that the aggressive response then occurs in a relatively automatic manner. Think of the effect of the "pain cues" in Baron's experiment. An external detail (information about the victim's pain) intensified the internal stimulation to aggression inside the angry subjects. What is equally important, however, is that a situational detail that seems to be entirely neutral in nature can have a similar aggression-stimulating effect because of its association with aggression in the attacker's mind.

I'll go into this matter more fully in Chapter 3, and here will only refer you to an experiment that Christopher Swart and I performed.[21] In this study, subjects who had been treated harshly by a fellow student in the first phase of the experiment then watched as their tormentor (the other student) received electric shocks during this other's part of the study. Some time later, when these subjects were required to punish *another* person (not the one who had angered them), they were especially punitive if they saw a neutral stimulus that *wasn't in itself indicative of pain but that had been present earlier when they learned of the annoying student's suffering*. In other words, they had seen something in the situation that reminded them of a gratifying injury that had been inflicted upon a bothersome individual, and this reminder apparently intensified the aggressive inclination remaining within them from the earlier provocation. For these subjects, this external stimulus was associated with a desirable state of affairs, a provocateur's injury, and it therefore heightened their existing aggressive urge.

Another major issue in the psychology of aggression is that some aggressive actions can be more (or less) severe than the aggressor consciously intended. The strong aggression in this last experiment was the subjects' reactions to a *neutral* person, someone who hadn't mistreated them before and whom they didn't especially like or dislike. They had no reason to want to get even with this person, and yet the mere presence of a situational stimulus associated in their minds with rewarded aggression tended to increase the intensity of their aggressive inclinations. Not being fully aware of what they were doing, they apparently reacted in a fairly automatic and impulsive manner to the stimulus associated with rewarded aggression.

In this experiment, as in many other instances of impulsive (or expressive) aggression, the relatively involuntary aspect of the behavior essentially "rode along" with the more controlled and voluntary component. The subjects in the Swart-Berkowitz study had been instructed to punish the second person and consciously acted to do what they were told. As they performed this behavior, however, another influence in the surrounding situation (the stimulus associated with gratifying aggression) operated to increase the severity of the punishment they gave. Think back to the example I used above—the man who is offended by his wife's remark. He wants to hit her and moves toward her threateningly. Then, let's suppose, he sees something that is connected in his mind with rewarded aggression (or with aggression generally): the souvenir army rifle he has hanging on the wall, a framed picture of himself as an amateur boxer, a magazine photo of Rambo holding a machine gun—or maybe his wife looking defiant as he approaches her. Any of these situational details might conceivably strengthen the aggressive urge which the woman's remark generated. The stimulus produces internal aggression-related reactions that add to the intensity of the ongoing aggressive inclinations created by the provocation. As a consequence, the man may then hit his wife harder than he consciously intends. Even if he doesn't actually strike her, he may become more verbally abusive than he initially wanted to be. Impulsive, involuntary reactions have added to the voluntary part of the behavior.

SOME WORDS ABOUT ANGER, HOSTILITY, AND AGGRESSIVENESS

I have been discussing aggression in general and in its various forms. What about "anger" and "hostility," two other terms that are also frequently employed in connection with aggression? What is their relationship to aggression? My answer to this question may be surprising.

Think again of the angry husband. He shouts at his wife and then punches her. Most people would say that he is "angry" and his aggression is a manifestation of his anger. The husband's aggressive act (hitting the woman) is not separated from his anger. The word "anger" in this case refers to both (1) an internal condition or drive state that impels the aggressive behavior and (2) the action. To complicate matters, however, "anger" sometimes refers to an emotional experience of particular feelings, and so in our example we may also say the man feels angry. Obviously, researchers will only confuse each other if the words they use have such widely different meanings. The scientific study of anger requires that we settle on a fairly clear and consistent definition of the concept of "anger."

"Hostility" is another term that has unclear implications in everyday speech. The abusive husband could be described as being very hostile toward his wife; but just what does this statement mean? Does the word "hostile" in this context refer to the man's underlying feeling at the moment or to a long-lasting negative attitude toward his wife, or does it describe his behavior? The term has been used in all three ways.

These different meanings for the words "anger" and "hostility" wouldn't be much of a problem if feelings, expressive reactions, stated attitudes, and open behavior always went together. As we all know, however, angry feelings aren't always accompanied by overt assaults, and we may express very unfavorable opinions of other people even when we don't have an urge to attack them.

I will make distinctions between the three words "aggression," "anger," and "hostility," in order to be as clear and precise as possible. When you are reading the balance of this book, you should keep in mind what I mean when I use these terms. The definitions I will give below will emphasize the differences between these concepts rather than what they have in common. There will be a cost, however. In striving for consistency and precision, I will have to depart from some of the meanings that are ordinarily attached to these concepts. You should be forewarned, then, that my notion of "anger" is not necessarily the same as the layperson's idea.

Anger Differs from Aggression

To begin, I believe it is especially advisable to distinguish between "anger" and "aggression." *Aggression* has to do with behavior that deliberately attempts to achieve a particular goal: injuring another person. This action is thus goal-directed. By contrast, *anger* (as I will use it) doesn't necessarily have any particular goal and refers only to a particular set of feelings—the feelings we usually label "anger." These feelings stem in large part from the internal physiological reactions and involuntary emotional expressions produced by the unpleasant occurrence—the motor reactions (such as clenched fists), facial changes (such as dilated nostrils and frowning brow), and so on—but are probably also affected by the thoughts and memories that arise at the time. All these sensory inputs are combined in a person's mind to form the "anger" experience. Whatever goes into this set of feelings, the experience isn't aimed at achieving a goal and doesn't serve any useful purpose for the individual in that particular situation. The important idea in all this, for the present purposes, is that anger, as an experience, does not directly instigate aggression but usually only accompanies the inclination to attack a target. However, the experience and the aggressive urge do not always go together. People sometimes try to hurt another person more or less impulsively and without being consciously aware of themselves as angry. The aggression is impelled by an internal instigation that is different from the experience. In my hypothetical example of the abusive husband, I wouldn't say that the man hits his wife *because* he is angry with her. I would hold, instead, that the husband's attack results from an instigation to aggression that was generated by an unpleasant event. The man might or might not have an anger experience at this time, but if he does, this experience only goes along with his aggressive inclination and does not directly create it.

Hostility

My perspective in this book is that *hostility* is a *negative attitude* toward one or more people that is reflected in a decidedly unfavorable judgment of the target. We express hostility when we say we dislike someone, especially if we wish this person ill. Further, a *hostile individual* is someone who is typically quick to voice or otherwise indicate negative evaluations of others, showing a general dislike for many people.

Aggressiveness

Finally, my preference is to say that *aggressiveness* refers to a *relatively persistent readiness to become aggressive in a variety of different situations.* Don't confuse this term with "hostility." People who are aggressively inclined, who often see threats and challenges, and who are quick to attack those who displease them may well have a hostile attitude toward others; but not every hostile person is necessarily assaultive. Thus, in my opinion, it's best to think of *aggressiveness* as a disposition toward becoming aggressive.

All in all, as I hope I've made clear, my approach has been to view the *instigation to aggression, aggression itself, anger, hostility,* and *aggressiveness* as separate, although usually correlated, phenomena. Researchers can investigate when and why any of these phenomena are strongly related to any of the others, and when and why there is little relationship among them. In my view, however, it would be a mistake to assume that they are the same thing or even that they are always closely interrelated.

SUMMARY

The ambiguities and imprecision of ordinary language usage impede the development of a truly adequate account of aggression. The scientific concept of "aggression" refers (as Robert Baron put it), to "any form of behavior directed toward the goal of harming or injuring another living being who is motivated to avoid such treatment." It should not be extended to "forcefulness," "assertiveness," or striving for mastery, even though these actions are frequently termed "aggressive" in everyday speech, unless there is good reason to believe that the people described have a desire to injure someone. Nor should this concept necessarily include the notion of socially illegitimate behavior, even though a layperson tends to call an action "aggressive" primarily when it is deemed to be "wrong," because people's characterizations of others' conduct as proper or improper are frequently arbitrary and relative.

An adequate analysis of aggression must also recognize the differences between the various kinds of deliberate attempts to injure or destroy another. At the very least, it is necessary to distinguish between *instrumental aggression,* in which the attack is primarily an effort to achieve an objective other than the target's harm or destruction, and *hostile aggression,* in which the primary aim is the victim's injury or death. Aggressive acts that are carried out to attain money or social status, to make a good impression on others, to control or coerce the victim, or to heighten one's sense of self-worth are instances of instrumental aggression. However, aggressors can also assault their targets chiefly out of a desire to injure or even destroy them. Since people are most apt to display hostile aggression when they are emotionally aroused, and especially when they are angry, in this book I will usually use the term "emotional aggression" when I discuss aggression that is aimed mainly at hurting another. It is important also to realize, however, that some persons have learned to enjoy inflicting pain on others because it gives them pleasure even when they are not emotionally aroused.

In a somewhat related vein, this chapter also argues that aggression is not always under attackers' complete and deliberate control, especially (but not only) when they are highly aroused. Whereas instrumentally oriented aggressors often have a definite purpose and match their actions to anticipated rewards, people who are engaged in hostile or emotional assaults sometimes attack their targets more strongly than they had consciously intended. Internal stimulation produced either by the emotional occurrence or by another instigating condition "pushes out" their aggressive reactions. Certain features of the external situation that have an aggressive meaning for the aggressors or that are associated in their minds with a provocateur's pain can intensify this internal, aggression-impelling stimulation, thereby strengthening the attack.

In conclusion, this chapter has offered definitions of "anger," "hostility," and "aggressiveness" in the interest of clarity and precision. *Anger* in common parlance typically refers to particular feelings, certain expressive-motor responses throughout the body, particular physiological reactions, and even overt physical and/or verbal assaults. However, since these different response systems are usually only weakly intercorrelated, I will use the term "anger" only in referring to experiences or feelings. *Hostility* is defined simply as a negative or unfavorable attitude toward one or more other persons, but it is recognized that this negative attitude is usually accompanied by a desire to see the attitude object suffer in some way. Finally, *aggressiveness* refers to a relatively persistent readiness to become aggressive in a variety of different situations. People who are high in aggressiveness in this sense are not necessarily angry, since they may not have recognizable angry feelings during much of the time that they are behaving aggressively.

*N*OTES

1. Straus, Gelles, & Steinmetz (1980), p. 3.
2. Storr (1968), p. x.
3. Buss (1961).
4. Bandura (1973).
5. See Kadushin & Martin (1981).
6. Straus, Gelles, & Steinmetz (1980), p. 31.
7. Patterson (1975, 1979).
8. See especially Tedeschi (1983).
9. Cited in Pagelow (1984), p. 77.
10. Gelles (1983). The quotation is from p. 157.
11. Toch (1969).
12. Felson (1978).
13. Dollard, Miller, Doob, Mowrer, & Sears (1939), p. 11.
14. Baron (1979), p. 7.
15. Feshbach (1964).
16. Front page story, *New York Times,* Nov. 2, 1990.
17. Baron (1977), pp. 260–263.
18. Chapter 14 provides an extensive discussion of this method of measuring aggression, as well as discussions of other procedures that are also frequently employed in research on aggression.
19. Dollard et al., (1939), p. 45.
20. Cited in Mulvihill & Tumin (1969).
21. Swart & Berkowitz (1976).

PART 1

❖

Emotional Aggression

ggression can be cold and calculated, an instrumental action carried out deliberately and to achieve a purpose other than injuring the victim, but it can also be an emotional reaction governed primarily by the desire to hurt someone. In either sort of aggression, the attackers may devote considerable thought to how they will accomplish their aggression goals, but they very often react impulsively and with little thought. Their assaults are propelled largely by the emotional agitation inside them and are steered, to some extent and in a fairly automatic manner, by the qualities of the available targets.

Here is an actual case that illustrates what I have in mind:

A mother [who was] reported for abuse lived with her husband and 4-year-old child in a rented, single back bedroom in the apartment of a friend. The landlady complained constantly about the child's behavior, claiming she was destructive.

On the early evening of the abuse event, the mother was cooking supper and the child went to the bathroom to wash up. The mother, a diabetic, was not feeling well ("It's been a long time since I knew what to feel good was"). After washing, the child, as reported by the mother, poured out the toothpaste and the shampoo and mixed a whole bunch of stuff in the sink, smeared lipstick over the bathroom toilet seat and pulled the curtains down in the bathroom. And the landlady came out screaming, "Look what your daughter did to my things. She done messed up this here, she done messed up that,' and I was already tired and just aggravated. I had been telling her all day long constantly, "Julia, don't do," and I had been talking all day and I just got tired of talking. So we went on and I—I just whupped her. I just got in that room, I picked her up, I'll never forget it—I was so mad at Julia I could have killed her."[1]

25

A sad story: A harried mother, ill and evidently worn down by poverty, loses her temper at her disobedient child, and lashes out in a burst of rage. There must be many hundreds of similar cases. Don't assume these are only rare incidents that have few counterparts in our own daily lives. Surely, like the mother in the case just cited, most of us have lost our temper at one time or another and have struck at an offending person—a child, a loved one, an acquaintance, or maybe even a stranger—either physically or verbally or both. The mother seemed to have a good excuse: She wasn't feeling well, and her daughter was downright naughty. Still, she overreacted, and she hurt her child severely. Haven't many of us also overreacted at one time or another (even though we may not have seriously injured anyone)? We have all seen people become strongly enraged by mild annoyances, perhaps because they were also bothered at the time by an external stress or by a headache, fatigue, or unpleasant heat. Sometimes, the result is a stronger attack than the person consciously intended. The mother in the case cited above probably hadn't wanted to hurt her daughter badly; she was probably carried away by her intense emotion.

WHAT IS EMOTIONAL AGGRESSION?

It is important for you to be clear on just how I conceive of emotional aggression. Let me summarize my thinking: I basically view this kind of aggression as being impelled by intense physiological and motor reactions within the individual.[2] Internal agitation is the instigation to aggression (or to an aggressive inclination) that "pushes out" the attempts to injure the target. If the person who makes such an attack is intensely aroused, I might even say, more dramatically, that a "fury" impels the physical and/or verbal assault.

Impulsive (or Expressive) Emotional Aggression

Remember, though, that this behavior is *emotional* (or hostile) aggression and is motivated more by an urge to injure the target rather than by a wish to achieve some other purpose. Moreover, I hold that in many cases (but not always) the aggressive action is carried out with relatively few complicated thoughts and plans—although hostile ideas and memories might well accompany the aggressive urge.

This means, first of all, that the attack isn't entirely premeditated. Julia's mother hadn't planned to beat her child. Also, the emotionally aroused attacker typically doesn't think of the long-term consequences, just as the mother didn't consider the possible long-term effects of her assault. Most homicides are of this nature. As one sociologist put it, the killings "are not morally self-conscious acts on the order of calculated political assassinations or coldly executed acts of vengeance. They emerge quickly, are fiercely impassioned, and are conducted with an indifference to the legal consequences. . . . The attacks are conducted within the spirit of a quickly developing rage."[3] In a phrase, the highly emotional action is largely impulsive.

Such impulsive (or involuntary or expressive) behavior is most likely to occur when the person is strongly aroused. The abusive mother was furious; and most murderers are enraged when they kill their victims. Even relatively unemotional and calculated aggressive activity can have an impulsive, expressive component.

Other Possible Aggressive Aims

Aggressors who are emotionally aroused and want strongly to hurt their intended target can have any number of other aims as well: eliminating a disturbing state of affairs, restoring a threat-weakened self-concept, regaining a sense of power and control, enhancing their social status, winning approval from others, and so on.[4] Their actions may even be motivated by a desire to assert their basic values—to preserve what they believe is right.[5] Child abusers often claim they struck their young victims to make them behave properly. Many of them think their victims deliberately violated their prescriptions, much as Julia had flagrantly disobeyed her mother, and they hit the youngster (they say) in order to assert their authority and preserve discipline.[6]

They May Also Want to Hurt

Whatever other goals highly aroused persons may have, we must remember that they also want to hurt their targets. They may be gratified if they can assert their power or control over their victim, or maintain their values, but deep down—and at times more than anything else—they are trying to hurt the persons they are attacking.

A good deal of evidence supports this idea. Chapter 1 showed that people who have been provoked can be pleased to learn that they are hurting their offenders. When they get this information soon after they start attacking, it can stimulate them to assault their tormentors even more severely. Later in this book you'll see that angered persons calm down and may even cease attacking their offenders when they think that they have done sufficient harm.

Of course, people don't always want to admit that they're seeking to injure their victims. It's more acceptable to cloak one's aggression in a moral purpose. Nevertheless, every once in a while an angry person will acknowledge the desire to hurt the offending party. Some years ago, in two separate studies, my associates and I interviewed violent criminals in English and Scottish prisons about the assaults for which they had been sentenced. Among other things, we asked these men what they had hoped to do when they struck their victim. Many of them (over 40 percent in both samples) indicated that they had deliberately tried to hurt the individuals. (Interestingly, in both groups the next most frequent desire was to protect themselves.)

Though it's important to recognize the difference between emotional aggression and instrumental aggression, many aggressive actions are a mixture of these two types, not one or the other. The abuse carried out by Julia's harried mother could well have been prompted both by her emotional agitation and by her desire to assert her authority over her rebellious daughter. Similarly, a highly aggressive boy might get into a fight with a classmate partly because he was infuriated by what he thought was the other child's insult but also because he believed he could gain status with his peers by showing how tough he was. By this point my argument should be clear: Just as it would be a mistake to think that all emotionally driven aggression is carried out entirely in a blind rage, we also would neglect an important aspect of this behavior if we thought it was only an attempt to satisfy some external purpose such as the attainment of power or status.

Even though acts of aggression serve a variety of purposes and are governed by many different influences, in Chapters 2 and 3 I will focus on instances in which the behavior is largely aimed at hurting someone. More than anything else, I will be concerned with factors affecting impulsive (or expressive) aggression which is done with little premeditation or planning and from which there is relatively little to be gained— other than the pleasure of doing injury. The largest part of this discussion will deal with the conditions that are at the root of this emotional aggression. Chapter 2 will give extensive consideration to the classic idea that emotional aggression is basically instigated by a frustration. Chapter 3 will modify this proposition by arguing that negative affect produces aggressive inclinations (but not necessarily open attacks). Chapter 3 will also demonstrate that the impulsive aspect of emotional aggression can be influenced by certain stimuli in the surrounding situation. The emphasis, in other words, will be on relatively nonthoughtful aggression. In a sense, this is our baseline: what people are apt to do when they are emotionally provoked and aren't thinking much about either the cause of their arousal or how they should react.

All this is not to say, of course, that thoughts have little influence on emotional behavior. Aroused persons obviously are affected by what they regard as the cause of their arousal and even by how they interpret their emotional state. Chapter 4 will therefore discuss the effects of thoughts, interpretations, and purposes upon people's responses to distressing events. I will also attempt to relate my analysis to contemporary psychological theories of emotion and therefore, I will offer you a brief summary of the latest theoretical formulations in this field before presenting my own conception of the development and operation of anger.

One final word. My dwelling on emotional aggression certainly does not imply that instrumental aggression is unimportant or rare. Obviously, people often assault their fellows in the hope of gaining some benefits, and indeed, I will discuss this type of behavior frequently throughout this book. Nevertheless, behavioral scientists and mental health professionals have not, in my estimation, given sufficient attention to emotionally impelled aggression. I am attempting to achieve a balance.

NOTES

1. Kadushin & Martin (1981), p. 154.
2. Some suggestive evidence indicates that certain specific motor reactions are involved in this instigation to aggression. Thus, in an experiment by Kelly & Hake (1970), youths who were unexpectedly deprived of anticipated monetary payments for a particular kind of behavior showed an increased tendency to punch an available object and a decreased tendency to merely press a button. In other words, humans may be "preprogrammed" to react to a sudden thwarting with a punching action. The internal stimulation involved in the instigation to aggression may thus consist partly of the internal motor reactions that lead to a punch. Of course, the instigation to aggression may have other components as well. Some of these may have to do with the motor reactions that lead to "angry" facial reactions. Thus, Hutchinson, Pierce, Emley, Proni, & Sauer (1977) have presented evidence that "in humans, jaw contractions appear to be a sensitive and valid measure of the propensity to attack" (p. 241).
3. Katz (1988), p. 18.
4. See, for example, Baron (1977), pp. 260–263.
5. See Berkowitz (1986), pp. 98–99.
6. Dollard, Doob, Miller, Mowrer, & Sears (1939). In this monograph the authors noted that William McDougall and Sigmund Freud, in his early works, had traced aggression to prior frustrations, even though they believed that other human actions were largely governed by inborn instincts (see pp. 20–21).

2

Effects of Frustrations

❖

The 1939 Frustration-Aggression Hypothesis ◆ *Definition and Basic Propositions*
◆ *Applying the Frustration-Aggression Hypothesis* ◆ *Do Only Some Kinds of
Frustrations Produce Aggression?* ◆ *Frustrations Can Lead to Aggression even when
the Thwarting Is Not a Deliberate Mistreatment* ◆ *Some Conditions that Increase the
Likelihood of Aggressive Reactions to Frustration* ◆ Revising the Frustration-
Aggression Hypothesis ◆ *Attributions Influence the Degree of Felt Displeasure* ◆
Can Frustrations and Insults Be Compared?

The most popular theory of aggression in the social sciences holds that people are driven to attack others when they are frustrated: when they are
unable to reach their goals, or they do not obtain the rewards they expect.
This theory would say, then, that the mistreatment cited earlier, the beating of a
daughter by an abusive mother, was caused by the thwartings the mother had
suffered: her failure to achieve the comfortable home life and material possessions she had hoped for and expected, the restrictions imposed upon her by the
absence of privacy and her landlady's demands, her daughter's disobedience,
and all the other ways in which her hopes had been dashed.

This theory deserves a fairly close look because of its historic importance in
the social sciences, because of the hundreds and hundreds of investigations it has
prompted, and, above all, because it is so widely accepted. I'll first summarize
what is undoubtedly the best-known and most precise statement of this theory,
and then I will offer a modification.

*T*HE 1939 FRUSTRATION-AGGRESSION
HYPOTHESIS

Although a number of writers dating back to the earliest days of scientific psychology have suggested that frustrations frequently produce aggressive reactions, a group of Yale University social scientists, led by John Dollard, Neal Miller, Leonard Doob, O.H. Mowrer, and Robert Sears, are the most famous proponents of this general idea. In a now classic monograph, *Frustration and Aggression,* first published in 1939, they spelled out clearly what they meant by "frustration" and listed some of the factors that they believed would influence the intensity of the resulting aggressive urge.

Definition and Basic Propositions

What Is a Frustration? Like "aggression," the word "frustration" has all too many different meanings. Even psychologists don't agree among themselves about just what is a frustration; for some the term refers to an *external barrier* that keeps someone from reaching a goal, while others think of "frustration" as an *internal emotional reaction* that arises from the thwarting (as when we say we "feel frustrated"). Dollard and his associates had the former meaning in mind. I can translate their technical terminology into everyday language by saying that they basically defined *frustration* as an external condition that prevents a person from obtaining the pleasures he or she had expected to enjoy.[1]

From this point of view, a frustration is not the same thing as the mere absence of a reward. The desirable outcome has to have been expected. Nor are privations necessarily frustrations. Poverty obviously keeps people from obtaining many of the good things of life, but, if we follow the Dollard group's definition, economic hardship is frustrating only to the degree that it prevents poor persons from getting what they had wanted and expected. Strictly speaking, we can't frustrate those who have no hope. The great nineteenth-century commentator on American society Alexis de Tocqueville voiced essentially this same conception of frustration when he noted that the lessening of tyranny can actually promote political unrest. A nation's citizens might "patiently endure" mistreatment as long as "it seemed beyond redress." However, de Tocqueville observed, once the possibility of having their grievances alleviated crosses people's minds, oppression becomes no longer tolerable. Whereas once they were only apathetic, now (from this perspective), with the coming of hope, they become actively resentful.[2] The student protests in China in May and June of 1989 can certainly be understood this way. The government's economic liberalization and the introduction of western technology had awakened the young people's hope for political liberalization. The political repression which they had previously suffered in silence became an evil which they could no longer accept.

The Frustration-Aggression Relationship. Dollard and his colleagues believed that *every* aggressive action could ultimately be traced to a previous frustration. However, as I have noted in several earlier papers,[3] this is much too sweeping a statement and fails to draw the important distinction between emotional aggression and instrumental aggression. Instrumental aggression can be learned, much as other instrumental actions are learned—by seeing that this behavior pays off—and need not be derived from some prior thwarting. It's probably better to restrict the frustration-aggression relationship somewhat, and to say that *a barrier to expected goal attainment generates an instigation to emotional aggression*—an inclination to hurt someone primarily for the sake of inflicting injury.

Having spelled out their basic proposition, the Yale theorists then turned to the factors that could influence the intensity of the thwarting-produced aggressive urge. I'll summarize their analysis, and then we'll see how well it applies to a situation most of you are familiar with.

Again rewording the original terminology, for Dollard and his colleagues the strength of the frustration-generated instigation to aggression is in direct proportion to the amount of satisfaction the thwarted individual had (1) anticipated and (2) failed to obtain. More specifically, they argued that when people are unexpectedly kept from achieving their goals, they will be more inclined to hurt someone (1) the greater was the satisfaction they had expected, (2) the more completely they are prevented from obtaining any satisfactions whatsoever, and (3) the more often their attempts to reach the goal are thwarted.

Open Aggression Is Not Inevitable: Alternative Responses to Frustration. The 1939 theorists recognized, of course, that not every frustration leads to open aggression. In their original monograph, they basically attributed the nonaggressive reactions to either a very weak aggressive urge or inhibitions against aggression aroused by the threat of punishment. Obviously, we'll hold back and not hit someone nearby if we think the action will get us into serious trouble. However, there's at least one more reason open aggression may not occur. Two years after the monograph was published, Neal Miller, an important member of the 1939 group, pointed to yet another factor that can also affect the likelihood of an aggressive response: whether the individual has developed other ways of reacting to frustrations. In his 1941 paper, Miller maintained that frustrations give rise to a number of different inclinations, only one of which is the instigation to aggression. A person who is prevented from reaching a goal might want to do several things at the same time, although not all to the same degree. He or she might, for example, want to escape from the unpleasant situation, to overcome the difficulty, to develop alternative goals, and to attack the obstacle. These other, nonaggressive inclinations might be stronger than the aggressive urge and thus might mask the aggressive tendency. However, Miller suggested, if the frustration were to continue, the alternative instigations would diminish in strength while the aggressive inclination would correspondingly intensify, and there would then be an increased probability of an open assault on an available target.[4]

Although Miller didn't come right out and say this, his modification obviously implies that people can learn nonaggressive ways of reacting to frustrations—and this is clearly true. For example, our childhood experiences may teach us that it pays to respond constructively when we are kept from achieving our goals. Later in life, then, we might apply this learning when we're frustrated; that is, we might try to overcome obstacles in a rational and nonemotional manner. On the other hand, we may find as we grow up that we often get what we want when we attack those who thwart us. As a consequence, we may be especially likely to become aggressive when our expectations aren't met. Even the rewards we obtain for nonaggressive conduct in general can influence what we do when our hopes are dashed. In general, children who have been rewarded for acting in a nonaggressive manner are relatively unlikely to become assaultive when they cannot get what they want.[5]

All this doesn't mean, however, that the frustration-aggression thesis is necessarily invalid. Learning and experience can *modify* the chances (that is, they can increase or decrease the likelihood) goal attainment will lead to open aggression, but there still can be *some* probability that a frustration will produce an instigation to aggression.

Applying the Frustration-Aggression Hypothesis

Now I'll apply this analysis to a situation that's familiar to most of us—a football game—and will try to show that many apparent exceptions to the theory actually can be understood from the perspective of the theory.

On any given weekend in the fall, millions of Americans watch two teams of young men repeatedly undergo a series of frustrations. They see the opposing players push, pummel, block, and batter each other. One team strives with force and determination to score a touchdown, and their rivals try equally hard to keep them from achieving their aim. Imagine a forward pass. A player races down the field, suddenly swerves to one side (leaving the defensive back following him far behind), and catches the football that is thrown to him, in a superb demonstration of athletic ability. Before the receiver can get very far, however, he is tackled by another member of the opposing team and hurled to the ground. Isn't he frustrated? He hadn't run more than a few yards with the ball, and he didn't even get close to the goal line. What does the pass receiver do, however, when he picks himself up? Does he assault his tackler or scream at him in anger? No, as most TV viewers can attest, there is a very good chance that he will only give his opponent a friendly pat on the behind and run back to his team in apparent good humor.

This commonplace occurrence seems to be a fairly severe test of the frustration-aggression hypothesis. Why don't the football players become increasingly aggressive as the game continues and they are repeatedly kept from reaching their goal? As I'll show you later, competition can generate an instigation to aggression. Instead of becoming violent, however, the contestants seem to have remarkably little antagonism toward each other. Of course, the players may have inhibited their aggressive tendencies because of the threat of penalties for "unsportsmanlike conduct," or they may have learned other, nonaggressive ways of reacting to frustrations. Nevertheless, in most games there's very little evidence that the players have aggressive desires.

One possibility is that the players aren't aggressive because they actually haven't been frustrated. As mentioned before, we can't say that people are frustrated unless they had been expecting to attain their goals. Maybe the pass receiver in this hypothetical example had only hoped to catch the ball and hadn't expected to gain much distance. From his perspective, then, not only was he not really thwarted when he didn't score a touchdown but also he obtained the gratification of catching the pass.

Then too, according to the 1939 analysis, we also have to wonder whether the players are strongly frustrated. Remember that the intensity of the aggressive urge produced by an interference with goal attainment is theoretically in direct proportion to the amount of satisfaction that had been expected. These anticipated pleasures should increase as the individual comes closer to the goal. Both theory and research tell us that we don't usually think much about the joys of goal attainment when we're far from a goal we desire, but that we do begin to anticipate these pleasures as we get closer to it. If we apply this point to the football game, we see that the players may not think much about the pleasures of victory at the start of the contest and, as a consequence, may not be especially bothered by their opponents' actions early in the game. Presumably, they would be much more aggressively aroused if they were defeated in the last seconds of the contest after having led their opponents up until that moment—if they had been strongly anticipating the joys of victory, but their hopes were suddenly dashed.

Do Only Some Kinds of Frustrations Produce Aggression?

I have indicated how the Dollard group's 1939 analysis would explain the relative absence of violent outbursts on the football field. Is this all there is to it? Are there any other reasons football players don't show high levels of frustration-produced aggression?

A number of social scientists were quick to criticize the frustration-aggression hypothesis practically as soon as the 1939 monograph was published.[6] One theme was frequently voiced in these objections: Only some kinds of frustrations produce aggressive tendencies. We don't become aggressive, these critics argued, simply because we're prevented from reaching our goals. We're provoked only when we believe the interference was unfair—arbitrary or illegitimate—or was directed at us personally.

Only Arbitrary (Illegitimate) Frustrations

Nicholas Pastore made this point in a study that is well known to aggression researchers.[7] Ten frustrating situations were described to college students. They were asked to imagine each one and then indicate how they would react. In one condition, the set consisted of ten "arbitrary" frustrations such as, "You're waiting on the right corner for a bus, and the driver intentionally passes you by." The other set, by contrast, listed ten "nonarbitrary" thwartings, including this variation on the bus incident: "You're waiting on the right corner for a bus. You notice that it is a special on its way to the garage." Not surprisingly, the students reported that they would be far more likely to become angry or have aggressive reactions in response to the "arbitrary" frustrations.

We can question some aspects of Pastore's study, including the validity of the students' reports; after all, they may not have wanted to admit that they would be provoked by the apparently legitimate frustrations.[8] Still, there's no doubt but that people are more strongly provoked when they regard interference with their goal attainment as unfair (or arbitrary or illegitimate) rather than in accord with social rules.[9] In the football example, critics might say the players aren't more aggressive during the contest because they view the frustrations they experience during the game as entirely legitimate. They know that their opponents are only following the rules in trying to stop them from scoring a touchdown. The players might become infuriated, however, if they thought an opponent was violating the rules and "playing dirty."

"Arbitrary" thwartings as violations of expectancy. Pastore tried to limit the frustration-aggression hypothesis by suggesting that only arbitrary thwartings which violate people's rules of conduct produce aggressive tendencies. However, the apparent arbitrariness of a frustration can actually be understood within the terms of the original 1939 formulation and thus doesn't really limit this analysis. More than a generation ago, John Kregarman and Philip Worchel pointed out that an arbitrary (or illegitimate) interference with goal attainment is usually unexpected. If we're waiting at a bus stop and see the bus "arbitrarily" pass by without stopping, as in one of Pastore's incidents, the bus driver's failure to stop is surprising as well as a violation of the rules.[10] Could it be, then, that we are strongly bothered by an illegitimate barrier to a desired goal at least partly because it is unexpected?

Failure to obtain anticipated pleasures as a determinant of aggression. According to the reasoning I have been spelling out here, when people expect to reach a certain goal or to obtain a certain reward, they are basically anticipating the pleasures this goal or reward would bring them. Furthermore, the greater the pleasure they are expecting, the more they will be provoked when their hopes are dashed. Very much in line with this analysis, an interesting experiment by Stephen Worchel indicates that a frustration will produce the strongest aggressive inclinations when (1) the obtained outcome is much less attractive than the preferred outcome and (2) the person had been anticipating the pleasures of achieving the desired result.[11]

In this study, the subjects, male undergraduates, were led to think they would receive one of three different prizes for serving in the experiment: an hour's credit for experimental service, a bottle of men's cologne, or $5 in cash. First the men rated the attractiveness of the prizes. Then the experimenter varied the extent to which the subjects anticipated the pleasure they would feel on obtaining the prize: One-third of the subjects were led to think about the satisfaction that getting this particular item would bring them. (Let's call this the *high satisfaction anticipation* group.) Another third were told that they would be given the item they had rated as most attractive but weren't otherwise encouraged to think of the prize. (We'll term this the *moderate satisfaction anticipation* group.) The remaining men were simply informed that the experimenter's assistant would give them one of the three available prizes, but which one was not specified. (This will be called the *no anticipation* group.)

Once these differences in anticipation were established, the experimenter created different degrees of disappointment: The men worked on several tasks and then, supposedly at the conclusion of the session, the experimenter's assistant "paid them off" by giving them one of the prizes. Within each anticipation group, one-third received the prize they had previously rated as most attractive, another third received their second most attractive prize, and the others were given their least desirable prize. The researcher ascertained the subjects' hostility by asking them to rate how well the experimenter's assistant had conducted the experiment. Figure 2–1 summarizes the findings.

As you can see, and very much in line with my analysis, the less attractive the outcome was to the subjects, the more hostile they tended to be toward the person who gave them the prize—but this was primarily true when they had been anticipating the satisfaction the preferred reward would bring them. The greater the disparity between what they

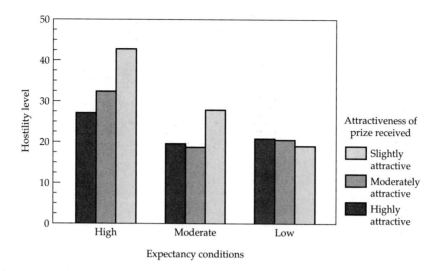

FIGURE 2-1

Hostility toward prize dispenser (indexed by subject's ratings of his performance in the experiment) as a function of reward expectancy. (Adapted from Worchel (1974), The effects of three types of arbitrary thwarting on the instigation to aggression. *Journal of Personality*, 42, copyright Duke University Press, 1974.)

had wanted and what they actually received, the stronger was the resulting hostility.

These results highlight an important phenomenon: A failure to obtained anticipated satisfactions can produce an urge toward aggression. I'm convinced that we see this type of reaction in many different areas of life, and I also think that this phenomenon is involved in the social unrest and even revolutions that can occur when rapidly rising expectations are not met. Because of the social significance of this matter, I'll have more to say about dashed expectations later. In the meantime, let's go on with objections to the original frustration-aggression hypothesis.

Thwartings Attributed to Another's Deliberate Misbehavior

Most of the objections raised nowadays against the Dollard group's analysis basically maintain that the thwarting has to be attributed to someone's deliberate misdeed if it is to provoke aggression. This argument says we're not bothered by a failure to reach our goals unless we think the frustrater intentionally—and improperly—sought to interfere with our efforts. If a would-be pass receiver in a football game is tripped by the defensive player racing alongside him, and if he falls down before he can catch the pass thrown in his direction, this player supposedly won't become aggressive if he believes the tripping was accidental but will be provoked if he thinks it was deliberate. Since this contention seems very plausible and is widely accepted, let's examine it a bit more closely.

Attributing the frustration. This alternative interpretation holds that people's *attributions*—that is, what they regard as the source of the barrier to their attainment of a goal—determine how they will react to a frustration. In the *attribution theory* language that many social psychologists use in this kind of analysis, the thwarted person (the pass receiver, in the example I am using) presumably will become angry with the individual who thwarts his goal attainment (the defensive player) only if he attributes that person's interference (tripping him) to a cause that has certain characteristics. Specifically, the cause has to be viewed as *internal* (i.e., as lying within the interfering individual—for example, as being caused by that person's motivation or personality—rather than as arising from an external, situational pressure on that person), *controllable* (i.e., the other person deliberately carried out the behavior or at least could have avoided doing it if he had wanted to), and *improper* (i.e., in violation of generally accepted rules of conduct).[12] (I'll discuss attribution theory more fully in Chapter 4.)

Here again, no one will be surprised to hear that intentional misdeeds are apt to produce aggressive reactions. Indeed, if we're asked to recall an incident in which we became angry, there's a good chance we'll think of a time when someone deliberately wronged us. Averill has reported research results showing just this effect. He asked the community residents and university students who participated in his study to answer a series of questions about "the most intense episode of anger" they had experienced during the preceding week. In Averill's words,

> The vast majority of subjects indicated that the incident was either voluntary and unjustified (51%) or a potentially avoidable accident or event (31%). Relatively few persons became angry [about] events which they considered voluntary but justified (11%) or unavoidable (7%).[13]

In appraising the provocative event as "voluntary" or "potentially avoidable," these people basically said that they believed the occurrence was brought about by something inside the responsible individual (e.g., an intention) and that they thought this person had control over what he did. Moreover, in the majority of cases the provocation was regarded as unjustified, a violation of generally accepted rules of conduct.

Why Attributions Can Influence Aggressive Reactions

Restraining aggressive inclinations. I'll go into this somewhat more fully in Chapter 4, but for now let me suggest some reasons these attributions often lead to relatively strong aggressive reactions. First, as I indicated in my discussion of arbitrary or illegitimate frustrations, many of us are apt to restrain ourselves when we attribute the thwarting to an accidental cause that was not directed against us personally. In my hypothetical football game, the pass receiver could believe it isn't socially proper to be angered by accidental events. Thus he might keep himself from assaulting his opponent and might even deny that he is angry, if he thinks the defensive player's interference is inadvertent.

An experiment by Eugene Burnstein and Philip Worchel, reported more than a generation ago, suggests the operation of this kind of inhibition against aggression. The researchers assembled groups of male undergraduates and required them to reach a unanimous decision on an assigned problem. In each of the two frustration conditions, the group found they could not complete their task within the allotted time because one person (who was actually the experimenters' confederate playing a part) persisted in asking questions. In the *nonarbitrary frustration* condition, the group members saw that this individual had an acceptable reason for his behavior (he wore a hearing aid, apparently because of a hearing difficulty), whereas there was no clearly acceptable reason for the interfering confederate's behavior in the *arbitrary frustration* condition. Burnstein and Worchel then obtained various measures of the group members' attitudes toward the confederate. What's most important for us here, the naive subjects were allowed to reject one member of their group and to prevent him from participating in a later session. The persons in the arbitrarily frustrated condition, who were thwarted by the confederate's seemingly inexplicable interruptions, unanimously, and publicly, voted to exclude him from future participation. By contrast, there was no such complete public rejection of the confederate when he seemed to have a good reason for his repeated question-asking, in the nonarbitrary frustration condition. Even so, however, these latter subjects expressed an unfavorable view of the frustrating confederate on a measure they believed would not be made known to the others in their group. They evidently were fairly hostile to him inwardly but didn't want to reveal this openly.[14]

Interpreting the thwarting as a personal attack. Attributions undoubtedly affect more than inhibitions against aggression. Isn't it also likely that a frustrater's supposedly deliberate and controllable action will be regarded as a personal attack? If so, the failure to get what was wanted can be especially unpleasant. Not only are the expected pleasures not obtained, but the thought that the frustrater was personally offensive can be especially disturbing. The resulting strong displeasure can lead to fairly strong aggressive inclinations, as Chapter 3 will demonstrate.

Frustrations Can Lead to Aggression Even when the Thwarting Is Not a Deliberate Mistreatment

Here is the point I want to make: Though people's beliefs about what caused their frustration can influence the likelihood that they will attack someone openly, they can become aggressive even when they are only legitimately or accidentally kept from their goal. The aggressive urge may not always be visible, but still, there are times when even socially proper thwartings generate an inclination to aggression.

Naturalistic Observations

Studies in natural settings outside the laboratory point to aggressive reactions to frustration. To take just one example, recall that, in Averill's investigation of angering incidents, which I mentioned earlier, 11 percent of the participants reported being angered by someone's deliberate but socially appropriate behavior, and another 7 percent admitted being provoked by an unavoidable accident or event. These people didn't believe that they had been intentionally mistreated, but they still became angry when they were kept from obtaining a desired outcome. Even more of the participants might have acknowledged having experienced such a reaction if they had been totally frank.

Competition. What about competition? Does rivalry for scarce resources produce aggressive tendencies, as the frustration-aggression hypothesis would lead us to expect? I've already noted that competitive situations can be viewed as frustrations. After all, the contestants realize that their opponents might deprive them of the prize (or outcome) they desire, and this anticipated thwarting could conceivably give rise to aggressive inclinations. Then too, in many competitions the rivals actively interfere with each other's progress toward the goal, and this interference could also be frustrating.

Contrast this reasoning with another view of competition: that the rivalry can be beneficial. Psychodynamically oriented theorists and others, who contend that the human personality is a reservoir of pent-up energies, believe that we can find a safe outlet for our accumulated aggressive urges by struggling to beat our rivals in a legitimate contest. Thus, years ago, the famous psychiatrist William Menninger stated that competitive games can bring about a needed release from the tensions created by "instinctive" aggressive impulses. This aggressive discharge could be achieved in active sports, he maintained, but he thought that even "sedentary intellectual competition" such as chess or checkers could also have this benefit.[15]

Though this view of competition is widely accepted, studies have repeatedly shown that competition is likely to produce hostility and aggression rather than friendship. Moreover, this antagonism can arise even when the competition is legitimate and the rivalry takes place within established rules of conduct.

Muzafer and Carolyn Sherif[16] have given us one of the best-known demonstrations of this negative effect. This investigation, conducted at an isolated boys' camp ("Robbers Cave" in Oklahoma) with well-adjusted youngsters from middle-class, white, Protestant families, was divided into three stages. In the first phase, which lasted three days, campwide activities were carried out so that the researchers could determine which boys were friends. These friendships were then deliberately broken up in the second stage, which lasted five days. The youngsters were divided into two groups by assembling them with others for whom they had previously shown little liking. The two newly formed groups (the Rattlers and the Eagles) were kept separate during this second phase, so that the boys in both groups developed fairly close ties. In the last stage of the experiment, the Rattlers and the Eagles competed with each other in a series of games, for attractive prizes.

The boys did not resume their earlier friendships in these contests; instead, they were openly hostile toward the members of the opposite group, whom they now treated as rivals. They started by insulting each other, and then, as the games continued (and the frustrations were repeated), the rivalry occasionally flared into open aggression. The opposing groups "raided" each other's cabins, threw food at each other during mealtimes, and even scuffled with each other. The aggression soon became so strong that the researchers tried to promote peace by setting up a fireworks display for the boys to watch, showing them movies, and even bringing them together at a "brotherhood dinner." All this was to no avail. The two groups used the dinner as an occasion to declare "war" on each other. Competition had apparently led to hostility and aggression. Enmity overrode the friendships that had previously existed.

Don't conclude from the Sherifs' study that it is only children who are affected in this way and/or that the rivalry-generated aggression is only playful behavior. Even adults can become seriously antagonistic toward those with whom they compete for scarce resources. For that matter, not only men but also women can become aggressive toward opponents. According to some reports, women in the African nation of Zambia are often overtly aggressive toward each other because of their competition for socially desirable men.[17]

Experimental Findings

Laboratory studies of competition. A considerable body of laboratory research also attests to the frequent negative effects of competition. I won't give you a survey of all the studies that show this outcome, but two are of special interest.

In one of these, Worchel, Andreoli, and Folger[18] created a carefully controlled laboratory analog of the Sherifs' field experiment and obtained conceptually similar results. In the part of their investigation that most concerns us here, university men and women who were assembled in a group developed ill will toward another group merely because they thought they were in competition.

A second experiment suggests that the competition's outcome can influence the strength of the rivalry-activated aggressive inclinations. In this study, pairs of first-grade children played either noncompetitively or competitively. In the competitive contests, the experimenter manipulated the outcomes, unknown to the players, so that one of them won most of the games while the other youngster lost. The children were then separated and each one played with a number of toys while observers recorded their actions.

The youngsters who had just engaged in competitive games displayed much more make-believe aggression in their solitary play than did those who had not competed earlier. Of course, the competitors who had lost most of the contests showed the greatest amount of make-believe aggression, but even the winners tended to be somewhat more aggressive than the control subjects who had not been involved in rivalry. The competition apparently had generated aggressive inclinations in the youngsters, and moreover, we again see that this happened even though the rivalry was apparently a fair one that followed accepted rules.[19]

Mood improvement, not "energy" discharge. Because there is so much evidence showing that competition increases aggression (although some other studies have obtained different results), you might ask why so many persons believe that competition can reduce aggressive urges. A major reason, I suspect, is that we sometimes feel better after participating in a contest, and we mistakenly attribute this improvement in mood to a release of our aggressive energies. In actuality, however, we probably are happier because (1) we enjoyed the competition (maybe because we won) and (2) we were so involved in the contest that we stopped thinking about the events that had provoked us, and thus stopped stirring ourselves up. In either case, aggressive inclinations were no longer activated.

It's important to keep these possibilities in mind. They tell us that our urge to aggression can be reduced when our mood improves and when we cease brooding about the wrongs that we think have been done to us. I'll have more to say about this in Part 4, in discussing the control of aggression.

Infants' angry reactions to restraints. Another type of evidence supporting the frustration-aggression hypothesis may be of interest to you. During World War I, John B. Watson, one of the founding fathers of

behaviorism, proposed that anger was an innate reactic
When he and J. J. B. Morgan prevented young infants fr
pressing their arms to their sides and holding their leg;
found that the babies displayed strong signs of what
called "rage" ("anger," in my term), usually kicking and
with their arms and legs. However, other investigators ;
cate these results, and many child psychologists quest
young infants did indeed become angry when they couldn't move freely.

Stenberg and Campos resolved this controversy by studying infants'
facial reactions to restraints. Over the years Paul Ekman and his associates have shown that many emotional states are accompanied by specific facial expressions that evidently are inborn, not taught. When people are angry, for example, whether they live in a relatively undeveloped society or in a highly technical western culture, "the eyebrows are lowered and drawn together, the eyelids are tensed, and the eye appears to stare in a hard fashion.[20] Making use of these findings, Stenberg and Campos[21] set up an experiment in which a researcher held infants' arms against their sides (for no longer than three minutes) until the infants became upset. Video cameras recorded the children's facial and bodily reactions, and the films were carefully analyzed.

How the babies responded depended on how old they were. The 1-month-old infants' expressions indicated only pain and distress, whereas many of the 4-and 7-month-old babies also showed angry facial reactions. (Interestingly, the scoring method excluded signs of pain and discomfort, so that it was clear that the babies in the older group were not merely exhibiting a general unhappiness.)

For our purposes, what's important in this study is the evidence of an innate linkage between frustration and anger. Of course, we have to assume, and I believe it is reasonable to do so, that the older infants' facial expressions were indicative of what might be called "angry feelings" and that the restraint imposed upon them kept them from doing what they wanted to do.

Some Conditions that Increase the Likelihood of Aggressive Reactions to Frustration

I've acknowledged several times that not every frustration leads to an open attack on an available target. Obviously, a variety of conditions can influence the chances that people will become assaultive when they are prevented from reaching their goal. Some of these conditions have already been mentioned.

For one thing, the aggressive inclinations evoked by the thwarting may be suppressed because the frustrated persons think they will be punished in some way (at least by disapproval) if they are openly aggressive. These inhibitions are especially likely to arise, I've suggested, when people believe that the frustration is in keeping with social rules and isn't a personal attack. In other words, we're apt to think it's wrong to become aggressive if we have not been mistreated and if we have been legitimately—or accidentally—prevented from obtaining the satisfaction we expected.

Then too, as Neal Miller recognized in his 1941 modification of the original frustration-aggression hypothesis, many persons have learned to respond to frustrations in a nonaggressive manner. When they find themselves unable to reach the goal they desire, their initial inclination may be to do something other than assault the obstacle before them. For example, they may choose to eliminate the difficulty rationally, to pursue a substitute goal, or to retreat from the frustrating situation. Nonetheless, if the interference persists and/or is repeated, the instigation to aggression is likely to mount in intensity. The aggressive tendency will then become stronger than the inclination to react in an alternative, nonaggressive way.

Also remember that not every thwarting gives rise to a strong aggressive inclination. A number of factors can affect the strength of the urge to be aggressive, including how much satisfaction is expected and not achieved, how completely the person is prevented from obtaining satisfaction, and how often the person has previously failed to fulfill his or her desires.

REVISING THE FRUSTRATION-AGGRESSION HYPOTHESIS

Let's think about the factors that affect the aggressive urge. Why is it that they influence the intensity of the aggressive reaction to a frustration? The answer is neither particularly mysterious nor especially profound. Many conditions can determine how unpleasant the failure to attain the desired goal will be for the individual. Obviously, we will be more unhappy about not getting what we want if we had anticipated great pleasure than if we had expected only a small satisfaction. Also, the more completely we are kept from having any satisfactions at all, the more unhappy we will be. It is because of this felt displeasure, I hold, that a frustration produces an instigation to aggression.[22] The negative affect is the fundamental spur to the aggressive inclination.

This proposition gives us the major reason (but not necessarily the only one) football players don't become aggressive when they're kept from scoring a touchdown: They don't feel bad enough at the time. Similarly, if people become creative rather than antagonistic when they are thwarted, there's a good chance that the frustration hasn't made them decidedly unhappy.

Attributions Influence the Degree of Felt Displeasure

The same idea can be applied to my earlier discussion of the effect of attributions on responses to a thwarting. I contended that people are especially bothered when they believe the frustrater intentionally kept them from reaching their goal. I suggested that this situation is doubly unpleasant; the thwarted persons are not only unable to get the satisfactions they expected but also distressed by thinking someone wanted to mistreat them. In other words, by attributing the interference with their goal attainment to a cause that was internal to the frustrater, controllable by him or her, and in violation of social rules, they make themselves especially unhappy. In my view, this strong negative effect leads to the aggressive reactions that are often provoked by arbitrary and/or illegitimate frustrations.

Can Frustrations and Insults Be Compared?

Several writers have maintained that thwartings are only weak instigators to aggression and that they are thus much less important sources of aggression than are insults or threats to the self. To buttress this argument, they cite experiments in which subjects became much more aggressive after being insulted than after being blocked from reaching their goals.[23]

However, if it's the unpleasantness of a frustration that produces the aggressive inclination, we can't draw any such conclusion about frustrations in general. Some insults might not be particularly upsetting and some barriers to goal attainment can be decidedly bothersome. It's the degree of negative effect they generate that matters, not whether they are an insult or a thwarting. Indeed, I go even further and propose that *both* insults and frustrations tend to evoke instigations to aggression, because they are unpleasant.

SUMMARY

The chapters in Part 1 of this book examine the most important determinants of emotional aggression, starting with frustrations. Dollard, Miller, Doob, Mowrer, and Sears advanced the best-known version of the oftenstated frustration-aggression hypothesis, which holds that frustrations produce aggressive inclinations. When this technical but somewhat outmoded theory is translated into more contemporary terms, its central proposal (as far as we here are concerned) is that barriers to the attainment of expected goals generate an instigation to emotional aggression. These psychologists later acknowledged that frustrations give rise to several inclinations, only one of which is aggressive in nature. This implies that people can learn either (1) to respond nonaggressively to thwartings or (2) that aggressive responses to thwartings often "pay off." The frustration-aggression hypothesis basically suggests, however, that learning only modifies the frustration-aggression relationship and is not responsible for it.

Many of the objections that have been raised against this formulation can be overcome by a thoughtful application of the analysis put forth by Dollard and his associates, especially if we remember that (1) a frustration occurs when anticipated pleasures are not attained, and (2) the intensity of the resulting instigation to aggression is in direct proportion to the magnitude of the satisfactions that had been expected. Thus, whereas critics have argued that only illegitimate or arbitrary thwartings produce aggressive reactions, aggressive reactions to "nonarbitrary" frustrations could be absent, in part at least, because the affected individuals had not been anticipating the pleasure of achieving their goals, or at least had not been expecting to achieve their goals completely. Theoretically, therefore, they were not greatly frustrated. It is also possible that the affected persons may have inhibited whatever aggressive inclinations they might have had when they were "legitimately" blocked from reaching their goals, believing that aggression in these circumstances might be punished (or at least might incur social disapproval).

Introducing a proposition that will be developed more fully in Chapter 3, I suggest that frustrations generate aggressive tendencies only to the degree that they are unpleasant. An unexpected failure to attain anticipated satisfactions is much more unpleasant than an expected failure to achieve these rewards. This proposition can also explain why affected persons' attributions can influence the likelihood that they will become aggressive: If we (1) attribute to the frustrater's controllable behavior a barrier that prevents us from attaining our goals, (2) believe that the behavior is aimed at us personally, and (3) consider the behavior socially improper, the displeasure we feel about not reaching our goal is heightened. From this perspective, competition can generate aggressive inclinations; indeed, it often does so, because the rivalry may be unpleasant. In cases in which aggression does not arise, other influences lessen the felt displeasure, such as the joy of victory and/or the enjoyment of the activities involved in the contest.

Chapter 3 will present evidence indicating that people as well as animals are disposed to become aggressive when they are having unpleasant experiences.

NOTES

1. More specifically, the Yale group defined a frustration as "an interference with the occurrence of an instigated goal-response at its proper time in the behavior sequence"[Dollard et al.] (1939), p. 7].

2. The classic 1939 version of the frustration-aggression hypothesis would therefore hold that privations do not generate an instigation to aggression unless they are the nonfulfillment of an expected goal attainment. By contrast, in my revision of this formulation, I maintain that privations will generate aggressive inclinations to the degree that they are unpleasant. However, since the dashing of hope is usually more unpleasant than the dull flatness of no hope at all, most frustrations would probably give rise to a stronger instigation to aggression than would many privations.

3. For example, see Berkowitz (1989).

4. Miller (1941).

5. See Davitz (1952).

6. For example, see the symposium on the frustration-aggression hypothesis published in the 1941 volume of *Psychological Review*.

7. Pastore (1952).

8. There are some suggestive data in this regard in a variation of Pastore's research carried out by Cohen (1955).

9. See Berkowitz (1989) for a list of some of the experiments testifying to this difference.

10. Kregarman & Worchel (1961).

11. Worchel (1974).

12. See Weiner (1985); Weiner, Graham, & Chandler (1982).

13. Averill (1982), p. 171.

14. Burnstein & Worchel (1962).

15. Menninger (1942).

16. Sherif & Sherif (1953).

17. Schuster (1983).

18. Worchel, Andreoli, & Folger (1977).

19. Nelson, Gelfand, & Hartmann (1969).

20. Ekman & Friesen (1975), p. 82.

21. Stenberg & Campos (1990).

22. See Berkowitz (1989).

23. For example, Buss (1963, 1966). Also see Baron (1977).

3

We're Nasty When We Feel Bad

---------- ❖ ----------

He who much has suffer'd much will know.
Odyssey, Book 15, line 436. Pope translation

It is not true that suffering ennobles the character; . . . it makes men petty and vindictive.

W. Somerset Maugham, *The Moon and Sixpence*

*H*ere are two different notions about the effects of suffering. The first one, dating back to the ancient Greeks and undoubtedly shared by many societies around the world, basically holds that suffering can be good for us. The hardships we've endured, the troubles we've experienced, have supposedly enriched us in some way and may even have made us better persons. The second statement, from a novel by the English writer W. Somerset Maugham, which was published in 1919, is skeptical of this view, to say the least, and contends that pain breeds hostility.

There's probably more justification for Maugham's view than for that of the ancient Greeks. I'm not sure why so many people subscribe to the idea that suffering improves character. Perhaps we're looking for compensation, hoping that something good will come out of the bad. Maybe there have been a few instances in which adversity improved someone's personality, but this is probably a relatively rare occurrence. A rapidly growing body of evidence indicates that unpleasant events are far more likely to make people hostile and aggressive than to make them kind and virtuous.

NEGATIVE AFFECT AS THE ROOT OF EMOTIONAL AGGRESSION

In my own papers on this topic I have referred to the aggression evoked by negative occurrences as "aversively stimulated aggression," since the causal events are occurrences the person ordinarily would attempt to avoid. Other psychologists have used different labels, such as "irritable" aggression and "annoyance-motivated" aggression. While these terms are probably more familiar, I will employ my own phrase in this book in order to highlight two main points: (1) the instigation to aggression is produced by an unpleasant state of affairs, and (2) a wide range of aversive occurrences can have this effect.[1]

Without going into all the research on this topic, this chapter will give you some of the evidence on which this formulation is based. However, we all know that people aren't always nasty when they're feeling bad. They can control themselves and inhibit their aggressive inclinations. This research review will therefore end with a brief discussion of one of the factors that can promote such self-restraint. Chapter 4, which will deal primarily with the effects of thoughts and cognitive processes on emotional aggression, will go into these exceptions more extensively.

Animal Studies of Pain-Elicited Aggression

The best-known demonstrations that unpleasant events can evoke aggressive reactions were the animal experiments conducted by Nathan Azrin, Ronald Hutchinson, Roger Ulrich, and their associates.[2] In these studies, which employed a variety of species, when two animals cooped up together in a small chamber were exposed to noxious stimuli (such as physical blows or electric shocks), they frequently began to fight. Open aggression under such circumstances seems to be an inborn reaction to the physical distress, since it occurs fairly regularly, doesn't require any prior learning, and persists even in the absence of obvious rewards. All in all, although this reaction is by no means inevitable, animals of many different species are especially likely to assault a nearby victim when they are in pain.

Several important issues are raised by this research, and they are worth delving into. Some general principles in this regard are highly relevant to human emotional aggression.

Fight and Flight Tendencies Can Occur Together

One issue is whether the pain-elicited behavior is actually an offensive attack. Some psychologists have argued that pain-stimulated aggression is a defensive response that has little actual resemblance to self-initiated assaults. The afflicted animals are presumably only trying to protect themselves from the noxious stimulus.

This criticism has been answered. According to at least one researcher, pain-evoked behavior aggression probably has both offensive and defensive components.[3] The animals could well be attempting to defend themselves, but at the same time they might also be trying to hurt the available target. Pain, in other words, could activate both an intention to assault *and* an intention to hurt. Suggesting this, some studies (which are too involved to go into here) indicate that pain can generate an "appetite for aggression." They have demonstrated, among other things, that afflicted animals will work to obtain a target they can attack and may even continue to assault a suitable victim after the noxious stimulation is turned off, as if their suffering had given them something of a desire for aggression.[4]

The pain-instigated aggressive urge isn't always seen, however. In some species, the afflicted animals usually prefer to flee from the noxious stimulus rather than to attack an available target, indicating that the aggressive (or fight) tendencies activated by the painful stimulation are often weaker than the defensive, escape, and avoidance (or flight) inclinations. However, the instigation to aggression could still be present, even though it is masked by the stronger urge to flee, and it might well be revealed when the distressed animals cannot get away from the unpleasant stimulus.

Is the Aim of Aversively Stimulated Aggression Only the Cessation of the Noxious Stimulation?

A question that is somewhat related to this point is, What are the animals trying to do when they attack something in response to the noxious event? Writers who view pain-elicited aggression as a defensive reaction obviously believe that the fighting is aimed at the reduction or elimination of the unpleasant stimulation. Using the technical language of psychology, they say the aggression is "negatively reinforced." This means that the organism's action is rewarded by a negative event, the lessening or absence of some occurrence—such as the reduction or cessation of the painful stimulus. To use a more specific example, in the child abuse case cited on page 25, the mother's aggression would be negatively reinforced if it forced her daughter Julia to stop annoying her (i.e., if the mother's punishment lessened the unpleasant event).

There's little doubt that pain-elicited aggression can be negatively reinforced. To cite only one bit of evidence, in an experiment with rats by John Knutson and his associates at Iowa,[5] if the fighting provoked by electric shocks was soon followed by the ending of the painful stimulation, the animals were more likely to act aggressively again the next time they received the noxious treatment. It's as if the rats believed their aggression had paid off—had eliminated what was bothering them—and this negative reinforcement then strengthened their tendency to react aggressively when they were again provoked.

However, the aggressive reaction isn't only an attempt to eliminate or reduce an unpleasant stimulation. Pained animals can also be *positively* reinforced by the opportunity to attack a suitable victim. The Knutson experiment mentioned above obtained one indication of this. In one condition tested in the experiment, though shocked rats fought with a peer, their attacks were not followed by the elimination of the painful shocks. These animals also were later relatively highly aggressive in response to further shocks, even though they had not learned that their attacks would end the unpleasant state of affairs. You'll see other evidence consistent with this finding throughout this chapter.

Human Aggression in Response to Aversive Events

People sometimes react to aversive conditions just as animals do. Moreover, in human beings, as in other animal species, an impressive variety of unpleasant events can provoke aggressive behavior.

The Great Variety of Negative Conditions that Can Evoke Aggression

Aggressive reactions to unpleasantly high temperatures. Take high temperatures as a case in point. Have you ever found yourself in a very hot room that you couldn't leave for several hours, for one reason or another? If you're like many other persons, according to a growing body of research,[6] there's a good chance that you became irritable and perhaps even openly hostile.

Shakespeare was aware of how tempers are frayed and irritability mounts when the weather is unpleasantly hot. Benvolio, a character in *Romeo and Juliet,* warns that the heat might lead to a fight with members of the rival Capulet family:

> I pray thee, good Mercutio, let's retire:
> The day is hot, the Capulets abroad,
> And, if we meet, we shall not 'scape a brawl;
> For now these hot days is the mad blood stirring.

Benvolio was right to be concerned. Fights become more likely as temperatures become extremely high, and indeed, all kinds of aggression become more frequent.

Riots and Heat: Urban Disorders in the "Long Hot Summers." In his 1989 movie *Do the Right Thing*, writer-director-actor Spike Lee vividly portrayed the onset of a race riot in a heat spell. If other conditions are right, unpleasantly high temperatures can promote urban disorders.

We actually saw this in the summer of 1967, when a series of riots broke out in a number of U.S. cities. As urban blacks protested against their underprivileged status in American society and as the violence spread from one community to another, the mass media spoke of "a long hot summer." Although the journalists may not have realized it, their phrase was more than a metaphor. Unusual heat apparently played a part in the violence. When Goranson and King checked the temperatures in the seventeen cities that had major riots that summer, they found a relationship between weather and violence. It had not been unusually hot in these communities until the day before the outbreak of the disorders, when, in fifteen of the seventeen cities, there was a sharp rise in temperature. The end of the heat waves may have helped to "cool things off," figuratively as well as literally. Temperatures generally dropped sooner in the cities that had shorter riots than in the communities that had longer disorders.

The hot weather's effect on the urban riots wasn't limited to 1967. Baron and Ramsberger determined what the temperatures had been during 102 instances of collective violence in the United States from 1967 through 1971, and found that the disorders had generally taken place in hot spells. Other social psychologists who have examined the analysis by Baron and Ramsberger have reported that there was indeed a regular relationship between very hot weather and the urban violence of these years.[7]

We can extend this idea even further. Other forms of antisocial behavior are evidently also spurred by unusual heat. You'll see in Chapters 8 and 9 that violent offenses tend to occur more frequently on very hot days.

Under the Heat in the Laboratory. Of course, evidence can be interpreted in a number of ways, and we can't really be sure, on the basis of the findings about urban riots, that high temperatures provoked aggressive tendencies. The heat may have driven more people out into the city streets in search of a cooling breeze, so that they came into contact with their neighbors and were readily influenced by what they saw and heard.

Only in laboratory experiments can such alternative explanations be ruled out.

In one of the first social psychological experiments to investigate the effects of unpleasant heat, Griffitt demonstrated that his subjects were harsher in their judgments of a same-sex stranger when they were in a high-temperature environment than when they were in a comfortably cool room. This general finding has been confirmed by other laboratory studies, both by Griffitt and by Robert Baron. For example, a 1975 experiment by Baron and Bell showed that nonangered university students who were in a hot laboratory room [between 92 and 95°F (33 and 35°C)] were more aggressive toward a peer when that individual made mistakes than were the control subjects in a more comfortable room.[8]

Aggressive reactions to other unpleasant conditions. I could go on to provide a fairly broad list of conditions that have been shown to produce increased hostility and aggression in humans. In a variety of experiments, employing many different procedures and measures, such factors as irritating cigarette smoke, foul odors, and even disgusting scenes have increased the punishment given to, or hostility displayed toward another person.[9]

Obviously, psychological stress is also unpleasant, and it too can lead to aggression. According to research by Simha Landau in Israel, as well as others researchers, in many (but not all) societies, various forms of social stress also heighten the amount of violent crime. Whether the stress is indexed by high unemployment, hyperinflation, or rapid modernization, or by more subjective matters such as how worried people say they are about the economic, security, and political conditions in the country, the resulting unpleasant social tension can promote antisocial behavior.[10]

The Aggression Is Aimed Not Only at the Elimination of the Unpleasant Event
Though all the findings mentioned above are in keeping with the formulation I am presenting, many of them are more than merely consistent with theory and actually provide very good evidence for the specific points I have been emphasizing. Besides testifying to the wide range of aversive conditions that can stimulate aggressive reactions, the results, especially those found through laboratory experiments, tell us that: (1) the aggression is *not only* an attempt to eliminate or lessen the unpleasant condition, and (2) the attack or hostility can be displayed even when the target hasn't done anything to provoke the suffering person.

It certainly isn't unusual for people to strike out in anger at those who have been bothering them, at least partly in an effort to stop the annoyance. Parents do batter their children at times in an attempt to control the offspring's disturbing behavior, much as Julia's mother "whupped" her daughter. Similarly, many youngsters hit a brother or sister in fury because they want to stop that child from bothering them. Because of the frequency with which this occurs, some psychologists have argued that aversively stimulated aggression is aimed only at eliminating the disturbing state of affairs. Laboratory experiments indicate, however, that this is not the only objective. In most of these investigations the afflicted subjects hurt a truly neutral person who couldn't be blamed for their discomfort and, furthermore, hadn't misbehaved in any way. They couldn't actually eliminate the bothersome occurrence by attacking this individual. Furthermore, even though people suffering from an aversive stimulation are especially likely to attack someone who had previously irritated them,[11] the target individual evidently doesn't have to be annoying for this aversively stimulated aggression to occur.

An experiment that I carried out with Susan Cochran and Marlowe Embree some years ago gives one example of how suffering persons can be very harsh to innocent bystanders, largely because they want to hurt someone. In this study, which ostensibly investigated how "harsh environmental conditions" influenced supervisory performance, female university students were asked to evaluate another student's work while they were exposed to an unusual situation: having to keep one hand immersed in a tank of water. Each subject was told that she was a supervisor and that she was to give the "worker" rewards and punishments in accord with her judgment of the quality of each of the worker's solutions to a series of business-world problems. The subjects could reward, punish, or ignore each of the worker's solutions by pressing the appropriate buttons on an apparatus. To reward the worker for "good" solutions, they could deliver anywhere from one to five nickels, and to punish her for "bad" solutions, they could give her from one to five blasts of noise.

There were two experimental manipulations, one varying the unpleasantness of the subjects' physical condition (the temperature of the water in the tank) and the other having to do with the supposed outcome of whatever punishment was administered. For the first of these manipulations, half the women found the water painfully cold [it was about 42°F (6°C)] throughout the 6-minute testing period, whereas for the others the water was at a more comfortable temperature (about room temperature). Equally important, within each of these two conditions, half had been told that punishment was likely to hurt the worker's performance, while the others were informed that punishment was apt to be helpful by motivating the worker to do better.

Figure 3–1 summarizes the main findings in the first of the two experiments using this procedure that were reported by Berkowitz, Cochran, and Embree. As you can see, the subjects clearly preferred to reward rather than to punish the worker, as if they were generally reluctant to mistreat her. Thus, when the subjects were not suffering very much (that is, when they were in the mild-water-temperature condition)

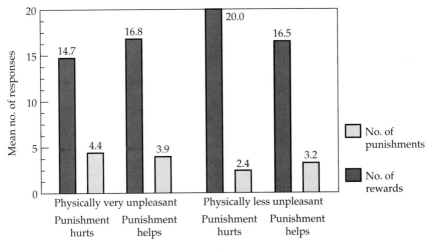

FIGURE 3-1

Number of rewards and punishments to a "worker" as a function of the aversive-
ness of the situation and whether the punishment will hurt or help the "worker."
(Adapted from Berkowitz, Cochran, & Embree (1981), Experiment 1. Copyright 1981 by the
American Psychological Association Adapted by permission.)
Note: For each condition, the maximum total number of responses possible was
fifty. The scores given are for all parts of the experiment.

and believed that punishment would hurt the worker, they gave her the
greatest number of rewards and the fewest punishments. Experiencing
relatively little discomfort, they didn't have a particularly strong desire
to injure anyone. By contrast, the women who were in pain because of
the cold water and who also thought that punishment would hurt the
worker were typically more punitive and less rewarding. Their suffering
apparently heightened their desire to inflict injury, and they took advantage of the opportunity to hurt their fellow student. Keep in mind that
the "worker" was not responsible for the subjects' pain and hadn't really
annoyed them in any way, and that the subjects' open hostility couldn't
get them out of the cold water any sooner.[12]

NEGATIVE AFFECT, AGGRESSIVE INCLINATIONS, AND ANGER

We come now to the core idea in the conception of emotional aggression
that I am presenting: Aggressive instigation is activated by unpleasant
feelings rather than by highly stressful events.

Negative Affect, Not Stress

Several behavioral scientists have noted that environmental stressors can evoke emotional aggression. Landau's previously mentioned research indicated that national stresses can contribute to the incidence of violent crimes in a country. Along much the same lines, Novaco has proposed that "anger can be understood as an affective stress reaction."[13] What these writers are basically saying is that people tend to become angry and aggressively inclined when they must face a highly bothersome state of affairs.

My analysis goes somewhat further than this, however. I hold that it is not the external stressor in itself but rather the negative affect aroused by the stressor that produces the aggressive tendencies and the felt anger. Indeed, my formulation offers a fairly strong (but still preliminary) working assumption: that virtually any kind of negative affect, any type of unpleasant feeling, is the basic spur to emotional aggression. The negative affect doesn't have to be intense, but the stronger the felt displeasure, the stronger will be the resulting instigation to aggression.

The effects of insults or threats to one's self-esteem can obviously be understood in these terms. We have all seen others become openly aggressive, verbally if not physically, and we may have even seen people lash out in rage, when they thought that they were being insulted or when their self-esteem was damaged. Highly aggressive persons provide an extreme example. They are typically very sensitive to possible affronts. They often become furious when they believe that their view of themselves has been threatened. I suggest that *these challenges to one's favorable self-image are especially likely to produce aggressive reactions because they're decidedly unpleasant.* It's not the injury to one's pride *in itself* that generates the urge to assault the offender, but the strongly aversive nature of the psychological wound.

Furthermore, however the negative affect arises, the aggressive urge may not be revealed openly since it might well be masked or restrained by stronger action tendencies. Even so, this analysis proposes, people who aren't feeling well are somewhat inclined to be aggressive.

A Brief Summary of the Present Theoretical Model

The sweeping notion that people who feel bad are inclined to be angry and aggressive may be difficult to accept, and, as a matter of fact, the relationship between affect and open aggression is a complicated one. Some of these complexities will be covered in more detail in Chapter 4. For now, I'll give you a brief summary of my thinking. It will be helpful if you will also look at the top part of Figure 3–2.[14]

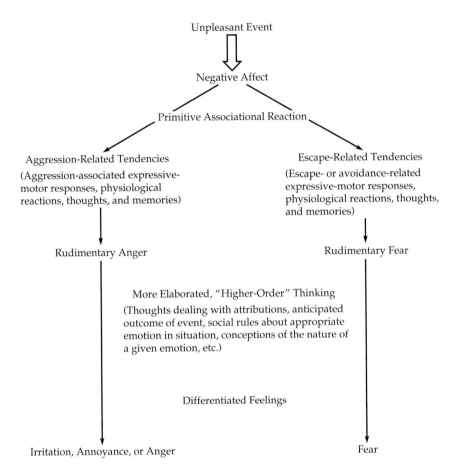

FIGURE 3-2
How negative feelings might produce anger.

Negative affect generates both fight and flight tendencies. As Figure 3–2 suggests, the present formulation posits several stages in the formation of emotional experiences and behaviors after a person has encountered an aversive event. The event itself obviously arouses negative affect, and theoretically, presumably because of our biological "programming," the unpleasant feeling gives rise automatically to a variety of expressive-motor reactions, feelings, thoughts, and memories. Some of these are associated with fight tendencies—that is, with the inclination to attack someone (preferably but not only the perceived source of the felt unpleasantness)—while other reactions (which occur at the same time) are linked to flight reactions—to the inclination to escape or to avoid the aversive situation.

In other words, negative affect generates *both* fight *and* flight tendencies, not one or the other. This is only speculation, but I suspect that many animal species are biologically disposed to cope with noxious stimuli in two ways: by escaping from the dangerous or unpleasant situation (the flight tendency) *and also* by destroying the source of the displeasure (the fight tendency). Of course, a variety of factors determine the relative strengths of these tendencies. One inclination may be stronger than the other because of genetic influences and/or past learning, and/or because of the perception of the immediate situation as either safe or dangerous for aggression.

My next suggestion may seem even more farfetched. The fight tendency may have two components: (1) an inclination to lash out at an available target (which is primarily an instigation to carry out the motor responses associated with aggression) and (2) an urge to hurt someone. Thus, from my point of view, when people are experiencing fairly strong displeasure, many of them (depending on their genetic inheritance and prior learning) are stimulated to perform the motor actions related to aggression (tighten their fists, clench their jaws, and so on), and they also want to injure someone or something. Both the research on pain cues mentioned in Chapter 1 and the experiment by Berkowitz, Cochran, and Embree which was described above testify to the existence of the urge to injure.

Feelings develop from these initial reactions. Theoretically, a primitive or rudimentary experience of anger grows out of the awareness of initial bodily, thought, and memory reactions, while a rudimentary fear accompanies the flight tendencies and presumably develops from the initial ideas, memories, expressive-motor reactions, and physiological sensations associated with the inclination to escape from the unpleasant situation.

In the next stage, as Figure 3–2 also indicates, more elaborate emotional feelings arise as a consequence of additional thought. Aroused persons attribute their feelings to particular sources, consider the likely outcome of the event, take into account their previous experiences and the social rules defining the appropriate emotion in the situation, and match their sensations and ideas with their conception of the kind of emotion that is likely to arise in their circumstances. The full emotional experience, then, is "constructed." The initial, rudimentary feelings are differentiated in a process in which some of them are intensified and enriched while others are suppressed.

The Initial Feelings Can Change with Thought. What this theoretical formulation suggest then, is that in the early stages of the emotion formation process, flight/fear and aggression/anger are apt to be blended together rather than sharply differentiated. However, when people are asked to report their feelings in particular emotional situations, or when their physiological and muscular reactions are recorded during emotional arousal, we find significant differences between the primary negative emotional states such as anger, fear, and sadness.[15] Is this a problem for the present theory? I think not. According to the formulation, cognitions (thoughts, attributions, and memories) can go into operation after the initial emotional reactions arise, and can substantially influence subsequent bodily changes, motor responses, and emotional experience. The relatively rudimentary emotional feelings and bodily reactions of the early stages become enriched, differentiated, intensified, or suppressed. My guess is that this sequence of changes—from (1) negative affect to (2) fear, anger, and perhaps several other primary negative emotions, and then to (3) more differentiated emotions such as jealousy or contempt—is facilitated by appropriate thoughts and memories.

Anger Parallels Aggressive Inclinations. The conception of anger as an *experience* that grows out of, and is constructed from, people's awareness of their aggression-associated physiological changes, expressive-motor reactions, and ideas and memories, has an important implication. It maintains that the instigation to aggression is derived from the internal aggression-related stimulation, but that it only parallels the feelings rather than being produced by the felt anger. Simply put, anger accompanies but does not cause emotional aggression.

The network model of emotion. In agreement with other recent analyses of emotion, the theoretical model I am presenting basically envisions each emotion as a network in which the various components are linked together associatively. Each emotional state is a collection of particular feelings, expressive-motor reactions, thoughts, and memories that are associated with each other. Because of their interconnections, the activation of any one component will tend to activate the other parts of the network in proportion to their degree of association.

The network model also has other implications. For one thing, it suggests that when we have aggressive ideas and memories, we're also apt to have the feelings and bodily reactions that are associated with aggression; that is, we are likely to experience anger. We can make ourselves angry, not only by brooding about the wrongs done to us but also by thinking again and again about how we'd like to hurt those who have mistreated us. Violence-associated thoughts and actions activate further aggressive ideas and angry feelings. As you will see when we consider the effects of make-believe aggression in Chapter 11, there's now a good deal of evidence that agrees with this interpretation.

Going further, this formulation also holds that unpleasant events that have no apparent connection with aggression can also activate hostile thoughts and memories. Remember, negative affect—the unpleasant feeling that would be produced by an aversive occurrence—is associatively linked to aggression-related ideas and recollections. There is evidence that we do have a greater than usual number of hostile thoughts when we are physically uncomfortable.

Subjects in one experiment were asked to write stories about certain emotional topics while sitting in a laboratory room that was either unpleasantly hot or at a comfortable temperature. The stories of the subjects who were exposed to the unpleasant heat expressed more aggressive ideas than did those of the control subjects who were in a comfortable room. Similarly, in a study carried out in my own laboratory, when subjects were asked to imagine themselves in a certain kind of emotional situation, those who were physically uncomfortable were more likely to voice ideas related to anger, annoyance, and hostility than were their counterparts in a more comfortable condition.[16] In both of these studies, the negative affect created by the physical discomfort activated ideas with an aggressive or angry meaning, which were revealed openly when the situation was appropriate to the expression of these thoughts.

Anger Often Accompanies Other Negative Emotions

Even after reading about this supporting research, you may still have serious doubts, especially in connection with my working assumption about the initial psychological equivalence of all negative affect (holding intensity constant): that virtually any kind of negative affect will tend to activate aggressive inclinations and a rudimentary anger experience before the person gives much thought to what has happened. "This can't be," you may say. "People aren't angry and aggressive when they're sad or depressed." Well, despite what many people think, sadness and depression apparently can produce angry feelings, hostile ideas, and aggressive tendencies.

Anger Often Coexists with Other Negative Emotions
One bit of evidence for this contention comes from the extent to which emotional experiences are often a blend of different feelings. When people are asked to describe how they felt on certain unpleasant occasions, they often report a mixture of emotions, with anger accompanying other negative states. It's as if unpleasant occurrences generate anger as well as more expected emotional states. In one study, as an example, the participants rated their feelings during emotional episodes for a period of weeks. According to the subjects' reports, at least some of the emotional incidents gave rise to both fear and anger. The participants were typically somewhat frightened, of course, when they faced threatening situations, but not a few of them said they also felt angry.[17]

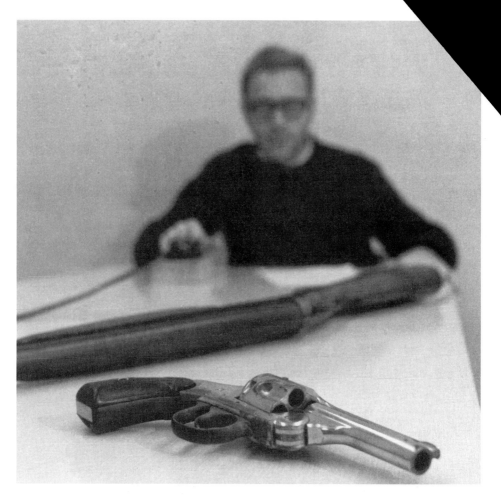

FIGURE 3-3

The experimental set-up employed in the original Berkowitz-LePage experiment. The subject has an opportunity to give his supposed partner from one to ten electric shocks using a telegraph key. On the table holding the telegraph key he sees a rifle and a revolver that, he is told, were left there by another experimenter who had been conducting another study. Later research indicates that the subject's awareness of the experimenter's interest in their reactions to the guns served to reduce, not increase, the number of shocks they delivered.

Sad events often produce anger as well as sadness.

"Oh yes," said Dalgliesh. "You can feel anger and grief together. That's the commonest reaction to bereavement."[18]

Even more impressive than the finding that anger coexists with fear, as far as I'm concerned, is the extent to which people become angry

lened by an unhappy occurrence. In his important text
Carroll Izard has noted the frequent mixture of anger
s, he reports, very much in line with the observation
P. D. James's fictional detective Adam Dalgliesh, per-
ing because of the loss of a loved one often describe
as well as sad and distressed.[19]

al survey of the psychological literature on mourning
and bereavement certainly confirms Izard's observations. You may be
surprised to discover how often people who are mourning someone's
death are also angry. According to one psychological paper, the young
students in a parochial school became unruly and even aggressive after
two of their schoolmates were killed in separate accidents during the
school vacation period. Even the teachers experienced some anger as
well as guilt and sadness when they thought about the children's deaths.
Other researchers have obtained quantitative evidence of this frequent
linkage between grief and anger, leading them to comment that it is not
uncommon for people who are bereaved to be angry and even to engage
in violent acts. In many instances, the mourners could not blame the
death on someone's misdeed or even on a human agent. Yet they were
angry.

Termine and Izard have recently carried this theme even further.
Besides noting that conditions eliciting sadness frequently elicit anger,
they demonstrated that infants often react to pain and separation with
facial expressions that indicate both sadness and anger.[20] The situations
that saddened these babies apparently also angered them.

From my perspective, then, the blending of anger with sadness is not
due simply to the suffering individuals' inability to recognize what they
are feeling. With Izard, I suggest that, in many instances (at least beyond
infancy), people know that they are distressed (and/or sad and/or
afraid), but they also realize that they are angry. Keep in mind, though,
that people can, and frequently do, differentiate among their various
emotional experiences. They may say they are sad or unhappy without
reporting any anger. The theory I am propounding is that this kind of
emotional differentiation begins to take place soon after the initial emotional reactions to an unpleasant incident occur, as people think about
the unpleasant incident, consider why it happened, and decide how they
ought to feel under the circumstances.

Is Anger Necessarily Always Focused on a Specific Target? People usually view anger as being directed at a specific target: They say they are
angry *with* someone or maybe *with* something. Izard (along with most
writers) takes this commonsense approach, maintaining that anger
accompanies other negative emotions because someone is blamed for the
unhappy event. In discussing the connection between anger and the distress experienced after a separation from a loved one, he proposes,
"Anger may also occur as a result of the individual blaming the absent or

lost loved one for deserting him or her or as a result of blaming someone else for the separation."[21]

My theoretical position is different from this popular view. There's no doubt that we typically attribute aversive incidents to particular causes. We believe that someone or something caused an event, and we direct our ire at the perceived source of our displeasure. This doesn't necessarily mean, however, that the resulting aggressive inclinations and experienced anger are *always and only* aimed at this particular cause. I noted earlier that people who are exposed to unpleasant stimulation— hot rooms, very cold water, foul odors, etc.—tend to become hostile and aggressive toward innocent bystanders whom they realistically can- not, and probably in fact do not, blame for the discomfort. If they were asked, the afflicted persons might also say they were irritable. (I regard irritability as a low level of felt anger.) Haven't you ever felt irritable when you had a headache, or when you were hot and sweaty during a continuing heat spell? This sort of irritability, annoyance, or anger is fairly general and may tend to be somewhat free-floating. It's not neces- sarily focused on a particular person or thing. The aggressive tendencies and angry feelings produced by negative affect can also be free-floating. Then too, when we do not feel well, we may have hostile thoughts about people who happen to be nearby. We may recall unpleasant things about them, think bad things about them, remember bad things they did to us, and even blame them to some degree for our unhappiness.[22] This blame can be the *result* of the hostile-aggressive process activated by the negative affect and *not the cause* of the hostile-aggressive inclina- tions.

Depression and anger. A substantial number of reports that note a connection between depression and aggression also provide support for the analysis I am presenting here. This linkage may not surprise you, since it has been discussed by many psychiatrists and psychologists, from Freud to the present. Mental health specialists have repeatedly observed that both child and adult depressives are apt to be hostile and may even be susceptible to intense outbursts of temper.[23]

Poznanski and Zrull saw a combination of depression and aggres- sion in a study of seriously depressed children. Most of the youngsters whom they observed displayed such a high level of fighting, biting, and destructive actions that this behavior, rather than the childrens' depres- sion, was the parents' and teachers' chief concern.[24] Less disturbed chil- dren can also exhibit both depression and aggression. A similar investi- gation of normal youngsters below 12 years of age found that children who had recently suffered depressive episodes were also apt to have been severely assaultive.[25]

Differences with Other Analyses. It seems to be quite clear, then, that depression often accompanies aggressive tendencies. What is much less certain is why this connection exists. Martin Seligman's highly influential cognitive theory of depression[26] would seem to suggest that depressives shouldn't be aggressive. Depressives are generally apathetic and passive, the theory emphasizes, so much so that they are frequently reluctant to undertake prolonged actions that require effort. We therefore wouldn't expect them to be deliberately assaultive. They presumably wouldn't want to exert themselves.

However, to say that depressives are unwilling to make the effort involved in carrying out a deliberate frontal attack doesn't mean that they won't have impulsive outbursts of emotional aggression. Nor does it mean that they won't express hostile opinions or that they won't curse or insult someone. As a matter of fact, whatever physical aggression a depressive displays is likely to appear in a fit of uncontrolled rage rather than as a calculated and deliberate action. Suggesting this, in their investigation of highly depressed youngsters, Poznanski and Zrull observed, "Frequently, the aggression was violent and explosive, occurring in short outbursts."[27] These children may not have planned and carried out direct, effortful aggression, but they did lash out at others quickly and thoughtlessly.

The theory I am presenting is clearly at odds with the traditional psychoanalytic conception of depression. Psychoanalytic formulations dating back to Freud maintain that depression grows out of inward-directed aggression, [28] while my model holds that depressed feelings generate aggressive inclinations. I don't deny that people in a depressed mood are apt to be harsh on themselves and even somewhat self-punishing, but a growing body of research has shown that depressed feelings in themselves can lead to anger and even to relatively strong attacks on an available target.

Evidence that Depressed Feelings Produce Aggressive Inclinations. Some of the research on the aggression-producing consequences of depressed feelings was carried out to test Seligman's theory of depression rather than to study aggression. Even so, the investigators unexpectedly saw their subjects become angry and hostile. Otherwise normal persons who were exposed to Seligman's learned helplessness procedure subsequently rated themselves as angry as well as depressed and also exhibited some hostility toward others.[29]

Some Qualifications and Limiting Factors
It's obvious that not every unpleasant occurrence produces an aggressive outburst, even in the absence of external restraints. Sad news can throw us into a "blue funk," in which we don't want to do anything and certainly don't want to assault someone openly. Depression often leads to apathy rather than activity. Even when we don't hold ourselves back, the conditions clearly have to be right if our inner aggressive inclinations are to be revealed in our overt behavior. (See Figure 3–4.)

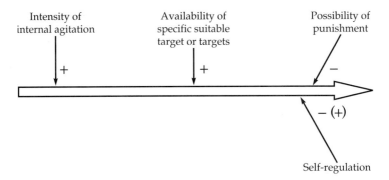

FIGURE 3-4

Factors influencing the probability that negative affect-generated instigation to aggresion will lead to overt aggresion.

Intensity of internal arousal. The instigation to aggression may be too weak to be shown openly. While my formulation suggests that even moderately unpleasant events can activate people's urge to attack someone, they may not be sufficiently aroused at the time for this urge to take command of their muscles. A sad event may be a "real downer," deadening people's feelings and dulling their emotional reactions so that they don't care to act at all. The more intense is the internal agitation created by the negative event, the greater is the probability that they will be assaultive.

Having a focused target. I also suspect that affect-generated instigation is more apt to be exhibited openly when a clear and definite target is available. We're fundamentally disposed to attack what we regard as the source of our displeasure, but as I've been arguing, we're also aggressively inclined even when there's nothing to blame for our unhappiness. Suppose you are feeling bad because, say, you have a toothache. The pain makes you irritable and even disposed to attack someone, but you may lack a definite *and suitable* object to assault. There isn't anyone or anything specific for your hostile thoughts and aggressive action tendencies to focus on, and so you show only a general and diffuse hostility and irritability. However, if someone then appears who is a definite and appropriate target, your anger and aggression-related feelings, ideas, and inclination will focus on this specific (and suitable) object, and there is a greater chance that your impetus to aggression will be displayed.

The self-control of negative affect-generated aggressive tendencies. The availability of a specific target only increases the probability of open aggression, however, and doesn't guarantee that it will occur. After all, most people have learned that it's wrong to assault someone who isn't to blame for their suffering. As a consequence, they often inhibit their affect-generated urge to be aggressive. While this point is quite obvious, the reader may be interested to learn that self-induced restraint can arise at times merely as a result of a heightened awareness of one's unpleasant feelings.

Several studies conducted independently of each other testify to this effect. Generally speaking, the experiments indicate, people who are in a negative mood are most likely to act on their negative inclinations when they act quickly, impulsively, after giving little or no thought to what they are doing and feeling.

Afflicted persons may consciously or unconsciously attempt to regulate their feelings and actions in keeping with social rules. Consider the teachers mentioned above, who were bothered by the accidental deaths of their two pupils. If they were fully aware of their anger, they may have tried to control their feelings and aggressive inclinations, thinking it wasn't right to be angry and aggressive when someone died accidentally. In other words, when social rules clearly define hostility and aggression as inappropriate under given circumstances, people who are aware of their unpleasant emotional state are less likely to act in keeping with their feelings than are people who are not thinking about their emotions at the time.

The formulation proposed here has some similarities to other conceptions of aggression but also is different from them in important ways. To make sure that you understand the differences very clearly, I recommend that you consider psychoanalyst Rollo May's interpretation of violence. In a book that was published a generation ago, *Power and Innocence*, May basically held that aggression was often spurred by a sense of powerlessness and therefore was frequently an effort to assert one's self-worth and significance. He also emphasized the impulsive nature of many violent reactions, as follows:

> In its typical and simple form, violence is an eruption of pent-up passion. When a person (or group of people) has been denied over a period of time what he feels are his legitimate rights, when he is continuously burdened with feelings of impotence which corrode any remaining self-esteem, violence is the predictable end result. Violence is an explosion of the drive to destroy that which is interpreted as the barrier to one's self-esteem, movement, and growth. This desire to destroy may so completely take over that any object that gets in the way is destroyed. Hence the person strikes out blindly. . . .
>
> Either because of the period of unseen build-up or [because of] the suddenness of the stimulus, the impulse to strike out comes so fast [that] we are unable to think, and we control it only with effort.[30]

According to my perspective, May's analysis is incomplete. I agree with it in some respects: Depressives typically regard themselves as powerless (as having relatively little control over the important events in their lives), and so there is indeed good reason to think that powerlessness can generate an urge to violence. However, I propose that this urge arises mainly because the sense of powerlessness and/or depression is decidedly unpleasant. The aggressive reactions of the powerless and/or the depressed are only special cases of the effect of negative feelings on aggressive inclinations. With this difference, though, I share Rollo May's view that the resulting urge to aggression can spur an impulsive and fairly nonthoughtful attack on other persons, especially on persons who are believed to be the source of the unpleasantness. Two experiments that provide evidence consistent with this argument are presented below.

Self-control due to self-awareness.

Impulsive Individuals May Reveal the Negative Influences of Their Negative Moods. In the first of these experiments, Daniel Hynan and Joseph Grush first divided their subjects, university men, into two groups based on their scores on a personality scale: subjects who were characteristically highly impulsive and subjects who were generally low in impulsiveness. Each subject first interacted briefly with a partner, who was posing as a fellow subject but actually was the experimenter's accomplice, and then was induced to have either a depressed or a neutral mood by means of a now standard laboratory technique (the Velten procedure[31]). After the desired mood was established, the naive subject was required to teach a certain concept to his partner using the Buss "aggression machine." This paradigm, which is described in Chapter 13, requires the subject to punish the "learner" whenever that individual makes a mistake, although the "teacher" is free to select the intensity of the punishment within a ten-step range. In this particular experiment, the subjects had twenty-five opportunities to punish the learner for making errors.

The results were pretty much as expected. In general, the most punitive men were those who (1) were made to feel depressed and (2) were also habitually highly impulsive and thus tended to react quickly without much thought. The depressive feeling apparently activated an aggressive inclination which was most clearly revealed by those who didn't think much about what they were doing.[32]

Attention to One's Feelings May Activate Self-Control. The second experiment of interest in this context, which Bartholomeu Troccoli and I performed, pursued a somewhat similar problem: the effect of people's thoughts upon their mood-influenced aggression. Whereas it can only be inferred that the impulsive men in the study by Hynan and Grush had not thought much about their actions or their feelings, in this investigation we deliberately varied the extent to which the subjects paid attention to their emotional states. As I have suggested, persons who realize that they are feeling bad may attempt to restrain the impact of their unhappy mood upon their judgments and actions if they think they have no good justification for being hostile and aggressive. This means that depressed individuals will be most likely to display their aggressive inclinations openly when they are not attending to their feelings.

Male university students who believed that they were participating in a study of the effects of thoughts on extrasensory perception (ESP) were induced to be either moderately depressed or happy, again employing the Velten procedure. Half the subjects in each of these two mood conditions were then led to be highly aware of their feelings by rating their moods on a questionnaire. The other half were distracted by being required to list whatever words came to mind when they were presented with a series of neutral nouns (e.g., table). Immediately after this experimental manipulation, the subjects were asked to think about certain colors that were shown to them. An "ESP receiver," who was supposedly in the next room, would try to guess what colors they were seeing. The subjects were also informed that they were to reward the ESP receiver whenever he guessed correctly by pressing the reward button on their apparatus anywhere from one to ten times. Each press supposedly would deliver 10 cents, so that the subjects could give the receiver as much as a dollar, every time he was right. Each subject had four opportunities to deliver money to the receiver. We assumed that the *less* money (the smaller the number of points) the subjects gave to the ESP receiver, the more hostile they were being toward him.

Figure 3–5 shows the mean number of points (or dimes) delivered to the receiver by subjects in each condition over the four opportunities combined. You can see that the findings are consistent with our expectations. When the men were distracted, so that they presumably were less aware of their feelings, the subjects who had been induced to be depressed delivered significantly lower rewards than did their happier counterparts. By contrast, when the subjects' attention was drawn to their feelings, their mood had no significant impact on how much money they gave the receiver. Apparently because their awareness of their moderately negative feelings prompted them to think about what was the right thing to do in this situation, these persons evidently tried to keep their bad moods from influencing their decisions.[33]

Are All Negative Feelings Alike?

As we have seen, many different kinds of unpleasant conditions can produce aggressive reactions, apparently because of the negative affect they generate. This seems consistent with my assumption that any type of negative feeling can activate aggressive inclinations and the rudimentary experience of anger—but is it really consistent? Psychologists who study emotions now differentiate between *high-arousal* emotional experiences,

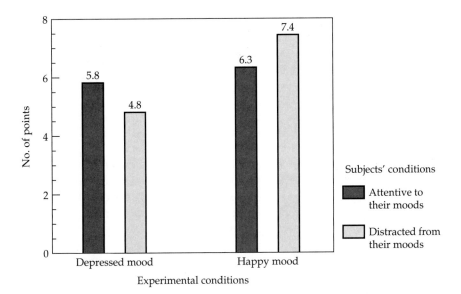

FIGURE 3-5
Number of points awarded to the "ESP receiver" as a function of subject's moods and degree of attention to their moods. (Data from Berkowitz and Troccoli (1990), Experiment 1.)
Note: The fewer the points awarded, the greater the hostility.

such as feeling "fed up," "jittery," or "nervous," and those at a *low arousal* level, including feeling "tired" and maybe "sad."[34] Isn't it possible that only the former kind of aroused displeasure has the aggressive effects suggested by the present theory?

My guess is that high arousal increases the chances that aggression and anger will become apparent; the more excited and agitated people are, the stronger will be their aggressive urge and experienced anger. However, even less aroused persons can be hostile and angry at times, as I have suggested. Someone who is melancholic and down in the dumps can easily flare up in an outburst of temper, indicating that she or he is at least ready to be aggressive.

PULLING OUT IMPULSIVE AGGRESSION: THE ROLE OF AGGRESSIVE CUES

Up to this point, I have been discussing what is probably the major cause of emotional aggression: the negative affect-generated internal stimulation that basically "pushes out" the aggressive reactions. As I suggested earlier, this urge may be composed of both a desire to hurt someone and an inclination to carry out aggression-associated motor actions.

However, emotionally engendered internal stimulation is not the only source of impulsive aggression. Externally derived stimulation may also contribute. Have you ever insulted, reprimanded, or even hit someone harder than you consciously wanted to? You may have had a more or less rational purpose in mind: to discipline a naughty child, to achieve power over someone who threatened your dominance and control, or to demonstrate that you are a worthy person who is not to be trifled with. Even so, for some reason you lashed out more strongly than you intended. This kind of impulsive (or expressive) aggression is not uncommon, and it can be revealed in extreme assaults as well as in relatively minor curses. When I introduced this type of emotional reaction in Chapter 1, I quoted a Dallas detective, to point out that many homicides are of this nature: "Tempers flare. A fight starts, and somebody gets stabbed or shot." The questions I will deal with here are: However often aggression that is not fully intended occurs, and whatever its specific form, why does it take place at all? What factors bring it about?

Reactions to External Cues

Much of my research and writing actually has been devoted to the questions posed above. I have argued that, in many cases, impulsive (or expressive) assaults are, at least in part, reactions to certain features of the surrounding situation. Nearby external stimuli essentially "pull out" responses that heighten the strength of the attacks.[35] This happens, I suggest, when the environmental stimuli either have an aggressive meaning for the attacker (i.e., are associated with aggression in the person's mind) and/or when they somehow remind the aggressor of decidedly unpleasant occurrences. Figure 3–6 summarizes this theory and identifies various conditions that can increase the ability of an external stimulus to evoke the stronger aggressive reactions. I will confine myself to discussing (1) stimuli that have an aggressive meaning and (2) stimuli that are associated with earlier unpleasant events.

The "Weapons Effect" as an Example of Reactions to Aggressive Cues
Weapons are obviously an excellent example of objects that have an aggressive meaning for many people. If we tend to think of guns (or even knives) as instruments that are deliberately used to hurt others, rather than as objects of sport and enjoyment, the mere presence of a gun or a knife may stimulate us to assault others more severely than we intend.[36]

The original demonstration of the weapons effect. An experiment that I carried out about twenty-five years ago with Anthony LePage was

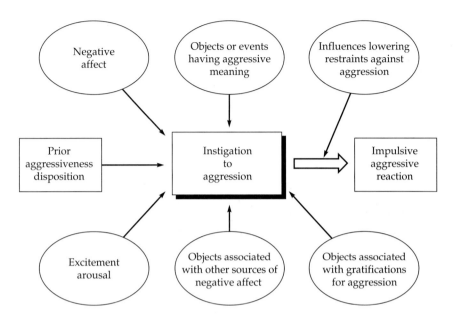

FIGURE 3-6

Factors that can influence the strength of open impulsive aggression. Negative affect and/or external stimuli having an aggressive meaning prime an aggressive inclination plus aggression-related feelings, ideas, and memories. The urge and other reactions are particularly strong if there is a strong previously established aggressiveness disposition and/or the person is excited at the time. The presence of situtational stimuli associated with other unpleasant events and with previously obtained gratifications for aggression will also intensify the aggressive reactions, leading to a relatively strong act of open impulsive aggression, particularly if restraints against aggression are low at the time.

the first to point to the weapons effect. In this investigation, each male subject was brought together with another student (the experimenter's confederate), and the two men were told that they were participating in a study of physiological reactions to stress. They would take turns in working on assigned problems, the experimenter explained, each knowing that his partner would evaluate his performance by giving him anywhere from one to ten electric shocks. After they were placed in separate rooms, the naive subject went first, wrote down his solutions to the problems, and received either one shock or seven shocks (all fairly mild), supposedly as his partner's judgment of the quality of his work. Needless to say, most of the men who got seven shocks became angry with the other person about the very unfavorable—as well as mildly painful—evaluation.

Then it was the subject's turn to evaluate his partner's ideas. He was taken to the "control room," shown the shock apparatus (a simple tele-graph key), and given his partner's answers to the assigned problems. Since the central question of the study was whether the mere presence of a weapon would heighten the subjects' aggression toward the person whom they had been set up to attack, some of the subjects saw a revolver and a shotgun lying on a table next to the shock key, while others saw two badminton racquets and some shuttlecocks on the table. With each subject, the experimenter pushed the objects aside, said that they had been left there by another experimenter who was engaged in a different study, and asked the man to give his judgments of his partner's work after the experimenter left the room. A third group of subjects were asked to make their judgments after seeing nothing but the shock key on the table.

The results, summarized in Figure 3–7, testify to the aggression-enhancing effects of the mere presence of weapons. The angered men (the ones who had received seven shocks from their partners) who saw guns on the table struck back at their tormentors more strongly than did angered men who saw neutral objects or nothing at all on the table beside the shock apparatus. The mere sight of the guns apparently stim-ulated the angered men to give their antagonist more shocks than they otherwise would have done.[37]

Confirming the existence of the weapons effect. I won't note here all the objections that have been raised against the experiment on the weapons effect and the interpretation I have offered, but mention of sev-

FIGURE 3-7
Mean number of shocks given as a function of presence of weapons. (Adapted from Berkowitz & LePage (1967). Copyright 1967 by the American Psychological Association. Adapted by permission.)

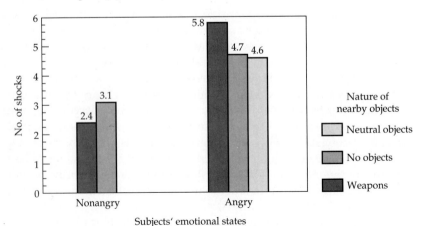

eral points will be worthwhile. First, as you will find in Chapter 13, which deals with research methodology, a clever experiment by Turner and Simons has shown that the angry subjects in the weapons condition were not, as some researchers have alleged, simply acting to confirm the experimenters' hypothesis. As a matter of fact, according to this later study, the more the subjects believed that the experimenter was interested in their aggressive reactions, the *less* punitive they were.[38] The increased aggression produced by the exposure to weapons came about *in spite* of the subjects' suspicions and *not* because of their awareness of the experimenter's interest in their aggressiveness.

Some Successful Replications. Equally significant, there have now been many successful replications of the original findings (as well as several failures to duplicate our results). Other social psychologists in a number of countries, including Sweden, Belgium, and Italy, have obtained comparable findings—an indication that the weapons effect isn't limited to middle-class university students in the American Midwest.

I will cite only one of these non-American studies, the Swedish experiment, which was carried out by Ann Frodi for her doctoral dissertation at the University of Göteborg. She showed that high school boys administered significantly more electric shocks to a fellow student (as a supposed evaluation of his work) when weapons were nearby than when a baby bottle and pictures of a nursing mother were present or when no neutral objects were on the table. This difference was obtained, furthermore, even when the boys hadn't been angered by the person they were "judging." The youths apparently were so willing to punish their peer that the weapons effect could be seen even when the subjects weren't emotionally aroused.[39]

In a study which demonstrated that the subjects were not merely going along with the experimenters' wishes, the heightened aggressiveness produced by the presence of guns was also obtained when the research participants weren't aware that they were taking part in an experiment. Thus, Charles Turner and his students set up a booth at a college-sponsored carnival. They invited students to throw sponges at a target person and allowed them to "assault" the target as often as they wanted. More sponges were hurled at the target when a rifle was lying nearby than when no weapon was present.

Finally, I should make it clear that a number of studies (for example, the Frodi and Turner experiments just mentioned) have shown that even nonangered persons can be stimulated to increased aggression when they see a gun. Emotionally aroused people may be especially susceptible to the weapons effect (because they're set to attack someone and are probably relatively uninhibited), but even nonaroused persons may become more aggressive than they otherwise would have been when weapons are nearby, especially if their inhibitions against aggression happen to be weak at the time.[40]

An Experiment with Children. A recent experiment with young children, conducted by Miomir Zuzul at the University of Zagreb in Croatia, is of special interest because it indicates why some investigations have failed to confirm the weapons effect. The 6-year-old boys and girls in this study were shown either real weapons, toy guns, or no weapons at all. They were then told a story implying that the adult had either a permissive attitude toward aggression; a stricter, less permissive attitude toward aggression; or no particular attitude on this topic. Next, some of the youngsters were frustrated by being forbidden to engage in an attractive activity, whereas the others weren't so thwarted. Finally, all the children were watched for half an hour in free play by observers who did not know what experimental conditions the youngsters had been exposed to.

Figure 3-8 reports the mean number of aggressive acts (mainly non-playful pushing and hitting) recorded for the frustrated children in each of the conditions. (The same trends were exhibited in the nonfrustrated group, although the trends were weaker and not statistically significant.) You can see that the youngsters were relatively restrained when the adult's story implied a negative attitude toward aggression. When no such attitude was conveyed, however, in the other story conditions, not only were the children generally more aggressive in their dealings with each other, but also they were especially apt to fight and hit each other after being exposed to the sight of weapons.

There are lessons here for researchers as well as for parents: For the

FIGURE 3-8

Children's aggression as a function of prior exposure to weapons and situational "atmosphere." (Data from Zuzul (1989), frustrated condition. Reprinted by permission.)

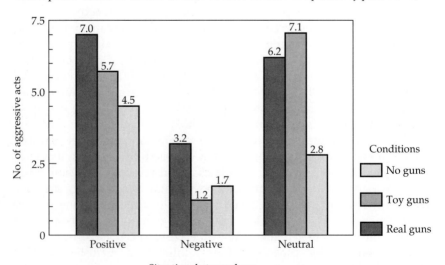

Situational atmosphere

former, Zuzul's findings indicate that situationally induced inhibitions could prevent researchers from seeing the increased aggressive tendencies produced by the presence of weapons. This kind of restraint may have been especially strong in the weapons studies that failed to obtain a significant weapons effect. For parents, this experiment, as well as others that could also be cited,[41] demonstrates that toy guns as well as real weapons can stimulate heightened aggression. Fantasy violence doesn't provide a "safe outlet" for supposedly pent-up aggressive urges. Children playing with make-believe pistols, rifles, or "death ray blasters" can become more aggressive and disorderly than they otherwise would have been.

However, the results also indicate that adults can dampen children's aggressive reactions by making it clear that aggression is wrong and has bad consequences. To put this more broadly; the results suggest that guns won't always stimulate overt aggressive reactions; people are often appropriately restrained in how they act. Nevertheless, we must also recognize that inhibitions against aggression are weak at times, maybe because of a strong emotional arousal or too much alcohol. It's on the occasions when restraints are low that the mere sight of a weapon can incite a stronger aggressive reaction than would otherwise have occurred.

One additional point. It's not only weapons that can have this effect. Anything that is clearly associated with successfully hurting others would presumably have similar effects. The stimulus might be a knife or an ax, or a violent scene in a movie or on television. Whatever the stimulus, its aggressive meaning heightens the chances that it will produce aggressive consequences.

Cues Associated with Unpleasant Events
Yet another factor, which seems to be greatly different, can also promote aggressive reactions: associations with unpleasant occurrences. This shouldn't surprise you. If aversive conditions can stimulate aggressive inclinations, stimuli that are linked to these negative events in our minds can also have this effect. They might generate bad feelings inside us, when we encounter them, by essentially reminding us of times when we have suffered. This negative effect could produce hostile thoughts and an aggressive urge. Then too, negatively associated stimuli could even work independently of unpleasant feelings to activate hostile or aggressive ideas and memories as well as aggression-connected motor reactions.

Empirical demonstrations. Animal research has demonstrated that stimuli associated with aversive events can lead to fighting. Suppose that, during a series of trials, we repeatedly sound a buzzer just before we deliver electric shocks to two rats that are cooped up together in a cage. The painful shocks will cause the animals to assault each other. After the buzzer has been paired with the shocks several times, its mere sound can also get the rats to start fighting. The buzzer has become a negative stimulus through its association with the aversive shocks, and, as a result, it can instigate aggression by itself.

This effect has also been shown in experiments with people. Adam Fraczek carried out an experiment in Poland in which men first learned to associate the color yellow either with cigarettes (a pleasant connection for these particular subjects) or with the receipt of electric shocks (an unpleasant association). Soon afterward, they were required to punish someone else in the presence of either yellow or another color. The men were most aggressive when they saw yellow *and* when this particular color had been linked with the painful happening. Here too, a feature of the environment (the color yellow) had become a negative stimulus through its connection with a painful event, and it could thus intensify aggressive reactions.[42]

The Available Target's Connection with Unpleasantness

Associations with aversive happenings play a very important part in determining what target is apt to receive the strongest attack. If we're feeling bad for some reason, we're obviously most likely to direct whatever aggression we display at the persons we blame for our distress. Rephrasing the proposition that Dollard and his colleagues at Yale advanced back in 1939, we can say (as is indicated in Figure 3–6) that the instigation to aggression aroused by an unpleasant event is most strongly directed at the agent perceived to be the source of the displeasure.

There are at least two reasons for this effect. The assault could be partly an attempt to eliminate or lessen the aversive stimulation. In addition, the perceived source is now associated with negative affect; as a result, his or her mere presence can evoke hostile thoughts and memories as well as the internal stimulation to aggression. This point can be phrased more broadly, as follows: People who have acquired a negative meaning (perhaps by being linked with earlier unpleasant incidents) are particularly likely to become the victims of aversively generated aggression.

Animal research supports this possibility. In at least one experiment, an animal became a likely target for aggression merely because it was present when the aggressor animals had previously been shocked. Humans can act the same way. As just one example, Riordan and Tedeschi demonstrated that subjects tend to become strongly hostile toward another individual who was simply present when the subjects were frightened (and who was not a fellow sufferer).[43]

Applying the analysis to interpersonal relations.

Displacement of Hostility and Scapegoating. Displacement of hostility is often at work, I believe, when an innocent person or a group is the victim of aggression aroused by another source. You've undoubtedly heard of this happening. We all know the story of the man who was angered by his boss and went home to shout at his wife, who then spanked her son for a trivial misdeed, who in turn kicked his dog. These people had all been provoked, but, unable or unwilling to attack the real tormentor, they *displaced* their aggression onto someone else. We sometimes say that the innocent victim is a *scapegoat.*

The usual interpretation of scapegoating holds that the victim is assaulted mainly because he or she is available and safe to attack, and this is partly true. The husband may well have spoken sharply to his wife simply because she was there (and maybe also because she did something that annoyed him). In my view, however, there's more to displacement of hostility than this. Why are some ethnic or minority groups especially likely to become scapegoats? I suggest that in many cases the target is also someone who is already disliked and thus has a negative meaning.

Whatever else is involved, this kind of process may contribute to the scapegoating of blacks and Jews.[44] An unpleasant state of affairs generates an aggressive urge, and this is directed at an available, safe, and disliked group.

Economic hard times evidently contributed to southern whites' assaults on blacks in this manner, up to the 1930s at least. Before the deep South's economy became as diversified as it is now, this area's economic well-being was tied directly to the value of its main cash crop, cotton. Whole communities suffered severe financial setbacks when the price of cotton fell. Investigators have found that, up to the late 1930s, sudden drops in the market value of cotton were not infrequently followed by an increase in the lynching of blacks in this part of the country.[45] Other statistics tell the same story. As an example, there were twenty-one lynchings in 1930. The southern counties in which these acts of violence occurred were more economically deprived than were the counties in which no lynchings occurred.[46] In all these instances, of course, the black victims may have done something to offend the whites. However, the poor farmers had also been taught to dislike blacks generally. They found a ready target for the aggressive inclinations produced by their economic plight in the blacks who had, they believed, "stepped out of line."

Isn't it possible that prior dislike has also contributed to the displaced hostility that has been directed against Jews through the centuries? People who have resented the privations and other hardships they suffered have attacked Jews, blaming them for their troubles, in large part simply because they had learned as children to hate this group. In other words, Jews (and certain other minority groups) draw displaced hostility at least in part because of their negative meaning— their previously established association with an unpleasant state of affairs.

Handicapped persons as aversive stimuli. Other people besides blacks and Jews can also be associated with unpleasantness. Think of people who are handicapped or afflicted by serious and long-standing ailments. For many "normals," these unfortunate people are also linked with a negative condition because of their incapacity and/or their ailment. Of course, most of us are sympathetic to the handicapped and the ill. We feel sorry for them and sometimes even inconvenience ourselves in order to help them. Deep down in our minds, however, we may also regard them negatively and have unpleasant associations to them, with the result that we are essentially ambivalent toward them. So far, I'm not saying anything original. A number of social scientists have noted this mixture of positive and negative feelings toward the handicapped.

I go further, however. Because of their negative meaning, the afflicted persons are occasionally mistreated by "normals," especially if the latter don't think much about what they are doing.

Evidence of thoughtless mistreatment was found in two experiments that I conducted with Ann Frodi.[47] In the second of these two studies, university women who had been previously insulted were asked to "supervise" a young boy whom they had watched on television. For half the cases, the TV monitor showed that the child was "funny-looking" rather than normal in appearance, and some of the subjects also heard the boy stutter when he talked. After the TV set was turned off, the child supposedly began a series of learning trials, and the women were informed each time he made a mistake. As supervisors, they had to give the boy a blast of unpleasant noise whenever he was wrong. Following the Buss "aggression machine" procedure, the subjects were free to select the intensity of the punishment (the noise) they delivered, on a ten-step scale ranging from very mild to decidedly unpleasant. It's important to point out that the women also worked on another task as they carried out this supervision, so that they weren't fully concentrating on what they were doing when they pressed the noise-delivering buttons.

Figure 3–9 reports the mean intensity of the punishment the aroused subjects gave to the boy over all ten trials in which he supposedly made a mistake. You can see that the somewhat distracted women were most punitive when they perceived the child as doubly afflicted: as funny-looking and also a stutterer. The unfortunate child who had both handicaps was particularly likely to be impulsively mistreated by the still-

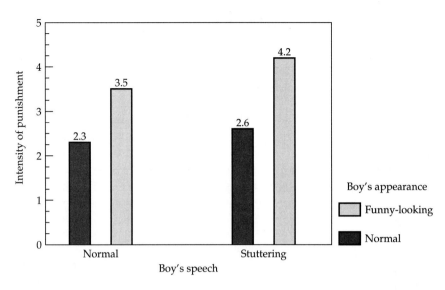

FIGURE 3-9

Mean intensity of punishment (noise blasts on a 10-step scale) given to boy as a function of boy's appearance and speech. (Data from Berkowitz & Frodi (1979). Copyright 1979 by the American Sociological Association. Adapted by permission.)

angry subjects, apparently because he had the most negative meaning for these women.

SUMMARY

Continuing the discussion of emotional aggression, this chapter focuses on the aggression-enhancing effects of negative affect. Research with humans as well as with other animal species indicates that many different kinds of aversive stimuli, including painful electric shocks, unpleasantly high temperatures, and foul odors, can instigate fighting and aggression. The aggression isn't inevitable, the afflicted animal or human may prefer to flee rather than fight, and the aggression displayed may have a substantial defensive component. In many instances, however, both people and animals that have been exposed to unpleasant stimuli tend to attack suitable targets, if they are present, and especially if alternative courses of action are not available. This happens, it's important to note, even when the aggression cannot lessen the aversive stimulation.

A theoretical model based on these observations suggests that both the anger experience and the display of aggression are affected by a sequence of processes. At the start, it is proposed, the negative affect generated by the aversive event instigates fight *and* flight tendencies. The relative strengths of these opposing tendencies are determined by biological, learning, and situational factors. The rudimentary anger experience stems from the negative affect-produced physiological, expressive-motor, and cognitive changes associated with the fight tendency, whereas the initial feeling of fear is based on flight-associated physiological, motor, and cognitive reactions. These feelings parallel their respective behavioral inclinations but do not cause them. From this view, anger accompanies rather than creates the instigation to aggression.

It is also proposed that in people at least, and possibly in other animal species as well, the expressive-motor inclination to strike at a target is accompanied by a desire to hurt or even destroy the target. Evidence is reported from an experiment with humans indicating that people in pain have an urge to hurt others. I suggest also that the negative affect is particularly likely to give rise to felt anger and aggressive inclinations, especially when the negative affect is intense and agitated, when specific suitable targets are available, and when the individual is not primarily intent on escaping from the unpleasant situation.

According to the analysis in this chapter, the first automatic and involuntary reactions to negative stimuli can be modified quickly as the aroused persons think about their feelings, the instigating events, their conceptions of what emotions they might be experiencing, and the social rules regarding the emotions and actions that may be appropriate under the circumstances. The initial rudimentary anger experience may be intensified, enriched and differentiated, suppressed, or eliminated altogether by these cognitions.

I maintain that it is helpful to conceive of an emotional state as a network of particular feelings, expressive-motor responses, thoughts, and memories, all so organized that the activation of any one component tends to spread, activating the other parts with which it is linked. Thoughts and/or memories that have an aggressive meaning thus are apt to generate angry feelings and even aggressive action tendencies.

Research findings consistent with this formulation indicate, for example, that aversive stimulation gives rise to hostile and/or anger-related ideas even when no one deliberately mistreated the subjects, that sad occurrences often produce anger as well as sadness, and that depression can generate anger and impulsive acts of aggression. However, by giving attention to their feelings, unhappily aroused people may also exert self-control, restraining their negative affect-produced aggressive urges and perhaps also lessening the anger they perceive in themselves.

Further extending the observation that emotional aggression is susceptible to automatic situational influences, the chapter then concludes with a more detailed consideration of the role of certain external stimuli ("aggressive cues"). I maintain that certain stimuli in the surrounding situation can intensify or even activate aggressive inclinations when the stimuli (1) have an aggressive meaning and/or (2) are associated with pain and suffering. Research on the weapons effect is an example of the first kind of influence, and quite a few studies have corroborated the original demonstration of this effect, especially if the subjects are relatively uninhibited at the time. The second type of influence is apparent in the impulsive and unthinking acts of aggression which "normals" often inflict upon handicapped persons, presumably because seeing these unfortunate individuals reminds the "normals" of suffering and other unpleasant states.

*N*OTES

1. See Berkowitz (1982, 1983, 1989).

2. For a convenient summary of much of this research before the mid-1960s, see Ulrich (1966). For more abbreviated discussion of this literature, see Berkowitz (1982) on aversively stimulated aggression, in *Advances in experimental social psychology,* and Berkowitz (1983) on the same topic, in *American Psychologist.* Interested readers who are looking for references to specific studies bearing on the points about animal research made in this section should consult these articles.

3. Brain (1981).

4. See Berkowitz (1982) for citations to these and other relevant studies; see especially pp. 263–264.

5. Knutson, Fordyce, & Anderson (1980).

6. See Anderson (1989).

7. See Berkowitz (1982) on aversively stimulated aggression, p. 266. See also Baron & Ransberger (1978); Carlsmith & Anderson (1979). Anderson (1989) discusses some of the statistical problems in these studies.

8. References to these and other experiments can be found in Anderson (1989), a review of the scientific literature; and also in Berkowitz (1982), pp. 266–267, and Baron (1977).

9. Jones & Bogat (1978); Zillmann, Baron, & Tamborini (1981); Rotton, Frey, Barry, Milligan, & Fitzpatrick (1979); White (1979); Zillmann, Bryant, Comisky, & Medoff (1981).

10. Landau & Raveh (1987); Landau (1988).

11. See Berkowitz & Holmes (1959, 1960).

12. Berkowitz, Cochran, & Embree (1981), Experiment 1. It's easy to see that relatively few punishments were delivered in any of the conditions and that the differences among the conditions were quite small. Nonetheless, I suggest that the women in this study were somewhat reluctant to give any punishments at all, probably because they didn't want the experimenter to think of them as overly aggressive. They might well have been much more punitive if they had been less restrained.

13. Landau & Raveh (1987); Landau (1988); Novaco (1986), p. 57.

14. This formulation was also outlined in Berkowitz (1983) and discussed in somewhat more detail in Berkowitz (1989), an article on my proposed revision of the frustration-aggression hypothesis. However, the most complete statement of this theoretical model can be found in Berkowitz (1990).

15. Ekman, Levenson, & Friesen (1983); Izard (1977); Schwartz, Weinberger, & Singer (1981); Sirota, Schwartz, & Kristeller (1987).

16. See Rule, Taylor, & Dobbs (1987); Berkowitz (1989, 1990).

17. Diener & Iran-Nejad (1986).

18. James (1989), p. 381.

19. Izard (1977).

20. See Berkowitz (1990) for a brief summary of several articles reporting displays of anger and aggression by people in mourning. The observation I quoted regarding the frequent association of anger and bereavement was made by Rosenblatt and his colleagues, cited in my 1990 paper. The observation regarding the connection between sadness and anger in infants was reported by Termine and Izard (1988).

21. Izard (1977), p. 308.

22. Demonstrating just this, when undergraduate women in one of our Wisconsin experiments were asked to recall significant incidents involving several people they knew (their mothers, their boyfriends, and a neutral person), those who were made to be physically uncomfortable at the time recalled more instances of conflict than did those who were not uncomfortable. See Berkowitz (1990).

23. Some references to studies demonstrating this relationship between depression and aggression can be found in Berkowitz (1983), a paper on aversively stimulated aggression.

24. Poznanski & Zrull (1970).

25. The investigation of children is summarized in Pfeffer, Zuckerman, Plutchik, & Mizruchi (1987). While many depressives are likely to be aggressive at times, research indicates that open aggression is more characteristic of some kinds of depressives than of others. A German study (Matussek, Luks, and Seibt, 1986) of the close relationships of adult depressives found that unipolar depressives (who have periodic episodes of deep gloom) were often arrogant and indirectly aggressive toward their partners. By contrast, bipolar depressives (whose moods swing from intense depression to strong elation) apparently were much more likely to inhibit their aggressive reactions.

26. Seligman (1975).

27. Poznanski & Zrull (1970), p. 13.

28. See Freud (1917/1955).

29. See Miller & Norman (1979).

30. May (1972), p. 182.

31. In this method, which is now frequently employed in research on depression, each subject reads a series of statements, all of which have a particular

emotional tone, and thinks of how each one applies to him or her. The men in the depressed condition thus read and thought about sixty statements, each one more depressing than its predecessor.

32. Hynan & Grush (1986).

33. Berkowitz & Troccoli (1990).

34. For example, see Mayer & Gaschke (1988).

35. This is a metaphorical statement, of course, and it is phrased in this manner only because I want to highlight the importance of the external stimuli. These stimuli probably work by activating thoughts, memories, and/or various expressive-motor reactions within the person that facilitate the open display of aggression.

36. I must emphasize that the effects of guns or weapons depend to a considerable extent on the meaning these objects possess for the person. Hunters might conceivably view guns as objects which they use only for sport (and not for hurting other people), so that they are reminded of the fun they have on autumn weekends when they hunt for wild game. For such people, seeing the weapons won't give rise to aggressive thoughts about people and shouldn't have aggressive consequences. However, a good many persons do assign aggressive meaning to weapons; this is true of adults as well as children, and in other nations as well as in the United States. As a result, these people are likely to have aggressive ideas when they see a gun. If their inhibitions against aggression are weak at the time, these ideas can be translated into impulsive aggressive actions (as well as other hostile thoughts and memories): clenched fists, thrown punches, quick pressure on a button that administers electric shocks, or maybe even reflexive squeezes of the trigger.

37. Berkowitz & Le Page (1967).

38. Turner & Simons (1974).

39. Frodi (1975).

40. Failures to confirm the weapons effect as well as many successful replications of the original experiment are discussed in Turner, Simons, Berkowitz, & Frodi (1977). The Belgian and Italian replications are reported in papers by Leyens and Parke (1975) and Caprara, Renzi, Amdini, D'Imperio, & Travaglia (1984). The Turner et al. carnival study is mentioned in Turner, Simons, Berkowitz, & Frodi (1977), p. 360.

41. For example, Turner & Goldsmith (1976).

42. The animal experiment is described in Ulrich & Favell (1970). The human study is summarized in Leyens & Fraczek (1983).

43. The animal experiment was reported in Ulrich, Hutchinson, & Azrin (1965). The human experiment was performed by Riordan & Tedeschi (1983).

44. Berkowitz (1962), Chap. 5. Also see Miller, N. E. (1948).

45. Hovland & Sears (1940). Also see Mintz (1946).

46. See Berkowitz (1962), pp. 136–137.

47. Berkowitz & Frodi (1979).

4

Does Thinking Make It So?

Cognitions and Emotion

———— ❖ ————

Theories of Emotion ◆ *What Determines the Emotional Experience?* ◆ *Cognitive Formulations of Emotion* ◆ *Experimental Demonstrations of the Role of Attributions in Emotions* ◆ Cognitions Don't Always "Make It So": Evidence of Noncognitive Influences upon Emotion ◆ *Effects of Expressive Reactions* ◆ *Bodily Reactions and Cognitions: An Associative-Network Interpretation* ◆ Thoughts Do Matter

Chapters 2 and 3 emphasized the relatively nonthoughtful and impulsive nature of many acts of angry aggression. It's obvious, however, that people can think about what has happened to them and what they might do under the circumstances, and that these thoughts can help to determine what they will feel and how they will act. In this chapter, I will focus mainly on the role of thoughts—or more generally, cognitive processes—in shaping both the nature of the emotional experience and the behavior that is displayed. Much attention will be given to a discussion of how people's beliefs about the causes of their emotional arousal and about what might happen next can influence their specific feelings and their actions. In addition, I'll also have something to say about the way the ideas we happen to have at a particular time can affect our interpretations of another person's behavior and how we behave toward this person. Even though the emphasis will be on cognitive processes, I will point out-

84

that bodily reactions also contribute to the emotional experience. Thoughts aren't everything.

This discussion obviously has a bearing on how we conceive of emotions generally, and so, to highlight the theoretical issues we will be facing, I'll present the research and my arguments within the context of contemporary theories of emotion.

THEORIES OF EMOTION

What Determines the Emotional Experience?

As a start, you should be clear about the difference between the views I will summarize in this chapter and the analysis I offered in previous chapters. I have suggested that when people encounter an unpleasant event (either something inherently unpleasant or something that they interpret negatively), they have a variety of reactions in their thoughts and memories and throughout their bodies. I have also suggested that ideational, physiological, and expressive-motor responses form the basis of emotional experience. Thoughts and beliefs presumably enter into the picture after the initial, basic emotional feelings arise. The cognitive formulations in this chapter will take a very different approach. Much more in line with everyday notions about emotions, and also in accord with the phrase from Shakespeare's *Hamlet*, which was paraphrased in the subtitle of this chapter, these analyses maintain that thoughts are the necessary determinants of emotional reactions. Presumably, we become angry only when we believe we have been wronged or deliberately threatened by someone, and we then want to hurt the other person because of our anger.

I certainly don't want to reject this kind of view altogether; it seems right to most of us and also has considerable empirical support. My contention, however, is that it is seriously incomplete. Paraphrasing another line from Shakespeare, we can say that there is far more to the development of emotional experience than is dreamt of by this cognitive/everyday approach. First, let's look briefly at how emotions are viewed from this cognitive perspective.

Cognitive Formulations of Emotion

What Interpretations Produce Anger?
Although the psychologists who take this cognitive stance don't agree in detail, they all start from the same basic supposition: The person's inter-

pretation of the arousing occurrence is all-important.[1] Let's use the following situation as an illustration:

> Jane Smith, a single woman in her mid-30s, has just met an attractive unmarried man at her place of employment. They seem to like each other, and they agree to have a drink together after work at a nearby restaurant. Jane arrives on time. After waiting about an hour, she realizes that the man has failed to keep their appointment.

How will Jane react? Common sense and the cognitive theories say that the feelings she will experience—whether she will be infuriated, saddened, or depressed—depend upon her interpretation of what has happened. This seems obvious. But what kind of interpretation will lead to an angry feeling and what will produce another emotion? First I'll summarize some of the ways cognitive theorists have answered this question, and later I'll offer my own views.

Appraisals and attributions. Unfortunately, not all cognitively oriented theorists use the same terminology when they try to explain what kinds of perceptions produce the different emotions. Some of the writers in this area speak of *appraisals*, referring to almost any kind of interpretation or assessment of the situation, while others prefer to talk about *attributions*, which generally have to do with a person's beliefs about the *cause* of an emotion-arousing event. Bernard Weiner's analysis of emotions provides a good example of the latter usage. He says that people are apt to become angry when they have an unhappy experience and attribute it to (1) an *external cause* (something other than themselves) that (2) *could have been controlled by the person or thing responsible*. In our example, Jane would be angry to the extent that she blamed the man for not showing up and believed that he could have kept the appointment if he had really wanted to.

One possible way to deal with the terminological confusion in this area is to adopt the distinction long recommended by Richard Lazarus.[2] He suggests that we should differentiate between "knowledge" and "appraisal." *Knowledge* refers to a belief about the facts of an encounter. Jane's interpretation of why the man did not show up is such a knowledge (or belief). Many attributions are instances of knowledge in this sense. *Appraisal*, on the other hand, according to Lazarus, should be confined to beliefs regarding the personal significance of the given event for the individual's well-being. Lazarus argues that strong feelings don't arise unless an appraisal of this kind is made. He would say, then, that Jane wouldn't be intensely aroused unless the man's behavior was personally highly significant for her, in that it had a bearing on her conception of herself.

Belief dimensions in emotional situations. Following Lazarus's usage, researchers who take the cognitive approach (such as Ira Roseman; Klaus Scherer; and Craig Smith and Phoebe Ellsworth[3]) have assumed that emotion-relevant knowledge (or beliefs) can be described in terms of a relatively small number of underlying dimensions. The location of any given belief along these cognitive dimensions determines the resulting emotional experience.

In an example of this type of analysis, when Smith and Ellsworth asked university undergraduates to recall and describe different emotion-arousing situations, they found that the situations perceived by their subjects could be characterized to a considerable degree in terms of (1) how pleasant they were; (2) how much effort was required to deal with them; (3) the extent to which the person had to attend to and consider the situations; (4) how certain the individual was about what was happening; (5) the extent to which the person, rather than someone else, was responsible for causing what occurred; and (6) the degree to which no one, someone else, or the subject could have controlled or influenced what happened.

Not all these dimensions are important in every emotion. Smith and Ellsworth are basically in agreement with Weiner's analysis of anger-provoking events. They found that when people feel angry they generally regard the emotion-arousing situation as being caused by someone's actions (i.e., someone was responsible for the unpleasant event), and they also think that the occurrence could have been controlled. However, they have added to Weiner's list the idea that most persons also view the angering situation as decidedly unpleasant and as requiring a good deal of effort. (Essentially, this means that the affected individual is intensely aroused and has to expend effort to deal with the event.) Jane would theoretically be angry to the extent that she believed the man was personally responsible for his failure to keep the appointment and could have controlled what had happened. The situation would also be exceedingly unpleasant for her and presumably would cause her to feel agitated and aroused.

Whether they speak of "appraisals" or "attributions," other theorists have argued that still other beliefs are necessary if a person is to become angry. As I noted in Chapter 2, James Averill maintains that anger is an accusation that one has been mistreated. We will supposedly feel angry not only because we have failed to get what we want and we blame someone for this unpleasant occurrence (i.e., we think someone was responsible and could have influenced what happened) but also because we believe the other person's action was unfair or violated social rules. In other words, according to Averill, Jane would be angry to the degree that she believed the man had deliberately wronged her. Lazarus goes even further. From his perspective, anger arises only when a negative event is regarded as personally significant and also when the affected person is uncertain about his or her ability to cope with the situation. Jane would experience anger only to the extent that she thought she was somehow threatened by the man's failure to show up.[4] The top half of Figure 4–1 lists the different types of appraisals and attributions that presumably give rise to anger.

But what if no one can be blamed? Though I want to defer my discussion of the shortcomings of this type of analysis, I should mention a point made by some cognitive theorists. As you undoubtedly know (and as I have pointed out), people sometimes become angry when no one in particular can be blamed. You can be irritated with your car if it breaks down on a highway, or furious with the weather if a thunderstorm spoils your picnic, and you might even shout with annoyance if a shelf you had just finished putting up collapsed. In these cases and many others, the unfortunate happening can't be attributed to anyone's intentional misdeed, but anger still arises. Why? A frequent answer is that unhappy persons actually think of a particular entity as being responsible for their disappointment. In their minds they momentarily regard a thing—a car, the weather, a shelf, or another object that bothers them—as a "being" or

FIGURE 4-1
Outline of two cognitive analyses of anger.

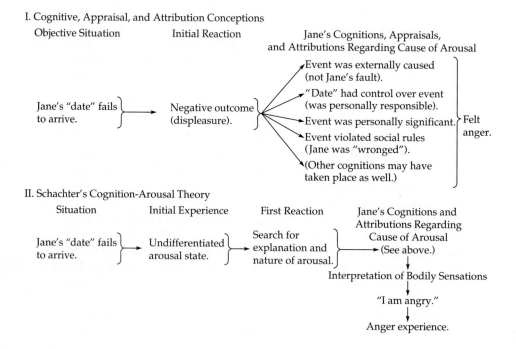

an "entity," and they blame the entity for misbehaving. "That damn thing has mistreated me," they presumably tell themselves, and then they are angry with the thing that "wronged" them.

Many of you undoubtedly agree with this possibility. Haven't we all had thoughts of this nature when something bad happened to us? Maybe we do tend to attribute our misfortunes to a specific entity even when an impersonal natural force was actually responsible—or maybe not. I'll return to this possibility a little later.

Experimental Demonstrations of the Role of Attributions in Emotions

Most of the empirical support for the analyses I summarized above has come from naturalistic investigations in which ordinary people were asked about their emotional experiences. These reports can be, and have been, a rich source of valuable information about emotions, but they are also susceptible to distorting influences: the subjects' wishful thinking, after-the-fact attempts to place the given event in the best possible light, previously acquired beliefs about the nature of a particular emotional experience, and so on. The only way to rule out these possible sources of error is to supplement the naturalistic studies with experiments in which the situational conditions are deliberately manipulated. Fortunately, social psychologists have conducted a fair number of experiments that demonstrate the effects of attributions upon emotional reactions.

The Schachter-Singer Two-Factor Theory of Emotions

Much current thinking about the role of attributions in emotions began with a very well-known cognitive theory of emotions which was published by Stanley Schachter and Jerome Singer in 1962.[5] (My own conception of how higher-order thoughts shape the formation of emotional experiences after the initial, relatively primitive, emotional reactions arise, which was spelled out in Chapter 3 and illustrated in Figure 3–2, has been influenced by this formulation.) Any consideration of the role of cognitions in the development of anger would be seriously incomplete without a discussion of this theory.

Schachter and Singer began their analysis by questioning the notion (advanced by William James and others) that specific emotions are a function of particular bodily reactions. According to Schachter and Singer, however, we don't feel angry because our muscles tense, our jaws clench, our pulse rates increase, and so on, but because (1) we are generally aroused, and (2) we have certain cognitions about the nature of our arousal.

Here's how the theory goes. When people encounter an emotion-exciting event, they supposedly first experience a neutral and undifferentiated physiological arousal. Theoretically, what happens next depends upon whether they know why they are aroused and what they are feeling. If individuals are unsure what emotion they are experiencing, they will presumably look for clues in the situation that might help to explain the nature of their sensations. "What am I feeling?" they ask themselves, perhaps at an unconscious level. "Am I afraid, excited, angry, or what?" They search for an answer. However, if they realize from the start what aroused them and what feelings they are having, they don't have to seek information about what is happening; they already know. In either case, according to Schachter and Singer, the aroused persons will then form a belief about the nature of their sensations, and this cognition will presumably mold the general, undifferentiated arousal state into the specific emotional experience.

The bottom half of Figure 4–1 applies this theory to Jane's feelings in the example I've been using. Theoretically, she was first generally aroused when she realized the man wouldn't keep their appointment, and quickly developed an idea of why she was aroused and what her feelings were: "I must be upset because he didn't show up. I must be angry with him." This belief shaped her emotional state so that she experienced a definite anger.

I'll briefly summarize part of the clever experiment Schachter and Singer carried out, to illustrate this theory in operation. Ostensibly because the researchers were studying the effects of a certain (fictitious) vitamin on vision, the subjects were told that they would be given an injection of the vitamin. In some cases the injection was a dose of epinephrine, which produces an autonomic arousal and sensations such as a pounding heart and a flushed face, while other subjects received only an innocuous saline solution that had little effect upon their nervous systems. (You'll recognize that the sensations caused by epinephrine are somewhat similar to the ones we have when we're angry.) Equally important, the experimenter also created differences in the participants' beliefs about the drug's side effects. In the part of the experiment that is of greatest concern to this discussion, half the people given the epinephrine were told what the side effects would be (for example, that they would feel their hearts pounding rapidly), whereas the other half were not given any information about the side effects. As a result, when the people in both of these conditions began to sense their drug-induced autonomic arousal, the aroused-informed subjects could attribute their sensations to the injection, while the aroused-uninformed subjects were presumably unsure what had aroused them and what their feelings meant. The nonaroused subjects who received the placebo treatment were also not told about the side effects.

After the "vitamin" injection had been administered to each subject, another person, who had supposedly received the same treatment but was actually the experimenter's accomplice, entered the room. Both were informed that they would have to wait about 20 minutes for the vision study to begin and were also asked to complete a questionnaire while they waited. The accomplice, who had been coached, began to express considerable annoyance about the personal nature of the questions asked in the questionnaire. The accomplice finally tore up the form and stormed out of the room. All the while, the real subject's actions were being recorded by an observer seated behind a one-way mirror. The object was to ascertain the degree to which the subjects displayed anger by emulating the accomplice and/or by making hostile statements about the study, the questionnaire, or both.

The two-factor theory makes a clear prediction about the effects of these experimental variations. The assumption was that the subjects in the aroused-uninformed condition were somewhat uncertain about why they were having strange sensations (the drug's side effects). Their cognitions about their feelings would therefore be readily influenced by seemingly appropriate situational cues, such as the accomplice's behavior. They would take this person's actions as clues to what they themselves must be feeling, as if they told themselves, "Since he's angry about the questionnaire, I must also be annoyed with it." Guided by this belief, they presumably would then experience anger and even display it openly in their behavior.

Although there were some ambiguities in the data, the naive subjects' actions were generally in accord with the theory's expectations. The observers' scoring system is too complicated to be described here, but in essence, as can be seen in Figure 4–2, the aroused-uninformed subjects were most strongly influenced by the accomplice's angry display and showed the highest level of expressed anger.

This intriguing experiment quickly attracted considerable attention and stimulated a considerable body of research. Some of the subsequent investigations have questioned various aspects of the theory and/or the study's procedure.[6] Nonetheless, the theory does seem to work under limited conditions—when the individual is only moderately aroused (rather than strongly so); is in an ambiguous, difficult-to-interpret situation; and isn't sure what produced the arousal.

The Misattribution Experiments
Psychologists have been especially taken by one implication of the Schachter-Singer research: Emotional experiences apparently can be readily influenced by attributions. Just as the subjects in this experiment presumably felt angry when (under the confederate's influence) they attributed their physiological arousal to an obnoxious, privacy-invading questionnaire, other people theoretically would not become angry if they believed their bodily sensations had been caused by something that ordinarily doesn't produce anger. Isn't it possible, then, a number of investigators asked, that we can lessen people's emotional reactions by somehow getting them to attribute their arousal to a nonemotional source?

We're dealing here with the possible emotion-changing effects of

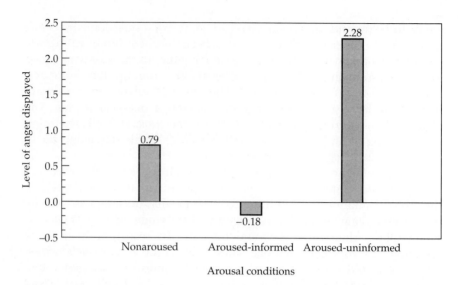

FIGURE 4-2
Level of anger displayed by subjects when accomplice acted angrily. (Adapted from Schachter & Singer (1962). Copyright 1962 by the American Psychological Association. Adapted by permisssion.)

misattributions (so named because the arousal actually produced by an emotion-evoking stimulus is incorrectly attributed to another, more plausible source). You can get an idea of what psychologists have in mind when they discuss misattributions by thinking back to Jane waiting for her date in the restaurant. She's emotionally aroused. However, let's also suppose that she had taken a new medication just before she left her office and had been warned by her physician that the drug might increase her heart rate and cause her to feel "butterflies" in her stomach—sensations similar to those experienced by angry people. The misattribution notion tells us that if Jane is aware of the possible side effects of the medication, she may attribute her physiological arousal to the drug rather than to the man's failure to show up. As a result, she may not believe she is angry ("It's the medication that's making me feel upset"), and consequently she won't be in an angry state.

The research on this topic has yielded uneven results, as I have indicated, but there have been some positive findings,[7] and the theory may hold true for certain limited circumstances.

You can see what these findings suggest. Let's say that you're trying to calm a boy who is very angry with his brother. Theoretically, according to this research, you might lessen his urge to attack his sibling if you could convince him that he had been aroused by something other than his brother—something emotionally neutral, such as a loud noise. As a matter of fact, Russell Geen has obtained results consistent with this notion. In the crucial condition of Geen's investigation, university men were provoked by the experimenter's confederate and then exposed to loud noise before they had an opportunity to retaliate. The people who had been provoked and who were led to attribute their arousal to the unpleasant noise tended to punish the confederate less severely than did subjects who didn't believe they had been aroused by the noise.[8] The former presumably didn't think of themselves as very angry and thus didn't act angry. However, as we all know (and as some studies have found), in many circumstances it can be very difficult to persuade insulted people that they aren't really angry.

Attributions in Excitation Transfer

The energizing effects of an irrelevant arousal. Generally speaking, we don't expect noise to promote aggression (unless the noise is annoying), but loud noise can actually heighten the strength of an attack. It can do this in several ways, some of which might involve attributions.

First, noise may be aversive. As you saw in Chapter 3, unpleasant stimulations—uncomfortable temperatures, foul odors, irritating cigarette smoke, or even raucous sounds—can generate aggressive inclinations. Second, noise can be generally arousing, and this arousal can energize aggressive tendencies that are already operating. Russell Geen and Edgar O'Neal[9] provided evidence for just this kind of effect by demonstrating that when people were disposed to be aggressive (in this case because they had watched a violent movie), those who were exposed to loud noises were subsequently more punitive to a fellow student than were others who had heard only mild noises. The loud sounds apparently were arousing, and the resulting general arousal intensified the subjects' movie-induced aggressive inclinations.

It's important to recognize that any arousing stimulation can have this effect, not only noise. We can be excited by many things, including physical exercise, certain drugs, the sight of others engaged in daring activities, rock music, and sexual scenes. Barclay, for example, showed that when subjects were sexually aroused in a laboratory experiment, they subsequently became more aggressive toward a target person than they otherwise would have been.[10] No matter what produces a heightened excitation, the arousal can energize whatever urge we may have to attack someone (assuming that the excitation doesn't put us in such a good mood that we're unwilling to hurt anyone).[11]

It's easy to think of other instances of this phenomenon. In the eighteenth and nineteenth centuries (and perhaps earlier), warriors in a number of American Indian societies performed exciting war dances before going off to battle. The drum beats, the shouting by dancers and onlookers, and the physical activity raised the warriors' feelings to a very high level and thereby intensified their existing aggressive inclinations. Much the same phenomenon occurs when ordinarily civilized and restrained people are so affected by the sights and sounds of an excited crowd that they become violent.

Excitation transfer theory. The energizing effect of arousal is a fairly primitive phenomenon that takes place without thought and can influence the behavior of practically every type of animal. However, another kind of arousal effect is evidently more dependent upon cognitive processes. According to Dolph Zillmann, who first identified this phenomenon, an attribution-mediated transfer of the excitation produced by an emotionally neutral event can strengthen reactions to another, more emotional occurrence.[12]

I will summarize Zillmann's theory very briefly. After we become physically aroused, the internal physiological excitation typically subsides with time, so that we are no longer fully conscious of our inner excitement, even though we may still be somewhat aroused. We may no longer even be thinking about what excited us in the first place. With the initial arousing event out of mind, it may be fairly easy to misattribute the moderate or low level of arousal we are still experiencing to another incident that occurs soon afterward. For example, suppose you come home after a bike ride. Your body may still be physiologically excited from the exercise, but after a while you're not fully aware of your arousal, and, in fact, you're no longer even thinking about your bike ride. You turn on the TV set and happen to see a newsflash about a politician you dislike. The sight of this person may produce a rush of feeling, which you interpret as strong anger. The residual physical excitation from your exercise has been transferred to the politician, adding to your normal distaste for this person. Moreover, according to Zillmann, you interpret your feeling as anger because you are more conscious of the more recent event (seeing the politician) than you are of the earlier event (the physiologically arousing bicycle ride).

Zillmann's excitation transfer theory isn't restricted to aggression. He has extended his analysis to other forms of behavior and other types of arousal, and has provided evidence that (among other things) the excitation left over from an earlier sexual arousal can heighten people's helpfulness or increase their enjoyment of music and appreciation of humor.[13]

Whatever the exact nature of their arousal and whatever kind of behavior they carry out, people who are still feeling the effects of an earlier excitation apparently tend to attribute their arousal not to the actual cause but to some other source (1) that *they are especially aware of at that time* and (2) *that could plausibly have produced the arousal they are experiencing.* A man who becomes sexually aroused when he sees an erotic movie may subsequently believe that a joke he hears is very funny. Very conscious of the joke but with the movie momentarily forgotten, he thinks that it was the joke that aroused him and that he must therefore be amused.

Attributions and the Effects of Mitigating Information

Attributions can work in other ways as well—for example, when we know that someone's annoying action wasn't really directed at us personally. Suppose you go to work one morning and are told by one of your coworkers to be careful in front of your boss. "He isn't feeling well today because of some family problems," your colleague warns you, "and he's been grouchy." Soon afterward, just as you're getting settled at your desk, your boss growls at you and accuses you of being late, even though you were actually on time. Ordinarily you would be annoyed. You would attribute his unwarranted criticism to a flaw in his personality. However, the information your coworker gave you explains that extenuating circumstances account for your superior's action. You therefore attribute his remark to external pressures rather than to his individual qualities, and you don't take his criticism personally.

There's nothing especially mysterious about this hypothetical event, and we don't need any research to tell us that this kind of thing does actually take place every once in a while. What is much more interesting is the studies that point to limitations on the effects of mitigating information and the resulting attributions.

This research also was initiated by Zillmann and his associates, and other investigators have provided corroborating evidence.[14] Let's go back to the example of your boss's nasty remark. Generally speaking, Zillmann's experiments have demonstrated that information about extenuating circumstances (in this case, that your boss had personal troubles) is *not* particularly effective in dampening the instigation to aggression when (1) the information is received some time after the unpleasant event occurs, and (2) the person is very strongly aroused.

The first point is demonstrated by the results of an experiment by Dolph Zillmann and Joanne Cantor.[15] All the participants in this study were provoked by an obnoxious experimenter, and most of them learned that there were mitigating circumstances—that the experimenter was distressed about an examination he was scheduled to take. However, some subjects were given this information *before* they were mistreated by the experimenter, whereas others received the information *after* they had been insulted. Of course, subjects in a third group were not told about the extenuating circumstances. To measure aggression, each subject was given an opportunity to file a complaint about the experimenter and was told that the complaint could affect his future.

None of the people who had been warned about the experimenter's distress before they were mistreated entered a complaint, and physiological measurements showed that they had not been greatly aroused by his obnoxious behavior. They hadn't regarded his action as a personal attack. On the other hand, telling the subjects about the mitigating circumstances several minutes after they were provoked was apparently telling them too late. The information didn't dampen their hostility toward the experimenter. When they learned why the experimenter had been so rude, their physiological arousal levels didn't drop much below the arousal levels of subjects in the no-mitigating-information condition, and they complained about the experimenter almost as much as did the subjects in the uninformed group.

Zillmann warns, however, that we should not assume that after-the-fact extenuating information never reduces the aggressive urge generated by a provocation. Citing the findings in a 1966 experiment by Shahbaz Mallick and Boyd McCandless,[16] he notes that reappraisal of a prior annoyance occasionally does lessen the subsequent aggression, though it may take some time for the "excusing" information to be absorbed and have an effect. The results in the Zillmann-Cantor experiment were based on measurements taken soon after the subjects had been mistreated. It's conceivable that, if they had been tested after their feelings subsided and they calmed down, these people might have thought more about the mitigating circumstances and readjusted their attitudes toward the experimenter.

However, even a long delay and ample time to consider the extenuating information may not eliminate provoked persons' aggressive inclinations altogether, if they are very strongly aroused at the time they are mistreated. Zillmann suggests that aggressive ideas developed in the intense "heat of anger" become firmly implanted and thus persist over time. Then, because the hostility (i.e., the negative attitude) continues, the provoked persons may attack their tormentor later, "in cold blood," when a suitable opportunity arises.[17]

Reinterpreting Attribution Effects from the Associative Network Perspective
Although the attribution research reviewed above seems at first glance to be very different from the associative network theory of emotional aggression I spelled out in Chapter 3, the attribution effects can actually be easily understood in the light of this alternative perspective.

First of all, contrary to the cognitive theorists' contention that certain kinds of appraisals and attributions (the ones listed in part I of Figure 4–1) are necessary if anger is to arise, I demonstrated in Chapter 3 that anger and aggression can occur even in the absence of these appraisals. It is apparently better to say that these cognitions typically only serve to intensify the anger experience and accompanying aggressive inclinations because they *heighten the felt unpleasantness* of the emotion-precipitating occurrence. Jane's belief that the man from her office deliberately failed to keep their appointment would obviously make her feel bad. She would feel even worse if, on top of that unpleasant idea, she also thought the man had changed his mind about their date because he considered her unattractive. The sense of having been wronged would increase her negative affect even further, and it would also lower her inhibitions about feeling and displaying anger. After all, many of us believe we are justified in being angry with those who have violated social rules. In sum, these appraisals and attributions would generate decidedly negative feelings and the resulting negative affect would lead to a fairly strong anger experience.

In this connection, I basically contend that aggressive inclinations will be stimulated as long as negative affect is experienced. This is why information excusing a deliberate affront is often ineffective when it is received too late. The insulted individual has already become displeased and, indeed, brooding repeatedly about the unpleasant incident before hearing about the extenuating circumstances may even have intensified the displeasure. Under such circumstances, people's residual negative feelings will have to be reduced substantially if their aggressive urge is to be completely eliminated.

The associative network analysis can also account for the effects of the self-perception emphasized by Schachter's two-factor theory and Zillmann's excitation transfer conception. Both of these formulations essentially maintain that we experience anger only after we think of ourselves as being angry. I suggest, however, that this self-labeling only heightens the existing negative affect-generated rudimentary anger feelings. Remember that aggression-related thoughts and memories are linked associatively to these negative feelings. The mere thought of oneself as angry can activate the feeling of anger to some extent, as shown in our ability to reexperience anger upon recalling an earlier, anger-provoking incident. Similarly, we feel somewhat sadder when we believe that we are experiencing sadness. The point, then, is not that emotional self-labeling is necessary for the production of an emotional experience but that it is one of several factors that contribute to the intensity of the emotion.

COGNITIONS DON'T ALWAYS "MAKE IT SO": EVIDENCE OF NONCOGNITIVE INFLUENCES UPON EMOTION

I have been describing the effects of fairly involved thoughts upon emotional reactions generally and upon angry or aggressive responses to unpleasant events in particular. Though our beliefs about what we are feeling and why we have been aroused can influence our emotional experiences and how we behave, these beliefs, appraisals, and attributions aren't necessary for emotional reactions to occur. Complex thinking doesn't always "make it so," at least not in emotional matters.

Effects of Expressive Reactions

The major rivals to the cognitive analyses of emotion are conceptions that emphasize the importance of bodily reactions in emotional experience. These ideas aren't new. For more than a century, some biologists, physiologists, and psychologists have held that feelings depend largely if not exclusively upon the changes that take place throughout the body—in the muscles, viscera, and so on. Charles Darwin took this position in his 1872 work, *The Expression of the Emotions in Man and Animals*, contending that "Most of our emotions are so closely connected with their expression, that they hardly exist if the body remains passive."[18] The best-known version of this line of thought is the classic *James-Lange theory* of emotions. It was named after the American philosopher-psychologist William James and the Danish physiologist Carl Lange, who each propounded the same notion somewhat independently about 100 years ago. I will go into this theory and its modern successors for at least two reasons: First, it will help you to gain a better understanding of what is involved in the formation of angry feelings. Second, it challenges the widespread belief in the psychological benefits of expressing feelings. Below is a brief outline of the James-Lange theory, based on James' writings.

The James-Lange Theory of Emotions

Bodily reaction, then emotion. William James started with a sharp departure from ordinary ideas about emotion (and from the cognitive theorizing just described). Most people (and cognitive theory) assume that emotions are produced by the person's interpretation of a psychologically significant situation. The appraisal or attribution supposedly determines what emotion will develop—what feelings will occur and what actions will take place. By contrast, James argued that "bodily changes follow directly the perception of the exciting fact, and that our feeling of the same changes as they occur *is* the emotion." He was well aware of the startling nature of his analysis.

> Common-sense [sic] says, we lose our fortune, are sorry and weep; we meet a bear, are frightened and run; we are insulted by a rival, are angry and strike. The hypothesis here to be defended says that this order of sequence is incorrect, . . . and that the more rational statement is that we feel sorry because we cry, angry because we strike, afraid because we tremble. . . . Without the bodily states following on the perception, the latter would be purely cognitive in form, pale, colorless, destitute of emotional warmth. We might then see the bear, and judge it best to run, receive the insult and deem it right to strike, but we should not actually *feel* afraid or angry.[19]

In outline, then, James's theory envisioned four steps in the production of an emotional experience: (1) The event is perceived. (2) Impulses travel from the central nervous system to muscles, skin, and viscera. (3) Sensations arising from changes in these parts of the body are transmitted back to the brain. (4) "These return impulses are then cortically perceived, and when combined with the original stimulus perception, produce the 'object-emotionally-felt.'"[20] Here is a clear difference with the cognitive theorizing described earlier. It's not a certain kind of appraisal that generates the emotional experience but our bodily reactions to this interpretation. We're afraid because we run, and we feel enraged because our muscles tense, our hands clench, we grit our teeth, and our stomachs churn.

More than visceral reactions. As is well-known, critics such as the great physiologist W. B. Cannon have faulted the James-Lange theory for a number of reasons, including the theory's supposed exclusive focus on visceral reactions. Cannon noted, among other things, that the viscera are generally too insensitive and too slow in response to be the basis of the often rapidly developing and quickly changing emotional experience. In actuality, however, James did *not* believe the viscera were the only determinants of the emotional experience. Although his later discussion of his theory did emphasize these autonomic responses, he maintained that changes in muscles, breathing, and even the skin contributed importantly to the emotions. "Can one fancy the state of rage," he wrote, "and picture no . . . flushing of the face, no dilation of the muscles, no clenching of the teeth?"[21] Thus, according to the *full* James-Lange theory, it is the total complex of physiological and muscular responses that produces the particular experience, not visceral changes alone.

Effects of Facial Expressions and Other Muscular Reactions
Cannon's criticism and psychology's changing interests led to an almost total rejection of the James-Lange theory. However, a newer version of the bodily reaction thesis came to the fore during the 1960s, when several psychologists, most notably (but not only) Silvan Tomkins and Carroll Izard, proposed that feelings are governed mainly by facial expressions.[22] In their analyses, facial reactions produce a sensory feedback to the brain which leads to much of the emotional experience. Other bodily responses contribute to the emotional feelings, Tomkins said, but the facial feedback—from the skin and facial muscles—plays the more important role, since the facial reactions are both more rapid and more complex than the reactions of the slower-moving visceral organs.

I won't go into the details of the *facial feedback hypothesis,* as this theory is often termed, nor even examine the intricacies of the research in this area and the controversies that have arisen. It's more important simply to note the essential validity of the facial feedback idea. People's facial movements can influence their subjective emotional experiences, especially when they aren't fully aware of the nature of their facial expressions. To illustrate this kind of effect, I'll tell you about one of the supporting experiments, a careful study carried out by Larry Rutledge and Ralph Hupka.[23]

After informing each subject that he was participating in a study concerned with the activity of facial muscles during a perceptual task, the experimenter put the man through a series of "trials." The subject was instructed to move some of his facial muscles in particular ways as he looked at an emotion-eliciting picture. In half the trials, randomly dispersed through the series, the experimenter arranged each subject's facial movements so that he seemed to be expressing joy, whereas in the other trials, he was induced to adopt the facial movements involved in the expression of anger. The scene presented to the subject while he maintained the indicated facial pattern showed either a joyous event (a sailor embracing a nurse), an anger-provoking incident (a woman who had been smeared with tar and tied to a stake), or a neutral occurrence. As the man looked at each picture, he rated his feelings on a number of standardized mood scales.

I should point out that the experimenter never told the subject the nature of the particular facial pattern that was established for any given trial, and as a matter of fact, when the men were questioned at the end of the session, the great majority of them hadn't realized what emotions they were expressing. I'll present the results that were obtained from this unaware group.

The men's reported feelings were affected by both the pictures they looked at and their facial expressions, but were especially affected when the pictures and the expressions were in alignment. They reported the strongest joy—and the least anger—when they saw the happy picture while maintaining a joyous expression, and they rated themselves as most angry—and least joyous—when they looked at the unpleasant scene with they had an angry expression.

It must be noted, however, that the subjects' facial expressions could not counteract the influence of the decidedly different emotional scene. A happy smile didn't make the men feel happy when they looked at the angering picture. The facial movements only strengthened the mood generated by the external emotional occurrence when they were compatible with the externally produced feelings. With Howard Leventhal and Andrew Tomarken, we apparently have to conclude that facial muscles aren't all-important or very powerful determinants of the emotional experience.[24] Nevertheless, what really matters is that facial expressions have *some* effect on feelings.

Another point should also be made here. Although researchers have devoted most of their attention to *facial* reactions, other bodily movements may also influence feelings. John Riskind and Carolyn Gotay have given us an example of this kind of effect in several experiments. They showed that subjects who were induced to adopt a slumped, hunched-over, depressed posture tended to act and feel more depressed than did control subjects who were told to take an expansive, upright posture.[25]

In sum, the evidence indicates that bodily reactions do contribute to feelings. The muscular movements we make during an emotion-arousing event can have an impact upon our emotional experience. It may well be that William James was right, at least in some respects. Think of the stereotyped high-status Englishman who insists upon keeping a "stiff upper lip" when confronted by adversity. He might conceivably be even more angry if he didn't restrain his facial expressions. A smile may not be an "umbrella" when something unpleasant happens (as the old song would have us believe), but a frown, grimace, or sneer may make us feel worse.

Bodily Reactions and Cognitions: An Associative Network Interpretation

We don't know exactly why bodily reactions influence emotional feelings. However, it certainly seems possible to interpret these effects in terms of the associative network ideas I have been advancing. If emotional states can be viewed as interconnected networks of thoughts, memories, feelings, and expressive-motor reactions, which is what I have been suggesting, the activation of any one of these components should activate the other components as well. Under limited but not completely understood circumstances, the performance of certain motor movements that are definitely associated with a particular emotional state might also bring the other components into operation. This, of course, would happen only to the extent that the motor actions were clearly linked to the emotional state and to the extent that there were no interfering thoughts.

Displaying Signs of Anger

The link between expressive-motor reactions and emotions is highly pertinent to the anger experience. Much as the associative network theory contends, the facial and bodily gestures that are associated with aggression—gritting the teeth, drawing the eyebrows down and together, tensing the muscles and clenching the fists, and so on—might well activate angry feelings and hostile thoughts.

Shakespeare recognized this type of influence. When his character King Henry V called on his soldiers to attack the French at the battle of Harfleur, he urged them to "imitate the action of the tiger" and adopt the physical expression of rage:

> Stiffen the sinews, summon up the blood . . .
> Then lend the eye a terrible aspect; . . .
> Now set the teeth and stretch the nostril wide,
> Hold hard the breath and bend up every spirit
> To his full height.

Showing rage in our facial expressions and bodily movements can sometimes make us angry, at least to some degree. Keep in mind, however, that facial and bodily movements generally don't have a very powerful influence upon feelings. We don't become highly enraged simply by gritting our teeth and snarling. The feedback effect is typically weak and sometimes doesn't occur at all. The associative network notion suggests why this might be: Other components of the emotional network are also linked to the feelings and the associated action tendencies (certain kinds of thoughts and memories and maybe even some types of physiological reactions), and these other components may not be in operation or may be activated only weakly. It's even possible that other ideas and recollections may interfere with the evocation of feeling. Some of the subjects in the Rutledge-Hupka experiment described above may have wondered what they were doing as they moved their facial muscles in response to the experimenter's instructions, and the questions in their minds could have interfered with the activation of their emotional networks. Similarly, we can imagine an English soldier at the battle of Harfleur worrying about being killed even though he adopted the aggressive physical pose urged by King Henry. He might have been asking himself, "What am I doing here? Why did I leave England? Am I going to die?" These thoughts too would have prevented the full activation of the anger-aggression network.

A caution about showing one's anger. Even with interferences from our thoughts, we may well stimulate some degree of anger and aggressiveness in ourselves when we express the physical signs of anger. There's a clear lesson here. We're often urged to show our feelings and not keep our anger bottled up. This recommendation is not very precise, but at the very least it seems to call on us to display the motor signs of anger openly in our face, arms, and body. The research and the theory I've reviewed here indicate that uninhibited *motor* expression of anger might actually do more harm than good. Instead of feeling better, we might intensify our anger. It may be beneficial to *talk about* one's feelings, but it isn't necessarily a good idea to shout, scream, and kick a plastic Bobo doll. I'll have more to say about this in Chapter 11.

Moods Can Influence Thoughts

Much as the associative network notion maintains, there is little doubt that people's moods can influence the thoughts and even the memories that come to mind at a given time. The effect of negative moods on cognitions is somewhat more complicated than the influence of positive moods, maybe because many persons try to avoid thinking about unhappy matters when they are feeling bad, but both types of feelings can have some impact upon what ideas occur to them, how they view the surrounding world, and what they remember at the moment.

We're undoubtedly all aware of how everything around us looks brighter and better when we're feeling good. Pleasant feelings are linked in our minds to positive thoughts and memories, with the result that we're likely to think favorably about all sorts of matters. We also tend to remember pleasant events relatively quickly when we're happy. Psychological experiments have demonstrated these effects in a variety of ways. They have shown (among other things) that when people are in a good mood, compared to when their feelings are more neutral in nature, they tend to regard themselves and even their possessions relatively positively, are less likely to view the world as dangerous, and are more willing to take moderate chances.[26]

Negative moods tend to have the opposite effects, although not as clearly so, perhaps because of the self-defensive mechanisms I mentioned. When people are feeling bad for one reason or another, quite a few of them are apt to remember unhappy events, think less well of themselves, and see more risks and dangers in the surrounding world.[27]

Robert Baron has demonstrated the negative effects of negative feelings in an experiment in which a job interview was simulated. After university students were induced to be in either a happy, a neutral, or an unhappy mood, they "interviewed" another student, who was playing the role of a job applicant, by asking a series of standardized questions. The men's subsequent ratings of the applicant were affected by their moods; they indicated that the applicant had the greatest "overall potential" and was most "likeable" if they were feeling good, and they gave him the lowest ratings if they were in a bad mood. More interestingly, their recall of information provided by the applicant was also influenced by their moods. When they were asked to recall what the applicant had said about himself, the subjects who were feeling bad remembered the fewest positive personal qualities, while the subjects who were in a positive frame of mind didn't remember any of the bad traits the applicant had admitted to possessing.[28]

Hostile Thoughts Can Result From Unpleasant Feelings
The theoretical analysis I am offering goes even further. It proposes that associations in our minds connect unpleasant feelings not only with negative thoughts generally but also with ideas and memories that have an angry or aggressive meaning. As a consequence, when we're in a negative mood there's a good chance that we'll have hostile thoughts and remember fights and conflicts that occurred in the past. Brenda Rule and her associates provided evidence for the first of these effects, as I mentioned in Chapter 3. Subjects in an uncomfortably hot room were especially likely to use hostile ideas when they wrote stories on emotional topics. Research carried out in my own laboratory has yielded similar findings. Undergraduate women who were made to be physically

uncomfortable were more likely than their comfortable peers to remember conflicts when they recalled a significant incident involving either their boyfriend or a neutral person. Physically uncomfortable subjects also tended to evaluate the neutral individual more unfavorably.[29]

All this is relevant to a point I have already mentioned, when I discussed the cognitive theories of emotion. In trying to explain why we are at times angered by an unfortunate twist of fate, such as a storm, a sudden gust of wind, or an automobile breakdown, appraisal or attribution theorists typically say that we think of the event as having been caused by a specific entity. In our minds, we believe we have been wronged by a definite "thing."

While this seems reasonable, another process might be at work to make us blame a natural force or an inanimate object for our troubles. The displeasure produced by the unpleasant occurrence could give rise to a variety of hostile ideas. Some, at least, of these thoughts could be directed at whatever is noticeable in the surrounding situation, including the perceived source of the negative affect. In other words, we have hostile thoughts along with our anger, and we think bad things about whatever attracts our attention. One result is that we blame whatever is most on our minds at that this time (the storm, the wind, the car, or whatever it is). The anger and the hostile thoughts could arise before the blame.

THOUGHTS DO MATTER

People think as well as act, of course, and their thoughts obviously can influence what they do and how they feel after they are emotionally aroused. Appraisals and attributions may not be all-important, but they can clearly have a substantial effect. At the very least, interpretations can determine whether the emotional occurrence is pleasant or unpleasant, how strong the resulting feelings are, and whether restraints come into play. We should also recognize that cognitions can operate in other ways as well, not only through appraisals and attributions. In the remainder of this chapter, I will discuss some of these other effects.

Keeping Hostility Alive: The Ill Effects of Brooding

More than forty years ago, Theodore Newcomb, a leading figure in social psychology, made an observation about why hostile attitudes are often so long-lasting. When someone bothers us, Newcomb pointed out, we're likely to turn away from that person and cut off further communication.[30] Our refusal to have anything to do with the offender may mean that we won't acquire any mitigating or favorable information about this person, and as a result we'll continue to view him or her in a bad light. Then too, as Abraham Tesser of the University of Georgia in Athens noted, our poor opinion might actually strengthen with the passage of time.[31] I wonder if the English poet, William Blake, had this kind of situation in mind when he wrote, in the poem "A Poison Tree":

> I was angry with my foe:
> I told it not, my wrath did grow.

Sharpening and Strengthening a Negative Conception

Why do people's negative opinions of others so often become stronger? One possible reason, favored by Tesser, is that as angry people continue to think about the person who provoked them, their conception of this individual becomes clearer. Because they receive no contradictory information, they forget the discrepant details that once clouded their picture of the other person. They become more certain of the central features of their angry image. The poet's wrath may have grown not because he didn't tell his feelings but because he (1) shut himself off from any positive information about his enemy and (2) repeatedly thought about this person, thereby strengthening his unfavorable conception.

Thoughts Can Stimulate Angry Feelings and Aggressive Inclinations

The associative network analysis also tells us that something else may happen: Just as angry feelings lead to hostile ideas, unfavorable thoughts about someone may activate angry feelings and even something of an aggressive urge. Thus, in "A Poison Tree," the poet may have kept himself stirred up and perhaps even stimulated himself to heightened anger by brooding about his enemy's bad qualities and/or improper behavior. Besides perpetuating his negative attitude (his hostility), his thoughts made him feel angry, prompted other hostile ideas, and made him want to hurt his foe.

In this connection, Albert Bandura has noted that people can become sexually aroused by erotic fantasies, can become frightened by imagining dangerous situations, and "can work themselves up into a state of anger by ruminating about mistreatment from offensive provocateurs." He illustrated this process by referring to the case of a husband who kept on thinking about his wife's supposed infidelities. The husband brooded for two years about a kiss he had seen his wife give to another man at a New Year's Eve party. Then, sparked by the sight of a killing shown on television, he shot the man he believed to be his rival.[32] As in all such instances, his emotional thoughts activated feelings, other ideas, and even tendencies to act—all factors that had much the same meaning and thus were associated with his thoughts.

The Concept of "Priming"

Psychologists who are interested in the operation of cognitive processes typically refer to the phenomena described above as instances of *prim–ing*. Basically, they say that the initial thoughts "prime" (make available to consciousness) other, semantically related ideas. Since these ideas are now readily accessible in the person's mind, there's a good chance that they will be employed if the situation is appropriate. What is especially important is that the primed thoughts are apt to bring a certain kind of conception, or interpretive schema, to mind and that this schema will determine how relevant information is understood. (The theoretical analysis I am offering in this book goes further, by suggesting that ideas are linked together in memory with feelings and expressive-motor reactions, so that the activation of any one of these components in the associative network by the priming operation will tend to activate the other components as well.)

Many social psychological experiments that have investigated priming effects are pertinent to aggression. By and large, they have demonstrated that even seemingly innocuous encounters with material that has a hostile meaning can give rise to hostile ideas, which can then shape our impressions of others.[33] Thus, if we happen to read some passages in a book that are full of hostility-related words, for a short time afterward we will be very likely to make unfavorable interpretations of other people's ambiguous behavior. Perhaps more important, priming can even lead to open aggression.

This effect can be seen in an experiment reported by Charles Carver, Ronald Ganellen, William Froming, and William Chambers.[34] In the priming phase of the study, the subjects were given thirty jumbled sets of four words, on the pretext that they were participating in an investigation of learning. They were asked to form meaningful three-word sentences out of the words in each set. For the people in the hostile priming group, 80 percent of the items they were given had a hostile content (e.g., "hits he her them"), whereas the subjects in the neutral priming condition found that 80 percent of their word sets were of a neutral nature (e.g., "the door open fix"). Soon afterward, they were introduced to the Buss "aggression machine" procedure (see Chapter 13) and required to administer electric shocks to a fellow student whenever that person made a mistake, in a series of twenty trials.

In line with theoretical expectations, the people who had been led to construct lots of sentences having a hostile meaning were more severe in their punishments than were the control subjects who had been exposed to only few hostile sentences. Whereas the mean shock intensity in the control group was 2.2 (on a scale of 1 to 10), the subjects who had been primed to have hostile ideas administered punishment at a 3.3 level, which was significantly higher.

A number of my own experiments have yielded similar results, although I didn't always interpret the findings from the priming perspective. Whatever terminology is used, such studies have also shown that exposure to material with a hostile-aggressive meaning—for example, violence on a TV or movie screen—tends to heighten people's subsequent unfriendliness to others and can even intensify whatever aggression is displayed openly. I'll go into all this more fully in Chapter 7, when I discuss the effects of depictions of violence in the mass media. Here I will mention only one experiment, which demonstrated that we are unlikely to experience a beneficial or "cathartic" purge of pent-up aggressive inclinations when we listen to hostile humor. As a matter of fact, exposure to nasty humor can even promote hostile treatment of others.

In this experiment, the female subjects listened to a tape recording of either a hostile or a nonhostile comic routine after hearing a female job applicant make either neutral or snide remarks about university women. They then rated the job applicant, believing that their ratings would affect the applicant's chances of being hired. The hostile comedy induced the insulted subjects to deal more harshly with the applicant. Although the two groups of subjects did not differ on how humorous they thought the comic routines were, those who had been offended by the job applicant rated her much more negatively after listening to the hostile humor than did those who heard the nonhostile comedy.[35]

These research findings can also help us to understand the actions of the jealous husband whom I mentioned earlier. He was ready to attack his supposed rival because he had kept himself emotionally stirred up by ruminating about the wrongs he imagined this man had done to him. The violent scene he happened to see on television gave him more aggressive ideas and strengthened his aggressive urge. He became even more infuriated and attacked his rival. Quite clearly, he had not drained off his anger by engaging in aggressive fantasies or watching other people beat each other up. Exposure to nasty material usually makes people nastier than they otherwise would have been.

Thoughts Influence Restraints on Aggression

Besides stirring us up, thoughts can also influence aggression by either weakening or strengthening inhibitions. I've been emphasizing the negative in this book—the conditions that can make us nasty and abusive—but have said little about the positive side of the human character. Any truly comprehensive account of human aggression has to recognize people's good qualities and especially the relatively civil way we usually behave in our daily lives. The great majority of people are only rarely assaultive. We don't walk around looking for a fight or trying to bully the people we encounter. If we attack others either verbally or physically, we do it only very infrequently. By and large and to a greater or lesser extent, most of us are reluctant to hurt others.

Part of the reason for this reluctance, of course, is that we fear punishment—disapproval if not outright retaliation—for whatever aggression we display. Indeed, as I will show in Part 4, the threat of punishment can effectively control aggression, under certain limited conditions. Our customary civility is due to more than the fear of punishment, however. Far more often than not, we hold back when we're prompted to strike at a person who has offended us, because we've learned that aggression is wrong—that it's not right to attack others verbally or physically. Being aggressive would violate our own social code as well as society's rules of proper conduct, and we would reproach ourselves for our misbehavior.

Anonymity, the Risk of Being Caught, and Self-Control
Skeptics might object to my saying that most people obey their own code of nonaggression. They might insist that relatively few people restrain themselves because of a strong internal sense of right and wrong. It's primarily the threat of punishment, they say, that preserves the social order. Sigmund Freud shared this pessimistic view of human nature. (In Chapter 12, Biology and Aggression, I will discuss his conception of the "death instinct.") He believed that force was necessary for the maintenance of civilized society. Without the threat of punishment, he thought, uninhibited primitive urges would break loose, resulting in an explosion of lawlessness.

Do we "let go" when we're free of social controls? How many times have we seen ordinarily law-abiding citizens turn into lawbreakers when they thought they could get away with it? This happened in many American cities during the urban riots of the 1960s. The nerves of many black people were smoldering with resentment about social injustices. Tempers were further inflamed by accusations of police brutality—and also in many cases, as you saw in Chapter 3, strongly irritated by unusually high temperatures. Mobs of blacks rioted under the cover of night, burning and looting the stores in their ghettoes. In Canada, whites who were usually peaceful and orderly have also shown darkness-cloaked outbreaks of lawlessness. When the Montreal police went out on strike in October 1969 and refused to carry out their normal duties, roving groups of apparently ordinary citizens ran wild, disrupting traffic, smashing store windows, looting, and setting fires, until order was restored by the Canadian army and the police officers' return to work.[36]

Is this really what most of us are like? Do we have a basic inclination to become violent and disorderly? Is this inclination only hidden by a thin, threat-induced veneer of civility? An experiment conducted by Philip Zimbardo, who was then at New York University in New York

City, appears to suggest that this is indeed the case. Zimbardo assembled four-person groups of university women and gave each group an assignment to listen to a psychologist interview female students and then judge the students. As you might expect, the interviewees' remarks followed a prepared script. They were conceited and obnoxious in one condition but very pleasant in the other cases. What is more relevant to the present discussion is that the subjects in half the groups wore large laboratory coats with hoods that completely covered their heads, much as if they were dressed in Ku Klux Klan costumes. Zimbardo termed this the "deindividuation" condition, because the women in these groups could not be personally identified. The subjects in the "individuation" condition, by contrast, were not cloaked, and the experimenter also made them highly self-conscious by giving them large name tags to wear and saying he was interested in their unique, individual reactions.

Keep this in mind: There were two aspects to these variations, one having to do with being either anonymous or identifiable to others, and the other involving differences in self-consciousness. We're dealing with the combination of these two aspects: anonymity plus little self-consciousness versus identifiability plus high self-consciousness.

After the women in each group had heard an interview with a female student, they withdrew to separate cubicles. Each subject was led to believe that she had been selected by chance to give the interviewee electric shocks, supposedly as her evaluation of that person. The principal shock measure was how long the subject pressed the shock button, on the average, each time she had an opportunity to punish the student.

How punitive the subjects were depended upon both the nature of the interviewee and how deindividuated they themselves were. The highly self-conscious, individuated women actually tended to be somewhat kinder to an obnoxious student than to a nice student. It was as if, very conscious of themselves and their moral standards, they leaned over backward in an attempt to be fair to an unpleasant person. The anonymous, deindividuated subjects, on the other hand, were highly punitive to the interviewee regardless of how nasty she had been, though on the whole, they did punish an obnoxious student more than a pleasant one. The essential point, however, is that they pushed the shock button twice as long for *both* types of targets as did their more identifiable and self-conscious counterparts—almost a second on the average, as compared to about half a second for individuated subjects.[37]

How should we understand this finding? The simplest explanation, which is in line with Freud's gloomy view, is that the anonymous women just "let loose." Hidden under their coats and hoods and realizing they couldn't be identified, they may have thought they were safe enough to give vent to their aggressive urges. For Zimbardo, though, it wasn't the deindividuated subjects' anonymity that mattered so much as their low self-consciousness. Other evidence from his research supports his emphasis on their low level of self-awareness. These women supposedly didn't control themselves because, since they were not thinking of themselves, they didn't care *at that time* what others thought of them. Their behavior was, as Zimbardo put it, temporarily "freed from obligations, . . . and the restrictions imposed by guilt, shame, and fear."

Other social psychologists have also investigated the effects of deindividuation (in Zimbardo's sense of this term) and some of their research supports Zimbardo's contention that people can become relatively aggressive when they're not highly aware of themselves. In one careful experiment along these lines, for example, Steven Prentice-Dunn and Ronald Rogers of the University of Alabama at Tuscaloosa established differences in self-awareness, while holding constant the subjects' belief that they would be held accountable for their aggression. The people in this study were nastier, as you would expect, when they thought they wouldn't be punished for being aggressive—but they were also more aggressive when their attention had been diverted from themselves.[38] It was partly their lack of self-consciousness, rather than only their fear of retribution, that led to stronger attacks on the target. What does all this mean? Do we reveal our inner brutality when we forget ourselves?

The evidence really doesn't warrant such a pessimistic and cynical conception of human nature. It is true, of course, that persons who are disposed to antisocial behavior for one reason or another are very apt to do as they want when they think they won't suffer the consequences. However, many of us don't always want to hurt someone. We're not all walking volcanoes full of repressed violent urges that we keep buried only because we fear punishment and are self-conscious. Relatively few of us want to inflict pain gratuitously, simply for the pleasure of doing harm, as some of the research described above seems to imply.

Reduced self-awareness doesn't always lead to crime and violence. Highly excited crowds also foster anonymity and the loss of self-consciousness, as Zimbardo noted, but not all excited crowds go on lawless rampages. Huge numbers of people attend sporting events and rock concerts, and on many of these occasions they forget themselves and get carried away with intense emotion. Yet we only rarely hear about such crowds turning into wild mobs. Apparently, not all sports fans and music lovers are harboring barely suppressed violent impulses that can easily be released. Anonymity and low self-awareness can reduce these people's inhibitions and weaken the influence of social controls, but other influences are necessary to incite them to antisocial conduct. At the very least, even though they're deindividuated, they would have to believe that it would be especially enjoyable to strike at, and/or to hurt and destroy, an available target, before they would turn into a mob—and they don't always believe this.

I choose to look at the research on deindividuation this way: Zimbardo and others are probably right in saying that people try to control themselves when they are highly aware of themselves, and that they may lose self-restraint when they forget themselves. What I would add is that this reduced self-control heightens susceptibility to influences in the immediate surrounding situation. Instead of saying that deindividuation produces a release of pent-up suppressed desires, it's better to suggest that persons in this kind of psychological condition may be easily carried away by the events around them.[39]

Heightened self-control due to increased self-awareness. While low self-awareness doesn't necessarily lead to antisocial conduct, heightened self-consciousness may promote socially approved behavior. According to a line of research initiated by Shelly Duval and Robert Wicklund about a generation ago, which is generally given the label *self-awareness theory,* we may indeed be more likely to act in a socially proper manner when we're paying attention to ourselves.

In these studies, when the research subjects were induced to focus their attention on themselves—for example, as a result of seeing their reflection in a mirror, because they thought other persons were looking at them, or because they felt conspicuous as an "outsider" in a group of "foreigners"—they tended to become highly conscious of (1) their established personal standards, and (2) the gap between these standards and what they were tempted to do in the immediate situation. Since these subjects, like most people, were rather committed to their existing personal values and code of conduct, they (3) were bothered by the temptation to deviate from their internal standards and (4) were therefore motivated to act in conformity with their own ideals.[40]

This reasoning certainly would suggest that since, in at least some of the experiments dealing with deindividuation, the subjects in the *individuation* condition were made highly aware of themselves, they may conceivably have become highly motivated to adhere to their own standards of conduct. Because they were "properly brought up," middle-class men and women, the chances are they believed aggression was bad. Consequently, they may have restrained their assaults on the available target.

It's important to remember that heightened self-awareness theoretically produces increased adherence to one's own established values and standards. Persons who don't oppose aggression are therefore not likely to try hard to avoid hurting others when they're highly conscious of themselves. As a matter of fact, they might even become more aggressive. We can see this in an early self-awareness experiment by Charles Carver. After selecting university students who either opposed or favored the use of electric shocks in experiments, Carver gave each of them an opportunity to punish a peer by means of shocks. Some of the subjects were induced to become very aware of themselves by situating them in such a way that they saw their reflection in a mirror. The self-aware subjects were most likely to adhere to their previously stated attitudes. The ones who had said they favored the use of shocks displayed the most aggression, and the ones who had opposed giving electric shocks were the least punitive.[41]

Before I discuss the implications of these studies, let me remind you of a related point. I noted in Chapter 3 that the reason many persons do not become aggressive when they're feeling bad is that they have become highly aware of their negative feelings. Inward attention evidently prompts them to restrain themselves. My guess is that a similar psychological process may work to inhibit aggression when we direct our attention to our relatively novel unpleasant feelings, as when high self-consciousness is created in the studies conducted by self-awareness theorists. In all of these instances subjects may be stimulated to think about what is happening and may, as a result, become more conscious of their personal values and standards (as emphasized by self-awareness theory). More generally, they may consider much of the information available to them about whether aggression is fair and appropriate.

At any rate, as I see it, there's good reason to believe that the great majority of our fellow citizens think aggression is generally wrong and to be avoided, whether the assault is carried out by others or by themselves. We also know, however, that it's the rare person indeed who has never deliberately hurt another human being. Who hasn't intentionally derogated a rival? Ordinarily well-behaved members of the middle class sometimes curse, threaten, or even hit those who have offended them. Parents sometimes beat their children. Soldiers try to kill their enemies in battle.

Why People Can Hold Nonaggressive Values and Still Be Aggressive

The undeniable existence of aggression as a significant aspect of human behavior is not really inconsistent with what I've been saying about most people's nonaggressive values and standards. The research and theorizing I have been summarizing point to at least two possible sets of reasons for people's failure to always live up to their professed beliefs, which are discussed below.

Out of Mind

First, and this follows clearly from the theories I have been describing, *our nonaggressive ideals aren't always fully in mind*. We are not always thinking about the values we hold and the codes of conduct we try to follow, and thus they aren't necessarily operative on a given occasion. On Sunday a churchgoer can truly believe that we ought to "turn our cheeks" to the blows delivered by our enemies, and yet, the next day, caught up in the very different world of business, he might want revenge for the unfair treatment he believes he received at the hands of a competitor. Because he is thoroughly immersed for the time being in his workaday world, with its unique pressures and strains, his noncompetitive social ideals don't come readily to mind. He is more likely to recall and adhere to values favoring harmony and forgiveness when he (1) is led to be highly aware of himself and (2) is in a situation that makes these ideals salient.

Not Seeing Any Inconsistency
Then too, according to theory, people who are disposed to attack someone have to *view their aggression as a significant violation of their rules of conduct* if they are to be bothered by the thought of wanting to hurt that individual. We don't always see our own inconsistencies. Most of us are very good at finding reasons that justify our assaulting those we dislike, and these excuses help us to believe that we haven't really done anything very wrong.

Consider the Nazi SS troops and their leaders who operated the concentration camps in which millions of Jews, gypsies, and other despised minorities were slaughtered during World War II. A number of Germans tried to halt the killings, but most of the guards and camp officials apparently weren't greatly troubled by what they were doing. In their minds, justifications were readily available.

Displacement of responsibility onto others. One rationalization they could offer themselves was repeatedly raised by the Nazi generals at their postwar trials in Nuremberg: They had only been following orders. It wasn't their responsibility, they insisted. They were just soldiers, and they were obeying the commands given them by their superiors.

Don't think that Nazis and SS troops are the only ones who "pass the buck" in this manner. Again and again through the centuries, law-abiding people have obeyed when they were commanded to kill particular persons who were innocent of proven crimes. In all these instances, the slayers denied to themselves and others that they were responsible for their actions. One now-forgotten case drew nationwide attention in Germany in 1921. Two sailors shot helpless passengers in a lifeboat when they were ordered to do so by a superior officer. Despite their claim that they had only been obeying a command, a German court convicted them of murder. Americans may think they are too independent-minded to submit to authority without thinking, but they should recall that Lt. William Calley and his soldiers brutally slaughtered the inhabitants of the Vietnamese village of My Lai in 1968 in obedience to orders from a superior. Lieutenant Calley was found guilty of this crime by an American military court.

In all these incidents, and in many others that I might also have cited, people were obedient because, like most of us, they were well conditioned to follow orders issued by superiors whom they regarded as legitimate authorities. If we have taken on a role that gives someone the right to tell us what to do, we're very likely to think, more or less automatically, that it's right to do what the authority says, as long as the orders are in line with the role we've adopted and there's no clear evidence that the orders are wrong. Employees generally believe that their bosses can properly tell them what to do in carrying out their work, and they are fairly ready to follow their bosses' orders, as long as the orders seem to be in keeping with the rules of the situation and aren't viewed as clearly wrong.

Stanley Milgram's deservedly well-known studies of obedience to authority show dramatically that many of us are prepared to follow seemingly legitimate commands even when they call on us to hurt another person. The authority's orders keep us from condemning ourselves for the pain we inflict, and as a consequence, we don't inhibit the behavior we would otherwise restrain.

In Milgram's experiments, which were conducted between 1960 and 1963, approximately a thousand adult men of different occupations, ages, and educational backgrounds were recruited for research on how punishment affects memory. When each man came to the laboratory, he was told that another person, the ostensible learner (who was actually the experimenter's accomplice), was in the next room trying to learn an assignment. The subject's role was to punish the learner whenever he made a mistake on a given trial. In the typical Milgram experiment, the first time the learner made an error, the experimenter (who was usually a young man) instructed the naive participant to deliver a very mild shock. He then ordered increasingly severe punishment each time the learner did something wrong. Eventually the shocks became exceedingly severe.

The subjects were typically quite willing to deliver the initial weak shocks. As the mistakes continued and the shocks became more and more intense, each subject would hear the learner start to protest and then cry out in pain. Apparently unconcerned, the experimenter commanded the subject to deliver ever more severe punishment. More often than not, the subjects obeyed. About two-thirds of the adults in the basic studies actually followed orders to the very end and administered the most severe shocks available on the apparatus, even though a sign on the apparatus clearly indicated that this high punishment level was extremely dangerous.

Milgram cited an example of one obedient subject's reactions as the experimenter ordered him to increase the severity of his punishment:

150 volts delivered: You want me to keep going?
165 volts delivered: That guy is hollering in there. . . . He's liable to have a heart condition. You want me to go?

180 volts delivered: He can't stand it: I'm not going to kill that man in there: You hear him hollering? . . . I'm not going to get that man sick in there. He's in there hollering. . . . I mean who is going to take responsibility if anything happens to that gentleman? [The experimenter accepts responsibility.] All right.

195 volts delivered: You see he's hollering. Hear that. Gee, I don't know. [The experimenter says: "The experiment requires that you go on."] I know it does, sir, but I mean—uh—he don't know what he's in for. He's up to 195 volts.

210 volts delivered.

225 volts delivered.[42]

The man was in conflict. He believed he was hurting a fellow human being severely, but he also felt obligated to follow the "authority's" commands. The orders seemed to be appropriate for the situation. He resolved his conflict by passing on the responsibility for whatever might happen to the experimenter so that, in his mind, he couldn't be blamed for any bad consequences. He himself hadn't done anything wrong, he could tell himself. He was only doing what a legitimate authority had told him to do. Surely, countless others have also justified their aggression in just this manner. Milgram certainly believed the man's actions were all too typical. In a later discussion of his research, Milgram drew this conclusion:

> The behavior revealed in the experiments reported here is normal human behavior . . . revealed under conditions that show with particular clarity the danger to human survival inherent in our make-up [sic]. And what is it we have seen? . . . The capacity for man [sic] to abandon his humanity, indeed, the inevitability that he [will do] so, as he merges his unique personality into larger institutional structures.[43]

On the other hand, maybe people can learn not to submit their individual wills to the commands of institutional authorities but, instead, to take personal responsibility for their behavior. Perhaps some steps have already been taken in this direction. After the trials of Nazi leaders, the Allies in World War II established the Nuremberg Accords to emphasize that individuals cannot avoid responsibility for the criminal actions they undertake. It was agreed that subordinates cannot be excused for their individual actions when they are commanded to be exceedingly inhumane, even when the orders come from the highest authorities. This principle is now gaining widespread acceptance, as we can see in Lieutenant Calley's conviction and also in the comments made by a German judge early in 1992 when he sentenced a former East German border guard to jail for having killed a man who was trying to flee to the West, three years earlier. "Not everything that is legal is right," the judge declared. "At the end of the twentieth century, no one has the right to turn off his conscience when it comes to killing people on the orders of authorities."[44]

(a) Shock generator used in the experiments. Fifteen of the 30 switches have already been depressed.

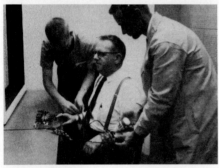

(b) The learner is strapped into a chair and electrodes are attached to his wrists. Electrode paste is applied by the experimenter. The learner provides answers by depressing switches that light up numbers on a box.

(c) The subject receives a sample shock from the generator.

(d) The subject breaks off the experiment. On the right, an event recorder wired into the generator automatically records the switches used by the subject.

FIGURE 4-3

Photographs of the obedience experiments. (Copyright 1965 by Stanley Milgram. From the film *Obedience*, distributed by the Pennsylvania State University, Audio Visual Services.)

Diffusion of responsibility. "Passing the buck" to higher authorities is not the only way to minimize personal responsibility. We can also reduce the blame to ourselves by saying that the other people with us were primarily at fault. "The others acted the same way," we insist. "They did as much harm as I did, maybe even more. I did only a small part." We've all encountered variations on this theme. In one way or another, people who use this excuse say, "The others did more than I did. I'm not really so bad."

Social psychologists have found that there is indeed a very widespread tendency to *diffuse responsibility*, in just this manner and in many different kinds of situations. The reason is quite understandable. Whenever people are required to do something that is psychologically costly, whether because it requires effort, because they might be punished, or because either their self-esteem or their esteem in others' eyes might be damaged, they are inclined to reduce the cost. Often they will take advantage of any opportunity to reduce the cost. If others are also obligated to carry out the activity, people may try to lessen their own costs by passing the responsibilities on to the others. If hard work is necessary, people are very likely to reduce their own efforts somewhat and to let others exert themselves. If other persons are nearby when an emergency occurs and someone needs help, people are apt to let the others provide the necessary assistance.[45] Similarly, even if they have joined with others in hurting another individual, they may attempt to lessen the psychological costs of the aggression (the possibility of being punished and/or suffering from guilt feelings, for example) by passing much of the responsibility along to the others.

By involving such alibis after they hurt someone, people can lessen their guilt feelings and their anxieties. Sometimes people even diffuse responsibility to others before the aggression takes place. If they are with other persons who are also going to attack someone, they tell themselves that they will play only a very small part in harming the target. Then, because they anticipate little guilt, they may not restrain their aggression, even though, individually they would not have been so nasty.

Albert Bandura, Bill Underwood, and Michael Fromson demonstrated this effect in an experiment with well-socialized college students. All the young men who participated in the study were required to shock a fellow student whenever he recommended an inadequate solution to an assigned problem. They were free to select the intensity of the punishment they delivered. The subjects who thought they were individually responsible for whatever punishment was given were relatively inhibited in shocking the supposed "problem solver" for his bad ideas, but those who believed that they and others were administering shocks together were much less restrained in delivering punishment.[46] A similar way of thinking may be operative among soldiers who are members of a firing squad. Each soldier alone might be somewhat reluctant to shoot the victim, but his reluctance is diminished when he and the other members of his squad are collectively responsible for the victim's death.

Dehumanizing the victim. I've described how restraints against aggression can be lowered by diffusing responsibility to others—superiors and/or peers engaged in the same behavior. Passing the buck reduces the guilt and anxiety that otherwise would inhibit harmful actions. Aggression-restraining guilt and anxiety can be decreased in other ways as well. We might, for example, try to convince ourselves that whatever pain and suffering we inflict is admirable rather than reprehensible, because it is in the interest of a noble or morally superior cause. I do not intend to debate the rights and wrongs of the various ways in which this can be done. I will only note that soldiers kill their enemies in the name of patriotism and/or the defense of freedom, that terrorists who hijack an airliner or blow up a bus carrying innocent civilians may claim to be fighting for the liberation of their oppressed compatriots, and that Rennaissance priests maintained that they were serving God when they burned people who didn't share their religious views.

We can also tell ourselves that our actions are not so terrible if our victims are inhuman, monstrous, or at least bad people who somehow deserve the harm we are doing them. If we make our victims less than human, we don't feel sorry for them, we don't feel their suffering, and we don't hold back in our attacks on them. My discussion would be seriously incomplete if I failed to offer a few words about the dehumanization process.

Many of the Germans involved in the Nazi campaign to exterminate Jewry during World War II clearly regarded Jews as less than human, or even as dangerous nonhumans who had to be destroyed. Joseph Goebbals, the Nazi Propaganda Minister, reflected this view. After Adolf Hitler told him that Europe must be cleansed of all Jews, "if necessary by applying the most brutal methods," Goebbels wrote in his diary,

> A judgment is being visited upon the Jews that, while barbaric, is fully deserved. . . . If we did not fight the Jew, they [sic] would destroy us. It's a life and death struggle between the Aryan race and the Jewish bacillus.[47]

The dehumanization of Jews—and also of Slavs, Poles, and gypsies—in the Nazi mythology made it easier for German soldiers to slaughter the innocent by the millions. Though there were undoubtedly peculiarities in the Nazis' thinking and beliefs that made it easy for them to categorize Jews and other non-Aryans as contemptible nonhumans, we have to recognize that people around the world have long used the same dehumanizing process to justify killing their enemies. Generations of Turks and Greeks have repeatedly characterized each other as horrible monsters. In the World War I, the Allies described their German opponents as "Huns" who were devoid of common moral values. Israelis and Arabs have viewed each other as uncivilized brutes who cannot be trusted. U.S. soldiers who massacred fleeing Indians in the American West in the late nineteenth century probably had somewhat similar thoughts when they continually repeated, "The only good Indian is a dead Indian." In all these instances, and in many other cases, victims are denied human qualities, so that it's not a "real person," not "someone like me," who is hurt or killed. The result is that the aggressors don't feel guilty when they think of attacking their victims, and thus they don't restrain themselves. The previously described experiment by Bandura, Underwood, and Fromson shows how readily devaluation of an opponent can lower inhibitions against aggression. The college men in this study who had been taught to regard the persons they were judging as "animals" and a "rotten bunch" were much more punitive than were their counterparts who were induced to have a more positive attitude toward the "problem solvers."[48]

SUMMARY

This chapter deals mostly with the effects of cognitive processes on emotional reactions, beginning with a summary of some of the better-known cognitively oriented theories of emotion. These conceptions hold that people become angry when they are afflicted by an unpleasant event, and when they also believe that the occurrence was externally caused and that an agent was responsible for the event and could have controlled what happened. Some theories go further and propose that other perceptions (or beliefs or appraisals) are also necessary if anger is to arise, such as, for instance, that the responsible agent violated social rules and that the unhappy event is personally significant.

The best-known cognitive analysis of emotion is a blend of the Schachter-Singer two-factor theory with attribution notions. This formulation basically maintains that the initial bodily arousal created by an emotional occurrence is affectively neutral until the affected persons attribute their arousal to a specific source. Guided by this attribution, they label their feelings accordingly. In order to feel angry, the aroused individuals must attribute their arousal to deliberate mistreatment and must infer that they are feeling angry. After summarizing some research findings consistent with this formulation, I note that this theory seems to apply mostly to occasions on which the arousing event is highly ambiguous and not especially strong.

From my perspective, this theory is seriously incomplete and does not adequately account for the anger-generating effects of unpleasant occurrences that are uncontrollable, not directed at anyone specifically, and not socially improper. I also argue that affected persons' attributions, by determining the unpleasantness of the negative event, influence the likelihood that they will become angry and emotionally aggressive. Next, I interpret Zillmann's findings on the effects of mitigating information (information excusing someone's perceived misbehavior). I suggest that after-the-fact provision of mitigating information is not especially effective in reducing the anger and aggressive inclinations produced by an incident, because strong negative affect has already been aroused.

Purely cognitive analyses of emotion are also incapable of accounting for the emotion-influencing effects of bodily reactions, especially (but not only) facial expressions. Extending the classic James-Lange theory of emotion, which held that bodily reactions enter into emotional experience, more recent researchers (following Tomkins and Izard) have shown that the movement of particular facial muscles, as well as certain other bodily muscles, can intensify and perhaps even activate the emotional states that are ordinarily associated with these muscle movements. I believe that these findings are best explained by an associative network conception of emotions. Associative linkages are posited among the various components of the network. Because of these connections, adopting an angry expression or making the other muscle movements that often accompany angry feelings can strengthen the anger generated by another event—unless one's thoughts intervene to counteract this effect. In accord with the associative network notion, positive feelings frequently give rise to positive thoughts, whereas negative moods tend to activate negative and even hostile ideas—unless a self-regulatory process aimed at lessening the negative affect is initiated which motivates the persons to avoid thinking "bad" thoughts. The concept of "priming," which maintains that particular ideas heighten the likelihood that other, semantically related thoughts will come to mind, is also relevant to this process.

The network conception also tells us that when people have hostile thoughts, and/or when they think of pain they have suffered or wrongs that have been done to them, there is a good chance that they will feel angry and will have aggressive inclinations. An important implication of this chapter, which will be discussed more fully in Chapter 11, Psychological Procedures for Controlling Aggression, is that it is inadvisable to carry out anger-related body movements, to cherish hostile ideas, or to display aggressive actions, if we wish to reduce our anger or lessen our aggressive tendencies. Encouraging any of these anger- or aggression-related reactions increases the chances that other components of the anger-aggression network will be activated.

No discussion of the influence of thoughts upon aggression would be complete without a consideration of how thinking can lessen people's inner restraints upon aggression, and I briefly sketch some of the ways in which this can happen. I argue that many persons possess values and codes of conduct that often keep them from assaulting others when they're tempted to do so. Effective as they are, however, these ideals aren't always operative. Sometimes they are inoperative because they're simply out of mind. They are also ineffective at times because most people are adept at justifying their behavior so that they do not regard their actions as a departure from their values. Some of the ways in which this is done, such as denying personal responsibility for one's aggression and dehumanizing the victim, are summarized in the chapter.

*N*OTES

1. Weiner (1985).
2. For example, see Lazarus & Smith (1989).
3. See Roseman (1984); Scherer (1984); Smith & Ellsworth (1985).
4. Averill (1982); Lazarus & Smith (1989).
5. Schachter (1964); Schachter & Singer (1962).
6. Several failures to replicate the Schachter-Singer experiment should be noted, e.g., Marshall & Zimbardo (1979) and Maslach (1979). A fairly comprehensive survey of the relevant literature can be found in Reisenzein (1983). Interested readers should also consult Leventhal's (1980) important discussion of this research. Also see Leventhal & Tomarken (1986).
7. See Leventhal & Tomarken (1986) and Reisenzein (1983) for two summaries of some of this literature.
8. Geen (1978).
9. Geen & O'Neal (1969).
10. Barclay (1971).
11. For one review of some of the experimental research on this point, see Rule & Nesdale (1976).
12. Zillmann (1978, 1979, 1983).
13. See Zillmann (1983) and especially Zillmann (1979) for a more complete discussion of this research, as well as for references to the relevant studies.
14. See Zillmann (1979). Also see Kremer & Stephens (1983); Johnson & Rule (1986).
15. Zillmann & Cantor (1976).
16. Mallick & McCandless (1966).
17. Zillmann (1979), p. 333.

18. Quoted in Buck (1980), p. 812.

19. This passage is taken from James (1890), pp. 449–450.

20. Quoted in Adelmann & Zajonc (1989), p. 253.

21. Quoted in Adelmann & Zajonc (1989), p. 252.

22. See Izard (1971) and Tomkins (1962, 1963). Also see Adelmann & Zajonc (1989); Leventhal & Tomarken (1986).

23. Rutledge & Hupka (1985).

24. Leventhal & Tomarken (1986), p. 580.

25. Riskind & Gotay (1982).

26. Alice Isen (1984, 1987) has discussed the pervasive benefits of a positive mood in chapters of several books.

27. Among the papers reporting these effects are Bower (1981); Johnson & Tversky (1983); Johnson & Magaro (1987); Snyder & White (1982); Teasdale (1983); and Wright & Mischel (1982).

28. Baron (1987).

29. Rule, Taylor, & Dobbs (1987). Also see Berkowitz (1990).

30. Newcomb (1947).

31. Sadler & Tesser (1973); Tesser (1978); Tesser & Johnson (1974).

32. Bandura (1973), p. 45.

33. Among the early demonstrations of this effect are Higgins, Rholes, & Jones (1977) and Srull & Wyer (1979).

34. Carver, Ganellen, Froming, & Chambers (1983).

35. Berkowitz (1970a).

36. *Time,* Oct. 20, 1969.

37. Zimbardo (1969).

38. Prentice-Dunn & Rogers (1982). Also see Diener (1979); Dipboye (1977); Johnson & Downing, (1979); Taylor, O'Neal, Langley, & Butcher (1991).

39. Since there don't appear to have been strong situational influences calling for aggression in Zimbardo's experiment, this could mean that the condition differences he observed are really due to *reduced aggression on the part of the individuated subjects* rather than to heightened aggression by those who presumably were deindividuated. That is, the women in the former group may have behaved differently than they normally would have done because they were extremely self-conscious and thus very aware of their standards of right and wrong. The possibility raised here is basically consistent with Diener's (1980) theory of deindividuation, which emphasizes the lessening of self-regulation as a consequence of very low self-awareness.

40. See Duval & Wicklund (1972); Wicklund (1975). Also see Carver & Scheier (1981).

41. Carver (1975).

42. The subject's remarks quoted here are taken from Milgram (1965), p. 67. Also see Milgram (1974); Miller (1986).

43. Milgram (1974), p. 188.

44. Margolick, *New York Times*, Jan. 26, 1992.
45. See Latané & Darley (1970).
46. Bandura, Underwood, & Fromson (1975).
47. Cited in Toland (1976), p. 709.
48. Bandura, Underwood, & Fromson (1975).

PART 2

❖

Aggressive Personalities

M ore than two decades ago, psychologist Hans Toch and his associates interviewed a number of men who were incarcerated in California prisons for crimes of violence. The researchers wanted to learn why these violent persons had attacked their victims. One of the cases in Toch's sample is particularly noteworthy:

> Jimmy was 23 years old, with a work record consisting of a successful career as a minor league pimp. Jimmy's "rap sheet" included many and diverse offenses, such as forcible rape, . . . kidnapping, intoxication, grand theft, and disturbing the peace. Most revealing, there were several instances of battery and assaults with deadly weapons, and two attacks on police officers. The police incident that Jimmy chose to discuss with us is not included on [his] record because it took place while he was in his pre-teens [sic] .[1]

Jimmy had told the researchers about having become annoyed with a police officer who had barred him from a school dance because of his reputation as a troublemaker. After throwing a can at the officer's feet, Jimmy had insulted him repeatedly, provoking the policeman to hit him with his billy club. In rage, believing that he had been wronged, Jimmy tried to shoot the officer with the weapon he had with him, and he had to be forcibly restrained.

Jimmy, of course, differs from other violent offenders in the details of his life story, but he is also similar to many of them in important respects, particularly in his frequent antisocial conduct and in the wide variety of ways he got into trouble with authorities starting when he was fairly young. Doesn't this case seem to be at odds with the analysis of aggression I have been offering? Chapters 1 to 4 focused largely on external influences that can affect the strength of displayed aggression—frustrations, unpleasant environmental conditions, stimuli in the surrounding situation, and so on. Were Jimmy's extremely antisocial and highly violent actions due *solely* to the frustrations and/or unpleasant conditions he encountered at a given time? Probably not. He apparently had some internal qualities that somehow led him to violent behavior again and again.

Part 2 will discuss relatively persistent aggressive dispositions. Highly violent men such as Jimmy have aggression-prone qualities, and we'll consider what makes these extremely aggressive personalities act as they do and how they might have become the way they are. In Chapter 5, I will be concerned with aggressive personalities in general, especially the aggressive personalities that you and I are apt to encounter in daily life. I will begin by reviewing some evidence that points to the existence of fairly stable dispositions to aggression, then will turn to a consideration of how a proneness to violence may operate to produce frequent open attacks on others. In Chapter 6, I will discuss the role of family and peers in the development of violence-prone personalities.

NOTES

1. Toch (1969), pp. 68–72.

5

The Identification of the
Violence Prone

❖

Are Some People Consistently Disposed to Be Aggressive? ◆ *Demonstrations of Different Forms of Contemporaneous Consistency* ◆ *Stability in Aggressive Behavior through the Years: Longitudinal Consistency* ◆ How Aggressive Personalities Operate ◆ *Different Kinds of Aggressive People*

ARE SOME PEOPLE CONSISTENTLY DISPOSED TO BE AGGRESSIVE?

The Controversy about the Existence of Traits

About a generation ago, several eminent psychologists argued that there actually were very few people like Jimmy who repeatedly displayed the same kind of behavior across widely different situations. A surprisingly large number of published studies had shown that many persons were quite inconsistent in how they acted from one time to another. For instance, an individual who was honest on one occasion might cheat, lie, or steal at other times, and there didn't seem to be a stable personality trait making for consistent honesty. Impressed by this evidence of inconsistency in many different forms of social behavior, psychologists such as Walter Mischel questioned whether most persons really possessed stable personality traits—in the sense of definite and abiding inner mental structures—that produced the same behaviors regardless of the situational context.[1]

These theorists didn't say that people are completely inconsistent. They did maintain, however, that behavioral stability is usually more limited than is commonly supposed and, in any case, is often more apparent than real. People's thinking about other persons presumably tends to exaggerate the degree of consistency that actually occurs. We have fairly stable conceptions of others whom we know well, and we regard them as having certain qualities. These conceptions, supposedly, induce us to "remember" these individuals as acting the same way from one occasion to the next, whereas they may actually have been quite inconsistent. The behavioral consistency that does exist, Mischel argued, pertains only to relatively similar contexts. Theoretically, then, in the case of aggression, people who are prone to violence will attack others only when the given situation has a certain meaning for them, such as (perhaps) when they regard themselves as being threatened or criticized.[2]

However one conceives of an aggressive disposition—as an abiding inner mental structure, an inclination to react in a particular way to certain kinds of situations, or something else—the research Mischel cited seemed to suggest that there is actually little consistency in the degree of aggression that is shown from one occasion to another. Yet the investigations he surveyed didn't deal with aggression, and we can rightly ask whether aggressive conduct is as variable across situations as are the other types of behavior involved in his research review.

Two Kinds of Consistency

Though I've been discussing the consistency of aggressive behavior from one occasion to another, I have said nothing about how far apart in time these occasions are. It's important to keep the time span in mind, however. Saying that the same actions will be carried out in different situations only a few minutes apart is not the same thing as contending that the same behavior will be exhibited on two occasions separated by a year or more. In the former case, the observed actions are *relatively contemporaneous*, whereas in the latter, there is *longitudinal consistency*, since the people and actions of interest are followed over a considerable period.[3] In making this distinction, I will first look at the relatively contemporaneous consistency of aggression. Basically, I will ask whether people who attack a target in a particular way are also apt to display other forms of aggression on another occasion soon afterward. After this, I will discuss the longitudinal consistency (or stability) of aggressive conduct over a fairly long time period.[4]

As you will see, the evidence essentially shows that *some* people are indeed apt to act the same way whenever an aggressive opportunity arises. If they are relatively free to do what they want in a given situation, there is a good chance that these individuals will behave in the same manner on many occasions. They will try to hurt someone if they have an underlying aggressive disposition, or they will not attack a target if they have a nonaggressive personality. These people, however, are likely to be at the extremes: disposed to be either *highly* aggressive or *very* nonaggressive. Most of us are not strongly inclined one way or another, and our behavior is more variable.

Demonstrations of Different Forms of Contemporaneous Consistency

Let's begin our discussion of the contemporaneous consistency of aggression by going back to Jimmy. Consider the wide variety of situations that could trigger a violent outburst from him: a barroom quarrel, a frustration that kept him from getting what he wanted, hearing someone boast, and lots of other things. In many seemingly different instances, Jimmy showed much the same kind of behavior: he physically assaulted someone. Psychologists sometimes account for this kind of consistency by referring to *stimulus generalization*. Basically, they are saying that a fairly broad range of stimulus situations evoke the same response (a physical attack in this example). Then too, Jimmy revealed his aggressive inclinations in many different ways. According to his case summary, he was often wild and uncontrolled; he tried to break into a dance hall where he wasn't wanted; and he threatened and insulted a policeman, threw an object at him, and then punched him. Jimmy exhibited different forms of essentially the same class of behaviors (all antisocial in nature) from one occasion to the next. This type of consistency can be viewed as a *response generalization*, meaning that when a situational stimulus activates the behavioral disposition, this underlying tendency can be manifested in a relatively wide variety of seemingly different responses. The precise nature of the response will depend upon how aroused the individual is at the time, what form of aggression is available to him or her at the moment, and what the possible costs of the action might be in the situation, but all the responses will have something in common. In this section we'll look briefly at both kinds of contemporaneous consistency. Keep in mind that these aggressive situations are generally fairly close together in time.

Consistency between the Laboratory and "Real Life"
One demonstration of contemporaneous consistency combines both stimulus and response generalization. As you will see in Chapter 13, laboratory experiments on aggression often measure aggressive behavior in terms of the intensity of electric shocks or blasts of unpleasant noise which the subjects administer to another person. Critics of this type of research have faulted these procedures as highly artificial. No one in the "real world" attacks someone else by delivering an electric shock, and the subjects' laboratory actions (such as pressing a button on a shock apparatus) obviously are physically very different from the aggressive behaviors shown in more natural situations.

Still, the laboratory measures can be defended, as Chapter 13 points out. The experimental subjects' intentions are more important than the specific nature of the physical movements they make. When they press a shock button or make a check mark on a questionnaire—or do whatever they are asked to do in the particular experiment—the subjects realize that they are deliberately hurting another individual, physically and/or psychologically. From their perspective, then, these laboratory responses are psychologically similar to hitting another person or insulting someone in a conversation (at least to the degree that they all injure their target), even though physically they are very different in form. All these behaviors have a common meaning. Researchers have found that, because of this shared meaning, (1) individuals who are often highly aggressive in their dealings with other persons in daily life are also apt to be highly punitive in the laboratory setting, and (2) studies employing very different laboratory procedures for assessing aggression have frequently yielded very similar results.[5]

These findings, then, give indications of both stimulus generalization and response generalization. A university psychology laboratory is certainly different from most ordinary situations, and subjects' laboratory behavior bears little resemblance to the way people usually strike out at one another. Even so, subjects who exhibit aggression relatively frequently in the everyday world are also apt to give another person fairly severe shocks in the experimental setting.

Consistency between Forms of Aggression (Response Generalization) in Everyday Life

Besides supporting the validity of certain laboratory measures, this evidence also indicates that highly aggressive people usually display their personal inclination in a variety of ways. We saw this in Jimmy's case. He would curse and insult those who thwarted him, or even lash out at them physically if they persisted in frustrating him. This kind of "response generality" is fairly common. Violence-prone people typically don't specialize in a particular way of trying to injure others, particularly when they're emotionally aroused. While there undoubtedly are some exceptions, persons who are quick to attack their opponents physically are also likely to be verbally offensive.

Research with young boys and girls has repeatedly observed this generality in aggression. Several investigators in the United States and Europe have asked schoolchildren to indicate which of their classmates exhibited certain kinds of behavior. For example, the youngsters were asked, "Who starts fights?" and "Who hurts another child when angry by hitting, kicking, or throwing something?" If a good many of the students in the class identified the same child as starting fights (indicating that this particular youngster had probably initiated quite a few battles), there was a very good chance that this child would also be listed by many of his classmates as "hurting another child when angry" and even as often being verbally abusive to others.[6] In other words, the children said that a highly aggressive child was likely to be harsh to others in a wide variety of ways.

The generalization of aggression is frequently broader than you might realize. People who are extremely aggressive, whether they are grownups or children and whether males or females, tend to be highly antisocial in many respects. Their unusually great readiness to hit others physically and verbally is accompanied by other antisocial tendencies, just as Jimmy drank too much and was a thief and rapist, as well as being violence-prone.

Consistency across Situations: Combining Stimulus and
Response Generalization
Generalization of aggression clearly involves both stimulus generalization and response generalization: Highly aggressive persons display their violent tendencies across a variety of situations, as well as through all the different antisocial actions they carry out. Before delving into this matter more deeply, I should remind you that it's the people with strongly aggressive dispositions who are most likely to demonstrate this kind of consistency.

Much as would be expected, then, a number of investigations have demonstrated that children who are consistent troublemakers in different situations, such as both at home and at school, are typically highly antisocial in the different settings. A study by Rolf Loeber and Thomas Dishion is illustrative. The psychologists divided the 9- to 16-year-old boys in their sample into four categories on the basis of ratings made by both parents and teachers: those who fought a great deal both at home and in school, those who were aggressive only at home or only at school, and those who had few if any fights in either setting. Figure 5-1 summarizes what the investigators found when they examined the juvenile court records to see whether any of the youths had been in contact with the police. As the figure indicates, the boys identified by both their mothers and their teachers as fighting a lot—in other words, who were highly aggressive both at home and at school—were the ones who were most likely to have gotten into trouble with the law.[7] The same strongly aggressive-antisocial inclinations that led them to behave aggressively across a range of situations also led them to have difficulties with the police.

All in all, we can see in many different ways that violence-prone people are very likely to react to an appropriate situational stimulus with an aggressive response. Almost any type of occurrence that is linked to aggression in the minds of these people is apt to generate fairly strong aggression-related ideas and motor reactions. Their tendency to react with aggressive thoughts and inclinations to an aggression-associated

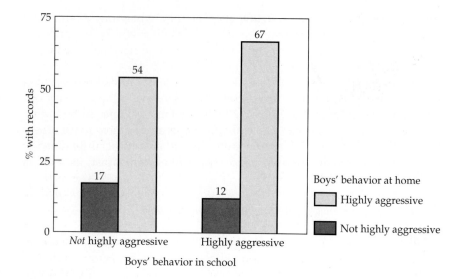

FIGURE 5-1

Percentage of boys in a group who had police records. (Data from Loeber &
Dishion (1984). Copyright 1984 by the American Psychological Association. Adapted by
Permission.)

stimulus has become so highly routinized, even automatic, that they
don't have to be actually threatened or consciously aware of dangers or
challenges in order to display an aggressive response. These people may
well have hostile thoughts and even aggressive inclinations when they
watch violence on a TV screen or even read a news report about a violent
incident. Furthermore, and very much in keeping with my discussion of
"pain cues" in Chapter 1, when highly aggressive persons attack someone, they are apt to be especially gratified when they learn that their victim has been hurt and/or defeated.[8]

We can make some guesses about Jimmy on the basis of these findings. Although his case history doesn't say so, his favorite TV programs
are probably the ones that feature a good deal of violence. It's likely that
he gets a special pleasure from seeing people hit and shoot each other.
Research evidence suggests that the consequences of allowing Jimmy to
have this enjoyment may be unfortunate, from society's perspective. The
violence on the screen not only "turns him on" but also gives him
aggressive ideas, and it may even activate his aggressive impulses.

Of course, merely seeing violence or reading an aggressive sentence
won't always incite highly aggressive persons to attack others openly.
The ideas and inclinations activated by the scene or sentence usually
aren't strong enough to prompt an overt assault. The aggressive
thoughts and action tendencies inspired by media violence may be held

inside, but they could still exist, in violence-prone persons and, to a weaker degree, in more ordinary individuals as well.

Consistency between personality tests and other behaviors. Because of these strongly developed stimulus-response associations, highly aggressive individuals can frequently be identified by personality tests (assuming that they are honest in their responses). An example of a consistency between personality test measures and reactions in other settings can be seen in the relationship between a test-measured propensity to become angry and arousal of anger in real-life situations.

The Reactions of People Who Report Frequent Strong Anger. A number of psychologists have developed measuring instruments designed to assess an individual's likelihood of becoming angry in social encounters. One of these is the State-Trait Anger Scale designed by Charles Spielberger and his associates at the University of South Florida in Tampa.[9] In this procedure the participants are given a series of ten items, such as "I am quick-tempered" and "I get angry when I'm slowed down by others' mistakes," and are asked to indicate how often each of the items applies to them. The possible answers range from "almost never" to "almost always."

Jerry Deffenbacher, Patricia Demm, and Allen Brandon administered this scale, along with a number of other tests, to their students at Colorado State University in Fort Collins. They also questioned the young men and women about their anger experiences. Among other things, each student was asked to describe a situation that had made him or her very angry, and to rate the strength of his or her anger at that time. The students were also asked to keep a log for one week, in which they recorded the most provocative incident that had occurred each day and rated the anger they felt when the event took place. By and large, the men and women who scored highest on the Spielberger anger scale—that is, who indicated that they became angry often—reported having the most frequent and most intense anger experiences during the survey week.[10]

The personality measure isn't always related to open behavior. I should introduce a note of caution about personality measures: They basically assess only a *readiness* to become very angry and/or to attack someone. Such readiness isn't always translated into overt aggression, and people who score high on a personality test don't always show their violent inclinations openly.

There are at least two fairly obvious reasons for this. First, the latent disposition to anger isn't always activated. Even people who are prone to violence have to experience something that has an aggressive or unpleasant meaning for them before their aggressive habits and/or emotional propensities will be set into operation. One of the qualities that distinguish these people is that they are very ready to detect aggression, threats, and dangers in the world around them. As I'll show later in this chapter, they're typically quick to interpret ambiguous actions as a deliberate affront or challenge, and are then strongly aroused emotionally. A recent newspaper article told the story of a serious fight between teenagers in a New York subway which began because one youth thought another was staring at him. This type of incident occurs more frequently than you might realize. It's not altogether unusual for violence-prone individuals to (1) think that someone nearby is looking at them too intently, (2) interpret the supposed staring as an insult or challenge, and (3) become intensely enraged.

Even if the violent inclinations of such people are activated, however, they may hold back on some occasions and not assault anyone, because they fear punishment. Jimmy probably wouldn't have attacked the police officer if the officer had drawn his gun when Jimmy started insulting him, or if other police officers or security guards had also been present. These clear dangers could have evoked inhibitions that might well have stifled his violent urge.[11]

Stability in Aggressive Behavior through the Years: Longitudinal Consistency

It's clear that aggressive behavior is impressively consistent over relatively brief time spans, but is such behavior also consistent over longer periods of time? It is especially important to know whether youthful aggressiveness can predict antisocial conduct later in life. We'd like to think that children can change with the passage of the years and that troublesome boys and girls typically outgrow their rebelliousness. However, some observers of humankind believe that character is more apt to persist than to improve over the years. The poet John Milton once wrote, "The childhood shows the man/As morning shows the day," and you may recall a similar line from William Wordsworth: "The Child is father of the Man." Both poets were saying the same thing, in effect, as a well-known folk saying: "As the twig is bent, the tree's inclined." Is the adult personality indeed shaped and maybe even fixed in youth?

The Olweus Review of Research on Longitudinal Stability of Aggression

According to an influential review of the pertinent research, which was published by Dan Olweus of the University of Bergen in Norway, we can't automatically assume that the "young leopard" (at least of the male gender) will "change his spots" as the years go by. Quite a few people who are aggressive troublemakers as children do "straighten out" with time, but many others do not.[12]

The American, English, and Swedish studies which Olweus examined first measured the aggressiveness usually exhibited by male subjects ranging from 2 to 18 years of age, and then repeated the measurements at intervals ranging from six months to twenty-one years later. A variety of procedures was employed in the behavioral assessments, including direct observations, teachers' ratings, and even reports from the subjects' peers. In all the investigations, the researchers computed the relationship between the initial and follow-up scores in each sample, asking whether the persons who were relatively highly aggressive at the time of the first measurement were still highly aggressive on the later occasion.

Olweus found a remarkable degree of agreement among the sixteen different samples of men involved in these studies. Generally speaking, there was a moderately high relationship between initial and follow-up scores, although the magnitude of the correlation tended to decline as the interval between the two measurements grew longer: The average correlation was over .7 when the follow-up was only a year or less after the first assessment and then fell regularly to about .4 when there was a twenty-one-year gap between the two measurements. Furthermore, aggression scores derived from observations of the subjects' actual behavior generally were just as consistent over time as were scores based on teachers' ratings, at least for the time periods involved in these particular studies.

Olweus drew an important conclusion on the basis of this survey. He believed that the boys who had persisted in being nasty had maintained their aggressiveness even though they were often under considerable pressure to adhere to social rules and even though the situations they encountered varied considerably with the passage of time. Like Jimmy, a number of these youngsters also acted aggressively in seemingly very dissimilar situations.

Olweus's argument seems very reasonable: Although many people do change, at least to some extent, there's a good chance that boys who exhibit a relatively high level of aggression when they are young will remain relatively aggressive (in comparison to the less aggressive boys who were studied along with them) as the years pass by.[13]

Two Noteworthy Investigations

The research on longitudinal stability of aggression tells us other things as well. As an introduction to these additional findings, I'll summarize two especially noteworthy studies. One is based on working-class youths from London, England, and the other deals with children from a largely rural county in upstate New York. Both are *prospective* studies in that the initial measurements were taken when the participants were relatively young and later assessments were carried out in periodic follow-ups over the years. Both investigations were included in Olweus's survey, but I'll extend my summary of his survey by describing later findings.

The Cambridge study of delinquent development. This project was initiated by Donald West of the Institute of Criminology at Cambridge University and later continued by his colleague David Farrington. It is a longitudinal survey of over 400 males from a densely populated working-class section of London, England.[14] When they were first contacted in 1961, the boys were about 8 years old. The study covered all the male pupils in their grade at six primary schools. Nearly every one was white and of British, working-class origin. Almost all were reinterviewed several times over the course of the years to determine what they were like at each of these times and what had happened to them. The youths' parents were also periodically interviewed by social workers, and their teachers were asked every few years to rate the boys' conduct. These data were supplemented by records of criminal convictions, which were obtained through repeated searches of files in the central Criminal Record Office.

Through the periodic follow-ups, it was possible to assess the study participants' aggressiveness when they were approximately 9, 13, 17, and 32 years old. In each time period, the subjects who were in the upper 25 percent of the aggressiveness distribution were called "highly aggressive" and were marked out for special study. For the present purposes, I'll also look at a group of twenty-seven violent delinquents who were identified in 1974, when they were about age 21, as having been convicted of at least one violent offense, such as an assault or violent robbery.

The Predictability of Aggressiveness. To simplify matters, I'll focus on how well youthful aggressiveness forecast later conduct. Figure 5-2 shows the amount of overlap between the subjects who were highly aggressive when they were quite young (at ages 9, 13, and 17) and those who were (1) in the highly aggressive quartile in late adolescence (at age 17) and/or (2) in the violent delinquent group at age 21. To read these data, consider the boys (in the top row) who were in the highly aggressive quartile at 9: 40 percent of these youths were also among the most aggressive boys eight years later at about age 17. (This is the "highly aggressive before" line in the figure.) In comparison, only 27 percent of the boys who were in the bottom three-quarters in terms of aggressiveness at age 9 (the ones who were "nonaggressive before") were in the highly aggressive group at age 17. According to this fairly crude measure, most of the boys had changed to some extent, but the ones who had been extremely troublesome when they were very young were least likely to modify their conduct substantially with the passage of time. These extremely aggressive individuals were the leopards who were most unlikely to have changed their spots.

Much the same conclusion can be drawn about the prediction of violent delinquency from high aggressiveness at age 9. Thus, as Figure 5-2 also indicates, 14 percent of the boys who had been the most aggressive

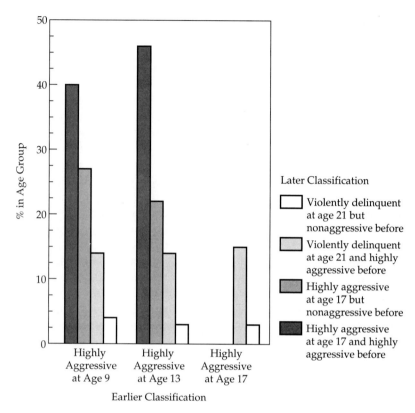

FIGURE 5-2
Percentage of highly aggressive boys in younger age groups who were classified as highly aggressive at about age 17 and/or who were classified as violent delinquents at about age 21. (Data from Farrington (1978). Adapted by permission from Farrington (1978), copyright Pergamon, Ltd. 1978.)

when they were very young had been convicted of a violent offense by age 21, as compared to only 4 percent of boys in the group who were nonaggressive at age 9. You can see that high aggressiveness in early adolescence, at age 13, was also significantly related to high aggressiveness four years later (at age 17), as well as to a record of violent delinquency eight years afterward (at age 21). All in all, then, while only a minority of youthful troublemakers are convicted of a violent crime by the time they reach adulthood, there's some risk that those who are extremely aggressive when they're young will have difficulties with the law as they grow older.

When Farrington and his interviewers went back to these men several years later, their newer findings only extended the earlier results.[15] Most notably, the people who had been highly aggressive in early adolescence were especially likely to have been convicted of a violent crime by the time they reached age 32. About 22 percent of the highly violent boys had such records, as compared to only about 7 percent of the less aggressive youngsters.

Studies conducted in other western countries have also demonstrated that early aggressiveness is a risk factor that forecasts the possibility of adult violence. In all these cases, even though aggressiveness was measured in widely different ways, there was a good chance that the persons who were identified as being extremely aggressive while they were young would also exhibit antisocial violence as adults and that they would even be convicted of violent crimes.[16]

Aggression as One Form of "Antisociality." These results do more than point to the continuity in some persons' behavior over the years. They also tell us, as West and Farrington maintained in 1977, that persistent and extreme aggressiveness is to a considerable degree "merely one element of a more general antisocial tendency." Although not all aggression has the same origin, and although people can become disposed to violence for different reasons, many people are quick to attack others. Those who do so relatively often are also inclined to reject other social rules. We saw this in Jimmy's case: Besides having a general history of violence, he had been guilty of rape, intoxication, and theft, among other things. Similarly, the highly aggressive boys in the Cambridge study were also apt to have violated many other social norms as they grew up. A relatively high proportion of them had also engaged in "drinking, gambling, drug use, sexual promiscuity, reckless driving," and vandalism.[17]

This doesn't mean, of course, that every antisocial individual is highly assaultive. Some people are quite ready to break laws if they think they can get away with it but aren't prone to violence. Furthermore, it also appears that there are different kinds of aggressive personalities. I'll have more to say about all these topics later.

The Columbia County twenty-two-year study. At about the same time that the Cambridge University project was getting under way, a team of psychologists led by Leonard Eron completed a survey of all the third-grade schoolchildren in Columbia County, a semirural area in upstate New York, with the goal of uncovering the origins of persistent aggressiveness. The researchers interviewed 870 boys and girls averaging about 8 years of age, as well as most of their mothers and fathers. About half the members of the original sample were reinterviewed in 1970, when the participants were about 19 years old, and more than 400 of them were again questioned when they had reached an average age of 30. Besides ascertaining whether the men and women had committed legal offenses and traffic violations, the investigators were also able to interview the spouses and children of some of the people in the sample.[18]

The Aggressiveness Measures. A peer nomination procedure was used to assess the participants' aggressiveness during their school years. All the boys and girls in the study were asked to indicate which of their class-mates were best described by each of a number of questions, such as "Who starts a fight over nothing?" and "Who says mean things?" A child's aggression score during this period was the percentage of times she or he was listed by the others in the class as behaving aggressively, out of the total number of times the youngster could have been named.[19] After the participants had left school, their aggressiveness was indexed in several different ways. The principal measure used was their self-reported aggressive inclinations. Their legal offenses and traffic citations (if any) were also recorded. If they were married, they were asked to describe how they disciplined their children, and their spouses were asked to rate their aggressiveness.

More Evidence of Consistency Over Time. Again, the participants' aggressiveness tended to be consistent over time. This tendency can be seen clearly when the childhood and teenage periods are compared: Both the boys and the girls who had the highest aggressiveness scores at age 8 were likely to be viewed as highly aggressive by their peers ten years later. Perhaps more important, their violent tendencies often continued into adulthood. One indication of this shows up in the relationship between the childhood scores and the adult participants' statements (at age 30) about how they disciplined their own children. When the persons who had children were asked how they would react to a display of aggression by their offspring, the participants who had been highly aggressive at age 8 were generally most likely to say they would punish the offending youngster. Even as adults they were apparently more like-ly to respond aggressively to aggression than were their less aggressive peers.

Generally "Bad" versus Generally "Good." Other findings support the West-Farrington notion of extreme childhood aggressiveness as basically an expression of general antisocial tendencies. When the Eron team traced the police records of the people in their sample in 1981, they found that the participants who had been most aggressive as 8-year-olds were three times more likely to have been convicted of a crime by age 19 than were their less aggressive counterparts. Furthermore, as can be seen in Figure 5-3, they tended to have the greatest number of criminal con-victions by the time they were 30 years old. This relationship held, more-over, whether the people involved were females or males. The highly aggressive youths' antisocial tendencies even led them to accumulate rel-atively large numbers of traffic offenses.

A hundred years ago, most people would have thought of the extremely aggressive persons in both the Cambridge and Columbia County studies as being "bad." Even today, with our greater psychologi-

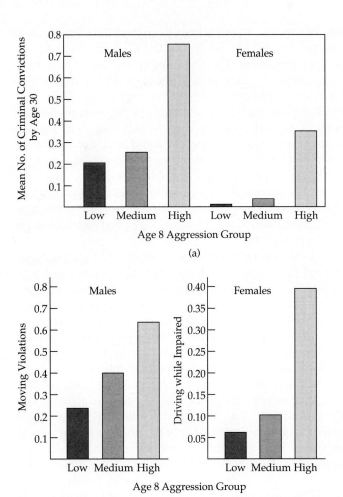

FIGURE 5-3

Relationships between peer-nominated aggressiveness at age 8 and convictions for (A) a crime or (B) traffic offenses by age 30. (Data from Eron (1987). Copyright 1987 by the American Psychological Association. Reprinted by permission.)

cal sophistication, many of us would agree with this characterization. Aggressive people are not nice. Like Jimmy, many of them are quick to hurt others and to violate many accepted rules of conduct.[20]

You should understand clearly, however, that the people we're dealing with here, including Jimmy, are *aggressively antisocial*. There are other kinds of antisocial persons, as I indicated earlier, who aren't especially assaultive, who aren't easily provoked, and who aren't quick to explode in rage. Rolf Loeber and Karen Schmaling have called our attention to two different kinds of antisociality, at least in children. After examining twenty-eight studies that sought to identify different types of antisocial conduct by children, they concluded that the youths' departures from socially approved patterns of behavior varied along an overt-covert continuum. At one end of this dimension were youngsters who were openly antisocial and who argued and fought a great deal—the sort of aggressive, norm-violating children who were identified in the Cambridge and Columbia County studies. At the opposite end of the overt-covert continuum, according to Loeber and Schmaling, were children who often hid their antisocial conduct. They stole, sometimes even set fires, and otherwise broke laws when they thought they could get away with it, but they weren't especially prone to violence.[21] It's the openly aggressive children who are the focus of this discussion.

The Concept of Aggressive Conduct Disorder. If I were to view the most extremely aggressive youngsters identified by the Cambridge and Columbia County projects from a mental health perspective, I might characterize them as having an *aggressive conduct disorder.* Consider how well this syndrome, as described in the American Psychiatric Association's *Diagnostic and Statistical Manual* (DSM-III), matches these youngsters:

> [They exhibit] a repetitive and persistent pattern of aggressive conduct in which the rights of others are violated, by either physical violence against persons, or thefts outside the home involving confrontation with a victim. The physical violence may take the form of rape, mugging, assault, or, in rare cases, homicide.

Jimmy certainly seems to fit this description, especially if we also take into account some of the syndrome's other features—such as "unusually early smoking, drinking, and other substance abuse . . . poor frustration tolerance, irritability, temper outbursts, and provocative restlessness."[22]

Are there gender differences in the consistency of aggressiveness? Before going on to the next topic, I should address a question that has probably occurred to you: Do males and females differ in how consistently they display aggression over the years? The answer, generally speaking, seems to be "no." Most of the relevant research has found little if any difference between the genders in this regard. In the Columbia County study, for example, consistency over time was comparable for the two sexes.[23]

Much the same conclusion can be drawn about possible gender differences in the degree to which early aggressiveness predicts later criminality. Here too, although there are some exceptions, a number of inves-tigations have supported the Columbia County findings reported above. Girls who are extremely aggressive before adolescence (when they are about 8 to 10 years old) seem to be at risk of having criminal records by the time they are teenagers.[24]

HOW AGGRESSIVE PERSONALITIES OPERATE

Having established that some people are persistently disposed to aggres-sion, my next task is to show how the personalities of these people oper-ate. To do this, we first have to recognize that there are actually two dif-ferent types of highly aggressive persons.

Different Kinds of Aggressive People

In describing highly aggressive individuals as basically antisocial, I don't mean to imply that every aggressive youngster is an incipient criminal or that each playground fight is a manifestation of a serious underlying psychological maladjustment. As I have pointed out, we're all inclined to be mean and nasty when we're not feeling well. At times we may even lash out impulsively in a burst of rage because we are intensely aroused and are not sufficiently self-restrained, for one reason or another. Also, some of us have learned in the course of growing up that aggression can pay off, that we can settle a dispute in our favor or get what we want by threatening others, and so we occasionally resort to aggression in a cal-culated effort to further our ends. It's the frequent and not the occasional aggressors who concern us here—the small minority of the population who are usually quick to attack, who act aggressively again and again, and who have little compunction about hurting others.

Emotionally Reactive versus Instrumental Types of Frequent Aggressors
Not even frequent aggressors are necessarily all alike. Although it's often difficult to draw sharp distinctions between the different kinds of aggres-sion, we can say—as I've proposed—that some assaults are largely instances of emotional (or hostile) aggression, while others are primarily acts of instrumental aggression. We can also apply this typology to fre-quent aggressors, as long as we realize that violence-prone persons don't always fall neatly into one category rather than the other. By and large, some persons are highly aggressive because they are emotionally reac-tive: often hot-tempered, easily enraged, and quick to "shift into over-drive." These hot-tempered people, however, sometimes attack others because they believe their aggression will pay off. Other aggressors can

be viewed as more instrumentally oriented, since their aggression is more frequently carried out in the service of other desires—to satisfy their urges to achieve power, status, monetary gain, and so on. However, these people can also lose their tempers occasionally and strike at someone in rage.

It's helpful to think of some highly aggressive youngsters as *mainly* displaying either emotionally reactive or instrumental aggression.[25] Let's look at some research that can be readily interpreted from this perspective.

Some Examples of Instrumentally Oriented Aggressors

Bullies as instrumentally oriented. Bullies are a good example of instrumentally oriented aggressors because they often try to intimidate or even assault others in a calculated attempt at coercion. There's evidence of this in Olweus's investigation of over 1000 Swedish schoolboys, all between 12 and 16 years old. Olweus asked the teachers he surveyed to identify the students in their classes who "oppressed or harassed" somebody else "either physically or mentally." On the basis of the results, he estimated that about 5 percent of the youngsters could be regarded as bullies. His data also suggested that the aggression these youths displayed was largely self-initiated rather than a response to specific, unpleasant conditions. They typically didn't hit out unthinkingly in rage but acted more coolly and deliberately, "selecting and creating" their aggressive encounters. Olweus believed that the boys weren't compensating for underlying feelings of inferiority. Nor were they especially likely to come from underprivileged, poor families. More often than not, they appeared to be self-confident and tough rather than anxious and unsure of themselves.[26]

It's not clear from Olweus's report just why the bullies acted as they did, but one possibility is that they were trying to assert their dominance and control over others. John Lochman, a psychologist at the Duke University Medical School in Durham, North Carolina, believes "that bullies have a strong need to control others. . . . Their need to be dominant masks an underlying fear that they are not in control." Whatever motive they had in mind, the boys evidently were not exhibiting an emotional reaction. They typically weren't angry when they threatened their victims. Rather, their behavior was a tactic; it was instrumental to the attainment of a goal other than simply injuring their victims.[27]

Instrumental aspects of the antisocial personality. Some aspects of the aggression displayed by very antisocial personalities can also be understood as instrumental behavior. One of the mental health authorities who helped to construct the American Psychiatric Association's diagnostic manual, DSM-III, Theodore Millon of the University of Miami in Florida, has described this personality type in the following way:

> Both the basic aggressive and overtly antisocial variants of this personality evoke hostility, not only as an incidental consequence of their behaviors and attitudes but because they intentionally provoke others into conflict. They carry a "chip on their shoulder," often seem to be spoiling for a fight, and appear to enjoy tangling with others to prove their strength and test their competencies and powers. Having been periodically successful in past aggressive ventures, they feel confident of their prowess. They may seek out dangers and challenges. Not only are they unconcerned and reckless, but they appear poised and bristling, ready to vent resentments, demonstrate their invulnerability, and restore their pride.[28]

This portrait seems to be similar to that of the school bully. In both cases much of the aggression that is exhibited is deliberately initiated, apparently in order to prove something in the aggressor's mind. According to Millon, antisocial personalities want to convince themselves that they are tough, strong, and powerful by being contemptuous of sentimentality, compassion, and tenderness. Having presumably experienced little affection and consideration themselves as they were growing up, Millon says, these persons "learned too well that it is best to trust no one. . . . By denying tender feelings, they protect themselves against the memory of painful parental rejections."

As Millon points out, the antisocial personality's hostile attitude has an unfortunate consequence: a self-fulfilling prophecy:

> [Their] aggressive, conflict-seeking behaviors only perpetuate their fears and misery. More than merely fostering distance and rejection, they have now provoked others into justified counterhostility. By spoiling for a fight and by precipitous and irrational arrogance, they create not only a distant reserve on the part of others but intense and well-justified animosity. Now they must face real aggression, and now they have a real basis for anticipating retaliation. . . . Their vigilant state cannot be relaxed.[29]

Obviously, not every school bully is so seriously antisocial that he or she can be labeled as an "antisocial personality" in the DSM-III sense. Nevertheless, in at least one respect the antisocial personality is an exaggerated version of the bully. Both are far more concerned with their own wishes and desires than with other persons' psychological needs, and both don't mind hurting others to get their own way.

The question of psychopaths. The antisocial personalities that I have been describing are certainly reminiscent of the classic notion of the *psychopath,* which once was very prevalent in psychiatric and criminologic literatures. You've probably heard of psychopaths and have some general idea of what they are supposed to be like. In their 1964 book on this kind of individual, William McCord and Joan McCord described what they regarded as a typical case, and the picture they present will undoubtedly sound somewhat familiar.

> He was a handsome man, slender, wavy-haired, and always immaculately garbed in the prison dress. The English accent to his speech, his theatrical gestures, his well-timed sense of the dramatic tabbed him as an actor, which once he was. Nothing on the surface revealed his career as a forger, robber, liar, homosexual—and ultimately murderer. . . .
> [After a spree of crimes in New York and California, including forgeries and robberies, he shot a man to death while committing a burglary.] During his imprisonment, several psychiatrists examined Borlov and agreed in diagnosing him as a psychopathic personality. His impulsive outbursts of aggression, his narcissism, and his lovelessness singled him out as pathologically different from other men. His lying indicated the possible existence of hallucinations. Yet all who knew him agreed that Borlov, unlike the psychotic individual, did not for one minute believe his own lies. He lied, the psychiatrists agreed, because he enjoyed it. If pressed, he would affably admit his prevarications.[30]

This man exhibits the signs the classic psychopath is supposed to possess, especially the outward charm and civility, a "mask of sanity," hiding an inner callousness and even brutality. McCord and McCord say that this type of individual "is an asocial, aggressive, highly impulsive person, who feels little or no guilt and is unable to form lasting bonds of affection with other human beings."[31] Along with many other mental health specialists, they believe that he is a major danger to society and the source of many violent crimes.

Other authorities, however, are seriously troubled by the looseness and imprecision of the classification, as McCord and McCord themselves acknowledged. Borlov had good manners, but other people who are labeled "psychopaths" are definitely not charming to those they encounter. More important, though impulsivity is often viewed as one hallmark of this personality type, several investigators have noted that "psychopaths can be planful and premeditated as well as short-sighted and impulsive." Because of this seeming inconsistency, it's not surprising that forensic psychiatrists haven't always agreed about exactly what characteristics psychopaths possess. According to one reviewer, in the past American specialists often stressed psychopaths' "charm, social skills, and vanity, as well as more damaging attributes," while German psychiatrists emphasized their "emotional coldness and lack of feeling for others," and the British gave greatest weight to their impulsiveness and aggression.[32] Indeed, the prevailing imprecision in the use of this term has been so great that the American Psychiatric Association's latest diagnostic manual, DSM-IIIR, doesn't even use "psychopath" as a classification and prefers instead to speak only of "antisocial personality disorder." There is a type of personality that gets into frequent trouble with the law and is prone to violence but, the manual seems to imply, it's not a good idea to call this type of person a "psychopath."

The Psychopathy Checklist. A number of researchers, however, haven't given up on "psychopathy" as a concept. They have shown that the psychopathic personality type can be identified reliably and with precision if the proper criteria are employed. One of the leaders in this endeavor is Robert Hare of the University of British Columbia in Vancouver, Canada. Hare and his associates devised the Psychopathy Checklist (PCL), a measure that originally included twenty-two items but has now been reduced to twenty items. These items refer to what the researchers regard as psychopaths' distinguishing characteristics. A selection of these items includes: (1) glibness and superficial charm, (3) a grandiose sense of self-worth, (5) pathological lying and deception, (9) callousness and lack of empathy, (11) poor behavioral controls, (15) impulsivity, and (20) failure to accept responsibility for their own actions. When investigators use this measure, they typically review whether or not the offender has each of the qualities listed on the PCL.[33]

Research by Hare and others who have employed the PCL clearly demonstrates the importance of the psychopathy concept in a complete picture of the role of personality in aggressively antisocial behavior. For example, studies have shown, criminals with extremely high scores on this checklist are much more likely to have been convicted of violent offenses than are other male criminals, and they also tend to engage in more violent behaviors while in prison.[34] They are indeed prone to violence.

In this discussion of the possibility of different kinds of violent dispositions, one other investigation is especially relevant. Williamson, Hare, and Wong first used the PCL to classify male inmates in several different Canadian correctional institutions as either high-scoring psychopaths or low-scoring nonpsychopaths, and then went over the police records of the men's most recent crimes to determine the natures of the offenses and the offenders' apparent motives for their actions. Figure 5-4 summarizes some of these researchers' major findings for the crimes in which there was a clear and definite victim (as contrasted to such crimes as fraud and drug trafficking, in which no one victim was involved).

It's interesting to note (although Figure 5-4 doesn't show this) that a significantly higher proportion of the *nonpsychopaths'* crimes in this sample involved murder, whereas the psychopaths were more likely to have committed robbery and property crimes. Consistent with this difference, as Figure 5-4 does show, the case histories indicated that the psychopaths were mainly interested in material gain when they carried out their crimes. By contrast, strong emotion arousal (such as jealousy, rage, and heated arguments) was more likely to have played a substantial role in the offenses committed by the nonpsychopaths. Considering all this, we're not surprised to learn from the researchers that the psychopaths and nonpsychopaths had different relationships with their victims. The victims of nonpsychopaths were typically people they knew, while the psychopaths' victims tended to be strangers.

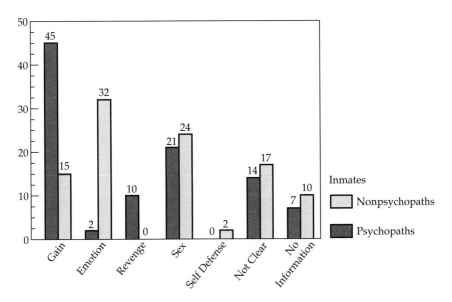

FIGURE 5-4

Percentages of psychopathic and nonpsychopathic inmates judged to have a particular motive for committing the offense. (Adapted with permission from Williamson, Hare, & Wong, (1987). Copyright 1987 by the Canadian Psychological Association.)

These findings indicate that many of the violent crimes carried out by the psychopaths are *not* highly emotional outbursts. Their violence, generally speaking, typically doesn't grow out of a highly charged argument with someone they know but is more likely to be an assault prompted in large part by the thought of achieving some benefit. Williamson and her associates believed that "psychopaths are more willing than are other criminals to put themselves in a position where violence might be needed," but that when they resort to aggression this behavior is "callous and coldblooded . . . without the affective colouring" of the other offenders' violence.[35] If much of psychopaths' aggression is instrumental behavior, as the studies cited here suggest, it appears that psychopaths have an instrumentally oriented, aggressively antisocial personality.

Insufficient Restraints: Toward a Detailed Understanding of the Psychopathic Personality. It's not enough to say that psychopaths are quite willing to attack others "in cold blood," though it's often true. As Hare and many other investigators have emphasized, these people are frequently also unable to restrain themselves when they're pursuing a goal they desire. Indeed, this inhibitory deficiency is one of the key features of the psychopathic personality, according to an interesting research program conducted by Joseph Newman at the University of Wisconsin in Madison.

For example, suppose a psychopath wants something, such as money or sex, on a certain occasion, and actively performs a series of behaviors aimed at achieving his objective. We can call this behavioral sequence his "dominant action tendency" in the particular situation. Let's also say that, though the psychopath might satisfy his desire, there's also a fairly good chance he will be caught and punished. As Newman sees it, on the basis of his experiments and experience with inmates of correctional institutions, psychopaths are characteristically defective in the ability to restrain their ongoing goal-oriented action tendency, even though it might lead to their being punished. As a result of their inadequate self-restraint in this kind of situation, moreover, they don't look at their behavior from other people's perspective or take into account other, long-range considerations (such as what their futures may be like if they continue to act in this way); it's the immediate possible gain that matters most.[36] If they think an assault might further their immediate purposes, or even if they think it would demonstrate their power, they will be all too apt to carry through with the attack, ignoring the trouble it may cause them in the long run.

Some Final Points. Since quite a few youths who could be viewed as having a conduct disorder do change as they grow older, nowadays psychiatrists and psychologists don't classify people as psychopaths unless they are over 18 years of age; youthful psychopaths continue to be aggressively antisocial as they move into adulthood. Moreover, not every psychopath—or, for that matter, every aggressively antisocial personality—necessarily has every one of the characteristics listed in the PCL. The more of these qualities they do possess, however, the more likely they are to be a violence-prone danger to society.

Emotionally Reactive Aggressors

Other people, both children and adults, are highly aggressive for noninstrumental reasons. They do not use aggressive behavior to gain something they want; rather, they behave aggressively because they are emotionally highly reactive and easily provoked. Very sensitive to slights or insults, they are quick to see threats and attacks that may not actually exist, and they are easily offended. Not surprisingly, then, they're all too apt to respond inappropriately to the events in their social world. As a consequence, they are often not very popular.

Evidence of the two types. Some readers, believing that all aggression is instrumental in nature, may be dubious about the distinction I've been drawing. Therefore, before looking further into the psychology of emotionally reactive aggressors, it may be helpful to examine some recent research that points to the difference between aggressive persons who are mainly instrumentally oriented and people who behave aggressively because they are easily affronted by actions or words that they see as threats and affronts.

In a series of investigations of schoolboys in first and third grades, Kenneth Dodge and John Coie used teachers' ratings to distinguish between youngsters who were mainly highly reactive aggressors and other children who seemed to be similar to the instrumentally oriented bullies. A child was classified as emotionally reactive if his teacher indicated that "When this child has been teased or threatened, he . . . gets angry easily and strikes back," while an instrumentally oriented child was described as threatening and bullying others and as using "physical force in order to dominate other kinds." Some boys could be easily placed in one or the other category, but of course other children were rated by their teachers as a mixture of the two types. For our purposes, we'll consider three categories of boys: those whose aggression was mainly instrumentally oriented (labeled "Instrumental only" in Figure 5-5) those whose aggression was largely reactive (labeled "Reactive only"), and others who displayed both kinds of aggression (labeled "Instrumental-reactive"). We'll compare these children with a fourth category, boys who (according to their classmates) were socially average (labeled "Average").

One of the things the researchers did was show these youngsters a series of twelve videotaped vignettes, each depicting a boy knocking down another child's building blocks. The actors in these vignettes had been carefully coached to behave in particular ways, so that the subjects would see three kinds of scenes: (1) intentional aggression, (2) accidents, and (3) incidents in which the frustrating child's intentions were ambiguous. After they saw each videotaped segment, the children were questioned individually about the scene, and asked how they would react to the depicted event.

Dodge and Coie then compared the four categories of boys in terms of how they perceived the videotaped incidents. Figure 5-5 shows that the groups were equally accurate in recognizing the clearly portrayed intentional hostility. Differences emerged, however, when the younsters couldn't be sure why the actor had knocked down the blocks. In these cases, both types of emotionally reactive boys—but especially the "pure" emotional aggressors—were particularly apt to attribute hostility to the actors (see the middle section of Figure 5-5). They apparently were disposed to interpret ambiguous behavior as hostile. Presumably because of this readiness to see hostility in the social world, when the youngsters were then asked what they would do, the two kinds of emotionally reactive boys—and again, especially the "pure" emotional aggressors—were most likely to say they would respond with some form of aggression (see the right-hand section of Figure 5-5).[37]

The results seem clear. Not all highly aggressive persons are alike.

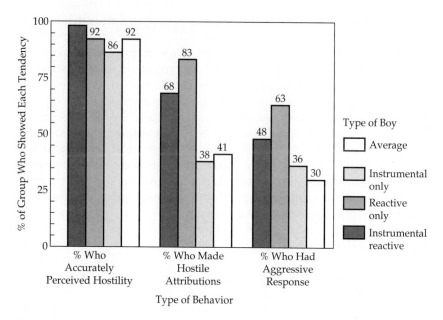

FIGURE 5-5

Percentages of boys who displayed different reactions: accurately perceiving hostility, making hostile attributions, and calling for an aggressive response to the incident. (Data from Dodge & Coie (1987). Copyright 1987 by the American Psychological Association. Adapted by permission.)

People who use aggression mainly for instrumental purposes—for example, to dominate and control others—tend to differ in important respects from relatively "pure" emotionally reactive aggressors who readily perceive hostility in others and are quick to make hostile attributions. This isn't to say that instrumentally oriented and emotionally reactive aggressors don't have any similarities. Indeed, they may have a number of characteristics in common, and both may believe that they are fairly skillful in assaulting their antagonists. Nevertheless, people who often employ aggression in a fairly calm manner and for the purpose of furthering their ends may be more likely to think that their aggression will have a positive outcome.[38]

Information processing and attributions in emotionally reactive aggression. The findings reported by Dodge and Coie are very much in line with Dodge's well-known *social information-processing model* of aggressive encounters, but they also highlight the limited nature of this formulation. This analysis is worth looking at in some detail, since it can undoubtedly be applied to many (though not all) violence-prone individuals.[39]

To understand this model, first think of the basic scene shown to the boys in the Dodge-Coie study: A boy knocks down another youngster's building blocks. Assuming that a watching child wants to understand this occurrence, the formulation says the first thing he has to do is *search the situation for relevant information and correctly detect whatever informative cues are available.* He might examine the actors' facial expressions and other nonverbal gestures for cues to the actors' attitudes and intentions. Some persons are better than others at reading subtle cues, although the nonverbal signals are occasionally so clear-cut that they are unmistakable. We saw that all four types of boys in the Dodge-Coie study were equally accurate in identifying *clear* signs of intentional hostility.

Once the child has detected whatever informative cues are available, *he has to interpret the cues.* This is the step to which the Dodge model gives the greatest emphasis (although other cognitive processes are recognized). Dodge has paid particular attention to the interpretations and attributions made by aggressive children. In the study we're considering, the emotionally reactive aggressors' interpretations and attributions reflected their conception of the social world as full of hostility. When it wasn't clear what the frustrater's motives were, these children typically believed that he had intended to hurt the other child.

After arriving at some understanding of the event, the person then has to *consider the possible ways of responding to the situation, select a particular response, and carry it out.* The individual presumably first thinks about the different possible ways of reacting to what has happened. The same range of alternatives won't occur to everyone. Whereas most well-adjusted people confronted by a problem situation will realize that they could do several different things, highly aggressive persons usually think of only a small number of possibilities, and they may think of only one (hitting) if they believe they have been deliberately wronged. Then, partly because of their limited repertoire of responses to interpersonal difficulties but also because their greatly dominant tendency is to react aggressively when they think they are threatened or mistreated, the violence-prone persons often choose to attack the perceived offender. The emotionally reactive aggressors in the Dodge-Coie research revealed their aggressive proclivities in deciding on an aggressive response as well as in their hostile attributions. Thinking they saw hostility, they believed it was appropriate to respond to the perceived aggression with their own aggression.

The Information-Processing Model's Limitations. Dodge's information-processing analysis identifies several important aspects of the psychology of the emotionally reactive aggressors: their tendencies (1) to interpret ambiguous actions as hostility and to attribute aggressive intent to others, (2) to think of relatively few alternative ways, other than aggression, of responding to disturbing events, and (3) to believe that it is desirable to respond aggressively to others' hostility. Clearly, however, this particular formulation neglects some other important considerations and cannot adequately account for the behavior of every highly aggressive individual.

First, *this particular model may not give sufficient attention to other cognitive processes besides hostile interpretations and attributions.* It's important to recognize that violence-prone persons are apt to have aggression-related thoughts when they encounter stimuli that have an aggressive meaning.[40] This is a significant point because it indicates that a wide variety of events (not only perceived hostility) can prime aggressive ideas in people who are disposed to assaultive thoughts and actions. As I noted earlier, these people can develop aggressive ideas when they hear words that connote aggression, see weapons, view a fight on a TV screen, or observe their peers in conflict. As a consequence, aggression-related memories, feelings, and action tendencies may arise, and may instigate acts of aggression soon afterward, if the circumstances are conducive to violence.

Thought processes can also operate over time to help form the propensity to aggression. Rowell Hucsmann and Leonard Eron have suggested that many of the aggressively inclined children in their studies

FIGURE 5-6

Although humorous in nature, this cartoon points to a phenomenon that can contribute to the occurrence of violence, especially by highly aggressive persons. On hearing words having an aggressive meaning for them, aggressive ideas and action tendencies might be activated within them that could lead to an impulsive assault on an available target if their inhibitions against aggression are sufficiently weak at that time. (Cartoon by Jim Borgman. Copyright by King Features Syndicate. Reprinted with special permission.)

had mentally rehearsed the kinds of aggressive encounters they frequently saw on television. Boys of this type might repeatedly think about the violence portrayed on the screen, perhaps imagining themselves as the heroes shown in the story, beating up their enemies. Cognitive rehearsal may help such youths to acquire aggressive patterns of conduct.[41]

Second, *the violent reactions of people who are prone to emotional aggression are affected by other factors, not just by their way of processing information.* Emotionally reactive aggressors as a group are not only easily and strongly aroused but frequently also deficient in self-control. As it is usually now presented, *Dodge's perspective doesn't give sufficient attention to emotionally reactive aggressors' frequent failure to restrain themselves adequately.* This point deserves considerable elaboration.

The absence of adequate restraints may result in a failure to control one's thoughts as well as an inability to hold back on one's motor reactions. Dodge suggested some years ago that his highly aggressive boys might tend to attribute hostility to others because they typically don't inhibit their attributional ideas. When someone bothers them, they don't catch themselves, so to say, and allow other possible interpretations of the disturbing person's behavior to come to mind.[42]

In addition, because of their generally weak inhibitions against aggression, emotionally reactive people may not adequately hold back on what they say and do in response to a perceived affront. Have you ever been so highly aroused by a provocation that you blurted out a hostile remark even though a part of your mind urged you to restrain yourself? Despite a small voice within you that may have cautioned, "Don't say it," perhaps you made the statement—and later regretted having said it. I'm suggesting that emotionally reactive aggressors frequently display this sort of failure to control themselves when they are extremely aroused.

Besides not holding back on verbal aggression, they may not adequately inhibit their urges to become physically aggressive. They may sometimes lash out in an impulsive assault upon a person who has offended them, regardless of the possible consequences. Jimmy, for example, acted just this way when he attacked a police officer at a dance because he was enraged by the officer's refusal to allow him entry.[43] Because of their weak restraints, furthermore, reactively aggressive persons may remain unable to control themselves once they get started on an aggressive interchange. They keep on attacking—cursing, pushing, or hitting—and they are oblivious to both the possibility of punishment and other people's entreaties. It's often difficult to get them to stop.[44]

Then too, to get back to a possibility I mentioned earlier, *emotionally reactive aggressors may well become highly aroused.* If we measured how people feel when they meet with a frustration, a threat, or a challenge, my guess is that the emotional aggressors, on the average, would tend to experience the strongest displeasure. In more technical language, it could be said that they would probably have rather strong physiological, expressive-motor, and ideational reactions of an aggression-related nature. Anger scales such as Spielberger's State-Trait Anger Scale, which was described earlier in this chapter, assess not only people's readiness to become angry when they are provoked but also the intensity of their feelings on these occasions. It's probably important to measure this intensity. If I am correct in arguing that unpleasant feelings tend to generate both an aggressive urge and an anger experience in proportion to the strength of this felt displeasure, it's clear that a truly comprehensive theory of emotional aggression must take this emotional intensity into account. In my view, the attributional model does not pay sufficient attention to individual differences in this respect, and to the likelihood that the reactive aggressors are prone to strong emotional reactions.

The Type A Personality as Reactively Aggressive
The notion of emotional reactivity is especially applicable to a certain kind of individual who is at risk for coronary disease: the well-known type A personality. It's interesting to look at this kind of individual from the perspective of research on aggression, but first let me give you some background.

The type A personality and heart disease. About three decades ago, Meyer Friedman and Ray Rosenman, two California physicians, became convinced that some people were particularly likely to develop chronic heart disease because of their emotional reactions to external stressors. On the basis of their clinical experience and initial research, they believed that a significant number of men who had serious heart ailments shared several personal qualities that could have led to development of their illnesses: They were highly competitive and very impatient; they were driven by a sense of great urgency to complete their tasks (and to win) as soon as possible; but they were also restless and all too ready to take on other tasks as well, as if they wanted to have lots of irons in the fire at the same time. Regarding these as the characteristics of the *type A personality,* Friedman and Rosenman then set out to determine whether people who possessed these traits would indeed be more likely to develop heart disease than would those who had the opposite qualities, which they called the *type B personality.*

Beginning in 1960, Friedman, Rosenman, and their collaborators studied more than 3000 middle-aged employees of eleven different corporations, with the goal of determining the kinds of risk factors (such as smoking, blood cholesterol level, and personality characteristics) that would predict the development of cardiovascular disease. The physicians' expectation was supported: The people who were classified as having type A personalities (on the basis of the researchers' initial interviews with them) were about twice as likely as were type B's to have some form of heart disease eight years later.

A great many other researchers have subsequently also sought to investigate the linkage between personality type and coronary illness. While there have been some exceptions, the general pattern of results (from prospective as well as concurrent studies) upholds the basic Friedman-Rosenman thesis: There is a modest, but not trivial, relationship between the type A personality and coronary heart disease. Furthermore, according to the evidence now available, the connection between personality and heart disease is about as strong for women as it is for men.[45]

What's most important in the context of this discussion is that the later research in this area qualifies the original Friedman-Rosenman analysis somewhat. It's not workaholics who are highly involved in their jobs and feel under great pressure to get the work done who are especially susceptible to heart ailments. Rather, it's people who are extremely competitive and prone to anger, hostility, and aggressiveness.[46] These individuals seem to be especially reactive to stressful events. When faced by a challenge or stressor, their sympathetic nervous systems tend to respond excessively. Their systolic blood pressure readings may be unusually high, as may their neurohormonal secretions, and their levels of low-density lipoprotein cholesterol may be elevated.[47]

To get a more specific idea of what's involved here, imagine this situation: You are driving and are almost late for an important appointment. Another car cuts in front of you but then slows down, so that you have to stop when the traffic light turns red. The drivers behind you seem to be annoyed and honk their horns. When you think about this situation, there's a good chance that your heart rate will accelerate more if you have a type A personality than if you are a type B, whereas your personality type would matter much less if you were imagining a neutral, nonstressful incident.[48]

Evidence of type A's as reactive aggressors. This discussion of the characteristics of type A personalities is obviously relevant to the notion of emotionally reactive aggressors. Not everyone who has a type A personality may be as extreme or as antisocial as many of the highly aggressive reactive individuals described earlier, and not every type A may be so strongly disposed to make the kinds of attributional errors that were emphasized by Dodge. Nevertheless, people who have this type of personality—particularly those who are high in the aggressive component— are typically highly reactive emotionally. They apparently are especially likely to become angry and aggressive when they are confronted by a decidedly unpleasant event. Several experiments indicate this likelihood fairly clearly.

One of these experiments was carried out by Charles Carver and David Glass. Male undergraduates at the University of Miami in Florida, each of whom had been previously categorized as either type A or type B, were placed in one of three conditions: (1) a *frustration* condition established by giving the subject a puzzle to work on that actually was insoluble while another student (the experimenter's accomplice) sat nearby; (2) an *insult* condition created by having the accomplice harass the subject as he tried to solve the puzzle; and (3) a neutral, *control* group in which the subject wasn't exposed to either of these treatments. After this, all the subjects were asked to be "teachers" in the Buss aggression machine procedure and were required to give the "learner" (i.e., the accomplice) an electric shock whenever he made a mistake on his assignment. As is standard in this procedure, the subjects were free to select the intensity of the punishment they administered.

To summarize the results briefly, the type A's administered much more severe shocks than did the type B's in both the frustration condition and the insult condition, but not in the neutral condition. (Note that the frustrated type A's had no reason to attribute hostility to the other student.) It was only when they were emotionally aroused that type A's tended to behave aggressively toward the available target.

Although Carver and Glass viewed the type A subjects' aggression as instrumental rather than as emotionally reactive behavior, a later experiment (conducted at the University of Utah in Salt Lake City by Michael Strube, Charles Turner, Dan Cerro, John Stevens, and Frances Hinchey) has shown that type A men are apt to be highly aggressive when they are frustrated *even when the aggression isn't instrumental to some other purpose.* Using male undergraduates who had been assessed as being either type A or type B, the Utah researchers first placed each subject in either a frustration or a no-frustration condition (using the same procedure that had been employed by Carver and Glass), and again each person supposedly had to be a teacher to a fellow student. This time, however, the teacher was to reward the learner on a scale of 1 to 9 for correct performance and to punish him for mistakes by imposing a fine of 1 to 9 points. The researchers also established an important—and somewhat subtle—experimental variation: Some of the subjects were led to think that they couldn't really influence the learner's behavior on the first few trials when they punished him for a mistake but could only hurt him; on these initial trials, these subjects were told, the learner wouldn't find out how much he had been fined for his errors, and thus they couldn't influence him any more by fining him heavily than by giving him only a small fine. The size of the fine would matter only to the subjects—if they wanted to hurt the "learner."

The results with this punishment measure were fairly clear-cut. Essentially, the subjects fined the learner more severely after suffering a frustration than after receiving neutral treatment. Again we see that a frustration can generate an urge to aggression, but what is more relevant to my present argument is that the aroused type A's were much more punitive than were the thwarted type B's. All in all, the type A men, being highly reactive emotionally, were likely to respond to the frustration with emotional aggression.[49]

A newspaper article that was published in 1990 described more research which adds to the picture of possible adverse effects of highly reactive aggressiveness upon a person's health:

> People who often explode in hostile rages or who sit around fuming over every perceived slight may be doing more than making themselves unpleasant. They may be killing themselves.
>
> Researchers have gathered a wealth of data lately suggesting that chronic anger is so damaging to the body that it ranks with, or even exceeds, cigarette smoking, obesity and a high fat diet as a powerful risk factor for early death.
>
> "Our studies indicate that hostile, suspicious anger is right up there with any other health hazard we know about," said Dr. Redford Williams, a researcher in behavioral medicine at the Duke University Medical Center.
>
> In results presented at a recent meeting of the American Heart Association, Dr. Williams reported that people who scored high on a hostility scale as teen-agers [sic] were much more likely than their more cheerful peers to have elevated cholesterol levels as adults, suggesting a link between unremitting anger and heart disease.
>
> In another recent study, Dr. Mara Julius, an epidemiologist at the University of Michigan, analyzed the effects of chronic anger on women over the age of 18. She found that women who [had] answered initial test questions with obvious signs of long-term suppressed anger were three times more likely to have died [by the time a second measure was taken] than those who did not harbor such hostile feelings. . . .
>
> Other researchers are teasing apart the complex welter of anger's physical effects on the body. They are finding that some people who are prone to anger have an overactive "fight or flight" response, generating excessive amounts of stress hormones when confronted by life's every bump.[50]

SUMMARY

Contrary to some psychologists' contention that there is much less consistency in particular modes of behavior across different situations than is commonly supposed, research has demonstrated that there is a remarkable stability in the tendency to be highly aggressive both across different settings within a narrow time span and over a considerable range of time. Individuals who are high in aggressiveness are apt to be assaultive in many different ways, if the situation confronting them has an aggressive meaning for them and if they are not sufficiently self-restrained. They are also more likely than are their characteristically less assaultive peers to display aggression on many different occasions.

Longitudinal research is described in this chapter, including such notable investigations as the Cambridge study of English urban working-class youth by Farrington and West and the comparable Columbia

County study of small-town American children by Eron, Huesmann, and their colleagues. This research shows stability in highly aggressive patterns of conduct from childhood into adulthood. (Keep in mind, however, that a good proportion of the children who are initially highly aggressive do change and become less extremely aggressive as the years go by.) These studies also demonstrate that unusual aggressiveness is often just one aspect of a general pattern of antisocial behavior, with the result that (although this isn't inevitable) a significant fraction of those who are highly aggressive in childhood acquire police records by the time they reach adulthood.

The chapter then turns to an examination of the personalities of highly aggressive individuals. Following the distinction between instrumental and emotional (or hostile) aggression which I drew earlier in the book, I suggest it may be helpful to differentiate between persons whose frequent aggression is mostly instrumentally oriented and those who are highly aggressive because they are emotionally very reactive to provocative situations. There is reason to believe that many schoolboy bullies are primarily instrumentally oriented, since their aggression is typically aimed at asserting dominance and control. The aggression often exhibited by people who have the antisocial personality described in psychiatric manuals may also have a very substantial instrumental component. Attention is also given in this chapter to the psychopathic personality. Although many authorities are troubled by the overly loose manner in which this concept has frequently been employed, studies have shown that it is possible to make reliable diagnoses of psychopathy if appropriate criteria are used. According to Hare, the developer of a well-known psychopathy scale, much of the aggression carried out by psychopaths is instrumental behavior prompted by the possibility of achieving some benefit rather than a highly emotional outburst. Newman's analysis of the psychopathic personality is summarized briefly.

Research by Dodge and Coie is then cited to document the existence of those who are mainly emotionally reactive aggressors. In accord with Dodge's analysis of violence-prone personalities on the basis of his information-processing formulation, this study found that emotionally reactive aggressive children (1) are relatively likely to attribute hostility to others when it is not clear why the others acted as they did and (2) tend to believe that aggression is an appropriate and even desirable response to perceived hostility. Accepting these results, I suggest that Dodge's formulation should go further and also recognize that emotionally reactive aggressors typically become intensely aroused when provoked, and that they are likely to be deficient in the ability to restrain their aggressive reactions.

The chapter concludes with a consideration of the type A personality's emotionally reactive aggression. Building on the original observations by Friedman and Rosenman, more recent studies now indicate that people who have type A personalities are susceptible to coronary heart disease because they are easily enraged when they believe they are challenged or threatened or are under stress. Two psychological experiments show that type A's are inclined to be aggressive when frustrated or insulted, even though they cannot gain any benefits from their assaults.

*N*OTES

1. Mischel (1968).
2. Wright & Mischel (1987).
3. Psychologists will recognize that the former type of research basically deals with the *concurrent validity* of the aggression measures, while the latter studies can be thought of as akin to the research on *predictive validity*.
4. See Olweus (1974), pp. 535–565.
5. See Berkowitz & Donnerstein (1982); Carlson, Marcus-Newhall, & Miller (1989).
6. See, for example, Olweus (1974); Pulkkinen (1987); Walder, Abelson, Eron, Banta, & Laulicht (1961).
7. Loeber & Dishion (1984).
8. See Wilkins, Scharff, & Schlottmann (1974).
9. Spielberger, Jacobs, Russell, & Crane (1983).
10. Deffenbacher, Demm, & Brandon (1986).
11. See Lesser (1957).
12. Olweus (1979).
13. See Caspi, Elder, & Bem (1987) for related and more recent supporting evidence.
14. For example, see West (1969); West & Farrington (1977); Farrington (1978, 1982, 1989a, 1989b).
15. See especially Farrington (1989b).
16. See Farrington (1989b).
17. Farrington (1989b), p. 97; Farrington (1989a), p. 27.
18. Eron (1987); Eron, Huesmann, Dubow, Romanoff, & Yarmel (1987); Eron, Walder, & Lefkowitz (1971); Huesmann & Eron (1984); Huesmann, Eron, Lefkowitz, & Walder (1984); Lefkowitz, Eron, Walder, & Huesmann (1977).
19. Studies conducted by Eron and his associates have amply documented the reliability and validity of this measure. For example, see Lefkowitz et al. (1977).
20. Also see Loeber & Dishion, (1983); Loeber & Schmaling, (1985).
21. Loeber & Schmaling (1985). The question of whether or not there is a single syndrome of "antisociality" is discussed at some length in Crowell (1987) and in Rutter & Garmezy (1983).
22. The description of the aggressive conduct disorder type is taken from the 1980 edition of the American Psychiatric Association's *Diagnostic and Statistical Manual* (DSM-III), p. 45.
23. Eron et al. (1987), p. 257. Also see Cairns & Cairns (1984).

24. Roff & Wirt (1984).

25. Although there is good evidence that many highly aggressive children are sufficiently similar so that they can all be understood as members of a single category (such as "conduct disorder"), as was indicated earlier, a number of authorities believe it is helpful to establish a finer differentiation. Thus, the DSM-III distinguishes between unsocialized and socialized forms of conduct disorder. Children who have unsocialized conduct disorder are much more likely to have poor interpersonal relationships. However, the research in this area hasn't led to any clear conclusions, and child psychologists and psychiatrists are not in agreement on the validity of this distinction. See Rutter & Garmezy (1983).

26. Olweus (1978).

27. This quotation is taken from an article on bullies written by Daniel Goleman, *New York Times*, Apr. 7, 1987. According to a recent review of quantitative studies of bullying carried out by David Farrington (1992), Olweus's characterization of bullies is supported by the findings from other investigations, mostly in western Europe. Summarizing the results obtained in many of these studies, Farrington concluded that, "Generally, bullies are aggressive, tough, strong, confident . . . derive pleasure from bullying and have a strong need to dominate" (p. 3). These individuals apparently intimidate and assault others in an effort to obtain a sense of having power and control over other persons. The term "bully" as used in this book refers only to such instrumentally oriented aggressors.

28. Millon (1981), pp. 212–213.

29. Millon (1981), p. 213.

30. McCord, W., & McCord, J. (1964), pp. 5, 6.

31. McCord, W., & McCord, J. (1964), p. 3.

32. Block & Gjerde (1986); Feldman (1977).

33. See Hare, Harpur, Hakstian, Forth, Hart, & Newman (1990).

34. Hare & McPherson (1984).

35. Williamson, Hare, & Wong (1987).

36. See Kosson, Smith, & Newman (1990); Newman (1987); Newman, Patterson, & Kosson (1987).

37. Dodge & Coie (1987).

38. Dodge & Crick (1990); Perry, Perry, & Rasmussen (1986).

39. See Dodge (1982).

40. See especially, Geen & George (1969); Simpson & Craig (1967). The cognitive processes involved in the behavior of these persons have to do with other matters, not just with making attributions.

41. Huesmann & Eron (1984).

42. Dodge & Frame (1982).

43. Dodge, in Dodge & Crick (1990), has also referred to highly aggressive children's frequent inability to restrain themselves when they are provoked by a peer.

44. See for example, Patterson, Dishion, & Bank (1984).

45. Friedman & Rosenman (1974); Booth-Kewley & Friedman (1987).

46. See Booth-Kewley & Friedman (1987); Baker, Dearborn, Hastings, & Hamberger (1984); Dembroski & Costa (1987); Chesney & Rosenman (1985).

47. See Chesney & Rosenman (1985); Weidner, Sexton, McLerrarn, & Connor (1987).

48. Baker, Hastings, & Hart (1984).

49. The first experiment reported in this section was conducted by Carver & Glass (1978). The second study, highlighting the thwarted subjects' desire to hurt their victim, was by Strube, Turner, Cerro, Stevens, & Hinchey (1984).

50. Angier, N., *New York Times*, Dec. 13, 1990.

6

Whole chapter

The Development of Violence Proneness

Familial and Peer Influences on the Development of Aggressiveness

❖

Childhood Experiences ◆ *Families Can Influence the Development of Antisocial Dispositions* ◆ Direct Influences on the Development of Aggressiveness ◆ *Rewards for Aggression* ◆ *Unpleasant Conditions Established by Parents* ◆ Indirect Influences ◆ *Conflict within the Family* ◆ *Modeling Influences*

C hapter 5 had a clear message: Some people have an abiding inclination to violence. Whether they use aggression instrumentally to further their purposes or are only quick to explode in intense rage, these troublemakers account for more than their share of the violence in society. Moreover, many of them show their aggressiveness in widely different situations and persist in this unpleasant conduct over the years. How did they become so aggressive?

There's no simple answer. Their violent tendencies could be the product of many different influences, including: too little love and affection from their mothers and fathers, harsh and erratic parental discipline during their formative years, genetic heritage and neurological makeup, the level of stress in their lives and the degree to which they have failed to satisfy their personal and economic wishes, the attitudes and values regarding aggression that are prevalent in their segment of society or that are shared by their friends and acquaintances, the extent to which they see others using aggression to solve their problems (in real life and/or on movie and TV screens), and how they have learned to view their social world. There is no one source of aggressive inclinations, just as there is no one way to develop a violent character.

Instead of looking at all of the factors that contribute to the development of persistent aggressiveness, this chapter will concentrate mainly on the roles of family and peers, especially in childhood. Mental health specialists have long viewed the family as both the crucible in which the individual character is forged and the chief source of antisocial proclivities. Indeed, on the basis of their pioneering 1926 study of some 2000 juvenile delinquents, William Healy and Augusta Bronner argued that parents were such an important influence on the development of delinquency that children should be removed from "bad homes."[1] Many would agree today. Nevertheless, my focus on the family does not imply that aggressive personalities are necessarily formed only in the home as a consequence of how mothers and fathers treat their offspring.

Although a child's aggressiveness can persist through the years, I am not suggesting that the violence-prone individual's personality is *always* fixed early in life. Many people can change their ways of behaving as they mature, at least to some extent.[2] Nor am I suggesting that children are generally fragile and easily damaged by their parents. Summarizing hundreds of studies and years of experience, developmental psychologist Sandra Scarr assures us that "The human organism is surprisingly resilient in the face of deleterious experiences. . . . Only the most pervasive and continuous detrimental experiences have lasting, negative effects on development."[3] You should keep in mind the resilience of the human personality as you read this chapter. Mothers and fathers are not necessarily turning their sons into criminals by frustrating them once in a while or by spanking them occasionally, particularly not if they reason with their youngsters, are consistent in their discipline, and, above all, are usually warm and affectionate. Highly aggressive personalities are typically the product of continuous strong and adverse influences.

I should acknowledge at the outset that Chapter 6 will talk about *masculine* aggression almost exclusively, much as Chapter 5 dealt with the identification of highly aggressive *males*. Female aggression is certainly not unknown, and women, like men, occasionally enjoy hurting others. Some women are even especially inclined to physically attack those who have provoked them. Yet, as Chapter 12 will show, aggression is more characteristic of men than of women, and most studies of aggression have focused on males. Only a relatively small number of studies have investigated the development of female aggressiveness. More research should be done on the sources of persistent aggressiveness in women, since the proclivity to hurt and attack may develop differently in the two sexes.

Finally, in this chapter you will see that persistent aggressiveness is at times indexed by antisocial modes of conduct. Evidence summarized in Chapter 5 clearly demonstrates that violence-prone men and boys are apt to violate many of society's laws and deeply held social norms, as if strong aggressive inclinations are only one component of a basically antisocial character. Youths who get into serious trouble with the law are likely to be much more aggressive than most of their same-age peers.

CHILDHOOD EXPERIENCES

Families Can Influence the Development of Antisocial Dispositions

A host of studies testify to the influence of family experiences on the development of antisocial inclinations. I'll start by summarizing some of the statistical analyses reported by William McCord and Joan McCord. You may be interested to know the background of their research, since I'll refer to the their findings a number of times in this chapter.

Just before World War II, an experiment was conducted in the Boston, Massachusetts, suburbs of Cambridge and Somerville to determine whether social casework could reduce young working-class boys' antisocial tendencies. About 230 youngsters between 5 and 13 years old were visited by social workers twice a month between 1939 and 1945. Unfortunately, at the end of the project there was no evidence that the counseling had succeeded in reducing juvenile delinquency.[4] Still, hoping that some use could be made of the social workers' records, McCord and McCord traced the participants between 1975 and 1979 to determine what had happened to them during the succeeding years. The researchers were particularly interested in learning whether the men's home lives in childhood, as described by the counselors, forecast their chances of becoming highly aggressive and antisocial by the time they were adults.

Rather than going into the details here, I will say only that McCord and McCord found that the parents' behavior toward their sons had apparently influenced the likelihood that the boys would be what I have termed "emotionally reactive aggressors" in their dealings with their peers and teachers. The youths' early home lives had evidently done much to determine how readily and how often they were assaultive when they saw themselves challenged or threatened. Joan McCord later reviewed the social workers' case histories to determine whether the parents' child-rearing practices, as recorded before the boys reached adolescence, were related to whether or not the men acquired criminal records in the following thirty years. A complicated statistical analysis based on the parents' characteristics and their behavior toward their children correctly identified, in almost three-quarters of the cases, the boys who grew up to become criminals. In other words, for some people at least, early family experiences can help to shape the paths they will follow as they mature and can even affect their chances of becoming lawbreakers. As a matter of fact, on the basis of her findings and the results from a number of other investigations in several countries, McCord concluded that child rearing often has "a long-term impact" upon the development of antisocial aggressiveness.[5]

What Kinds of Child Rearing Promote the Development of Antisocial Tendencies?
What kinds of family influences can have such adverse impacts? Specifically, what kinds of parental qualities increase the likelihood that a son will become nasty and antisocial? Looking at a particular case will show that there's no simple answer to such questions.

More than thirty years ago, Albert Bandura and the late Richard Walters interviewed the parents of fifty-two boys in central California, in order to study the roots of adolescent aggression. Among other things, they asked the mothers and fathers whether they had ever encouraged their sons to fight. One of the women in the sample told how her husband had urged her son to hit back when he got into a battle with other children. When her son Glen was about 6 or 7 years old, the mother said,

> All the kids were fussing and fighting, and he would never fight. His sister would always have to take up his battle for him. . . . So one day my husband took off his belt and said, "Listen, you're coming home and crying all the time, saying 'Somebody hit me.'" So my husband was watching through the bedroom window one day, and he saw two little boys. They were really fighting him [Glen]. So he went up, took off his belt, and he said, "Glen, I'm going to tell you something. You're going to whip these boys or else I'm going to whip you." So he made him stand up and fight both of them.[6]

There's more in this case than you might realize at first glance. To start with, you probably think that the parents were right to be concerned about Glen. "The boy should stand up for himself," you may say. "He should learn to fight back when he is attacked." No matter how much you may agree with the parents' aggression-for-aggression policy, however, their urging Glen to fight may well have had some consequences you won't favor: The child actually may have learned to resort to violence whenever he had problems with others. It is important, though, to realize that any number of factors may contribute to boys' aggressiveness. Empirical research can best tell us what family characteristics have the greatest influence on the development of violent tendencies. Some of the principal findings obtained in such research will be summarized in this chapter.

I will begin with a brief discussion of the direct positive influences that not only encourage people to attack others but also tend to maintain this type of conduct, and will then turn to the negative (unpleasant) factors that also seem to foster persistent aggressiveness. I will conclude with a brief look at some of the indirect influences that may also contribute to the development of this behavior pattern.

Something to keep in mind. I should warn you that this chapter could be somewhat misleading if you read it too casually. It will take what is sometimes termed a "single-variable" approach, in that most of the sections will consider the effects of one factor at a time, such as the rewards parents provide when their sons are aggressive, or their rejection of the child, or the punishments that mothers and fathers administer. Think of how Glen's father treated his son: He apparently not only encouraged the boy to fight but also rewarded him (at least with praise) when he did fight, and he was quick to beat the youngster when he failed to meet his demands. Any one of these actions alone might conceivably have strengthened Glen's aggressiveness. However, the effects of any of these child-rearing factors may depend upon what other conditions are also present. For example, one of the McCord findings indicates that even though Glen was often spurned by his mother, he was not likely to become antisocial as long as she was also clear and consistent in the rules she spelled out for the boy. The eminent British child psychiatrist, Michael Rutter, has highlighted the advisability of a "multiple-variable" perspective in his review of the effects of maternal deprivation. Research has shown, Rutter pointed out, that "it is not separation alone but separation in conjunction with other risk factors, for example, family stress, that leads to later antisocial behavior."[7]

Single variables as possible risk factors. Nevertheless, it is worthwhile to look at the possible consequences of any one kind of parental action, because we can think of each such an action (e.g., the mother's rejection of her child) as a *risk factor* that could increase the likelihood of later antisocial conduct, even though other conditions (e.g., the clarity of the parents' rules) can affect this probability. Much the same thing can be said about other aspects of child rearing. You may be surprised to learn that fewer than half the youngsters who are battered by their mothers and/or fathers grow up to be abusive parents themselves.[8] This does not mean that parental abuse doesn't contribute *at all* to the development of aggressive inclinations. It can be one of many influences, and its adverse effects can be moderated by other factors. Just as cigarette smoking is a risk factor in the development of lung cancer and heart disease, being abused by one's parents can be a risk factor that heightens the probability of aggressiveness and antisocial tendencies.

DIRECT INFLUENCES ON THE DEVELOPMENT OF AGGRESSIVENESS

Rewards for Aggression

Some of those who are prone to violence continue to be aggressive over the years because they have been rewarded for such behavior. They have attacked others fairly often (in essence, they have "practiced" being assaultive) and have found, much of the time, that their aggressive behavior paid off.

We're all generally aware that rewarded behavior tends to persist, but you may not know how powerful and pervasive the effects of rewards can be nor what kinds of events can reinforce aggressive conduct. In this section, I'll examine the role of different kinds of rewards, proceeding from the most to the least obvious of these gratifying circumstances.

Rewards can influence behavior in two somewhat different ways: A reward can operate as an *incentive* to spur an action, or it can be a *reinforcer* that serves to maintain a particular type of behavior. In the first case we anticipate the pleasure we would experience upon receiving a reward, and this anticipation stimulates us to do what we believe will be necessary to actually achieve the desired outcome. Glen may have regarded his father's approval as an incentive in this sense. Wanting the praise and affection his father could give him, he was motivated to fight back when another child assaulted him. Since Glen's aggression was prompted by the hope of gaining an external reward—his father's approval—it could also be said that the boy's behavior constituted instrumental aggression.

On the other hand, when Glen's father praised him for hitting those who attacked him, this parental approval might have automatically strengthened the boy's tendency to react aggressively to provocations, thereby maintaining Glen's aggressiveness. As a reinforcer, the reward promotes the more or less thoughtless acquisition of aggressive reactions to certain kinds of situations and thus increases the chances that the aggressive behavior will be repeated.

The discussion below will place somewhat more emphasis on rewards as reinforcers than on rewards as incentives, but only because most readers are less familiar with the automatic, habit-strengthening influence of positive outcomes, and I'd like to correct for this unfamiliarity. Both types of reward effects are important. We tend to repeat actions that have previously led to favorable consequences, sometimes in conscious anticipation of obtaining these positive outcomes again and sometimes because the behavioral tendency has become habitual.

Rewards Provided by People Other Than the Victim

The caretakers' approval.
Increasing the Likelihood of the Directly Rewarded Behavior. Psychologists have given countless demonstrations of how rewards can heighten the probability that a reinforced action will be repeated. For example, in an experiment by Joel Davitz, which was conducted about two generations ago, a caretaker's rewards influenced the likelihood of openly aggressive reactions to a frustration.

Groups of four youngsters first went through a series of brief training sessions in which they were praised for certain kinds of behavior—for making aggressive responses in one condition or for playing constructively and cooperatively in the other condition. When the children were later frustrated, the ones who had been verbally rewarded for their aggressive actions during training displayed the most aggressive behavior, whereas the boys who had received approval for acting cooperatively were least antisocial in response to the thwarting.[9]

In other words, appropriately dispensed rewards can modify a youngster's natural inclination to react aggressively to an unpleasant frustration. Rewards for constructive behavior can lower the chances that the child will become violent, and rewards for aggressive behavior can raise the likelihood of aggression.

Reinforcing Related Behaviors. Rewards can also have an even broader influence. Glen's father, as I indicated earlier, might have taught his son to be generally aggressive by praising him whenever he struck back at his antagonists (as long as the boy's aggression didn't have any negative consequences for him). He didn't try to turn his son into a bully. He only wanted the boy to "be a man," to stand up for himself and not let other youngsters "push him around." However, by encouraging his child to fight back and praising him when he did so, the father basically taught Glen to act aggressively in other situations as well, even situations in which the boy wasn't being tormented by others. Put simply, rewards can have a much more pervasive influence than one might realize. They can also strengthen not only the intended actions but also other tendencies of the same general nature.

Generalization of reward effects can be seen in an experiment with 7-year-old Canadian schoolboys. In this study, Richard Walters and Murray Brown asked whether the systematic reinforcement of make-believe aggression in playful attacks on a toy can increase the probability of real aggression in other situations. They first established three different "aggression training" conditions in which each subject practiced hitting a big, plastic Bobo doll over a series of "learning trials" in two separate sessions. One group of boys received marbles as a reward each time they struck the Bobo toy (this was the continuous reward condition), another group were given marbles only intermittently after each six hits (in the intermittent reward condition), and a third group didn't get any marbles at all (in the no-reward condition). A fourth condition was also established: another control group in which the subjects had no contact with the Bobo doll.

Two days after the second training session, the researchers began to show all the youngsters an interesting movie. In order to create differences in how frustrated the subjects were at that time, thwarted and non-thwarted conditions were established. Some boys were permitted to see the film through to the end, whereas, for the others, the movie projector apparently broke down halfway through the film. Immediately after this experimental variation, each boy was invited to play two competitive games with another child of his own age, while being observed by an adult who didn't know what training condition the subject was in. The adult observers recorded every aggressive action that each boy made. I'll report the results for the measure that was based on the number of times each child assaulted his partner by butting, kneeing, elbowing, kicking, or punching him.

Extrapolating from what psychologists have already discovered about the learning process (which we cannot go into here), Walters and Brown had predicted that the subjects who had been rewarded *intermittently* for engaging in make-believe aggression (hitting the Bobo doll) would be most likely to transfer this learning to the later competitive situation. You can see from the results summarized in Figure 6–1 that this prediction was confirmed. The boys who had been rewarded only once in a while for punching the Bobo toy were subsequently more aggressive in their competition with the other child than were any of the other subjects. Having been rewarded for aggression—even though the rewards were given only occasionally and only for make-believe aggression—they became more aggressive in a later, more realistic situation.

Interestingly, as Figure 6–1 also indicates, the frustrated boys in the intermittently rewarded condition were the most aggressive of all. The unpleasant thwarting they had just experienced increased their inclination to carry out their intermittently rewarded aggressive tendencies.[10]

All in all, then, parents may be doing more than they intend when they encourage their boys to fight. They may only want their sons to retaliate when they are bullied by other youngsters, but they could be unwittingly reinforcing a wide range of aggressive actions. To limit this effect, parents ought to make sure that their children understand that

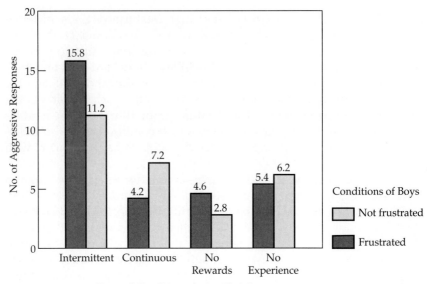

FIGURE 6-1
Mean number of aggressive responses not required by games in a later situation. (Data from Walters & Brown (1963). Copyright 1963 by the Society for Research in Child Development.)

they should fight only under very restricted circumstances and that there is a great difference between standing up for oneself and other kinds of aggressive behavior. Even then, however, adults should realize that they are running the risk of heightening their offsprings' general aggressive inclinations when they teach their sons to fight back.

Rewards from peers. Parents aren't the only socializing agents whom boys encounter in their lives, even when they are fairly young. Children's friends and acquaintances also teach them how to act in certain situations, by serving as models and by rewarding them with acceptance or even open approval when they behave in what the others regard as an appropriate manner.
Group and Gang Influences. It's no mystery that many youths are especially susceptible to influence by their peers. Wanting to be valued by others of their own age, they are often eager to seek the company of other youngsters who might appreciate them. This is even true of a high proportion of children who get into frequent fights with their peers. The bullying and assaultiveness of these belligerent boys can drive many of their classmates away, but most of them do find friends—other youngsters who are similar in aggressiveness and lifestyle.[11] These youths then support each other. Their conversations and the actions they take togeth-

er strengthen the interests and attitudes they have in common and reinforce their shared antisocial inclinations. These friendships may heighten the conflicts that such boys have with the adult world. Whereas individually they are relatively powerless, together they can threaten the social order, especially in schools. Teachers and principals would do well to try to break up hostile groups, if they can.

These observations, of course, are especially true of many antisocial youth gangs.[12] In these deviant groups, the members find acceptance and status; they're important in the gang, whereas elsewhere they're nothing. They also find reassurance that the perceptions and attitudes they have in common are right, and that the dangers they fear may be overcome.

These reassurances can play a significant role in youthful crimes. Any one socially deviant boy might not dare to break the law alone, but when he is with his fellow gang members, he feels brave and secure. Not surprisingly, a fairly high proportion of youthful offenses, including violent ones, are carried out by groups of boys acting together. The aggression that these groups display can be serious.[13]

Adherence to a Gang Code of Conduct. The gang's influence obviously isn't limited to strengthening the members' attitudes or providing them with a sense of security, status, and personal value. In their contacts with each other the youths also establish rules of conduct defining how any one of them should act under certain circumstances. These shared attitudes and values can have a powerful impact on the individual members' conduct. They realize that, whether they are alone or with others, they can either win the approval of their fellow gang members by adhering to the gang's standards or be rejected by them if they don't live up to the gang's expectations.

Violent teenage gangs are a particularly noteworthy example of this kind of social influence. At least partly because of the great value they ascribe to "masculinity," many of these groups insist that their members must be tough in asserting themselves and preserving their pride. Two investigators at the Institute for Juvenile Research in Chicago put it as follows, on the basis of their experience with a Chicano gang from the inner city of Chicago:

> Gang members subscribe to a code of personal honor that stresses the inviolability of one's manhood and defines breaches of interpersonal etiquette in an adversarial idiom. Any act or statement that challenges a gang member's "right" to deferential treatment in face-to-face relations is interpreted as an insult and hence as a potential threat to his manhood. For these [youths], honor revolves around a person's capacity to command deferential treatment (i.e., "respect") from others.[14]

This code seems to be an exaggerated version of the principle that Glen's father wanted his son to follow: A "real man" stands up for himself and doesn't let others push him around. It's important to realize, though, that this gang norm doesn't necessarily call for a repudiation of customary societal values or insist that the gang members have to continually fight outsiders or each other. Rather, it usually only defines the desirable way to behave when a gang member's "honor" (or identity) has been impugned: In order to prove his manliness when his conception of himself has been threatened, a member has to be tough and punish those who have offended him.[15]

Whatever its exact nature and the conditions under which it comes into operation, the belief in the desirability of aggressive behavior under certain circumstances serves as both an incentive and a reinforcement for violence. The individuals who share this belief are motivated to live up to their agreed-upon code of conduct and are therefore spurred to be violent when they think their honor (or self-image or identity) is at stake. When they "practice" aggression, their fellows give them the approval they desire, thereby rewarding the behavior and increasing the chances that the youths will act the same way again. Of course, if the young men in a gang are extremely antisocial and seriously alienated from society, they may well approve many forms of antisocial conduct besides violence. In one study of institutionalized delinquents, individual boys were rewarded by the other delinquents when they deviated from societal rules and were punished to some extent when they were judged by their peers to be too compliant with the authorities' standards.[16]

Rewards Provided by the Victim
In the instances discussed above, aggressors were rewarded by outsiders who were not directly involved in the altercation, usually their parents and/or their peers. Sometimes, however, they can also be gratified by their victims' reactions.

Negative reinforcement. As I've pointed out many times, much of the aggression we display is a reaction to a disturbing state of affairs. We can be especially upset, of course, when someone bothers us, and very often, at such times, we lash out at the offender to stop the annoyance. You may recall from Chapter 1 that several psychologists, such as Gerald Patterson and his colleagues, believe that a considerable amount of aggression arises in just this manner—as a crude effort to coerce others to become less bothersome.[17]

For many years, these investigators at the Oregon Social Learning Center have sought to determine how mothers, fathers, and children affect each other in daily life. By visiting families in their homes and recording family interactions in close detail, they have traced sequences of actions and reactions as the members responded to each other. These psychologists have even been able to calculate the probability that a certain kind of behavior would be followed by another family member's aggressive response, as well as the chances that this response would lead in turn to each of various kinds of reactions from the others around them.

I'll go into the Oregon group's findings more fully later in this chapter. For now, I'll only mention one of Patterson's central conclusions: Much aggression in the home arises out of attempts to control other members of the family. Moreover, the aggressor's attempted coercion is often aimed at ending the target's annoying behavior. A good (though stereotyped) example is the young boy who is angered by his sister's teasing and strikes at her in an attempt to get her to stop bothering him. If the sister then does stop tormenting her brother, this outcome is rewarding. Using the language of psychology, we can say that the brother's hitting is *negatively reinforced*, in that his action has terminated an unpleasant (i.e., negative) state of affairs.

The Oregon researchers' probability estimate regarding negative reinforcement is interesting. Over all the family interactions they observed in which a youngster acted the way this hypothetical brother did in attempting to coerce another family member, the aggressive behavior was successful in ending the other's disturbing conduct in four out of every ten instances. This suggests that a substantial portion of the aggressiveness displayed by children in their homes is negatively reinforced. All kinds of children are reinforced this way, but highly aggressive boys are especially likely to find that their behavior pays off in this manner.[18] Maybe because the family members have learned how difficult it is to control them, these boys are evidently relatively successful in using aggression to get their own way.

One of Patterson's early studies clearly demonstrates how negative reinforcements can foster aggressive behavior. Young boys who had been repeatedly victimized by other youngsters were given several opportunities to punish the children who had assaulted them. Not surprisingly, many took advantage of these occasions and did retaliate. In about two-thirds of the cases, their counteraggression successfully convinced the tormentors not to attack again. The previously submissive children had responded to aggression with aggression, and their behavior paid off in that it lessened further assaults on them. What's most important, however, is that this negative reinforcement heightened the likelihood that these boys themselves would later attack other children, even when they were not being bullied. The more often their counterattacks had been successful, in other words, the more frequent was *their own later* aggression. Instead of becoming peaceful because they knew how unpleasant it is to be a victim of aggression, their rewarded aggression tended to make them become more bullying themselves.[19] This effect is another demonstration of how hard it is to keep rewarded aggression within narrow limits.

The victim's pain and/or defeat as a reinforcement. Yet another type of reaction by a victim is also often rewarding to an aggressor: the victim's display of pain and/or defeat. Think back to the discussion of the goals of aggression, in Chapter 1. People who have undergone an unpleasant experience are often motivated to hurt someone, and they are gratified to some degree when they find that their intended target has been appropriately injured.[20] What's important in the context of the present discussion is that information on the target's injury can reinforce the sort of behavior that led up to the receipt of the information.[21]

Richard Sebastian obtained evidence consistent with this line of reasoning in an experiment dealing with provoked men's reactions to their tormentor's pain. Some of the male subjects in this study first were deliberately provoked by the experimenter's accomplice, then had an opportunity to get even with him, and finally were given information about how much they had hurt this person. The higher the level of pain the subjects had supposedly inflicted upon their tormentor, the more they reported enjoying the experiment. They apparently liked the chance to hurt the man who had hurt them. Even more important results were obtained the next day, when the subjects were required to punish *another student* for his mistakes. The more they had enjoyed the previous day's opportunity to retaliate, the more intense was the punishment they gave to this innocent person. In sum, it appears that the angered men whose aggression had been rewarded by their tormentor's suffering in the first session were generally quite willing to hurt another—blameless—individual on a later occasion.[22] Their aggressive inclination had been strengthened. Getting even, successfully following the ancient precept "An eye for an eye, a tooth for a tooth," can reward aggression and thereby increase the chances of further aggression, even when there's no desire for revenge.

These conclusions are relevant to the distinction I've been drawing between instrumental aggression and emotional aggression. Clearly, some people are persistently aggressive because they have learned that assaultive behavior often pays off by getting them what they want. For these people, aggression is primarily instrumental behavior, a means to achieve another end. Since the victim's suffering isn't their main goal, they aren't necessarily satisfied by the pain they inflict unless the pain means they will get what they want. However, as I emphasized in Chapter 5, there are also some persons whose aggressive disposition has a more emotional basis. These individuals actually enjoy hurting someone when they are emotionally aroused, and they are gratified when they can do harm. The satisfaction they feel when they inflict pain may even reinforce their inclination to be generally aggressive in many different situations. At the very least, they are relatively unlikely to be disturbed by the thought that their behavior could injure someone.[23]

Unpleasant Conditions Established by Parents

If unpleasant feelings produce an instigation to aggression, as I have suggested, it may be that persons who are frequently afflicted by unhappy events while they are growing up then develop a disposition to be highly aggressive when they reach adolescence and adulthood. Such individuals may become emotionally reactive aggressors. They are often quick to anger, and they may lash out at others who bother them. Whether these people are emotionally reactive aggressors or instrumental aggressors, it is undoubtedly true that many children who are victimized by decidedly unpleasant family conditions do indeed become prone to violence.

Parental Mistreatment

Mistreatment is often general. Parents can mistreat their offspring in a variety of ways—for example, they may be cold and indifferent toward their children, they may inflict brutal punishment when the children do not obey adults' commands, and/or they may not be clear and consistent in specifying what they expect of the children. It's important to realize that few caretakers specialize in one way of wronging their children. If they mistreat their sons and daughters in one way, for example by being frequently indifferent to them, they tend to be negative toward them in other respects as well. Highly punitive mothers and fathers are usually also cold to the youngsters and inconsistent in their methods of discipline.[24] Glen's father seems to have been very severe with his son and quick to beat the boy when he was angry with him. If so, there's a good possibility that the man also was not very affectionate with Glen and was inconsistent in how he treated him.

Findings that were published by Dan Olweus of the University of Bergen in Norway (whose work was introduced in Chapter 5) illustrate how different kinds of parental mistreatment tend to go together and contribute jointly to the development of aggressiveness. As part of his research on schoolboys, Olweus interviewed the parents of seventy-six youths who were about 13 years old and who resided near Stockholm, Sweden. On the assumption that the mothers were the principal caretakers and that the fathers were more active in disciplining their sons, ratings were made of a number of parental qualities including: (1) the mothers' *negativism* when the boys were less than 5 years old (i.e., how negative, cold, and indifferent they were toward the children), and (2) the mothers' *permissiveness in regard to aggression,* and (3) the extent to which *both parents employed harsh, punitive discipline* in trying to control their sons. In addition, the *boys' temperaments* when they were very young (principally how hot-tempered they were) were also rated on the basis of the interviews with their parents. Finally, the youths' aggressiveness was also assessed by having their classmates rate the degree to which they were physically and verbally assaultive in their dealings with peers and teachers. The classroom aggressiveness data were collected twice, first when the boys were in sixth grade and again, three years later, when they were in ninth grade.

The results of a statistical analysis of the relationships between these various measures (termed a "path analysis") are summarized in Figure 6–2. The first thing to note is that the child-rearing ratings were intercorrelated to some extent. The mothers who indicated that they were cold and rejecting when their sons were very young also tended (along with their husbands) to be harsh and punitive toward their offspring when the boys were older. Also, perhaps because of their frequent indifference, the highly negative mothers said they were somewhat likely to tolerate the boys' display of aggression in the family (i.e., these women were often permissive about this kind of behavior).

Even though the measures were intercorrelated, the analytic procedure investigated how well any one of the child-rearing measures predicted the boys' aggressiveness by statistically controlling the influence of all the other variables. The results of this analysis are also depicted in Figure 6–2. As you can see, the women who were cold and rejecting

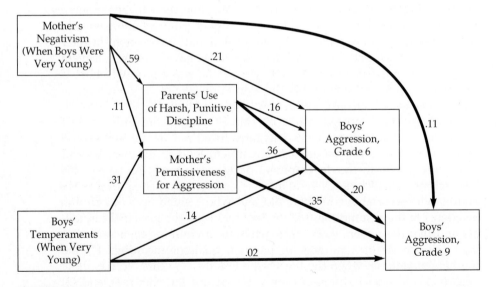

FIGURE 6-2

Inferred influences upon the aggressiveness of a sample of Swedish boys in grade 6 and also, 3 years later, in grade 9. The numbers reported are the path coefficients (beta weights) indicating the direct causal effect of one variable on another when all other causal variables are held constant. (Data from Olweus (1980), Figs. 1, 3. Copyright 1980 by the America Psychological Association. Adapted by permission.)

when their sons were less than 5 years old tended to produce boys who were relatively aggressive in school in sixth grade and also, to a somewhat lesser extent, in ninth grade. Similarly, the more harshly punitive the parents were toward their sons, the greater was the chance that these boys would be aggressive at both ages.[25]

The main point for purposes of this discussion is that when parents mistreat their offspring, they typically do it in a variety of ways. This means that, in many studies of children's aggressiveness, it is unclear whether the boys' conduct was the outgrowth of any one type of child-rearing practice. Even so, because there is widespread interest in such matters as parental neglect and punishment, and because of the possibility that some kinds of parental behavior may be risk factors for the development of antisocial tendencies, I will briefly describe what seem to be the consequences of some specific forms of child rearing.

Parental rejection. Parental rejection is obviously painful to young children, and it's therefore not surprising to find that many highly aggressive boys have had cold and indifferent parents.[26] For example, according to McCord, McCord, and Howard, the mothers and fathers of the aggressive youths in their sample were generally less affectionate toward their sons than were the parents of the better-behaved boys. Joan McCord pursued the matter further. Asking whether the parents' child rearing was related to their sons' later criminality, she found that half the participants who had been rejected in childhood by unaffectionate parents had been convicted of serious crimes by the time they reached adulthood—even though they hadn't been physically abused. Other research has obtained comparable results.[27]

All in all, the evidence is fairly consistent. Remember, however, that the antisocial effects of parental rejection can be counteracted by other influences. Thus, in the Massachusetts study, boys with unaffectionate mothers were not particularly likely to become criminals if these women were also self-confident and consistent in their discipline.[28] The cold but consistent mothers evidently defined clear rules for their sons, and the boys tended to adopt the rules (perhaps because they were very insecure and felt highly dependent on their parents). The rejected youths apparently developed open aggressiveness primarily when they lacked firm internal standards to guide them along socially approved paths. Thus, it's not parental coldness and indifference alone that leads boys to reject society but the parental rejection combined with other adverse influences.

Harsh parental treatment. Adults obviously can make their offspring feel bad by abusing them as well as by turning their backs on them. Again, it's not surprising to see—in Olweus's study and in much of the research literature generally—that harsh, punitive parents are somewhat likely to produce highly aggressive and antisocial boys. I'll mention only a few findings that reveal this relationship.

First, consider, the evidence obtained by the McCord researchers in the Massachusetts project. About 20 percent of the participants who were identified in the case records as having been abused as children were convicted of serious crimes by the time they reached adulthood, as compared to only 11 percent of boys who had been consistently loved by their parents. Farrington has reported comparable findings in his follow-up of the youths in the Cambridge longitudinal project. Although only a small number of these working-class Londoners had been convicted of violence by adulthood, those who had such records of assaultive crimes were especially likely to have had parents who possessed "cruel attitudes" and employed harsh, punitive discipline.[29]

The national survey of violence in American homes mentioned in Chapter 1 also points to a process in which violence breeds violence. According to the researchers' interviews with family members, the more children are hit by their parents, the more frequently they assault not only their brothers and sisters but also their parents.[30] (I'll tell you more about this in Chapter 8, Domestic Violence.)

Extremely aggressive youngsters apparently are especially likely to react aggressively when they are beaten by their mothers and/or fathers. John Reid, a psychologist at the Oregon Social Learning Center, has shown this in a statistical analysis of interactions between family members in their homes. In his sample there was only about one chance in seven that normal children would respond with some kind of aggression to a parent's punitive action. By contrast, this probability was much greater (about 35 percent) for youngsters with a history of antisocial conduct, and it was more than 50 percent for the highly antisocial children in the sample who had been severely abused by their parents.

On the basis of these and other findings, Patterson has commented that "Antisocial boys are significantly more likely than normal boys to continue being [aggressive] when mildly punished by parents." Equally important, not only are the problem youngsters apt to persist in their aggression, but this behavior often pays off for them. There's a good chance that they will get what they want. Their aggression is reinforced and is thus likely to be repeated.[31]

How Effective Is the Use of Punishment in Disciplining Children?

Is all "power-assertive" discipline bad? Does the research cited above imply that parents should never spank their children, even when the youngsters deliberately defy them? Child development experts disagree on the answer to this question. While some specialists believe there is a place for the appropriate use of corporal punishment, others urge mothers and fathers never to hit their offspring in an attempt to control the children's behavior.[32]

The authorities who strongly oppose physical punishment sometimes refer to virtually any use of punishment as a *power-assertive* method of child-rearing, through which the caretakers attempt to get their own way by force. From this perspective, power-assertive tactics are likely to backfire, producing rebelliousness and aggression rather than acceptance of society's moral standards. The findings I've summarized so far seem to support their contention, but let's look more closely at these studies and see what the evidence actually says.

Most of the research I've discussed so far in this chapter hasn't really investigated the consequences of a single kind of parental behavior. The parental punishment assessed in many of the studies was mixed with other factors. Remember that many of the abusive mothers and fathers were also fairly cold toward their children, at times even openly hostile to them, didn't take much time to reason with the youngsters, and were all too frequently inconsistent or overly permissive in how they managed their offspring. The abusive parents in a now-classic study by Robert Sears, Eleanor Maccoby, and Harry Levin did more than hit their children fairly often; they were also apt to be inconsistent and even unduly permissive at times. The parental punitiveness investigated by the Oregon researchers was also blended with other qualities. As Patterson has emphasized repeatedly, the mothers and fathers of the problem boys he and his associates studied were *ineffective* disciplinarians rather than simply being punitive. They weren't sufficiently selective and consistent in choosing the actions they rewarded or punished, and they tended to nag, scold, and threaten indiscriminately.[33]

The implications are clear: The bad effects attributed to parents' use of punishment may actually be due, in part anyway, to *inconsistent, indiscriminate, unduly extreme,* and/or *unreasoned* punishment, not to the punishment itself. There's also a difference between wide-ranging and emotional parental aggressiveness and more selective and well-controlled use of physical punishment. There's even a difference between an impulsive blow with a fist or belt and a relatively calmly delivered spanking. Not all the supposed power-assertive methods are alike.[34] Under the right circumstances, mothers or fathers can use corporal punishment effectively in disciplining their children without leading the youngsters to develop an abiding tendency toward aggressiveness. Every spanking isn't necessarily a step toward juvenile delinquency.

Inconsistent discipline. As I've already suggested, a good many extremely punitive parents are inconsistent in managing their children. A distinction advocated by Ross Parke and Ronald Slaby will be useful in this discussion.[35] In their review of the research on the development of aggressiveness, these writers differentiated between "intra-agent" inconsistency and "interagent" inconsistency, noting that researchers haven't always given adequate attention to the difference. In intra-agent inconsistency, the caretakers don't treat "violations in the same manner each time they occur" and/or don't follow "through on threats of punishment." Perhaps because they don't care very much for their offspring (or because they may even be somewhat hostile toward them) and/or because they're preoccupied with their own troubles, these people punish their children for certain actions on some occasions and ignore the same actions on other occasions. McCord and McCord attempted to assess this type of consistency in their analysis of the Massachusetts boys' case histories. They found that many of the youths who acquired criminal records had mothers who were punitive some of the time but lax on other occasions.[36]

On the other hand, in families in which there is *interagent inconsistency*, the "different socializing agents, such as two parents, [don't] respond in a similar fashion to rule violations." Obviously, this type of inconsistency could arise when the mother and the father are in conflict, or it might arise when one parent plays a much more dominant role than the other in family decisions. Whatever the reasons for parents' disagreement, it too seems to contribute to the development of antisocial tendencies. Thus, in the Cambridge longitudinal study, there was less harmony between the mothers and fathers of the boys who became violent delinquents several years later than between the parents of boys who did not later get into trouble with the law. Similarly, McCord tells us that boys in the Massachusetts investigation "whose parents got along reasonably well and were not aggressive had low rates of criminality."[37]

Interestingly, even though it is possible to distinguish between these two types of inconsistency, Parke and Slaby concluded that both types can lessen the effectiveness of parental discipline.[38] In both cases, the children may be torn by inner uncertainty about what to believe and how best to act. Again, there's a possible lesson here: Parents don't necessarily create aggressive lawbreakers by spanking their children, as long as they do it consistently whenever the youngsters violate clear-cut and reasonable rules.

Explaining the punishment. Psychologists who condemn the use of power-assertive methods of child rearing don't by any means oppose the establishment of firm standards of conduct. Parents, they typically say, *should* spell out rules for their offspring and should clearly explain why it is to the youngsters' benefit to adhere to these principles. Moreover, if the children do violate the rules, the adults should also make sure that they understand what they have done wrong. Above all, however, these psychologists emphasize the overriding importance of parental love and affection. They maintain that the standards should be enforced "psychologically" rather than with physical force. Besides giving reasons for their actions, the parents should clearly and consistently indicate their disapproval when the children break a rule, perhaps by withdrawing privileges or even by implicitly threatening to withhold their love (temporarily).[39]

Diana Baumrind's well-known comparison of authoritative, authoritarian, and permissive parents illustrates how parental standards can be maintained firmly and reasonably, without damaging the children. On the basis of her observations, she divided the mothers and fathers of the 4-year-olds in her sample into the three categories summarized in Table 6-1. Whereas the *permissive-indulgent* mothers and fathers didn't clearly communicate their rules to their children and didn't do much to enforce whatever standards they held, the *authoritarian* parents tended to insist that the children follow their rules in a fairly rigid manner, but they did not explain the rules clearly. They were harsh and punitive in

TABLE 6-1 THE THREE TYPES OF PARENTING STYLES IDENTIFIED BY BAUMRIND AND THE CHILD BEHAVIOR PATTERNS THAT PRESUMABLY RESULT

Parental style	Child's behavior
Authoritarian parent	*Conflicted-irritable*
Enforces rules rigidly.	Is fearful, apprehensive.
Does not explain rules clearly.	Is easily annoyed.
Uses harsh, punitive discipline.	Alternates between aggressive and sulky withdrawal behavior.
Is low in warmth and involvement.	
Shows anger and displeasure.	Is moody, unhappy.
Authoritative parent	*Energetic-friendly*
Enforces rules firmly.	Is self-reliant.
Communicates rules clearly.	Has high energy level.
Does not yield to child's coercion.	Is self-controlled.
Shows displeasure and annoyance in response to child's bad behavior.	Is cheerful, friendly with peers.
	Is cooperative with adults.
Shows pleasure with and support of child's constructive behavior.	Copes well with stress.
Permissive-indulgent parent	*Impulsive-aggressive*
Does not communicate rules clearly.	Is resistant, noncompliant.
Does not enforce rules.	Is low in self-reliance.
Yields to coercion or crying by child.	Is low in self-control.
Provides inconsistent discipline.	Is aggressive.
Is moderately warm.	Is impulsive.
Glorifies free expression of impulses.	Is aimless.

Source: Table modified from Baumrind (1973).

their discipline, and they were easily angered when their children offended them. *Authoritative* mothers and fathers, by contrast, were warm and involved with their children, but they also specified clear standards for their offspring, tended to maintain the standards consistently, and didn't give in to the children's coercive attempts. They displayed their displeasure and annoyance openly when the youngsters were bad, and they seemed to be willing to employ corporal punishment.

These different parental styles evidently lead to different patterns of child behavior (as Table 6-1 also indicates). The children in the permissive and authoritarian families were generally "conflicted and irritable," in that they were easily annoyed and showed a mixture of aggressive and sulky withdrawn behavior, whereas the children who had authoritative parents were much more likely to be friendly, cooperative, and self-reliant.[40]

On the basis of these conclusions about the effects of different parenting styles, I can accept an emphasis on parental use of love and reason in disciplining children without insisting on the total avoidance of all corporal punishment. Spankings may not have adverse consequences if they are adequately explained and appropriately administered. A reanalysis of some of the data from the Straus, Gelles, and Steinmetz survey of

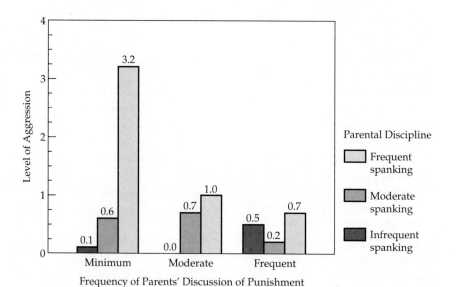

FIGURE 6-3

Mean aggresion toward parents as a function or frequency of parents' discussion of punishment and frequency of spanking. (Data from Larzelere (1986), Table I, "Moderate spanking: Model or deterrent of children's aggression in the family," *Journal of Family Violence*, 1. Copyright by Plenum Publishing Corp. Adapted by permission.)

violence in American families seems to support this idea. These New Hampshire researchers asked the parents in the study to say how often they physically punished a particular one of their preadolescent children and how frequently they discussed the punishment with the child. Still another investigator looked at the possible consequences of the parents' discipline by determining how aggressive the youngsters were toward the adults. As Figure 6–3 shows, it was only when the parents seldom discussed the punishment with the youngsters that frequent spankings seemed to produce fairly strong aggression toward the parents.[41]

Some characteristics of effective punishment. Since the corporal punishment employed in real life is often accompanied by other potentially adverse factors, psychologists have to turn to the experimental laboratory to determine when physical punishment free of other influences can be an effective disciplinary procedure. Although laboratory research has provided some useful information, the findings are relatively complex, and I can give you only a brief and somewhat simplified summary.

Generally speaking, the evidence suggests that caretakers can use corporal punishment effectively if—in addition to being consistent and providing an explanation—(1) their timing is right, (2) an attractive alternative course of action is available to the youngsters, and probably also, (3) the children's self-esteem is not damaged.[42] Suppose a young boy persists in running into a busy street even though his mother has repeatedly explained why it is dangerous and has insisted that he must remain in the backyard. A spanking may be effective, and may not provoke an undue aggressive reaction, if it is administered properly. This means that the mother must spank the child soon after he violates the prohibition (and preferably before he can enjoy the forbidden pleasures of playing in the street) and that there must be an attractive substitute for the forbidden action (that the backyard must provide a suitable playground).

An Integration: Patterson's Social Learning Analysis
Even though several kinds of parental behavior may contribute to children's antisocial patterns of conduct, we should keep in mind that the youngsters don't merely accept passively whatever their mothers and fathers do to them. They react to their parents' actions, and their responses in turn can affect what the adults do next. Family life is a series of actions and reactions, in which the members continually influence and are influenced by each other. Any truly adequate account of the origin of persistent aggressiveness must deal with these interactive sequences. As I have indicated, Gerald Patterson, John Reid, and their colleagues at the Oregon Social Learning Center have been attempting to develop such an account.[43] I'll briefly review some of the major conclusions these investigators have drawn from their research, partly as a way of summarizing a number of the points I have been making.

The family as the root of antisocial conduct. The Patterson analysis starts out with a fairly strong assumption: Many children are basically trained to become aggressive through their interactions with other members of their family. Patterson recognizes that stressful conditions acting on the family, such as unemployment or conflict between the husband and wife, as well as the parents' education, income, and ethnic background, can also influence the developing child. However, he contends that these factors operate largely by affecting how the youngster is reared. If a boy becomes aggressively inclined because of his interactions with family members, he will tend to act in socially inadequate ways outside the family. The resulting series of social and scholastic failures will heighten his antisocial disposition. Figure 6–4 outlines this hypothesized sequence.

Bad family managers. The first step in the chain of adverse family influences, according to Patterson and his associates, has to do with the way a child's unwelcome behavior is controlled. After more than a decade of home observations, these researchers concluded that the parents of the antisocial youngsters are deficient in four important "management" functions: (1) they don't effectively monitor the activities of their offspring both inside and outside the home, (2) they fail to discipline antisocial behavior adequately, (3) they don't reward prosocial conduct sufficiently, and (4) they, together with other family members, aren't good at problem solving. These deficiencies tend to occur together, as noted earlier, so that one kind of parental failure is often accompanied by the other parental deficiencies. The mothers and fathers who don't

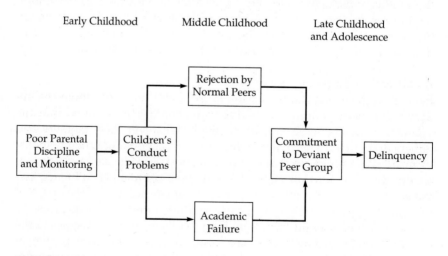

FIGURE 6-4

Patterson's formulation of the development of children's aggressiveness and antisocial conduct. (Patterson, DeBaryshe, & Ramsey (1989), p. 331. Copyright 1989 by the American Psychological Association. Reprinted by permission.)

supervise their offspring adequately are frequently bad at disciplining their sons, and similarly, the parents who are inept disciplinarians tend not to reinforce the boys' prosocial conduct. It's as if there is a "trait" of being a bad manager generally.

The microsocial analysis of family interactions.

Inadequate Control and Nondiscriminating Reactions. Let's look more closely at what is involved in bad parental management. According to Patterson, inept parents are especially likely to allow the members of their families to interact in ways that reinforce their children's aggressive behaviors. The adults' poor control over what happens is reflected in a relative lack of discrimination and selectivity in how they respond to their offspring. In comparison to "normal" mothers and fathers, they are more apt to blur the difference between prosocial and antisocial conduct by frequently rewarding their children's coercive behavior—for example, by paying attention to the children when they try to get their own way by behaving coercively, and sometimes even giving them approval—while failing to consistently reward their children's friendly, constructive actions. Even when they do punish their children's aggression, they don't always clearly connect their discipline to the misbehavior.[44]

Provoking Aggression. As if being ineffective in controlling their off-springs' conduct isn't enough, the parents of the antisocial youngsters are also especially likely to provoke their children by being harsh and punitive. These mothers and fathers are generally more unpleasant to their children, the Oregon researchers tell us, than are other parents, not only by nagging and scolding them frequently but also by punishing and even hitting them often and severely. A good many of the antisocial youngsters then reveal their aggressive tendencies through the ways in which they react to their parents' mistreatment. In comparison to normal boys, they are more likely to match aggression with aggression. They even persist in their assaults over a longer period of time.

Negative Reinforcement of the Child's Aggression. However the antisocial boys' aggression arises, their behavior is all too often successful in eliminating the conditions that disturb them. The Oregon researchers' microsocial analyses show that an aggressive child's siblings are especially important in providing this negative reinforcement. In many instances, they found, a brother or sister provoked the boy but ceased annoying him when he struck back, thereby teaching him that aggression paid.

Rejection and failure.

Rejection by Peers. Patterson suggests that the likely consequences of an aggressive child's unfortunate early learning experiences are that he is not only ready to be threatening and assaultive but also unlikely to have acquired adequate social skills.[45] He doesn't know quite what to do when he meets someone new, isn't particularly sensitive to the other person's opinions and needs, and may also lack the ability to capture the new person's interest. The boy is especially apt to misunderstand the actions of the other youngsters he encounters, as you will remember from Dodge's research (which was summarized in Chapter 5). He may perceive threats and challenges where none exist and may mistakenly attribute malicious intent to others. As a result of these deficiencies, Patterson continues, there's a good chance the antisocial child will be rejected by his more normal peers, and indeed, such a boy's aggressiveness is more likely to be the cause than the result of his social rejection.

Failure at School. Antisocial children are also likely to have difficulty in school. As Patterson points out, a number of investigations have found that youngsters who get into trouble with the law have also tended to do poorly in school, and he believes that this tendency is due, at least in part, to their unfortunate personalities. Because they are impulsive and undercontrolled, they are restless and easily distracted. They are often unable to sit still, don't pay sufficient attention to the teacher and the tasks before them, and frequently fail to complete their homework.

Membership in deviant groups. Because of their poor performance in school and their rejection by relatively well-socialized peers, many of these children are drawn to other youngsters who not only have similar personalities but also are inclined to reject society's traditional norms and values. Newcomers to these deviant groups are often taught to engage in antisocial conduct and may even be encouraged, implicitly if not explicitly, to abuse illegal substances. Thus, lawbreaking brings them the popularity they cannot gain in other ways.

Clearly, Patterson does not attribute delinquency solely to either parental mismanagement or the bad influence of socially deviant peers. Both family and peers, and perhaps other factors as well, contribute to the formation of antisocial patterns of conduct.[46] Patterson does suggest, however, that the deviant peer group's influence usually serves to maintain and perhaps even to accentuate the learning acquired in the family.

*I*NDIRECT INFLUENCES

So far, this chapter has dealt with some of the direct influences on the development of aggressiveness: actions carried out by parents and/or peers that are aimed at the young boy and contribute to the formation of a persistent disposition to violence. However, the youngster's personality can also be affected, at least to some degree, by indirect influences that are not intended to have an impact on him specifically.

Though any number of factors may operate in such a manner, including cultural norms and poverty and other situational stressors, I will confine the discussion here to only two such indirect influences: parental discord and the presence of antisocial models.

Conflict within the Family

Do Broken Homes Breed Delinquency?
Crime and delinquency are frequently attributed to the ill effects of a broken home. Quite a few social scientists and ordinary persons alike believe that many delinquents are the socially distorted victims of abnormal family conditions. Because they have not only grown up in poverty but also have had only one parent rather than two, they are thought to have not learned to adopt society's traditional norms and values.

You may be surprised to find out how little solid evidence there is for this widespread assumption. Studies are not in agreement about whether delinquents are more likely to come from broken homes than are nondelinquents, as Joan McCord has in a sizable number of investigations in both the United States and Great Britain, emphasized. Indeed, she points out that boys from low-income broken homes actually had no higher incidence of delinquency than their counterparts from equally poor but intact homes. What really matters, McCord argues (on the basis of all the research), is not whether one parent is gone from the family but how the broken home came about. In her words, "homes broken by the death of a parent are less criminogenic than those broken by divorce or separation." All in all, she says, a broken home "appears to be a proxy for other more potent variables."[47] Other factors that often accompany family breakdown may actually be responsible for the child's antisocial tendencies.

Conflict between the mother and the father. McCord is one of several researchers who believe that parental discord is the main source of whatever "criminogenic" tendencies grow out of broken homes. The Cambridge project gives one example of the available evidence. Some of the English youths were not especially aggressive before adolescence but became violence-prone in their late teens. When Farrington looked at the family backgrounds of these particular boys, he found that, in a disproportionate number of cases, their mothers and fathers had quarreled and fought with each other during the children's early adolescence. Further, the parents' quarrelsomeness apparently preceded the boys' strong aggressive dispositions. Family tension had evidently heightened the youngsters' aggressive inclinations. Several American studies also highlight the aggression-generating effects of parental disharmony.[48]

It's easy to explain why sharp disagreements between parents can arouse aggressive inclinations in their offspring: Youngsters can be distressed by antagonism between their parents. Years ago, a very young and unusually articulate girl described this disturbance when she told me how she felt when her parents were in conflict. She said she thought of her mother and father as bookends that held her upright between them. When her parents argued bitterly, the bookends pulled apart, withdrawing their support and leaving her standing alone and unsteady.

We know from laboratory experiments as well as from observations in home settings that young toddlers are indeed emotionally upset when they see angry adults in conflict. The more fighting they witness, the more distressed they are. As in other realms of human behavior, children's strong displeasure can produce aggressive reactions. Even witnessing adults whom they don't know in an angry exchange can stimulate young children to hit, kick, and push each other, evidently because of their inner emotional turmoil.[49] If youngsters react this way to strangers quarreling, it's likely that they will be even more bothered and become even more aggressive when they watch their parents in conflict.

Conflict and Divorce. When parental conflict is so severe that it leads to the breakup of the marriage, it is often highly disturbing to children and can thus provoke aggression. Mavis Hetherington of the University of Virginia in Charlottesville has reported such aggressive reactions in her well-known longitudinal study of the effects of divorce on children. She and her colleagues assessed the social behavior of a sample of 4-year-olds—both boys and girls—over a two-year period after their parents' divorces. (In all these cases, the mothers had been awarded custody of the children.) Since this chapter is focusing on male aggression, I'll discuss only the findings regarding boys (although, by and large, the girls showed somewhat similar patterns).

Many of the boys in the Hetherington study seemed to be upset by the breakup of their families, and their disturbance persisted for a period of time. In comparison to their counterparts from intact homes, the youngsters with divorced parents exhibited higher levels of both emotional and instrumental aggression, physically as well as verbally, even a year after the separation. Another indication of these children's emotional turmoil was that they were not only more likely than their counterparts to display angry outbursts but also tended to be less effective in using aggression to get what they wanted.

Two years after the family breakup, however, the picture changed, to some extent. The psychologists no longer saw any differences between the two sets of boys, although the children's peers still regarded the boys from the broken homes as more aggressive than those from nondivorced families. One possible interpretation of this discrepancy is that the youngsters from divorced homes were now somewhat less easily provoked than they had been a year earlier (so that they didn't assault anyone when the psychologists were nearby) but still weren't as friendly to their peers as were the children from intact families.[50]

Again, however, I suggest that the boys' aggression was not caused

by their fathers' absence. Rather, it stemmed from the emotional disturbance that had been generated by parental conflict. Another longitudinal
study attests to this interpretation. Making use of personality measurements of children as they were growing up, the researchers compared
children whose parents were *later* divorced or separated with other
youngsters whose parents subsequently remained together. The boys
from the families that were to break up later tended to be more impulsive, overactive, and aggressive than the others, *even several years before
the family breakup*, as if they were already greatly disturbed by their
mothers' and fathers' disharmony. As the investigators put it, "the
behavior of conflicting, inaccessible parents during the preseparation
period may have serious consequences for personality development,
especially for boys."[51]

The implication, of course, is that children aren't necessarily severely
upset by their mothers' and fathers' divorce or separation in itself. The
degree of stress the youngsters experience may well depend upon the
level of parental conflict. They may not be seriously bothered, or at least
they may get over their felt disturbance fairly quickly, if their parents do
not in engage in open warfare and if they dissolve their marriage amicably. Hetherington and her associates have provided some encouraging
evidence on this point. When they compared the children of divorced
and nondivorced parents two years after the breakup, they found that
the boys from conflict-ridden but intact families were actually more
aggressive than were the sons of peacefully divorced parents. As the
researchers commented, "In the long run, marital discord may be associated with more adverse outcomes for children than is divorce."[52] A calm
and mannerly dissolution of the marriage may damage children less
than repeated exposure to parental tension and conflict over a considerable period of time.

Modeling Influences

"Do as I Do": Providing Examples for Children to Copy
Besides the factors described above, examples that others provide for
children can also influence the children's aggressive inclinations,
whether or not the others want to be copied. It was Albert Bandura who
did the pioneering research and theorizing in this area.[53] Bandura and
other psychologists usually refer to this phenomenon as *modeling*, defining it as the influence that occurs when people observe someone else (the
model) act in a certain way and then imitate this person's behavior.

Peers and parents as models for socially deviant behavior. Children can be influenced by any number of different models. Their peers
often serve this function, showing them what clothes to wear, what

music to listen to, how to talk and act, and even how they should deal with conflict and other social problems. It is particularly important to recognize that socially troubled youths can employ antisocial groups as models to emulate and, especially, that they may strive to copy other boys who have a high standing in the gang. A leader's influence isn't confined to direct commands. It frequently occurs because members who are relatively low in status simply copy the behavior of their attractive higher-status leader. Joe may begin to wear a gold chain around his neck because he sees that Duke, the gang leader, has such a chain, and he may also begin to swagger when he walks in imitation of his prestigious friend. What is much more serious as far as society is concerned is that Joe may also emulate Duke's cocaine smoking and other illegal actions.

Children can also use their parents as models, and, not surprisingly, research indicates that some antisocial youths may well have copied a socially deviant parent. Farrington's Cambridge project provides an example. A significant number of the London boys who acquired criminal records by the time they were young adults had parents who were convicted of lawbreaking before the sons reached adolescence.

Joan McCord reminds us, however, that not every deviant father traces a path for his son to follow. After she identified the Massachusetts fathers in her sample who were alcoholics or had criminal records, she found that more than half of these particular men also had criminal sons. Nonetheless, other factors moderated the chance that the boys would copy the adults' antisocial lifestyle. The youngsters were less likely to have become lawbreakers if their socially deviant fathers were affectionate to them and had a good relationship with their mothers. About half the boys who had unaffectionate, socially deviant fathers became criminals, as compared to only about one-fifth of the boys whose fathers also were criminals and/or alcoholics but were warm and loving to their sons. If some of the antisocial fathers had served as models for their sons, this influence apparently had occurred only under special, limited circumstances.[54]

Some conditions that affect the model's influence. McCord's findings deserve further comment. At the very least, they show that children don't always copy someone else's actions; other conditions apparently must also be present to make youngsters ready to follow a model's example. Let's speculate about what some of these facilitating conditions might be.

Being Predisposed to Act in a Similar Fashion. One reasonable possibility, it seems to me, is that persons who are watching a model are most likely to imitate the model's behavior if they are already disposed to behave the way the model is behaving. The youths in McCord's sample who evidently copied their deviant fathers may have had fairly strong antisocial inclinations. After all, their fathers were unaffectionate to them and were in frequent conflict with their mothers.

Laboratory experiments also point to the importance of such a disposition to follow a model's example. In at least two studies, children who saw an aggressive adult attack someone were especially apt to copy the adult's behavior if they had just been frustrated. The thwarting undoubtedly increased their aggressive tendencies so that they were readily swayed by the aggressive adult model.[55] Outside the laboratory, youngsters who are exposed to frequent frustrations and harsh parental treatment may be very ready to emulate their socially deviant father's antisocial conduct.

The Model's Power over the Watching Child. Yet another factor may have contributed to the socially deviant Massachusetts fathers' influence upon their sons. Think of how the sons may have viewed their cold and unaffectionate parents. Perhaps the youngsters were yearning for their fathers' love and support, and maybe the men were affectionate to their children every once in a while. However, they probably also thwarted and punished their sons frequently. If so, the boys may have viewed their fathers as sources of both rewards and punishments and thus as persons who had considerable power over them. Well, as Albert Bandura, Dorothea Ross, and Sheila Ross have demonstrated experimentally, adults who are powerful in this sense—who dispense both rewards and punishments—are especially likely to be copied by young children who are dependent upon them.[56]

SUMMARY

The common assumption that the roots of persistently antisocial modes of conduct can be traced, in many (but probably not all) cases, to childhood influences has received considerable empirical support. This chapter summarizes research that examines ways in which experiences both in the family and with peers can affect the development of highly aggressive antisocial dispositions. The discussion focuses largely on the effects of single variables, such as the adult caretakers' punitiveness, but it also emphasizes (1) that the influence of any one factor upon a developing child usually depends upon other conditions that may also be present at the time, and (2) that parents who are bad for their children in one way tend to treat their offspring badly in other ways as well.

The first variables considered can be regarded as influences operating directly upon the young children. I start by looking at the effects of rewards for aggression and noting that these rewards can have a much more general effect than most parents realize. Thus, when the grownups praise their sons for fighting back when bullied, there's a good chance that, unless they are very careful, they may also be strengthening their offsprings' general aggressive tendencies. Growing children obviously are also susceptible to the rewards provided by peers, and these influences are briefly considered. Further, I point out that youngsters' aggression can be reinforced by their victims' reactions, in at least two different ways: (1) the victims may cease annoying or disturbing the aggressor, thus negatively reinforcing the aggressors' actions; and/or (2) the victims' pain and suffering may be gratifying, especially if the aggressors are emotionally aroused at the time, so that the assaults are positively reinforced.

Caretakers can also help foster childhood aggressiveness by exposing their young charges to repeated decidedly unpleasant conditions. Although those who mistreat their children tend to do so in a variety of ways, the discussion in this chapter singles out adults' rejection and harsh treatment of the youngsters for special attention. Many of the adverse effects that are usually attributed to corporal punishment per se may actually be caused by the combination of spanking, for example, with other conditions such as parental inconsistency. Available research indicates that corporal punishment (and power-assertive disciplinary methods in general) can be more effective and can have fewer unfortunate side effects than is commonly supposed if it is administered (1) consistently, (2) with an adequate explanation to the children about why they are being punished, (3) before the children obtain a good deal of pleasure from the disapproved behavior, and (4) when attractive approved alternatives are available.

Gerald Patterson's social learning analysis of the development of childhood aggressiveness is summarized in the chapter as a way of integrating many of the above observations. This formulation assumes that social conditions, such as poverty, that are usually linked to the growth of antisocial conduct operate mainly by affecting the caretakers' treatment of their children. It also holds that the parents of highly aggressive and/or antisocial youngsters are typically poor managers who do not effectively monitor and discipline their offsprings' aggressive behavior and who also fail to adequately reinforce their prosocial conduct. Patterson also maintains that the children of such parents are likely to lack social skills, besides being aggressive, and that, as a consequence, they are apt to be rejected by their more normal peers and to have difficulty in school.

The chapter concludes with a brief overview of some indirect influences on the development of childhood aggressiveness. The most attention is given to the possible role played by broken homes, and evidence is cited indicating that, in many cases, it is parental conflict rather than having only one parent at home that heightens the chances of childhood aggressiveness. Modeling, in which children emulate the actions of others, is also considered briefly. I suggest that youngsters are especially likely to copy others' behavior when they are already disposed to act the way the models act and when the models have considerable power over the children.

NOTES

1. Healy & Bronner (1926). [Also, quoted in McCord, (1986), p. 343.]
2. As just one example, only about 59 percent of the 93 highly aggressive 8- to 10-year-olds in the Cambridge longitudinal study were classified as extremely aggressive in young adolescence, and even fewer (40 percent) were in the most aggressive quartile in late adolescence (Farrington, 1978; West & Farrington, 1977).
3. Scarr, Phillips, & McCartney (1990), p. 27.
4. The Cambridge-Somerville project and its initial results are described in Powers & Witmer (1951).
5. McCord, J. (1979, 1986); McCord, W., McCord, J., & Howard, A. (1961).
6. Bandura & Walters (1959), p. 107.
7. Quotation from Scarr, Phillips, & McCartney (1990), p. 28.
8. See Widom (1989).
9. Davitz (1952).
10. Walters & Brown (1963). On the basis of the data given in this paper, I have found that the frustrated and intermittently rewarded group made a significantly larger number of aggressive responses than did the group in the non-frustrated and intermittently rewarded condition ($p = .05$).
11. Cairns, Cairns, Neckerman, Gest, & Gariepy (1988).
12. Giordano, Cernkovich, & Pugh (1986).
13. Farrington, Berkowitz, & West (1982).
14. Horowitz & Schwartz (1974), p. 240. Also see Klein & Maxson (1989).
15. Erlanger (1979a) suggests that the gang's code of machismo only facilitates the occurrence of aggression when other violence-predisposing circumstances exist.
16. Buehler, Patterson, & Furniss (1966), as cited in Patterson, DeBaryshe, & Ramsey (1989), p. 331.
17. E.g., Patterson (1979, 1986).
18. See, for example, Patterson, Dishion, & Bank (1984); Perry, Perry, & Rasmussen (1986).
19. Patterson, Littman, & Bricker (1967).
20. As was noted in Chapter 1, Baron (1977) and Swart & Berkowitz (1976) provided evidence that information about the intended target's pain can be rewarding to angered people.
21. Also see Feshbach, Stiles, & Bitter (1967).
22. Sebastian (1978).

23. See Perry & Bussey (1977).

24. Farrington (1978); Olweus (1980); Parke & Slaby (1983).

25. Olweus (1980).

26. In a number of investigations, parental behavior was measured at about the same time that the child's aggressiveness was assessed, which means that we cannot be sure whether the child rearing caused the youngster's conduct or was mainly a reaction to the way the child acted. As Parke & Slaby (1983) have pointed out, developmental psychologists are increasingly aware that child rearing is interactive and doesn't necessarily proceed in one direction; children's behavior can have a great influence upon how they are treated by grownups. Nevertheless, for simplicity I will assume in the following sections that the parents' actions were largely responsible for the offsprings' conduct. This assumption seems warranted in many instances, since: (1) in a number of the investigations, the child rearing was described before the children's behavior was measured; and (2) even when the child-rearing practices and the youngsters' conduct were assessed concurrently, the obtained relationship was much the same as when the parental behavior clearly preceded the children's aggressiveness.

27. McCord, W., McCord, J., & Howard, A. (1961); McCord, J. (1983).

28. See McCord, J. (1986), p. 352.

29. The Massachusetts findings are reported in McCord, J. (1983, 1986), whereas the results obtained in the Cambridge longitudinal project are reported in Farrington (1989a, b) and in West & Farrington (1977).

30. Straus, Gelles, & Steinmetz (1980). Also see Erlanger (1979b).

31. Patterson's comment as well as the data obtained by Reid were taken from Patterson, Dishion, & Bank (1984).

32. For comprehensive discussions of the possible effects of punishment on child development, see Berkowitz (1973a); Hoffman (1970); Parke & Slaby (1983); Walters & Parke (1967).

33. The references for this paragraph, in order, are Sears, Maccoby, & Levin (1957); Patterson (1986a, 1986b); Patterson, Dishion, & Bank (1984); Patterson, DeBaryshe, & Ramsey (1989).

34. Baumrind (1973).

35. Parke & Slaby (1983), p. 581.

36. McCord (1986).

37. McCord (1986), p. 353; Farrington (1978), p. 87.

38. Parke & Slaby (1983), p. 581.

39. See Hoffman (1970).

40. See Baumrind (1973).

41. Larzelere (1986).

42. For more comprehensive discussions of the use of physical punishment in disciplining children, see Berkowitz (1973a); Walters & Parke (1967); Parke & Slaby (1983).

43. Patterson (1986b); Patterson, DeBaryshe, & Ramsey (1989); Patterson, Dishion, & Bank (1984).

44. Suggesting that the parents' poor discipline often gave rise to the children's misbehavior and wasn't only a response to this misconduct, Patterson referred to a study by Forgatch indicating "that changes in parental discipline and monitoring were accompanied by significant reductions in child antisocial behavior" (Patterson, DeBaryshe, & Ramsey, 1989, p. 330).

45. Patterson, DeBaryshe, & Ramsey (1989), p. 330.

46. Hundleby & Mercer (1987) reported that *both* certain adverse experiences in the home (particularly having antisocial parents and/or lacking parental affection) *and* friends' attitudes and actions were significantly associated with drug use.

47. McCord, J. (1986), pp. 344-345.

48. A number of pertinent studies are cited in McCord (1986), p. 344, while Farrington's findings are summarized in Farrington (1978). Also see Loeber & Dishion (1984).

49. Cummings, Iannotti, & Zahn-Waxler (1985).

50. Hetherington, Cox, & Cox (1979, 1982). Also see Parke & Slaby (1983), pp. 588-589.

51. Block, Block, & Gjerde (1986).

52. Hetherington, Cox, & Cox (1982), p. 262. The parents' warmth and love might also serve to buffer the youngster against the stresses and strains of the family breakup. For example, see Hodges, Buchsbaum, & Tierney (1983).

53. Bandura (1965, 1973).

54. Farrington (1986); McCord (1986).

55. Hanratty, O'Neal, & Sulzer (1972); Parker & Rogers (1981).

56. Bandura, Ross, & Ross (1963b).

PART 3

---- ❖ ----

Violence in Society

Number of Killings Soars in Big Cities across U.S.

PHILADELPHIA, July 17—After an alarming increase last year, homicide rates have continued to soar this year, and experts attribute the rise to an increase in drug disputes, deadlier weapons, and a tendency among more young people to start careers in crime with a gun. . . .

The statistics have alarmed the police and prosecutors across the country, some of whom describe the situation in dark terms. "Our homicide rate is going through the roof," said Ronald D. Castille, the Philadelphia District Attorney. "Three weekends ago, 11 people were killed in a 48-hour period."

"What's causing most of the increase," he said, "is the ready availability of powerful handguns and the effects of drugs on human beings."

. . . In 1988 there were 660 killings in Chicago. Last year [1989], the number rose to 742, including 29 child-abuse homicides, seven accidents and two mercy killings. The police attributed about 22 percent of the killings to domestic disputes and 24 percent to drugs.

M. D. Hinds, New York Times, July 18, 1990

T his distressing testimony to the violent crimes afflicting contemporary U.S. society was published on the front page of the *New York Times*. The next three chapters of this book are concerned mainly with some of the major societal influences on aggression generally and violent crimes in particular. Chapter 7 explores the possible effects of movies and television, asking whether the depiction of people attacking and killing each other on movie and TV screens can induce viewers to become aggressive themselves. After this, the causes of violent crimes are explored, beginning with an examination of domestic offenses (such as wife battering and child abuse) in Chapter 8 and concluding with a discussion of the general causes of homicide, both outside and within the family, in Chapter 9.

7

Violence in the Media

Entertaining, Informative, Instructive, . . . and Dangerous?

❖

Violence on the Screen and Printed Page: Immediate Effects ◆ *Copycat Crimes: The Contagion of Violence* ◆ *Experimental Investigations of the Short-Lived Effects of Media Violence* ◆ The Prolonged Influence of Repeated Exposure to Media Violence ◆ *Shaping Children's Conceptions of the Social World* ◆ *Acquiring Aggressive Inclinations* ◆ *Understanding Why: The Formation of Social Scripts*

Each year advertisers spend [billions of dollars] in the belief that television can influence human behavior. The television industry enthusiastically agrees with them, but nonetheless contends that its programs of violence do not have any such influence. The preponderance of the available research evidence strongly suggests, however, that violence in television programs can and does have adverse effects upon audiences.

National Commission on the Causes and Prevention of Violence,
Commission Statement, *Sept. 23, 1969*

*I*n the movie *Taxi Driver,* the mentally disturbed protagonist informs a teenage prostitute that he will kill a certain political candidate if she rejects his love. This scene may have prompted another deranged individual to shoot an eminent politician. In March 1981, some time after he saw this film, John W. Hinckley, Jr., attempted to assassinate President Ronald Reagan, wounding him, apparently in the hope of winning a woman's love. Investigators later found a letter in his hotel room addressed to Jodie Foster, the actress who had portrayed the prostitute. The would-be assassin, evidently infatuated with Ms. Foster, had written that he was going to kill President Reagan for her. The news media and mental health specialists speculated that Hinckley had been acting out a fantasy inspired by the movie.[1]

Can the violence depicted on motion picture and TV screens actually incite aggression? Let's assume that John Hinckley was emulating the character in the *Taxi Driver* story. Do violent movies influence only those who are mentally disturbed or who have extremely aggressive personalities? Or can the sight of people fighting stimulate even relatively normal people to become somewhat more aggressive than they otherwise would have been?

The public at large suspects that movie and TV viewers do not have to be mentally ill to be affected by what they see on the screen but still thinks that the possible ill effects of television and movie programming are restricted—to children. Youngsters presumably learn that aggression pays and that people can use violence successfully to achieve their ends.

Concern about this possibility was widespread a generation and more ago. Three committees of the U.S. Senate, a Presidential Commission, and the National Institute of Mental Health, as well as various psychological and psychiatric organizations, all expressed serious misgivings about the heavy doses of violence to which children are exposed on commercial television. Numerous experts testified that children can acquire aggressive inclinations through being exposed to a steady diet of violence on television. The experts' agreement was so great and the research findings seemed so clear that in 1972 the Federal government's highest medical officer, U. S. Surgeon General Jesse Steinfield, concluded that:

> . . . there is a causative relationship between televised violence and subsequent antisocial behavior, and that the evidence is strong enough that it requires some action on the part of responsible authorities, the TV industry, the Government, the citizens.

Even television industry officials appeared to share this view. The president of the American Broadcasting Company promised that the industry would reform:

Now that we are reasonably certain that televised violence can increase aggressive tendencies in some children, we will have to manage our program planning accordingly.[2]

This consensus soon disintegrated, however, and controversy now swirls about the question of how much of an impact televised violence has on frequent viewers. There certainly hasn't been much of a reduction in the amount of shooting, fighting, and killing shown on our TV screens. According to frequency counts made by George Gerbner and his associates at the University of Pennsylvania, network television has presented about five to six violent acts per hour to its prime time audiences since 1967. The Gerbner team also calculated that in 1989 about 70 percent of the prime time network programs portrayed at least some violence and that this figure rose to 90 percent in the hours children were most likely to watch.[3]

Does all this aggression in the media have an effect? If so, are children and mentally ill people the only ones who are influenced by violent movies and TV programming? Just what has the research into this problem actually shown?

You'll see in this chapter that certain depictions of violence in the mass media increase the likelihood of further aggression by grownups as well as children, and by relatively normal people as well as by those who are emotionally disturbed. You'll also see that this heightened chance of aggression can be due to temporary influences as well as to a more persistent learning. Although TV programming has not changed over the years and although criticism has been leveled against much of the research on media effects, behavioral scientists have actually learned a great deal about the possible consequences of the violence portrayed on TV and movie screens. I will summarize their findings in this chapter.

My research review will be divided into two main parts. The first section will cover the immediate, or relatively temporary, effects of the depiction of assaults and murders in the broadcast media, starting with a consideration of copycat crimes. I will devote much attention to this initial topic in order to make two main points: First, the mass media can have a more extensive influence on social aggression than is commonly realized, by simply reporting news as well as by providing entertainment. Second, some of the same psychological processes that promote aggressive reactions to fictional movies also operate in copycat cases. I will review experiments that have investigated the short-run consequences of exposure to scenes of fighting and killing on movie and TV screens. The major focus will be on the conditions that make it more or less likely that televised violence will have aggression-enhancing effects. The second main section of the chapter will examine the long-term consequences of repeated exposure to a heavy diet of TV violence.

I'll conclude with suggestions about how these adverse effects might be lessened.

VIOLENCE ON THE SCREEN AND PRINTED PAGE: IMMEDIATE EFFECTS

Copycat Crimes: The Contagion of Violence

"Epidemics of Crime Follow the Line of the Telegraph"
John Hinckley's case is a fairly good example of how subtly and how pervasively the mass media can influence the level of aggression in contemporary society. Not only was his attempt to kill President Reagan apparently incited by a movie but also this action, which was widely reported in the press and on radio and television, evidently prompted others to imitate his aggression. According to a spokesman for the Secret Service (the government agency charged with protecting the President), there was a substantial increase in threats against the President's life in the days after the shooting. This was not unusual, the Secret Service official said. Attempts to kill a President have often been followed by a jump in the number of spoken and written threats against him.

Indeed, just such an increase also occurred six years earlier, in September 1975, after Lynette Fromme tried to shoot President Gerald Ford. Statistics released by the Secret Service indicated that the agency received 320 threats against President Ford in the first three weeks after the attempted assassination, as compared to the customary 100 threats for this time span. Each such threat has to be taken seriously, of course, since some persons might try to translate their words into action—and, indeed, about two weeks after Lynette Fromme's assassination attempt, Sara Jane Moore also shot at President Ford. Assassination attempts are apparently a hazard that all prominent politicians must face. Hubert Humphrey, who was vice-president under Lyndon Johnson and himself three times a presidential candidate, commented after the second attempt on President Ford's life, "There is a certain number of people who, for some reason or another, the minute they see an attempt or hear of an attempt. . . . They like to get in on the act."[4]

Other anecdotal reports also attest to the contagion of violence as news is spread of sensational crimes. Several murders which occurred in 1966 are especially pertinent to an analysis I'll offer later in this chapter. Richard Speck murdered eight nurses in Chicago, Illinois, in July 1966, and Charles Whitman shot forty-five people from a tower at the University of Texas at Austin in August of the same year. About three months later, Robert Smith, an 18-year-old high school senior, walked into an

Arizona beauty school and killed four women and a child. He later told the police he had gotten the idea for a mass killing after reading the news stories about Speck and Whitman. Smith also said that he had been planning the shootings from the time his parents had given him a target pistol as a birthday present.[5] I'll come back to this point later in this chapter.

We now hear a great deal about copycat crimes, and social scientists have long been aware of this phenomenon. Back in 1890 the French sociologist Gabriel Tarde wrote about "suggesto-imitative-assaults," saying that as reports of a violent crime spread (over the telegraph lines of that era), susceptible members of the public developed aggressive ideas and some of them even openly imitated the described behavior. Tarde believed the famous Jack the Ripper killings in London in 1888 had such an effect:

> In less than a year, as many as eight absolutely identical crimes were committed in the great city. This is not all; there followed a repetition of these same deeds outside . . . the capital (and abroad). . . . Infectious epidemics spread with the air or the wind; epidemics of crime follow the line of the telegraph.[6]

Statistical Evidence of the Contagion of Violence

Evidence shows that copycat crimes are not necessarily rare events. They apparently occur with some regularity, although they also aren't inevitable. More than a generation ago, my colleague Jacqueline Macaulay and I obtained crime data for forty American cities from the Federal Bureau of Investigation (FBI), in order to determine whether sensational acts of violence led to a jump in violent crimes across the country. We formed an index of violent crimes based on homicides, aggravated assaults, rape, and robbery, and we employed statistical procedures to control for variations in crime rates due to such matters as city size and month of the year, and found that there were sudden and unusual changes in this index after President John F. Kennedy was assassinated in late November 1963. Although violent crimes generally have increased over the years, the President's murder was followed first (the month after the assassination) by a relative drop in such occurrences and then by an abrupt rise above the trend line for the next several months. (I'll later offer a possible reason for this initial decrease and then spurt in violent crimes.) Interestingly, the index of nonviolent crimes (larceny, burglary, and auto theft) which we had developed did not reveal the same pattern. Further support was added to these results when the Speck and Whitman crimes were also followed by a sudden jump in rates of violent crimes above the figures that would have been expected on the basis of the general trend. Robert Smith was not the only person who was influenced to become violent by these news stories.[7]

We can't be sure just why these abrupt increases in violent crimes came about. What we can say, however, is that the FBI did not know of any sudden changes in police procedures or rules that could have been responsible for the jump in reported crimes. I suppose the assassination of President Kennedy may have heightened police agencies' concern about law and order so that they became more attentive to violent events, but it's hard to believe that the Speck and Whitman incidents also aroused a nationwide police concern. More than likely, the sudden and temporary jump in violent crimes was a reaction to the news reports.

Phillips' Studies of the Contagion of Violence

Perhaps the best-known and certainly the most controversial investigations of the contagion of violence have been carried out by sociologist David Phillips of the University of California in San Diego. Although some of his findings have been criticized, others have been confirmed by independent researchers. It will be worthwhile to look at several of his studies in some detail, because of their theoretical as well as their practical implications. They indicate that factual news reports as well as fictional movies and TV programs can have socially unfortunate effects on people in the audience, that these consequences can be relatively temporary and are not necessarily due to a long-lasting learning of aggressive modes of conduct, and that adults as well as children can be influenced by the mass media.

The contagion of suicides. Phillips began his studies by asking whether there were many imitative suicides. After establishing a list of some thirty-five nationally reported suicide stories from 1947 through 1968, he used official records to determine the number of suicides in the United States during three periods: the month before each story appeared, the month of the suicide, and the month afterward. As Figure 7–1 shows, when the thirty-five widely publicized incidents are considered together, a greater number of people took their own lives than would ordinarily have been expected in the month of the famous person's death. This "excess" number of suicides wasn't especially high on a per-case basis—on the average there were only about fifty-eight more suicides nationwide than would otherwise have taken place—but the news reports evidently had a definite (and statistically significant) influence.

The contagion of suicides isn't limited to the United States. Phillips carried out a similar analysis of British statistics and obtained the same general results. Widely publicized suicides led to a significant rise in the number of people who apparently followed suit in the United Kingdom, as in the United States. To cite only one example, you may be interested

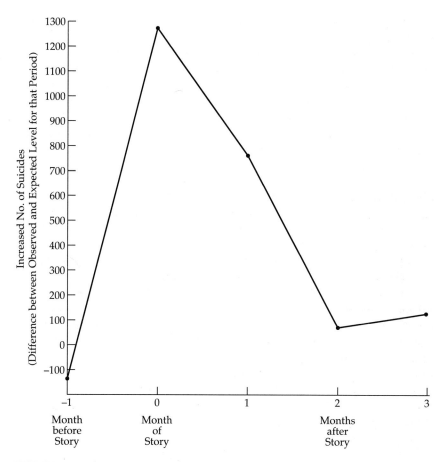

FIGURE 7-1

Fluctuations in the number of suicides in the United States before, during, and after the months of nationally reported suicides, over all cases. (From Phillips (1974). Copyright 1974 by the American Psychological Association. Adapted by permission.)

to hear that Marilyn Monroe's suicide in August 1962 was followed by a 12 percent increase in self-killings above the expected number in the United States and close to a 10 percent rise in Great Britain. Furthermore, in both countries, the greater the amount of coverage the national newspapers gave to any given suicide, the higher was the above-expected number of other people who also killed themselves.[8]

Phillips argues that the contagion of suicides is more common than most people suspect. Even some automobile and airplane crashes, he maintains, could be news report-instigated deliberate suicides. One of his investigations noted that automobile fatalities increased by more than

30 percent after a publicized suicide, with the rise reaching its peak three days later. Like his earlier, previously cited study, this analysis also showed that the wider the audience was for these news stories, the higher was the increase in motor vehicle deaths.[9]

Though a number of Phillips' studies have been questioned, Phillips has refuted several of the critics' arguments.[10] Taken together, his research papers provide pretty good evidence that some suicides are prompted by newspaper and television stories about well-known persons who take their own lives. The "imitators" undoubtedly had been thinking of killing themselves for some time, but a few of them might have changed their minds and gone on living if they hadn't encountered the publicized suicide stories.

The impact of publicized aggression upon homicides. Encouraged by his success in accumulating evidence of the contagion of suicides, Phillips then investigated whether widely publicized reports of aggressive encounters would have a significant impact upon the incidence of homicides in the United States. He realized, of course, that not every violent event would necessarily be followed by an immediate increase in the number of killings. A spectacular act of violence might not spur others to act aggressively themselves, Phillips reasoned, when the news media showed that the perpetrators were clearly punished for their offenses.

Prize Fights Give People Violent Ideas. Championship prize fights are good examples of socially sanctioned aggressive encounters that aren't punished by society, and Phillips therefore expected these sporting events to actually lead to rises in violent crimes.

Carrying out a complicated statistical analysis (in which he controlled for time of year, holidays, and day of the week) to test this audacious hypothesis, Phillips examined the fluctuations in daily homicides in the United States before and after every heavyweight championship fight between 1973 and 1978. The fights, he found, had a small but significant effect, in which the maximum impact occurred three days later. Each bout in his sample led to approximately twelve more homicides (in national statistics) than would otherwise have been expected. In line with his theory, there were more "excess" homicides when the championship fight was reported on the network evening news than when it didn't get this national coverage.[11]

Think of it. Sporting events are intended to entertain their audiences, and, indeed, quite a few people do enjoy watching them. However, if Phillips' findings can be accepted—and I believe they can—a number of persons apparently get violent ideas from the TV and newspaper reports of these aggressive encounters, and some of them even translate their thoughts into violent actions. I'll provide more detail about this process later in this chapter.

Experimental Investigations of the Short-Lived Effects of Media Violence

Does Media Violence Increase the Likelihood of Aggression?
I've suggested that news reports of violent events can induce some people in the audience to become violent. The same statement can be made about the effects of movies, which are intended to be entertaining rather than informative: The depiction of people attacking, fighting, and killing each other can heighten some viewers' aggressive inclinations. Some psychologists, however, have questioned whether this is indeed the case. Jonathan Freedman, for one, has insisted that available "evidence does not support the idea that viewing television violence causes aggression." Other skeptics have contended that witnessed aggression has only a slight influence on the observers' behavior—at most.[12]

The results of laboratory experiments. I believe, however, along with some other writers, that a considerable body of experimental research indicates that violent movies can increase the likelihood of aggressive behavior to an extent that ranges from small to moderate. Andison's statistical analysis of the findings obtained in thirty-one laboratory experiments summarizes some of this evidence. Most of the studies demonstrated that the violence witnessed in movies led to a higher level of aggression than did the control films. More than half the studies showed that the violent movies had a moderate impact upon the subjects' behavior.[13]

Studies assessing more realistic aggression. The somewhat similar analysis conducted by Wendy Wood and her associates, at Texas A&M University in College Station, may be even more convincing to you. Because doubts have been raised about the supposed artificiality of laboratory measures of aggression, the Wood group focused on twenty-eight separate experiments in which the subjects had been able to assault other persons freely and naturally.[14]
Leyens' Belgian Experiment. An experiment conducted by Jacques-Philippe Leyens and Leoncio Camino of the University of Louvain in Belgium is a good example of the kind of study the Texas psychologists examined. In this investigation, making use of teenage boys residing in four cottages within a Belgian minimum-security penal institution, trained observers first measured each boy's normal level of aggressiveness toward the others in his cottage. After a week of this, in the second phase (which lasted five days), each cottage was shown a commercially available movie every evening. In one condition the movies shown were aggressive in nature while the cottages in the other condition saw nonaggressive films. The observers again recorded the boys' behavior. Finally,

the youths' actions were again observed every day during the following week, when no movies were shown. I'll tell you only about the teenagers' aggression during over the five evenings of the second, movie-watching week, since Wood and her associates concentrated on the subjects' behavior immediately after seeing a film. And to keep the discussion brief, I will confine it to the boys' physical attacks on each other.

You can see from Figure 7–2 that the violent movies increased the youths' physical aggression above their baseline ("normal") level, whether they had initially fought a lot or a little in their cottage. By comparison, the boys who were shown the neutral films either decreased or remained constant in how often they assaulted each other. Leyens also found, it's important to note, that the heightened aggression exhibited in the cottages that watched the violent movies was not caused simply by an increased activity level; the boys had been specifically stimulated to be aggressive.[15]

Wood's Findings Over All the Studies Surveyed. Leyens' Belgian results are not atypical by any means. The findings obtained in the studies surveyed by Wood and her associates were generally similar to those obtained in the studies Andison examined, even though the Texas survey concentrated exclusively on investigations utilizing only "natural" forms of aggression. Seeing violent movies led to greater aggression than did seeing nonaggressive, control films, in about 70 percent of the experiments reviewed by the Texas group. Moreover, calculating from the magnitude of this difference, Wood and her colleagues concluded that "the mean effect of exposure to violent media on unconstrained aggression is in the small to moderate range," typical of social psychological predictors.[16]

Don't misunderstand the implications of the phrase "small to moderate," as some of the critics of media research have done. Wood points out that even a small influence isn't necessarily trivial. On the basis of statistical analysis, she estimated that a substantial minority of the youngsters who watched violent movies could become more aggressive than they otherwise would have been. This fraction has to be considered in light of the huge size of the media audiences. Because millions of people are being exposed to broadcast films, there might be several hundred more serious acts of violence in the country in any one week than would ordinarily have occurred.

Placing Media Violence under the Microscope: When and Why Violent Movies Have Aggressive Consequences

For most investigators of media violence effects, then, there's no longer a question about *whether* viewing violent events in the mass media enhances the likelihood of further aggression. The real problem has to do

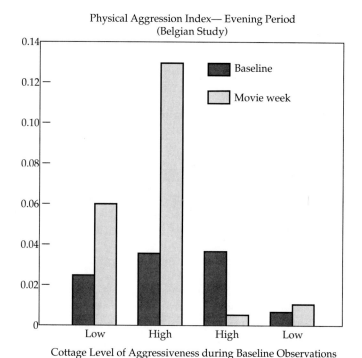

FIGURE 7-2

Mean levels of physical aggression among teenage boys soon after seeing movies, in low- and high-aggression cottages. (Data from Leyens, Camino, Parker, & Berkowitz, (1975), as reported in Parke, Berkowitz, Leyens, West, & Sebastian (1977), p. 155. Copyright 1975 by the American Psychological Association. Adapted by permission.)

with *when and why* this effect comes about, and it's this problem to which I will now turn. You'll see that not all violent movies are alike and that only some kinds of aggressive scenes are apt to have aggressive aftereffects. As a matter of fact, some depictions of violence may even dampen viewers' urges to attack their enemies. Besides spelling out the conditions that limit the adverse influences of media violence, I'll offer a theoretical analysis of media effects that will attempt to account for the exceptions and will also help to explain both the copycat effects discussed earlier and the consequences of fictitious movie violence. Because of space restrictions, the research review I'll present will be highly selective, and many interesting and important experiments will not be considered.[17]

The priming effect of aggressive scenes: people get ideas. Before going further, I should remind you that I am now dealing only with the relatively immediate and transient effects of seeing violence on TV and movie screens or reading about it on the printed page—not with the long-term consequences of repeated exposure. Even short-term effects can be fairly complicated, and they are undoubtedly influenced by a variety of different psychological processes. Nevertheless, I believe it will be helpful to explain these aftereffects in terms of the "priming" concept I introduced in Chapter 4. Let me remind you of what's involved in priming.

The Concept of Priming. The central notion of priming is that when people encounter a stimulus (or an event) that has a particular meaning, other ideas occur to them that have much the same meaning. These thoughts in turn can activate yet other semantically related ideas and even tendencies to act.

One of the experiments cited in Chapter 4 illustrates this principle at work. Charles Carver and his associates asked their subjects to assemble sets of four words into meaningful three-word sentences. In the "aggressively primed" condition, 80 percent of the word sets given to the students contained a word that had an aggressive connotation. One set, for example, was "hits her he them," so that a likely sentence formed from these words would be "He hits her." Immediately after the subjects finished this sentence construction task, they were required to punish a fellow student for his mistakes. The subjects in the aggressively primed condition were significantly more punitive than were those in any of the other groups. The aggressive thoughts that were activated in the subjects as they formed the aggressive sentences apparently led to a hostile assessment of the other student's work and perhaps also to aggressive inclinations.[18]

Applying the Priming Notion to Media Violence. As Chapter 4 suggested, just this type of phenomenon contributes to the aggressive behaviors that results from exposure to a violent movie or TV program or the news report of a violent incident: People in the audience get aggressive ideas. Many people are aware of this kind of effect. Years ago a journalist asked the leader of a teenage gang in New York City what kind of TV programs the youth most enjoyed. The boy listed the shows full of shooting and killing, but then added that he didn't like to see rape portrayed on television. He claimed that such scenes "[give] many guys wrong ideas. . . . They go out and do it just for the hell of it."[19]

The teenager could be right. Whether they did it "for the hell of it" or not, many of the people who threatened President Reagan after he had been shot, or who assaulted someone criminally following President Kennedy's assassination or after a widely publicized championship fight, had probably been aggressively primed by the media stories of the initial aggressive incident and then had translated their violent thoughts into violent actions.

An experiment carried out by Charles Turner and John Layton at the University of Utah, Salt Lake City, can help to show what may happen, psychologically, in this process. After the researchers gave their male subjects certain kinds of word lists to memorize, they required each man to punish another student for his mistakes on a sham learning assignment. The most punitive subjects in this task were those who had previously learned lists of easily visualized words which had clear aggressive connotations (e.g., "gun," "punch," and "smash"). The subjects who had memorized less easily visualized aggressive words (e.g., "anger," "enemy," "punishment") or who had learned only neutral words (whatever their imagery value) were less punitive.[20]

Let's now apply this finding to a much more common occurrence. Suppose we hear that two men attacked and injured another person. We can easily imagine what happened. Easily visualized events such as this are apt to be readily recalled at a later time. (Turner and Layton as well as other investigators have demonstrated this effect.) If the incident has a preponderantly aggressive meaning for us—so that we don't become anxious or regard the attack as reprehensible—not only will we be fairly quick to remember it, but also there's a pretty good chance that the memory may activate other aggression-connected ideas, feelings, and action tendencies. Violent movies could operate in a similar manner. They are usually easily recalled because of their visual, highly dramatic, and conceptually simple nature. When the memories come to mind, their aggressive content could prime additional aggression-related thoughts, feelings, and motor reactions. We might then do something in line with these primed reactions, especially if our inhibitions happened to be weak at the time.

More recent research by Brad Bushman and Russell Geen provides still more empirical support for my analysis of the way in which viewing violence enhances the likelihood of further aggression. Their subjects wrote down the thoughts that had come to mind as they looked at a brief movie scene. The more violent the scene had been, the greater was the number of aggressive ideas the subjects listed. Interestingly, and in further corroboration of my theorizing, the people who were shown the most violent film also had the strongest increase in their anger-related feelings (as compared with how they had felt at the start of the session), as well as the greatest rise in systolic blood pressure.[21] The priming experience, then—in this case, witnessing a violent movie—can generate physiological and emotional reactions as well as particular thoughts.

The meaning of witnessed violence. My discussion of the Turner-Layton experiment touched upon an important point that should be made explicit: People who are exposed to violent scenes won't have aggressive thoughts and inclinations unless they interpret the actions they see as having to do with *aggression.* In other words, they basically have to think they are watching people intentionally trying to hurt or even kill each other.

Are Contact Sports Violent Games? This notion can be applied to contact sports such as American football. Football is frequently regarded as a violent game, and, indeed, for some people a football contest can have some of the same consequences as a violent movie. Jeffrey Goldstein and Robert Arms interviewed the sports fans at two athletic events, a football game and a gymnastics meet, to assess the fans' hostility levels before and after the contests. Whereas the gym meet did not have any detectable effects, the football spectators did exhibit a significant rise on the hostility measure, and this was true whether they supported the winning or the losing team.

However, football doesn't have to be viewed as an aggressive sport. Rather than thinking of the contestants as trying to hurt each other, it's possible to look at the players merely as skilled athletes who are energetically pursuing victory. People who interpret the game in this nonaggressive manner shouldn't have many aggressive thoughts as they watch the contest (unless they're greatly bothered by how the game is progressing), and thus they shouldn't become aggressively stimulated. Joe Alioto and I demonstrated this experimentally. The subjects were first deliberately insulted by a confederate of the experimenters and were then shown a movie of either a professional football game or a prize fight. They were led to regard the contest in one of two different ways: The opponents were described to one group of subjects as bitter rivals who were seeking to hurt each other and to another group as professionals who were unemotionally going about their business. Only the subjects in the first group thus watched a contest with an *aggressive* meaning. When the men later had opportunities to shock the person who had insulted them previously, the subjects who had believed that the athletes were trying to injure their opponents were more punitive than were their counterparts who had watched the supposedly less aggressive events.[22]

Observed aggression is in the mind of the beholder. Only if people interpret the action they see as aggression will the event activate strong aggression-related ideas and make them aggressively inclined.

Is the Witnessed Aggression Punished? Even if viewers think of a witnessed occurrence as aggressive, they still may not develop aggressive tendencies if they are also clearly reminded that aggression is very apt to be punished. Let's say that we watch someone knock another person down, and then we see the bully suffer for his misdeed. As Albert Bandura has emphasized, there is little likelihood that we'll copy the offender's behavior, and we may not even have many thoughts favorable to aggression. This point can be extended to crime reports. When you read the discussion of capital punishment in Chapter 10, you'll see that news

of a murderer being executed or sentenced to life imprisonment apparently can produce a short-term drop in homicides—a drop that will persist as long as the news of the punishment remains fresh and timely.

Is the Observed Aggression "Bad"? There may be much the same outcome when we think of the aggression we observe as morally reprehensible. In the same hypothetical example, suppose that we learn that the
person whom we saw being knocked down later died of the injuries sus-
tained in the assault. This reminder that aggression can have exceedingly
unhappy or even tragic consequences could also activate our inhibitions
against aggression and even keep us from striking at someone who had
just tormented us.

This outcome is definitely pertinent to movie violence. A highly
aggressive film won't promote aggression-enhancing thoughts and
motor reactions when the viewers regard the fighting, shooting, and
killing in the movie as morally wrong. But most violent movies don't
really question the aggression they portray. A good many old-fashioned
Westerns were very unfortunate in this respect. For all the fighting that
went on in these movies, the people who were shot in them were never
shown suffering or even seriously wounded. The characters only fell
down, and the watching public was never reminded of the death and
destruction that gunfire could bring. Today's violent movies, of course,
are much more likely to depict bodies being bloodily torn open by bullets and knife slashes, but even so, by the story's end the audience still
finds that much of the portrayed violence is in a good cause. However
gory the film, it ultimately communicates the message that violence can
be entirely proper.[23]

Whatever the outcome of the filmed aggression, however, we may
regard the behavior portrayed on the screen as "wrong" because we disapprove of the aggressor's reason for attacking his victim. Here's an
example of what I have in mind: Have you seen the old movie *Bad Day at
Black Rock?* The protagonist (portrayed by Spencer Tracy) goes to a small
western community to find out why a friend of his has mysteriously died
there. He is repeatedly bullied by several townspeople. Some viewers
may actually enjoy seeing the "bad guys" push Spencer Tracy around,
because they like the sight of aggression generally and/or because their
moral sense is not affronted by this kind of behavior. These people don't
think of bullying behavior as bad, and they could well get aggression-
promoting ideas and feelings from watching the bullies' actions. In much
the same vein, a small minority of Americans probably weren't bothered
by the assassination of President Kennedy or by the attempts to kill President Ford and President Reagan. Such people may have been primarily
responsible for the increased aggression and threatened violence that
occurred soon after these spectacular crimes were committed.

My guess, however, is that most persons react very differently when
they see bullies in action. The majority of people who watch *Bad Day at*

Black Rock undoubtedly regard the villains' behavior toward the character portrayed by Spencer Tracy as morally improper, and the overwhelming preponderance of Americans were horrified by the attacks on Kennedy, Ford, and Reagan. Their negative opinions of the depicted violence may have stifled whatever aggressive ideas and inclinations might otherwise have been activated.

However, the typical violent movie does more than portray obviously improper aggression. It usually goes on to show the hero triumphantly beating up the bad guys at the end of the story. This is certainly the case in *Bad Day*. After being picked on throughout most of the film, Spencer Tracy finally decides he has taken enough and (accompanied by the cheers of many members of the audience) turns on his oppressors. As Victorian writers would have put it, he gives the villains a sound thrashing. Audiences love this ending. They enjoy seeing the wrongdoers receive the treatment they deserve—and the thoughts activated by this gratifying violence may actually increase the chances that at least some persons in the audience will assault another individual soon afterward.

I'm fairly confident about this prediction because of the results obtained in at least nine separate experiments, starting with a study Edna Rawlings and I published back in 1963. This study was replicated in my own laboratory as well as elsewhere. In all the investigations, angry male subjects were most aggressive toward a person who had provoked them earlier after they watched a movie villain receive the beating he supposedly deserved. An experiment I reported in 1965 is typical.

When each subject arrived in the laboratory, he was told that he would be working on several tasks with a fellow student, ostensibly as part of an investigation of physiological reactions to various kinds of activities. The two men were then hooked up to the supposed physiological recording apparatus. The first phase was introduced as a new intelligence test, and the "other student," who was actually the experimenter's accomplice, either disparaged the naive subject's performance (thus angering the man) or acted in a relatively neutral manner. In the next phase, which followed immediately afterward, the two men watched a six-minute prize fight scene from the movie *Champion* in which a character portrayed by actor Kirk Douglas received a bad beating. Before the film began, however, the men were given a brief summary of the movie story, supposedly so that they could better understand the scene. This synopsis led the subjects in one condition to regard the Douglas character as a basically nice person, whereas in the other condition he was described much more unfavorably as someone who had long mistreated and exploited everyone he knew. The people in the second condition presumably came to think of the beating Kirk Douglas received in the prize fight as justified aggression; he was getting his "just deserts." In the condition in which he was described as a nice guy, by contrast, the harsh punishment he was given was seen as less justified.

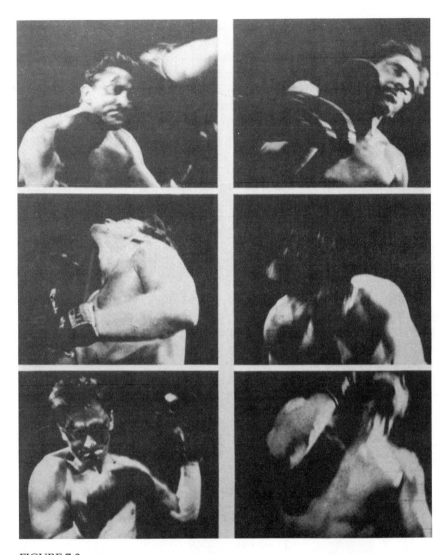

FIGURE 7-3

Filmed aggression shown in author's experiments was from the motion picture *Champion* and included these scenes in which Kirk Douglas receives a bad beating. Watchers had been given certain kinds of information about the movie protagonist and/or their coworker in the session before they saw the film.

In the last phase of the study, the "other student" was ostensibly given an assignment to work on several problems in another room. The naive subject was informed that his job was to evaluate each of the other man's problem solutions by giving him from one to ten electric shocks for each problem, depending upon how bad he thought the particular answer had been. A few minutes later the subject was shown the other student's supposed work (which consisted of standard products that were used throughout the experiment). Figure 7–4 reports the mean number of shocks administered to the accomplice in each condition, with a greater number indicating stronger aggression.

As you can see, the men who had been provoked by the accomplice's insulting remarks punished this person more severely than did their nonangered counterparts. More important, the people who were most aggressive were the ones who had just watched "good aggression" on the screen, as if seeing the movie "bad guy" getting a deserved thrashing led them to believe (for a while) that it would be proper for them to attack the bad guy in their own lives.[24]

This finding can be extended to an audience seeing *Bad Day at Black Rock* (or any movie in which the hero is shown beating up the villain).

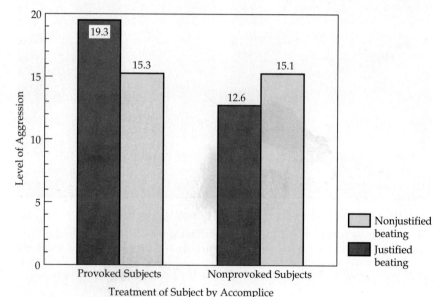

FIGURE 7-4

Mean aggression toward an accomplice after seeing a movie character receive either a justified or a less justified beating.

The aggression scores are for the sum of the shock number and shock duration measures. (Data from Berkowitz (1965). Copyright 1965 by the American Psychological Association. Adapted by permission.)

The movie writers and producers may argue that their film has conveyed a valuable lesson; such as "Crime doesn't pay" or "Justice will triumph." A number of viewers, however, may well leave the theater with a somewhat different thought: that aggression is warranted at times. Having just witnessed aggression that is portrayed as justified, these people may believe, for a short time anyway, that it would be entirely appropriate for them to hurt others who provoked them.

Identifying with a Movie Aggressor. Viewers' identification with movie or TV characters also influences the degree to which they are affected by what they see on the screen. In identifying with one of the characters in the story they are watching, they are essentially imagining themselves to be this person. As a consequence, they react emotionally to whatever happens to the character. If the character is a man battling with others, they think of themselves as fighting along with him, hitting and shooting with him in his struggle with his movie opponents. As they imagine themselves aggressing, the violence they see easily activates a broad range of aggressive ideas and action tendencies.

Jacques-Philippe Leyens and Steve Picus have provided a good demonstration of enhanced aggression resulting from an identification with a movie aggressor. These researchers asked some of their University of Wisconsin—Madison students who participated in the study to think of themselves as one of the two fighters in a brief prize fight scene they were to see (the character who subsequently won the bout). After the subjects watched this particular man give the other fighter a bad beating in the film, they themselves were much more punitive toward a person who had provoked them earlier than they otherwise would have been.[25]

Psychologically Distancing Oneself from Movie Violence. Where psychological closeness to a movie aggressor can increase viewers' later aggressiveness, the opposite effect can occur if viewers distance themselves psychologically from the fighting on the screen. This psychological stepping back apparently reduces the likelihood that the observed aggression will activate aggressive ideas and action tendencies.

One way to achieve a distancing effect is to focus one's attention on the nonviolent aspects of the movie. For example, Leyens, Cisneros, and Hossay led some of their Belgian subjects to concentrate on the aesthetic qualities of aggression-related pictures. When all of the men later had opportunities to shock a person who had insulted them before they saw the pictures, the subjects who had been concerned about the aesthetic qualities of the pictures were less punitive than were the other people. Because they focused on matters other than aggression, the aggressive content of the pictures they saw didn't strongly arouse aggressive thoughts and inclinations.[26]

We here have one reason, I believe, why professional movie critics are rarely bothered by the assaults and murders which are so frequently d in many present-day films. When they watch a movie, their is apt to be centered on the aesthetic and artistic aspects of the on, so that they don't become aggressively aroused. What they don't realize is that some other viewers will have very different interests, may get caught up in the violence they see, and may be stimulated to become aggressive by the fighting and killing they see on the screen.

Realizing the Violence Isn't Real. People in the audience can also distance themselves from a movie by telling themselves that the events they're watching are only fictional, or make-believe. "That's not real," they think, and in their minds they step back from what they see and are less affected by it.

Some people intuitively know how to achieve this beneficial psychological distancing when they look at a disturbing movie. A journalist once described how she loved to watch horror movies when she was a child but would always become terror-stricken by the frightening events unfolding on the screen. Her aunt, with whom she saw these films, would then calm her down by reminding her that the story was only fictional. "'Remember,' she said in a reassuring voice, 'there are lights and cameras and makeup people and a director standing all around, just off the screen where you can't see them.' In other words, it's only make-believe."[27]

The aunt was right in trying to draw the child's attention to the horror movie's unreality. Awareness of the make-believe nature of things that happen on the screen can lessen the emotion-arousing capacity of these events—and can lower their ability to activate aggression-related ideas and urges. Experiments with children and young adults have demonstrated that aggressive scenes are less likely to promote heightened aggressiveness when viewers are reminded beforehand that they will see only playacting. Seymour Feshbach, for instance, showed a movie of a campus riot to children after telling some of them that the film was a fictional portrayal. The other youngsters were informed that they were seeing a newsreel of an actual occurrence. When the children were given opportunities to punish one of their peers soon afterward, the subjects who had been told that the violence they would see was make-believe were less aggressive.[28] Their awareness that they weren't seeing people really attack each other apparently reduced the impact of the witnessed aggression.

This finding doesn't mean that make-believe violence is always less aggressively arousing than realistic fighting and killing. In order for psychological distancing to occur, viewers have to be fully aware that the characters on the screen aren't actually trying to hurt each other. This awareness isn't always present. Sophisticated members of the audience may spontaneously remind themselves of film's fictional nature as they watch, but young children are probably less likely to remember that what they're seeing isn't real. Furthermore, research tells us, youngsters from underprivileged families are less apt than children from more advantageous backgrounds to tell themselves that a movie is only make-believe. Maybe it's because they've met many disappointments in the real world and because the reality of their lives has been exceedingly harsh that they want to think fantasies can be true-to-life. Whatever the reason, underprivileged children may be the ones who are most "at risk" when violent TV programs are shown.[29]

Keeping the influence of media violence alive. Let me remind you that the aggressive thoughts and tendencies activated by the depictions of violence in the mass media usually diminish in strength fairly quickly with the passage of time. Phillips found, you'll recall, that the flurry of copycat crimes after the first widespread reporting of a violent incident tends to disappear in about four days. Similarly, in one of my laboratory experiments the increased aggressiveness generated by watching a violent movie seemed to be gone within an hour. (Experimental investigations have also observed a weakening of priming effects with time.)[30]

Yet the influence of media violence is not always so short-lived. Robert Smith, the murderer whom I mentioned at the beginning of this chapter, is a case in point. Though Smith claimed that the Speck and Whitman crimes had given him the idea of carrying out multiple killings himself, he still waited three months before he shot up an Arizona beauty school. Why did the news stories about the Speck and Whitman atrocities have such a persistent effect? Also, why did the assassination of President Kennedy lead to an increase in crimes of violence a month later?

Something apparently happened in these particular instances to prolong the aggression-enhancing influence of the crime stories. We can guess how this may have occurred. Robert Smith had probably kept his news-activated aggressive tendencies alive by engaging in periodic violent fantasies. As he practiced firing the target pistol which his parents had given him, during the months after the Speck and Whitman incidents, he may have imagined shooting people—until one day he decided it was time for him to act. Make-believe aggression is much more likely to perpetuate aggressive thoughts and inclinations, and even to strengthen them, than it is to bring about a cathartic reduction of violent urges.[31]

The mass media were probably responsible for the prolonged influence of the assassination of President Kennedy. There's a paradox here. Print and broadcast journalists obviously had to tell the world about this tragic event (just as they have the duty to report other important violent occurrences). However, by relating the story, by replaying tapes of the assassination again and again, and by continually speculating about whether it was really Oswald who killed the President (and, if so, why he did it), the news media may have inadvertently given some violence-prone people aggressive ideas and may have helped to keep these aggressive thoughts and inclinations active as the days and weeks went by.

The Reactivating Influence of Aggression-Associated Cues. The priming-effect analysis of media influences that I am advancing here can readily account for the findings described above. Basically, this formulation says that aggressive thoughts brought to mind by another activity soon after an earlier aggression priming through news reports or violent movies can reactivate the aggressive ideas and inclinations that were produced by the media experience. Thus, Robert Smith's violent fantasies as he practiced shooting his pistol presumably reawakened and prolonged the aggressive priming that news stories of the Speck and Whitman crimes had generated.

What is more surprising is that certain kinds of apparently neutral stimuli in the surrounding environment can also reactivate an earlier movie-produced priming effect, even though the stimuli aren't obviously aggressive in nature.

Let me give you one example. After President Kennedy was killed in 1963 and his brother, Robert Kennedy, was shot in 1968, quite a few people seemed to believe that their surviving brother, Senator Edward Kennedy, would also be a likely target for an assassination attempt. The assumption was that the Senator's association with his murdered brothers could somehow prompt an emotionally disturbed person to attack him. To put this in another way, simply because of his name, either the sight of Ted Kennedy, or a story about him might reactivate the aggressive ideas and urges that had been evoked earlier by the reports of his brothers' deaths.[32]

Several Wisconsin experiments which I conducted with the help of my students suggest that this sort of reactivation was a very real possibility, but I will describe only the study Russell Geen and I published in 1966.

At the start of each experimental session, each male university student who participated in the study was first introduced to the experimenter's accomplice, who was posing as another subject. This "other student" was given one of three names—Bob *Kelly,* Bob *Dunne,* or Bob *Riley*—in order to vary the accomplice's name-mediated connection with a soon-to-be-shown aggression victim. In all cases the accomplice then provoked the naive subject by giving him a harsh evaluation of his performance on an assigned task. After this, following our usual procedure in this line of research, the subject was shown a six-minute film clip, either our standard prize fight scene from the movie *Champion* showing Kirk Douglas being beaten or an exciting but nonaggressive track race. At the end of the movie, he was given an opportunity to punish the accomplice with electric shocks (supposedly as his judgment of the quality of the accomplice's work on his task).

The accomplice's name associated him with one of the characters in the fight movie. When he was introduced as "Bob Kelly," his name essentially connected him with the *victim* of the witnessed aggression, since Kirk Douglas, the beaten fighter, was called "Midge Kelly" in the film. On the other hand, he was associated with a *successful aggressor* when his name was given as "Bob Dunne," because it was a character named "Dunne" who beat up Midge Kelly. Finally, since there was no one named "Riley" in the fight movie, "Bob Riley" had no name-mediated connection with the prize fight.

Figure 7–5 shows that the insulting accomplice's name actually influenced how many shocks he was given, but only after the subjects had watched the fight movie. All in all, he was attacked most severely when he was associated with the *victim* of the filmed aggression (a mean of 5.4 times, as compared to only slightly over 4 times for subjects who weren't dealing with a "victim-associated" target). The angry subjects in this experiment wanted to get even with their tormentor, had a good opportunity to do so, and set out to obtain their revenge—and their target's connection with someone they had seen being beaten up intensified their attacks upon him. It may be that, as they thought of this person, his association with someone else who had been aggressively injured strengthened their existing urge to hurt him.[33]

This experiment and other studies in which comparable results were obtained send a clear message: The aggressive tendencies generated by

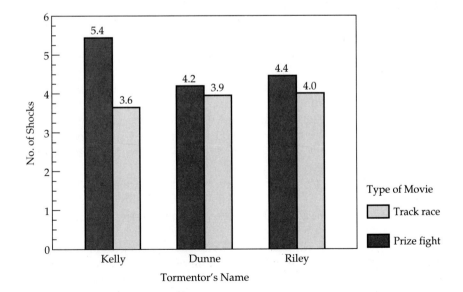

FIGURE 7-5

Mean number of shocks given to a tormentor as a function of his name and the type of movie he had previously seen. (Data from Geen & Berkowitz (1966). Name mediated aggressive cue properties, *Journal of Personality*, 34, copyright Duke University Press 1966. Reprinted with permission of the publisher.)

violent movies are not necessarily directed equally at everyone who happens to be present. Some kinds of people are more likely to be attacked than others.[34]

To return to the matter of Ted Kennedy, we don't know why he has, fortunately, escaped being the target of a crazed assault. Whatever may have protected him in the first few years after his brothers' deaths, my guess is that, with the passage of time, people have come to no longer automatically associate him with his brothers. The weakening of this spontaneous association lessens the chances that he will suffer the same fate.

One more point: Movie-activated aggressive thoughts and inclinations can also be reawakened by the sight of an inanimate object that just happens to be connected with the film. The object reminds the viewers of what they saw—and also revives the ideas that had occurred to them at that time as well as the feelings and motor tendencies they had then possessed. An experiment conducted by Wendy Josephson of the University of Manitoba in Winnipeg demonstrates the operation of external aggression-related cues.

Small groups of second- and third-grade Canadian schoolboys watched a short TV program that was either violent (a police action drama showing a SWAT team killing snipers) or nonviolent (a depiction of police officers coaching a motorbike racing team). The subjects were then taken to the school gym for a game of floor hockey. (All the children had also been frustrated earlier, supposedly by accident.) Just before the game began, an adult observer (who was blind to the group's experimental condition) interviewed each of the youngsters in the manner of a play-by-play sports announcer. The interviewer used a tape recorder with some subjects and a walkie-talkie with others. The important aspect of this variation is that a walkie-talkie was prominent in the violent movie. Presumably, the boys who had seen the violent film would be reminded of the aggression they had witnessed when they were interviewed with the walkie-talkie. Once the brief interviews were completed, a nine-minute hockey game began and two observers independently recorded every aggressive action they saw.

Josephson's major findings, simply put, showed that the most aggressive boys were the ones who had watched the violent film and then were exposed to the walkie-talkie (the aggression-associated cue). These youngsters didn't merely imitate the aggression that had been portrayed on the screen; they also elbowed, hit, and kneed each other. Of course, some of the children were especially susceptible to the influence of the aggressive stimuli. On examining her results more closely, Josephson suggested that the condition of TV violence plus the walkie-talkie reminder had led the most violence-prone boys in each group to become aggressive pretty quickly, and that their assaultive actions had provoked others to retaliate. For these boys, at least, the sight of the walkie-talkie had apparently reactivated the aggressive thoughts and motor tendencies that had been primed in them by the movie violence. These reactions were quick to occur, perhaps because of the frustration the children had experienced some minutes earlier as well as because of their aggressive personalities.[35]

Disinhibiting and Desensitizing Effects of Observed Aggression
The theoretical analysis I've been presenting obviously emphasizes the *inciting* (or instigating) influence of the violence depicted in the mass media: Witnessed or reported aggression activates (or generates) aggressive thoughts and action tendencies. Other writers, such as Bandura, have favored a somewhat different interpretation, contending that movie-produced aggression arises because of a *disinhibition*—a lowering of the viewers' existing inhibitions against aggression. It's as if the sight of others fighting makes it easier for aggressively disposed people in the audience to attack those who bother them, at least for a short time afterward.[36]

These two accounts of the effects of media violence seem different. Indeed, they can lead researchers in different directions—but they can also be reconciled, if we remember that the sight of people fighting can bring aggressive ideas to mind. I will present such a reconciliation in the next major section of this chapter, but first, let me call your attention to yet another effect of observed aggression.

Emotional blunting. Some experiments on media violence effects have yielded findings that may surprise you, because they seem to contradict the argument I have been advancing. According to several investigations, witnessed fighting and killing can give rise to an "emotional blunting," or *desensitization,* in which the audience becomes relatively indifferent to aggression. How can this be, if the viewers are supposedly stirred up by the mayhem and murder presented on the screen?

Research by Margaret Hanratty Thomas, Ronald Drabman, and their colleagues provides some of the best demonstrations of this desensitization effect. In one of their studies, children who had just watched an aggressive movie were later not especially concerned about other youngsters' fighting. In comparison to their counterparts in the control condition, they were fairly slow in attempting to stop the serious fighting between other children in an adjoining room. Consider how the viewers' thoughts could have led to this apparent indifference to aggression. With aggressive ideas actively in mind, the subjects who had watched the battling on the screen might have believed (temporarily) that it was fairly common for people to fight.

Just so, in yet another experiment, when schoolchildren were asked how other youngsters their age would react to several different conflict situations, the children who had been previously shown an aggressive movie expected their peers to be more aggressive than did their "controls" who had seen a neutral, nonviolent film.

Thomas and Drabman then went on to provide another indication of this seeming desensitization. If people believe aggression isn't unusual, they may not be shocked or even emotionally upset when they see others attacking and hitting each other. Consistent with such an argument, a prior viewing of a fictional aggressive scene led male college students to be less aroused physiologically by a news film showing an actual street riot. Interestingly, the researchers also found, the people who watched the greatest amount of violent television in their daily lives tended to exhibit the weakest physiological arousal in response to both fictional and realistic aggression.

The investigators' conclusion about this emotional change is a reasonable one. Their findings, they suggested, "lend credence to the suspicion that the excessive display of violence on television may be contributing to a population becoming increasingly inured to violence."

Movie-generated indifference to aggression, however, certainly does not mean that the viewers are less apt to attack someone else. Lessened arousal in response to the sight of fighting only indicates that the people in the audience are now not strongly bothered by aggression. As a matter of fact, since they are less anxious about violent behavior, they may actually be more likely to assault someone who provoked them earlier.[37]

Disinhibition and desensitization due to primed aggressive thoughts. Indications of movie-produced desensitization to aggression can be explained in priming terms. All kinds of aggressive ideas are undoubtedly activated when people see fighting, shooting, and killing portrayed on the screen. As long as the viewers aren't repelled or made anxious by what they see, a violent movie may well generate hostile thoughts about others. Some viewers may be led to think that many people are apt to behave aggressively, and a disinhibition may even be produced in these viewers, because of their temporary belief that aggression is proper and acceptable in lots of different situations. It's because of instigated thoughts such as these that violent TV programming may be contributing to an increasing desensitization to violence in the population as a whole.

THE PROLONGED INFLUENCE OF REPEATED EXPOSURE TO MEDIA VIOLENCE

If parents could buy packaged psychological influences to administer in regular doses to their children, I doubt that many would deliberately select Western gun slingers [sic], hopped-up psychopaths, deranged sadists, slapstick [sic] buffoons, and the like, unless they entertained rather peculiar ambitions for their growing offspring. Yet such examples of behavior are delivered in quantity, with no direct charge, to millions of households daily. . . . Today's youth is being raised on a heavy dosage of televised aggression and violence.[38]

This passage is a clear indictment of television programming. Even back in 1963, Bandura was convinced that at least some children acquire socially unfortunate values and antisocial modes of conduct by watching the behavior of the "Western gun slingers, hopped-up psychopaths, deranged sadists . . . and the like" who are so frequently depicted on network TV. Though psychologists are still debating about just how strong this adverse influence really is, the research that has been conducted in the three decades since Bandura wrote this statement does not require any substantial change in his argument.[39] A "heavy dosage of televised aggression" can shape many youngsters' abiding view of their social world and their beliefs about how it is best to act in dealing with others.

Shaping Children's Conceptions of the Social World

The Cultivation Thesis

I've already noted that children's ideas about other people can be temporarily affected by violent movies. After watching aggression on the screen, many of them believe that their peers are also apt to act aggressively when they are in conflict with others. In the Thomas-Drabman experiment described above, this expectation was produced by only one film and was probably short-lived.[40] Isn't it likely that the expectation of aggression will become even stronger if children see violence on their TV sets day after day? The commercial networks in the United States certainly do paint a picture of a world full of murder and mayhem. According to George Gerbner and his associates at the University of Pennsylvania's Annenberg School of Communication, in 1989 seven out of ten prime-time TV programs showed at least some violent actions.

Doesn't all this violence have an impact upon children's conception of the people around them? According to the Gerbner team, the answer is decidedly "yes." The frequent depictions of evil and violence on television, they say, "cultivate" a long-lasting impression of the world as untrustworthy, wicked, and hazardous.

Gerbner's *cultivation thesis* seems reasonable, but it may be overstated. These Pennsylvania researchers have reported several surveys showing that people who watch a great deal of television tend to overestimate the amount of violence in society and to believe the social world is generally dangerous. In contrast, similar studies by other investigators in the United States, Australia, Canada, and Great Britain have noted important exceptions. In sum, some people who look at much television do have an exaggerated impression of the dangers in their social environment, but this "paranoid" picture of the world isn't as widespread as the cultivation thesis implies. The truth may be, then, that television can influence one's general beliefs about the surrounding world but that the cultivation effect is fairly modest across the television audience as a whole.[41]

Still, it's a mistake to say that television has no influence on children's impressions of the world about them. Consider an experiment by Bryant, Carveth, and Brown, in which undergraduates were asked to look at specially selected TV programs with a specified frequency over a six-week period. Some of the students were given a light schedule, calling for relatively little viewing, whereas the others were assigned a much heavier schedule, emphasizing at least twenty-eight hours a week of action-adventure programs. At the end of the six weeks, the subjects who had been exposed to the heavy dose of action-adventure programs (which of course contained a good deal of violence) had come to think of the world as more dangerous than had their light-viewing counterparts. As compared to the "controls," the heavy viewers believed that there was a greater chance that they themselves would be victims of violence.[42]

These findings should be understood in a broader context. Television is one of many possible sources of information about the social world. Some persons don't watch television often and thus have less chance to absorb its image of society as full of evil and danger. Others may see much more television, but the people they know—their parents, friends, and neighbors—don't act like the characters in the TV stories: the TV characters are aggressive and untrustworthy, while the people in *their* social world are friendly and supportive. Because these viewers consider TV stories to be decidedly unreal, they reject television as an accurate depictor of life.

Some other people, however, are much more susceptible to the information conveyed by TV programs. These viewers are apt to be youths from underprivileged families. Relatively young and uneducated, they are inclined to think of the TV stories as realistic. They readily accept television's portrayal of people as untrustworthy, mean, and dangerous, especially if the significant people in their lives also behave inconsistently and harshly toward them. The more often such children encounter network television's negative picture of the social world, the more strongly this picture becomes implanted in their minds, particularly since they are not concurrently acquiring other, clearly contradictory information.[43]

Acquiring Aggressive Inclinations

Besides conveying an impression of what the world is like, television can also teach susceptible youngsters how to act in such a threatening environment. The National Commission on the Causes and Prevention of

Violence pointed this out in 1969. When the leading characters in TV stories assault someone, the Violence Commission noted, more often than not the attack produces a successful outcome. "Violence is [frequently] . . . portrayed as a legitimate means for attaining desired ends."[44] Some children take this lesson to heart.

The Eron-Huesmann Group's Research on the Long-Term Effects of TV Violence The Violence Commission's conclusion is now supported by a considerable body of research too detailed and too numerous to be reviewed here. In the interests of brevity, I'll concentrate on the findings obtained by Leonard Eron, Rowell Huesmann, and their colleagues in studies conducted in the United States and other countries.[45]

The Columbia County study. The Columbia County study, which was summarized in Chapter 5, offers some of the best evidence of the long-term consequences of a heavy dosage of televised violence. The Eron team, you'll recall, collected a good deal of information about the daily behavior of all the children in the third-grade population of Columbia County, New York, a semirural area in the Hudson River Valley, from the youngsters themselves, from their classmates, and from their parents. The children were then followed up to see how they acted as they grew up and what happened to them by the time they reached adulthood. As I have already said, the principal measure of each subject's usual aggressiveness was based on how this individual was seen by his or her schoolmates. What is especially important in the context of the present discussion is that the researchers also ascertained (in the third grade and again ten years later) the extent to which the children liked to watch violent TV shows.[46]

As a number of other investigators also found, the most aggressive third-graders in Columbia County—girls as well as boys—were the ones who most preferred violent TV programs. But does this mean only that aggressive children liked watching people assault each other? Or did the sight of fighting contribute to the youths' aggressiveness? To answer this question, the psychologists went to a subsample of 211 boys for whom they had complete data and calculated the correlation between the third-grade viewing preferences of these boys and their aggressiveness ten years later. The findings are interesting. The boys' aggressiveness in third grade did *not* forecast their TV preferences ten years later. Their levels of aggressiveness had tended to persist over the decade, but their tastes in television programming had changed by the time they were 19 years old. Nevertheless, the third grade boys who exhibited the strongest preferences for violent shows—who presumably watched the violent programs often—grew up to be the nastiest and most assaultive young men in the sample. The researchers also demonstrated that a preference for violent programming in third grade was a significant predictor of the boys' aggressiveness ten years later, even when their initial level of aggressiveness was held constant statistically—a finding that provided additional support for their theoretical position. The frequent viewing of televised violence had apparently contributed to the development of a pattern of assaultive conduct, independently of how aggressive the youths were as very young boys.

Figure 7–6 carries this analysis further. As you'll remember from the discussions of aggressive personalities in Part 2, highly aggressive individuals tend to be antisocial in a variety of ways and are more likely to engage in illegal behavior than are their better behaved peers. Frequent exposure to violent TV shows might therefore be expected to contribute to a criminal tendency as well as to a violent disposition, and this is evidently the case. The 8-year-old boys who had the strongest preference for violent programs were the ones who were most likely to have been convicted of a serious crime by the time they reached age 30.

The results of cross-national research: the five-nation study. Eron and Huesmann didn't stop with the findings I described above. Since most studies of the effects of media violence have been carried out in the United States, they wanted to know whether the same results would be obtained in other nations. They realized that other societies might have very different attitudes toward aggression and that the frequent sight of people fighting might therefore not have the same consequences everywhere.

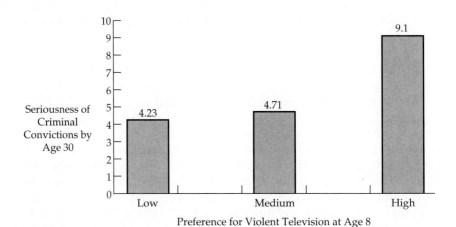

FIGURE 7-6

Relationship between a boy's preference for violent television shows at age 8 and the seriousness of his criminal convictions by age 30. (From Huesmann (1986). Copyright 1986 by Society for the Psychological Study of Social Issues. Reprinted by permission.)

Working with psychologists from four other countries, Eron and Huesmann organized a collaborative, three-year investigation in Australia, Finland, Israel, and Poland, as well as in a suburb of Chicago, to see whether the Columbia County results could be replicated. As in the earlier project, schoolchildren and their parents were repeatedly interviewed and tested. At the end of the project, in 1982, the researchers found that the new results duplicated their earlier findings in important respects—but that there were also some intriguing and suggestive differences.

Several of the TV viewing measures were positively related to the children's aggressiveness in all the countries, although the correlations weren't always significant (partly because some of the samples were fairly small in size). Across the entire project, the most assaultive children, in comparison to their less aggressive counterparts, exhibited the following characteristics: They tended to (1) watch more television in general, (2) were more apt to prefer violent programs, (3) typically identified themselves with the TV characters to a greater extent, and (4) thought that the violent actions shown on television were more lifelike.

Although these correlations were an encouraging confirmation of the Columbia County findings, the psychologists sought better evidence that watching television plays a part in the development of children's antisocial conduct. Since a person's aggressive disposition tends to be fairly stable over the years, they realized, any given child's assaultive behavior at the start of the study should predict *to some extent* how aggressive he or she would be three years later. They sought to discover whether information about the youngster's initial TV viewing would increase the accuracy of this forecast above the predictability achieved by knowledge of initial aggressiveness alone. If so, it would appear that the children's exposure to television had contributed something to their later antisocial behavior pattern.

Although there were some exceptions, the researchers did obtain the evidence they wanted: "In the United States, Poland, [and] Finland, and among Israeli city children, early TV habits significantly predicted the aggressiveness of [the] children even when the children's initial aggressiveness was statistically controlled."[47]

These results do not mean, of course, that television is the only or even the major influence on the growing child's conduct. As a matter of fact, the psychologists who conducted this collaborative study found that parental behavior was also related to the youngsters' assaultiveness. In most of the countries that participated in the project, the more aggressive children tended to have harsher, and particularly more rejecting, mothers and fathers. Judging from the statistical analysis, the parents' treatment of their offspring was affected by how the children acted toward them. Even so, the frustrations and punishments the parents administered undoubtedly also influenced the youngsters' aggressiveness, at least to some degree.

Understanding Why: The Formation of Social Scripts

The results, together with the findings of other studies that have reported similar outcomes, provide support for the fundamental validity of the stance I have taken in this chapter. Repeated exposure to a heavy dose of violence on television has no social benefits and may even help to form antisocial modes of conduct. However, as I've noted several times, witnessed aggression does not always promote aggressive behavior. Moreover, since the relationship between TV viewing and aggressiveness is far from perfect, it can also be said that the frequent sight of people fighting on television doesn't *necessarily* lead to development of a highly aggressive personality in a given person. In order to understand why frequent heavy doses of TV violence influence some children's aggressive tendencies and what circumstances weaken, or heighten, this effect, we must establish an adequate theory of the learning that occurs when children see people hit, shoot, and kill each other on TV screens.

A "Script-Theoretical" Conception of the Effects of TV Violence

Rowell Huesmann has recently advanced an analysis of the effects of media violence that seems very promising.[48] Making use of psychological concepts of how people receive, process, and retain information, Huesmann basically holds that young TV viewers develop a way of understanding aggression as they watch assaults and fighting on the screen. Cognitive psychologists would say the viewers develop a script that guides their expectations in relevant situations—in this case, expectations about what produces aggression as well as expectations about the likely consequences of this behavior—and thus provides a strategy for dealing with certain social problems. When these youngsters next encounter a difficulty with other persons, the aggression script predicts what is likely to happen and prescribes the best way to act under the circumstances. People who have developed strongly aggressive scripts are likely to choose an aggressive course of action as the best way of resolving a problem.

Agreeing with Bandura's earlier "social learning" formulation, Huesmann emphasizes that children's social strategies (i.e., their scripts) can be derived at least partly from observation of other people's behavior, whether they see this behavior "in the flesh" or on the television screen. Huesmann also recognizes something else that is in accord with Bandura's analysis: that certain prerequisites are necessary if televised violence is to give rise to these aggressive conceptions. First, the viewers have to *pay attention* to the actions depicted on the screen. They don't have to notice and think about *everything* that's happening before them, but the violent events have to stand out in their minds. Very much in accord with my own analysis of the factors that influence reactions to media violence, Huesmann proposes that an aggressive scene will be highly salient to certain observers if they regard the occurrence as realistic and if they identify with the make-believe aggressor.

They also have to *interpret* (or "encode") what they see in an appropriate manner. The youngsters are particularly likely to form an aggression-facilitating script in their minds, for example, if they think of the aggression they see as "good" and "successful" behavior.

However, whatever its exact nature, this conception may well fade from memory if the TV watchers don't occasionally "rehearse" the notions they have developed. Thus, it is also necessary to consider what influences the children's *retention* of the TV-induced script. The more the viewers practice and remind themselves of what they have learned, either in their imaginations or in realistic behavior, the more strongly the script becomes implanted in their memories. Further, the more varied the nature of their rehearsals, the greater will be the range of situations to which they will apply the script. For example, Robert Smith (the man who shot up the Arizona beauty parlor) rehearsed the violent script he had acquired from the Speck and Whitman news stories as he practiced shooting his pistol.

It's not enough, though, for the script to be only stored in memory. It must be *activated* in order to exert an overt influence. In accord with the priming analysis offered earlier, Huesmann holds that certain cues (or features of the surrounding environment) can bring a viewer's existing script to mind and set it into operation. Merely the sight of people fighting or of a weapon can activate an aggressive behavior script which has been acquired through the years. Similarly, soon after a person has looked at a violent TV show, relevant situational cues can reawaken the already established script very easily, because it is still somewhat fresh in the person's mind.

All in all, Huesmann concludes, media violence "provides examples of new aggressive scripts to be acquired, and cues the use of existing specific or general aggressive scripts."[49] You can see why it is highly aggressive people who are most strongly affected by violent movies. They have the most strongly learned and the most generalized aggressive scripts stored away in their memories, and their existing scripts are readily activated by the fighting on the screen (the aggressive cue). However, don't forget that most people, even those among us who are not highly aggressive, have acquired *some* aggressive conceptions and strategies in the course of growing up. Violent films can activate our scripts as well, at least to some degree, especially if we don't have any interfering thoughts at the time.

It should be clear from this summary that not only is script theory entirely compatible with the priming analysis advanced earlier in this chapter but also the priming formulation can be encompassed within the more general script approach. The priming stimulus is a cue that activates certain ideas and action tendencies, which are located within a relevant, already acquired script. These two theoretical conceptions were presented separately because the priming notion emphases the short-term consequences of observed aggression, whereas script theory focuses on the long-term effects. Despite the different emphases of these two lines of analysis, they are highly compatible.

Mitigating the Harmful Influence of Violent Television
Both Huesmann's theoretical analysis and the findings he, Eron, and their colleagues have obtained (as well as the results other researchers have reported) suggest a number of factors that can affect the degree to which repeatedly observed violence contributes to antisocial patterns of conduct. The five-nation study which I mentioned earlier points to one possibility.

TV viewing wasn't related to children's aggressiveness level in Australia, nor was it related among Israeli children from a kibbutz (although the relationship did exist for Israeli city dwellers). While it's not clear what dampened the effects of television in the Australian sample, the researchers suggested (very reasonably it seems to me) that the kibbutz society's attitude toward aggression had overcome the adverse effects of the witnessed violence. Not only did the kibbutz youngsters see relatively few aggressive programs, but when these violent shows were encountered, there was apt to be a group discussion of the social implications of fighting, shooting, and killing.[50] Whatever ideas the violent programs might have instilled in the children at first, the subsequent discussions probably left them with little doubt that it is improper to resolve one's social problems by attacking other people.

Isn't there is a lesson here for all of us? When children watch a TV program full of assaults and murders, shouldn't adults remind their young charges that aggression isn't a desirable way to deal with one's interpersonal difficulties?

An experiment with Chicago-area schoolchildren, reported by Huesmann, Eron, and others as part of the five-nation project, also testifies to the importance of young viewers' attitudes toward televised violence. Following their script-theory formulation, these psychologists carried out two training sessions in which children were induced to become highly aware of the undesirability of imitating the aggressive behavior portrayed on television. This was done mainly by having the youngsters develop and then think about reasons why the depicted violence was bad. Four months later, when the researchers compared these youngsters with peers in a control condition, the psychologists found that the trained children were less aggressive in dealing with classmates than were their counterparts. What is equally important theoretically is that in this experimental condition there was no correlation between how much violence the children watched on television and how assaultive they were, although such a relationship did exist among the untrained, control group youngsters. The two training sessions had apparently inoculated the trained children against the harmful effects of the fighting and killing depicted on TV. Though they had been exposed to the same amounts of violence as the untrained children, they were less apt to accept TV's socially unfortunate messages because they had developed an unfavorable attitude toward violent behavior.[51]

Now that you have accompanied me on this journey through the research literature, I wonder whether you don't share my agreement with two concluding comments made by the National Commission on the Causes and Prevention of Violence. One statement rebuked the commercial networks: "Television entertainment based on violence may be effective merchandising, but it is an appalling way to serve a civilization." The other advised parents: "Parents should make every effort to supervise their children's television viewing and to assert their basic responsibility for the moral development of their children."[52] Research and common sense tell us that parents—and educators—can do a great deal to minimize the harmful influences of TV programming. At the very least, they can help children to realize that aggression is undesirable, even when it is carried out by a "hero," and that it is far better to solve our problems peaceably.

SUMMARY

The public at large and even some media specialists believe that depictions of violence on movie and TV screens and in the print media have at most a very minor effect on audience members. Further, they think that only children or mentally deranged viewers are susceptible to even this minor effect. However, the majority of researchers who have investigated media effects and/or who have carefully studied the pertinent research literature believe otherwise. In this chapter, I show that: (1) Portrayals and even news reports of violence increase the chances that people in the media audience, adults as well as children, will behave aggressively themselves. (2) This influence is not trivial, especially when one considers that many millions of persons are ordinarily exposed to the media. (3) Psychological concepts that are becoming well accepted can help to identify the factors that heighten or weaken the likelihood of aggressive reactions.

The mass media can have both short-lived and long-lasting influences on their audiences. This chapter starts with a consideration of the immediate and transient effects of media violence. I first note the growing evidence of copycat crimes, focusing largely on David Phillips' investigations of the "contagion" of suicides and homicides, in order to show how pervasive and subtle the media's influence can be. I then turn to experimental investigations of short-lived effects, citing several research reviews which indicate that witnessed aggression can have a small to moderate influence on subjects' behavior. This effect has been demonstrated both when the actions involved were realistic and when subjects in experiments have been asked to perform acts in the laboratory that were supposedly artificial in nature.

Applying the priming-effect concept, I suggest that media reports or depictions of violence can activate aggression-related ideas and action tendencies in the audience members. These aggressive ideas and inclinations will be activated, however, only to the extent that the media-presented material has a relevant meaning for the recipients. According to available research, witnessed violence is most likely to increase the probability of aggressive behavior by people in the audience under the following conditions: (1) They don't see the violence being punished or having adverse consequences for the aggressor. (2) They don't regard the violence as improper or unjustified. (3) They identify with the observed aggressors, imagining themselves to be the aggressors. (4) They focus their attention on the aggression rather than on other aspects of the witnessed occurrence. (5) They do not distance themselves psychologically from what they see or hear, for example by telling themselves the observed event isn't real.

Even though the primed ideas and behavioral inclinations usually subside with the passage of time, later happenings can reactivate the thoughts and action tendencies. Situational cues that remind viewers of violence they have previously seen, read about, or heard about can reawaken earlier aggression-related cognitions and impulses, at least to some degree.

I suggest that the frequently discussed desensitizing and disinhibiting influences of media violence may well be caused by primed aggressive thoughts. Observed aggression may make viewers relatively indifferent to violence generally and/or more willing to assault others in their own lives. Because the violent scene has given them aggression-related ideas, they are led to believe, for a short while, that aggression is both fairly common and often appropriate.

Next, I discuss the possible consequences of repeated viewing of violent scenes. I propose a modified and less extreme version of Gerbner's cultivation thesis. I hold that people who are frequently exposed to violent events in the mass media will tend to believe that violence is more prevalent in their social world than is actually the case, but that this perception will develop only to the extent that they do not encounter other, contradictory information from the people they know in the real world.

Repeated exposure to violent scenes on television may also help to foster aggressive modes of conduct among children. Although a number of investigations have pointed to such a possibility (and some others have reported contrary findings), I employ the results of the Columbia County project and the five-nation replication by Leonard Eron, Rowell

Huesmann, and their associates to document this thesis. Generally speaking, and although there are some exceptions, there is a significant chance that children who watch a good deal of violent TV programming will grow up to be unusually aggressive adults.

Huesmann's script-theory formulation (which is somewhat similar to Bandura's earlier social learning analysis) is useful in pulling together the various ideas presented in this chapter. Youngsters who frequently watch portrayals of violence in the media can learn aggressive scripts which tell them that aggression is a common and appropriate way of dealing with interpersonal problems. Children are especially likely to acquire these scripts if they pay close attention to the witnessed violence and if they are not told by the important persons in their lives that aggression is undesirable behavior. Parents, educators, and the mass media can and should take steps to mitigate the harmful consequences of heavy doses of violence on TV and movie screens.

NOTES

1. *Wall Street Journal*, Apr. 2, 1981.
2. See statements by the Surgeon General, TV industry officials, and several researchers in testimony before the Subcommittee on Communications of the U.S. Senate, March 21–24, 1972 [Communications Subcommittee (1972)]. The Surgeon General's Advisory Committee on Television and Social Behavior recognized that there were ambiguities and even flaws in individual studies but nevertheless concluded that the *total pattern* of the findings of hundreds of investigations, which employed diverse samples of participants and greatly different procedures, pointed to a "causal relationship between extensive viewing of violence and later aggressive behavior" [Rubenstein (1978), p. 686].
3. These statistics are taken from George Gerbner's report, *Violence profile 1967–1989: Enduring patterns,* as summarized in the *Wisconsin State Journal,* Jan. 26, 1990.
4. *Wisconsin State Journal*, Apr. 3, 1981; *Capital Times*, Apr. 1, 1981.
5. These cases are cited in Berkowitz & Macaulay (1971).
6. Tarde (1912), pp. 340–341.
7. Berkowitz & Macaulay (1971).
8. Phillips (1974). Besides reviewing a number of sociological studies of the possible role of suggestion in suicides, this paper provides the details of Phillips' analytic procedures, such as how he estimated the amount of newspaper coverage given to any single story. Also see Phillips (1986). The news media sometimes play a role in the contagion of adolescent suicides. In an investigation that made use of national statistics, Phillips & Carstensen (1986) demonstrated that news or feature stories about suicides on the three major TV networks led to a higher-than-expected nationwide increase in the number of adolescents who took their own lives during the following week. Moreover, this effect did not occur only in response to newspaper coverage;

the greater the number of TV news programs that carried the story, the greater was the subsequent increase in teenage suicides around the country.

9. Phillips (1979). A disproportionate share of the higher-than-expected number of deaths occurred in single-vehicle accidents rather than in multiple-car crashes.

10. For example, among several other critics, Kessler & Stipp (1984) maintained that there was a serious methodological flaw in a study by Phillips of the effects of fictional suicide stories in daytime TV soap operas (this study was not mentioned in this chapter). Phillips (1986) has answered some of the major criticisms leveled at his research.

11. Phillips (1986).

12. Freedman (1984) has questioned the adequacy of the evidence that points to the aggression-enhancing effects of movie violence, mostly by emphasizing what he regards as inconsistencies in the findings. His critique has been answered by Friedrich-Cofer & Huston (1986) and by Phillips (1986), p. 236. In my view, Freedman did not give sufficient weight to the degree to which the results of various studies (which employed different kinds of viewers, different movies, and different measures) converged to demonstrate somewhat similar effects.

13. Andison (1977).

14. Wood, Wong, & Chachere (1991).

15. Leyens, Camino, Parke, & Berkowitz (1975). A report on the larger Wisconsin project, which described two field experiments carried out in Wisconsin as well as the Belgian study described here and four laboratory experiments, can be found in Parke, Berkowitz, Leyens, West, & Sebastian (1977).

16. Wood, Wong, & Chachere (1991), p. 379. That the findings obtained with the more natural-appearing aggression measures are similar to those obtained with the supposedly "artificial" laboratory indicators of aggression supports the validity of the laboratory indexes. Additional evidence of the validity of laboratory indexes is presented in Chapter 13 of this book, as well as in Carlson, Marcus-Newhall, & Miller (1989).

17. The most detailed statement of my theoretical formulation can be found in Berkowitz (1984). Other psychologists, needless to say, have advanced somewhat different interpretations of the effects of filmed violence. See, for example, Bandura (1973); Zillmann (1979); Huesmann & Malamuth (1986).

18. Carver, Ganellen, Froming, & Chambers (1983).

19. Gale, W., *New York Times,* Mar. 30, 1975.

20. Turner & Layton (1976).

21. Bushman & Geen (1990). The researchers also found that the men who had relatively strong inclinations to be physically assaultive, as assessed by the Buss-Durkee assault scale, were especially likely to have aggressive thoughts when they were exposed to the moderately violent scene. Wann & Branscombe (1989) explicitly employed the priming concept in their investigation of the effects of sports. Instead of having their subjects actually watch a certain kind of game, they gave the participants a sentence construction task that brought either aggressive sports (e.g., boxing) or nonaggressive sports (e.g., golf) to mind. When the subjects later judged an ambiguous target person, the subjects who had been primed with the names of aggressive

sports were more likely to regard the target as having both a hostile personality and a strong preference for aggressive activities.

22. The first-mentioned football study was conducted by Goldstein & Arms (1971). Arms, Russell, & Sandilands (1979) also found indications of increased aggressiveness after a hockey game and a wrestling match but not after a swim meet. The second experiment mentioned here was conducted by Berkowitz & Alioto (1973).

23. As summarized in Berkowitz (1984), p. 421, Richard Goranson found that people who saw a prize fight tended to become *less* aggressive than did subjects in the control condition, when they were told that the loser in the prize fight died as a result of the beating he had received in the contest. A reminder that aggression can have very unfortunate consequences apparently activates restraints against hurting someone else.

24. The original experiment showing that viewers who have watched supposedly "justified" aggression are more willing to assault another person than they otherwise would have been is described in Berkowitz and Rawlings (1963). The experiment reported in this particular section is Berkowitz (1965), Experiment III. The studies that obtained comparable findings are listed in Berkowitz (1984), p. 421.

25. Leyens & Picus (1973).

26. Leyens, Cisneros, & Hossay (1976).

27. James, C. *New York Times,* May 27, 1990.

28. See Feshbach (1972); Geen (1975); Geen & Rakosky (1973). Also see Berkowitz (1984), pp. 422–423.

29. See Liebert & Sprafkin (1988), pp. 89–90. The *Commission Statement on Violence in Television Entertainment Programs,* which was published by the National Commission on the Causes and Prevention of Violence, made an observation in 1969 that is still relevant a generation later: "Many young children are inclined to believe that the world they see portrayed on television is a reflection of the real world. The ability to differentiate between fact and fiction naturally increases with age and maturity, but it also appears to be a function of the child's particular social environment. . . . Young children and a large proportion of teenagers from low income families believe that people behave in the real world the way they do in the fictional world of television" (1969a, p. 6).

30. Buvinic & Berkowitz (1976) reported a diminution in the effect of observed violence within an hour, while Doob & Climie (1972) obtained similar results with nonangered subjects. Yet another demonstration of how quickly the priming effect can disappear in social situations is provided by Wilson & Capitman (1982).

31. In the study by Buvinic & Berkowitz (1976), the overt aggression displayed by insulted subjects who saw a violent film clip did not lessen after an hour if the subjects were given an opportunity to express their preliminary opinions of their tormentor following the film but before they had the opportunity to attack the tormentor. The symbolic verbal aggression apparently helped to prolong the aggressive thoughts and inclinations that had been activated by the sight of the filmed violence.

32. According to the journalist Tom Wicker (1991), Robert Kennedy suspected

that he might be a target for assassination. He had told a French writer that he might be killed "through contagion, through emulation" of other murders (p. 326). Senator Kennedy's association with his slain older brother conceivably could have helped implant the idea to kill him in his murderer's mind. There's some evidence that the youngest Kennedy's (Ted's) name-mediated association with his martyred two older brothers had raised the chance that he too would be the victim of criminal violence. Writing in 1972, the syndicated newspaper columnist Hy Gardner (in his column "Glad You Asked," Sept. 17, 1972) reported that Ted Kennedy received more threats in the period between his brother John's assassination in late 1963 and the end of 1971 than did anyone else in the nation. According to the Secret Service, 355 of these threats seemed to be so serious that they were investigated.

33. Geen & Berkowitz (1966). Also see Berkowitz (1984), p. 422; Carlson, Marcus-Newhall, & Miller (1990).

34. As yet another demonstration of this effect, more than a generation ago [Berkowitz (1965), Experiment III], I found that a person who had an aggressive meaning, because he supposedly was a member of the University of Wisconsin's boxing team, tended to evoke the strongest attacks from people who had just watched a prize fight movie. This happened, furthermore, even when the subjects had not been provoked by this individual. His mere connection with aggression evidently strengthened the aggressive ideas and inclinations that had been activated by the aggressive scene.

35. Josephson (1987).

36. See Thomas, Horton, Lippincott, & Drabman (1977); Liebert & Sprafkin (1988), p. 138.

37. Evidence for this can be seen in Thomas (1982). The above quotation is from Thomas, Horton et al. (1977), p. 457.

38. Albert Bandura wrote this in 1963. Cited in Liebert & Sprafkin (1988), pp. 9–10.

39. Cook, Kendzierski, & Thomas (1983) suggested that television may possibly have harmful effects but that its adverse influence may be somewhat less than many psychologists suppose. Freedman (1984) and McGuire (1986) voiced even stronger doubts, contending that television has, at most, only a "trivial" influence on subsequent aggressiveness. Friedrich-Cofer & Huston (1986) answered many of Freedman's arguments. Liebert & Sprafkin (1988) reviewed many studies that had investigated the possible long-term effects of repeated exposure to TV violence. They generally concluded that there is fairly good evidence that a heavy dosage of TV violence can have socially unfortunate consequences. Turner, Hesse, & Peterson-Lewis (1986) also looked at the published investigations and attempted to reconcile the negative and positive findings. They too maintain that repeated exposure to media violence tends to enhance the likelihood of aggressive conduct.

40. Experiment by Thomas & Drabman (1977), summarized in Liebert & Sprafkin (1988), p. 138. Also see research by Harvey Hornstein, which was cited in Berkowitz (1984).

41. For the relevant citations, see Berkowitz (1984); Liebert & Sprafkin (1988); Rule & Ferguson (1986). Also see Cook, Kendzierski, & Thomas (1983) for a somewhat skeptical view of the cultivation thesis.

42. Reported in Liebert & Sprafkin (1988), pp. 139–140.

43. Jerome Singer and Dorothy Singer (1986) found that the youngsters who were the most frequent viewers of TV action-adventure programs tended to be disproportionately poor, nonwhite, and of below average IQ.

44. National Commission on Causes and Prevention of Violence (1969), p. 194.

45. See in particular, Eron (1982); Eron, Huesmann, Lefkowitz, & Walder (1972); Huesmann (1986); Huesmann & Eron (1986).

46. The children's preferences for violent programming during the third grade were determined on the basis of the mothers' reports of their offsprings' three favorite TV shows, while their preferences ten years later were based on the subjects' own reports of their favorite programs at that time. The resulting scores reflected the number of violent TV shows among the three favorite programs. See Eron et al. (1972).

47. See the article by Huesmann in Huesmann & Eron (1986), p. 242.

48. See Huesmann (1986). Also see the chapters by Huesmann and Eron in Huesmann & Eron (1986).

49. Huesmann (1986), p. 133.

50. Huesmann & Eron (1986), p. 242.

51. Huesmann, Eron, Klein, Brice, & Fischer (1983).

52. National Commission on the Causes and Prevention of Violence (1969a), pp. 11, 10, respectively.

8

Domestic Violence

———— ❖ ————

Explaining Domestic Violence ◆ *Perspectives on Domestic Violence* ◆ *Factors that Can Promote Domestic Violence* ◆ *Research Indications*

W e like to think of our families as providing shelter against the stresses and strains of an uncertain world. Whatever threats may exist outside the home, we hope to find safety and support in the love of those with whom we have our most intimate relationships. "Where can one better be than in the bosom of one's family," says an old French song. For many individuals, however, this yearning is not fulfilled. The people with whom they live are a source of danger rather than security.

Chapter 1 gave you an indication of this. According to the National Family Violence Survey—a study of a nationally representative sample of American families, which was carried out by New Hampshire sociologists Murray Straus, Richard Gelles, and Suzanne Steinmetz—in more than one U.S. household in six, a spouse physically struck his or her partner at least once during the year 1975. Children were beaten in 60 percent of homes. The second National Family Violence Survey, which was conducted a decade later, in 1985, found approximately the same incidence of physical violence among American couples. Most of the violence was relatively minor, and was restricted to pushing, shoving, or slapping, but some aggressive incidents were much more serious and involved kicking, punching, biting, or even choking. On the basis of their findings in the 1985 survey, Straus and Gelles estimated that more than three million married couples experienced one or more severe assaults in which there was a relatively high risk of injury. They also calculated that one out of eight American women had been assaulted by her husband or partner in the twelve months covered by the survey. The women had been attacked, on the average, about six times during the year. Family life isn't necessarily more peaceful for children. Judging from other information collected in the 1985 survey, one out of ten American children is severely assaulted each year.[1] Some of the major findings obtained by Straus and Gelles are shown in Table 8-1.

The Bureau of Justice Statistics publishes results of still other measures of violence in U.S. homes. I'll mention only one figure. According to the bureau's 1987 national survey of crime victimization, when a person was illegally assailed by another individual, the offender was a relative in approximately 20 percent of the cases.[2]

We really shouldn't be surprised at the high levels of domestic violence. People who live together in a close relationship will inevitably rub each other the wrong way every once in a while. Families are highly interdependent, social scientists would say, and are bound to disappoint each other or come into conflict at one time or another. Yet the potential for violence isn't always realized; quite a few families remain relatively harmonious, or at least don't develop open civil war. Why this difference?

EXPLAINING DOMESTIC VIOLENCE

Perspectives on Domestic Violence

Social workers and physicians have been largely responsible for the nation's current concern about domestic violence, starting in the 1960s and early 1970s. Not surprisingly, because of these professionals' training and outlook, the initial attempts to analyze wife beating and child abuse were typically couched in individual-oriented medical or psychiatric terms, and much of the early research sought to determine what personal qualities drove abusers to assault their spouses and/or offspring.

The focus broadened, however, as other social scientists, and especially sociologists, turned their attention to aggression within families. There was a greater recognition of the part played by societal influences, especially by society's norms and values regarding who should be dominant in the family and how authority could properly be enforced. To mention only one example, in *Violence against Wives*, which was published in 1979, Emerson Dobash and Russell Dobash attributed wife beating in large part to men's learning that they could beat their spouses in order to preserve their traditionally superior position. "Men who assault their wives," Dobash and Dobash maintained, "are actually living up to cultural prescriptions that are cherished in Western society—aggressiveness, male dominance, and female subordination—and they are using

TABLE 8-1 ANNUAL INCIDENCE RATES FOR FAMILY VIOLENCE AND
ESTIMATED NUMBER OF CASES BASED ON THESE RATES

Type of intrafamily violence[1]	Rate per 1000 couples or children	Number assaulted[2]
A. Violence between husband and wife		
Any violence during the year (slapping, pushing, etc.)	161	8,700,000
Severe violence (kicking, punching, stabbing, etc.)	63	3,400,000
Any violence by the husband	116	6,250,000
Severe violence by the husband ("wife beating")	34	1,800,000
Any violence by the wife	124	6,800,000
Severe violence by the wife	48	2,600,000
B. Violence by parents—children aged 0–17		
Any hitting of child during the year	Near 100% for young child[3]	
Very severe violence ("Child Abuse-1")[4]	23	1,500,000
Severe violence ("Child Abuse-2")[5]	110	6,900,000
C. Violence by parents—children aged 15–17		
Any violence	340	3,800,000
Severe violence	70	800,000
Very severe violence	21	235,000
D. Violence by children aged 3–17		
Any violence against a brother or sister	800	50,400,000
Severe violence against a brother or sister	530	33,300,000
Any violence against a parent	180	9,700,000
Severe violence against a parent	90	4,800,000
E. Violence by children aged 15–17		
Any violence against a brother or sister	640	7,200,000
Severe violence against a brother or sister	360	4,000,000
Any violence against a parent	100	1,100,000
Severe violence against a parent	35	400,000

[1] *Section A* rates are based on the entire sample of 6002 currently married or cohabiting couples interviewed in 1985. *Section B* rates are based on the 1985 sample of 3232 households with a child aged 17 and under. *Sections C and D* rates are based on the 1975 National Family Violence Survey, because data on violence by children were not collected in the 1985 survey.
[2] The "Number assaulted" column was computed by multiplying the rates in this table by the 1984 population figures, as given in the 1986 Statistical Abstract of the United States. The population figures (rounded to millions) are for 54 million couples and 63 million children between age 0 and age 17. The number of children between age 15 and age 17 was estimated as 11.23 million. This was done by taking 0.75 of the number between age 14 and age 17, as given in the Statistical Abstract, Table 29.
[3] The rate for 3-year-old children in the 1975 survey was 97%.
[4] "Child Abuse-1" involves parental acts "universally regarded as abusive," such as kicking, biting, punching, beating up, and even attacking with weapons.
[5] "Child Abuse-2" adds hitting the child with an object.
SOURCE: From Straus & Gelles (1990), *Physical Violence in American Families;* Table 6-1, pp. 97–98. Data based on the 1975 and 1985 National Family Violence Surveys. Copyright 1990 by Transaction Publishers. Reprinted by permission.

physical force as a means to enforce that dominance." Going even further along these lines, some family researchers argued that societal norms basically define who is powerful and who is weak in the family. They saw domestic violence as a manifestation of power differences in a male-dominated, patriarchically oriented society.[3]

Even the societal perspective has proved to be too narrow. Researchers and theorists now increasingly emphasize the interactional nature of the factors that produce violence in the home. Conditions outside the family, such as unemployment, low income, or culturally derived beliefs and values, can impinge upon the members of the household and affect relationships within the family. Even a victim's behavior can have a significant influence on an attacker's conduct. Moreover, as a growing number of investigators have also noted, a good deal of what has been learned about other aspects of human aggression can also help to explain the causes of spouse battering and child abuse. A dispute between a man and woman who are living together obviously differs in important respects from an argument between two strangers in a tavern, but many of the same conditions can heighten the likelihood that violence will erupt.[4]

Factors That Can Promote Domestic Violence

I will look briefly at the evidence for each of the viewpoints described above. Essentially, though, I will adopt the newer approach to domestic violence and will devote most of my attention to a review of the multiplicity of conditions that can heighten or lower the chances that people who reside in the same household will assault each other. For convenience, I will take up these factors very much as they are organized in Figure 8–1. (I make no claim that the factors listed in this figure are the only ones at work or that the figure indicates the only causal influences.)

Two other preliminary points may be helpful. First and most important, as a reminder, I am using the terms "aggression" and "violence" to refer to deliberate attempts to injure someone. In my view, aggression rarely involves acts of omission (unless the motive is to do harm). Intentionally hurting a child is not the same as failing to care for the youngster properly, and violence and negligence occur for different reasons. Neglectful adults are typically quite different from caretakers who beat their charges. However much I may deplore child neglect, to call parental indifference "violence" would imply that the same psychological processes give rise to both modes of conduct, and to foster this mistaken implication could create serious confusion.[5]

Second, and also in accord with my general approach, the review in this chapter will emphasize features common to the various forms of

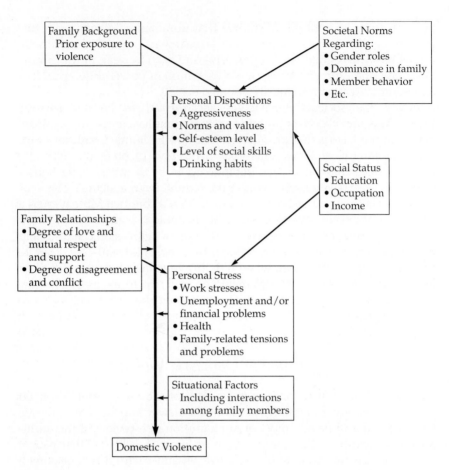

FIGURE 8–1

Factors that can promote domestic violence.

domestic violence. While I will occasionally discuss wife battering and child abuse separately, I don't consider them to be altogether different kinds of behavior, and my analysis will point out that the same conditions can give rise to both. Murray Straus has provided some of the best evidence for this position, and he describes it as follows:

> The results show that the same factors which explain child abuse and wife-beating [sic] also explain ordinary physical punishment and minor violence between spouses. Thus . . . it seems that violence is violence—irrespective of the severity of the attack and irrespective of whether the violence is normatively legitimate (as in the case of physical punishment) or illegitimate (as in the case of child abuse and wife-beating.)[6]

Research Indications

Societal and Community Norms and Values

Male dominance in family and society. Quite a few students of the American family believe that society's conception of the man as the head of the household is an important contributor to wife abuse. The democratic ideal is now more widespread than ever, however, and increasing numbers of men say that women should be equal partners in the family's decisions. Even so, as Straus and Gelles have commented, "many, if not most," husbands implicitly assume that they should have the final say in whatever choices the family makes, simply because they are men. If a man and a woman cannot reach agreement in a dispute, the male thinks that he is justified in using force to assert his authority—thus assuring that he will get the final word. One husband, who was quoted by Straus and Gelles, might have been speaking for many of his peers when, after talking about having slapped his wife, he told the interviewer, "And we haven't had any trouble since."[7]

Writers who emphasize the role of social expectations in wife battering basically fault society at large rather than the individual abusers. Women are brutalized, they maintain, largely because we all live in a patriarchal system which is governed by rules and standards that support male domination of women. In the words of Dobash and Dobash, "The problem lies in the domination of women. The answer lies in the struggle against it."[8]

Very much in line with this type of analysis, many of the abused women identified in the 1975 National Family Violence Survey were so insignificant in their households that they had little influence on family decisions. Wife abuse occurred in about 11 percent of couples in which the husband was clearly dominant, as compared to only about 3 percent of couples in which the man and the woman were approximately equal in influence.

Female Dependency and Male Domination. The man is especially apt to be the dominant member of the household when his spouse is highly dependent upon him, either *economically,* because he provides the major (or only) economic support for the family, or *psychologically,* because she would suffer more than he if the marriage were to break up. The 1975 National Family Violence Survey found that violence against wives was most likely to occur when both kinds of dependency existed.

Interestingly, the magnitude of the dependency-violence relationship varied according to the nature of the women's dependency and the severity of the violence. The stronger the wives' psychological dependency on their husbands, the greater was the chance that they would be the recipients of minor violence (such as pushing, shoving, and slapping): Only about 5 percent of the more psychologically independent women were assaulted in this way, as compared to about 14 percent of the most dependent group. By contrast, economic dependency was associated with much more severe violence. About 4 percent of the women who could take care of themselves and their families financially had been severely beaten, as compared to 7 percent of the women who were greatly in need of their husbands' financial support. In both forms of dependency, the researchers concluded, "wives who are highly dependent on marriage are less able to discourage, avoid, or put an end to abuse than are women in marriages [in which] the balance of resources between husbands and wives is more nearly equal."[9]

Does the Marriage License Permit Wife Abuse? In the early 1970s, Gelles and Straus offered a variation on the social norm theme. They proposed that, for many men, "the marriage license was a hitting license." Common law dating back to medieval times, the sociologists noted, gave husbands "the right to physically chastise an errant wife." Though this supposed "right" hasn't been legally recognized in the United States since the middle of the nineteenth century, Gelles and Straus maintained that the principle behind it may still live on in popular culture, at least to some extent.[10]

I wonder, though, whether this conjectured "hitting license" is indeed an important contributor to wife abuse. If such a social rule did have a major role in domestic violence, we would expect married men to be more assaultive than their nonmarried counterparts who were living with women. The unmarried men in these couples theoretically should be less likely than married men to believe they have "permission" to beat their troublesome women. In 1985, however, when Straus and his associates conducted the second National Family Violence Survey, they compared the violence rates of married couples to those of cohabiting couples, and found more fighting and aggression between unmarried than between married couples. This was the case whether the assaults were carried out by the men alone, the women alone, or both partners. Furthermore, this difference was obtained for both minor and severe violence and for blue-collar as well as white-collar families.

In my estimation, there's little support for the "hitting license" idea. Indeed, the researchers themselves speculated that the married men and women may have given in to their partners' wishes more than their counterparts in the cohabiting couples did. Married people, they suggested, were more apt to think they had to "make sacrifices or compromises for the sake of keeping the relationship intact."[11] The marriage license apparently does more to elicit compromise and accommodation than it does to allow a man to beat his wife to "keep her in her place."

Expectations about Parental Authority and Child Abuse. Social expectations about who should control the family undoubtedly play a major part in bringing about child abuse (as abuse is now defined legally).

Society has long viewed children as belonging to their parents and as having few rights of their own. Especially in earlier centuries, fathers and mothers were accorded almost unlimited control over their offspring. Since most of our forebears also believed that youngsters were apt to go wild and had to be tamed—that "sparing the rod spoiled the child"— parents in years past were prone to punish their offspring severely when they thought their children had misbehaved.

As a matter of fact, scholars have noted that youngsters were often seriously mistreated by their parents up until fairly recently. Lloyd DeMause, a well-known student of the history of childhood, has remarked, "The evidence which I have collected on methods of disciplining children leads me to believe that a very large percentage of children born prior to the eighteenth century were what would be today termed 'battered children.'" Another authority not only agrees but also thinks that harsh treatment of children was widespread at least until the nineteenth century. "Forms of punishment considered proper and even wholesome in Elizabethan or Victorian days," he said, "would be considered . . . abuse today."[12]

Although children are now afforded considerably more legal rights, and although parental authority is correspondingly much more limited, society still allows mothers and fathers to punish their offspring physically—within bounds. A Harris Poll survey conducted in late 1988 found that 86 percent of Americans approved of physical punishment in the home. School teachers, by and large, also don't frown on this type of discipline. According to Alfred Kadushin and Judith Martin, two-thirds of the elementary schoolteachers questioned by the National Education Association (NEA) in 1972 favored the use of corporal punishment in schools, while more than half the teachers surveyed in a more recent Gallup Poll supported their right to punish children physically in school.[13]

Because of the widespread belief in the necessity—and efficacy—of physical punishment as a way of controlling children, many parents obviously will hit their offspring at least once in a while when they believe the youngsters have violated their rules. Parental aggression is usually relatively minor, as Kadushin and Martin point out, but it can also be severe at times. Table 8-1 shows that, as recently as 1985, according to the second National Family Violence Survey, more than 2 percent of American children ranging in age from infancy to 17 years old were struck so seriously that they could be regarded as abused. This figure increases to 11 percent if we add instances in which the child was hit with an object, such as a paddle, to the other aggressive actions in the index. So many children are bruised (to some degree) by their caretakers' punishment that at least one government survey of child abuse chose to confine the definition of physical abuse to those cases in which "the injury or impairment [was] serious enough to persist for at least 48 hours."[14]

My point is that in quite a few of these instances the parents believed that they were justified in striking their children because the youngsters had defied them or had done something very wrong. Kadushin and Martin tell us that in their survey of child abuse cases which Wisconsin protective service workers had reported to the authorities, the great majority of the child victims had misbehaved in some way. And moreover, in fully 21 percent of the incidents, the youngster had not merely transgressed but was aggressive before the caretaker struck him or her. Other data Kadushin and Martin collected give us still more information along these lines. When they closely interviewed a sample of men and women who had been reported for child abuse, the researchers found that more than 60 percent of parents believed that they were justified in having punished their youngsters severely. In the adults' eyes, the children had defied them. They, as parents, were only doing what was "right." They were asserting their authority, as societal norms supposedly permit.[15]

The implications of those findings are interesting, by the way. Since many Americans think it's proper to punish a misbehaving child, they don't regard themselves as abusers when they hit a youngster who has violated their rules. Most of them don't even believe that their parents' severe punishment of them when they were children was abusive. "Abuse" is wrong, but justified slapping, spanking, or hitting is not bad. Even though it's fair to say that abuse is to a considerable extent in the eyes of the beholder, I'll follow Murray Straus's definition of the term "abuse" as referring to injurious or potentially injurious behavior.

Don't get me wrong. I'm not defending people who strike their young children and certainly am not saying their aggression is warranted. I also believe that there often is more involved in child abuse than conformity to societal norms. Many abusive parents are also highly aggressive toward their partners, and some of them are even prone to violence outside the home.[16] I'll have more to say about the qualities of abusive parents later.

Power differentials. Yet another version of the societal norms explanation of domestic violence holds that this aggression is caused largely by power differentials. One person in the household, the husband and/or father, has the capacity to force the others to do his will because of societal norms and his greater physical strength. His female companion and children aren't economically, psychologically, socially, or physically strong enough to withstand him. This power differential presumably enables the dominant individual to assault the weaker members of the family when they don't comply with his wishes.

Child Abuse as the Abuse of Power. It is easy to view child abuse as the exercise of power. According to the 1975 National Family Violence

Survey, parents are increasingly less apt to assault their children as their offspring grow older, presumably because the adults' relatively greater power lessens with the passage of time. Furthermore, some other findings suggest that, whereas boys rather than girls are the main victims before adolescence, more girls than boys are physically punished as the offspring become teenagers. Apparently, as sociologist Mildred Pagelow puts it, "Parents' power diminishes relative to boys' increasing power, but remains substantial relative to [girls' power]. It is likely that some parents who [have] focused most of their abuse on their sons [will] turn their aggression on their previously unabused daughters once the boys grow to a size sufficient to [enable them to] strike back."[17]

Wife Battering. Pagelow and other authorities also believe that power differentials can account for much of the violence directed against women in the family. They look upon the statistics showing the relationship between male domination and wife beating as a testimony to the unfortunate domestic consequences of differences in power. According to Pagelow,

> These [and other] findings argue against the ideas of some people who believe and claim that women are most likely to be beaten when there is fierce competition for domination and control between husband and wife. . . . To the contrary, the Straus et al. findings show that the less power the wife has, the more likely the husband is to abuse his greater power; conversely, the more egalitarian the relationship, the less likely [it is that] spouse abuse will occur.[20]

Norms Are Not Enough

Societal norms and power differentials undoubtedly play a part in domestic violence. However, in most instances there's far more involved in violent behavior than just social rules which proclaim a man's dominance in his household. Norms alone don't adequately account for a number of the findings researchers have obtained in their investigations of the aggression within families.

Some frequently obtained findings. A few years ago, Gerald Hotaling and David Sugarman examined fifty-two studies in which battered women and their husbands were compared to a matched group of nonabused wives and their husbands, trying to determine just how the women and men differed between these two kinds of couples.[19] I'll list only some of the major results of these comparisons:

- *More battered wives than nonabused women:* (1) had witnessed violence in the family while growing up (in 73 percent of the studies that investigated this factor) and (2) had themselves been victims of violence while growing up (in 69 percent of the studies that made this comparison).

- *More abusive husbands than nonabusive husbands:* (3) were violent to their children (in 100 percent of the studies that looked at this characteristic), (4) had witnessed violence in the family while growing up (in 88 percent of the studies that investigated this factor), and (5) had experienced violence while growing up (in 69 percent of the studies that made this comparison).
- *More couples in which there was violence than other couples:* (6) had frequent arguments (in 100 percent of the studies that investigated this characteristic), (7) were more likely to include a wife who had more education than her husband (in 67 percent of the studies that looked at this factor), and (8) had relatively low family incomes and/or were low in socioeconomic status (in 78 percent of the studies that inquired into this factor).

Let's think about some of these differences. First, I suspect it's important that the battered women were especially apt to have been exposed to violence when they were children, both as observers and as victims (characteristics 1 and 2). This early experience doesn't necessarily mean that these women had grown up to be passive and unwilling to assert themselves, as the power differential theory might say. Many of them stood up for themselves often enough so that they had frequent arguments with their husbands (characteristic 6). Isn't it possible that the women's early exposure to violence increased the likelihood that they would behave violently, at least in response to provocation?

The husbands of the battered women were probably generally prone to violence. These men were abusive to their wives, of course, but they tended to beat their children as well (characteristic 3). Further, they too had been frequently exposed to violence when they were young—again both as observers and as victims (characteristics 4 and 5).

What these statistics seem to suggest, then, is that in at least some cases of domestic violence, both members of the couple were disposed to be aggressive. Then too, since a good proportion of the beaten women were better-educated than their husbands (characteristic 7), we can guess there was at least a potential for conflict between husband and wife about which of them would dominate.[20]

All in all, whereas Pagelow seems to minimize the struggle for domination and control as a cause of wife abuse, there's reason to believe that this kind of competition could contribute to many instances of domestic violence. Quite a few abused women do suffer because of their subordinate status in the household, but others are beaten in altercations that grow out of conflict-ridden relationships.

Women also can be assaultive. Another important point about the male-female relationship in violence-prone families is that women also can be assaultive. They may be generally less disposed to engage in physical violence than men are, but they can be aggressive at times. This may happen mostly when they're provoked or so threatened that they have to lash out in self-defense, but—however they are aroused—not a few of them do hit, kick, and even beat up their domestic partners.

You may be surprised to discover how many women can act this way. When Murray Straus and his associates looked at the couples in the 1975 National Family Violence Survey in which only one spouse had been violent, they discovered that the husband had been the only aggressor in about 28 percent of these cases and the wife had been the only aggressor in 23 percent. The statistics on frequency of aggression give much the same picture. Again according to the 1975 survey, wives assaulted their husbands—in both minor and serious ways—about as often as husbands attacked their wives. Women in the survey were the recipients of about 8.9 acts of serious violence per year, whereas men were the recipients of a mean of about 8.0 such acts.

In many different ways, then, whatever the gender differences in violence statistics outside the home, within the family women were *not* less likely than men to hit, kick, or beat up their spouses, nor were they less likely to threaten their spouses with guns or knives.

Straus and Gelles assure us that this is by no means an unusual finding. Women were shown to be just as aggressive as their male partners in the 1985 survey, and maybe even a little more so, as the top section of Table 8-1 indicates. Other investigators, studying different samples, have also reported that women as a whole "are about as violent within the family as men."[21]

R. L. McNeely and Gloria Robinson-Simpson stressed the absence of husband-wife differences in a controversial paper which they published in a leading social work journal. Their summary of the findings they obtained in an independent interview study will give you an idea of their message: "Wives reported hitting their husbands almost as frequently as husbands reported hitting wives, and a higher proportion of men reported having been hit by their wives than vice versa." In sum, the writers argued, it's not only women who are abused; "men often are the victims of spousal violence."[22]

What can we make of these statistics? Of course, as Straus and Gelles emphasized, if a man and a woman exchange blows in a domestic brawl, the chances are the man will inflict more injury because of his generally greater size and strength. However, people don't necessarily fight only with their hands and feet. They may also use a physical object—maybe a knife or (since firearms are so readily available in our country) even a gun—which can do more damage than a bare fist. Moreover, in many instances it's the woman who wields the weapon. A study by McLeod cited by McNeely and Robinson-Simpson examined more than 6000 cases of domestic violence (which had been reported either to law enforcement authorities or to the National Crime Survey, sponsored by the federal government, in 1973, 1974, and 1975) to see which member of the couple tended to sustain more serious injuries in a fight. According to the researcher, a weapon was employed in about a quarter of the cases in which the woman was the victim but in over 80 percent of the instances in which the man was victimized. As a result, the man was actually more likely to be seriously hurt. McLeod concluded, "Clearly, violence against men is much more destructive than violence against women. . . . Male victims are injured more often and more seriously than are female victims."[23]

I'm not saying here that women are the main aggressors nor that they always start fights. Quite often they only respond to men's insults or brutality. Whoever initiates the brawl, however, women can hurt their spouses severely. One of the wives interviewed by Richard Gelles provides an example:

> He wants different things [the woman said]. Like if I'm there. They're not simple demands—like "clean the house" at three in the morning. If I don't do it he'll toss everything around. He threw lamps, sometimes tables at me. . . . I went after him with a knife once and I did it. . . . He went to the hospital and had to get sewed up.[24]

Regardless of who suffers more, what's important for this discussion is the relatively high level of aggression some women display in their families. They aren't necessarily always the helpless victims of a male-dominated society that prescribes violence as a way of "keeping them in their place." This isn't to say that social norms don't have a role in family violence—only that these rules and expectations probably don't operate in quite the manner that a number of theorists have maintained. If a husband's assault on his wife is affected by the norms and values of his social group, the chances are this happens because: (1) he thinks he is expected to be the dominant member of his household, and (2) he is greatly disturbed when he believes that his dominant status is threatened. He may believe that social rules permit him to punish the woman, but what is more important, it seems to me, is that the rules themselves are a source of discontent. He is emotionally aroused because he sees himself as not having the position in his family that he thinks he ought to have and/or because he believes that his authority is being challenged.

Family Background and Personal Dispositions

In line with the approach I've taken throughout this book, I view domestic violence as being in large part an emotional reaction to a state of affairs that the person perceives as disturbing. Much of the violence in families is similar in important ways to much of the aggression that takes place outside the home. Any truly adequate account of aggression in families must deal with the emotional reactions that are the sources of the aggressive arousal and with the nature of the people who are particularly apt to respond aggressively. I'll begin by describing the personalities of the people who are quick to assault other members of their families, since this is a topic to which researchers have given considerable attention.

Violence begets violence. Quite a few family researchers have pointed to the same characteristic of family abusers: Many of these people were abused themselves when they were growing up. As a matter of fact, this has been noted so often that it's now commonplace to speak of the *cycle of violence* or, more technically, the *intergenerational transmission of aggression*. Violence breeds violence, these family researchers argue. People who are exposed to aggression in their formative years tend to become aggressively inclined themselves. Of course there are exceptions, and some family specialists have questioned whether there is really good evidence that violent modes of conduct are transmitted over the generations.[25] The accumulating research, however, gives us more and more confidence in the fundamental validity of the cycle of violence thesis. An admittedly selective review of studies supporting this notion is given below.

Spouse Beating.   I mentioned some of the evidence earlier, in my description of the Hotaling and Sugarman survey of research on wife battering. In 88 percent of the studies these writers examined, you will recall, abusive husbands were more likely than nonabusive men to have witnessed violence in their families while they were growing up. Similarly, in 69 percent of the relevant investigations, the men who beat their wives had been beaten themselves during their childhoods.

The 1975 National Family Violence Survey gives more detailed information. Straus, Gelles, and Steinmetz asked the men and women in their national sample to recall how often they had been physically punished by their parents (for example, by being slapped or hit) when they were about 13 years old. The researchers then counted how many male and female respondents at each level of childhood punishment had assaulted their spouses during the survey year. The results are shown in Figure 8–2. The childhood experience–adult behavior relationship for men is shown in part A, and the same relationship for women is shown in part B.

The top line in both charts indicates ordinary violence such as slapping, pushing, and throwing things. Both the women and the men who had been punished most often as children were most likely to engage in this relatively minor aggression. More important, much the same kind of relationship exists for the more serious acts of violence, although there are some fluctuations which are probably due to chance. The

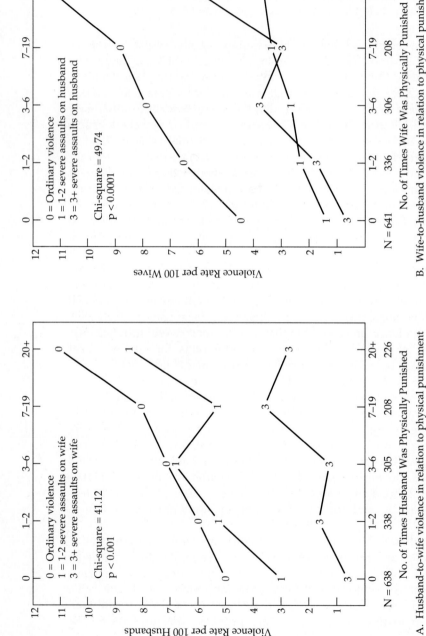

FIGURE 8–2

Relationship between respondents' rate of spouse abuse and the frequency with which they were punished as 13-year-old children. (From Straus (1983), Figs. 13.7, 13.8, pp. 227, 228. Adapted with permission of the publisher, Sage Publications.)

more frequently these men and women had been punished as young-sters, the greater was the probability that they would assault their spouses severely.[26]

Child Abuse. Now let's turn to the question of whether the people who beat their children are also apt to have been mistreated by their parents when they were growing up. Here too, aggression tends to beget aggres-sion.

A study of people at a mental health clinic, which was reported by John Knutson and his associates at the University of Iowa in Iowa City, is illustrative. An examination of the case records of 169 children who had been referred to the University of Iowa's Child Psychiatry Service because of various behavior problems revealed that about a quarter of the youngsters had been unequivocally abused by one or both parents. When the investigators interviewed the mothers and fathers of these children, they found that the abusive parents were especially likely to have been frequently punished during *their* childhoods. If both the moth-er and the father reported having been severely beaten when young, there was a 50 percent chance that they would abuse their child. In com-parison, if only one parent had been exposed to severe parental punish-ment, there was about a 32 percent probability that the offspring would be abused, and there was only a 17 percent likelihood of child abuse when neither the mother nor the father reported having been beaten often in childhood.[27]

The 1975 National Family Violence Survey demonstrates that the violence-breeding effect of childhood punishment isn't confined to peo-ple who are seen at a psychiatric clinic. In this national sample, the par-ents who had been physically punished most frequently when they were young (according to their own recollections) were the ones who were most likely to assault their own children severely.

Abused Children Are Apt to Become Generally Aggressive. I have cited only a brief selection from a fairly large number of studies. Though there are exceptions, and though there have been methodological problems in much of the research on this topic, the preponderance of findings sup-ports the notion of a cycle of violence. This isn't surprising if you recall the research on the behavior and development of aggressive personali-ties which was reported in Chapters 5 and 6. Parents who treat their off-spring harshly and punitively tend to have aggressively inclined chil-dren. Moreover, not only are a high proportion of these aggressive youngsters assaultive to the other children around them, but also they continue their aggressive ways through adolescence and into young adulthood.

The research on family violence has yielded somewhat similar find-ings. For example, the 1975 investigation by the Straus team documents the general aggressiveness of repeatedly abused children. Three-quarters of the youngsters who were beaten frequently by their parents assaulted their siblings severely and often during the survey year, while only 15 percent of the youngsters who had nonpunitive parents acted this way. General aggressiveness can also extend into adulthood. Being prone to violence, quite a few of the men in the 1975 study who were treated harshly as children tended to be abusive toward both their spouses and their offspring. As I have already mentioned, Hotaling and Sugarman found in their literature survey that *every* study they examined which compared abusive and nonabusive husbands showed that more of the wife-battering men were also aggressive toward their children.

These people's violent tendencies aren't always confined to the home (as would be the case if the abusers' aggression was only an attempt to maintain dominance in the family). Although comparatively few researchers have looked into this topic, in at least one study a significant proportion of wife-battering men who were themselves the victims of child abuse also tended to be aggressive toward nonfamily members.[28]

Straus, Gelles, and Steinmetz were impressed by the evidence which they found of a continuity of aggression between one generation and the next. They drew this conclusion:

> Each generation learns to be violent by being a participant in a violent family. We traced this learning process through three generations. The more violent the grandparents, the more violent the couples in our study are as husbands and wives, and the more abusive they are to their children. The children of these couples, in turn, tend to follow the pattern of their parents. The more violent the couple we interviewed, the more violent their children are to each other, and to their parents. "Violence begets violence."[29]

In general, then, I can say the same thing about the effects of child abuse that I said previously about the influence of harsh parental discipline: Being the victim of child abuse is a *risk factor* for the development of adult aggressiveness. This is a probability, not a certainty. Not all persons who are severely punished in childhood grow up to mistreat their own children. The studies cited above show this, and so do other investigations. As a matter of fact, when two researchers examined all the studies that had inquired into the intergenerational transmission of abuse, they estimated there was a 30 percent chance that adults reared by abusive parents would be harshly assaultive toward their own offspring. This probability undoubtedly varies with all sorts of factors, such as the level of open conflict in the family and how much stress the parents are under at the time. Nevertheless, in general, having had early experience of aggression increases the likelihood of adult aggressiveness, even toward one's own family.[30]

However, just as parental mistreatment doesn't mean that children will necessarily grow up to be abusive mothers and fathers, not every harshly punitive adult has been the victim of parental abuse in childhood.

People can acquire aggressive tendencies in a variety of ways, as noted in Chapter 6. For example, they may have watched the important persons around them behave aggressively again and again, and may have taken these individuals as models.

Witnessing Parental Violence.   The case histories of some violent men certainly suggest that they were exposed to aggressive models. A convict who had been imprisoned for criminal violence once told a psychiatrist about having long accepted violence as a way of life, in part because he had repeatedly seen other people be assaultive. Here are his words:

> Violence is in a way like bad language—something that a person like me's been brought up with, something I got used to very early on as a part of the daily scene of childhood. . . . As long as I can remember I've seen violence in use all around me—my mother hitting the children; my brothers and sisters all whacking our mother or other children; the man downstairs bashing his wife and so on.[31]

Indications of this modeling influence are also shown in the literature on domestic violence. According to the 1975 National Family Violence Survey, men who had watched their parents fight when they were children were 2 ½ times more likely to be abusive husbands than were men who hadn't seen parental aggression. This kind of finding certainly isn't unusual. In the Hotaling-Sugarman research survey, for example, almost 90 percent of the studies examined found that wife-battering men were more apt than their nonabusive counterparts to have witnessed aggression in their families when they were growing up. This survey also noted that battered women were especially likely to have watched the members of their family fight when they were young.

Why childhood exposure to violence promotes adult aggression. Because of this book's interest in all aspects of aggression, it's worthwhile to ask why people who have seen violence in their families as they were growing up are so likely to be aggressive toward their own spouses and/or children. Undoubtedly, there are several reasons. One is suggested by the remarks of the violent criminal whom I quoted above (as well as by some of the research on the effects of TV and movie violence): People who watch lots of aggression may become relatively indifferent to violent behavior. Their inhibitions against aggression may be fairly weak because they don't believe it is especially bad to attack others to further their own interests.

Albert Bandura's well-known analysis of observational learning goes further. As I mentioned earlier, Bandura demonstrated that children often learn the right way to act in a given situation by observing what others do. When youngsters see adults fight, they learn that they too can solve their problems by attacking the people who are bothering them.

This process may have contributed to the results reported by Zaidi, Knutson, and Mehm in a study with University of Iowa students. The researchers showed their subjects pictures of children who were doing various annoying things (ranging from spilling grape juice on a carpet to puncturing a car tire with a knife). For each picture, they asked the students to indicate what they would do to the child in such a situation. When the psychologists later divided the subjects (on the basis of their self-reports) into students who had been severely punished by their parents and students who hadn't been treated so harshly, they found that the severely disciplined students were more likely to have said that they would use physical punishment in disciplining the young offender.[32]

The subjects may have been copying their parents. When their mothers and fathers had beaten them in childhood, they were implicitly saying, "Do as I do." Thus they taught their offspring that children had to be punished severely for violating rules. They may also have taught them that aggression was an effective way of solving problems. In a study carried out for the National Commission on the Causes and Prevention of Violence, it was found that people who had observed a good deal of violence in their youth tended to favor the use of violence in their adult dealings; among other things, these people not only approved of spanking disobedient children but also were apt to believe it was all right for a husband to slap his wife if they had an argument or if she insulted him.[33]

Parental Mismanagement and Conflict.   Youngsters who see lots of aggression in their families are probably affected by other factors besides observational learning. It's quite possible, for example, that their parents do not discipline them effectively. The research conducted by Gerald Patterson, John Reid, and their associates at the Oregon Social Learning Center (which was summarized in Chapter 6) suggests that many abusive and quarrelsome mothers and fathers are so inept at managing their offspring that they actually train them to become highly aggressive. Besides treating the youngsters harshly, these parents are all too prone to reward antisocial conduct without adequately encouraging positive forms of behavior.[34]

Adults' fighting can also affect their children independently of direct mistreatment. Chapter 6 indicated that parental discord can be very disturbing to watching youngsters—so stressful and emotionally upsetting, in fact, that the offspring may become violently and even antisocially inclined. Social workers have corroborated these observations on the basis of their experience with conflict-ridden families. Their case descriptions document some of the symptoms that the distressed children of strife-torn families can develop: bed-wetting, nightmares, depression, psychosomatic complaints, temper tantrums, frequent fights with siblings and schoolmates, and even delinquency. These reports have been so consistent that two writers concluded that "open marital conflict . . . is a primary determinant of childhood problems in discordant families."[35]

I hasten to add that parental warfare doesn't seriously wound every youngster. Some children apparently aren't seriously affected, or at least not in ways that are immediately obvious to outside observers. Even so, open fighting between mother and father can be regarded as a risk factor that heightens the likelihood that their children will become aggressive adults.

Other personal characteristics: social class and problem drinking. So far, in considering the personal qualities of people who assault members of their families, I've focused on the long-standing aggressive tendencies of these individuals. Other characteristics of such persons have also been investigated, however. Two of these factors which may be related to the occurrence of domestic violence are: the abusers' social class and the extent to which they are problem drinkers.

Social Class Background. The mass media repeatedly tell us that domestic violence occurs in every segment of society. Blue-collar workers and unskilled laborers are not the only ones who beat their wives and abuse their children. Professional men and business executives also engage in this sort of aggression, or so the popular articles report. These statements are correct—if we take them literally—but this does not necessarily mean that family violence is equally likely to occur on every socioeconomic level. People whose occupations, education, and/or income are low on the social ladder have a greater probability of being assaultive than do people who rank higher.

This likelihood is suggested by the nature of the households in which child abuse is most likely to be reported. Kadushin and Martin tell us that a high proportion of abusive families have "insufficient income," because the fathers and mothers have relatively little education and few employment skills. "Although abuse is found among all socioeconomic groups," these writers commented, "it is most frequently reported among the poor." We should not dismiss this social group difference as being due entirely to a greater willingness to accuse underprivileged families of violence. Kadushin and Martin say there is good reason to believe that "even after allowing for . . . justifiable explanations of discrepancies in reporting, lower socioeconomic groups are disproportionately represented among maltreaters, so that it is not, in fact, a 'classless' phenomenon."

The Hotaling-Sugarman research review indicates that wife battering also may not be "classless." In the sample of studies which these investigators examined, spouse-beating men tended to have lower-level occupations and less education than did nonabusive men. This difference is corroborated by a statistical analysis of the data from the 1975 National Family Violence Survey. Here too, blue-collar men were shown to be more likely to assault their wives than were white-collar men.[36]

Alcohol Usage. Whatever opinions we may hold on social class differences in family violence, all of us have heard stories about working-class men who went home drunk after a binge in the local tavern and beat up their wives and children. Reports of alcohol-induced assaults on family members were fairly common in American history and literature before World War II. Is there any hard evidence to indicate that drinking contributes to domestic violence in more recent times?

There's no easy answer to this question, since the research findings haven't always been consistent. Most of the results do indicate, however, that use of liquor is often involved in domestic disorders. In the Hotaling-Sugarman review of research, for example, more than two-thirds of the studies that looked at the possible influence of drinking on wife abuse concluded that such an effect existed. Though there were some exceptions, wife beating was usually associated with frequent alcohol usage.

Researchers on domestic violence, however, also want to know whether there is any support for the stereotype of the abusive, alcohol-besotten working-class man. More specifically, is consumption of liquor especially likely to lead to violence in less affluent, low-socioeconomic homes? Glenda Kantor and Murray Straus believe, on the basis of their analysis of the data from the Straus team's 1985 National Family Violence Survey, that a link of this sort does exist.

The male respondents in this survey were subdivided into different groups according to: (1) their occupations (whether they were blue-collar or white-collar), (2) how often they drank alcohol, and (3) whether they were more or less approving of aggression toward wives (i.e., whether there were situations in which they would approve of a husband's slapping his wife). As Figure 8–3 indicates, each of these factors was related to the proportion of men in the group who acknowledged having assaulted their wives during the year of the survey. In general, no matter what the respondents' occupational levels and attitudes toward wife slapping were, the men who drank often were more likely to have hit their wives than were the men who used alcohol only infrequently. What's most important in the context of the present discussion is that the highest violence rate occurred among blue-collar workers who approved of a husband's slapping his wife and who occasionally went on alcohol binges. These men were almost eight times more likely to have struck their spouses than were white-collar men who did little drinking and did not favor hitting one's wife.[37]

In short, there's little doubt that many violent crimes are committed under the influence of alcohol. Chapter 12 will discuss why this may be true. For now, I'll say only that many domestically violent men apparently drink to forget their problems. They hope that liquor will lessen their worries, ease their pains, and reduce the stresses and strains in their lives.[38] This doesn't always happen, however. In many instances, the

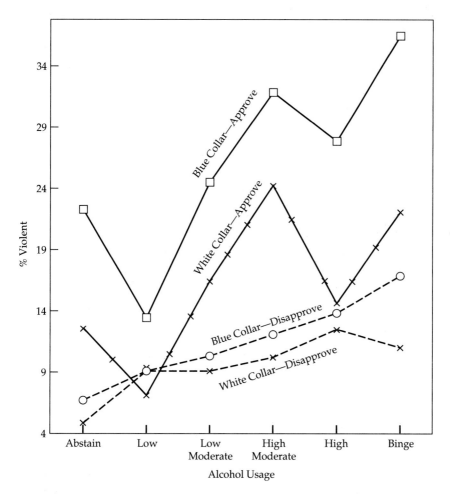

FIGURE 8–3
Violence rate as a function of drinking type, occupational status, and violence norms. (Straus & Gelles (1990), *Physical Violence in American Families.* Based on Table 12.2 in Chap. 12. Copyright 1990 by Transaction Publishers. Adapted by permission.)

men's emotional turmoil doesn't cease. They don't find the peace they seek in the bottle, and in fact, they may become even more emotional. The result is that, in one way or another, the alcohol raises the chances that they will attack other people who bother them.

Stress and Negative Affect as Contributors to Family Violence
The link between alcohol and aggression leads to a very important consideration: Much aggression in the home is a reaction to stress of one kind or another. Although this point may seem fairly obvious, I think it's

worth discussing the many ways in which stress contributes to conflicts that occur behind closed doors.

As I've said before, this book's central thesis is that much aggression we see around us is an emotional reaction to an unpleasant state of affairs. People who are decidedly unhappy for one reason or another are apt to experience anger and to become aggressively inclined. I've applied this proposition to many different forms of violence, and I can also extend it to the present topic. Basically, I suggest, many (but certainly not all) of the instances in which a husband abuses his wife and children, and/or his spouse attacks him, could be largely impulsive emotional outbursts impelled by the negative affect the assailants are feeling at the times of the assaults. As I have also pointed out, however, the negatively instigated impulse to assault someone is often inhibited. The exceptions occur when people's restraints against aggression are weak and/or their aggressive dispositions are fairly strong.

I will spell out this theme in greater detail by pointing to some of the many ways in which family members may develop unpleasant feelings that turn them, in effect, into tinderboxes that can be easily set on fire by a spark.

Economic and life stresses. Clearly, economic privations and problems can be a major source of unhappiness. Blue-collar men may be quick to lash out at their wives at least partly because of their money troubles. Bothered by their inability to buy many of the things they and their families desire, and perhaps also disturbed by the significance of this failure for their self-esteem, their nerves are raw, and they may be easily affronted by their wives and children. Their urges to strike people who offend them can readily lead to open attacks, if: (1) they have comparatively strong aggressive dispositions because of their childhood experiences, (2) they're under the influence of alcohol at the time, and (3) their self-restraints are weak because they believe that husbands have the right to hit their wives and parents have the right to beat their children.

Much of this discussion of stresses applies, of course, to women as well. The family's financial problems are hard on the wives as well as the husbands and may contribute to the women's aggressive tendencies. As the Hotaling-Sugarman research review pointed out, relatively low-income couples are more likely to fight a lot and to hit each other than are their more affluent counterparts.

Jobs can also be significant stressors, and not only because of troubles with coworkers or supervisors. Pressures to accomplish or to get the work done on time can be upsetting, as can boring and seemingly endless routine work. Blue-collar workers on a mass-production assembly line may feel the strain of their monotonous activities, and may come home tired and somewhat out of sorts. Even uncertainty about what is required to carry out one's responsibilities can be bothersome. In one investigation, mothers tended to punish their children most intensely when the youngsters interrupted their work on an assigned task if the women weren't clear about what they had to do in order to accomplish the work.[39]

Economic and work difficulties aren't the only sources of stress, of course. We can also be upset if a loved one has died or if someone close to us is ill or is acting in a hostile manner. We can even be disturbed to some extent by changes in our daily routines brought about by new job responsibilities or by the family's move to a different house or apartment. The resulting emotional turmoil can heighten our sensitivity to threats, challenges, and disappointments. These things can shorten our fuses and can raise the chances that we will be provoked by something a family member does.

Many people have difficulty in dealing with such stresses, as Murray Straus indicated on the basis of data from the 1975 National Family Violence Survey. The greater the number of stresses the respondents said they were experiencing (out of a list of eighteen possible life events, including the types of stresses mentioned above), the greater was the probability that they would report having assaulted their spouse that year. Though this was true for both men and women, the findings suggested that the number of stresses seemed to have the greatest effect on the wives' violence. Women who had few troubles were half as likely to be assaultive as were equally unbothered men, but at the high end of the reported stress continuum, far more wives than husbands had attacked their spouses severely. Whatever operates to produce this difference, at the very least it can be seen that both men and women may easily become enraged by their marital partners if they're emotionally bothered at the time.[40]

Situational stress may also contribute to many instances of child abuse. In the Kadushin-Martin interviews with adults who had been reported to Wisconsin authorities for beating their children, 68 percent of the respondents indicated that they were under considerable strain when they hit the youngsters, because of unemployment, financial difficulties, illness, and/or personal problems. Some of the caretakers were experiencing so much stress that even a trivial misdeed could trigger a violent outburst from them. A single mother who was caring for four young children described such a situation:

> It was on a Sunday night. I felt very down. I laid in bed that morning because my kids refused to clear the table for me. They refused to help me. And I felt very down. I was very tired and very upset. I've wanted to get a break from my children, to send them to this camp, and they won't go. I felt really down and really rather overwhelmed—I felt it was really like I had given so much and received nothing in return. And life at work has not been

too rewarding. And I was having difficulty putting up the aluminum siding on my house, which I am trying to finish and didn't, and what I put up was wrong. I really felt I was really down. I was at a low, low ebb. We were eating and he said he had a bone in his mouth, he goes [the child blew the bone out of his mouth] and I said, "You don't do that." And I put the knife to him. Well, I pressed it in him. I was so damn mad.[41]

Interestingly, a later analysis of the Kadushin-Martin interviews suggests that many of the abusers were ashamed of having hit their children in a fit of temper while they were experiencing emotional distress. They seemed to differentiate between aggression that was applied to enforce rules and emotional aggression that was spurred by internal problems. It was all right to strike a willfully disobedient youngster, they indicated, but it was wrong to "fly off the handle" and beat the child when they were feeling upset.[42]

Another source of negative affect: weather and pollution. There is nothing surprising in the idea that troubled people tend to be irritable, maybe even angry, and that they are easily provoked to violence. What is not so obvious is that almost anything that bothers us can also activate aggressive tendencies and thus may contribute to domestic disorders.

When I first introduced this notion in Chapter 3, I pointed to some of the unpleasant things that can promote aggression, such as uncomfortably high temperatures and social stresses. Let me add to this list: High levels of atmospheric pollution can also be aversive, and as a consequence, can also increase family violence.

As part of a systematic research program investigating the psychological effects of atmospheric pollutants (in both laboratory and natural settings), James Rotton and James Frey recorded the number of family and household disturbances that were reported to the Dayton, Ohio, police each day during 1975. They also recorded the daily level of air pollution in the city during this period, as measured by a local environmental protection agency. After performing a very sophisticated statistical analysis of the data, the researchers concluded that the police received the largest number of complaints about domestic assaults *on or right after* the days on which temperatures were relatively high, wind speeds were low, and ozone levels were also high. The investigators pointed out that irritating pollutants were at their peak when ozone was high and there was little wind to blow the noxious chemicals away.

Rotton and Frey maintained that these findings shouldn't be attributed simply to increased interactions among family members. Many sociologists and criminologists have argued that weather and atmospheric conditions influence the rate of violent crimes by heightening the frequency of social contacts. The more often people encounter others, they say, the greater is the chance of conflict. Rotton and Frey, however, noted that the members of a given household should have the most contact with each other in cold weather when they're all at home, and that cold days led to the fewest reports of domestic assaults. Apparently a better explanation is that the air pollution was unpleasant for many persons in the city and that their resulting negative affect heightened the probability that they would act aggressively.[43]

The Precipitating Encounter

Although an aroused person's unpleasant feelings can in themselves spur an inclination to assault someone, this impetus is often too weak to produce an open attack. Frequently, the violent urge has to be strengthened in some way, perhaps by another bothersome event or perhaps by seeing something that is a reminder of earlier negative occurrences and/or something that brings aggressive thoughts to mind.

An argument or an unpleasant encounter can serve this function. Richard Gelles collected many examples in interviews with the members of violent families. Many husbands and wives told of how either they themselves or their spouses complained, nagged, or insulted their partners, provoking violent reactions. Nagging sometimes led to such an outburst, "depending on the context and the amount of stress the partner [was] under at [the] particular time," and some of the women admitted that they might not have been beaten if they had kept quiet. "I can't blame it all on me," one of them said, "but there [were] many times that I could have just shut my mouth. I'd keep at him and at him until he reached his breaking point." Very often, however, wives maintained that their husbands were at fault, at least to some degree, either because of something they did do (e.g., drink too much, gamble, or insult her) or because of something they didn't do (e.g., bring in enough money for the family's needs, look for a job, or talk to their wives when they came home from work). Gelles also reported that in some cases strong dissatisfaction was expressed about "deficient sexual performance or sexual appetites of the partner."[44]

Whatever the specific source of the discontent, the resentment would sometimes lead to an argument. Bitter words would be exchanged as the dispute intensified, and the conflict might then heat up to the degree that open violence would occur. In a sequence of this sort, any aggression that's displayed, whether in the form of words or through physical blows, is apt to provoke counteraggression. Indeed, counteraggression is very common, according to findings of the 1975 National Family Violence Survey. A spouse's attack is typically a more important determinant of the partner's aggressive reaction than is the partner's attitude toward this kind of behavior generally. Intensely aroused by the other's aggression, more often than not the partner doesn't stop to think of what she or he believes about the overall propriety of hitting a spouse in a fight but impulsively strikes back in retaliation.[45]

Murray Straus has pointed to this kind of aggressive interchange in objecting to the "Let it all hang out–express your feelings openly" school of marital therapy. When he asked his university undergraduates to describe recent conflicts between their mothers and fathers, he found that, when any one parent attacked the other verbally, there was a good chance that this aggression would soon be followed by physical assaults. Instead of the disputants "discharging" their rage by yelling at each other or even smashing an inanimate object in fury, verbal or symbolic aggression was more likely to lead to physical aggression than to peace and harmony. Furthermore, this was true whether the aggressor was the husband or the wife.[46] (I'll discuss these effects more fully in Chapter 11, Psychological Procedures for Controlling Aggression.)

This kind of acceleration of violence also occurs in at least some instances of child abuse. Kadushin and Martin have drawn a distinction that is very much in accord with the analysis of aggression which I am presenting in this book. On the basis of their interviews with child batterers, they held that there is a difference between "expressive" beating (what I term "emotional aggression") and consciously purposive, better controlled, rule-enforcing aggression. Most of the adults in their sample (more than 60 percent of them) had apparently displayed purposive aggression by hitting their young charges in what they claimed were attempts to teach the youngsters a lesson and change their behavior. Almost a quarter of the caretakers, however, described their actions in more expressive or emotional terms, indicating that they had lashed out impulsively, because of their strong emotional state, or because they wanted to hurt the children. One mother acknowledged that her own aggression was of this kind, by saying she hadn't set out to hit her child with a conscious purpose in mind. "I really didn't think about it," she reported. "It was an impulse reaction for me to do it."

Whatever their initial intentions, in a number of instances the adults became highly aroused emotionally once they started striking the children, and their assaults mounted rapidly in intensity. The abusive mother whom I first quoted in Part 1 indicated that this had happened in her case, partly in reaction to her daughter Julia's initial, somewhat aggressive response to the punishment:

> And I grabbed her and I looked at her. She wouldn't even look at me. [But] you know, she did look at me. She looked at me like I was poison. And I whupped Julia and I whupped her and I whupped her and it looked like the more I whupped her, the more I wanted to whup her. I couldn't whup her enough.[47]

Clearly, there would be many fewer abusive incidents if we could somehow lessen susceptible persons' emotional distress and/or teach them how to reduce or control their emotional turmoil after they become aroused in a disturbing interchange with family members. Chapter 11 will summarize some procedures through which these ends may be achieved.

SUMMARY

Social science discussions of family violence have broadened from an initial focus on the supposedly "defective" personalities of the abusers to consideration of the role of societal norms and values and, more recently, to a growing recognition of the interacting influences of a multiplicity of factors. Research has now demonstrated that conditions in society at large, in the personalities of the individual family members, in the family relationships, and even in the immediate situation can all operate together to affect the chances that any one person will assault others in the household. Continuing with the theoretical orientation that was employed earlier in the book, in this chapter I examine these interacting factors. The assumption is that many instances of domestic violence are basically similar to the other acts of aggression that were discussed previously. Many of the same conditions which affect the probability that one person will attack another outside the home can also influence the chances that fighting and assaults will occur within the household.

This survey begins with an examination of the role played by societal and community norms and values, especially the ones that deal with male dominance and power within the family. While the adult man's traditional dominance and relatively great power over others in his family can contribute to the likelihood that he will be abusive, a growing body of research shows that societal norms and values are by no means the only or even the major causes of family violence. We now know, among other things, that women as well as men can be assaultive, that violence can be the result of conflict within the family, that a significant proportion of abusers were themselves exposed to violence during their formative years, and that many batterers tend to be aggressive not only toward their wives and children but also toward other people.

In fact, not a few highly abusive adults have a persistent disposition toward aggression. There is now considerable evidence to indicate that aggressive modes of conduct are often transmitted from one generation to the next—a finding that is consistent with the research on the formation of aggressive personalities summarized in Chapter 6. Besides citing some findings in support of this thesis which have been obtained in investigations of family violence, this chapter provides some explanations of why childhood exposure to violence promotes adult aggressiveness. The influences of other personal characteristics are also discussed, and it is noted that a disproportionate share of abusers come from low-socioeconomic backgrounds and that a substantial fraction of them are also problem drinkers.

Situational stress, either alone or, more likely, in conjunction with personal dispositions, can also promote aggression within the home. In keeping with my contention that negative affect is the primary source of emotional aggression, I suggest that unpleasant feelings generated by economic hardships and other difficulties (and even by annoying environmental conditions) can increase the chances that conflict and other bothersome events will lead to aggressive outbursts, especially by people who have strong inclinations toward aggression and/or weak inhibitions against aggression.

Any truly comprehensive account of domestic violence must recognize that domestic aggression is precipitated by the encounter between assailant and victim. Personal dispositions and situational stresses only create a readiness for aggression. This readiness has to be activated by an unpleasant event. Although few investigators have given sufficient attention to the precipitating encounter, the available research shows that fighting frequently leads to still more fighting and that one party's aggression is all too likely to stimulate the other party to counteraggression. There are many different senses in which violence begets violence.

NOTES

1. On the basis of their 1975 data, Straus, Gelles, & Steinmetz (1980) estimated that 60 percent of American women will be battered at least once in their lifetimes. Calculating from her well-known study of battered women, Lenore Walker (1979) came up with a somewhat similar estimate: 50 percent. Straus & Gelles (1990) present a comparison of their 1975 findings with data collected a decade later. The Straus team has focused on physical violence in a wide range: from throwing something at another person, at the low end of the scale; through pushing, shoving, slapping, and hitting; to using a knife or a gun, at the high end. In all instances, the actions were "carried out with the intention or perceived intention of causing physical pain or injury," although there needn't have been any physical injury.

2. Data from Bureau of Justice Statistics (1988), Table 3.36, p. 310.

3. Dobash & Dobash (1979). Also see Gelles (1987); Kadushin & Martin (1981); Pagelow (1984); Straus & Gelles (1990).

4. Straus and his associates [e.g., Straus & Gelles (1990), Straus et al. 1980] have been particularly insistent upon the necessity of such an interactional approach, as were Kadushin & Martin (1981). Also see Wolfe (1985).

5. Pagelow (1984) views parents' neglect of children as violence, saying, "Children who are physically or emotionally neglected . . . are denied their individual rights to develop their human potential to the fullest" (p. 21). In Chapter 1, I discuss the reasons for my belief that defining *aggres-*

sion or *violence* as counternormative behavior creates considerable conceptual confusion. Wolfe, (1985), has summarized research on the differences between neglectful and abusive parents. Some of the studies he cites indicate that neglectful caretakers tend to be more irresponsible, apathetic, and generally troubled than child-abusive adults are. More generally, the antecedents of child abuse are often quite different from the precursors of child neglect.

6. Straus (1983), p. 231.

7. Straus & Gelles (1990), p. 514.

8. Dobash & Dobash (1979), quoted in Straus & Gelles (1990), p. 385.

9. See Kalmuss & Straus in Straus & Gelles (1990).

10. This notion is discussed more fully in Straus et al. (1980).

11. See the chapter by Stets & Straus in Straus & Gelles (1990). The quotation is taken from p. 242.

12. The first quotation, from Lloyd DeMause, is taken from Kadushin & Martin (1981), p. 1, while the second quotation, from Mildred Arnold, appears in Kadushin & Martin (1981), p. 5.

13. The NEA survey results are reported in Kadushin & Martin (1981), p. 7. The Harris and Gallup Poll findings were kindly reported to me by Professor Kadushin in a personal communication. More than 80 percent of respondents in the 1975 National Family Violence Survey conducted by Straus et al. (1980) indicated at least some approval of slapping or spanking a 12-year-old child, as compared to only a little more than a quarter who considered slapping a spouse acceptable.

14. See Department of Health and Social Services Publication No. 81–30326, October 1981.

15. See the section entitled "Parents' intentions in the abuse event" in Kadushin & Martin (1981), pp. 188–199. See also the reanalysis of the Kadushin & Martin interview data in Dietrich, Berkowitz, Kadushin, & McGloin (1990).

16. Wolfe (1985) has published a useful review of studies that document this point.

17. Pagelow (1984), p. 76.

18. Pagelow (1984), p. 77.

19. Hotaling & Sugarman (1986).

20. In a pioneering interview study of eighty New Hampshire families, Gelles (1987) found that domestic violence was more prevalent when the husband's occupational and educational level was lower than his wife's. Gelles suggested that this status discrepancy "contributed to the husband's becoming quite sensitive to the legitimacy of his status as the head of the family." See pp. 137–139.

21. See Straus & Gelles (1990), pp. 119–120, for a list of other studies that support the New Hampshire researchers' findings. To give you some more statistics, when Stets & Straus [in Straus & Gelles (1990), p. 234] combined the data from the 1975 and 1985 surveys to determine who was the dominant aggressor (when only member of the married couple was the primary

abuser), they found that this person was more likely to be the wife than the husband.

22. McNeely & Robinson-Simpson (1987), p. 486.

23. Quotation from McLeod (1984), cited in McNeely & Robinson-Simpson (1987), p. 487. A number of writers have disputed the contention that men are more often seriously injured than women are in family disputes. See Berk, Berk, Loseke, & Rauma (1983). It would seem, then, that there are some groups in which the battered woman is the primary victim, although this is not always the case.

24. Gelles (1987), p. 163.

25. E.g., Pagelow (1984); Widom (1989).

26. Straus (1983).

27. Zaidi, Knutson, & Mehm (1989).

28. Fagan (1983). Nonetheless, we have to recognize that there are some abusive men whose violence is confined to their families, while other men are assaultive only outside the home. See, for example, Shields, McCall, & Hanneke (1988).

29. Straus et al. (1980), pp. 121–122.

30. The 30 percent probability estimate is from Kaufman & Zigler (1987), cited in Zaidi, Knutson, & Mehm (1989), p. 138.

31. Steele (1977), quoted in Straus et al. (1980), p. 121.

32. Zaidi, Knutson, & Mehm (1989). Also see Wolfe, Katell, & Drabman (1982).

33. Owens & Straus (1975).

34. Besides the evidence cited in Chapter 6, see the other studies mentioned by Wolfe, D. A. (1985).

35. Fantuzzo & Lindquist (1989), p. 78; also see Kempton, Thomas, & Forehand (1989).

36. Kadushin & Martin (1981), pp. 10–11. The reanalysis of the survey data collected by the Straus team in 1975 was reported by Howell & Pugliesi (1988).

37. Kantor & Straus, in Straus & Gelles (1990). Nevertheless, Kantor & Straus also emphasize that not every assault was preceded by drinking and that drinking did not always lead to aggression. The careful review of the research on the relationship between alcohol consumption and crimes of violence published by Murdoch, Pihl, & Ross (1990) provides still more evidence that drinking increases the likelihood of "physical marital conflict."

38. Fagan, Barnett, & Patton (1988).

39. Passman & Mulhern (1977).

40. Straus (1980b). The eighteen life stresses ranged from "Death of someone close" (experienced by about 40 percent of the respondents) to the least prevalent "Got arrested or convicted of something serious" (1.3 percent of the sample). They included such other stresses as "Serious problem with the health or behavior of a family member" (26 percent), "Troubles with other people at work" (20 percent), "Being a lot worse off financially" (14 percent), and "Moved to a different neighborhood or town" (17 percent). Straus reports that each source of stress was related to the domestic assault rate,

although "spousal stress" and "economic plus occupational stresses" seemed to have the strongest impact on the rate of domestic violence.

41. Kadushin & Martin (1981), p. 228.
42. Dietrich et al. (1990).
43. Rotton & Frey (1985).
44. Gelles (1987), pp. 158–163.
45. Dibble & Straus, in Straus & Gelles (1990).
46. Straus (1974).
47. The quotes are from Kadushin & Martin (1981), pp. 189, 196, respectively.

9

Murder

Whole Chapter.

❖

An Introduction to Murder ◆ Conditions that Influence Murders ◆ *Personal Dispositions* ◆ *Social Influences* ◆ The Violent Interaction

Record for Killings in Year Is Set in 8 of Nation's 20 Largest Cities

In 1990, young city dwellers killed for drugs, for clothes, for small amounts of cash, for love, for hate and for no discernable reason. They killed friends, relatives, and innocent bystanders. They turned poor neighborhoods into virtual prisons for law-abiding citizens."

New York Times, Dec. 9, 1990

This picture of the murders in American cities is certainly different from the one which crime novels present. The killings portrayed by novelists are usually calculated actions either impelled by passion or carried out cooly in the hope of achieving a substantial gain. In keeping with fictional accounts, this passage says that many murders are spurred by the expectation of profit (perhaps through a robbery or drug trafficking), but it also indicates that people are sometimes killed for seemingly trivial purposes: "for clothes, for small amounts of cash, . . . and for no discernable reason." Can we make sense out of these diverse reasons for murder? Why does one person take another's life?

In this chapter I will offer a brief overview of what social scientists have learned about murder. The coverage will be quite restricted in scope. It will concentrate on murders in the United States, much as the other chapters have also focused on violence in this country. This focus has been chosen partly because of the availability of a good deal of information about criminal homicides in this country but also because the deliberate killing of others is a far more serious social problem in the United States than in most other technologically advanced

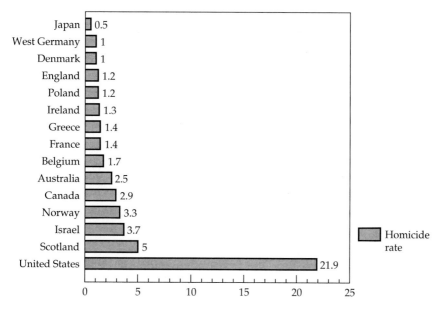

FIGURE 9–1
Number of killings per 100,000 men 15 to 24 years old (1986 or 1987). (Data from Fingerhut & Kleinman (1990), *Journal of the American Medical Association.* Vol. 263, pp. 3292–3295.)

nations. A critical observer of American society remarked in the mid-1960s that violence is "as American as apple pie." The statistics summarized in Figure 9–1 seem to be in keeping with this cynical comment. The number of killings by young men between age 15 and age 24 (an age group that is, in this country, especially prone to lethal violence) is far higher in the United States than in any other developed nation.[1]

I'll say nothing here about bizarre killings by obvious psychotics, such as paranoid schizophrenics who hear "voices" commanding them to slay or gruesome persons who lure young children to their deaths. Unfortunately (from my perspective), I will also have to neglect serial killers. I will confine this discussion to the more usual types of killings which account for the great preponderance of murder statistics.

*A*N INTRODUCTION TO MURDER

As a foundation for the discussion, I will first define some of the most relevant legal concepts, and then will summarize, in general terms, the principal statistics that will be explained later in the chapter.

Law, Homicide, and Murder

Legally speaking, *homicide* refers, very broadly, to any killing of one person by another. Not all deaths, obviously, are equally reprehensible in the eyes of the law. A slaying doesn't result in a criminal prosecution if the authorities deem it to have been justifiable or excusable. Justifiable homicides arise from adherence to legal demands, as when a police officer shoots a fleeing suspect who ignores the officer's orders to halt, whereas excusable deaths result accidentally from lawful acts, as when a car runs over a child who suddenly darted into traffic and was killed before the driver could stop. Only a *culpable homicide*, for which someone is held criminally responsible, leads to prosecution.

The seriousness of a culpable homicide, as far as the law is concerned, depends upon whether it is regarded as *murder* or *manslaughter*. The difference is a function of how much premeditation and malice aforethought were involved in the taking of the life. In a case of *manslaughter*, the death was presumably caused unintentionally or unknowingly even though the outcome could reasonably have been anticipated. A motorist is guilty of manslaughter if he or she has killed someone while driving a car in an obviously reckless manner. By contrast, if an offender is to be convicted of murder in the first degree, authorities have to prove that the perpetrator not only intended to commit the crime and planned its execution, *but also wanted to kill the victim.* For second-degree murder, on the other hand, only the desire to kill (malice aforethought) has to be proved. This discussion will focus mainly on murder, whether in the first or in the second degree, although some of the statistics I'll mention combine both murder and nonnegligent manslaughter (since the *Sourcebook of Criminal Justice Statistics*, which is published by the U.S. Department of Justice, doesn't separate these two kinds of offenses).

What Most Murders Are Like in the United States

Crime statistics can give a pretty good idea of what most murders in the United States are like, since the great majority of them are cleared by an arrest and the basic information about these cases is readily available. It's clear, for example, that they are usually one-on-one incidents, in which a single person kills one other individual. It's also clear that the majority of murderers are relatively young—a point that you'll encounter repeatedly in this chapter. Then too, both the killer and the victim are apt to be men. To give you an indication of how much more dangerous males are than females, in 1987 the offender was a man in about 86 percent of the 10,000 incidents in which one individual killed another person. This proportion has not changed very much over the years. Moreover, more than 70 percent of the victims were also men.[2]

Rather than simply continuing to cite statistics, I'll organize the introductory discussion according to the findings of the eminent criminologist Marvin Wolfgang in his classic 1958 investigation of homicides.[3] These findings raise a number of issues that must be confronted in an attempt to understand why people deliberately take another's life.

Murder in Philadelphia and other cities.

Background Statistics. Wolfgang went through the files of the Philadelphia police to collect statistics on the 588 criminal homicides that were known to the authorities during the five years from 1948 through 1952. He soon found that the data fell into regular patterns, even though the killings were unplanned in the overwhelming majority of cases.

Some of the regularities had to do with the backgrounds of the crimes. Most of the homicides occurred on weekends, and fully a third took place on Saturday nights. Furthermore, as you might expect, consumption of alcohol was involved in nearly two-thirds of the cases.

The findings regarding the nature of the offenders and their victims are more interesting in the context of this chapter. It appears that, in most instances, one or both of the participants had long-standing dispositions toward violence. A relatively high proportion of the male murderers had been arrested previously, particularly for crimes against the person. This doesn't mean that the killings were inevitable or that almost anyone could have been a victim. Far more often than not, the perpetrators killed someone similar to themselves. Both offender and victim were especially likely to be poor and/or working-class, and also, in more than 90 percent of the instances, murderer and victim were from the same ethnic and racial group. It's important to note in this regard that blacks were greatly overrepresented—a point to which we'll come back later. Even though only about 18 percent of the city's residents in the years studied were black, three-quarters of the perpetrators and almost as high a proportion of the victims were from this racial group. Then too, in keeping with a statistic I mentioned above, the majority of Wolfgang's offenders were young, between 20 and 30 years of age, and their victims were typically about the same age or a bit older.

Finally, in many instances the two parties knew each other before the murder occurred, and many of them even had close relationships. They were friends or relatives in more than half the cases, and almost 60 percent of the male victims were killed by someone who had been psychologically close to them.

Victim-Precipitated Violence. Wolfgang did more than compile these background statistics. He also demonstrated that a substantial fraction of the victims had played active parts in the violent encounters that led to their deaths. This point was new. Before Wolfgang published his report, I think it's fair to say, most sociological investigations had focused on the offenders and their cultural and physical backgrounds. The victims' possible roles in the killings had been comparatively neglected. In the words of one team of psychologists, "homicide victims had simply been regarded as passive and subordinate individuals whom fate had nominated as the recipients of fatal assaults by the active and central participants in these events: the offenders."[4]

Wolfgang provided a needed corrective to this one-sided view by arguing that a substantial minority of the victims might actually have initiated the violent episodes. His examination of the case records indicated that the slain persons had been the first to brandish a weapon or use force in about a quarter of the incidents. Adopting a phrase from an earlier writer, he said these were *victim-precipitated homicides.* To further document this thesis, he noted that the victims in many of these cases had previously been arrested for criminal assaults. Apparently they hadn't been the passive and innocent targets of brutal murderers.

Motives for the Crime. Wanting to do more than describe the settings and the persons involved in the violent episodes, Wolfgang also tried to determine what motives might have prompted the killers' actions. Judging from the case records, he concluded that most of the homicides had resulted from altercations that grew out of either domestic quarrels, arguments over money, or jealousy. Only a minority of the incidents seemed to have been largely or entirely cold-blooded and unemotional.

Similar Findings from Other Studies. A number of other researchers have carried out comparable investigations in other U.S. communities over various periods, ranging from shortly after World War II to the mid-1970s. The results, by and large, have been similar to those reported by Wolfgang, though not always exactly the same in detail.[5]

Some of the differences in detail may be very important. One study of homicides in Houston, Texas, separated Hispanics from other whites (a distinction that Wolfgang had not made) and reported that this ethnic group had a high rate of homicide offenders and victims. In other words, other socioeconomically disadvantaged groups besides blacks feel the slings and arrows of violence. In addition, an analysis of criminal homicides in Chicago in 1965 found a higher proportion of gunshot-caused deaths than Wolfgang had tabulated more than a decade earlier. A still later survey of homicides in Chicago between 1965 and 1970, carried out by Richard Block and Franklin Zimring, found that the rate of killings rose substantially in the city during the five years. The greatest increases in this period, proportionally, were for killings of young black males between age 15 and age 24, for deaths resulting from robberies, and for murders caused by firearms.[6]

Different Precipitating Events for Killers

The killing of strangers versus the killing of people known to the murderer. These statistics mentioned above suggest there has been an upsurge in the deliberate slaying of strangers. This change, if it does exist, has important implications. The killing of someone the perpetrator knows is probably very different, at least in many instances, from the murder of a stranger; it is apt to be the result of an intense emotion arousal generated by an argument or a strong personal conflict. By contrast, when killers take the lives of persons they hadn't met before, they are likely to do it in the course of a burglary, a robbery, or a motor vehicle theft, or maybe when they're engaged in drug trafficking. The victim's death isn't the primary aim but is more or less incidental to some other objective. The suggested increase in killings of strangers may thus mean that there has been a rise in "secondary" or "incidental" killings.

Several lines of evidence are consistent with this analysis. Let's distinguish between deaths resulting from altercations or intensely emotional conflicts, on the one hand, and deaths arising from felony crimes, such as burglary, theft, robbery, or even arson, on the other. (Employing the concepts I introduced earlier in this book, we might think of the latter crimes as being primarily instrumental activities, since they are typically carried out to achieve a purpose other than the injury of the victim.) Sociologists Kirk Williams and Robert Flewelling of the University of New Hampshire in Durham drew a similar distinction when they studied offender-victim relationships in different types of death-producing crimes.

Confining themselves to statistics from U.S. cities with populations of over 100,000, since lethal violence against strangers is most likely to occur in large urban centers, they studied the approximately 48,000 officially recorded one-on-one murders and nonnegligent manslaughter cases that took place in these cities between 1980 and 1984. The investigators divided the death-causing events into two categories: conflict occurrences, such as lovers' triangles or arguments, and felony crimes, which I'll label "instrumental crimes." They then determined the offender-victim relationships in these two types of situations. Figure 9–2 summarizes their findings.

You can see that relatively few of the people killed in the conflict crimes were strangers to the perpetrators. As a matter of fact, fully 87 percent of the 21,000 victims had been previously known to the slayers. On the other hand, strangers were far more likely to have been the victims in the "instrumental" death-causing crimes.[7]

More recent national data, which are not confined to large cities, reveal a somewhat similar pattern. According to the 1988 *Sourcebook of Criminal Justice Statistics,* in all the approximately 18,000 murder and nonnegligent manslaughter cases of which the police were aware in 1987, the victim and the perpetrator were members of the same family in more than 16 percent of the instances, and they were friends or acquaintances in about 40 percent of the cases. In only 13 percent of these fatal incidents were they strangers to each other. Their relationship was unknown in the remaining cases. More important, the victim was much more likely to have been a stranger when the perpetrator had been engaged in a felony than when the violent incident grew out of an argument or romantic troubles. Thus, the person who was killed was

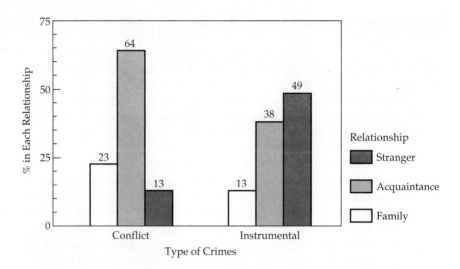

FIGURE 9–2

Distribution of victim-offender relationships in murder and non-negligent manslaughter cases arising from conflict and instrumental crimes. (Data from Williams & Flewelling (1988), Table 1. Copyright 1988 by the American Sociological Association. Adapted by permission.)

unknown to the slayer in about 31 percent of clear felony cases, as compared to 11 percent of lovers' triangle crimes, 7 percent of financial argument incidents, and 9 percent of other argument situations.[8]

Crime statistics document an increase in homicides in which strangers are killed. In Chicago, for example, the victim was someone the offender knew in about three-quarters of criminal homicides in 1965. Ten years later, however, the slayer knew the person he killed in only 58 percent of the homicide cases. Statistics also show a marked growth in felony-related homicides. In 1960, only about a fifth of all homicides were felony murders, but by the end of the decade, the figure had grown to about 30 percent. Toward the end of the 1970s, as Franklin Zimring observed, "while the majority of all killings are still committed by friends or acquaintances of the victim, a substantial and increasing proportion of the 'new American homicide' is the outcome of robbery—an event [in which] victim and offender are usually strangers."[9]

Just what is going on? Why has there been such an upsurge in felony-precipitated deaths? The increase is probably due to a number of different factors. The Philadelphia District Attorney who was quoted at the beginning of Part 3 blamed much of the increase on "the ready availability of powerful handguns and the effects of drugs on human beings." This may be too simple an explanation. While drug use and drug dealing probably do play a part in violent crimes, much of the growth in homicides seems to be independent of drugs. According to the Washington,

D.C., Police Department, drug dealing and addiction wer
about two-thirds of the homicides in that city in 1988 but
39 percent of the murders in 1990, *even though the total nu
increased substantially over those two years.* Much the same
seen in the New York City crime data for the same perioc
are more apt to be killed these days, it's probably not s......,
there are more people involved with drugs.

A better case can be made for the role of weapons in the growth of
felony-produced deaths. When Zimring analyzed the police-reported
robberies in Detroit during the years 1962 through 1974, he found that
there had been (1) a substantial rise in the number of robberies over this
period but (2) a much more substantial upsurge in the rate at which
these offenses led to a killing. A very considerable proportion of the
growth in robbery-related deaths was due to the increased use of guns.[11]
To generalize from these findings, it may well be that the marked rise in
the slaying of strangers over the past two decades stems partly from the
increased use of firearms in felonies.

Interestingly, Zimring also estimated that there was about 1 death
for every 150 robberies in Detroit at this time, and he suggested that
many of the killings had been "accidental" rather than instrumental
to the furtherance of the offenders' aims. Something may have happened during these encounters that stimulated the criminals to shoot.
Maybe the victims resisted or were slow to do what the robbers wanted. Emotionally aroused and with their nerves on edge, in at least
some of these cases the offenders may have fired their weapons impulsively.

One other finding in Zimring's data is worthy of special note: In the
public's mind, the typical robbery consists of a black offender stealing
from a white victim. Indeed, in the early 1960s most of the people who
were killed in Detroit robberies were whites slain by blacks. However,
there was an abrupt change in the last part of the decade. By 1974, almost
two-thirds of the people who died in Detroit robberies were blacks, and
the great majority of these victims were murdered by other blacks. This
pattern continues to the present.

Black homicides. Citizens, police authorities, and social scientists
have been concerned for generations about the high rate of homicides
committed by blacks. The statistics are truly depressing. In Wolfgang's
study of Philadelphia homicides, you'll recall, almost three-quarters of
the offenders and approximately the same proportion of the victims
were black, even though only about 18 percent of the city's residents
were black at the time. These figures yielded a homicide rate of almost 42
offenses per 100,000 population for black males, as compared to a rate of
about 3 per 100,000 population for the white men of the city. Other studies of criminal homicides in American cities, as I mentioned earlier,
obtained very similar findings.

The overrepresentation of blacks in homicide cases, both as victims and as perpetrators, continues to this day. As just one indication of this, out of approximately 10,000 incidents in 1987 in which a single offender killed one person and the slayer's race was known to the police, about half the killers were black—even though this racial group constitutes only about 12 percent of the U.S. population. The victims were also apt to be black; 88 percent of the people slain by blacks in these one-on-one cases were also black.[12]

It's important to keep in mind, though, that this exceptionally high homicide rate is concentrated mainly in a particular segment of the black population: young males. According to the U.S. Centers for Disease Control (CDC), the homicide rate for young black males from 1978 through 1987 is "four to five times higher than for young black females, [and] five to eight times higher than for young white males." Figure 9–3 shows the homicide rate (per 100,000 population) for black men between age 15 and age 24 in this ten-year period, and also indicates that firearms accounted for about three-quarters of the killings.

The CDC has recently brought these statistics up to date. Homicide rates continued to rise from 1987 to 1990, as the newspaper articles I've cited also indicate. Most of the upsurge was accounted for by black male teenagers, and fully 95 percent of the homicides in this recent increase have involved guns.

It is important also to realize that the great majority of the people slain are also blacks and are of about the same age as the killers. The

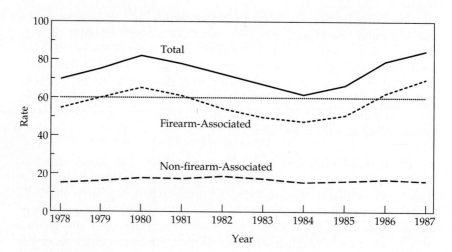

FIGURE 9–3

Firearm- and non-firearm-associated homicide rates per 100,000 population for black males 15 to 24 years of age (United States, 1978-1987). (Report from the Centers for Disease Control. *Journal of the American Medical Association*, Jan. 9, 1991, p. 183.)

killings are now so numerous, the epidemiologists at the CDC have calculated, that homicide has become the leading cause of death for young black men between 15 and 24 years old. As one of the CDC epidemiologists observed, "In some areas of the country it is now more likely for a black male between his 15th and 25th [birthdays] to die from homicide than it was for a United States soldier to be killed on a tour of duty in Vietnam."[13] Think of the implications. Right now the inner areas of many large American cities are more dangerous for these young people than were the jungles and rice paddies of Vietnam for their fathers or brothers or uncles during the Vietnam war.

Other conditions also may influence the black homicide rate besides age and gender. A high proportion of homicide offenders, both white and black, are on the lower rungs of the socioeconomic ladder. Furthermore, there's a good chance that alcohol plays a major part in the frequent killings that continue to plague this segment of the population. Putting all these facts together, according to Lawrence Gary of Howard University in Washington, D.C.:

> One can argue that, in homicides among lower-income persons, the murderer is typically a black man under 30 years of age, and alcohol is implicated in more than 50% of the cases. . . .Alcohol-related homicides were rare among middle- and upper-income black males.[14]

CONDITIONS THAT INFLUENCE MURDERS

A major task that now confronts society is to understand and use the statistics that I have been citing in this chapter. We especially need to learn why such a high proportion of American murderers are poor and black. Is this violence a result of the resentment generated by a life of poverty and discrimination? If so, do other social factors also contribute? What social conditions promote the likelihood that people will assault each other? What about the role played by the offenders' personalities? Do murderers tend to have certain personal qualities which heighten the chances that they will take someone's life, perhaps in an explosion of temper?

Figure 9–4 summarizes the way I will organize this discussion, which is much like the scheme employed in Chapter 8. I will start with an examination of personal dispositions to violence and then will turn to some of the major social conditions that promote violence by generating aggressive inclinations and/or by lowering restraints against violent actions. Finally, I will briefly discuss the interaction between the offender and the victim.

As I indicated at the start of this chapter, this review is neither complete nor even truly comprehensive; it obviously neglects, for example, the important influences of the offenders' psychiatric and neurological

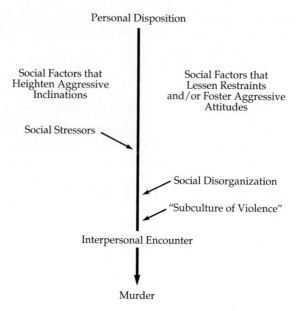

FIGURE 9–4
Factors that influence the incidence of murder.

conditions. However, I believe that the available evidence is quite good for the factors that will be considered.

Personal Dispositions

Are Murderers Prone to Violence?

Years ago, the former warden of a well-known penal institution wrote a popular book about the convicted murderers whom he and his family employed as servants in their residence on the prison grounds. These men weren't dangerous, he told his readers. Rather, driven by extremely stressful circumstances beyond their control, they had exploded in one-time outbursts of violence. They were unlikely to become violent again since their lives were now calmer and more peaceful.

This is a comforting portrait of murderers, in a way. However, the warden's characterization of the prisoners he knew does not fit most people who have deliberately taken another's life. Many homicide offenders are not at all like the men the warden described; instead, they have records of frequent violence and antisocial conduct. In Wolfgang's classic study of Philadelphia homicides, for example, nearly two-thirds of the killers had been arrested before, most often for a "crime against the person." They were evidently violence-prone as well as antisocial.

Other investigations give us much the same image of the homicide offender. When Miller, Dinitz, and Conrad examined the criminal careers of a large sample of Ohio men who had been found guilty of serious violent crimes (such as murders and aggravated assaults), they found that only about 30 percent of these people had ended their criminal careers after committing only one violent offense. As the researchers commented, these individuals' "personal problems or inadequate modes of coping" led them to develop a continuing pattern of antisocial behavior that often lasted into middle age.[15]

We can also see this criminal history in many highly assaultive men. In Chapter 8, I noted that a high proportion of the people who abuse the members of their families have persistent inclinations toward violence, and the research on aggressive personalities which was summarized in Chapter 5 shows that violence-prone individuals are apt to exhibit a wide variety of antisocial actions. Adding to this picture, when sociologist Ann Goetting looked into the backgrounds of Detroit men who had killed their wives or girlfriends in 1982 and 1983, she found that about two-thirds of the offenders for whom data were available had been arrested at least once before.[16]

Different Personality Types?
Is it possible that there are different kinds of murderers? Many killers have a history of violence and antisocial conduct, but perhaps others are quite different. On the surface at least, they may be ordinarily law-abiding and peaceful citizens.

The overcontrolled murderer. Edwin Megargee has proposed that this type of violent offender is fairly common. Impressed by the not-infrequent newspaper reports of totally unexpected outbursts of violence by people who had previously seemed to be quiet and inoffensive, Megargee maintained that these people were *overcontrolled aggressive personalities,* in contrast to the better-known and more expected *undercontrolled aggressive personalities.* The overcontrolled personalities, he says, carry around within them buried but active instigations to aggression, although they repress every outward manifestation of their violent urges.

> The extremely assaultive person is often a fairly mild-mannered, long-suffering individual who buries his resentment under rigid but brittle controls. Under certain circumstances he may lash out and release all his aggression in one, often disastrous act. Afterwards [sic] he reverts to his usual overcontrolled defenses.[17]

Megargee's contention has received some support from a number of studies in England and this country. The English psychologist Ronald

has extended the analysis even further. On the basis of his
he suggests that there may be two types of overcontrolled mur-
"overcontrolled repressor" with strong "impulse control" and
open signs of emotional problems and a "depressed inhibited"
with strong inhibitions who also tends to be quite depressed and
full of self-blame.[18]

Much more has to be learned about the overcontrolled aggressive
personality. So far as I know, this type of individual has been defined
more by scores on personality tests than by measurements of actual
behavior. It would be nice to know whether such persons really don't
show any overt signs of aggression at all until their "disastrous" explo-
sions of violence occur. Furthermore, contrary to Megargee's interpretation, my guess is that these persons are apt to brood a great deal about
the threats and injustices which they believe they have suffered, so that
they are often emotionally aroused even if their resentment isn't revealed
openly. Frequent recall of unhappy and aggressive thoughts may well be
major contributors to the violent outbursts of these people.

The reactive, undercontrolled murderer. Whatever is involved in
the behavior patterns of the overcontrolled personality, and however
prevalent this type of violent personality may be, many murderers lack
the strong restraints the "overcontrolled" aggressors presumably possess. Following the portrait of the emotionally reactive, violence-prone
individual sketched out in Chapter 5, and also in accord with the contention by James Wilson and Richard Herrnstein that many dangerous
offenders are highly impulsive, I suggest that most murderers have a
combination of extreme antisocial tendencies and weak inhibitions
against aggression. Psychopaths certainly seem to possess these qualities,
as noted in Chapter 5, and even nonpsychopathic but highly reactive
persons have them to a considerable degree.[19]

An important theoretical issue is involved here. From my perspective, relatively few violent offenders are continually driven to assault
others; they don't have a constant urge to kill or hurt. Instead, the essential point is that *they are reactive.* They may be quick to get aggressive
ideas and/or especially apt to interpret other people's actions in an
unfriendly manner, but they will do this mainly under special circumstances: when they encounter things that have an aggressive meaning for
them, when they are emotionally aroused because they can't get what
they want, when they are challenged or threatened, or maybe when they
just aren't feeling well. These arousing conditions may also activate relatively strong aggressive inclinations within them that are fairly difficult
to suppress *once they get under way.*

The phrase "once they get under way" is important. Highly aggressive persons often find it difficult to hold themselves back once they

have become emotionally aroused, but they can restrain themselves if they're not too excited at the time and if they have a strong incentive to restrain themselves.

Do some people enjoy hurting others? Let me speculate some more. While I think most violence-prone persons have the qualities described above, I also suspect that a growing number of highly aggressive people attack others primarily because they don't care how much they hurt others. They may even enjoy inflicting pain. My discussion in Chapter 1 of the 1989 "wilding" spree in Central Park in New York City raised this possibility. This was the incident in which six to twelve youths assaulted a woman jogger who just happened to be running by, and they did it at least partly, some teenagers said afterward, "just for the hell of it." Also remember the gang mentioned in Chapter 1 that had savagely attacked several homeless people. According to the police, the young men had beaten the derelicts, killing one of them, just for thrills, "because they were getting their jollies attacking the homeless." Whatever else was involved in these incidents, the assailants apparently also sought the pleasure of making other people suffer.

This kind of desire may also have been involved in some of the killings mentioned at the start of this chapter, which were done "for no discernable reason." Consider two occurrences, one all too real, the other make-believe. First, picture in your mind a gang of young toughs bursting into a subway train and intimidating the middle-class commuters. The youths parade up and down the aisles, playing their radios at full blast and shoving any of the subway riders brave (or foolish) enough to look at them. Second, remember (or imagine) the brutal violence in Stanley Kubrick's 1972 movie *A Clockwork Orange*—an imaginative but terrible vision of a futuristic Britain. In one scene, the "hero" Alex and his teenage pals break into an elderly couple's home and assault the hapless man and woman. Evidently their goal is not sex or money but the pleasure of demeaning, frightening, and even hurting the terrified victims.

Of course, any number of influences may contribute to such seemingly senseless violent incidents. Some mental health specialists would say Alex had psychopathic qualities. Whatever their diagnosis, these aggressors are so emotionally callous that they fail to empathize with their victims. As far as they're concerned, what matters is *their* goal and *their* pleasure. They may also welcome the illusion of power which they derive from frightening and injuring others. They are anxious about their lack of consequence in the world, and they want to prove that they are worthy of respect. When they beat someone up, they see themselves as strong and forceful, as a "Master of the Universe."

I wonder, however, whether the people who make these random

attacks are seeking only to demonstrate their power and enhance their self-identities. The aggression displayed by the young toughs on the subway might well have been motivated by their desire for a sense of power and control. They seemed to be more interested in dominating the commuters than in injuring them. Alex and his gang may also have had this motive to some extent. However, they appeared to want to hurt as well as control. Could Alex really think of himself as dominant and masterly—as "a real man"—because he had terrified and beaten an elderly couple? What about the real-life young men who attacked the homeless derelicts? Did they kill their victim, a helpless man who couldn't fight back and didn't challenge them, to prove they were strong? My guess, which coincides with the police officer's opinion, is that besides asserting themselves, the assailants sought the extra thrill, the additional pleasure, which they could obtain from hurting their victims and even destroying one of them.

Some Observations on the Prediction of Dangerousness
I've noted several times in this book that a relatively few people are responsible for many of the serious acts of violence that plague our country. Couldn't we make use of what we know about these people's personalities to identify and watch them—*before* they commit crimes?

The U.S. legal system has long expected mental health experts to be able to identify highly aggressive individuals. In the well-known book *Predicting Violent Behavior*, author John Monahan, who is a psychologist and a professor of law, psychiatry, and public policy at the University of Virginia School of Law in Charlottesville, observed that "every society in history" has engaged in the preventive confinement of presumably dangerous persons. These people are imprisoned or otherwise restrained, not because they have been convicted of past criminality but because they are "thought likely to cause serious injury in the future."[20] The U.S. Supreme Court has also held that it is constitutional for states to impose the death penalty for some kinds of murders when the offenders are believed to be apt to become violent in the future.[21] Can psychiatrists and psychologists do what the legal system supposes: accurately predict whether a given individual is "likely to cause serious injury" or become violent on a future occasion?

Just determining how good mental health specialists are at predicting dangerousness is really quite complicated, and any truly adequate discussion of this matter would have to examine a host of issues, ranging from the statistical to the legal and ethical problems. On the basis of all of these considerations, however, a number of authorities have now concluded that society is unduly and unrealistically optimistic about mental health experts' ability to foretell how dangerous any one individual is likely to be.

The main difficulty is that these experts are essentially being asked to predict very rare occurrences. The high levels of violence in the United States are well known, and indeed, far too many people are murdered in this country. However, suppose you're a psychiatrist and are being asked to say whether a particular 19-year-old man is dangerous. Is there a good chance he will kill someone in the future? Look at Figure 9–1 again. Even though the U.S. homicide rate is much too high, only about 22 out of every 100,000 young men of this approximate age take someone else's life. Homicides are still quite unusual, and unusual events are very difficult to forecast.

The problem doesn't lessen much even when a person has a criminal record. Imagine that you, as a psychiatrist, are asked to judge whether a certain inmate of a penitentiary is too dangerous to be granted the parole he is requesting. He is a convicted felon, and the relevant statistics indicate that 68 percent of felons with his kind of criminal record will be rearrested in the future. Is he likely to criminally assault someone if he is released from jail? After evaluating a considerable body of data, researchers have calculated that only about three out of a hundred convicted felons will subsequently be charged with homicide or rape. In other words, even among people in high-risk groups, the chance is still quite low that any one person will commit murder.[22] Psychiatrists and psychologists can estimate the probability of serious violence by people who have certain characteristics (e.g., the ones who score high on a certain personality test, who belong to a certain ethnic or racial group, or who have a record of criminal offenses), but the probability is typically much too low to allow them to say with confidence what any one individual is apt to do in the future.

Another major reason for the difficulty of forecasting dangerous violence, besides the relative rarity of the behavior, is that aggression is highly susceptible to situational influences. More often than not, violent behavior is a reaction to particular conditions. In order to make accurate predictions, then, mental health specialists would have to take the activating conditions into account—and no one can really say if unknown future conditions will occur.

Whether they base their judgments on clinical interviews or on standardized personality tests, psychiatrists and psychologists are often wrong in their attempts to forecast whether someone will become seriously violent in the future.[23] All too frequently, they come up with "false positives"—predictions of violence that are not fulfilled. Most people who appear to have a strong inclination toward aggressiveness when they are interviewed and/or tested will not actually show open aggression in their later dealings with other persons. Measurement procedures are generally valid enough for research purposes. They can provide important information about the origins and functioning of people's disposition to violence. On the whole, however, they cannot be used to foretell whether *any one individual* will or will not engage in serious anti-social behavior on a future occasion.

Social Influences

The way in which we can make the greatest progress toward reducing violence in America is by taking the actions necessary to improve the conditions of family and community life for all who live in our cities, and especially for the poor who are concentrated in the ghetto slums. It is the ghetto slum that is disproportionately responsible for violent crime. . . .

To be a young, poor male; to be undereducated and without means of escape from an oppressive urban environment; to want what the society claims is available (but mostly to others); to see around oneself illegitimate and often violent methods being used to achieve material gain; and to observe others using these means with impunity—all this is to be burdened with an enormous set of influences that pull many toward crime and delinquency. To be also a Negro, [a] Puerto Rican, or [a] Mexican-American and subject to discrimination and segregation adds considerably to the pull of these other criminogenic forces.[24]

In this statement, the National Commission on the Causes and Prevention of Violence has listed the major social factors that contribute to the high level of criminal violence in American society. We see the indictment of adverse family influences and also note that extremely violent conduct is associated with being young and male. More than anything else, however, the commission's statement emphasizes the part played by what I term "social stressors"—harsh social conditions that cause distress and suffering. As I've been suggesting, unpleasant conditions can activate hostile thoughts, generate violent inclinations, and facilitate the development of antisocial modes of conduct.

Socioeconomic Stressors

Social scientists have long attributed much of the violence in U.S. society to economic privations and the social disorganization that often accompanies them. We know, for example, that a disproportionate share of violent offenders come from working-class or lower-class backgrounds. More than half the Detroit men who murdered their wives or girlfriends, in the sample by Goetting which was mentioned earlier, were relatively low in social status. Nearly two-thirds of them were unemployed. The demographic characteristics of the city areas with the greatest numbers of killings also point to the criminogenic effects of poverty. According to an illustrative investigation which was made in metropolitan Cleveland, Ohio, the highest homicide rates occurred in the poorest sections of the city. These areas were characterized by low average incomes, low educational levels, residents who worked on the bottom rungs of the occupational ladder, and dilapidated and overcrowded housing.[25]

Studies of the relationship between crime rates and the social and economic characteristics of metropolitan areas throughout the country have shown comparable findings. This research is especially interesting because it seems to offer some relatively new insights.

Judith Blau and Peter Blau correlated the 1970 murder and assault rates in the 125 largest metropolitan areas of the United States with various social and economic statistics. They found that the communities with the most poor people as well as the greatest concentrations of blacks tended to have the greatest numbers of killings relative to population size. What was more intriguing, this association between poverty and the homicide rate tended to disappear when the sociologists took the amount of income inequality in the area into account. In other words, the amount of violent crime in a given community seemed to be more a function of the disparity in incomes in the area than of the proportion of poor people residing in it.

Blau and Blau also found, as did many other investigators, that the greater the proportion of the population of any one metropolitan area that was black, the higher its murder rate tended to be. Wondering whether the relationship between race and violent crime could be due to racial inequalities in access to the good things of life, the sociologists computed an index of the socioeconomic inequalities between the whites and the blacks living in each metropolitan area. This measure did indeed account for much, but not all, of the association between the proportion of blacks in the area and its level of criminal violence.

Considering these results, Blau and Blau concluded,

> High rates of criminal violence are apparently the price of racial and economic inequalities. In a society founded on the principle "that all men are created equal," economic inequalities . . . [especially those associated with race] violate the spirit of democracy and are likely to create alienation, despair, and conflict. . . . Socioeconomic inequalities, between races and within them, are positively related to high rates of violent crime.[26]

This emphasis on socioeconomic inequalities as a source of social stress appears to be quite valid, but these researchers may have been too quick to minimize the adverse effects of poverty in itself. Other researchers have obtained better evidence linking the amount of poverty in a geographical area to its level of lethal violence. Thus, Kirk Williams confirmed the Blaus' finding regarding the connection between high homicide rates in an area and the existence of sharp racial inequalities in socioeconomic status, but he found that poverty alone was also associated with relatively substantial numbers of killings. The previously mentioned study by Williams and Flewelling of homicides in large American cities provides still more evidence of poverty's influence on homicides. Using some of the same indices that Blau and Blau had employed, these investigators found that the communities having the greatest numbers of killings per capita also tended to have the highest percentages of poor people residing in them, as well as the greatest population densities. In sum, then, there is good reason to believe that poverty helps to produce violent crimes.

Note, however, that these unfortunate social consequences are not caused only by economic privations. As I've been arguing throughout this book, anything that makes people exceedingly unhappy could conceivably have the same violence-generating effects. We can certainly view income inequalities as sources of displeasure. People who are unable to enjoy the comforts most of us take for granted may well resent the difference, and their resentment is all too apt to produce aggressive inclinations. Then too, according to some research, even inflation-produced economic uncertainties and anxieties, as well as high levels of unemployment, may contribute to the country's economic distress and thus add to the homicide rate.[27]

Also remember that oppressive heat can also be a source of stress. Violence tends to mount when atmospheric conditions are decidedly unpleasant. Psychologist Craig Anderson of the University of Missouri in Columbia has been pursuing this line of research for some time now and has reported the best evidence that is available to date on the aggressive effects of high temperatures. One study, which he carried out with Dona Anderson, is especially relevant to the present discussion. These researchers determined the numbers of aggressive crimes (murder and rape) and nonaggressive crimes (robbery and arson) in Houston, Texas, on each day over a two-year period (1980–1982), and then investigated whether these crime frequencies were correlated with high temperatures. They discovered that, whereas nonaggressive crimes were unaffected by temperature, the numbers of highly violent crimes were greatest on the very hottest days.[29]

It's a mistake, I believe, to dismiss this finding as being due to only a greater number of people out on the streets during hot weather. There's now pretty good evidence from laboratory experiments, as well as from research in natural settings, that unpleasantly high temperatures can indeed activate aggressive inclinations.[30] Is it not possible, then, that a person suffering from the heat—and perhaps also from other unpleasant conditions, such as poverty, unemployment, and racial discrimination—can be easily offended by what he regards as another individual's misbehavior? If the afflicted person also has a strong aggressive disposition, if his restraints are weak at the time, and if a weapon happens to be available, he may kill the offender in a fit of temper.

Social Disorganization

Besides maintaining that aggression is often a response to unpleasant conditions, I have repeatedly emphasized the importance of restraints in controlling aggressive reactions. Most of my attention has been given to individual differences in the strength of these inhibitions, but it's also obvious that the external social world can influence both the strength of restraints and the frequency with which they are loosened. Circumstances can tell people, either explicitly or indirectly, that aggression is morally wrong and/or that they are very likely to be punished if they become violent. On the other hand, in other situations the same people may come to believe that it's entirely proper to strike at others who have offended them and/or that there isn't much chance that they will be punished for the assault by either their peers or the authorities.

Social disorganization tends to lessen inhibitions against aggression. As sociologists have long recognized (and as some theorists have emphasized), informal as well as institutionalized social controls help to maintain the social order. Persons who are disposed to break the law—to loot, to steal, or to assault their enemies—are kept from acting illegally to a considerable extent by the threat of punishment. The influence of social control agents (who include a person's family, neighbors, and coworkers as well as law enforcement agencies) is typically weakened by economic and social stressors. People who are suffering from aversive conditions may well become distrustful, especially of strangers. Their distrust can arise partly because they are surrounded by real dangers, but it may also grow out of the individuals' anger and hostile thoughts. Because they are preoccupied with their own frustrations and anxieties, they are relatively indifferent to the views of others in the community. Some of them are even apt to develop attitudes and values favorable to crime. Society isn't to be trusted, these persons may believe. The world they see is replete with greed, deceit, graft, and immorality. They think they have to make their own rules and fend for themselves if they are to get what they want. Society at large tends to disparage them, thus adding to their problems, and even legal authorities may give them as little time and attention as possible.

A number of sociologists in Chicago are well known for their pioneering studies of social disorganization in the central areas of many large American cities. In the words of two of these writers, these "are areas of physical deterioration, congested population, . . . economic dependency, rented homes, . . . and few institutions supported by the local residents."[31] These conditions obviously exist in many black urban ghettos, and social controls are correspondingly often relatively weak in these particular areas. "American society in the wider sense is not a presence in the ghettos except on television," one writer has commented. "Policemen don't walk the beat, most schools don't teach, fathers don't live at home, crime goes unpunished."[32]

Besides the overcrowded and deteriorating housing, the disorderly schools, and the one-parent families that are prevalent in ghettos, social disorganization is also manifested in other ways. Some sociologists have also pointed to conflicting norms and values as prime contributors to

icators of social disorganization. People don't know what
can become confused, anxious, and resentful when society
y should be law-abiding and work hard in order to succeed
yet they also see that some people who work hard get
hereas people who indulge in criminal activities gain money
status. When individuals are torn by such opposing beliefs,
the.. rence to conventional rules weakens. Disorganization is also
shown in the large numbers of youngsters who drop out of school before
graduation; in the high rates of childbirths by unwed mothers; and even,
according to two studies, in very high divorce rates.

Whatever the specific indicators, according to sociologists from the
time of Emile Durkheim (who was active in the late nineteenth and early
twentieth centuries) to the present, and especially according to the so-
called Chicago school of criminologists, social disorganization gives rise
to widespread crime and high homicide rates. This effect can be seen in
the statistical relationship between the frequency of divorces and the
number of killings that occur in an area. Separate studies conducted by
Judith Blau and Peter Blau and by Kirk Williams and Robert Flewelling
showed that the metropolitan areas with the highest divorce rates also
tend to have the most homicides per capita, even when income level is
ruled out as a factor. Apparently, in the communities in which families
break down most frequently, all sorts of societal rules and standards are
weak, and aggression is all too likely to be unrestrained.[33]

Subcultural Influences, Shared Norms, and Values

How can we account for blacks' high homicide rates? A truly adequate discussion of the social and economic influences on homicides
must account for the very high rates of murders and nonnegligent
manslaughters committed by blacks. Virtually every investigation of the
social factors that affect lethal violence has noted the relatively high frequency with which blacks kill and are killed by other blacks. Besides
Wolfgang's classic study, which I mentioned earlier, other researchers
who have examined the homicides in America's cities have found similar
results. In addition to these depressing observations, more recent investigations have also found that the U.S. metropolitan areas with the highest
homicide rates also tend to have comparatively large proportions of
blacks.[34]

More than Poverty. The relationship between racial composition and
homicide rate is not a simple and direct function of poverty alone. The
studies cited above tell us that metropolitan areas having a high concentration of blacks are still high in killings even after their income levels are
statistically adjusted, and other research has yielded comparable results.
One authority has concluded, "Social class and income level do not

account for all the disparity between minorities and whites in rates of committing serious violent crime and delinquency."[35]

Social Inequalities. It's obvious, then, that other kinds of social factors, in addition to poverty, must also be at work to produce the differences in murder rates. One of these extra factors could be social inequalities, as I've already mentioned. Let me give you some more evidence that suggests such an influence.

In their pioneering study of the relationship between the business cycle and homicide rates, Andrew Henry and James Short found that, in the years between 1900 and 1947, the effects of economic hard times were different for whites and blacks. Generally speaking, business contractions in this period led to an increase in homicides by whites, as well as to an even greater rise in the number of whites who took their own lives. It's as if economic hardships had increased whites' aggressive inclinations to some extent (especially among lower-status whites, Henry and Short suspected) but had also caused quite a few of them to blame themselves for their financial difficulties.

By contrast, declines in business activity actually led to drops in the rates of killings by blacks and had comparatively little impact upon their suicide rates. Could it be that, when times were bad during this era, underprivileged blacks saw less difference between themselves and others? Economic recessions were levellers, so to say. It was *most* people who were having financial problems, not blacks alone. As a consequence, blacks' self-esteem suffered less than in good times, and they had less free-floating resentment and readiness for aggression than before.[36]

Are there subcultures of violence? In his analyses of ethnic and racial group differences in homicide rates, Wolfgang attributed minority groups' relatively frequent killings to widely shared attitudes and beliefs within these communities that are favorable to aggression. These groups have *subcultures of violence,* Wolfgang maintained—sets of beliefs and norms that teach their members how to interpret particular situations and then prescribe how they should respond. Thus, according to this eminent criminologist, persons who grow up in a violence-prone subculture are typically easily angered because they are quick to define altercations or other interpersonal difficulties as provocations, and they then realize they must react aggressively if they are to maintain their standing with the others around them. Men in this kind of subculture thus presumably attack others mainly because they believe they are expected to do so. If they have been provoked, the only way they can receive respect and approval is to lash out at the offending party.

Wolfgang does not believe that poor blacks are the only ones who hold violence-favoring beliefs and attitudes. As he sees it, most minority groups with high incidences of violence, as well as a substantial segment of the lower class, probably also possess norms of this kind. Other theorists have also employed this line of reasoning to account for the frequent aggression displayed by some groups in U.S. society, whether youth gangs in urban ghettos or an entire region of the country.[37]

Does the South Have a Subculture of Violence? The different sections of the United States do not suffer from the same degrees of lethal violence. Relative to the population in their area, white people are much more apt to be murdered in the South than in, say, New England or the North Central states, and this has been the case for the past century. Thus, in 1958, the same year in which Wolfgang published his study of Philadelphia homicides, the *Uniform Crime Reports* of the Federal Bureau of Investigation (FBI) noted that the homicide rate in the South Atlantic region was six times higher than the rate in New England. Although the gap is narrowing, the South continues to be a comparatively deadly part of the country, especially for young white men. In 1987 a number of southern states, particularly Texas, Florida, and Alabama, were well above the national average in their rates of lethal violence by young white males between 15 and 24 years old. (Interestingly, the homicide rates for blacks of this age in the South were generally quite low.)[38]

Sociologists differ in how they explain the high rates of killings by southern whites. Some attribute this phenomenon to the poverty and economic inequalities that are endemic to this part of the country, but others argue that the killings are fostered by a "regional culture." We can readily picture such a culture in operation. As one historian has commented,

> In various guises, the image of the violent South confronts [us] at every turn: dueling gentlemen and masters whipping slaves, flatboatmen indulging in a rough and tumble fight. . . . The image is so pervasive that it compels the attention of anyone [who is] interested in understanding the South.[39]

This image is more than just a stereotype, some sociologists contend. Substantial numbers of Southerners are thought to hold attitudes and beliefs that promote violence. The same historian suggested that "violence in the South is a style of life that is handed down from father to son along with the old hunting rifle and the family Bible." With this perspective in mind, it is easy to imagine a young white man in a rural community in the South who has had a serious argument with someone else. Easily affronted by words or actions that he regards as a threat to his pride, he is quick to anger, and moreover, he believes his honor requires him to take violent action against the person who he thinks has insulted him.

The proponents of the subculture-of-violence interpretation of the South support their argument with complicated statistical analyses.

Although the studies that have been done offer somewhat contradictory findings, they have basically demonstrated that the incidence of homicides in a particular section of the country (a metropolitan area or a state), especially by whites, is positively correlated with the proportion of the white population in the given area that has come from the South. This relationship holds, furthermore, even when poverty and socioeconomic inequality are taken into account. One team of researchers has thus concluded that a subculture of violence "is partially responsible for the high levels of lethal violence in the South."[40]

These findings, however, while they are suggestive, offer only indirect support for the subculture-of-violence thesis. To my knowledge, no direct evidence is available that shows that beliefs, attitudes, and values conducive to violence are actually more prevalent in the South than in other sections of the country. There's some reason to think that Southerners as a group are more favorable to the use of violence to maintain "law and order" than are other Americans, but this doesn't mean that they believe it is proper to use violence to settle arguments or to protect their honor. Indeed, several researchers who have looked for South versus non-South differences in such attitudes have failed to find them. Maybe then, as some writers have suggested, the hypothesized southern cultural tradition condones only *lethal* violence, rather than all kinds of physical assaults, and only under very specific circumstances.[41]

Some Narrowly Defined Groups Could Possess Subcultures of Violence. It's certainly plausible that some group and regional differences in homicide rates are caused by attitudes and values that are favorable to aggression. Some evidence is consistent with this possibility. Nonetheless, empirical research has now shown that violence-supporting beliefs and attitudes are not as widespread throughout the poorer sections of society, including black communities, as Wolfgang and others had supposed. It's even likely that the values of toughness and machismo are not as prevalent among violent offenders as the subculture thesis contends.[42]

Even though the great majority of people who are socially and/or economically underprivileged don't condone aggression as a way of solving interpersonal problems, it is possible that some persons within these segments of society do have an outlook on life that is conducive to violence. As I noted in Chapter 6, quite a few violent teenage gangs in U.S. inner cities subscribe to a code of personal honor that stresses the inviolability of one's manhood and defines breaches of interpersonal etiquette in an adversarial idiom. Because they share these beliefs and values, gang members are easily insulted when they are not given the respect they insist upon. They believe that they must assault offenders in order to prove their manliness and preserve their honor. With deadly guns in their possession or readily available, they can easily kill those who they think have wronged them.

What's worse—and what's seemingly all too apparent these days—

some young men, especially in the poorer and minority sections of society, have an even more extreme view of aggression. They appear to have become quite indifferent to the pain and death of others. These callous, uncaring aggressors are full of barely submerged resentment and hostility. Their focus is totally on themselves and their desires. They evidently aren't troubled very much, if at all, by seeing or even causing another person's suffering. When several of them get together, they support each other's callousness and violence. They agree that it's OK, and even a good idea, to go on a wilding. It's fun to assault the rich joggers in the park, they tell themselves, or to attack and rob teenagers who are wearing the leather jackets and Nike sneakers they want, or even to beat up some old drunks.

We don't know how many of these young people there are in the United States. The police reports and newspaper articles which I've cited suggest that they may be increasing in number. A city dweller recently told a journalist how his inner-city neighborhood has changed over the years. When he was young, he said, the residents weren't so easily affronted by accidents and minor disputes. "Now," he related, "if you touch someone's car, you get killed." Though this statement may be exaggerated, it is very much in keeping with a criminologist's observation that growing numbers of homicides are caused by inner-city youths' "casual attitude about human life." It's quite possible that these uncaring aggressors are the product of a growing but still relatively small and restricted subculture of "profound disillusionment and routine violence" that community workers who are familiar with urban ghettos see developing in the inner cities.[43]

Effects of Growing Up in a Violent Environment. The norms, values, and beliefs characteristic of a violence-prone subculture don't necessarily arise in the same ways in which conventional societal norms develop and are transmitted. Instead of being handed down from father to son "along with the old hunting rifle and the family Bible," these beliefs and attitudes could well be the more indirect product of life in a harsh, uncaring, and violent environment.

You saw earlier in Part 2 that cold and unloving parents are apt to have highly aggressive children. Obviously, the severely stressed and chaotic world of the urban ghetto is not conducive to adequate parenting. With their inadequate education, the stresses and strains of a poverty-stricken life, and the discrimination and social disorganization to which they are often exposed, it's no wonder that so few of these adults give their children the love and attention they should have, nor that they are even neglectful of and/or unduly harsh toward their offspring.

In addition to feeling the ill effects of inadequate parenting, mounting numbers of inner-city children have witnessed extreme violence. John Richters, a researcher at the National Institute of Mental Health, has given an idea of how frequently such children may be exposed to violence. On interviewing children and mothers who resided in a low-income "moderately violent" section of Washington, D.C., Richters found that 72 percent of the fifth- and sixth-graders had witnessed violence to someone else, 11 percent had seen someone shot, and 6 percent of them had themselves actually been shot at. Four percent had seen a murder.

This witnessed killing and shooting must be highly disturbing to children. In Richters' Washington sample there was a significant relationship between the amount of violence the children had seen and the number of adverse psychological symptoms they had. What's worse, as you saw in Chapter 6, emotional turmoil can generate violent tendencies. Researchers from Columbia University, in New York City, who went to Lebanon to study the children of war-torn Beirut, found that an inordinately high proportion of these children were not only anxious and highly stressed but also aggressive.[44]

Urban blacks and other minority youths thus don't have to be explicitly taught by their peers and elders to favor violence. A significant number of these young people suffer from mistreatment and thwartings, both at home and in the general environment of the ghetto. They live in a relatively lawless, disorganized, and violent social environment, surrounded by aggressive models and peers. Quite a few of these youngsters could easily come to see their social world as a jungle in which only crime and aggression pay. Ready access to guns heightens the already too high chances that they will assault and even kill someone else.

Short-lived influences on violent attitudes. So far in this chapter, I have described only influences that can produce relatively long-lasting beliefs and attitudes which are conducive to aggressive behavior. However, society also exposes its members to more transient influences that can make at least some of them more favorably disposed to violence for a short time.

In Chapter 7, Violence in the Media, I discussed these temporary effects at length. People can get short-lived aggressive ideas from violent movies and TV shows and even from news reports of violence, and some audience members who have weak restraints against aggression can translate these thoughts into open assaults upon others. Consider the impact an extremely violent movie could have upon teenagers from the poorer sections of U.S. cities. The fighting depicted on the screen might easily activate aggression-related ideas and motor tendencies in youngsters who: (1) have relatively strong aggressive inclinations toward and weak inhibitions against antisocial conduct; (2) are intellectually unsophisticated, thus are not apt to tell themselves the movie events are only fictional in nature, and anyway, are disposed to accept the violent world portrayed on the screen as real; (3) are inclined to identify themselves with the violent hero, at least partly in order to give themselves a sense of power and mastery; and (4) interpret the hero's violence as justified and in a good cause, thus temporarily heightening the likelihood that they will regard their own aggression as also justified.

Besides movies and TV shows, news reports of people fighting, shooting, and killing each other can also increase the probability that susceptible persons in the audience will become more aggressive. It should come as no surprise, then, that nations tend to have an increase in violent crimes after wars.

At least as far back as Emile Durkheim's pioneering examination of the aftereffects of the Franco-Prussian War (1870–1871), social scientists have speculated about what conflict between nations does to the social order in the combatant countries. It is of particular interest in the context of this discussion that some theorists have proposed that the citizens of the warring nations experience a catharsis through their country's battle with the enemy. They supposedly drain off their own violent urges as they think about the fighting, and then behave more peacefully toward the others they encounter in their own families and neighborhoods. Movies don't have this beneficial effect, as shown in Chapter 7, but maybe real killing does offer a release for aggressive energies.

Dane Archer and Rosemary Gartner tested this possibility, as well as others that theorists had suggested, by comparing homicide rates in a large sample of countries before and after they had participated in wars. Table 9-1 summarizes one set of analyses by these sociologists. Regardless of whether the nations were victorious or defeated, and regardless of whether they suffered many or relatively few deaths in battle, over all the countries combined there was likely to be an increase rather than a decrease in homicide rates after the conflicts.

However, heightened postwar violence certainly isn't inevitable. You can see that it didn't occur in the United States after World War II (although there was such a rise following the Vietnam war). All in all, according to Archer and Gartner,

> Most of the combatant nations in the study experienced substantial postwar increases in their rates of homicide. These increases did not occur among a control group of noncombatant nations. The increases were pervasive and occurred after both large and small wars, with several types of homicidal indicators, in victorious as well as defeated nations, in nations with improved postwar economies and nations with worsened economies, among both men and women offenders, and among several age groups.[45]

Rather than providing a discharge for pent-up aggressive urges, a nation's war is apt to heighten its incidence of violent crimes. Much as movie scenes of supposedly justified aggression can make people in the audience believe that their own aggression is proper, the nation's conflict implicitly also tells some of its citizens that assaulting their personal enemies is legitimate.

TABLE 9-1 POSTWAR HOMICIDE RATE CHANGES AS A FUNCTION OF BOTH THE LEVEL OF COMBAT DEATHS AND THE OUTCOME OF WAR

		Homicide rate change		
		Decrease	Unchanged	Increase
More than 500 battle deaths per million prewar population	Victorious nations	United States (II)*	Canada (II)* England (I) France (I) Japan (1904, Russo-Japanese War)	Australia (II) Belgium (I) England (II) France (II) Italy (I) Netherlands (II)* New Zealand (II) Norway (II) Portugal (I) South Africa (II) United States (I)
	Defeated nations	Finland (II) Hungary (I)		Bulgaria (I)† Germany (I) Hungary (II) (1956, Soviet conflict) Italy (II) Japan (II)
Fewer than 500 battle deaths per million prewar population	Victorious nations	Israel (1956, Sinai campaign) Italy (1896, war with Ethiopia) Italy (1935, war with Ethiopia)	Japan (1932, conflict with Manchuria)	Israel (1967, Six-Day War) Japan (1894, First Sino-Japanese War) Japan (I) Pakistan (1965, second war over Kashmir)
	Defeated nations	India (1962, border war with China)	Egypt (1956, Sinai campaign) India (1965, second war over Kashmir)	Jordan (1967, Six-Day War)

*For the United States (II), Canada (II), and the Netherlands (II), the data include murder and manslaughter.
† For Bulgaria the data refer to crimes against the person, including homicide.
NOTES: I = before and after World War I.
    II = before and after World War II.
SOURCE: Archer & Gartner (1984), Table 4.5, p. 88. *Violence and Crime in Cross-National Perspective.* Copyright 1984 Yale University Press. Reprinted with permission of the publisher.

*T*HE VIOLENT INTERACTION

So far in this chapter, the discussion has only set the scene for murder. I've identified a variety of factors which influence the chances that a person will deliberately take someone else's life. Before a killing can occur, the potential offender has to encounter the individual who will become the victim, and the two people have to interact in a way that leads to the victim's death. The nature of the violent interaction is the topic of this section.

Different Kinds of Violent Interactions

As you read this section, you should keep in mind the difference between instrumental aggression and impulsive, emotional aggression. Instrumental killings, in which the offender is primarily interested in attaining some objective other than the target's death, are not the same as emotionally impelled murders. Several students of criminal homicides have argued for a similar distinction. As I said earlier in this chapter, Williams and Flewelling differentiated between felony homicides (what I term "instrumental" killings) and homicides that stem from intense interpersonal conflict. In much the same vein, Richard Block spoke of "two models of behavior." In his analysis of Chicago homicides, he wrote:

> The first model, instrumental action, assumes that the victim and [the] offender are both acting to maximize their benefits and minimize their costs in a dangerous situation. Robbery is analyzed as instrumental action. The second model, impulsive action, assumes noninstrumental behavior. There is no weighing of costs and benefits, only the desire to injure or kill.[46]

Killing a Stranger: Instrumental Aggression

As I proposed earlier, the interpersonal interactions that lead to instrumental violence may be different in important respects from the interactions that give rise to more emotional attacks. The instrumentally oriented aggressor is more interested in achieving an external objective than in injuring or killing the victim for the gratifications that might be obtained from the harm or destruction itself. With Block, I can say that murders committed in the course of a robbery are usually instrumental actions; the felons believe that they can best further their criminal purposes by slaying the victims. The victim of instrumental aggression is an impediment who has to be gotten out of the way or someone who threatens the safety of the aggressor and thus has to be removed.

This doesn't mean, of course, that instrumental killings are always coldly calculated and entirely deliberate. Robbery deaths are most likely to occur when victims resist armed assailants.[47] Remember Franklin Zimring's contention that a substantial proportion of these murders come about because the offenders are highly emotional at the time. They react impulsively to perceived threats, such as the victims' seeming resistance. Nevertheless, because they are primarily interested in safely obtaining the victims' money or other possessions, the criminals kill mainly in pursuit of this objective.

While I have suggested that many of the people who are slain in instrumentally oriented homicides hadn't had close relationships with their killers beforehand and may even have been total strangers to them, you certainly shouldn't conclude that there are no instrumental aspects to some murders of relatives, friends, or lovers. People have been killed in reality, as in fiction, by murderers whom they knew and who expected to gain from their victims' deaths. News reports soon after the Gulf War told of a young soldier just back from the war who was killed outside his relatives' home as he was loading his car with household goods. Although the initial news stories indicated that he had been a robbery victim, it soon turned out that his wife and her lover had been the actual culprits and that they had hoped to benefit from his death. The killing was a calculated effort to further the murderers' purposes. Though the homicide was dictated by the hope of sexual and financial benefits, it did not arise from an emotional outburst of rage and passion, and it was more instrumental than emotional in nature.

Killing a Known Person in a Conflict: Emotional Aggression
The intense conflict that usually leads to the slaying of a family member, a friend, or an acquaintance typically produces a very different kind of interaction. The victim usually plays a much more active role in this type of situation and, as Wolfgang and others have reported, may even at times precipitate the aggressive exchange. No matter who starts such an exchange, however, it quite often heats up to a point at which tempers explode in violence.

As I indicated in the discussion of domestic violence in Chapter 8, some writers view this aggressive interaction between people who know one another as a struggle for power or dominance. According to this theory, a large proportion of persons with violent dispositions fear that they are insignificant in the world's eyes and think of themselves as having little control over what happens to them. When a man, for example, who sees himself this way gets into an argument with a neighbor, he will attempt to compensate for his perceived weakness by trying hard to assert his power and to show his neighbor who's boss.

Other theorists have advanced a somewhat different interpretation, holding that both disputants are excessively concerned about saving face. David Luckenbill has given us a good example of such an interpretation in his analysis of seventy murder cases. According to Luckenbill, one of the parties involved in the interaction starts the aggressive exchange by doing something the other individual regards as "an offense to 'face,' that image of self a person claims during a particular occasion or social contact." This is often an offensive or belittling remark, but it can also be a refusal to comply with the other's wishes. The offended individual doesn't withdraw or try to placate the other party, presumably because he thinks this would cause him to lose even more face. Instead, he tries to salvage his respect and honor by expressing anger and/or contempt, thereby supposedly signifying his opinion of the other "as an unworthy person." The interaction escalates because each person doesn't want to show weakness or lose face. Luckenbill also comments that each essentially defines the situation as one in which violence is an appropriate reaction.[48]

I don't doubt that the desire to save face (and/or to assert one's power) is involved in many conflict-ridden violent exchanges. One of Luckenbill's cases is illustrative:

> *Case 4* The offender, [the] victim, and three friends were driving in the country [and] drinking beer and wine. At one point, the victim started laughing at the offender's car, which he, the victim, [had] scratched a week earlier. The offender asked the victim why he was laughing. The victim responded that the offender's car looked like junk. The offender stopped the car, and all got out. The offender asked the victim to repeat his statement. When the victim repeated his characterization of the car, the offender struck the victim, knocking him to the ground. [The victim was killed soon thereafter.][49]

My contention, however, is that quite a few violent actions are much more impulsive in nature. They are relatively thoughtless reactions and are impelled by strong internal agitation. In my view, these reactions are not uncommon in violent crimes. As a matter of fact, when my associates and I interviewed seventy-one incarcerated violent criminals in Scotland, we received few clear indications that these men had been concerned about saving face. When they were asked what they had wanted to accomplish in the fights that landed them in jail, most replied that they had primarily wanted to hurt the other person. Only 12 percent of the men in the sample indicated a desire to protect their reputations or to gain approval. The ideas the offenders expressed during the course of the interview were even more revealing. Whereas the majority talked explicitly about having wanted to injure their opponents and/or to protect themselves, only about 20 percent made explicit mention of having sought self-satisfaction or social approval.[50]

Whether or not the urge to hurt or destroy the opponent is a frequent factor in homicides, it also can be seen in another case cited by Luckenbill, as follows:

> *Case 28* As the offender entered the back door of the house, his wife said to her lover, the victim, "There's—." The victim jumped to his feet and started dressing hurriedly. The offender, having called to his wife without avail, entered the bedroom. He found his wife nude and the victim clad in underwear. The startled offender asked the victim, "Why?" The victim replied,

"Haven't you ever been in love? We love each other." The offender later stated, "If they were drunk or something, I could see it. I mean, I've done it myself. But when he said they loved each other, well that did it."[51]

My guess is that the offender lost his temper when he heard the victim's statement. If we accept the offender's later explanation, he apparently wasn't bothered too much by his wife's unfaithfulness. (Shouldn't he have lost face by being cuckolded?) What did provoke him, evidently, was the threat of losing the woman. "That did it," as he himself said. Exceedingly disturbed by this idea, he seems to have exploded in rage and killed his rival.

We can't be sure that this was the way it happened or just what motivated the homicide; but surely, many murders, like many other violent actions, are highly emotional outbursts, driven by strong passion.

SUMMARY

Focusing on criminal homicides in the United States, which has the highest murder rate of any country in the technologically advanced world, in this chapter I offer a brief overview of the most important factors that lead people to deliberately take others' lives. Although considerable attention is given to the role of violence-prone personalities, no analysis of the more extreme mental disorders or of serial killers is offered.

The basic statistics that need to be explained have been well known since Marvin Wolfgang's classic 1958 analysis of Philadelphia homicides: More often than not, both offender and victim are especially likely to be low-socioeconomic-status young males from the same ethnic or racial background. Both are disproportionally black, in relation to the population, and they typically knew each other before the crime occurred. Alcohol use is involved in the great majority of instances. In a substantial fraction of the cases, moreover, the killings seem to be victim-precipitated, in that the slain persons apparently played active roles in the fatal encounters. According to Wolfgang's data, in most cases the encounters were highly emotional in nature; only a minority of homicides seem to be cold-blooded and unemotional.

Although other studies have generally corroborated Wolfgang's findings, more recent statistics suggest that there has been an upsurge in the killing of strangers in the past several decades. The murders of strangers are probably different in important respects from the slayings of people whom the murderer knows. On the basis of concepts used throughout this book, I propose that killings of strangers are especially apt to be instances of instrumental aggression, whereas murders of people whom the killer knows are more likely to be acts of emotional aggression. Evidence consistent with this interpretation is cited in the chapter, along with findings which suggest that the growth in the proportion of persons killed during instrumental, felony-related crimes (notably robberies) is largely caused by increased use of firearms.

I attempt to account for the statistics mentioned above by describing offenders' personal dispositions, as well as social factors that heighten aggressive inclinations and/or weaken restraints upon violence. Findings from a number of studies, including Wolfgang's, show that many murderers have histories of aggressive offenses and are violence-prone. While some researchers speak of an "overcontrolled aggressive personality," the evidence for the existence and frequency of such a personality type among murderers is not fully convincing. It appears that most people who are guilty of serious violent crimes are apt to be emotionally reactive, undercontrolled aggressive personalities. I also maintain (somewhat tentatively) that there may be an increasing number of people who are not only indifferent to others' suffering but who also enjoy hurting merely for the sake of inflicting pain. However, no matter what is the nature of the people who are prone to violence, and no matter how much is known about them, it is exceedingly difficult (and maybe even impossible) for psychiatrists and psychologists to use the information to predict whether an individual will commit a violent offense in the future, largely because these acts are exceedingly rare.

The role of social conditions, especially conditions which serve as social stressors, is also examined. Generally speaking, homicide rates tend to be highest in the areas of the country that have the lowest average incomes, dilapidated and overcrowded housing, and high proportions of black residents. While socioeconomic inequalities between whites and blacks in a given area apparently contribute to high rates of violent offenses, it is also true that poverty in itself seems to produce violent crimes. In keeping with the thesis of this book, I propose that any condition that generates substantial displeasure—whether poverty, racial inequalities, overcrowded housing, or oppressive heat—can give rise to aggressive inclinations that may lead to murder.

The social conditions that promote high homicide rates typically do more than activate aggressive urges, however; many of them also serve to reduce inhibitions against aggression. Social disorganization results in weak social controls, and such disorganization is all too characteristic of poverty-stricken, physically deteriorating, and overcrowded areas. Social disorganization may even exist to some degree in areas with high divorce rates, since the incidence of family breakups is associated with homicide rates even when income level is statistically held constant.

In this chapter I also discuss the possibility that subcultural influences, meaning principally the norms and values shared by particular groups of people, may affect homicide rates. One relevant question in this regard is whether the high homicide rates that are typically found in metropolitan areas with high concentrations of poor blacks are due at least partly to the existence of subcultures of violence which encourage or at least permit aggression. According to various statistical analyses, the relatively frequent killings in these particular communities are not adequately explained by poverty and social inequalities. I suggest that, if subcultures of violence do exist—and there is no good direct supporting evidence for their existence—their influence may be confined to relatively small segments of the community: small numbers of inner-city youths who are favorably disposed toward violence because of their resentment and their alienation from the mainstream society. Modifying the usual interpretation of these possible subcultures, I propose that the violence-favoring attitudes and values held by these youths have not necessarily been deliberately taught to them by their elders. Instead, these young men may have developed such attitudes and values as a result of having grown up in a harsh and frustrating environment in which violence is all too common.

While the discussion in this chapter focuses largely on long-standing dispositions to aggression, I do point out that short-term influences can also contribute to the taking of another's life. Research by Archer and Gartner which indicates that homicide rates tend to rise shortly after wars provides one example of short-term influences. However, the effects of short-term influences can be better seen in the violent interactions that lead to murder. To some degree in instrumental, felony-related crimes but more often in highly emotional encounters with people whom they know, aggressively inclined persons are somehow stimulated to assault others. Highly reactive and deficient in self-restraints, such assailants may kill others whom they perceive as enemies, especially when weapons are readily available.

Notes

1. Data from Fingerhut & Kleinman (1990).
2. The gender distribution statistics were taken from the U.S. Department of Justice (1988). *Sourcebook of Criminal Justice Statistics*. Washington: U.S. Department of Justice. p. 453.
3. Wolfgang (1958, 1967).
4. Braucht, Loya, & Jamieson (1980), p. 316.
5. See Braucht et al.; (1980); Gibbons (1987).
6. The studies mentioned in these two paragraphs are cited in Braucht et al. (1980).
7. Williams & Flewelling (1988). It should be recognized that the conflict crime category is somewhat broader than the present discussion implies. It includes children killed by a baby sitter, lovers' triangles, brawls over alcohol or drugs, and arguments. The "other" category includes rape, burglary, larceny, robbery, motor vehicle theft, vice crimes, violation of drug laws, gambling, and gang killings.
8. From U.S. Department of Justice (1988), op. cit., p. 448.

9. The data pointing to the drop in the proportion of Chicago homicides in which the victim was known to the slayer come from Block (1977), p. 40. The statement about the growth in felony-related homicides in the 1960s is taken from Rose (1979), pp. 10–11, and the last quotation is from Zimring (1979), p. 31.

10. Statistics taken from the editorial, "Fight guns, not just drugs," in the *New York Times*, Dec. 8, 1990.

11. Zimring (1979).

12. U.S. Department of Justice (1988), op. cit., p. 453.

13. The statistics cited here come from the summary of the CDC Weekly Morbidity and Mortality Report, as reported in the *Journal of the American Medical Association*, Jan. 9, 1991, pp. 183–184. The epidemiologist's remark was quoted in a *New York Times* article on the CDC report, Dec. 7, 1990. Adding to the dismal figures given in this section, Richters (1992) noted that in 1988 black male adolescents were eleven times more likely to be killed by guns than were their white counterparts.

14. Gary (1986), p. 25.

15. Miller, Dinitz, & Conrad (1982), p. 106.

16. Goetting (1989). Also see Palmer (1960).

17. From Megargee (1966) and from Megargee & Mendelsohn (1962), as quoted in Megargee & Hokanson (1970), p. 111.

18. See Hollin (1989), pp. 75–78, for a summary of some pertinent studies including the research by Blackburn.

19. See Wilson & Herrnstein (1985).

20. The quotation is from an article by Dershowitz (1974), cited in Monahan (1981), p. 21.

21. Monahan (1981), p. 23.

22. The figures cited here are taken from Steadman (1987), p. 8.

23. See Monahan (1981, 1988) for careful reviews of the pertinent research literature. Although he offered several suggestions about how the predictive efficacy might be improved, Monahan concluded that psychiatrists and psychologists are all too frequently in error even when they take previous history of violence and mental illness into account.

24. From the final report of the National Commission on the Causes and Prevention of Violence (December 1969). *To establish justice, to insure domestic tranquility.* Washington, D.C.: U.S. Government Printing Office, pp. xxi–xxii.

25. Bensing & Schroeder (1960), summarized in Braucht et al. (1980), p. 319.

26. Blau & Blau (1982), p. 126.

27. Williams (1984); Williams & Flewelling (1988). Devine, Sheley, & Smith (1988) have reported that national increases in unemployment are typically accompanied by rises in the country's homicide rate.

28. Devine, Sheley, & Smith (1988).

29. Anderson & Anderson (1984).

30. See Anderson (1989).

31. Sutherland & Cressey (1960), pp. 159–160.

32. Lemann (1991), p. 20.

33. Blau & Blau (1982); Williams & Flewelling (1988).

34. E.g., Blau & Blau (1982); Williams (1984); Williams & Flewelling (1988).

35. Curtis (1989), p. 140.

36. Henry & Short (1954). I can speculate that blacks may be disturbed by unfavorable comparisons between themselves and other blacks as well as between themselves and whites. Both disparities could be lessened in times of business recession. In this connection, Blau & Blau (1982) found that intraracial as well as interracial inequalities were positively related to homicide rates in metropolitan areas.

37. Wolfgang (1967); Wolfgang & Ferracuti (1967).

38. Fingerhut & Kleinman (1990) report the homicide rates for young white and black males in many U.S. states in 1987. It's worth noting that the homicide rate for young white men is comparatively high in several western states, such as (besides Texas) Arizona and Colorado. Greenberg, Carey, & Popper (1987) have given us more information about the high death rate for young white males in the western part of the United States. Besides showing that the rural western states had the highest death rates *from all causes* for young males between age 15 and age 24, they report that "the overall white male violent death rate in the 6 most dangerous rural western counties was 13% higher than the comparable black rate in 6 eastern inner cities."

39. Hackney (1969), p. 505.

40. Huff-Corzine, Corzine, & Moore (1986), p. 921. Also see Blau & Blau (1982).

41. Erlanger (1976).

42. See Ball-Rokeach (1973); Erlanger (1974).

43. The city dweller's statement and the criminologist's observation were reported in the *New York Times,* Dec. 9, 1990. The community workers' observations regarding the development of a subculture of disillusionment and routine violence in urban black ghettos are from Pally & Robinson (1988).

44. Richters' findings are reported in Richters & Martinez (1992). Another summary of his results and the observations regarding the Beirut children can be seen in Shuchman, *New York Times,* Feb. 21, 1991.

45. Archer & Gartner (1984), p. 96. In this research the investigators compared the homicide rate in the five years before each war to the rate in the five postwar years.

46. Block (1977), p. 9. The previous reference is to Williams & Flewelling (1988).

47. Block (1977).

48. Luckenbill (1977).

49. Luckenbill (1977), p. 182.

50. Berkowitz (1986).

51. Luckenbill (1977), p. 180.

PART 4

❖

Controlling Aggression

T here's no need to repeat the dismal statistics. The sad fact is all too apparent: Crimes of violence are becoming ever more frequent. How can society lessen the horrendous amount of violence with which it is plagued? What can we—government, the police, citizens, parents, and educators, all of us—do to make our social world a better, or at least a safer, place?

The Different Prescriptions

Specialists in the study of human behavior have offered widely different formulas. Many consider it only common sense to punish the criminals who violate our laws. This is the *deterrence* policy, widely favored in our society by much of the public, as well as most police agencies, many lawyers, and also quite a few social scientists. If behavior can be controlled by its consequences, as the social scientists generally say, we can lower the rate of crime by showing potential wrongdoers that their misdeeds will have a negative outcome for them.[1] Sigmund Freud was also sympathetic to the deterrence approach. He held that civilization is ultimately based upon force, not upon love and charity. Law is basically socially condoned violence "ready to be directed against any individual who resists it."[2] The threat of punishment preserves law and order, and it is the foundation on which society is built.

Quite a few jurists and legal scholars share this view. Wickedness should be penalized, they insist, in order to prevent further wrongdoing (although of course this is not the only justification for severe sanctions). The failure to treat

309

miscreants harshly only encourages further misdeeds. An Englishman once put it this way: "Men are not hanged for stealing horses, but that horses may not be stolen."

Advocates of punishment, of course, are not the only voices to be heard on this matter. Other people maintain that punishment is by no means as effective in lessening crime as is widely supposed, and that it only rarely brings a positive good. "The world does not grow better by force or by the policeman's club," they say. The threat of capital punishment doesn't really stop people from killing those they hate and certainly doesn't teach them to resolve their quarrels in an amicable and constructive manner. Worse, according to this argument, when we call for a murderer's death, we are only insisting on vengeance and revealing the primitive side of our nature. "When we execute a murderer," a writer once remarked, "it may be that we fall into the same mistake as a child that strikes a chair it has collided with."

How can this mistake be avoided? Some mental health practitioners believe the ideal solution to the problem of criminal violence is to seek a "purge" or "release" of a supposedly pent-up impetus to violence. They contend that people can lower their urges to attack others by engaging in various forms of aggression, of either an imaginary or a realistic nature, or even by practicing a substitute type of aggression, such as competition. I call these therapists "ventilationists," because of their belief in the benefits of venting feelings. Psychologists also say that these therapists have a *hydraulic* conception of motivation, since they basically believe that people have within them a reservoir of accumulated aggressive energy that constantly presses them to assault someone.[3]

Some of the mental health specialists who take the hydraulic position think, with Freud and his disciples, that the urge to violence is instinctive and that it accumulates all by itself, as a result of unidentified biological processes. Others don't posit an aggressive instinct but nevertheless believe people to be walking storehouses of repressed violent urges. According to them, we carry around within us the remnants of whatever aggressive impulses have been generated by the threats and frustrations we experienced in our lives, and it's advisable, for the sake of our mental health, to release this pent-up aggressive drive. One ventilationist, Fritz Perls, a cofounder of Gestalt psychotherapy, put the argument in these terms:

> If a person suppresses aggression . . . if he bottles up his rage, we have to find an outlet. We have to give him an opportunity of letting off steam. Punching a ball, chopping wood, or any kind of aggressive sport, such as football, will sometimes work wonders.[4]

The more extreme proponents of this approach have gone much further. They attribute many of society's ills to the absence of sufficient outlets for the aggressive drive. "If society is in danger," one of them once said, "it is not because of man's aggressiveness, but because of the repression of personal aggressiveness in individuals."[5] Suitable ways supposedly must be found to discharge the aggressive energies that build up inside us.

What are the alternatives if this conception is wrong? Considerable research does indicate that it is indeed seriously in error. What can be done if we cannot rehabilitate violent criminals or tame them through soccer games, white-water canoeing, or mountain climbing? Maybe another kind of psychological intervention is required, one that emphasizes education and treatment. Karl Menninger, the internationally recognized cofounder of the Menninger Clinic, was so repelled by traditional ways of dealing with criminals that he entitled one of his books *The Crime of Punishment*. "And just so long as the spirit of vengeance has the slightest vestige of respectability," he wrote, "so long as it pervades the public mind and infuses its evil upon the statute books of law, we will make no headway toward the control of crime."[6] According to Menninger and many others, the best way to reduce crime is by rehabilitating or treating the criminals.

Part 4 will be devoted to these three basic approaches to the control and/or reduction of violence: threatening to punish people who behave aggressively, "discharging" violent urges through various forms of aggression, and fostering new learning. Many complexities are involved in each of these approaches. In Chapter 10, I will focus primarily on the effectiveness of external societal controls, and will describe the research on punishment, on the death penalty, and on restricting the availability of firearms. In Chapter 11, I will deal with the psychologically oriented interventions, procedures that essentially try to alter the individual's urge to assault someone. In this connection, I will concentrate mostly on the approaches that encourage people to express their feelings and emotional urges, as well as on other psychological methods that generally try to bring about new learning.

Notes

1. Wilson & Herrnstein (1985), among other social scientists, favor this approach to controlling criminal behavior and spell out their argument with considerable thought.

2. Freud (1933/1950).

3. See Zillmann (1979), pp. 118–122; Berkowitz (1970b, July 1973b); Geen & Quanty (1977); Feshbach (1984).

4. Perls (1969), p. 116.

5. Storr (1968), p. 109.

6. Menninger (1968), p. 165.

10

*P*unishment and *S*ocietal *C*ontrols

❖

*U*SING PUNISHMENT TO DETER VIOLENCE

The Pros and Cons of Punishment

Chapter 6, The Development of Violence Proneness, described the effects of punishment in some detail, with a focus on the role of punishment in the development of relatively persistent modes of violent conduct. In this chapter, I will ask whether the threat of punishment can minimize the likelihood of displays of aggression, mainly by convincing the would-be aggressor that an attack wouldn't pay off.[1]

Even with this difference, much of the theory and research that was spelled out in Chapter 6 is also applicable here. A review of the major points will be useful.

Arguments against Punishment as a Deterrent

Quite a few educators and mental health specialists condemn the use of punishment in an attempt to influence children's behavior. Proponents of nonviolence question the morality of using physical force, even in a socially worthy cause. Other professionals insist that punishment is unlikely to be effective. The injured victims, they say, may stop carrying out the disapproved behavior, but the suppression will be only temporary. According to this view, if a mother spanks her son for hitting his sister, the boy may halt his aggression for a while. However, there's a good chance he'll hit the girl again, especially when he thinks his mother won't see him doing it. What's worse from the disciplinarian's perspective, he may even become more highly aggressive.

Opposing physical punishment in schools. The same objections, especially the possibility of undesirable side effects, have been leveled against the use of corporal punishment in schools. More than inflicting physical pain, the opponents say, the beatings hurt the youngsters' pride and may even heighten their rebelliousness. Besides, hitting a child on the buttocks with a wooden paddle doesn't resolve anything. Faced with these protests, twenty U.S. states have now outlawed corporal punishment in schools; nine of these prohibitions were enacted in the period between 1987 and mid-1990. The opposition to this practice is even more uniform in Europe. As of this writing, no European nation except Great Britain allows its teachers to punish pupils physically for violations of discipline.

Threats of bombing and shooting often don't coerce the enemy. If physical punishment is often counterproductive with children, it can frequently be even more futile when used on adults. To give you an example that may not have occurred to you in this context, the American bombing of North Vietnam during the Vietnam war shows how ineffective punishment can be in many instances. Of course, the U.S. military might have done even more: it might have destroyed all organized opposition by blasting the enemy with nuclear bombs. Even without going this far, however, the United States still inflicted tremendous punishment on the North Vietnamese, hitting them with a greater weight of bombs than was dropped on Germany in World War II. All this was to no avail. The North Vietnamese continued their battle in spite of all the death and destruction. As we know, they eventually drove the United States out of southeast Asia. Despite all the harm we did to the enemy, we still couldn't bend them to our wishes, and for all we know, the bombardment may have actually strengthened their resolve.[2]

The possible dangers of labeling. Sociologists have also identified another possible shortcoming in the use of punishment as a social control procedure. A sociological conception known as *labeling theory* maintains that many people become deviants as a consequence of being labeled "wrongdoers." Because they are treated as bad persons by society, their self-identities are altered. They come to think of themselves as being outside the law, and they act accordingly. From this perspective, people who are punished by the criminal justice system are all too apt to be labeled—by themselves and by others—"deviants" and "lawbreakers." Instead of deterring them from breaking the law again, their punishment heightens the likelihood that they will commit further crimes as they live up to this self identity.[3]

Punishment is often ineffective with psychopaths. Whatever one's stance on the issues I've just discussed, it is undeniable that the threat of punishment may be particularly ineffective with some kinds of people, especially psychopaths. As I pointed out in Chapter 5, these people tend to be highly impulsive. According to Joseph Newman's research, psychopaths often persist in the behavior they are disposed to enact at the time, regardless of any information that is made available to them indicating that their mode of conduct is inappropriate and probably won't pay off. It's reasonable to suggest, then, that when psychopaths are strongly inclined to assault someone, they may well be insensitive to information on the threat of punishment. Focusing on their urge to hurt the one who provoked them (their aggressive goal), they don't restrain themselves sufficiently to think of the possible negative consequences of their behavior.[4]

Punishment Can Be an Effective Deterrent—Sometimes
The objections to the use of punishment can't be dismissed out of hand. They are valid—a good deal of the time but not always. As I noted in Chapter 6, under certain conditions the expeditious delivery of negative consequences, either physical or psychological in nature, can deter antisocial conduct without producing serious adverse side effects.

I listed these conditions earlier, but they are so important that I'll repeat them here. Punishment works best, according to psychological theory and research, when it is: (1) severe; (2) delivered quickly, before the persons whose behavior needs to be controlled can enjoy the pleasures that they might gain from the disapproved behavior; (3) administered consistently and with certainty, so that there is little doubt that the disapproved action will have at least some negative consequences; (4) attractive alternatives to the disapproved behavior are available; and (5) the people who are punished have a clear understanding of the reasons for the discipline.

Theory and research also tell us, however, that we can't always make others behave properly by threatening them with dire outcomes if they misbehave. The ideal conditions listed above don't always exist, and indeed, they may be relatively rare. The United States punished North Vietnam severely, as I said before, and the North Vietnamese leaders undoubtedly were well aware of the reasons for the U.S. actions (although they didn't accept the reasons). The alternatives presented by the U.S. government (stopping the struggle and acquiescing to a separate, noncommunist South Vietnamese state) were not attractive to the North Vietnamese leaders, and many of their disapproved actions (such as delivering supplies to their forces in South Vietnam and killing U.S. and South Vietnamese soldiers) were not punished soon enough or with sufficient certainty. In essence, the North Vietnamese leaders believed that they had a fairly good chance of getting away with doing what they wanted in spite of the U.S. opposition.

There are some additional difficulties involved in using punishment effectively to control aggression. One such difficulty has to do with the rewards aggression can bring. It is sometimes impossible to prevent aggressors from being rewarded by their actions. People who are emotionally aroused are gratified simply by being able to hurt their targets. Let's say a boy is provoked by his sister and hits her in retaliation. If the mother wants to punish her son, she obviously shouldn't wait until the father comes home from work. That's much too late. But even if the mother spanks the offender right away, the punishment may come after the girl has shown she is hurt. The victim's pain has thus rewarded the aggressor before he is punished by his mother.

Yet another problem stems from the negative affect generated by punishment. The unpleasant feelings produced by punishment are all too likely to spur later attacks unless the persons who have been disciplined (1) think of the punishment they might suffer, (2) can restrain their aggressive impulses, and (3) have attractive alternative courses of action available to them.

Does Punishment Deter Violent Crimes?

All this psychological theorizing seems plausible, you may be thinking, but how well do these ideas work in the real world? In essence, the threat of punishment does appear to reduce the rate of violent offenses *to some degree*, at least *under some circumstances,* although the evidence is not as airtight as would be desirable.

An Example: Arrests Deterring Domestic Violence
An important real-world experiment involving domestic violence was carried out jointly by the Police Department of Minneapolis, Minnesota,

and the Police Foundation (a private organization concerned with research into all aspects of police performance). Police officers don't like dealing with family brawls and are often reluctant to take any steps at all when called to the scene of a fight. Around the country in the mid-1980s, it has been estimated, they made arrests in only about 1 percent of the cases in which wives were assaulted.[5] Even if the police officers are sure a legal offense was committed and even if they arrest the aggressor, they also know that the courts are unlikely to impose legal penalties. Besides, domestic problems seem to them to be basically beyond solution. Even if they were willing to take action, they would be uncertain about what to do.

Various experts advise the police freely, but they don't all prescribe the same courses of action. Some psychologists and social workers believe that the police should be active peacemakers—that the officers who investigate a domestic conflict should try to settle the dispute as amicably as possible, rather than make arrest, and should even counsel the warring man and woman. This recommendation is strongly criticized by other people, especially members of militant women's groups, who have little sympathy for male assailants. They argue that the men should be punished (i.e., arrested) rather than counseled.

The Minneapolis experiment sought to learn whether counseling or arrest was more effective in reducing the likelihood of further domestic abuse. When the police officers who were participating in the study arrived at a scene of domestic violence, they first determined whether the case fit the experiment's criteria: Both members of the couple had to be present, the assault must have occurred within the past four hours, and the offense had to be only a misdemeanor (that is, the battering had to be bad enough to warrant arrest but not so severe as to cause serious injury or be life-threatening). Appropriate cases were then randomly assigned to one of three conditions: (1) the assailant was arrested; (2) the officers listened to the disputants and tried to advise them on how to settle the conflict; or (3) the officers separated the man and the woman, sending the offender away for at least several hours. (It's important to realize that the arrested subjects weren't jailed for very long; more than 40 percent of them were released within a day, and almost 90 percent were out of jail in a week or less.) All the cases were then followed up over the next six months to see what happened next and, particularly, whether the domestic abuse was repeated.

As Figure 10–1 indicates, arrest seemed to be the best deterrent to further abuse. According to the official police records, only 10 percent of the men who were arrested for assaulting their domestic partners during the "intervention" period were rearrested within the next six months for battering them again. This low rate of repeated abuse contrasts with 19 percent of advised assailants and 24 percent of "separated" men who were subsequently arrested for further violence against their domestic partners.

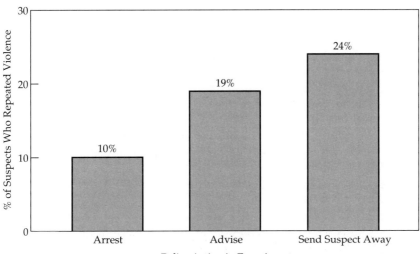

FIGURE 10–1

Percentage of repeat violence over 6 months for each police action, according to official records. (Data from Sherman & Berk (1984b), Fig.1. Reprinted with permission of the Police Foundation.)

These findings clearly have important implications for social policy, and the experiment has attracted nationwide attention. The Minneapolis Police Department was so impressed by the results that it has modified its policies regarding domestic assaults. The researchers themselves suggested that it might be desirable to empower the police to make arrests in cases of simple domestic assaults "unless there are good reasons why an arrest is not likely to be appropriate."[6]

The limited deterrent value of arrests. We have to be cautious in drawing lessons from the Minneapolis results, however. I have pointed out that punishment is an effective means of control only under limited circumstances, and we therefore shouldn't expect arrests to be widely successful deterrents to criminal conduct. This limited effectiveness can be seen in the Minneapolis domestic violence experiment itself and, more clearly, in some of the attempted replications of the original study.

Only Some Persons May Be Deterred. First of all, there is the obvious possibility that arrests may be a much more effective deterrent to further misbehavior for some people than for others. Keep in mind that the arrested men in the Minneapolis experiment hadn't seriously injured the women. This suggests that they probably hadn't been extremely excited and hadn't lost all conscious control over their behavior. It may be, then, that most of them were neither extremely reactive emotionally nor psychopathic aggressors. Because they were not highly aroused, they were able to hold back and to think about the possible negative consequences of violence. On later occasions, when they were again provoked, they could remember that they might be rearrested if they struck their companions, and they therefore restrained themselves.

The Deterrent Value of Arrests May Diminish With Time. By and large, the threat of punishment dissuades people from misbehaving only to the degree that they are thinking of this possible negative consequence when they're tempted to transgress. This suggests that, for many persons at least, prior arrests for wrongdoing could cease to be an effective deterrent to further law violations as time goes by. The punishment they had received earlier fades from memory and isn't readily recalled.

A reanalysis of the data obtained in the Minneapolis investigation gives us one indication of how the passage of time can lessen the degree to which arrests exert a controlling influence on domestic violence. When a team of researchers looked closely at the results from this study, they found that "the deterrent effect of arrest was short-lived; most of the deterrence occurred initially, and the effect decayed by the end of the six month follow-up period."[']

Other research on the use of arrests in domestic assaults points in the same direction. The National Institute of Justice, encouraged by the initial findings from the Minneapolis experiment, had sponsored a series of studies in other U.S. cities, including Omaha, Nebraska, Charlotte, North Carolina, and Milwaukee, Wisconsin, to determine if an arrest policy would lower the prevalence of domestic violence in these communities as well. The results from these later investigations were decidedly mixed and there was no consistent evidence that arrests could lower the reoccurrence of misdemeanor domestic assaults. More relevant to the present discussion, whatever deterrent effect there was seemed, over all, to be relatively short-lived.

The findings obtained in the carefully designed and well conducted Milwaukee experiment carried out by Lawrence Sherman and his associates at the Crime Control Institute (a research organization) in Maryland are especially suggestive. When the Milwaukee police officers in the research team encountered a misdemeanor domestic battery case that could have led to an arrest, they randomly assigned the suspect (a male in almost all instances) to one of three conditions: (1) a *full arrest* condition in which the suspect was told he was arrested for battery, was handcuffed, and was in custody for approximately 11 hours; (2) a *short arrest* condition in which the suspect was also charged and handcuffed, but was informed he "may be released in a few hours" and subsequently was in custody only for about 3 hours; and (3) a *warned* condition in which no one was arrested but the people involved were told "someone will go to jail" if the police officer has to return. Over 1000 couples from four poverty-stricken black neighborhoods were involved in the experiment.

Interviews with the participants about a month after the incident showed that both the full and short arrest procedures had reduced the risk of any repeat violence. Thus, where 17 percent of the warned men were reported for another assault within the next month, only 6 and 7 percent of the "full" and "short" arrested men were so reported. However, the arrests lost their deterrent value as the months went by; approximately 30 percent of the men in each condition were said to have repeated their violence some time during the six months following the initial incident. As their earlier experience receded into the past, in the heat of an altercation with their partner the arrested men apparently didn't stop to think about the consequence they might suffer, and thus were not especially apt to restrain themselves.[8]

The Severity and Certainty of Punishment

However right I am in this interpretation of the arrest for domestic violence experiments, the severity and certainty of punishment could be very important in determining how well legal sanctions deter crimes. Indeed, *deterrence theory*, the well-known criminological conception mentioned earlier, says just this. Society can presumably lessen illegal conduct by showing potential wrongdoers that they are almost certain to suffer serious negative consequences if they break the law. Though this seems obvious, you might be surprised at some of the results criminologists have obtained in research on punishment.

The findings on punishment severity may be especially startling. In the United States, public demands for harsh treatment of criminals are usually translated into long prison sentences for serious offenders. It's by no means certain, however, that the threat of spending a long time in jail actually discourages crime. According to a research review commissioned by the National Academy of Sciences, there's little good evidence showing that longer sentences have much of a deterrent effect. Whether the offenses are marijuana use, theft, driving while intoxicated, or even homicide, studies "question the assertion that crime may [better] be deterred by increasing penalties."[9]

Certainty of punishment seems to be more important. The research review just mentioned suggests that criminality tends to decline as the perceived probability of arrest and incarceration becomes greater. The punishment apparently has to be severe enough to hurt, but it's the likelihood of punishment more than its absolute intensity that seems to count in deterring crime.[10]

Deterrence can never be perfect, however, in part because not every offense is punished. Many violations of the law are not detected. Even when the violations are detected, the perpetrators are not caught and punished. This is true of violent crimes as well as traffic offenses and business frauds. Contrary to the impressions conveyed by fictional police stories, most arrests for criminal violence are made because a witness can identify the offender and/or because the police arrive on the scene quickly and can catch the lawbreaker practically red-handed. Since attacks on strangers are less likely to be witnessed and/or to come quickly to the attention of police than are domestic assaults, they are less apt to lead to arrests. As a matter of fact, a good proportion of violent offenses don't lead to arrest and punishment. A decade ago, according to Peter Greenwood, though almost three-quarters of reported murders in the United States were "cleared by arrests," only about 59 percent of aggravated assaults, 48 percent of forcible rapes, and one-quarter of robberies had the same outcome.[11] The percentages will be even lower if the present trend toward increases in violence against strangers continues. You can see what this might mean to people who are thinking of assaulting others. Even when they are aware of the possible adverse consequences, they will know that there's some chance their aggression won't be punished by the legal system.

Does Capital Punishment Deter Homicides?

What about the ultimate penalty? Does society reduce the incidence of homicides when it prescribes death for murderers? This question has been hotly debated. Hundreds of books and articles have been written on the morality, wisdom, and effectiveness of the death penalty, and dozens of empirical studies have investigated whether would-be murderers are deterred to any significant extent by the threat of capital punishment.

These investigations have been of various kinds. Some have involved comparisons of countries (or U.S. states) that do and do not practice capital punishment. In a well-known study of this type, Thorstein Sellin examined the homicide rates of various sets of U.S. states in the period 1920–1958. He basically compared states that differed in their policies toward capital punishment but were otherwise similar, geographically and demographically. Sellin tells us that the threat of being put to death for taking someone's life did not seem to influence a state's homicide rate. The states that imposed the death penalty did not have fewer murders per capita than did comparable states that did not practice capital punishment. Other studies of this kind have reached much the same conclusion.[12]

We can also look for evidence on the possible effects of the death penalty by asking what happened to the country's homicide rate after a national hiatus in the use of capital punishment. Although the U.S. Supreme Court had previously forbidden executions on the grounds that they were cruel and unusual punishment and were thus unconstitutional, the Court reversed itself to a considerable extent in 1976 and allowed the use of this penalty under certain circumstances. This change has not reduced the rate at which people in the United States kill each other, according to sociologists Ruth Peterson and William Bailey. After carefully examining the relevant statistics, they concluded, "There is no indication that the national return to capital punishment . . . has had a systematic downward impact on homicide."[13]

Sellin's research has also addressed another, related question: whether the police are particularly endangered by the absence of the death penalty. After all, they're on the front line, so to speak, and are frequently confronted by armed lawbreakers. Maybe criminals are more reluctant to shoot at police officers when they know they could be executed for killing them. In another comparison of states which do use capital punishment with states which do not, Sellin again found no difference in the rates at which police were murdered in the line of duty. Again, the results are supported by other investigations. We cannot say, Sellin argued, "that the states which have abolished the death penalty have thereby made the policemen's [lives] more hazardous."

International comparisons also have failed to find evidence that the death penalty lowers a country's homicide rate. A methodologically sophisticated analysis of this type employed data from nine countries that used capital punishment and eleven countries that did not. After controlling for such factors as degree of industrialization, unemployment, and illiteracy, the study found that the nations that executed murderers tended to have the highest homicide rates.[14]

The studies which I have been describing have basically looked into the long-term effects of the death penalty. Other investigations have examined the short-run influences, asking whether the publicized execution of a murderer reduces the occurrence of homicides for a fairly brief time afterward. There could conceivably be such a temporary effect. Just as some persons seem to get aggressive ideas from the violence reported on television and in the print media, widely publicized news stories of the execution of a murderer might remind potential killers of the extreme penalty that could be imposed upon them if they took another person's life. They might therefore restrain their violent inclinations, at least for a brief time.

David Phillips, whose work was mentioned in Chapter 7, Violence in the Media, has obtained indications of such a homicide suppression effect. Using as an index the amount of coverage the British press gave to the most notorious executions between 1858 and 1921, he found that newspaper coverage did seem to influence the homicide rate in London. In general, as shown in Figure 10–2, there was a statistically significant drop in the number of murders in London during the weeks of the highly publicized executions. Interestingly, and in accord with his other findings, the magnitude of this decrease was significantly correlated with the amount of attention the press gave to the execution. A number of killings that might otherwise have taken place apparently did not occur, as if some potential murderers, very aware of the extreme penalty they might suffer, had restrained themselves.

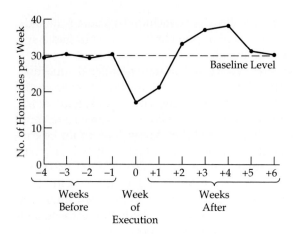

FIGURE 10–2

The frequency of weekly homicides before, during, and after 22 publicized executions (London, 1858–1921). (From Phillips (1980b), *American Journal of Sociology*, 86. Copyright 1980 University of Chicago Press. Adapted with permission.)

However, their self-restraint was only temporary. According to Phillips, the London homicide rate shot up beyond its baseline level two weeks later, perhaps because the temporarily deterred would-be killers had decided to carry through with their original violent plans. The threat of capital punishment evidently suppresses further homicides only when this extreme penalty is fresh in the public's memory.[15]

Obviously, proponents and opponents of capital punishment can draw different lessons from these findings, but they might also want to consider the implications of a later investigation, by Phillips and Hensley, of the aftereffects of U.S. homicides during the 1970s. Here again, capital punishment was followed by a temporary drop in the number of subsequent killings. After each death sentence, there were on the average approximately three fewer homicides across the entire country than otherwise would have been expected. However, Phillips found, this decrease came about only if the penalty was widely publicized on national TV news programs. Furthermore, the widely publicized imposition of a life sentence led to approximately the same size decline in homicides as did a death sentence or an execution.[16]

In sum, there isn't much evidence at all that the death penalty can deter homicides for a substantial period of time. Phillips' findings point only to a temporary effect—and his results are at best only suggestive. As a matter of fact, other studies along the same lines have come to somewhat different conclusions, and indeed, at least one investigation has reported an *increased* frequency of murders following executions.[17] Maybe all we can say, as some writers have argued, is that no airtight mathematical proof for or against the deterrent value of capital punishment is available at present. No one can insist with certainty that the threat of the extreme punishment definitely does lower the incidence of murder in the United States.

This statement may be surprising. Much of the public consider it only a matter of common sense that the death penalty successfully lowers the homicide rate. However, this view neglects two important considerations which I've been emphasizing in this chapter: first, that many violent actions are carried out impulsively with little thought of the possible negative consequences, and second, that even if the attackers are aware at the time that they might be punished, they have reason to believe they might escape punishment. This point holds for murder as well as for other aggressive offenses. Only about seven in ten homicides brought to the attention of the police result in arrests. Of these cases, according to the same statistics, only a further 70 percent are convicted, although not necessarily for first-degree murder. Some persons do get away with their crimes. Not every homicide is punished by execution, even in the jurisdictions that have the death penalty.

In any event, because of the uncertainty about whether capital punishment has a deterrent effect, the suggestive evidence that prolonged jail terms have as much of a restraining influence as the death penalty, and the serious moral and social questions about whether a government should deliberately kill its citizens, most technologically advanced societies no longer execute murderers. The United States is increasingly alone in its use of capital punishment.

WOULD GUN CONTROL LESSEN VIOLENT CRIMES?

Few people really want to read about the social ills of the United States. We don't want to learn how many people in our society are poor, homeless, or dying of AIDS, and we especially would rather not be told about the incidence of crime. The dreary figures only point to problems that seem beyond our control. Statistics on violent crimes involving guns, however, do command our attention, because they suggest that a solution might be found for at least one of the social ills that are so troubling to society.[16]

According to a U.S. Department of Justice study of victim-reported crimes in the United States between 1979 and 1987, about 640,000 crimes were committed with handguns *each year* during that period. More than 9000 of these offenses were murders, and more than 12,000 were rapes. In more than half the cases of murder or nonnegligent manslaughter, the killings carried out with handguns occurred during an argument or a fight, and not during a robbery. (I'll say more about use of firearms later in this chapter.)

Also, consider how the United States compares to other nations. The

National Center for Health Statistics tells us that, in 1987, three-quarters of the homicides in this country involving young males were committed with firearms, as compared to the mean of 23 percent for a sample of other technologically advanced nations. Here's a specific instance of this difference: Even though a U.S. city and a Canadian city—Seattle, Washington, and Vancouver, British Columbia, Canada—have similar overall rates of criminal activity, the homicide rate is considerably higher in Seattle than in its Canadian neighbor. Virtually all the difference is due to gun-related killings in the U.S. city.

According to crime reports as well as common knowledge, when a weapon is used to take someone's life *in this country* the chances are quite good that the weapon will be a firearm. As shown in Figure 10–3, a gun was used in over 60 percent of the U.S. homicides that were reported to the police in 1988.

The question is, could the government reduce the rate of violent crimes, and especially of murders, by lessening the availability of guns in general and handguns in particular?

More and more police officials favor such restrictions. Heads of many major police organizations have joined together to publish their names in newspaper ads calling on Congress to impose federal gun control laws. Police commissioners in some of the largest U.S. cities have also publicly urged imposition of such restrictions. Willie L. Williams,

FIGURE 10–3

Types of weapons used in U. S homicides (1988.) (Data from the *New York Times*, Aug. 1990.)

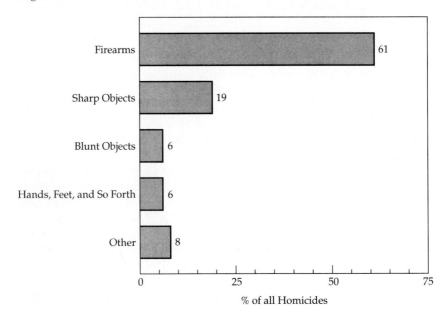

% of all Homicides

formerly Commissioner of Police in Philadelphia and the new Police Chief in Los Angeles, stated several years ago that rigorous gun control would help to curb the number of killings in Philadelphia (which reached 489 in 1989). He spoke of being particularly appalled by the increasing use of semiautomatic assault weapons in criminal violence, and he strongly supported the proposals introduced in the U.S. Senate to ban these weapons. However, Chief Williams also said that it is too late for such a ban to significantly cut the incidence of homicides. "There are so many of these weapons around," he said.[19]

Some Objections to Gun Control

Whatever the police may think about gun control, up until a few years ago at least, a number of sociologists and criminologists questioned whether gun control would actually reduce the rate of violent crimes.[20] Let's look briefly at some of their major objections to restrictions on gun ownership (without going into the legal and constitutional arguments).

"There are so many guns". Opponents of these restrictions often point out, first of all (as Chief Williams acknowledged), that there are already so many firearms in the hands of the public that gun controls would be ineffective. About a decade ago, sociologists James Wright, Peter Rossi, and Kathleen Daly estimated that there were *then* probably over 100 million guns in private hands and that about half of American homes contained at least one firearm. With this vast pool of weapons already in existence, they argued, it was too late to do anything realistic: "The existing stock is adequate to supply all conceivable criminal purposes for at least the entire next century. . . . Just how are we going to achieve some significant reduction in the number of firearms available?"[21]

"Guns provide protection". Most of the guns in U.S. homes are used for legitimate purposes, of course—a high proportion for hunting and sports, as well as many for self-protection. Residents of the United States seem to be especially interested in the security which they believe their weapons provide. According to public opinion surveys, even people who use guns mainly for recreational purposes are apt to believe that their homes are safer because of the weapons they own. Restricting the availability of guns, according to the argument used by opponents of gun controls, would frustrate hunters and sportsmen seriously and would also interfere with people's ability to protect themselves.

"Some other weapon will be used". Another argument which is often raised by people who object to gun controls is especially important in the context of this discussion. We're told that the unavailability of firearms will only lead persons who are intent upon killing someone to find substitute weapons. Criminologist Marvin Wolfgang put it this way, on the basis of the findings in his now classic 1958 study of Philadelphia homicides: "Few homicides due to shooting could be avoided merely if a firearm were not immediately present. . . . The offender would select some other weapon to achieve the same destructive goal."[22] If most killings are done with guns, he maintained, this is because the murderers prefer guns over other weapons rather than because the firearms are primarily responsible for the deaths. This statement by Wolfgang is basically in agreement with the well-known argument by the National Rifle Association (NRA): "Guns don't kill people. People kill people."

Some Answers to the Objections
This is not the place for a detailed discussion of the complex issues involved in the weapons controversy, but the above-mentioned objections to gun control can be answered. I'll begin with the widespread belief in this country that guns provide protection and then turn to the proposition "Guns don't kill people"—the belief that firearms don't really in themselves contribute to violent crimes.

As part of its continuing campaign against all efforts to restrict the availability of firearms, the NRA likes to publicize incidents in which ordinary people use weapons to defend themselves against armed criminals. The NRA has even insisted that legally owned firearms save the lives of many more Americans than are lost to guns. *Time,* the weekly newsmagazine, has challenged this claim. After selecting one week in 1989 at random, the magazine found that there were 464 deaths by firearms in the United States during the seven-day period. In only 3 percent of cases was the death the justifiable result of defensive action, while 5 percent of the deaths were due to accidents and almost half were suicides. If a firearm kills someone, in other words, the victim is overwhelmingly more likely to be a noncriminal gun wielder than a person who has criminal intentions.[23]

These statistics are supported by a close analysis of gunshot-produced deaths in homes. Epidemiologists Arthur Kellermann and Donald Reay examined the circumstances surrounding the 743 firearm-related deaths that occurred from 1978 through 1983 in King County, Washington, using official records as well as interviews with the investigating police officers. They discovered that 54 percent of the deaths had occurred in the residences where the firearms, which were usually handguns, were kept. The great majority were suicides, and only about 2 percent of the others could be considered to be legally justified—that is, to have come about through self-protection. All in all, Kellermann and Reay calculated that there were about 43 legally unjustified deaths by firearms (suicides, accidents, and criminal homicides) for every incident in which a gun was used to kill someone in self-protection. As the epidemiologists asked, doesn't this raise the question "whether keeping firearms in the home increases a family's protection or places it in greater danger"?[22]

What I'm saying is not that guns don't provide *any* protection but that the availability of firearms for self-defense has a considerable social cost. This becomes even more apparent when we consider the limited usefulness of guns in preventing crime. As *Time* pointed out, the overwhelming majority of all crimes in homes take place when the victims are away, and so the victims don't even have opportunities to use their weapons in self-defense. Then too, as a sociologist who was quoted by the magazine added, violent crimes often occur in the streets, and guns

FIGURE 10–4

Cause or effect? Handgun sales and the homicide rate.

Why have the sales of handguns in the United States paralleled the incidence of homicides in this country? Firearm sales obviously might increase or decrease as people become more or less concerned about violent crimes in their neighborhoods. However, the sales of these weapons can also contribute to the occurrence of these crimes. On the basis of a growing body of evidence, the present book argues that the ready availability of handguns increases the chances that innocent people will be killed by persons wielding a firearm. (Chart from *New York Times*, Apr. 3, 1992; data from Bureau of Alcohol, Tobacco and Firearms and the Centers for Disease Control. Copyright 1992 by the New York Times Company. Reprinted by permission.)

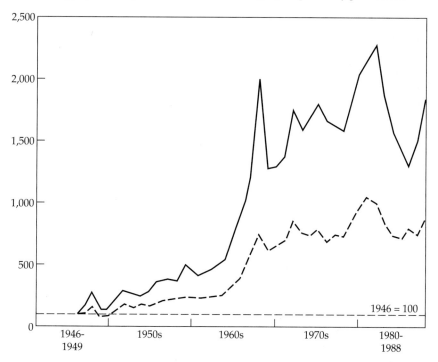

- - - Homicides caused by handguns   ——— New handguns produced/imported

are rarely available for use in attempting to stop these offenses (unless of course, people took to carrying firearms with them at all times). Only a tiny fraction of the population actually have chances to employ guns for self-protection, and there are far more firearms available than this very small minority actually require.

There's also the question of what kinds of guns should be legally available. Experts have noted that handguns are poorly suited for self-protection; they are very difficult to shoot accurately, and, authorities tell us, "only an extremely accurate shot will immediately incapacitate an assailant."[25] Of course, a rapidly firing semiautomatic assault weapon is much more likely to accomplish this purpose—but think what harm these guns are already doing to society. Police officials believe that a considerable part of the recent rise in homicide rates can be attributed to the spread of semiautomatic weapons, and many criminologists agree. Lawrence Sherman, one of the chief designers of the Minneapolis and Milwaukee domestic violence experiments discussed earlier in this chapter and also president of the Crime Control Institute, a research organization, has commented that "the number of bullets these guns fire, the speed [at which the bullets] travel, and the damage they do is driving the homicide rate up."[26] Sometimes the killings are multiple murders, a drive-by execution of a rival gang, but at other times single victims are shot, their bodies torn apart by the high-powered bullets.

It's also increasingly apparent that not only criminals are killed. Innocent bystanders are also hit, people—young children as well as grownups—who just happen to be in the wrong place at the wrong time. According to statistics collected by the *New York Times*, 253 people were shot in New York City alone between 1977 and 1988, simply because they unfortunately happened to be nearby when shootings occurred. The numbers of such deaths are increasing as the years go by and as assault weapons become more common. How many of these tragedies would not have occurred if the NRA and other gun devotees hadn't insisted on being able to buy assault weapons freely and without restrictions?

A great number of firearms of all kinds are already widely available in the United States. Any criminal can undoubtedly obtain a gun of his or her choice, but I do not see this as a valid argument in favor of making still more firearms available. The more weapons there are in our country, the greater the probability that someone will be shot unintentionally. Correspondingly, the fewer the number of firearms that are readily available, the smaller is the chance that an innocent person will be badly hurt or killed by being shot.

These probabilities can be seen in operation in Florida. The number of children killed by firearms in that state increased markedly in the months after the legislature, in October 1987, made it easier for residents to buy and carry concealed weapons. A veteran homicide detective from the Miami area was convinced that the rise in shooting deaths was due mainly to the increased availability of guns. "There are so many guns lying around in people's homes and cars," he said, "that naturally kids are going to get into them." Other statistics also testify to these tragic odds. *Time* has estimated that about 135,000 children bring their guns to school every day. It shouldn't be surprising, then, that a child is killed or injured by a firearm at the rate of about one child every thirty-six minutes.[27]

Finally, let's turn to the contention that all homicides are intentional. Quite a few people, social scientists and laypersons alike, assume that most murderers would have obtained a knife or another substitute weapon if firearms hadn't been available. I question this assumption, on the basis of my differentiation between instrumental and emotional aggression. I have repeatedly argued that many violent actions are relatively impulsive outbursts which are propelled by strong internal agitation. Persons carried away by the intense passion within them might well seize nearby guns and fire at the individuals who have offended them, thinking of little but their desire to destroy their tormentors. Moreover, as the "weapons effect" research summarized in Chapter 3 has demonstrated, the mere sight of a gun may serve to intensify an aggressor's violent urge. A wife who is enraged by a bitter argument with her husband, and who is passionately caught up in her hatred of him because of his repeated mistreatment of her, might see the pistol they have in the house, become even more furious, and shoot the man in the heat of the moment. Her impulse to attack and destroy might have been weaker and thus better restrained if she hadn't noticed the weapon.

Researchers who share my general position, such as Franklin Zimring and Richard Block, point to particular crime statistics to support this line of argument. In many homicides, they note, the murderers and their victims were either members of the same family, friends, or acquaintances (although the proportion of all homicides involving strangers has been increasing greatly in recent years). Zimring reasoned, then, that the murderers were unlikely to have planned to kill the person with whom they had this fairly close relationship. Rather, he believes, the killings probably grew out of a quarrel that intensified rapidly and got out of control.[28]

There is still better evidence that quarrels do indeed play a major role in homicides. As I mentioned before, the Justice Department's National Crime Survey indicates that more than half of all the handgun-produced murders and nonnegligent manslaughter killings in the United States between 1979 and 1987 occurred during arguments or fights.

Other kinds of statistics are also consistent with Zimring's thesis. As Block pointed out, "Opponents of gun control legislation . . . [assume] that persons who commit homicides are basically different from those who commit other violent crimes." Supposedly certain personal qualities the killers possessed, and which other violent but nonlethal offenders lacked, led the killers to take their victims' lives. Contrary to this assumption, in his analysis of Chicago homicides from the late 1960s to the mid-1970s, Block concluded (in agreement with several other investigators) that there were fewer differences between homicides and other injury-producing violent crimes than is widely supposed. The offenders who were arrested for killing someone were similar in important respects to those who were arrested for aggravated assault. The two kinds of crimes seem, on the average, to have arisen in somewhat similar settings. There was at least one major difference, however: Firearms were much more likely to have been present in the situations in which deaths occurred.[29] Isn't it likely that in a substantial fraction of the cases in which someone was killed, one of the parties to the conflict snatched up an available gun and used it impulsively?

Sociologists Wright, Rossi, and Daly acknowledged this possibility in their thoughtful examination of the gun control controversy, but they expressed doubt about whether impulsive killings are as frequent as I have suggested. According to them, the findings obtained in a study conducted by the Police Foundation in Kansas City questioned whether many domestic homicides are actually caused by outbursts of passion. According to this investigation, "no fewer than 85% of all homicides involving family members had been preceded at some point in the past by some other violent incident sufficiently serious that the police were called in." This means, they argued, that the killing in a particular case of this sort was "the culminating event in a pattern of interpersonal abuse, hatred, and violence that stretches well back into the history of the parties involved." For example, a wife who murders her husband has presumably developed such a great hatred for the man that she intends to kill him sooner or later, and one day she does it. If she doesn't have a pistol in the house, she may use a knife.[30]

It seems to me that there's an easy answer to the sociologists' objection: Rather than contradicting the possibility of an impulsive act of violence, the prior history of conflict and aggression surely increases the chances that later quarrel will produce an emotional outburst. A wife who has been frequently mistreated by her husband in the past may become quickly enraged by a further act of abuse. We can easily imagine what may happen next: Knowing that there's a pistol in the bedside table, in her fury the woman may run to get it, seize the weapon, and shoot her husband. Moreover, the sight of the firearm, or perhaps even the thought of it, may have heighten her violent urge even further, so that she didn't think of the consequences. She may have thought only of her desire to destroy her tormentor.[31]

Who knows how often this kind of scenario may occur in homicidal encounters? The only thing that is certain, I believe, is that emotional outbursts of violence, in which weapons are employed impulsively, are probably not at all infrequent. I can go even further: However often one person attacks another in a fit of rage, it undoubtedly happens frequently enough to justify lowering the availability of firearms. Moreover, however intent would-be killers are upon murdering their victims, it's probably far better for society if they use knives rather than guns. Among other reasons, they are less apt to also murder innocent bystanders if they don't have high-powered assault rifles or even pistols.

SUMMARY

There's little agreement in U.S. society, to put it mildly, about possible methods for controlling criminal violence. In this chapter, I discuss the potential effectiveness of two methods: punishing violent crimes very severely and outlawing firearms.

Starting with an examination of the pros and cons of corporal punishment as a disciplinary procedure with children, I note the growing opposition to the use of physical punishment in schools both in the United States and abroad, as well as the valid ethical and psychological reasons for this opposition. I also point out (maintaining a position I took earlier in the book) that punishment can be effective, and that strong adverse side effects can be avoided, under certain limited circumstances—most notably, when the punishment is sufficiently severe, when it is delivered before the punished individual can benefit from the disapproved activity, when it is administered consistently every time the disapproved behavior is carried out, when the recipient understands the reasons for the punishment, and when attractive alternatives to the disapproved behavior are available.

The Minneapolis Police Department's experiment on the use of arrests to reduce domestic violence provides one example of the possible deterrent value of punishment. Under the particular conditions of this investigation, men who had battered a woman (seriously enough to warrant arrest but without doing grievous injury) were less likely to repeat the abuse within the next six months if they were arrested than if they were only warned or counseled by police officers.

Since punishment is effective only under the right circumstances, it is important to determine how the criminal justice system can best employ punishment in the deterrence of crime. Available research indicates that potential lawbreakers would be better controlled by an increase in the certainty that society would inflict negative consequences upon them for their offenses than by an increase in the severity of the consequences.

I turn next to the ultimate social punishment, asking whether society can reduce the incidence of homicides by prescribing death for people who deliberately take others' lives. After reviewing various studies, I conclude that there is no clear evidence that the threat of capital punishment lowers the murder rate. Some of David Phillips' findings suggest, moreover, that while widely publicized executions can lessen the number of killings in a country for a short while (apparently only as long as the executions are fresh in the public's memory), the same temporary reduction might be achieved by imposing long jail sentences.

Finally, I examine the question of whether the incidence of violent crimes would be lowered if fewer guns were readily available. Although reasonable arguments against gun control have been advanced, some of which are summarized in the chapter, I argue in favor of a gun control policy. Along with other writers and many police officials, I contend that: (1) the rapidly increasing availability of automatic weapons is responsible for much of the rise in homicides over the past several decades; (2) handguns do not actually provide much protection for citizens and these people are more apt to use their guns to kill family members than to shoot illegal intruders; and (3) it isn't necessarily true that murderers would employ other weapons if firearms weren't available. Guns can contribute to impulsive crimes of violence. The more firearms, and especially the more handguns, that there are circulating in society, the greater are the chances people in general, and not necessarily lawbreakers, will be killed.

NOTES

1. See especially Parke & Slaby (1983); Solomon (1964); and Blanchard & Blanchard (1986) for other discussions of punishment.

2. Karnow (1983) assesses the results, in his history of the Vietnamese conflict; as follows: "Operation Rolling Thunder, the American air strikes against North Vietnam, went on almost daily from March 1965 until November 1968, dropping a total of a million tons of bombs, rockets, and missiles—roughly eight hundred tons per day for three and a half years. . . . One objective of Operation Rolling Thunder was to crack the morale of the Hanoi leaders, and compel them to call off the southern insurgency; the other was to weaken the Communists' fighting capacity by impeding the flow of their men and supplies to the south. But neither goal was even remotely achieved. . . . Secretary of Defense McNamara, an architect of the air offensive . . . asserted, . . . 'Enemy operations in the south cannot, on the basis of any reports I have seen, be stopped by air bombardment—short, that is, of the virtual annihilation of North Vietnam and its people'" (p. 454).

3. Gibbons (1987) and Sherman & Berk (1984a) discussed this conception.

4. See for example, Newman (1987).

5. See Straus & Gelles (1990).

6. See Sherman & Berk (1984a, 1984b). Berk & Newton (1985) reported later findings that support the Minneapolis results. Police arrests in California wife-battery cases apparently reduced the likelihood of further arrests for domestic assaults during the twenty-eight months of the study.

7. As cited in Sherman et al. (1991), p. 833, the reanalysis of the Minneapolis experiment's data was carried out by Tauchen et al. (1986).

8. Sherman et al. (1991). According to the investigators, there were indications in the year-after follow-up data that the short arrest procedure had led to a long-term "criminogenic" effect, i.e., a greater number of reported cases of domestic violence in the short arrest condition than in the warned group. Sherman and his colleagues also noted (pp. 842–843) that the arrest "treatment" in the Omaha and Charlotte experiments also seems to have had a criminogenic effect. Their interpretation was that, as they put it, "The consistent pattern of decaying initial deterrence suggests that short arrest produces some fear that wears off quickly. Then sooner (as in Charlotte and Omaha) or later (as in Milwaukee) anger takes over, and the memory of the previous arrest may become a challenge to prove how 'hard' a man the suspect is . . . " (pp. 843–844).

9. The National Academy of Sciences review is cited in Greenwood (1982). The quotation at the end of this paragraph is from Waldo & Chiricos (1972). The evidence indicating that we cannot be sure that increased sentence severity reduces drunk driving is based on a literature survey by Ross that was cited in Blanchard & Blanchard (1986), p. 144.

10. Greenwood (1982) has concluded, "To the degree that these studies find relationships that are consistent with the deterrence hypothesis, they suggest that the probability of incarceration is much more important than the length of time served" (p. 338). However, see Piliavin, Gartner, Thornton, & Matsueda (1986) for contrary observations.

11. Greenwood (1982), p. 324. Crime statistics cited by Blanchard & Blanchard (1986, p. 146) indicate that about half of all violent crimes in the United States are reported and that, of these, only about 43 percent lead to an arrest. In about 70 percent of the cases that come to trial, a conviction results.

12. The two articles by Sellin are reprinted in Bedau (1967). Sellin's procedure and findings in the two studies cited here and below are summarized in Shin (1978), and the quotation in the next paragraph is also taken from Shin (1978). Ehrlich (1975) argued that Sellin's research was seriously flawed in that its capital punishment states included states that provided for the death penalty but had not actually carried out any executions. Using data for the United States between 1932 and 1970, Ehrlich did a statistically more sophisticated analysis and concluded that the use of the death penalty had a significant deterrent effect. His study supposedly influenced some of the Supreme Court justices when the Court decided to reinstate capital punishment in 1976. However, other authorities, including a panel established by the National Research Council, insist that Erlich's research is methodologically and substantively questionable. Outsiders such as Nathanson (1987) have concluded that the criticisms "effectively undermine Ehrlich's alleged vindication of the superior deterrent force of the death penalty" (p. 26).

13. Peterson & Bailey (1988).

14. Shin (1978).

15. See Phillips (1986). The temporary drop in homicides followed by a sudden jump in the number of these crimes is somewhat similar to the pattern

reported by Berkowitz & Macaulay (1971) after the slaying of President Kennedy. It may be that the sudden decrease in homicides in December 1963 was caused by the punishment given to Lee Harvey Oswald, the accused assassin, at the end of November: his murder by Jack Ruby in a jail in Dallas, Texas, while the entire nation watched on television. Oswald's "execution," which was shown again and again on national television for the next several days, was a highly dramatic demonstration of homicide being punished. However, even this lesson was apparently forgotten after a few weeks.

16. See Phillips (1986), pp. 242–246, for a brief summary.

17. Bowers & Pierce, as cited in Nathanson (1987), pp. 28–29.

18. In the immediately following paragraphs, the statistics on handguns are from the Bureau of Justice Statistics' National Crime Survey, as reported in the *New York Times* on July 9, 1990, while the international comparisons are from Fingerhut and Kleinman (1990) of the U.S. National Center for Health Statistics.

19. Hinds, *New York Times*, July 18, 1990.

20. Wright, Rossi, & Daly (1983) have published a scholarly review of the pertinent literature in which they basically question the advisability of gun control legislation. Lester (1984) has also concluded that there is no good evidence that such legislation would reduce the homicide rate. Kates (1979), a law professor, is also skeptical of the value of handgun prohibitions.

21. Wright et al. (1983), p. 320.

22. Wolfgang (1958), p. 83.

23. The NRA statement and *Time*'s discussion of it, as well as the figures cited in this paragraph, can be found in *Time*, Aug. 21, 1989, pp. 25–26. More recently, criminologists McDowall, Lizotte, & Wiersema (1991) have published a careful statistical analysis that also questions whether the widespread possession of weapons actually deters crime. Employing a sophisticated statistical procedure, they examined burglary and/or robbery rates in five different U.S. cities before and after these communities took steps to either encourage or discourage the use of firearms by their citizens, and found no evidence of a deterrent effect. For example, after Morton Grove, Illinois, passed an ordinance in June, 1981 prohibiting the possession or sale of handguns within the city, Kennesaw, Georgia, countered with its own law requiring every household in the city to maintain a firearm. The mayor and police chief of Kennesaw claimed that their city's action led to a substantial reduction in burglaries in the next seven months. However when McDowall and his associates looked closely at the crime records, they could not conclude that the city's pro-gun ordinance had lowered its burglary rate. Rather, there apparently had been an unusual jump in the number of burglaries in Kennesaw during the first few months *before* the ordinance was passed, and the supposed "decrease" when the law went into force evidently was a drop to the city's "normal" level of burglaries. Nor, on the other side, had the Morton Grove anti-gun law resulted in a rise in robberies in that city, as several gun advocates had predicted.

24. Kellerman & Reay (1986).

25. Hemenway & Weil, quoted in the Madison, Wisconsin, *Capital Times*, May 17, 1990.

26. Cited in the *New York Times*, July 18, 1990.

27. The statement made by the Miami detective was quoted in the *New York Times*, Oct. 10, 1988. The estimates of the number of children taking guns to school and the number of shootings are from *Time*, Oct. 8, 1990, p. 42.

28. Zimring (1968).

29. The statistics cited in this paragraph are from Block (1977) and the quotation from Block is from p. 33 of his monograph. Adding to my general argument here, McDowall, Lizotte, & Wiersema (1991, p. 542) cited a study by Philip Cook (1979) indicating that gun prevalence has little, if any, effect on the prevalence of robberies but is related to the frequency of homicides in robberies. The presence of firearms apparently increases the chances that someone will be killed during a highly emotional robbery.

30. Wright et al. (1983), p. 193.

31. Wright et al. (1983, p. 202) also expressed misgivings about my weapons effect research, citing several early failures to replicate the Berkowitz & LePage (1967) results. However, there have been a fair number of successful confirmations of the weapons effect in the United States and elsewhere [Turner, Simons, Berkowitz, & Frodi (1977); Caprara, Renzi, Amolini, D'Imperio, & Travaglia (1984)], including Zuzul's Yugoslavian study that was summarized in Chapter 3. [Also see Carlson, Marcus-Newhall, and Miller (1990), for relevant evidence.]

11

Psychological Procedures for Controlling Aggression

❖

Catharsis: Reducing One's Violent Urges by Aggressing ◆ *Ventilating Feelings* ◆ *The Catharsis Hypothesis* ◆ *The Aftereffects of Realistic Aggression* ◆ Developing New Ways of Behaving ◆ *Teaching that Cooperation Pays: Improving Parental Management of Problem Children* ◆ *Lessening Emotional Reactivity* ◆ *Does Anything Work with Incarcerated Offenders?*

*A*ggression can be controlled by force—at times. Under the right conditions, society can lessen the rate of violent crimes by threatening potential perpetrators with punishment. However, the right conditions aren't always present. In many instances, would-be criminals realistically believe that they have a good chance of escaping punishment altogether. Even when they are penalized, the noxious consequences are usually inflicted on them after they've had the pleasure of hurting their intended victim, and thus their aggression has been reinforced.

It's not enough, then, to rely only on deterrents. Society may well have to use force on occasion, but it should also attempt to reduce violent persons' aggressive inclinations. The correctional system should somehow lessen the assaultive tendencies of these individuals. Psychologists have offered different prescriptions as to how this might be done.

336

CATHARSIS: REDUCING ONE'S VIOLENT URGES BY AGGRESSING

> Traditional ethics have prevented the open expression and even enjoyment of . . . personal aggression. The repression of aggression begins with parental admonitions not to raise one's voice, talk back, argue, yell, or rebel. When aggressive communication is blocked and inhibited in relationships, whether they be transient or intimate, individuals enter into . . . reality-distorting dishonest [contracts] with each other. . . . Aggressive feelings that have been blocked from conscious expression within the normal flow of the relationship suddenly emerge in indirect, intense, and uncontrollable forms. The presumed "harmonious" relationship suddenly turns sour, as accumulated, hidden resentments and hostilities come pouring through.[1]

Ventilating Feelings

Over the years, but especially in the 1960s and 1970s, quite a few psychotherapists called for the free and open expression of "aggressive feelings" as a remedy for many of society's ills. These "ventilationists," as I labeled them,[2] claim that it is undesirable, or even unhealthy, to bottle up one's emotions. If someone has annoyed us, they say, we should reveal our anger by "telling the offending party off." "Let it all hang out," as the saying goes. We'll be better off as a result, and if we don't show our emotions, they may only intensify. Recall these lines from William Blake, which I quoted in Part 1: "I was angry with my foe:/I told it not, my wrath did grow." Then too, we are told that when we express our feelings, we lessen the chances that our bodies will suffer ill effects from the repressed aggression. Several researchers have indicted inhibited aggression as a causal factor in the development of heart disease,[3] maintaining that it's unhealthy to keep one's anger locked inside.

I'm sure you're all familiar with this prescription for physical and mental health. Many years ago, a psychologist put this notion in very simple terms for her audience:

> When pus accumulates and forms an abscess, the abscess must be opened and drained. If it isn't done the infection spreads. . . . Just so with feelings. The "badness" must come out. The hurts and fears and anger must be released and drained. Otherwise, these too may destroy the individual.[4]

The thinking in this analogy here is simple and easy to grasp; but how valid is it?

What's Involved in Revealing One's Feelings?

Just what do people have in mind when they call for the ventilation or open expression of feelings? In what ways can the "badness" come out?

In Chapter 3, I used as an example an incident between a woman named Jane and a man who did not keep an appointment with her. If I asked you how Jane might reveal her emotional state, you probably would list most of the following ways:

- *Jane might report her experience (or feelings).* She could conceivably tell the man, or anyone else, that she had been offended and was angry. In the pure case here, Jane only describes how she feels in an unemotional manner.
- *She might display the physiological and expressive-motor reactions that usually accompany the anger experience.* Whatever Jane might or might not say, she could show the muscular reactions we usually associate with anger: eyebrows drawn together, muscles tensed, and jaws clenched. She might also show the physiological changes that typically take place when people are affronted: red face, increased blood pressure, and speeded up heart rate. Jane could even exhibit the excited, agitated actions that sometimes go along with the anger experience: On returning home that night, she might slam her front door, kick a small stool that's in her way, and throw her coat and purse on the couch.
- *She might express her hostile thoughts and attitudes verbally.* Without really trying to hurt anyone, she might voice the negative ideas and attitudes that often come to mind when an individual is provoked. Jane might make a disparaging remark about the man's poor taste in clothes or tell a woman friend that men are childish and selfish.
- *She might assault someone, either verbally or physically.* Jane might engage in instigated aggression; she might deliberately try to hurt someone, whether the man who stood her up or another person.

Of course, Jane could also display any combination of the reactions listed above, since they are interrelated and often go together.[5] However, these anger-related reactions are also partially independent, and some of them may not appear on a given occasion. Let's suppose that Jane really doesn't have any conscious experience that she could call "anger," but she then criticizes the man's performance on the job. To what extent would she be expressing her anger openly? On the other hand, what if she tells a friend she felt angry with the man but never attempts to hurt him? Would Jane be showing her anger openly in this instance?

It should be clear from these questions that I'm not at all sure what people are saying when they urge us to express our anger. Are they recommending that we pay conscious attention to our bodily reactions and feelings? Are they telling us to talk to others about our feelings? Are they insisting that we ought to hit people who provoke us, verbally if not physically? Each of these reactions can have very different consequences. It's one thing to inform someone who has offended you that you are angry, but it's something quite different to scream at the person in rage.

Since the different emotional reactions listed above don't always appear together, we can reduce the confusion by giving them different names. Along with several other psychologists, I believe that there are advantages to restricting the term "anger" to an individual's feelings (or experience). The physiological and motor reactions that frequently accompany these feelings may be labeled "anger-related bodily reactions." I think of "hostility" as a negative attitude and "aggression" as behavior aimed at hurting—or destroying—another person or an object.

The Catharsis Hypothesis

This chapter, by and large, will be concerned with the consequences of *aggression*—behavior that is intended to injure someone or something.[6] The aggression can be either a physical or a verbal assault, and it can be as realistic as a punch in the face or as make-believe as shooting a toy gun at an imaginary enemy. Furthermore, it should be clear, even though I'm using the term "catharsis," I have *not* adopted the hydraulic conception. All that I have in mind is a *decreased instigation to aggression*, not a discharge of a hypothetical pool of energy. Thus, for me and most laboratory researchers—but not for every psychotherapist—the *catharsis* notion basically holds that any aggressive action reduces the likelihood of later aggression.

The questions that I will be investigating in this section are: Does catharsis really occur, and if so, under what circumstances?

Catharsis through Imaginary Aggression

As you undoubtedly know, a good many people, mental health practitioners as well as ordinary persons, subscribe to a very general version of the catharsis doctrine. They think that a wide variety of actions can be substituted for direct attacks on a target and can thus drain off one's supposedly pent-up aggressive drive. Orthodox psychoanalytic theory, with its hydraulic conception of motivation, takes the position that people can discharge their accumulated violent urges in various ways: surgeons by wielding their knives in medical operations, salespersons by assertively trying to persuade unwilling customers, mountain climbers by seeking to scale steep mountain peaks, and so on.

Typically, though, most proponents of this generalized catharsis hypothesis believe that it's beneficial to act in an aggressive manner even if no one is really assaulted. Imaginary aggression presumably will do nicely. Otto Fenichel, a well-known psychoanalytic theorist and the author of a classic text in this field, assured his readers that children can benefit from play therapies through a catharsis process.[7] The youngsters can release the impetus to violence that is locked up inside them by tearing their dolls apart in play, thus making believe that they are destroying their parents or their sibling rivals. Even therapists who do not explicitly tie themselves to psychoanalysis believe that their patients should "discharge" or "release" their inhibited emotional energies or urges by practicing imaginary aggression. Here is an example:

> A woman subject is given a tennis racket and directed to beat the bed. While [she is] doing this, she is asked to make an appropriate verbal statement such as "I hate you," "You bitch," "Son of a bitch," or "I'll kill you." The group, observing the subject's actions . . . [encourages] her to be more aggressive, to let go, to let it out.[8]

Psychotherapists of this general persuasion aren't the only ones who believe that a beneficial release can be achieved through make-believe aggression. A manufacturer has sold toy machine guns to adult motorists by telling them that if they were angered by other drivers, they could discharge their rage right away by raking the offenders with simulated machine gun fire. Similarly, violent games have been popularized as providing a psychologically healthy outlet for pent-up aggressive desires. In one of these "sports," the players—adults as well as children—put on futuristic helmets, breastplates, and power packs, and run through dimly lit corridors shooting at their opponents with electronic guns. A young man who was participating in this game described the supposed benefits this way, according to a newspaper account: "You can take out all your frustrations here. . . . It's shooting and killing without the guilt."

Even academic research psychologists, such as John Dollard, Neal Miller, and their associates at Yale University, have also believed that it was possible to reduce the instigation to aggression in this manner. In their 1939 monograph on the frustration-aggression hypothesis, the Dollard group held that "the occurrence of any act of aggression" will lessen the aggressive inclinations generated by a thwarting. They did point out, however, that "this reduction is more or less temporary and the instigation to aggression will build up again if the original frustration persists."[9] Still, according to these psychologists, any kind of aggressive behavior, including insulting other people or even making a "gory drawing," can have a cathartic effect.

There's no doubt, then, that the catharsis doctrine is widely accepted. Broad agreement isn't serious enough for students of human behavior, however. Consider how many people had believed in the past that the earth was flat or that the sun circled the earth. Scientific investigations want better evidence than shared opinions. What does empirical research actually show? I'll first consider the effects of fantasy aggression, focusing on imaginative play with toy weapons, and then will turn to the consequences of more realistic behavior. After this, I'll have more to say about expressing one's feelings.

Does Make-Believe Aggression Reduce Aggressive Inclinations?
I've already discussed the effects of make-believe aggression in this book, and you've seen how consistent the research findings have been. Thus, the experiment by Richard Walters and Murray Brown which was cited in Chapter 6 showed that fantasy violence can heighten realistic aggression. Boys who had been intermittently rewarded for punching a large plastic doll were relatively more aggressive when they competed with a peer several days later (see Figure 6–1). Their fantasy assaults had not made them friendlier. Similarly, in Miomir Zuzul's experiment with Yugoslav children (which was summarized in Chapter 3), the youngsters who had played with toy weapons, were fairly aggressive soon afterward in their playground interactions with their classmates (see Figure 3–8).

Other studies along these lines have yielded very similar results. For example, in two experiments conducted by Charles Turner and Diane Goldsmith with preschool children, play with toy guns led to a greater increase in antisocial aggressive behavior than did play with either novel toys or the children's usual toys.[10]

The children hadn't been provoked in the Turner-Goldsmith investigations, but don't think that make-believe aggression would have a more positive effect if the youngsters had been emotionally aroused at the time. Research by Shahbaz Mallick and Boyd McCandless is informative here.

Each of the third-grade boys and girls in the study worked on a block-construction task with another child of his or her own sex. What the subjects didn't know was that the other youngster was the experimenter's accomplice who either allowed the subjects to complete their assignment or frustrated them by being very clumsy. Immediately after this initial experience, each subject performed an intervening activity for about eight minutes. These activities were the crucial experimental variation. Some of the subjects, in both the frustrated and the nonfrustrated conditions, carried out imaginary aggression during the eight minutes by shooting a toy gun at a target, while, as a control condition, other frustrated and nonfrustrated youngsters spent the time in a neutral talk with the experimenter. Still another group was used to determine how aggressive the subjects would be if they learned that their partners' misdeeds hadn't been aimed at them personally; some of these frustrated children chatted with the experimenter during the eight minutes and were told that their partner had been tired and upset.

When the intervening phase was completed, the experimenter's accomplice went into another room, supposedly to work on another block-construction task. Each naive subject had an opportunity to help or hurt the accomplice's work by pushing specified buttons on an electronic apparatus. The aggression measure was the number of times the subject pushed the "hurt" button in an attempt to interfere with the partner's work (twenty pushes were the maximum possible). No differences were found between boys and girls, and I'll report the main results for the two genders combined.

Figure 11–1 clearly shows that the frustration increased the children's aggressive inclinations (even though their partner presumably hadn't intended to block their activity). The experimenter's explanation of why the other child had been so clumsy significantly lowered the children's urge (or willingness) to hurt their frustrater. Now that they thought better of their partner, either they didn't want to hurt him or her too much or they restrained their aggressive impulses. The aggressive play, on the other hand, produced no reduction in the number of attacks on the frustrater. Thus the aroused children hadn't experienced a beneficial catharsis through shooting their toy guns.[11]

The evidence is conclusive. It is safe to completely reject the notion that children—and adults—can purge their aggressive drives by engaging in make-believe violence. Motorists will not become less aggressively inclined as a result of shooting a toy machine gun at another driver, and children won't become friendlier and nicer by playing with toy weapons.

FIGURE 11–1
Number of aggressive responses after intervening activity (neutral talk, explanation, or aggressive play). (Data from Mallick & McCandless (1966), Study II. Copyright 1966 by the American Psychological Association. Adapted by permission.)

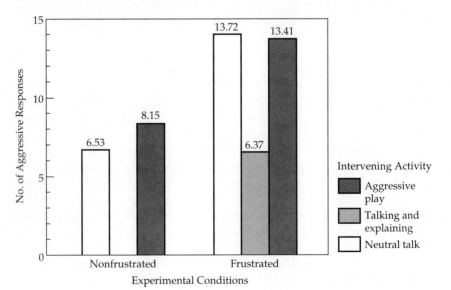

Indeed, as I've argued throughout this book (and as the studies cited above demonstrate), aggressive games can even increase the likelihood of further, more realistic aggression by giving the players aggressive ideas and by allowing aggressive behavior to be rewarded.

We have to agree with a woman who, some years ago, wrote a letter objecting to the advice a newspaper columnist gave to one of her readers. A mother had asked this columnist for advice on how to cope with her son's temper tantrums and had been told to provide a punching bag for the child to hit so that he could "get the anger out of his system." The letter criticized this recommendation, reporting what had happened in her own family:

> My younger brother used to kick the furniture when he got mad. Mother called it, "Letting off steam." Well, he's 32 years old now and still kicking the furniture—what's left of it, that is. He is also kicking his wife, the cat, the kids, and anything else that gets in his way.[12]

It certainly is plausible that this happened (see Chapter 6, The Development of Violence Proneness). As he kicked the furniture, the brother's fantasy aggression was apparently rewarded so that his violent disposition was strengthened and he became more likely to attack whoever bothered him. Much the same process can occur whenever people practice behaving aggressively, no matter what form the behavior takes. It's time that mental health professionals stopped recommending make-believe violence as a way of lessening aggressive tendencies.

Some other considerations. Two additional points are important in this context. First, people's moods can affect their aggressiveness: They are more aggressively inclined when they're feeling bad and, correspondingly, are less apt to be assaultive when they're in a good mood. This means the games they play can temporarily influence their behavior toward other persons by influencing their moods. People who have had a pleasant time shooting pistols at targets or running through darkened corridors zapping "enemies" with electronic light guns may well become friendlier in the next minutes or hours, not because they've drained their violent urges but simply because they've had fun and are feeling good for the time being. Their increased friendliness will last only as long as their pleasant moods.

Second, many children, and especially boys, obviously enjoy playing with toy weapons. Countless parents have found it difficult if not even impossible to stop their young sons from engaging in fantasy aggression. If parents don't provide boys with toy guns, the children are apt to use sticks or even their fingers to emulate guns, as they imagine themselves shooting at make-believe targets.

Boys do this sort of thing not necessarily because they're innately aggressive but probably because of their desire for mastery over their environments. They are showing, in a way that seems appropriate to their immature masculine minds, that they want to have control over their social worlds. As they pretend to blast alien creatures from outer space, they're imagining themselves destroying all sorts of dangerous forces and even having a considerable say in determining their own futures. I believe they're manifesting much the same wish that young children often express when they insist on pressing the control buttons in an elevator. It seems to me that mothers and fathers might well recognize boys' desires to achieve control over their environments by allowing their children to play with toy weapons if they insist. This doesn't mean, however, that parents should encourage their sons to engage in aggressive play. Furthermore, they can certainly teach their offspring that it's wrong to hurt others deliberately.[13]

Imaginary acts and mere complaints don't attain the aggressive goal. There's no mystery involved in why make-believe aggression rarely lessens the impetus toward further aggression: No one has been injured. Let's say that Jane is angry with the man who stood her up. Kicking a Bobo doll or striking a bed with a tennis racquet doesn't gratify her aggressive wish; she has no reason to think that her behavior has actually hurt the man who offended her. As a matter of fact, Jane wouldn't even achieve a satisfactory catharsis by criticizing this man to a friend unless she thought the criticism had somehow injured him. Suggesting just this, when a team of psychologists interviewed disgruntled men who had just been laid off from work, the angered employees became even more hostile toward the company that had discharged them after they were given opportunities to criticize the firm. Since they didn't believe they had actually injured the company—and since they also hadn't gained an understanding of the company's side of the story—they had only stirred themselves up all the more.[14] We only enflame ourselves further when we brood about the wrongs that have been done to us, imagine how we will get even with our tormentors, or even attack them verbally—if we don't think we have successfully hurt them.

The Aftereffects of Realistic Aggression

Even though imaginary aggression doesn't reduce aggressive tendencies (except by putting the aggressors in a good mood), under certain conditions more realistic attacks *can* lessen the desire to inflict further injury.

How this can happen is no simple matter, however, and you should understand some of the complications that can be involved.

Some Factors that Spur Heightened Aggression

Inhibitions on aggression can be frustrating. Since people who are aggressively aroused want to hurt the persons who they believe have offended them, it follows that they're frustrated when they're unable to achieve this goal. This is true even when they themselves are responsible for the restraint—when they are holding themselves back.

We can see indications of such a frustration in some experiments that were carried out several decades ago. In the earliest of these experiments, deliberately angered men who were briefly prevented from replying to a provocateur later exhibited more aggression than did a comparably insulted group who had been permitted to respond right away. The temporary interference with the provoked subjects' aggressive reaction had apparently heightened their aggressive inclinations. Some years later, I showed that the blocking of the insult-generated aggressive urge is especially frustrating when the emotionally aroused people had expected to be able to retaliate. Wanting to get even and expecting to be able to do so, the subjects in the study were thwarted all the more when they couldn't fulfill their aggressive desires.[15]

In these cases, the restraints were established by external influences, but my guess is that a comparable kind of frustration exists when the thwarting is largely self-produced. The consequences also may be similar: Through suppressing their aggressive desires, whether for external or for internal reasons, people may experience heightened tension and may become even more strongly instigated to attack someone.

Some therapists regard suppressed aggression as a major psychological problem because they see the resentment and hostility that are generated by the inhibitions. Many of their patients are furious with other people and want to strike out at them. For one reason or another, however, they are too fearful to attack, with the result that they seem to become all the more emotionally disturbed. We must recognize, nevertheless, that these patients' tension and increased aggressiveness arise from the blocking of an *activated* instigation to aggression. The patients wouldn't be experiencing this internal conflict if they weren't emotionally aroused and didn't *actively* want to hurt other people (in their thoughts at least).

The escalation of aggression. On some occasions, aggression escalates. Instead of being satisfied with their initial blows, the attackers strike harder and harder. They start hitting and then get carried away with what they're doing. Their assaults mount in fury until they tire or realize their goal has been reached. The consequences can be tragic.

Edward Byrne Jr., 28 years old, was executed in Louisiana in June 1988 for murdering a woman during the robbery of a gasoline station. Byrne had dated the woman he killed, and planned to rob her because he knew she handled large sums of money on her job. But he insisted he had not intended to murder her. When he carried out the robbery, he maintained, he had only wanted to knock her unconscious with the hammer he had with him. However, his first blow wasn't altogether successful, and he kept on hitting the woman again and again—until he killed her.

Assuming that Byrne was telling the truth and hadn't wanted to kill his victim, why did he keep on hammering at the woman? His first blow didn't knock her out, but did he have to hit her so many times and so hard, just to render her unconscious? Byrne apparently didn't have full control over his actions.

This kind of automatic escalation of aggression isn't really unusual. There is a counterpart, for example, in laboratory experiments in which subjects are required to punish a "fellow student" in a nearby room. As the subjects repeatedly punish the (nonexistent) person in the other room, their attacks frequently mount in severity. This happens, moreover, even when they haven't been provoked by their victim or even by the experimenter. As in Byrne's case, their assaults rise in intensity as they continue to strike at the victim.[16] Why does this occur?

Psychological Processes that Promote the Escalation of Aggression. There are undoubtedly all sorts of reasons for this mounting aggression, and I'll mention only some possibilities. As a start, aggressors may become *increasingly excited* and agitated as they continue lashing out at a target, so that their own excitement gives their actions an even greater impetus, at least for a while. Ed Byrne may have become more and more excited as he struck the woman. He may have been carried away by the audacity of what he was doing, the danger he was confronting, the anxiety he was feeling, and maybe even the pleasure he was experiencing.

Then too, *inhibitions against aggression may well weaken*. After Byrne hit his victim the first few times, he may have thought less and less about the possible future consequences of his behavior, perhaps because of the emotional turmoil within him, so that he didn't hold back in striking the woman.

I wonder whether a *self-stimulation* process doesn't also take place. I've noted several times in this book that thoughts and words with an aggressive meaning can prime other ideas that have much the same meaning and can even activate aggressive tendencies. People who are thinking about deliberately hurting someone—and who aren't worried about the consequences—can give themselves all sorts of aggressive ideas and can thus prompt themselves to make stronger attacks than they otherwise would have made.[17] Ed Byrne may have primed himself in a similar manner. He undoubtedly had violent thoughts as he struck his victim, and these ideas may have stimulated him to even greater violence.

Then too, Byrne may have been incited by the anticipation of achieving his aggressive goal. The analysis I am presenting helps to explain why this happens. Attackers' reactions to their own aggression depend partly upon how close they come to fulfilling their aggressive purpose. Especially if they're emotionally aroused and want to inflict pain, the first information they receive indicating that they are beginning to hurt their target gives them a taste of the pleasure they seek and should therefore incite them to even stronger attacks. When they find they have reached their goal and injured their target enough to suit their own purposes, they should be gratified and cease their assaults. In the absence of other influences (such as fear of punishment or guilt), aggressors should strike harder as they come closer to their goal and then should finally stop attacking when they think they have reached their objective.

Escalation of Violence in the Family. Sociologist Murray Straus of the University of New Hampshire in Durham, whose work has been cited several times in this book, has pointed out that family fights often show this acceleration of aggression. When he asked his students to describe how their mothers and fathers had responded to three recent "important conflicts or disagreements" between them, Straus found that the parents' fights frequently were not confined to just one type of aggression. The more intense was the adults' verbal conflict, as it escalated from heated arguments to insults and yelling to stomping out of the room, the greater was the likelihood that they would also engage in physical aggression. For both the mothers and fathers, "as the level of verbal aggression increases, the level of physical aggression increases dramatically."[18]

Entirely in agreement with my stance, Straus used his findings to question the ventilationists' approach to marital counseling. Some therapists of this persuasion, he noted, had insisted that "couples who fight together are couples who stay together"—as long as they "fight properly" and don't attack each other personally and directly. Within these limits, these therapists told their readers, they should drop their inhibitions, cease being civil to their partners, and have it out with each other.[19] The main problem with this kind of advice is easy to see: It's difficult to keep aggression within bounds. Fights escalate, all too often. Whether it's because the disputants antagonize each other and/or because they prime themselves to heightened aggression, criticisms can quickly lead to insults, and insults are easily transformed into physical attacks. I'm not saying, of course, that we shouldn't tell our close partners when they've done something that bothers us, but I do think we should try to give them the information calmly, with civility, and in a nonaccusatory manner. We don't have to be hurtful and combative.

Why Do People Stop Attacking? A question must have occurred to you by this time: If aggression often leads to an escalation of further aggression, why does it frequently stop before it gets completely out of hand? Ed Byrne didn't catch himself before he hammered his victim to death, but most of us do halt our attacks before they become damaging, even when we're highly aroused.

It's partly a matter of differences in individuals' ability to restrain themselves. Chapter 5, The Identification of the Violence Prone, noted that some people, particularly those whom I term "emotionally reactive aggressors," tend to develop a full head of steam very rapidly when they're challenged or provoked, and they often find it difficult to inhibit their violent impulses. Other, more fortunate, persons have greater self-control. When they see what they're doing, and when they aren't carried away by intense feelings, their inhibitions against aggression begin to operate, and they can then stop themselves. Ed Byrne probably didn't have this amount of self-control. (I'll have more to say about self-regulation later in this chapter.)

Other factors probably also contribute to the halting of aggression, especially the perception of goal attainment. As I noted above, in the absence of restraints, people will continue striking at their victims until they believe they've accomplished their purposes. They will stop attacking when they think they've reached their aggressive goals—when they've hurt their opponents sufficiently.

Let's look at some relevant evidence.

Evidence of a Postaggression Reduction in the Instigation to Aggression
The research on aggression catharsis is unusually complex, and a comprehensive review of the experimental literature on this topic will quickly reveal the often puzzling inconsistency in the research results.[20] It's difficult to reconcile the seemingly contradictory findings, I believe, mainly because of the absence of unequivocal indicators of the strength of the subjects' *instigations* to aggression. All we see is what the research participants do, not why they are more or less assaultive. This means we can't be sure that any weakening in the subjects' open attacks after their initial punishment of the target is actually caused by a lessening of their impetus to aggression (i.e., to a catharsis). As Russell Geen and his students at the University of Missouri, Columbia, have emphasized, the subjects' lowered aggression might be caused by guilt and/or by anxiety, causing them to restrain themselves from continuing to strike the victim.[21]

Despite this uncertainty, I think that several studies have obtained results which definitely suggest that a catharsis process has occurred—under limited circumstances. You may be interested in two of these experiments, but remember that this highly selective presentation is not representative of all the research on this topic.

As long as the tormentor is hurt.   The first investigation I'll summarize here was carried out by Anthony Doob and Lorraine Wood at the University of Toronto in Ontario, Canada. It is very much in line with the theoretical analysis I've been advancing. Each subject in the study, which used both male and female students, was first annoyed or treated in a neutral manner by a woman student (who was actually the experimenter's confederate) as they worked on a card-sorting assignment. Immediately afterward, in a supposedly "different" part of the research, the confederate was required to learn numbers that had been paired with particular words.

This fictitious learning task was used to give some of the subjects the impression that the confederate could be hurt. Two-thirds of the subjects were told that the learner (that is, the confederate) was to receive an electric shock whenever she made a mistake, whereas the other third were the control group. Since the researchers wanted to determine whether it mattered who hurt the tormentor, half the experimental subjects were to administer the punishment, whereas in the other instances the experimenter would deliver the shocks. In both instances, the confederate was ostensibly punished to exactly the same degree whenever she committed an error. Nothing was said to the subjects in the control group about punishment. All the subjects' final levels of aggression were assessed in the last phase of the experiment by giving them opportunities to shock the confederate to indicate their judgments about the "creativity" of her work on yet another task.

Figure 11–2 reports the mean number of shocks the subjects in each condition delivered to the confederate. The students' final punitiveness

FIGURE 11–2

Level of aggression toward a confederate after the confederate was shocked and not shocked. (Data from Doob & Wood (1972). Copyright 1972 by the American Psychological Association. Adapted by permission.)

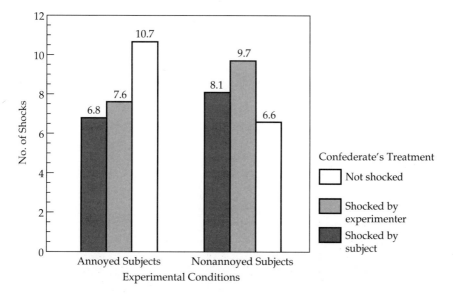

depended not only upon their own emotional states but also upon whether the confederate had been hurt earlier. Thus, when the subjects *hadn't* been provoked by the confederate, they apparently found it easier to shock during the final learning trials if she had been punished earlier—by either the experimenter or themselves. Maybe they believed that these earlier severe treatment of the confederate legitimated their punishing her again fairly harshly.

The students' reactions were very different, however, if they had been provoked by the confederate. The subjects in this condition who believed that the woman had been hurt earlier—either by the experimenter or by themselves—attacked the confederate *less* than did those who thought the confederate had not previously been punished. They seemed to be satisfied because their tormentor had been injured by *someone*. It apparently wasn't especially important for *them* to have hurt her personally.[22]

Is the difference due to brooding-heightened aggressiveness? So far so good, but let's now consider what else might have happened in the annoyed condition in the Doob and Wood experiment. The subjects who hadn't shocked the confederate during the intervening activity period had simply sat still, waiting to do something else. In his 1973 discussion of catharsis research, Albert Bandura questioned whether subjects who underwent this kind of waiting period really constituted an appropriate "control group." The provoked subjects conceivably might have spent the waiting time brooding about the mistreatment done to them, so that their aggressive inclinations would have remained strong or even increased. The people in the supposed catharsis conditions (who punished the frustrater) might have been less punitive toward the target at the end of the study only because they had been too busy to ruminate about the prior insult, and thus hadn't stirred themselves up.

Other catharsis research was also conducted at the University of Toronto, this time by Vladimir Konecni, who is now at the University of California, San Diego. Konecni addressed the control group problem which had been raised by Bandura. His results provide still more information about the conditions affecting the likelihood of an aggression catharsis, and this research is worth describing in some detail.

In the first of several experiments, Konecni required his subjects (male and female high school students) to work in individual sessions on a number of assignments with a peer (the experimenter's accomplice), much as in the Doob and Wood study just described. In the first phase, the "other student" (that is, the confederate) either was neutral to the naive subject or behaved in an obnoxious and insulting manner. Next came the intervening activity conditions. Again, as in the Doob and Wood study, there was a middle period in which (1) some of the subjects gave the experimenter's accomplice electric shocks whenever that person made a mistake on a learning task, while (2) others sat alone for standard periods of time, waiting for the final part of the experiment. In addition, (3) there was yet another condition, in which the subjects didn't attack the accomplice but were given a job to occupy their minds; they worked alone on a series of math problems, supposedly only to determine how difficult the items were. Konecni also introduced another experimental variation that's important to consider: Because he wanted to see whether the provoked subjects would calm down simply with the passage of time, the intervening activities went on for either seven or thirteen minutes. Finally, each naive subject had an opportunity to deliver "moderately painful" shocks to the confederate as his or her judgment of the creativity of the other student's ideas on another task.

Konecni found, first, that the effect of the intervening activities depended upon the subjects' emotional states. Figure 11–3 summarizes the means involved in this interaction for the subjects who had been given a *brief* (7-minute) intervening assignment. The nature of this fairly short task didn't significantly influence the number of shocks delivered by the nonangered students. They basically didn't punish the other student much, no matter what job they had just worked on.

The aroused subjects, on the other hand, were affected by the nature of the activity. The annoyed subjects who merely sat and waited were

FIGURE 11–3

Number of shocks administered to an accomplice by annoyed and nonannoyed subjects after brief intervening activity. (Data from Konecni (1975b). Copyright 1975 by the American Psychological Association. Adapted by permission.)

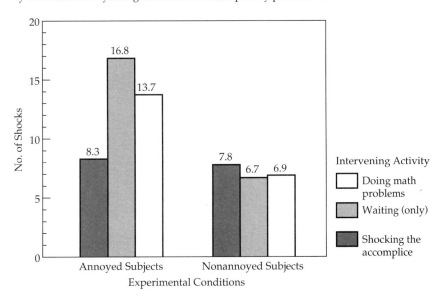

the most punitive people in the experiment, while the people who had been given the distracting mathematics problems tended to be less aggressive. Much as Bandura had suggested, it's as if the annoyed subjects had brooded about the accomplice's insults while they waited for the next part of the study, thus keeping their ire up or even increasing their aggressive inclinations. The distracted subjects, on the other hand, evidently hadn't kept themselves incensed but had calmed down somewhat because their minds had been on the math problems. Whereas the rumination had presumably maintained the provoked subjects' aggressiveness, the subjects in this group who had previously punished their tormentor were less aggressively inclined. In fact, they were now the least aggressive of the subjects in the three annoyed conditions and were no more punitive than their nonannoyed counterparts. They seem to have undergone a cathartic reduction of their instigation to aggression as a result of their prior attacks on their tormentor.

These results should not be construed to mean that we have to attack people who bother us if we're to be rid of our aggressive urges. "Many an ill has time repaired," Virgil remarked long ago, and Konecni's results indicate that the Roman poet was right, at least under some conditions. At the end of the study, the annoyed subjects who had engaged in the longer neutral intervening activities (for *thirteen minutes*), either waiting alone or working on the math problems, were much less aggressive than their equally insulted counterparts who had been allowed only seven minutes before they delivered the final shocks. Their aggressive inclinations had apparently subsided to some extent simply with the passage of time.[23]

Turn our minds to peaceful matters. This finding conveys an important message. We don't have to assault the persons who offended us to experience a "cathartic effect" (defined as a reduced likelihood aggression). Time itself can make us more peaceful, unless of course, we repeatedly brood about the wrongs we have suffered and don't turn our minds to other matters. Before the start of the twentieth century, a young man interviewed by the pioneering psychologist G. Stanley Hall spoke of how he coped with anger-arousing situations. One of his remarks is pertinent here:

> Once when I was about 13, in an angry fit, I walked out of the house, vowing I would never return. It was a beautiful summer day, and I walked far along lovely lanes, till gradually the stillness and beauty calmed and soothed me, and after some hours I returned repentant and almost melted. Since then, when [I am] angry, I do this if I can, and find it the best cure.[24]

Wouldn't it be nice if all of us could find our own "lovely lanes" to walk along when we've been offended?

The Long-Term Dangers of Aggressive Satisfactions

It's not necessarily a good idea to attack those who provoke us, no matter how satisfying this aggression might be. If we do attack, we may initially be pleased by what we've done: Besides attaining our aggressive goal, we may believe that we've taught our tormentors a lesson and also shown others (and maybe ourselves as well) that we're not to be pushed around. However, these pleasures could have a cost. The people we attack could strike back in retaliation, producing a chain of aggression and counteraggression. There's another, more subtle possibility as well. As I pointed out in Chapter 6, The Development of Violence Proneness, aggressors are often rewarded by finding they've successfully injured the people they set out to attack. Because of this reward, they are then all too likely to lash out at other people in the future, even under different circumstances. And so, while our aggressive urges may diminish after we hit those who provoked us, there is only a *short-term* reduction in the probability that we'll aggress again. Over the *long run,* the chances are we'll become even more aggressive than we had been in the past.

It Could Be Beneficial to Talk about One's Troubles

You may be unconvinced by the argument I have been spelling out so far in this chapter. You may be thinking, "There wouldn't be such a widespread belief in the benefits of expressing angry feelings openly if emotional expression didn't have some value." I want to make sure that you understand exactly what my thesis is.

I've pointed out that feelings can be revealed in several different ways. I have questioned only the form of expression of anger in which the provoked person attacks or threatens someone else. I do not object to the open display of angry emotional states in facial and bodily reactions (unless these motor responses are clearly threatening) or to the nonconfrontational reporting of feelings. Think back to the other lines by William Blake which I quoted earlier: "I was angry with my friend:/I told my wrath, my wrath did end." Maybe what the poet did was tell his friend how he felt without verbally assaulting him.

The benefits of confiding in others. My point here is that Blake wasn't necessarily *emotionally expressive* in the sense of ranting and raving at his friend. Instead, he may have been *informative,* talking about his feelings and also about the facts—what his friend had done to annoy him. An impressive research project conducted by James Pennebaker at Southern Methodist University in Dallas, Texas, highlights the difference between these two ways of revealing emotional states. Pennebaker's findings demonstrate that one of these ways of showing emotions can be far more beneficial than the other.

Some of us are exceedingly reluctant to tell others about the traumas we have suffered or the tragedies or disappointments that have befallen us. Thinking that these incidents are our private business, that we might somehow cast ourselves in a bad light by talking about the unfortunate occurrences, or that other people simply aren't interested in hearing about our troubles, we try not to show our feelings and don't say anything about what has happened to us. Most mental health workers disapprove of an unwillingness to confide in others, and Pennebaker's research indicates that they are right to disapprove. Silence may add to our emotional turmoil and thus may be physically as well as psychologically costly.

In one study, Pennebaker questioned the surviving spouses, all between 25 and 45 years old, of men and women who had died suddenly, either in an automobile accident or by committing suicide. The unexpected death was clearly stressful for most of the people in the sample, as might be expected, and many of the survivors indicated that their health had worsened in the year after the tragic event. The subjects who developed the least serious problems tended to be the ones who said that they had talked to others about their spouses' deaths. Interestingly, according to the data, the more they had confided in others, (1) the less likely it was that their health had declined and (2) the less likely they were to ruminate about their spouses' deaths in the year afterward.

Encouraged by findings such as these, Pennebaker and his students embarked upon a series of naturalistic studies as well as experiments investigating the physical health, psychological, and even neurophysiological and biochemical consequences of telling others about the traumas one has suffered in the past. One of their experiments is especially pertinent to the analysis I have been advancing.

For four consecutive days, healthy undergraduates wrote either about trivial matters (this was the control group) or about the most traumatic and stressful experiences of their lives. The people who wrote about their traumatic experiences were further subdivided into three groups: (1) The "trauma-fact" group reported the facts of the traumatic incidents in their lives but said nothing about their feelings. (2) The "trauma-emotion" group described only their feelings at the times of the traumatic incidents. (3) The "trauma-combination" group wrote about both the facts and their feelings at the times of the incidents.

When asked how they felt immediately after completing their writing assignments, the subjects who had written about their emotional states at the times of the stressful events (that is, the people in the trauma-emotion and trauma-combination conditions) were most upset; they also showed the greatest increases in systolic blood pressure. They had been stirred up emotionally by the recollection of their earlier feelings.

The emotional arousal seemed to be beneficial, however, only for the students who had been fully informative. When the psychologists inquired into the students' health six months later, the subjects who had reported both the facts *and* their feelings indicated that they now felt healthier, had fewer illnesses, and had visited the student health center less frequently than the students in any of the other conditions. The data for frequency of health center visits are summarized in Figure 11–4. In other words, what seemed to be important was not expressing their feelings alone but talking about their feelings within the context of what had happened.

Let's now go back to the first Pennebaker study I cited and ask why the uncommunicative people's health suffered after their spouses' sudden death. Pennebaker says the major reason was that they were experiencing considerable stress. Besides not telling others about the traumas they had suffered, they were probably also trying not to think about their tragic losses. It took a good deal of mental effort on their part to suppress the unwanted ideas and memories, and this psychological work was physiologically wearing. Because of their struggle to block the unhappy thoughts, they couldn't relax. They had to be on the alert all the time. So as to stop themselves from consciously thinking about their tragedies,

FIGURE 11–4
Number of visits to a health center for illness per month as a function of writing topic. (From Pennebaker & Beall (1986). Copyright 1986 by the American Psychological Association. Reprinted by permission.)

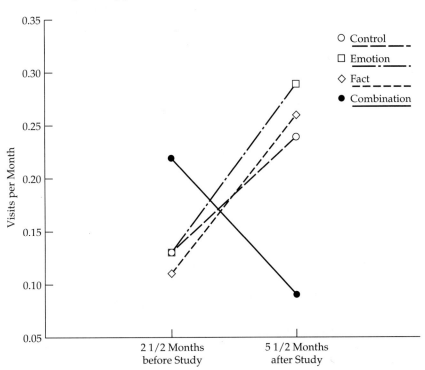

they had to keep their losses in mind virtually all the time, although below full awareness. Because dangerous ideas and recollections were usually lurking in the backs of their minds, the survivors were physiologically stressed without fully realizing it. The more communicative widows and widowers presumably didn't experience this additional stress. Having consciously confronted the reality of their loved ones' deaths, they didn't have to work so hard and so often to keep themselves from remembering what they had lost.

The second Pennebaker investigation just summarized suggests what else is involved in a more adequate acceptance of a trauma. According to Pennebaker, when people inhibit their thoughts and feelings about unhappy events, they do more than keep themselves under tension. They also fail to fully integrate the sad memories and feelings into their functioning psychological systems. Telling others about the traumas, even if only in writing, can promote this beneficial integration. It may be, then, that as the subjects in the second study wrote about the disturbing incidents in their lives and about their feelings at the times of the incidents, they achieved a better understanding of the occurrences, became better able to cope with the consequences of what had happened, and developed more adequate controls over their feelings. Putting this another way, they became better able to accept the reality of the events and, in Pennebaker's words, to "attain closure of the experience." In the first study, the survivors who had talked about their tragic losses tended not to ruminate about their dead spouses. They had attained closure.

Pennebaker's studies show that the benefits to be derived from revealing one's emotions to others do not stem from venting the feelings. What's important is not displaying emotions or discharging a pool of supposedly suppressed energy but attaching words to the distressing incidents and the accompanying emotions. Contemporary psychoanalytic theory recognizes this. According to many present-day psychoanalytic therapists, patients improve not through achieving catharsis but by attaining insights. When they achieve understanding, their memories of unpleasant events they suffered and the unhappy feelings they had at the time are no longer isolated from the rest of their personalities. Their recollections and emotions become accepted parts of themselves, and thus their feelings become more controllable.[25]

Self-Awareness and Self-Control
Self-awareness can undoubtedly help people to restrain the hostility and the aggressive impulses which are activated by unpleasant feelings. Imagine that you're functioning as someone's supervisor and have to judge the quality of this person's work. Let's also suppose that you have a mild toothache at the time and are trying to keep on with your job anyway. The low-level pain you're experiencing might make you irritable (that is, the negative affect might produce an impetus to aggression, as

well as hostile thoughts and felt anger). As a consequence, you could be inclined to give your subordinate an unfavorable rating. Consider, however, what might happen if you become very conscious what you said about the other person and that you would then deliberately try not to allow it to affect your judgment?

A series of experiments that Bartholmeu Troccoli and I conducted (and which were discussed in Chapter 3) indicate that awareness-produced self-control is indeed quite likely to occur. Adding to the summary of this research provided earlier, in one of our experiments (not mentioned before), we asked half of our female university students to extend their nondominant arm outward and unsupported for several minutes while listening to another woman talk about herself (supposedly as part of a job interview). Their other half of the subjects merely rested their nondominant arms on a table while listening to this woman. The students whose arms were extended soon felt considerable muscular discomfort in their outstretched arms, but the other subjects were in no pain. We then asked half of the subjects in each group to rate their feelings at the time they kept their arms in the same position, in order to heighten their awareness of their feelings. The other people in each of these two groups were given another brief task to work on so that their attention would be turned away from their feelings. Finally, all the subjects completed a questionnaire in which they (1) judged the job applicant's personality by saying what traits they believed she possessed and (2) rated how uncomfortable they felt at the end of the session. The hostility measure was the number of socially undesirable qualities which the subjects attributed to the applicant, from a list of positive and negative traits.

Figure 11–5 shows the results, which are in accord with the findings of the other experiments in this series. The degree of attention which the subjects had been induced to give to their feelings significantly affected the relationship between the magnitude of their discomfort and their negative judgments of the target person. Generally speaking, the more discomfort the women who had been distracted had experienced, the more hostile they were toward the job applicant. Presumably because they weren't trying to control themselves, their negative affect apparently led directly to a fairly strong expressed hostility. This wasn't the case, however, for the women who had been made aware of their unpleasant feelings. As you can see in Figure 11–5, the worse these particular subjects felt, the *less* negative they were toward the target person, as if they had leaned over backward not to be unfairly harsh to her.[26]

The uncomfortable subjects' prior attention to their moderately unpleasant feelings evidently prompted them to restrain themselves and do what they thought was socially desirable under the circumstances. My guess is that their awareness of their somewhat unexpected emotional state caused them to think about the situation they were in, so that

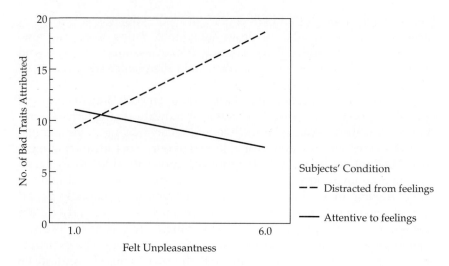

FIGURE 11-5

Relationship between negative feelings and expressed negative judgment as a function of attention to feelings. (Based on data from Berkowitz & Troccoli (1990), Experiment 2.)

they considered all the available information and decided to do what they believed was right.

DEVELOPING NEW WAYS OF BEHAVING

If the interpretation offered in the previous section is correct, people won't restrain themselves when they become aware of their aroused emotions unless they believe it's wrong to be hostile or aggressive in the given situation and capable of inhibiting their aggression. Some persons, however, are slow to question their right to derogate or attack others, and they may also be relatively unable to hold themselves back when they're provoked. Merely showing these highly aggressive individuals that they're being offensive is not enough. They also have to learn that it is often better to be nonaggressive rather than assaultive. It may even be beneficial to teach them how to behave in a socially skillful manner and how they can restrain themselves when they're aroused.

In the past generation or so, psychologists have developed a number of different programs designed to promote this kind of learning. These programs vary, partly because their originators don't think of aggression in exactly the same ways. Psychologists who see aggression as primarily instrumental behavior, which is carried out in pursuit of some other purpose and is repeated because the attackers have learned that aggression pays, typically concentrate on teaching highly assaultive persons that antisocial conduct is apt to be punished (or at least is unlikely to produce favorable outcomes) and that socially desirable behavior is more likely to achieve their aims. This approach, which is frequently (but not only) employed with children and teenagers, is often termed *behavior modification* (or *contingency management*). Its proponents assume that approved behaviors can be increased by associating them with rewards and that unwanted actions can be decreased by linking them either with punishments or with a lack of favorable outcomes.

Other psychologists are generally more impressed by the rapidity with which many highly aggressive persons lose their tempers and by the difficulty which such persons have in restraining themselves. Therapists taking this perspective therefore usually focus on altering the assaultive individuals' emotional reactivity. Since the procedures they employ typically emphasize changing the individual's thoughts and interpretations, their training programs are often viewed as being *cognitive* (or *cognitive-behavioral*) in nature.

Teaching that Cooperation Pays: Improving Parental Management of Problem Children

The first training program we'll look at was devised by Gerald Patterson, John Reid, and their associates at the Social Learning Center of the Oregon Research Institute. The chapter on the development of aggressiveness (Chapter 6) summarized many of the findings they had obtained in their research on antisocial children and, you will recall, emphasized the part played by inadequate parenting. According to the Oregon investigations, in many instances the mothers and fathers had helped to form their youngsters' aggressive personalities by being bad managers. They tended to be highly erratic in disciplining their offspring—often nagging the children, failing to reward desirable behavior, and punishing the youngsters inconsistently when they misbehaved.

Adopting a general behavior modification stance, Patterson and his colleagues basically sought to teach parents to become better at dealing with their children. Though they didn't slight the importance of parental love and support, they emphasized that love wasn't enough. They told the parents in their program that adults occasionally have to discipline and manage their offspring, and that some mothers and fathers need to learn to be more effective in these tasks.

Disciplining and managing children can be very difficult, partly because some children are serious troublemakers. For example, the Oregon group described a child named Maude as follows:

Maude was only 10 when [she was] referred to [the Oregon Research Institute] at the behest of the school. In addition to frequent stealing episodes, and even more frequent lies, she was almost totally without friends. Her "entrance" into a game being played on the playground could be marked by her shouted commands and freely dispensed kicks and blows to those who [didn't comply]. What was most infuriating to peers and teachers alike was her ability to look an accusing adult in the eye and say, "No, I didn't take the money," even though [she was] faced by three eyewitnesses (including the teacher). . . . [Though Maude was] only four feet tall, she could reduce most adults half again her size to smoldering impotence.

Her parents fared no better [than did the teachers]. Her presence in the home consisted of running battles with both of her older sisters. What she did not accomplish by verbal invectives could be won by stealthy attacks upon their belongings. . . .

The parents listed the following as problems of greatest concern to them:

1. Steals
2. Lies
3. Swears at home and school
4. Fights with peers
5. Not liked by other children
6. Teases siblings
7. Does not mind[27]

Patterson and his colleagues generally assume that Maude and other problem children can be reeducated by employing the principles of instrumental learning—that is, by rewarding desirable behavior. Although they believe that everyone in the family has to participate in the process of change, the psychologists place particular emphasis on the parents' rewards and punishments.

I can offer only a brief and greatly oversimplified summary of the three- to four-month training program at the Oregon Research Institute. In presenting this summary, I'll use Sally, a troublesome young girl similar to Maude, as an example. (The same principles would apply in dealing with a boy.)

Sally's parents, like many couples who have aggressive children, had all too frequently failed to treat her differently when she did things they liked and when she behaved in ways they disapproved. The child's proper behavior had thus not been adequately reinforced, while her antisocial conduct had been too often rewarded. To rectify this problem, both her mother and her father were taught at the outset of treatment to identify, monitor, and record any behaviors which Sally carried out that were especially bothersome and disruptive. They then learned how to reward her for actions of which they approved and to punish her consistently and with discrimination when she refused to comply.[28]

As a part of this program, Sally had to learn to distinguish very clearly between right and wrong—that is, she had to know what she should do and what things she should not do. She also had to have a clear idea of the consequences of both acceptable and unacceptable behavior. In order to provide her with this clear understanding, the counselor helped the adults and the child to work out a behavioral contract—a formal agreement in which the parents spelled out a few specific things that they wanted Sally to do. They had to take care not to make excessive or unrealistic demands, and they also specified the rewards Sally would receive if she complied with the terms of the contract. In the initial contract, they said they would like Sally to make her bed every morning, clear the table after the evening meal, and do her homework for one hour on every weeknight. Since Sally, like other highly aggressive youngsters, would have been unwilling to do what her parents wanted simply in order to get their approval, they had to offer her more definite incentives. She was told, then, that she could earn points daily for meeting the specified objectives. The points would be her "pay" for doing her chores, much as grownups are paid for their work. She could earn a total of ten points a day, five for minding her parents and five for carrying out her particular assignments. Noncompliance would bring punishment: the loss of points or even "time out" in which she would be sent to another room (such as the bathroom) and would have to sit still for a specified period of time (e.g., fifteen minutes or half an hour).

The number of points earned by the end of the day would determine which of several previously agreed upon incentives Sally could obtain. The contract for the first week stated that for ten points, she could stay up until 9:00 and watch television; for eight points, she could remain up until 8:30 and have a special dessert; if she had only four points, she would have to go to bed at 7:30; and if she had earned no points, she would be required to wash her dishes and go to bed at 7:00.

In the Oregon training program, if the first contract is successful, the counselor then helps the family to negotiate a second contract, in which new behaviors are added for the child to carry out and the point requirements are readjusted. In Sally's case, a later contract stipulated that she would lose three points each time she swore and two points for every act of noncompliance. It was also agreed that her mother would read to her for thirty minutes if she earned ten points, that six points would allow her to stay up until 8:30, and that she would have to go to bed at 7:30 if she didn't end up with any points at the end of the day.

The counselor in this program does much more than help the family to negotiate contracts. Throughout the process, the counselor checks frequently on how well the training program is proceeding, consults with the adults often, and rewards them for effective parenting behaviors (such as smiling, touching, the absence of put-downs, and so on). Keep in mind, in this connection, that difficulties do occur in such programs; the difficulties may include parental misunderstanding and/or resistance, stubborn if not openly rebellious children, and barely submerged

but strong hostilities. These problems can complicate the relearning process, and the counselor may need to exercise great tact and persistence.

If all goes well, Patterson's theory maintains, the problem children in
the training program will soon come to want their parents' general
approval as well as the more specific points and rewards they can obtain
by meeting the contract terms. Finding that good behavior pays and that
rebelliousness and aggression do not, the youngsters will become less
disruptive and less aggressive in the family, and will be on the way
toward becoming better-socialized members of society.

This optimistic projection does not always come true, of course. The
Oregon group is one of the few organizations in the field of family learning and therapy that makes regular and systematic attempts to assess
clients' progress. In addition to frequent telephone conversations with
the parents, direct observations are made of the family members' behavior toward each other at the very start, in the middle, and at the end of
the program, partly so that the observer can provide feedback to the family but also to determine the success of the training. Patterson and his
associates have estimated from the records of these observations that the
basic Oregon Research Institute program is effective with only about one
out of three children. Additional programs are required for the other two
thirds. Sometimes relearning procedures are provided in the classroom
setting, and at other times more emphasis is given to resolving marital
conflicts. With a combination of these various procedures, the Oregon
Research Institute program evidently does help more than a few families
and children.[29]

Lessening Emotional Reactivity

Though behavior modification programs, which attempt to teach aggressive individuals that they can achieve desirable outcomes by behaving in
a friendly, cooperative, and socially approved manner, are useful to
some people, other persons are prone to violence primarily because they
are easily aroused and cannot restrain themselves. A growing number of
psychological training programs seek to alter this sort of emotional reactivity.

Novaco's Study of Anger Control Methods
Raymond Novaco of the University of California, Irvine, developed one
of the best-known programs for controlling anger or aggression. Perhaps
of equal importance, he also reported on one of the earliest systematic
tests of such a program's efficacy. In this endeavor, Novaco took a decided cognitive position that is in some ways consistent with my analysis of
aggression. Although he defined anger in commonsense terms, as having
to do with both feelings and actions, he believed that this emotion is

basically a reaction to experienced stress (an unpleasant state of affairs). He also emphasized that anger can be intensified by unfortunate expectations and repeated ruminations. His position differs from mine in that he maintained that aversive events won't produce anger unless they are appraised as personal threats.

Novaco wondered whether a person's anger reactions could be lessened by changing both the appraisal and the way in which the person thought about the provocative event afterward. In line with the reasoning followed by other cognitively oriented psychotherapists, Novaco believed that it is especially important to teach emotionally reactive persons to talk to themselves (in their minds, of course) in a nonangering manner about the provocative situations which they encounter. Psychologists sometimes refer to programs that attempt to alter people's internal statements to themselves as *self-instructional training*.[30]

I'll give you a greatly abbreviated description of Novaco's procedure by telling you about the experiment he conducted. The subjects were eighteen men and sixteen women between 17 and 42 years old who acknowledged having serious difficulties in controlling their tempers (and indeed, some of them had strong outbursts of anger during the course of the study). The treatment sessions were held twice weekly for three weeks in all the four conditions that were established for the study. There were several additional meetings at the beginning and at the end, during which various measurements were made.

The relaxation condition. Since Novaco's conception of anger control concentrated on lessening the emotion arousal generated by a provocative event, he decided to compare the results of his cognitive (or self-instructional) procedure with a widely used relaxation technique. To establish relaxation, some of the subjects were initially informed that anger "was a high-arousal state accompanied by agitation that leads to impulsive behavior" (note that this statement is very much in accord with my formulation), and that it was important to be able to relax both physically and mentally. The subjects were then put through a series of fairly standard relaxation exercises during the course of their training. They were asked to imagine especially provocative incidents, and they practiced taking deep breaths as well as tensing and then relaxing particular muscle groups. Nothing was said about the role of thoughts and appraisals in the generation of anger.

The cognitive treatment. I'll describe Novaco's cognitive condition in more detail, since he was primarily concerned with the effectiveness of this procedure. The experimenter began by giving the subjects in this condition a rationale for the study along with a way of understanding anger. Besides describing to the subjects how emotions could be aroused by thoughts, this rationale explained that anger could be both constructive and destructive. It also emphasized that the program's goal was to help the subjects learn to use anger to further their personal goals without being self-defeating. During the course of the treatment, and at home as well as in the treatment room, the subjects practiced assigned exercises: making certain specified statements to themselves as they imagined and enacted particularly bothersome events.

The thoughts which the participants rehearsed dealt with what Novaco regarded as the four stages of the provocation sequence; as follows:

> *Preparing for a provocation.* The subjects rehearsed statements such as: "If I find myself getting upset, I'll know what to do" and "I can manage this situation. I know how to regulate my anger."
>
> *Confronting the provocation.* The thoughts used in this stage were along the lines of: "Stay calm. Just continue to relax," "You don't need to prove yourself," and "It's really a shame that this person is acting the way she is."
>
> *Coping with the arousal and agitation.* The subjects said to themselves statements such as: "My muscles are starting to feel tight. Time to relax and slow things down," and "I'm not going to get pushed around, but I'm not going haywire either."
>
> *Reflecting on the provocation.* The statements in this stage dealt with both unresolved conflicts and concluded conflicts. An example of the kinds of statements used with unresolved conflicts is: "These are difficult situations, and they take time to work out." The statements with concluded conflicts included: "That wasn't as hard as I thought" and "It could have been a lot worse."

Other treatment conditions. There were two other conditions in the experiment. The subjects in one, the control group, were not given either the cognitive or the relaxation training but were asked to pay attention to their anger experience. The other was a combined treatment condition in which the subjects practiced both the relaxation exercises and the self-instructional statements.

Effectiveness measures. Novaco employed several measures of changes in anger to test the effectiveness of each treatment condition in lessening anger. He assessed the participants' anger tendencies before the training sessions started, using a number of different methods. These methods included asking the subjects to rate how angry they believed they would be in response to several provocations they imagined and recording their systolic and diastolic blood pressure as they thought about the bothersome incidents. The same measures were used again at the completion of the training program, and Novaco calculated the amount of change between the pretreatment and the posttreatment assessments.

Figure 11–6 reports the mean change scores in the four conditions for the measures mentioned above: felt anger ratings and blood pressure readings in reaction to imagined provocations. (Quite a number of Novaco's other indexes also produced significant condition differences.) In general, as Figure 11–6 indicates, the best results were obtained from the treatment that combined the self-instructional and the relaxation exercises. The people in this condition experienced the greatest drop in both felt anger ratings and systolic and diastolic blood pressure relative to their pretreatment levels. The cognitive procedure alone also seemed to be somewhat effective (as was the relaxation training on some of the measures), but the joining of both techniques together evidently was better than either alone. I'll say more about this shortly.

Some Recommendations and Implications

Other psychologists also have reported research results supporting the efficacy of combining cognitive and relaxation methods in anger control.[31] Clearly, then, at least some people can become less aggressive by

FIGURE 11–6

Changes from pretreatment level in anger self-report and blood pressure in reaction to imagined provocations. (Data from Novaco (1975). Copyright by Raymond W. Novaco. Adapted with permission of the author. The results reported are for the anger self-report and blood pressure measures in the imaginal provocation condition.)

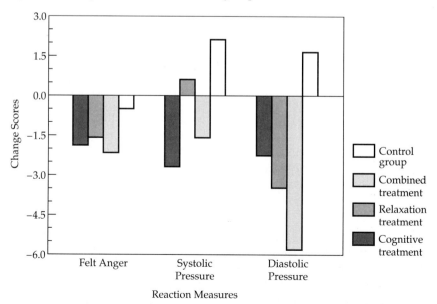

learning how to lessen their emotional arousal and agitation when they are provoked. We must recognize, however, that this treatment procedure will not work for every emotionally reactive aggressor. Jerry Deffenbacher of Colorado State University, Fort Collins, is one of the leading investigators of anger/aggression control techniques. He has suggested that this training may be best for young adults who are somewhat aware of their own anger and who want help for the problem. He believes that other kinds of interventions (perhaps including the ventilationist therapies mentioned earlier in this chapter) may be more helpful to people whose aggressive inclinations are severely inhibited and greatly repressed.

Deffenbacher has also made some important observations about how the therapist should act in the training program. Whereas my summary of Novaco's procedure seems to imply that the therapist takes a somewhat inactive role, Deffenbacher emphasizes that the psychologist should be active, persistent, supportive, and at times even confrontive. People who are prone to strong anger and aggression are often highly challenging, usually quick to jump to conclusions, and highly abrasive. Deffenbacher thinks that a therapist can best deal with these persons by challenging their usual interpretations and their blaming tendencies in a supportive but persistent manner, as well as by teaching them how to control themselves.

Although some research suggests that either the cognitive treatment alone or relaxation training alone would do just as well as the combination of the two methods, Deffenbacher believes, with Novaco, that it is best to employ the combination.[32] This opinion certainly makes considerable sense from the perspective employed in this book: Since a good many attacks are emotional reactions impelled by strong internal agitation, it is clearly important to teach people who are especially reactive in this mode how to lower their emotional arousal when they are under stress.

Many of us should learn to do this, but especially quick-tempered persons who are susceptible to chronic heart disease. As the discussion of the Type A personality in Chapter 5 pointed out, people who frequently explode in rage or who fume about the slights they think they've suffered are especially prone to heart disease. Increasing numbers of researchers now believe that these persons would do well to change their thought patterns so that they wouldn't see themselves as being affronted again and again, and so that, when they were aroused, they could calm down fairly soon. A newspaper article on the adverse effects of chronic anger offered the following advice:

> Researchers say that most, if not all, consistently crabby people can shift the balance of hormones in their favor by training themselves not to let every snag nettle them. Scientists say that, by recognizing irrational anger at the

outset and coping with it intelligently, a person can perhaps block the cas-
cade of stress hormones before it tumbles out of control.

Dr. [Redford] Williams [a specialist in behavioral medicine at the Duke
University Medical Center] . . . suggests that whenever a person feels irritated by a thoughtless shopper in the supermarket, or by a balky elevator,
the person acknowledge that a fit of pique is pending. The person might
then seek distraction by reading a magazine or chatting with someone else,
he said.[33]

Besides trying to distract herself or himself, as Dr. Williams proposed, the individual might also benefit from attempting to reinterpret
the arousing event in a manner that is less personally upsetting. Above
all, she or he should try not to brood about what happened.

Does Anything Work with Incarcerated Offenders?

So far, I've been talking about relearning procedures that can be, and
are, used with relatively well-socialized persons—people, that is, who
aren't in trouble with the law. What about individuals who commit violent crimes so serious that they are sent to jail? Can they be taught to
reduce their violent inclinations through any means other than force and
punishment?

The Doubts

For many years, quite a few correctional system administrators as well as
academically oriented social scientists believed that society cannot rehabilitate most lawbreakers who are imprisoned or otherwise legally
restrained. It's an illusion, they maintain, to hope that correctional institutions can remake offenders into better citizens.

There seemed to be considerable justification for this pessimistic
view. A substantial body of research indicates that rehabilitative programs are generally not especially effective in lowering the likelihood
that incarcerated criminals will be returned to jail for later offenses. This
apparently holds true whether they are carried out with groups or with
single individuals. A research review published by Robert Martinson
about a generation ago certainly pointed in this direction. After reviewing 231 studies of prison rehabilitative programs, Martinson concluded,
"With few and isolated exceptions, the rehabilitative efforts that have
been reported so far have had no appreciable effect on recidivism."[34]

James Wilson and Richard Herrnstein have given special attention to
behavior modification programs (employing procedures similar to those
used by Patterson and his colleagues at Oregon Research Institute) and
have generally come to much the same conclusion. They describe, for
example, a widely copied behavior modification program (which was
initially called "achievement place" but now is often termed the "teach-

ing-family model") in which specially trained foster parents administer rewards and punishments to eight or so teenage delinquents, who are with the foster parents. The goal is to teach the youths to take care of their rooms, study hard in school, and generally act in a socially desirable manner. According to Wilson and Herrnstein,

> There seems to be little doubt that the teaching-family system alters the behavior, including the delinquency, of [teenagers] in the group homes. But there is no evidence that it alters the rate at which the youth commit offenses one year after their release from treatment, or that it has any greater effect on delinquency than do other community-based programs.[35]

Because so much negative evidence has been accumulated, many correctional officials and social scientists alike have lost hope in the possibility of rehabilitation. Some have even argued that social science and mental health specialists have misled the correctional system into believing they can do a great deal to reform offenders.

But Is There Hope?

However, the issue isn't really settled. A number of psychologists, psychiatrists, and social workers have objected to the sort of pessimistic conclusions which I have summarized, saying that such reviews have neglected relevant considerations. Adding to this rebuttal, a recent careful statistical analysis of the research results, incorporating later investigations and making use of sophisticated statistical procedures, shows that some rehabilitation programs can indeed be effective.[36]

C. J. Garrett surveyed 111 studies of adjudicated adolescent delinquents which had been carried out between 1960 and 1983. In each of these studies, the youths who had been exposed to a treatment program were compared with an appropriate nontreated control group. (There were a total of more than 8000 delinquents in the treated conditions and almost 5000 in the control groups, and three-quarters of the subjects were males.) When all the outcome measures used in these investigations (including adjustment measures and academic improvement, as well as recidivism) were combined, and over all types of settings, delinquents, and treatments, Garret found that the delinquents who had been exposed to the training procedures were moderately apt to have done better than the untreated controls. This relative improvement was somewhat greater for behavior modification and cognitive programs than for psychodynamically oriented programs, and comparatively young delinquents and females were more likely to have profited from the interventions than were older delinquents and males.

Following a line of investigation that is much more relevant for the purposes of this discussion, Garrett also asked whether the treatment programs had been equally effective for all types of delinquents. He found that this had not been the case. Youths who had been convicted of crimes against the person (largely aggressive crimes) were evidently somewhat more likely to have benefited from the psychological interventions than were those who had committed property crimes.

Garrett's analysis offers some hope, but it's obviously only a beginning. Herbert Quay, an eminent investigator of juvenile delinquency, has commented, "She [Garrett] has demonstrated that some interventions do work, and that in some instances these interventions work quite well." However, investigators will have to find out much more before these results will be truly useful. They will have to determine just what kinds of reeducation procedures are best for what kinds of offenders. Moreover, what has not yet been determined is whether it's possible to teach highly aggressive adult criminals to become less prone to violence.[37]

SUMMARY

Several different psychological approaches to the control of aggression, other than the use of punishment, are considered in this chapter. The first school of thought which I discuss maintains that inhibited anger is at the root of many personal and social ills. Mental health professionals of this persuasion call upon people to express their feelings freely and thus to achieve catharsis. In order to examine this thesis adequately, it is necessary first to have a clear understanding of what is meant by "free expression of anger," which can have any of several different meanings. It can refer to (1) an informative report on one's feelings, (2) a display of physiological and expressive-motor reactions, (3) an expression of hostile ideas and attitudes, and/or (4) a verbal and/or physical assault on another person. These different responses are far from perfectly correlated and can have different consequences for the actor as well as for the recipient. In the first section of this chapter, I focus mainly on the aftereffects of aggression, and specifically on whether an instigation to attack is lowered by realistic or make-believe aggression.

Although the findings of experimental research on the aftereffects of aggression are complicated and even somewhat inconsistent, I cite evidence indicating that, in the absence of restraints against aggression: (1) Make-believe aggressive actions often tend to increase rather than to lower the likelihood of further aggression, unless the actions are enjoyable to carry out and thus lessen the attackers' negative affect: (2) Since emotionally aroused aggressors are motivated to hurt their targets, their assaults tend to reduce their instigations to aggression only to the degree that they believe they have sufficiently injured the people whom they wanted to harm. (3) The reduced urge to commit further aggression is usually relatively short-lived, however, since successful attainment of the aggressive goal is reinforcing. Successful aggression thus heightens the chances that an aggressor will again attack someone in the future.

In reviewing the pertinent research, the chapter also notes that people can stir themselves up by ruminating about the wrongs they think have been done to them. It is usually beneficial, therefore, for the aroused persons to turn their minds to other matters and think of pleasanter events, rather than brooding about others' misdeeds. However, this doesn't mean that people who have been victimized by tragic occurrences shouldn't talk to others about these sad incidents. Studies indicate that people who refuse to tell others about the blows which fate has visited upon them are apt to experience considerable psychological and even physiological tension, presumably because of the strain they feel in trying to suppress thoughts of their tragedies. Confiding in others lessens the strain, according to Pennebaker, and also facilitates a more effective psychological coping process.

Thus, though I am not in favor of the free expression of anger in the sense of an open assault upon a target, I do believe that it is often desirable for emotionally aroused persons to tell others about their feelings as well as about the events that produced their emotional states. I also suggest in this connection that people can better control their emotional states. I also suggest in this connection that people can better control the impact of their negative affect upon their verbal and physical actions when they are highly aware of their unpleasant feelings.

The chapter next provides brief summaries of two other, and very different, methods of reducing aggressive inclinations—both interventions which attempt to train highly aggressive persons to be less assaultive. The first, employed by Gerald Patterson and his associates at the Oregon Research Institute, takes an instrumental learning approach. The assumption is that highly aggressive children will tend to become less aggressive when they learn that aggressive and uncooperative behaviors do not pay off and that constructive, prosocial actions are more apt to produce the outcomes they want. The second type of psychological intervention, typified by Raymond Novaco's anger control program, is much more cognitively oriented. It focuses on lessening the emotional impetus to aggressive outbursts rather than on altering the rewards for aggression. Both approaches are apparently successful in some but not all cases.

The chapter concludes with a very brief look at psychological programs that attempt to rehabilitate incarcerated offenders. Although the conventional wisdom holds that these programs are not effective, several recent analyses of treatment programs dealing with adolescent delinquents have been more optimistic. Both behavior modification (i.e., instrumental learning) and cognitive procedures seem to have been somewhat more successful than psychodynamically oriented interventions.

NOTES

1. Bach & Goldberg (1974), pp. 114–115.
2. Berkowitz (1973b).
3. E.g., Gentry (1985); Spielberger, Krasner, & Solomon (1988).
4. Baruch (1949), pp. 38–39.
5. Spielberger et al. (1988) believe that it is worthwhile to think of an "anger, hostility, and aggression syndrome" (which they call the "AHA syndrome"), even though they recognize that these components are somewhat separate. They prefer to think of "anger" as a specific set of feelings. Spielberger's State-Trait Anger Scale attempts to assess the intensity of the angry feelings that are usually experienced and how often these feelings arise.
6. I will not review the research on a somewhat different conception of "catharsis": as a reduction in general physiological arousal. When people are frustrated or otherwise provoked, their autonomic nervous systems are usually activated, thereby producing vascular changes and especially marked increases in their blood pressure and heart rate readings. It could be important to ask, then, whether their aggressive reaction helps to bring their autonomic activation down to their normal levels, as if they had calmed down physiologically. The research bearing on this question has yielded intriguing and potentially exceedingly important findings, as Geen & Quanty (1977) have noted in their thoughtful survey of this literature. However, because of the problems and ambiguities in this research into the main body of this book.
7. Fenichel (1945), pp. 565–566. Although Fenichel believed that it was possible to purge one's repressed impulses through fantasy activities, he also thought that catharsis was generally of limited therapeutic value in treating neuroses. Many contemporary psychoanalysts agree and also place the greatest emphasis on the insights the patient achieves in the course of the therapy, particularly as a result of the analyst's interpretations.
8. From Alexander Lowen, cited in Berkowitz (1973b).
9. Dollard, Doob, Miller, Mowrer, & Sears (1939), p. 50.
10. Turner & Goldsmith (1976).
11. Mallick & McCandless (1966), Study II. Note that while the aggressive play had tended to increase the nonfrustrated youngsters' aggressiveness somewhat (but not significantly so), there was no such rise in the thwarted group after the aggressive play. The frustrated children in this particular condition may have realized that they had already been quite aggressive and may have been reluctant to become even more hurtful.

12. From the Ann Landers column of April 8, 1969, as cited in Berkowitz (July 1973b), p. 24.

13. Some additional comments may also be of interest. First, some therapists use fantasy aggression in teaching their patients to become more assertive. With many other psychologists, I believe that a person can become more assertive without becoming more aggressive (in the sense that "aggression" is defined in this book). We don't have to teach people to enjoy hurting others in order to make them willing to stand up for themselves. Then too, make-believe aggression is sometimes fun. The people playing an aggressive game may enjoy the activity. The resulting pleasant feelings may lower their aggressive inclinations *at that moment*, but this doesn't mean they are less likely to be assaultive some time in the future.

14. Ebbesen, Duncan, & Konecni (1975).

15. The first experiment mentioned here was carried out by Thibaut & Coules, and I did the second study. See Berkowitz (1966).

16. Goldstein, J. H., Davis R. W., & Herman, D. (1975).

17. See Berkowitz & Heimer (1989) for evidence consistent with this possibility.

18. Straus (1974).

19. Bach & Goldberg (1974) took just such a position.

20. Geen has documented these inconsistencies in Geen & Quanty (1977) and in Geen (1990).

21. For more comprehensive discussion of this complexity, see Geen & Quanty (1977); Geen, Stonner, & Shope (1975). Also see the answer offered by Konecni & Ebbesen (1976).

22. Doob & Wood (1972).

23. Konecni (1975b). Bandura's discussion of the catharsis experiments can be found in his 1973 book, cf. especially p. 151.

24. Quoted by Tavris (1989), p. 135.

25. A fairly complete description of Pennebaker's research and theorizing can be found in Pennebaker (1989). Supporting Pennebaker's contention that people are stressed when they attempt to block unwanted thoughts, Wegner, Shortt, Blake, & Page (1990) have demonstrated experimentally that suppression of an emotion-arousing thought leads to a heightened activation of the sympathetic nervous system, as indexed by increased skin conductance. An experiment by Costanza, Derlega, & Winstead (1988) indicates that it may be more beneficial to talk about what one can do than about one's feelings alone. The subjects were best able to cope with stressful events after they had discussed with a friend how they would deal with the occurrences. Just talking about their feelings before the disturbing event took place, but without discussing their possible actions, made them even more anxious and depressed.

26. Berkowitz & Troccoli (1990), Experiment 2. A multiple regression analysis of the relationship between (a) the subjects' ratings of how uncomfortable they felt at the end of the session (e.g., tense, hurt, distressed) and (b) the number of bad qualities they attributed to the woman job applicant revealed that the distraction versus attention-to-feelings manipulation significantly moderated this relationship. The lines in Figure 12–5, which were

calculated from the regression analysis, depict this interaction. [The regression analysis is not reported in Berkowitz & Troccoli (1990).]

27. Patterson, Reid, Jones, & Conger (1975), p. 31.

28. The Oregon Research Institute's social learning program is described in detail in Patterson et al. (1975).

29. Needless to say, psychologists have developed many other intervention programs intended to reduce children's aggressiveness. See Goldstein, A. P., Carr, E. G., Davidson, W. S., & Wehr, P. (1981); Shapiro & Derr (1987).

30. See Novaco (1975); Goldstein, A. P. (1988), especially Chap. 5.

31. See for example, Deffenbacher (1988); Hazaleus & Deffenbacher (1986); Goldstein, A. P. (1988).

32. Deffenbacher's comments and observations were made in a talk at the 1989 American Psychological Association convention in Atlanta, Georgia. The talk was entitled "Cognitive-Behavioral Approaches to Anger Reduction: Some Treatment Considerations."

33. Angier, N., *New York Times*, Dec. 13, 1990.

34. Martinson (1974), p. 25. Wilson & Herrnstein (1985) have also looked at the research in this area, and they are dubious about the value of psychological rehabilitative programs.

35. Wilson & Herrnstein (1985), p. 383.

36. See especially Bartol (1980); Quay (1987).

37. Garrett's meta-analysis is reported in Garrett (1985) and summarized in Quay (1987).

PART 5

❖

Some Special
Questions

*T*he next, and penultimate, section touches briefly on two topics that haven't been discussed up until now and are apt to be of special interest to the reader. First, I will look at some biological influences on aggression. Although this book has focused on psychological processes and on situational factors operating in the immediate present and/or in the past, we should recognize that aggression, in humans as in other animal species, is also affected by physiological processes in the individual's body and brain. There now has been considerable research into the part played by these biological determinants, but the following chapter has to be very selective and will take up only a little of what has been learned about the role of biological influences on aggression. After a brief review of the notion of aggressive instincts, I will examine the question of whether heredity has an impact on people's proclivity to violence, and then will consider the possibility of gender differences in aggression because of the effect of sex hormones. The chapter then will conclude with a brief summary of how alcohol may influence the likelihood of committing an assault. The following chapter will be concerned primarily with methodological issues. Many of the ideas and propositions advanced in this book are based on laboratory experiments conducted with children and adults, and the discussion will therefore concentrate on the logic behind the use of experiments in behavioral research.

12

Biology and Aggression

PHOTOCOPY ALL 18 pgs.

❖

A Lust for Hatred and Destruction ◆ Are People Instinctively Driven to Violence? ◆ *What Is an Instinct?* ◆ Critique of the Traditional Instinct Conception ◆ Heredity and Hormones ◆ *"Born to Raise Hell"? Hereditary Influences on Aggression* ◆ *Gender Differences in Aggression* ◆ *Hormonal Influences* ◆ Alcohol and Aggression

A "LUST FOR HATRED AND DESTRUCTION"?

In 1932 an agency of the League of Nations invited Albert Einstein to arrange an exchange of views with any eminent person of his choice on an important issue of the day. The organization proposed to publish the exchange as part of its attempt to further communication among the leading intellectuals of the period. Einstein agreed to take the assignment and decided he could best advance the League's goals by inquiring into the causes of international conflict. With the carnage of World War I still vivid in his memory, he believed that no question was more crucial than whether there was "any way of delivering mankind from the menace of war." The great physicist undoubtedly expected to find no simple answer to this question. Suspecting that strife and violence were rooted in human psychology, he solicited the opinion of Sigmund Freud, the founder of psychoanalysis. How is it, Einstein asked the pioneering explorer of the human mind, that propaganda devices succeed so well in rousing men to war? Might it not be that people have within them a "lust for hatred and destruction" which ordinarily is latent but can be aroused and raised to "the power of a collective psychosis"?[1]

This was a relatively new question for Freud. He hadn't thought very much

376

about the sources of human aggressiveness until the previous decade. With a few exceptions, his case histories up to that time had discussed anger and hate only in relation to sexual urges, and (in the words of his disciple, Erich Fromm), "he simply failed to attach much importance to the problems of aggressiveness."[2] But now, after the horrors of the first World War, the violence in human behavior was all too obvious. Depressed by the conflict and with an increasingly dark view of the human condition, by 1920 Freud had changed his interpretation of aggression so that he believed what the physicist only suspected. Yes, he replied to Einstein, people were indeed driven to hate and kill. An "active instinct for hatred and destruction" resides in the depths of the human personality.[3]

Can we deny Freud's gloomy conception? Is humanity destined always to bear the mark of Cain? War of one kind or another seems unavoidable. World War I, with its millions of deaths and even greater numbers of people permanently maimed, was followed, only a generation later, by an even greater worldwide conflagration which produced more death and destruction—and the battles have not stopped. According to one estimate,[4] at least 17 million people have died in the wars that have taken place since 1946. There were twenty-five different wars around the globe in 1987 alone. In the fourteenth century, a troubador sang that his heart was "filled with gladness" when he saw "both great and small/Fall in the ditches and on the grass/And . . . the dead transfixed by spear shafts. . . . Lords," he exclaimed, "mortgage your domains, castles, cities/But never give up war!"[5] Even now, in the late twentieth century, do people's hearts continue to sing with gladness at the sight of slaughter?

Even when combatants do not attack each other with the latest in high-technology weapons, muggings and murders abound in many city streets. Besides all this, how can we explain the millions of war toys sold each year—G.I. Joes, Masters of the Universe, robots, monsters, and space ships, all bearing weapons for destroying enemies? Grownups as well as young children apparently have a taste for violence. Does this appetite account for the great popularity of movies and TV programs featuring violence and brutality, such as Clint Eastwood's Dirty Harry pictures and Sylvester Stallone's Rambo films, to say nothing of *The Texas Chainsaw Massacre*? Do these toys, movies, and programs appeal to an abiding appetite for violence, a continuing lust for hatred and destruction that can be traced back to humanity's biological past?

Through the centuries, various observers of human behavior have believed in the existence of a drive to violence. Even in recent years, not a few theorists, including professional zoologists and psychiatrists, have insisted that we are born with a compelling urge to hate and destroy. One such theorist was Konrad Lorenz, the Nobel prize-winning founder of ethology, the study of the behavior of animals in their natural habitat.

In a book that attracted considerable attention throughout the western world during the turbulent mid-1960s, when protests and riots were erupting in many American and European cities, Lorenz argued that humans, like other animal species, possess an innate aggressive drive.[6] Who could reasonably deny this, Lorenz asked? He knew that some people would dispute his view—people who had what he believed was an unduly optimistic liberal belief in the perfectibility of man. These people were pursuing an illusion, Lorenz insisted: They wanted to attribute social ills—such as violence—to external flaws that might be remedied, and refused to recognize (according to Lorenz) that these social problems were actually due to intractable human nature.

It obviously matters whether people are innately driven to violence or not, and we must evaluate the claims for such a drive. I'll begin by briefly considering what an "instinct" is, and will then examine what Freud, Lorenz, and other theorists had in mind when they used the term.[7] I will then argue that there may indeed be inherited influences on behavior, but that they do not necessarily operate in the ways proposed by Freud, Lorenz, and others.

ARE PEOPLE INSTINCTIVELY DRIVEN TO VIOLENCE?

What Is an Instinct?

In order to evaluate the idea of an instinctive drive to aggression, it is necessary first to clarify the meaning of the term "instinct." The word is used in many different ways, and it is not always possible to be sure exactly what someone has in mind when she or he talks about instinctive behaviors. We sometimes hear that a person "acted instinctively" in responding to a sudden emergency. Does this mean the individual reacted in a genetically preprogrammed manner—or that he or she responded to the emergency with relatively little thought? Musicians are occasionally described as having an "instinct for music." Are the speakers saying that the musicians have an innate talent and sensitivity, which were developed by training and practice—or that the musicians were born with a drive to play and hear music? Women are often said to have a "maternal instinct." Does this statement refer to an inborn urge to have and nurture children—or to an interest, shared by many women, in a variety of matters related to children?

Darwin's Conception
Laypersons aren't the only ones who talk of "instincts" in a loose and ambiguous manner. Specialists and scholars often disagree among them-

selves about just what they mean by this term. Not infrequently, they even disagree with themselves as their definitions change over the years. Even Charles Darwin, whose nineteenth-century publications still have a tremendous influence on modern analyses of animal behavior, wasn't consistent in his usage. C. G. Beer, in an article in the authoritative *Encyclopedia of the Social Sciences*, has described how Darwin's view of instincts shifted: He viewed instincts variously as drives impelling particular types of behavior, as behavioral tendencies (such as courage) or feelings (such as sympathy), and more in keeping with contemporary analyses, as species-specific stereotyped behavior patterns (such as bees' hive building).[8]

Most discussions of instincts, however, including those published by Freud and other psychoanalysts, have employed a conception of instincts basically similar to the one used by Darwin in his classic 1871 work, *The Descent of Man*.[9] In this book Darwin essentially envisioned an *instinct* as a drive or urge compelling an animal to seek a particular goal. It is the goal more than anything else that defines the nature of the instinct, he maintained, rather than the specific activities that are carried out. An animal doesn't always exhibit exactly the same behaviors in trying to obtain food, a mate, or shelter. What matters most is the animal's objective. Further, according to Darwin, instincts are not necessarily aimed at seeking pleasure and avoiding pain. He thought it is more "probable that instincts are presently followed from the mere force of inheritance, without the stimulus of either pleasure or pain."[10]

Freud's Notion of the "Death Instinct"
Freud's notion of instincts had important similarities to Darwin's conception. Like Darwin, he believed inner urges drive a person toward particular goals, and also like the great evolutionist, he thought the instinctual aim is not always simply a search for pleasure. Indeed, he published his post-World War I analysis of humankind's presumed striving for death and destruction under the title *Beyond the Pleasure Principle*.[11] What all life ultimately wants, according to Freud, is not the gratification of fundamental biological needs for survival but rather to die.

Deeply pessimistic about human nature as a result of both the horrendous violence and destruction in the war and his own personal troubles (including arguments with several of his former followers), Freud had come to believe that the instinct to live is countered to some degree by an opposing instinctive force which seeks death. He grounded the "death instinct" in a biological mechanism common to all living forms. Every organism, he speculated, wants the reduction of nervous excitation to the lowest possible level. Death is the complete elimination of internal tension, and thus, all organic life seeks to die. However, the striving for total internal peace is countered by an opposite force, a life instinct. In Freud's words, "the libido has the task of making the destroying instinct innocuous, and it fulfills the task by diverting that instinct to a great extent outwards . . . towards [sic] objects in the external world." The death instinct, then, is manifested in aggression toward others. Freud saw the struggle for existence as a cruel paradox. People can save their own lives only by attacking others. "It really seems," he said, "as though it is necessary for us to destroy some other thing or person in order not to destroy ourselves. . . . A sad disclosure indeed for the moralist."[12]

People don't necessarily have to make this choice, however, according to Freudian theory. To a certain extent, there are alternatives. Orthodox psychoanalysis holds that the aggressive drive can be lessened (that is, redirected or sublimated) by engaging in substitute actions that involve neither violence to others nor one's own destruction. We can find a constructive outlet for our aggressive energies by striving to dominate others, by overcoming the difficulties which confront us, or by mastering the environment. However, Freud wasn't altogether hopeful about how well such diversions operate. His "final vision was bleak."[13] People cannot escape the continual struggle between their life and death instincts. Perhaps the drive toward hate and destruction can be weakened, but it cannot be eliminated altogether.

In Chapter 11, Psychological Procedures for Controlling Aggression, I pointed out that there is little empirical support for the notion of "redirected" aggressive energy. Nor have many of Freud's followers taken up his conjecture that the urge toward violence is grounded in a striving for one's own death.[14] Nonetheless, present-day psychoanalysts typically do share the essential features of his views on aggression. Also with Freud, they generally believe that humans have to reconcile their opposing sexual and aggressive instincts. For many contemporary Freudians, these drives are alike in important respects: Both are inborn, both are constantly pressing for expression, and both can be diverted into other channels. This conception is so widespread that even some psychologists who do not view themselves as orthodox psychoanalysts accept it. A California psychologist recently told the press that "children are born with aggressive drives." However, she went on, presenting her version of orthodox psychodynamic theory, "in a loving home" these drives can be channeled into "healthy aggressiveness: competition and ambition."

Lorenz's Conception of the Instinct to Aggression

Konrad Lorenz, an eminent investigator of animal behavior, interpreted aggression from the perspective of his energy model of animal motivation (to employ Hinde's characterization[15]). His formulation is worth discussing at some length, because it raises a number of issues that are exceedingly important for an adequate understanding of aggression, including human violence.

Throughout his long and distinguished career, Lorenz maintained that instinctual actions are largely endogenously determined in both animals and human beings, and are not primarily reactions to external events.[16] An unknown substance or excitation builds up spontaneously in instinctual centers within the nervous system of an organism and impels the organism to respond in a specific way to particular stimuli in the surrounding situation. It's theoretically important to note that Lorenz did not conceive of these situational stimuli as drawing out the behavior in reflex fashion. The organism isn't stimulated by the external happenings. Rather, the situational stimuli supposedly only "unlock" (or "release") inhibitory mechanisms in the nervous system, thereby allowing the internal drive to "push out" the instinctive action.

Lorenz's formulation made an important point in this connection, one that has profound implications for the control of aggression. He held that if an organism does not encounter occasional releasing stimuli at appropriate times, it may act inappropriately, behaving in ways that really aren't called for by the immediate situation. The instinctual behavior will go off all by itself because of the pressure of the pent-up drive. A male dove that is prevented from courting and mating with a female of its species will start bowing and cooing not only to a stuffed pigeon but even to the corners of its cage.[17] This "vacuum activity," Lorenz argued, is due to an excess of instinctive energy that has accumulated within a specific instinctive center. I'll come back to this argument shortly.

Lorenz's energy model is obviously similar in important ways to Freud's general motivational approach, and the pioneering ethologist acknowledged the "correspondence" between his and Freud's views. In the case of aggression, although he did not accept Freud's idea of a death instinct, he did believe, with the psychoanalyst, that people possess an inborn urge to attack others. He also thought that this drive can impel actions which appear, on the surface, to have little connection with aggression.[18]

What really matters in the context of this book is Lorenz's contention that the aggressive urge, like other instincts, is spontaneously generated inside the person and is continually seeking expression. He was very explicit about this in his 1966 book, *On Aggression,* which was written for a general audience. Generalizing from his energy model, he argued that "it is the spontaneity of the [aggressive] instinct that makes it so dangerous."[19] The aggressive drive supposedly builds up all by itself and not as a reaction to frustrations or external stresses. We cannot substantially lessen people's aggressive inclinations by easing their lot in life or reducing their disappointments, he insisted.

Are humans especially dangerous? Lorenz also believed that people are more seriously affected by the aggressive instinct than other animal species are. Unlike human beings, he claimed, many species possess instinctive mechanisms that can control and inhibit assaults on others.

These inhibitory processes are most likely to be found, he said, in animals which can readily kill one of their own kind in a fight. Thus, Lorenz maintained, lions, wolves, and even dogs have a kind of inborn "switch" that can automatically check their attack on an opponent once the inhibitory mechanism is activated, and can thus keep them from slaughtering enemies in their own species. Appeasement gestures typically have this effect, according to Lorenz. When two animals of the same species are engaged in combat, after a while the losing animal, in danger of being killed, will submit to the victor by making an appeasement gesture. A wolf fighting with another wolf in a bitter struggle and about to be defeated will show submission by turning over on its back and exposing its unprotected belly. The appeasement gesture quickly blocks the victor's aggression and thereby prevents the dominant animal from fatally assaulting its victim. People don't have instinctive blocks against killing their own kind, Lorenz said. Their attacks on others can't be turned off so easily and quickly. As a consequence, the instinctive drive to aggression is far more dangerous in humans than in other species.

Is there a need for a "safe outlet"?   Lorenz did not think, however, that all is necessarily lost even if people don't have inborn checks on their violent urges. Along with Freud and orthodox psychoanalytic theory, he believed it is possible to redirect the aggressive drive into other, nonaggressive activities and thereby to discharge the pent-up aggressive energy. Indeed, he argued that society has to furnish its members with socially acceptable ways of discharging the aggressive force inexorably building up inside them, or else there will be uncontrollable outbursts of violence. For Lorenz and others who share his viewpoint, civilized people today suffer from an insufficient release of their accumulating aggressive urges.

Let's look at this particular notion in more detail since, in one form or another, it is still widely accepted. Lorenz's thesis holds that certain groups of people have especially strong instinctive drives because of past evolutionary influences. It is presumably very important for these groups to find suitable outlets for the aggressive energy within them. For example, Lorenz maintained that the high rates of maladjustment, neurosis, and even accident proneness which prevail among present-day Ute Indians of the western plains in North America are caused by their inability to discharge the intense aggressive drive that was bred into them through the centuries.[20] He also believed that expeditions to distant areas have been plagued with serious dissension because the explorers have been isolated from other people and thus have lacked specific targets outside their groups for their pent-up aggressive urges. They have had to attack other members of their expeditions because of the destructive pressures which had built up inside them. Lorenz offered some advice to people who find themselves in similar circumstances: "The man of perception finds an outlet by creeping out of the barracks (tent, igloo) and smashing a not too expensive object with as resounding a crash as the occasion merits."[21]

Here is the familiar argument for a "cathartic discharge" of supposedly pent-up aggressive energy, which is so often advocated by psychodynamically oriented mental health workers. They don't all share Freud's and Lorenz's belief in the existence of a spontaneously generated instinctive spur to violence, and indeed, most of them probably think of the drive to aggression as building up during a lifetime of frustration and stress. With Freud and Lorenz, however, they claim that there must be periodic releases for the accumulating aggressive urges. If the drive isn't redirected into substitute activities, such as competition or a striving for mastery, or discharged in make-believe forms of aggression, such as Lorenz's recommended vase breaking, they believe that it will inevitably burst out in uncontrolled violence.

CRITIQUE OF THE TRADITIONAL INSTINCT CONCEPTION

The preceding summary has described some of the main features of the traditional notion of an aggressive instinct, especially as this conception is spelled out in Freud's and Lorenz's theories. Rather than attempting a detailed examination of these theories, I will only highlight a few of the theoretical and empirical flaws in this traditional instinct doctrine.[22]

Inadequate Empirical Support
The basic problem with the traditional instinct notion is that it doesn't have a sound empirical basis. Specialists in the study of animal behavior have seriously questioned a number of Lorenz's confident statements about animal aggression. Take his remarks about automatic restraints upon aggression in other animal species, for example. Lorenz claimed that, with the exception of human beings, most animals which are capable of easily killing others of their own species have instinctive mechanisms that can quickly quell their attacks. People lack these mechanisms, and ours is the only species in which there is a substantial killing of one's own kind. In actuality, however, as a number of researchers have pointed out, Lorenz unduly minimized the amount of within-species aggression that goes on throughout the animal world. Lions, wolves, and even dogs kill other members of their species far more often than Lorenz indicated.[23]

The Questionable Notion of Spontaneously Generated Instinctive Drives
There are other problems with the traditional view of aggressive instincts that are even more serious. No one has been able to find even a sign of

the drive reservoirs in either the body or the brain that are assumed by this type of notion. Specific brain areas are involved in many aggressive actions, but these areas seem to govern reactions to emotional situations rather than serving as reservoirs of an accumulation of aggression-spurring excitation or chemical. Moreover, investigators have also criticized the idea that aggressive behavior pops out all by itself (Lorenz's conjectured "vacuum activity"), supposedly because of the pressure of too much pent-up drive. Quite to the contrary, research indicates that supposedly spontaneous aggression and other instances of seemingly "vacuum" instinctive behavior as well are much more likely to be responses to stimuli in the surrounding situation than actions that are only "pushed out" by internal forces.[24]

In the late 1950s, J. P. Scott, a widely respected scholar and researcher in the area of animal behavior, objected to the notion of a spontaneously generated instinctive drive to aggression on the basis of the evidence that was then available:

> There is no physiological evidence of any spontaneous stimulation for fighting arising within the body. This means that there is no need for fighting . . . apart from what happens in the external environment. . . . We can also conclude that there is no such thing as a simple "instinct for fighting" in the sense of an internal driving force which has to be satisfied. There is, however, an internal physiological mechanism which has only to be stimulated to produce fighting.[25]

Research in the succeeding years has provided still more nails for the coffin in which the traditional view of an instinctive, internally produced drive to aggression should be buried. On the basis of this evidence, a number of renowned scientists trained in disciplines ranging from anthropology to zoology signed a statement first initiated in Seville, Spain, in 1986 and which directly contradicts Freud's ideas about an instinctive drive to war. The Seville Statement on Violence points out:

> It is scientifically incorrect to say that we have inherited a tendency to make war from our animal ancestors. . . .
> It is scientifically incorrect to say that war or any other violent behavior is genetically programmed into our human nature. . . .
> It is scientifically incorrect to say that in the course of human evolution there has been a selection for aggressive behaviour [sic] more than for other kinds of behaviour. . . .
> It is scientifically incorrect to say that war is caused by "instinct" or any single motivation. . . . Biology does not condemn humanity to war.[26]

Different Types of Aggression

Another serious problem with the traditional instinct doctrine has to do with its assumption that there is basically only one drive to aggression. The people who hold this view believe that every attack on others, whatever its form and whatever its objectives, is carried out for the same underlying purpose—the discharge of the internal aggressive drive—and is governed by the same biological mechanisms. Indeed, the proponents of this doctrine often go even further, as I noted in Chapter 1, and contend that many nonaggressive actions are also powered by this instinctive urge.

Does the aggressive drive spur assertiveness and the striving for mastery? Since this idea is so common, let me go back to some statements made by the author of a popular book on human aggression, which I quoted in the first chapter. "There is no clear dividing line," the writer maintained, "between [the] forms of aggression which we all deplore and those which we must disown if we are to survive."[27] Aggression isn't all bad, he argued. It is the "aggressive, active side" of human nature that spurs people to try to influence the world around them. They are being aggressive, according to this view, when they strive for independence, seek to influence others, or try to master the difficulties confronting them. Their efforts in all these worthwhile endeavors are supposedly driven by the same underlying urge that otherwise leads to destruction and violence.

Many agree with these statements. After all, isn't it often said that people are "aggressively" pursuing their objectives when they try hard to reach their goals or forcefully attempt to convince others that they are right? Ordinary speech equates assertiveness with aggression, and the assumption is that the same drive is involved in both cases. Similarly, don't we hear of a man's "sinking his teeth" into a question or a woman's "attacking" a problem? Maybe this means that attempts to overcome a difficulty are spurred by aggressive impulses.

In actuality, however, ordinary speech doesn't really prove that the same motives power aggression, assertiveness, the search for independence, the striving for achievement, and the struggle to overcome external difficulties. All these actions are at times given the label "aggression" which may reflect a widely held folklorish belief about the source of these behaviors, but the belief is certainly wrong. Studies of achievement, dominance, independence, and mastery show that these motives typically develop in complex and different ways and generally have little in common with the origin of persistent aggressiveness.[28]

Categories of aggression. The more closely researchers have looked into the causes and consequences of aggression, the more they have realized that people (and animals) try to injure or destroy their opponents for a variety of reasons and that there different kinds of aggression. However, they don't entirely agree about what the different kinds of aggression are.

I've noted throughout this book that it's necessary to distinguish between two types of aggression, depending upon the aggressors' main purposes in striking at their targets: *emotional* (or *hostile*) *aggression*, in which the attackers are mostly interested in hurting their victims, and *instrumental aggression*, in which assaults are carried out to achieve other, noninjurious objectives. It's important to recognize this difference but also to realize that blows are frequently struck for both hostile and instrumental purposes. Husbands are often furious when they assault their wives; they may hit the women both for the pleasure of hurting them (to satisfy the goal of hostile aggression) *and* to assert their dominance (to achieve a goal other than injury).

Investigators of animal aggression (with the exception of Lorenz and his followers) generally draw even finer distinctions between the different kinds of aggression, based on the biological functions that are served by the given behavior. Kenneth Moyer, for example, has suggested that the following types of aggression exist in the animal world: *predatory, intermale, fear-induced, irritable, territorial defense, maternal, instrumental,* and *sex-related*.[29] Other writers have questioned the adequacy of his classification, and have argued for somewhat different categories. There seems to be a common theme in at least some of the classes of aggression that have been proposed. John Archer,[30] a highly knowledgeable student of animal behavior, thinks of aggression as only an animal's attempt to solve a problem. He maintains that it is best to distinguish between aggression which is prompted by *competition for scarce resources,* such as food or a mate, and aggression which is carried out as a *defensive reaction.* Taking a somewhat different tack, Burr Eichelman, Glen Elliott, and Jack Barchas relied on neurological and biochemical evidence to propose two other (but perhaps related) categories: *predatory* and *affective* aggression. Predatory aggression occurs when there is "destruction of prey, usually for food." In affective aggression, on the other hand, "threatening stimuli initiate an intense and patterned activation of the autonomic nervous system," along with threatening and defensive actions.[31]

Present knowledge doesn't yet allow investigators to determine the best way to classify the different kinds of animal aggression. However, I'm inclined to regard instrumental aggression as a broad category which encompasses several of Moyer's types; Archer's competitive aggression; and the predatory aggression described by Eichelman, Elliott, and Barchas. With Eichelman and his colleagues, I view irritable, fear-induced, and even defensive aggression as falling within the general category of hostile or emotional aggression.

Whatever labels are applied to these different forms of behavior, however, it's important to note that all the researchers I've cited distinguish between emotional (irritable, hostile) attempts to injure others and calculated attacks which are carried out to accomplish an objective other than the injury of the victims (instrumental, predatory aggression). For my present purposes, it really doesn't matter what the specific kinds of aggression are. The main point is that there isn't only one type of aggression propelled by just one underlying drive.

There are many reasons to discard the conception of an instinctive drive to aggression, as espoused by Freud and Lorenz. However much their followers have clung to this traditional view, it has remarkably little empirical support. People have a *capacity* for aggression and violence but not a biological urge to attack and destroy others that is continually building up inside them.

HEREDITY AND HORMONES

"Born to Raise Hell"? Hereditary Influences on Aggression

In July 1966, a disturbed young man named Richard Speck killed eight nurses in Chicago. This horrible crime attracted nationwide attention, and the press reported the incident in great detail. One of the things the public learned about Speck was that he had a message tattooed on his arm: "BORN TO RAISE HELL."

Early Genetic Conceptions: Lombroso's Theory
We don't know whether Richard Speck was indeed born with murderous tendencies that led him inexorably to this crime—whether his parents had passed on to him "violent genes" that somehow gave rise to his murderous actions—but I can raise a more general question: Is there an inherited disposition to violence?

Several investigators have argued that criminal tendencies can be transmitted genetically. One of the best known was the late-nineteenth-century Italian criminologist Cesare Lombroso. Influenced by Darwin's ideas, which were then gaining popularity, Lombroso held that some people were evolutionary throwbacks who were biologically inclined toward antisocial conduct. He based his argument on the mistaken notion that these "born criminals" had distinctive primitive features (sloping foreheads, long arms, unusual faces, and the like) which were indicative of their genetically dictated antisocial tendencies. Subsequent research has demonstrated the errors in Lombroso's thinking, and his theory has now been swept into the wastebasket of history.[32]

Unfortunately, however, Lombroso's crude ideas have tended to discredit all research on the possible heritability of crime. Even today, many social scientists are likely to dismiss such investigations as only contemporary versions of Lombrosian doctrine. It could well be wrong, nevertheless, to turn away from the possibility of genetic transmission of criminal tendencies without a second thought. The traditional notion of a spontaneously generated inner drive to death and destruction is erroneous, but there may be some biological influences on aggression, and people's genetic makeup may have an influence on their likelihood of striking out at others. A growing number of studies indicate that an individual's heritage may indeed affect the chances that he or she will commit a crime.

Modern Evidence of Genetic Influences

The family has some influence. Empirical research dating back to Lombroso's time leaves little doubt that a person's family background has an effect on the probability that he or she will engage in criminal conduct. In an English study, for example, about 40 percent of the sons of criminal fathers were convicted of crimes themselves, while only 13 percent of the sons of noncriminal fathers had criminal records.[33] The problem is how to determine what proportion of familial influence occurs through genetic transmission rather than through learning experiences.

Twin studies. In order to get a clearer picture of genetic effects on crime and violence, investigators have conducted studies comparing identical and fraternal twins. The logic behind this line of research is clear: Both identical and fraternal twins are exposed to the same prenatal influences within their mother's wombs, and both also (although this is not always certain) probably had very similar family environments after birth. However, the two kinds of twins differ in terms of genetic similarity. Since identical twins are genetically identical because they develop from a single fertilized egg, they are therefore termed "monozygotic twins" by geneticists. Fraternal twins, on the other hand, come from two eggs that were separately fertilized, (and are called "dizygotic twins"). On the whole, fraternal twins are no more genetically similar than ordinary brothers and sisters. To the extent that a given trait is heritable (i.e., capable of being passed down genetically from parents to offspring), therefore, identical twins should be much more alike in their possession of the trait than are fraternal twins.

Research comparing monozygotic and dizygotic twins, which goes back at least to the 1920s, has consistently demonstrated that a proclivity to criminality may indeed be heritable. Consider the *concordance* rates, the extent to which members of a pair within the population being studied display the same characteristic. If monozygotic (identical) twins have a 67 percent concordance on a particular trait, this means that in two-thirds of these pairs the pair members have the same characteristic. One review of the research on the relationship between genetics and crime, which had been published between 1929 and the 1940s, found an average concordance rate of about 75 percent for monozygotic twins as compared to only about 24 percent for dizygotic twins. In later investigations, which used more precise methods of determining whether the twins were identical or fraternal, the concordance rates were 48 and 20 percent, respectively. Whatever the exact degree of concordance, there does seem to be a genetic influence on crime.[34]

The Danish Studies of Genetic Influences

An even better demonstration of genetic effects has been found in research conducted in Denmark. This country provides an admirable setting for studies of crime, because it permits qualified investigators to gain access to any citizen's criminal record. Taking advantage of the accessibility of this information, Karl Christiansen of Copenhagen University first selected almost 800 pairs of Danes from a sample of approximately 3900 twins who had been born around the turn of the century. In each of the pairs selected, at least one twin had been convicted of a crime. He then looked to see if the other twin in each pair also had a criminal record, and whether the concordance was greater for identical than for fraternal twins. In this sample, Christiansen reported, both sets of twins were more similar in the incidence of recorded criminality than would be expected by chance. More important, the concordance between pair members was greatest when they were identical twins and were guilty of crimes against the person rather than of property crimes. Though he was not willing to say that environmental influences had no role at all, Christiansen concluded that "the combined influence of heredity and environment is greater for crimes of violence than for property crimes."[35]

There are problems with these twin studies, and scientists are not in agreement about exactly what conclusions may be drawn from them. At the very least, however, these investigations indicate "a substantial genetic component in criminal behavior."[36]

The influence of biological versus adoptive parents. If science were the only consideration, the importance of heredity in the development of criminality might be gauged by conducting a harsh and unfeeling experiment: Infants could be taken away from their biological parents as soon as they were born and raised by other sets of parents, who would be chosen randomly. Researchers could then periodically examine the children as they grew up to see whether they resembled the natural or the adoptive parents more closely by assessing them with both psychological and behavioral measures. If the children's criminal records were more like their natural parents' records than their adoptive parents' records, we could conclude that heredity had affected the likelihood of illegal offenses.

It's obvious that this kind of experiment will never be carried out in any society that espouses humanitarian values, but approximations are obtained in investigations which compare the criminal records of adopted persons with the records of their biological and their adoptive parents. Although a number of investigations along these lines have been conducted,[37] I'll describe only one of the best, which made use of a large sample of adoptees.[38]

Capitalizing on the extensive information that Denmark gathers about its citizens, a team of researchers led by Sarnoff Mednick examined the offense records of over 14,400 Danish men who had been adopted when they were very young and hadn't known their natural parents. Because of the completeness of the information, the investigators could determine the identities of both the biological parents and the adoptive parents of the persons in their sample, as well as how often each individual had been arrested and convicted for a criminal violation.

Not surprisingly, the adoptive parents' criminality had an effect on the likelihood that their sons would also have criminal records, but this influence was relatively small—less than that of biological parents. If neither the biological parents nor the adoptive parents had been arrested and convicted, only about 13.5 percent of the men were guilty of committing crimes. The crime rate rose to only about 15 percent if the adoptive parents had criminal records but the biological parents did not. By contrast, about 20 percent of the men who had noncriminal adoptive parents but at least one convicted biological parent were themselves criminals. There was the greatest chance of criminal conviction when both the hereditary family and the adoptive family contributed antisocial influences: A quarter of the sons who had both biological and adoptive parents with criminal records had themselves been arrested and convicted.

To accumulate further evidence of hereditary influences on criminality, the investigators then singled out the men who had not been exposed to antisocial parental influences while they were growing up (because they had had noncriminal adoptive mothers and fathers). In this sample, those whose biological parents were frequent offenders (who had had three or more convictions) were three times more likely to be criminal than were men whose biological parents had had no convictions.

This is not to say that the men who had "bad inheritances" were doomed to lives of crime. Fully three-quarters of those born to highly criminal parents did not develop criminal records. Even so, the sons of frequently offending natural parents who did become chronic offenders themselves were evidently "bad apples." Although they represented only 1 percent of all the adoptees who had highly criminal biological parents, they accounted for almost a third of the convictions in the entire sample of men who had noncriminal adoptive parents. The implication may be that genetic influences contribute relatively little to all the crimes committed but have a substantial effect on the behavior of the most antisocial segment of society.

In describing this study, I have been referring to all types of offenses. The relevant question in the context of this book is whether frequently offending biological parents transmitted a tendency to violent crimes as well as other kinds of wrongdoings. Figure 12–1 provides a more detailed analysis of the strength of the genetic influence in relation to the nature of the sons' crimes, for the sample of men whose adoptive parents were not criminal. The figure shows that the natural parents' criminality was more strongly related to the likelihood of property offenses by their sons than to the chances that the offspring would engage in violent crimes, but there seems to be at least some relationship between genetic inheritance and both types of antisocial conduct.[39] Christiansen's findings, in his study of identical and fraternal twins, also suggest that the proclivity to violent crimes may well be heritable.

Taken together, the results of these Danish investigations suggest that some men inherit a tendency to engage in antisocial behavior, perhaps including violent crimes. The data also indicate, however, that biological parents' criminality doesn't always lead to criminal conduct by

FIGURE 12–1

Relationship between biological parents' criminality and sons' crime convictions. Percentage of adopted boys who were convicted for property crimes or violent crimes in relation to the number of such convictions for their biological parents. In this sample, none of the adoptive parents had *any* convictions. (Modified with permission from Mednick, Gabrielli, & Hutchings (1987). Copyright 1987, Cambridge University Press.)

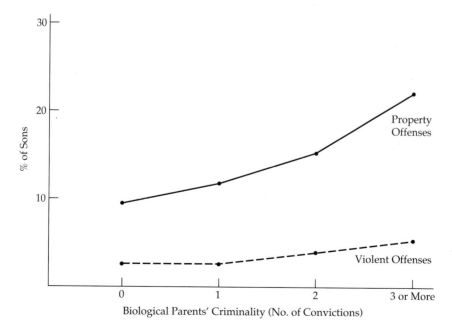

their offspring. Only a minority of male adoptees with criminal biological parents became criminal themselves, even when their adoptive parents were lawbreakers. It may be that if the sons had inherited "bad
genes" from their antisocial mothers and/or fathers, in most (but maybe
not all) cases the genetic disposition was somehow countered by learning and other environmental influences. The point that should be
stressed is that the genetic inheritance constitutes only a potential for the
development of criminal tendencies. The potential will be fulfilled only if
the appropriate learning and environmental conditions are also present.

Gender Differences in Aggression

Gender differences in human aggression have been the subject of a good
deal of controversy in recent years. Many readers may be surprised to
learn that there is any disagreement about this topic, because it seems
perfectly obvious that men are more apt to strike out in anger than
women are. However, a number of psychologists have argued that this
difference is not as pronounced as many persons suppose and that at
times it doesn't appear at all.[40] Let's look at the research on these differences and on the part which sex hormones may play in producing
aggression.

Some Research Findings

Animal research. There is little disagreement about the findings
obtained in animal research. In most of the species investigated, from
mice to humans, males tend to be more aggressive than females. Under
some conditions, of course, females in many species do display intense
aggression, especially when they are fighting off a dangerous predator,
and there may be no sex differences on such occasions. Usually, however, males are more likely than females to attack and to fight.[41]

Male-female differences in crimes of violence. What about human
beings? People's actions are much less governed by biological constraints
than animals' actions are. Are men and women equally likely to become
aggressive? One way to answer such a question is to compare the rates of
crimes, and especially violent crimes, committed by men and women.
These statistics are instructive—and provocative. Predictably, the great
majority of persons arrested for a criminal offense are males, and this
seems to be true around the world.[42] Furthermore, when women are
arrested for criminal offenses, they have more often been engaged in
property crimes (such as larceny, forgery, fraud, and embezzlement)
than in violent attack on other people (such as murder or aggravated
assault). Women were arrested for only about 13 percent of the murders

and aggravated assaults that were reported to the FBI in 1981, as compared to 29 percent of larceny and theft arrests.[43]

My interest in gender differences, however, extends beyond crime rates. I want to know whether the differences are due only to cultural and historical forces or whether they also reflect biological differences between males and females to a substantial extent. Changes in the rates of violent crimes committed by men and women over the past few decades may be informative in this context. Social definitions of desirable masculine and feminine behavior have altered dramatically in many areas of life since the 1960s. Women are now asserting themselves in ways that were previously thought to be improper. It would be possible to argue that, if there has been a recent increase in the proportion of violent offenses by women, the increase is probably due to societal changes in the conception of appropriate feminine conduct. Such an increase would be evidence of an overriding influence of social standards upon gender differences.

However, there is no good evidence of a narrowing of the gap between men and women in their rates of violent crimes. Recent years have seen some reduction in the difference between the genders but only for the offenses that have traditionally *not* been highly "masculine" in nature. Consider larceny, a crime that has long drawn a relatively large number of female offenders. Women accounted for only about 8 percent of arrests for this type of crime in the period just before World War II but for almost a third of larceny arrests in the late 1970s. On the other hand, for criminal homicide—an offense that is historically very "masculine"—the arrest rate for women grew during the same period only from about 10 percent of arrests to about 14 percent.

Statistics for the number of arrests in a particular crime category per 100,000 population show much the same pattern. During the 1970s, the rate at which men were arrested for property crimes grew by 20 percent, whereas there was a 35 percent increase the arrest rate for women for property crimes during the same decade. By contrast, the arrest rate for violent crimes by females showed approximately the same percentage increase as did the arrest rate for men who committed this type of offense (about 30 to 35 percent).[44] All in all, crime statistics have provided little support for the contention that gender differences in rate of violent crimes are caused by women's customary adherence to traditional nonaggressive female roles, but it may still be too early to come to any definite conclusions about this matter.

Other forms of aggressive behavior. Are males also more apt to be aggressive than females in less extreme forms of aggressive behavior? The answer to this question seems to be yes, but there is still some disagreement about why this is so.

In their well-known 1974 survey of the research on children's behav-

ior, Eleanor Maccoby and Carol Jacklin noted that the expected sex difference in aggressiveness has been found repeatedly in studies dating
back at least to the 1930s. With only a relatively few exceptions, in field
research as well as in laboratory experiments and employing many different kinds of measures, boys have been found to be typically more
aggressive than girls. Furthermore, this difference exists across social
classes and in many cultures.

I'll describe only two examples of the research cited by Maccoby and
Jacklin. In one, a study that had been conducted by Whiting and Pope,
observers watched interactions between children in seven different cultures. Although youngsters in these samples didn't engage in many
physical assaults, in every one of the cultures more boys than girls insulted their peers, and more boys also counterattacked when they were
aggressed against. In a second study, carried out by Omark, Omark and
Edelman, the investigators observed children on school playgrounds in
the United States, Switzerland, and Ethiopia. Defining *aggression* as
pushing or hitting another person without smiling, the researchers found
that in all three societies boys exhibited more of this behavior than did
girls.[45]

To pull together all the evidence, Maccoby and Jacklin performed a
careful statistical analysis of the findings from observational studies of
children's aggression, based on thirty-one different samples. All the children were under age 6, and they came from a wide range of social class
backgrounds. The results again showed that boys were typically more
aggressive than girls. One aspect of this analysis is particularly noteworthy. Contrary to the suggestions by some psychologists that the male-
female difference in aggressiveness is largely confined to physical
assaults, and that girls are just as likely as boys to attack others verbally,
Maccoby and Jacklin found that the gender difference was just as pronounced for verbal aggression as for physical aggression, over all the
studies which they reviewed.[46]

The research which I have mentioned so far has dealt with the
behavior of young children. What about adults? Alice Eagly and Valerie
Steffen believed that the differences observed in studies with youngsters
would be much smaller in the case of grownups.[47] They statistically analyzed the gender differences that had been found in sixty-three field and
laboratory studies which had used subjects who were college-age or
older and which had employed behavioral measures of aggression
(rather than projective test or make-believe aggression). Eagly and
Steffen singled out several findings for special emphasis. First, although
men were somewhat more aggressive than women on the average, the
difference wasn't consistent across all the studies reviewed, and it generally seemed to be somewhat smaller than the sex differences that had
been obtained in studies of other types of social behavior, such as helping or nonverbal reactions. Second, the tendency for men to be more

aggressive than women was most apparent when the subjects' actions could hurt their targets physically (for example, when they administered electric shocks). In this connection, Eagly and Steffen noted that, when the investigations had inquired into the subjects' reactions to their own behavior, the females seemed to express stronger guilt or anxiety and also appeared to be more empathically concerned about the harm they might have done to the victim.

Why are men and women different in aggressiveness? *Masculine and Feminine Roles.* Few researchers dispute the kinds of findings that I summarized above, but there is some controversy about how the gender differences in aggressiveness should be explained. A good many social scientists, including Eagly and Steffen, believe that the differences are caused primarily by the social roles that have been traditionally assigned to men and women. Think of all the ways in which modern western society, for example, teaches children that fighting is far more appropriate for men than women. Popular literature and the mass media consistently show men but not women fighting. Parents buy toy weapons for their sons and dolls for their daughters. Parents are more likely to approve of and reward aggressive behavior in boys than in girls. Again and again, directly and indirectly, youngsters learn that males are aggressive and females are not—that it's all right for boys and men to strike out at others to defend their rights or to correct wrongs, but that girls and women shouldn't behave this way. Not surprisingly, because their aggression is more frequently rewarded as they grow up, more men than women approve of the use of force and aggression in many walks of life, including social control, law enforcement, and even interpersonal relationships.[48]

Besides being less likely to favor the use of aggression to solve problems, females may also be more attentive to the possible consequences of aggressive behavior for themselves and for others. Eagly and Steffen suggested that when women are inclined to hit people who have offended them, they generally are quicker then men to think of what the outcomes might be: that their victims might suffer unduly, that long-standing relationships could be destroyed, that their own reputations might be harmed, and so on. Because they have the possible negative consequences more clearly in mind, they are presumably more likely to hold back.

It's More than Gender Role Learning. Is cultural learning the only reason males are more often aggressive than females? According to Maccoby and Jacklin, among others, biology also contributes to the difference. They made the following four points in support of their contention:

1. Males are more aggressive than females in all human societies for which evidence is available.

2. The sex differences are found early in life, at a time when there is no evidence that differential socialization pressures have been brought to bear by adults to "shape" aggression differently in the two sexes. . . .
3. Similar sex differences are found in man and subhuman primates.
4. Aggression is related to levels of sex hormones.[49]

Hormonal Influences

Let's turn to the last point in the Maccoby-Jacklin list: the role of sex hormones in aggressive behavior. It's obvious that sex hormones can influence animals' aggressiveness. Just look at what happens when male animals are castrated. A wild stallion is transformed into a docile horse, a savage bull becomes a plodding ox, and a rowdy dog is turned into a sedate pet. This effect can also be turned around. When testosterone is injected into castrated male animals, their aggressiveness is likely to increase again.[50] Is human aggression as dependent on male sex hormones as animal aggression is?

How Male Hormones May Operate

Though this book is not the place for a detailed review of research on the influences of sex hormones, a few comments will be helpful. There are actually several male sex hormones and several female sex hormones, but the most important in the study of aggression is testosterone, the hormone that is secreted in a man's testes and that stimulates the development of masculine characteristics when it begins to circulate in quantity at puberty. The influence of testosterone is not limited to this period of life, however. Researchers who have done work in this area tell us that hormones affect human conduct in two ways: (1) by organizing the developing human brain in such a way that particular modes of response become more likely and (2) by activating the physiological mechanisms that help to govern certain behavior patterns.[51] It is important to keep the two kinds of influences separate. Let's look at some of the evidence.

The brain-organizing influence. In human beings, as in other animal species, an individual's gender is not entirely fixed at conception. The growing fetus is usually inclined in one direction or the other, but its development can be affected by the concentration of male and female hormones circulating within it. A relatively high concentration of testosterone can push its central nervous system in a masculine direction, and in some species (such as rodents) this can happen shortly after birth as well as in utero. Whenever masculinization is induced, whether before or shortly after birth, the individual develops masculine physical characteristics and also tends to act in a "malelike" manner at times. Robert Goy and his associates demonstrated such an effect when they administered testosterone to pregnant monkeys, thereby exposing the fetuses to relatively high amounts of the male hormone. After birth, as the babies grew up, the female offspring not only had masculine-appearing genitalia but also behaved somewhat like males in playing, for example by engaging in more rough-and-tumble activities than is characteristic of young females.[52]

Similar findings have been reported in people. Erhardt and Baker studied young girls who had been exposed to relatively high levels of male hormones before birth because their adrenal glands had prenatally malfunctioned. Even though surgery during infancy had eliminated the malelike genitalia with which they were born, it was found that they engaged in more masculine play and also tended to initiate more fighting than did their sisters.[53] Their high levels of male sex hormones before birth had apparently inclined them toward masculine behavior patterns in childhood.

The question is, however, what kind of behavior is influenced? Does the testosterone promote aggression fairly directly (for example, by somehow heightening the chance that a man will react aggressively to a provocation rather than trying to resolve the dispute more peacefully)? Or is the effect more roundabout in nature (say by influencing a man to be dominant and competitive so that he then comes into frequent conflict with others)? The knowledge available to date doesn't present a clear choice between these alternatives, but evidence does suggest that male sex hormones may raise the probability of aggression in a relatively direct manner.

Some of the evidence for this direct influence comes from an investigation of the behavioral effects of prenatal exposure to progestin, a synthetic hormone which is sometimes given to pregnant women to lessen the possibility of miscarriage. Knowing from existing research that progestin can have masculinizing effects on developing fetuses, June Reinisch wondered whether it would also heighten the aggressiveness of children who had been exposed to the hormone while they were in their mothers' wombs. She therefore administered a psychological test that assessed aggressive dispositions to twenty-five youngsters (seventeen girls and eight boys) whose mothers had taken the synthetic hormone during pregnancy. The test was administered also to the brothers and sisters of the twenty-five children, who had not been exposed to progestin before birth.

In the test, the child was asked to indicate how he or she would respond to six different conflict situations, such as an argument over a game. When Reinisch compared the exposed children's responses with the answers given by their nonexposed brothers and sisters, she found that both gender and progestin exposure influenced the youngsters' reactions to the conflict situations. The results are summarized in Figure 12–2, in which a high score indicates physical but not verbal aggression. Overall, as you can easily see, the boys were much more likely than the girls to select physically aggressive responses. Within each gender, however, the children who had experienced the synthetic hormone as fetuses chose physical aggression more often than did their siblings who had experienced a more normal fetal environment. The progestin evidently had influenced their developing brains before birth in such a way that they seemed disposed toward physically aggressive reactions to conflict while they were growing up.[54]

Is there an activating influence? Although there seems to be clear evidence for a brain-organizing influence, the question of whether male sex hormones can activate aggression presents a far muddier picture. There has been no unequivocal demonstration of such an influence because, for ethical reasons, it isn't possible to do the kind of experiment that would be required to establish such proof.

FIGURE 12–2
Mean physical aggression scores for children in the Reinisch study.
The scores reflect the frequency of choosing a physically aggressive action in response to described conflict situations. The maximum possible score was 18 if a subject chose to be physically aggressive in all of these conflict situations. (Data from Reinisch (1981). Adapted with permission. Copyright 1981 by the American Association for the Advancement of Science.)

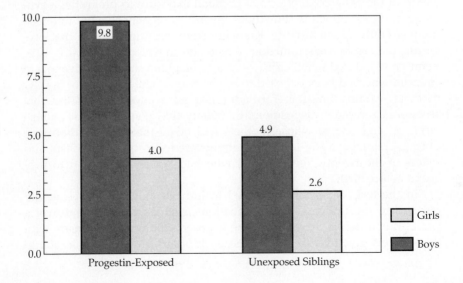

Most of the studies that have investigated the possible aggression-activating effects of male hormones have followed the same logic. They typically ask whether men who are known to differ on a measure of aggressiveness also differ in terms of the levels of testosterone that are circulating in their blood. For example, Dan Olweus carried out a statistically sophisticated investigation with a group of normal male adolescents in Stockholm, Sweden. He found that the boys' reports of how physically and verbally aggressive they would become in response to a frustration or a threat were significantly related to their testosterone levels. (Interestingly, testosterone level was not associated with unprovoked aggression.)[55] Similarly, an examination of young prison inmates showed that men with histories of violent crimes in adolescence had higher average testosterone levels than did less aggressive inmates.[56]

A large-scale study of almost 4500 male U.S. military veterans seems to point in the same direction. The U.S. Centers for Disease Control (CDC) collected a great deal of data on these men—medical, psychological, and physiological—in order to assess the long-term effects of participation in the Vietnam war. James Dabbs and Robin Morris of Georgia State University, Atlanta, made use of this huge pool of information to determine whether the veterans' testosterone levels, as measured by the CDC, were related to the incidence of antisocial behavior. The psychologists did indeed uncover such a relationship, but they also found that the connection between hormone level and antisocial conduct was influenced by the men's socioeconomic status. Among veterans who were below average in income and education, the men who had the very highest testosterone levels were twice as likely as their "normal" hormone-level counterparts to have engaged in antisocial behaviors and to have used hard drugs. This difference between the highest-testosterone group and the "normals" didn't exist among veterans who were above average in income and education.

The researchers' explanation for these results seems plausible. All the men who had very high testosterone levels may have been very prone to aggressive and/or antisocial modes of behavior, regardless of their socioeconomic status. However, the men who were from better-educated and higher-income backgrounds may have developed stronger inhibitions against antisocial inclinations and therefore may have been more apt to restrain themselves, thus presumably weakening the hormone's influence.[57]

While this evidence is interesting and important, its implications are unclear. For example, when the testosterone exerted its influence is unknown. Had the men with high levels of circulating testosterone in adolescence (or later) also had high concentrations of this hormone while their central nervous systems were developing prior to birth? If so, their brain development may have been affected in such a way that they were inclined to react aggressively to provocative situations.

Do castrations reduce violent crimes? The only way to determine whether male hormones have an activating effect independently of a prenatal brain-organizing influence would be to carry out an experiment in which testosterone concentrations were deliberately lowered. Such a study obviously would be unethical, but several rough approximations of this kind of investigation have been made. In some European countries, including Germany, Switzerland, and Denmark, men who had been convicted of certain violent crimes, including sexual assaults, voluntarily agreed to be castrated in order to obtain quicker releases from prison. Researchers have followed up on the subsequent thoughts and activities of these men, seeking to learn whether they had been measurably changed by the castrations.

According to one summary of the findings,[58] the artificially reduced levels of male sex hormones did lessen the men's sexual thoughts and actions, and even led to a reduced likelihood that they would make sexual assaults. However, there was little good evidence that castrations reduced nonsexual violence.

In Conclusion

It appears that the masculine and feminine central nervous systems are organized somewhat differently, in part because of the effects of sex hormones on the developing brain. Because of this biologically determined differentiation, as well as cultural influences which define the kinds of behavior that are appropriate for men and women, males are somewhat more likely than females to show direct aggressive reactions to provocations or threats. However, even if the male hormones have a fairly direct effect on aggression, and even if they thus facilitate assaults, this doesn't mean that these hormones are the source of the mysterious "instinctive drive to aggression" that was postulated by Freud and Lorenz. The hormones don't "push out" aggression. Rather, as a number of writers have suggested, they somehow affect the relationship between the perceived instigating event and the aggressive response. Contrary to what the orthodox instinct theory says, aggression—or at least emotional (or hostile) aggression—is a reaction to something that happens in the environment.

ALCOHOL AND AGGRESSION

O thou invisible spirit of wine, if thou hast no name to be known by, let us call thee devil! . . .

O God, that men should put an enemy in their mouths to steal away their brains! that we should, with joy, pleasance, revel and applause, transform ourselves into beasts!

—[*Cassio, in* Othello, *Act II, Scene iii.*]

The last topic in my brief survey of biological influences on aggression is the effects of alcohol. It has long been known that people's actions can change dramatically when they've had a few drinks, that alcohol can "steal away their brains," as Shakespeare's Cassio put it and perhaps even "transform [them] into beasts." Crime statistics point to a strong association between alcohol and violence. Studies of the relationship between intoxication and homicide, for example, have estimated that alcohol was involved in between half and two-thirds of all the murders that have been reported to police in the United States in recent years. Liquor is also implicated in a wide range of antisocial behaviors, including domestic violence. On this point, Chapter 8 noted that men who imbibe frequently, and especially binge drinkers, are more apt to hit their wives than are men who drink less often or who abstain from alcohol altogether. Moreover, this research also found, the wife batterers had been drinking just before the abusive incident in one out of four cases.[59]

Questions about the Effects of Alcohol
Clearly, then, alcohol consumption increases the likelihood of aggression. However, there are also some serious questions about this influence. Think of all the exceptions. Even though the heavy drinkers in the National Family Violence Survey were especially apt to be wife abusers, the investigators also emphasized that "about 80 percent of the men in both the high and binge drinking groups did *not* hit their wives at all during the year of this survey." Drinking does not inevitably lead to violence. Alcohol use, these researchers said, "is far from a necessary or sufficient cause of wife abuse."[60] Similarly, heavy drinking certainly doesn't always result in taking someone's life. The effects of alcohol seem to be inconsistent in other ways as well. Drinking sometimes promotes aggression, but on other occasions, it increases altruism. It can heighten anxiety and apprehension, but it can also relieve tension and provide comfort.

How is it possible to account for the apparent contradictions presented by the use of alcohol?

Theories of alcohol effects. Not surprisingly, given the importance of wine, whiskey, and other alcoholic beverages in social life over the centuries, social scientists have proposed a number of theories to explain the effects of alcohol on people's feelings and actions. I'll confine this discussion to the influence of alcohol on aggression and will offer only brief summaries of some major themes in the analyses I'll be describing.

Few if any contemporary theories propose that alcohol consumption provides a direct biochemical stimulus to aggression. Wine all by itself doesn't "transform [us] into beasts." Apparently, other factors also have to be present.

One obvious possibility, of course, is that a drinker won't become aggressive unless he or she is provoked in some way. In *Othello*, Cassio became assaultive not only because he had drunk several cups of wine but also because someone had prevented him from doing what he wanted. The usual interpretation of such events is that alcohol lowers the aroused individual's inhibitions by dulling certain brain centers. As a result, the person becomes more willing to engage in socially disapproved behavior. Cassio simply didn't restrain the violent urge his frustrater had evoked.[61]

As simple and as popular as this explanation is, it can't account for all the complexities which researchers have reported. It's also necessary to consider the social situation. Attempting to do this, various theorists have pointed out that most people have an expectation of how our behavior may be affected by drinking beer, wine, or whiskey. We know that we may become more boisterous and perhaps even more aggressive. Equally important, we also know that others expect liquor to have this effect on us. If we attack someone when we're intoxicated, we know that onlookers may attribute our aggression to the alcohol rather than to our personal characters. Have you ever heard a man, for example, try to excuse the disorderly conduct he exhibited while drunk by blaming it on the alcohol he had imbibed? He was basically saying that it wasn't *he* who had misbehaved; rather, it was the liquor that had been at fault. The "social expectation" argument assumes that quite a few drinkers think of this kind of alibi and suggests that people sometimes feel free to be aggressive when they're drunk because they believe they can blame the liquor and thus avoid responsibility for any harm they might do. They're less restrained because they believe they have an excuse and not because of the alcohol's direct effect on their brains and their thinking processes.

Glenda Kantor and Murray Straus speculated that this process could account for their findings about the relationship between drinking and wife abuse. From these sociologists' perspective, even some men who ordinarily disapprove of hitting a woman believe that the liquor they had ingested gives them a socially acceptable "time out" from normal rules of conduct. Such a husband presumably feels free to assault his spouse if she antagonizes him, because he can attribute his violence to the alcohol.[62]

A number of psychologists, including (most notably) Alan Marlatt and his associates, have offered a very similar explanation of why liquor often promotes aggression. I'll summarize a laboratory study that was conducted by Alan Lang, Daniel Goeckner, Vincent Adesso, and Alan Marlatt as an example of the experimental evidence which supports their thesis, and also to show how sophisticated the research on alcohol effects has become. Investigators now realize it's important to control for people's expectations. If subjects know they have imbibed alcohol, their reactions may be influenced by their beliefs about how they will be affected. The participants are therefore not always accurately informed about what type of beverage is given to them.

In the experiment by Lang and his associates, as a case in point, when the male university students came to the laboratory, believing they were going to serve in a study of the effects of alcohol "on various behaviors," half of them were told they would be asked to drink a mixture of vodka and tonic. However, some of the men in this "alcohol expectation" condition were given only tonic water so that (unknown to them) they didn't ingest the alcohol they expected, whereas the others did get the anticipated vodka. Similarly, other students were informed that they would receive only tonic water (thus creating a "no alcohol expectation" group), but half of them were actually given vodka in their drinks. Immediately after each subject drank his beverage, he interacted with "another student," who was actually the experimenter's accomplice, and was either deliberately insulted or not insulted by this person. Finally, all the subjects had opportunities to punish the "other student" by giving him electric shocks.

In this study, only the subjects' expectations had a significant influence on how aggressive they were toward the accomplice. Whether they had been provoked or not, and also whether they had imbibed vodka or only tonic water, the men who knew or thought that they had drunk alcohol were more punitive to the other student than were the men who believed they had received only tonic water. It may be that the subjects who knew or thought that they had drunk vodka believed that the vodka gave them a legitimate excuse to be nasty, and it may be that they thus felt free to punish the other man severely.[63]

I've summarized this experiment to show some of the complexities involved in research on alcohol effects and to indicate that people's expectations can influence their behavior *to some extent* when they've been drinking. However, these results are not to be taken as the last word on alcohol research. In recent years, there have been at least two highly sophisticated statistical reviews of all the published research on the effects of alcohol expectations. Both of these reviews concluded that liquor can affect social behavior even when the drinkers aren't aware of the nature of their beverage. If wine did promote Cassio's assault on his frustrater, it didn't have this effect only because he knew what he had drunk and what the effect might be.[64]

More and more psychologists are now coming to believe that alcohol influences people's thoughts and behavior primarily by impairing their mental processes. Claude Steele, now at Stanford University in California, perhaps the leading exponent of this theory, speaks of an intoxication-induced "myopia," a deficient and "shortsighted information processing." Steele and Josephs have spelled this effect out more specifically. Alcohol intoxication, they maintain, has two main effects:

1. *Drinking restricts the range of cues that we can perceive in a situation.* We pay attention to, and think about, only the most obvious and central aspects of the situation confronting us,

and we neglect other information that might also be important, even though it is out in the "periphery."

2. *Drinking reduces our ability to process and to extract meaning from the cues and information we do perceive.* In other words, we don't think much about the information we receive, and thus we fail to relate the information to other knowledge and ideas we already possess.

The result of all this, according to Steele and Josephs, is that

> Alcohol makes us the [captives] of an impoverished version of reality in which the breadth, depth, and time line of our understanding is constrained. It causes what we have called an *alcoholic myopia,* a state of shortsightedness in which superficially understood, immediate aspects of experience have a disproportionate influence on behavior and emotion, a state in which we can see the tree, albeit more dimly, but miss the forest altogether.[65]

The findings in an experiment carried out by Kenneth Leonard can be used to illustrate this "alcoholic myopia" at work. Male subjects who agreed to serve in a study of the "influence of alcohol on perceptual-motor skills" were individually given a beverage that contained either alcohol or no alcohol. (The men were told whether they had received alcohol or not.) After this, each subject was placed in a competitive reaction-time situation with another student; at the receipt of a signal, each was to try to press a shock button as quickly as possible, knowing that only the slower student would receive the electric shock the other had set for him. The aggression measure was the shock intensity level the subject set just before each reaction-time trial. What's important to this discussion is that, before the first trial got under way, half the men in both the alcohol condition and the no-alcohol condition were clearly told that their opponents had said they intended to give them severe shocks if they lost the race, whereas the other subjects were told that their opponents wanted to administer only mild shocks.

Regardless of whether the subjects had received any alcohol or not, how aggressive they were on the first trial depended upon the other person's supposed initial intention; those who thought their opponent wanted to shock them severely set a high level of punishment for him in return. However, whatever the other student's supposed initial intention, all the subjects were then informed that their opponents had actually tried to give them only *very weak* shocks on the first trial. Since this later information was somewhat less obvious than the opponents' earlier statements about the shock levels they wanted to administer, the statements can be called "peripheral cues." The question was whether the subjects would moderate their behavior in line with this less obvious information.

The sober subjects did take in the later information; the men who had been highly aggressive on the first trial reciprocated their partners' mildness and reduced the punishment intensity they set for the next trial. By contrast, and consistent with Steele's analysis, the initially highly punitive intoxicated subjects continued being highly aggressive on the second trial. They had evidently failed to absorb the new information about their opponent's actual peacefulness, or at least they didn't realize the full significance of the peripheral cues, and thus didn't regulate their behavior accordingly.[66]

Maybe this helps to explain why Cassio became so aggressive after several cups of wine. He reacted only to the "central cue" in the situation (that someone was preventing him from doing what he wanted) and failed to consider less obvious cues (which in his case included his frustrater's peaceful motive and his commander's rules against fighting).

This summary of alcohol research shows once again that human aggression can be influenced by biological and chemical processes as well by cultural and personal learning.

SUMMARY

In this chapter, I examine several ways in which biological processes can affect aggressive behavior. I start by looking at the traditional notion of an aggressive instinct, particularly as this concept is employed in Sigmund Freud's psychoanalytic theorizing and in the somewhat similar ethological formulation advanced by Konrad Lorenz. Although the term "instinct" is exceedingly imprecise and has a number of different meanings, both Freud and Lorenz thought of an "aggressive instinct" as an inborn and spontaneously generated urge to destroy someone. In summarizing the Freudian and Lorenzian conceptions, I note that both theories maintain that the innate aggressive drive can explode in uncontrolled violence unless it is released through socially appropriate substitute activities.

My discussion emphasizes that this traditional notion lacks empirical support and is seriously in error in important respects. Thus, not only have researchers failed to locate the supposed reservoirs of "aggressive energy" anywhere in the animal or human organism but also, as shown in Chapter 11, there is no good evidence that substitute aggressive activities will have cathartic benefits and lessen the subsequent impetus to aggression. Perhaps equally important, whereas the Freudian and Lorenzian conceptions posit a single aggressive drive (although this unitary urge supposedly powers many different kinds of activities), the great majority of investigators now recognize the existence of several types of aggression which have different origins and are governed by different biological and psychological mechanisms. At the very least, it is necessary to differentiate between instrumental and affective or emotional aggression.

Although I criticize the traditional notion of an aggressive instinct, I certainly do not dismiss the role of biological processes. Many studies which were conducted in Denmark indicate that there can be a hereditary transmission of a disposition to crime, perhaps even to violent crime. Individuals who inherit a very strong disposition in this direction are not doomed to a life outside the law but are at risk of engaging in criminal conduct under particular situational circumstances.

Biological influences can also be seen in gender differences in aggression and crimes of violence. Although there can be little doubt that cultural learning contributes to these differences, I agree with Eleanor Maccoby that these differences are not caused by prior learning alone. Research indicates that males tend to be more aggressive than females in all primate species and in all human societies for which evidence is available. There is evidence that male sex hormones can affect the proclivity to aggression. On summarizing some studies which point to such an influence, I note one way in which hormones seem to affect the likelihood of aggressive reactions; it seems clear that male sex hormones circulating throughout the body before birth (and in some species even shortly afterward) help to organize the developing brain in a way that heightens the probability of aggressive responses to provocations. By contrast, we don't have any clear evidence that these hormones help to activate an impetus to aggression once the nervous system is fully developed.

The last biological influence examined in this chapter is alcohol. Chapter 8, Domestic Violence, and Chapter 9, Murder, reported that many violent offenders are drunk when they commit their assaults, and it is frequently suggested that alcohol serves to lower restraints on socially disapproved behavior. While there seems to be some validity to this interpretation, I find considerable merit in Claude Steele's notion of an intoxication-induced "myopia." This conception holds that alcohol restricts the range of information which a person can absorb and integrate in the immediate situation, and that it also reduces the person's ability to process and extract meaning from the available information. An experiment is cited which supports the applicability of Steele's formulation to aggression.

NOTES

1. Einstein (1933).
2. Fromm (1977), cited in Siann (1985), p. 99. For a fairly comprehensive survey of the development of Freud's ideas about aggression, see Stepansky (1977).

3. Freud (1933/1950).

4. Reported in James Reston's column, *New York Times,* June 3, 1988.

5. Bertrand de Born, quoted in Tuchman (1978), p. 16.

6. Lorenz (1966).

7. In this brief review, I will not discuss the conception of aggression which was advanced by E. O. Wilson (1975) and other sociobiologists, not only because it is exceedingly imprecise but also because Wilson, unlike Darwin and Lorenz, has deliberately chosen to say nothing about the motivational mechanisms through which genes presumably affect behavior and social structure. While I disagree with Wilson's formulation in a number of ways, I'm sympathetic to his suggestion that aggression "is a set of complex responses . . . programmed to be summoned up in times of stress" (p. 248). I also don't altogether disagree with Wilson that the components of the aggressive reaction pattern have "a high degree of heritability," although I give more weight than he does to learning and other environmental influences.

8. Beer (1968), pp. 363–372.

9. Darwin (1871/1948).

10. Darwin (1871/1948), p. 477.

11. Freud (1920/1961).

12. Both quotations are from Fromm (1977) and are cited in Siann (1985), p. 103.

13. Siann (1985), p. 104.

14. Siann (1985), p. 105.

15. Hinde (1960).

16. See Lorenz (1966); Eibl-Eibesfeldt (1979).

17. Lorenz (1966), p. 52.

18. Unlike Freud, however, Lorenz attempted to integrate his conception with Darwin's evolutionary doctrine. Lorenz proposed that aggression had yielded at least three evolutionary benefits. It had brought about the dispersal of animals within the same species over a given territory, thereby balancing the number of species members with the available resources; it had led to the selection of the strongest members in their fights with rivals; and it had promoted the defense of the young.

19. Lorenz (1966), p. 50.

20. Lorenz (1966), pp. 244–245.

21. Lorenz (1966), pp. 55–56.

22. Contrary to what some laypeople believe, Lorenz's views are not shared by many zoologists and ethologists. Two eminent students of animal behavior who have very different conceptions of instinctive behavior are Hinde (1982) and Barnett (1967). A very sophisticated discussion of animal aggression can be found in Archer (1988).

23. Marler (1976). Also see Wilson, E. O. (1975).

24. See Berkowitz (1969a) and, especially, Hinde (1960).

25. Scott (1958), p. 62.

26. More information about the 1986 Seville Statement on Violence can be

obtained from Prof. David Adams, Psychology Department, Wesleyan University, Middletown, CT.

27. Storr (1968), p. xi.

28. For a summary of some of the research on these different motives and forms of conduct, see Endler & Hunt (1984).

29. Moyer (1976).

30. Archer (1988).

31. The quote at the end of the paragraph is from Eichelman, Elliott, & Barchas (1981), p. 57. Summarizing some of the evidence of a difference between predatory and affective aggression, Eichelman and his associates stated that, "It appears that the role of a given neuroregulator [e.g., dopamine, norepinephrine] depends on the type of aggression being studied, arguing against nonspecific activation of the systems during aggressive acts. On one hand, increased norepinephrine release correlates with—and may even trigger—affective aggression. . . . On the other hand, increased activity of this same neuroregulator appears to inhibit predatory aggression" (p. 67).

32. It is only fair to recognize that Lombroso believed that only about a third of all offenders are born criminals. He also maintained that adverse environmental conditions give rise to crime, although he focused much of his attention on genetic determinants. See Wilson & Herrnstein (1985), p. 73.

33. Osborn & West (1979).

34. Cited in Hollin (1989), pp. 25–26.

35. Christiansen (1974).

36. Wilson & Herrnstein (1985), p. 93. Writers who are skeptical about the findings obtained in these studies have argued that identical twins may actually grow up in psychologically more similar environments than fraternal twins do, because identical twins may evoke more similar reactions from other persons. Furthermore, it's possible that identical twins may have closer relationships than fraternal twins have, so that they influence each other to a greater extent and are more apt to take on each other's behavioral styles, including their antisocial actions. See Hollin (1989), p. 26.

37. For generally sympathetic reviews of this kind of research, see Wilson & Herrnstein, (1985), pp. 95–100, and especially Mednick & Christiansen (1977).

38. A convenient summary of this research can be found in Mednick, Gabrielli, & Hutchings (1987).

39. I should acknowledge that the relationship between the biological parents' criminality and that of their offspring is statistically significant for property crimes but not for crimes of violence. Mednick concluded that there is evidence only for the heritability of a disposition to engage in property crimes. Still, the Christiansen findings as well as other evidence obtained by the Mednick group suggest that there may be an inherited disposition to commit violent crimes in a small fraction of the population. In a later close examination of the Danish records, Moffitt (1987) found that biological parents' psychiatric histories were related to their sons' chances of being convicted for violent crimes. The inherited proclivity to violence even in these

extreme cases is probably only a *potential* which is not revealed in open behavior unless other environmental influences are present that strengthen and/or activate the potential.

40. For example, see Frodi, Macaulay, & Thome (1977).

41. See Moyer (1976) and especially Archer (1988).

42. Wilson, J. Q., & Herrnstein, R. J. (1985), pp. 104–107.

43. Bureau of Justice Statistics (1983).

44. Statistics taken from Wilson & Herrnstein, (1985), pp. 109–111, and from Bureau of Justice Statistics (1983), p. 35.

45. Of all the studies cited by Maccoby & Jacklin (1974), the comparatively few that did not find boys to be more aggressive obtained no sex differences. The two studies summarized here are reported on p. 228.

46. Maccoby & Jacklin (1980).

47. Eagly & Steffen (1986). Among the reasons for the Eagly-Steffen belief that gender differences in aggressiveness would be less apparent in adulthood was the conclusion drawn by Frodi, Macaulay, & Thome (1977) that college-age men and college-age women displayed relatively little difference in aggression, in laboratory experiments.

48. See Eagly & Steffen (1986), pp. 310–311.

49. Maccoby & Jacklin (1974), pp. 242–243.

50. The classic research along these lines was conducted by Elizabeth Beeman (1947).

51. Rubin (1987).

52. Young, Goy, & Phoenix (1964). Also see Goy (1970).

53. See Money & Erhardt (1972). The experiments mentioned here are also summarized in Maccoby & Jacklin (1974), p. 243, and in Meyer-Bahlburg & Ehrhardt (1982).

54. Reinisch (1981). In connection with this kind of prenatal influence, it is of interest to note that children who had been exposed before birth to MPA, a chemical that suppresses the production of male sex hormones and that is sometimes given to pregnant women, evidently tend to be relatively nonaggressive in their relationships with their mothers. See Meyer-Bahlburg & Ehrhardt (1981).

55. Olweus (1986).

56. Kreuz & Rose (1972), cited in Rubin (1987).

57. Dabbs & Morris (1990). The high-testosterone group was in the upper 10% of the hormone level distribution, while the "normals" were the remaining 90%. The antisocial actions included such things as assaulting their partners in marital or other intimate relationships, committing acts of violence, getting into trouble on their jobs, and committing traffic offenses. All these actions had occurred after age 18.

58. Rubin (1987).

59. Bushman & Cooper (1990) cite McDonald's (1961) review of the research in this area, indicating that "the proportion of murderers who had been drinking before their crimes ranged from 0.19 to 0.83, with a median of 0.54."

Steele & Josephs (1990), citing a report of the National Commission on the Causes and Prevention of Violence, say that alcohol was involved in 65 per cent of the murders. In a detailed review, Pernanen's (1981) research survey indicates that either the perpetrator, the victim, or both had been drinking in half of all officially reported violent crimes. Similarly, in their comprehensive survey of the research, Murdoch et al. (1990) noted that alcohol is far more likely to be involved in violent as compared to nonviolent offenses. The study of the association between alcohol consumption and family violence was reported in a chapter by Kantor & Straus, in Straus & Gelles (1990). This chapter also provides a review of the sociological research on the aggressive effects of alcohol consumption, including domestic violence, as well as several of the more prominent sociological analyses of alcohol effects.

60. Kantor & Straus, in Straus & Gelles (1990), p. 216.

61. There is considerable evidence that alcohol consumption promotes aggression primarily after an instigation to aggression is activated. See for example, Taylor, Schmutte, Leonard, & Cranston (1979).

62. Kantor & Straus, in Straus & Gelles (1990).

63. Lang, Goeckner, Adesso, & Marlatt (1975).

64. Hull & Bond (1986) concluded that expectations had only a weak effect, if any, while Bushman & Cooper (1990) suggested that the heightened aggressiveness results only from the combination of the psychological and pharmacological effects of alcohol consumption.

65. Steele & Josephs (1990), p. 923. Steele & Josephs point out that other theorists, such as Pernanen (1976) and Taylor & Leonard (1983), have interpreted the influence of alcohol on aggression in a similar manner.

66. Leonard (1989). The competitive reaction-time procedure is employed in Stuart Taylor's research program and is mentioned in Chapter 13.

13

Aggression in the Laboratory

❖ ────────

The Typical Laboratory Procedure ◆ Some Considerations in Support of
Laboratory Experiments

Much of the research described in this book was carried out in the laboratory. The scientific adequacy of the arguments presented here thus rests to a considerable extent on the validity of the experimental procedures and it is therefore important to consider both the advantages and disadvantages of laboratory research.

*T*HE TYPICAL LABORATORY PROCEDURE

The Buss Aggression Machine
First, you should have a clear idea of just what's involved in laboratory research. I'll give you a concrete example of the procedure that has been followed in many experiments by briefly describing the best-known method for the laboratory study of physical aggression: the "aggression machine" procedure devised by Arnold Buss more than three decades ago.[1] The summary below is based on the way Buss measured aggression in a series of studies on the effects of frustration, but the same methodology has been used in hundreds of other studies by Buss and others, sometimes with minor modifications.

Upon entering the laboratory in each experiment, the subject met the experimenter and a fellow student who was posing as another subject but was actually the experimenter's accomplice. (In the great majority of investigations, both subject and accomplice have been males.) The experimenter first provided the "cover story"—information about the study's ostensible purpose. He told the two men that they were going to take part in an investigation of the effects of punishment on learning, and that one of them would serve as the teacher, while the other would be the learner.

The naive subject was selected to be the teacher, supposedly by chance, and was then taken to the control room where he was shown how to transmit the material to be learned to the other student and how to record the learner's responses. The subject was also told that, on each trial, he would have to let the learner know whether his response was correct or not. The teacher would only flash a light signal when the learner gave a right answer, but he was to punish the learner's mistakes by giving him electric shocks. The subject's attention was then called to the apparatus in front of him, a small box with ten buttons in a row, the "aggression machine." (One version of this apparatus can be seen in Figure 13–1.) The first button, the experimenter explained, would give the learner a very mild shock, and the succeeding buttons would deliver ever more intense punishment, up to a very painful level at button 10. The subject was told that he had to punish the learner for each mistake but that, as the teacher, he was free to select whatever shock intensity he wanted to administer. The experimenter then gave the subject a few sample shocks at level 5 and below, so that he would have some sense of the punishment he would deliver (and also to convince him that he would actually be giving shocks). After this, the learner (the experimenter's accomplice) was brought into the room and given instructions about the material to be learned. The naive subject was asked to attach the shock electrodes to the learner's finger.

The learning trials then got under way, and the experimenter's accomplice made errors on a previously set number of trials that was the same for every subject in the experiment. In a typical Buss experiment, after an initial "warm-up" series the naive subject would have, say, twenty-six opportunities to punish the learner out of sixty trials. The measure of the subject's aggressiveness was the intensity of the shocks he administered.

Of course, there is no "other subject" in most of the experiments that employ this procedure, and the subject does not administer any shocks. What's important is that, from the subject's perspective, his or her actions are deliberate attempts to hurt someone else.

Modifications and Variations

A number of researchers have modified the aggression machine procedure because increasing numbers of the college students whom experimenters often use as subjects have heard about the use of electric shocks

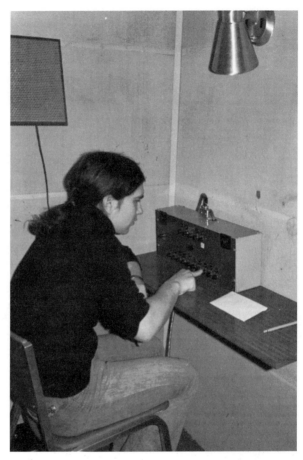

FIGURE 13-1
Subject using "aggression machine."

in psychological research. Some of the modifications have involved only substitution of other forms of noxious stimulation for electric shocks. For example, subjects are sometimes told that they will administer blasts of unpleasant noise to the other person. In another variation, whatever the specific nature of the punishment, some investigators have recorded how long the subject holds the punishment button down as well as the intensity of the punishment that is selected, assuming that duration is another reflection of the strength of the subject's inclination to hurt the other person.

People who have read about the research using the aggression machine paradigm have raised questions about the procedure, and I'll be discussing some of them in this chapter. One such question is: Just what is the subject's motive when he punishes the supposed learner? Although investigators regard the intensity of the punishment as an index of the strength of the subject's desire to hurt the other person, a given subject may have another motive for administering punishment— perhaps to help the learner by giving him feedback and motivating him to do better or maybe even to help the experimenter. Is it possible to know whether the subject really intended to harm the other individual? In order to lessen this possible ambiguity, some researchers indicate in the cover story that punishment will not aid the learner.[2]

Other procedures involving physical harm. Other procedures have also been employed in the experimental study of aggression, although they are less popular than the one devised by Buss. For instance, subjects may be required to press a button (or a telegraph key) a number of times rather than to select the intensity of the punishment.

In many of my own early experiments, for example, the subjects were led to think that they were evaluating a fellow student's performance on an assigned task. They were told that the other person had been given a problem to solve, knowing that his work was going to be judged. Each subject in turn was shown the other person's solution and asked to evaluate it by giving the "worker" from one to ten electric shocks (or, in later experiments, blasts of unpleasant noise). One shock meant that the work was thought to be very good, while ten shocks indicated a very unfavorable judgment. The assumption was that, since all the subjects saw the same somewhat ambiguous solution, the subjects who administered the most shocks generally had the strongest desire to hurt the worker.[3]

There have been a number of variations on this basic method, as well as some other techniques that are totally different from the Buss and Berkowitz paradigms. One that is of interest is the competitive reaction-time procedure used by Stuart Taylor and his associates (which was described briefly in Chapter 12).[4] In this type of experiment the subject is led to believe that he and another person are competing in a series of trials to see which of them is faster in administering an electric shock to the other upon receipt of a "go" signal. The subject is allowed to vary the strength of the shock he will give to his rival on each trial, and the measure of aggression is the intensity level the subject sets.[5]

How important are the differences in procedure? Because there are so many possible differences in laboratory methods, you may wonder whether all the aggression measures really do tap the subjects' aggressive inclinations. Are measures based on *intensity* of punishment really similar to measures based on, say, the *number* of punishments? Do both measures deal with the same kind of aggression?

I believe I can set your mind at ease on this point. These procedures do have much in common. In each case, the subjects believe that they are deliberately injuring another person. All aggression involves the intentional harm of another person, and the measures are all indicators of aggression in this sense (to a greater or lesser extent). Furthermore, studies employing these different methods have often yielded very similar results.[6]

The intensity selection and punishment number techniques, however, are different in one respect, and the difference may be important in some situations (but is not necessarily important in others). On some occasions at least, subjects may be more impulsive—less aware of exactly what they are doing—when they press a shock key a number of times than when they decide which intensity button to push. The conscious choice of a particular intensity could conceivably be controlled to a greater extent by a person's beliefs about what is socially permissible than would the number of times the same person would press a shock key.[7]

Is laboratory behavior "real" aggression? Some critics have insisted that the shocks or noise blasts delivered by the subjects in laboratory studies are actually poor indicators of the aggression that takes place in everyday life. In the real world, these critics maintain, no one administers shocks to another person. Laboratory behaviors are obviously very different from the ways in which one individual attacks another in the home or on the street. How, then, can researchers generalize from the subjects' actions to more realistic aggression?

SOME CONSIDERATIONS IN SUPPORT OF LABORATORY EXPERIMENTS

The Problem of Validity

Objections based on the supposed "unreality" of laboratory procedures basically refer to the problem of *validity*, or the extent to which a particular measure does indeed assess the intended process or characteristic. Determining validity is not a simple matter.[8] Let's say that an investigator wanted to ascertain the validity of the measures she could obtain from the aggression machine procedure. Just how she would proceed would depend upon the specific type of validity she wanted to assess. Psychologists differentiate among several types of validity, but three types are especially relevant to laboratory indicators of aggression: *face validity*, *construct validity*, and *criterion-related validity*.

Face validity. *Face validity* refers to what a particular indicator, score, or test appears to measure rather than to what it actually assesses;

in other words, it refers to the degree to which the indicator "looks" valid. This is, of course, the main problem with laboratory procedures. In the eyes of many members of the general public and even of some social scientists, laboratory measures are low in face validity. Pressing a button to deliver a shock obviously doesn't resemble the aggression that takes place in everyday life.

For experimentalists, however, face validity isn't the ultimate criterion. They believe that their aggression measures can be justified and do capture the essence of what they mean by "aggression."

Construct validity. *Construct validity* has to do with the relationship between the measure of interest to the researcher and other variables. More generally, it has to do with the extent to which the scores on the particular indicator are indeed related to other variables in the way that theory predicts. The hypothetical investigator mentioned above would certainly expect subjects who had been deliberately insulted by another student to be more aggressive toward the other student than subjects who had not been provoked by the student would be. If shock intensity reflected the urge to assault a target, then, the insulted subjects in an experiment should administer more intense punishment to the offender than their noninsulted counterparts should. Finding that this was indeed the case would increase the investigator's confidence in the construct validity of the punishment intensity measure. In other words, the construct validity of the shock score would be supported if the scores were affected by the experimental manipulation (the degree of provocation, in this case), much as the investigator's theory had led her to expect.

Criterion-related (or empirical) validity. *Criterion-related validity* is somewhat similar to construct validity. In both, evidence of validity has been obtained when the researcher finds that the measure of interest (for example, the level of punishment delivered) is related in much the expected way to another variable. However, when test-development specialists speak of criterion-related validity, they are usually thinking, more narrowly, of the measure's relation to a *criterion*—that is, they are thinking of an outcome that is of concern to them. For example, the researcher would be assessing the criterion validity of the shock intensity scores in this sense if she tried to determine whether the subjects' laboratory aggressiveness could be used to predict how aggressive they would be in other situations or even their proclivity to engage in antisocial behavior.

Evidence of the Validity of Laboratory Procedures.
Considerable evidence supporting the construct validity of laboratory measures of aggression is now available. In a great many different experiments, only some of which have been discussed in this book, the results

obtained were quite similar to what was predicted on the basis of both theory and earlier research. The subjects in these studies typically reacted to the experimental condition they were in by giving someone shocks or noise blasts or other types of unpleasant stimulation, very much as we would expect if they were behaving aggressively.

Psychologists Michael Carlson, Amy Marcus-Newhall, and Norman Miller of the University of Southern California, Los Angeles, demonstrated the construct validity of laboratory measures in a careful and comprehensive statistical analysis of the results reported in more than a hundred publications. They noted, first of all, that the three common indicators of physical aggression—the intensity of the punishment the subjects selected, the number of punishments they gave (that is, how many times they pressed the shock key), and the length of time they held the shock button down—tended to be intercorrelated, indicating that they all reflected the same behavioral tendency to a considerable extent. Experimental conditions "that heighten one mode of [physical] aggressiveness," they concluded, "also increase alternative forms of [aggressive] responding [to] the same target."

Perhaps more important, the statistical analysis performed by these psychologists also showed that, over all the studies examined, variations in experimental conditions led to the expected condition differences on the laboratory aggression measures. Whether the subjects had been deliberately and personally provoked or had been frustrated, those exposed to unpleasant experimental treatment tended to score higher on the aggression indicator than did the subjects who had been treated in a neutral manner.[9]

As a reminder, I'll mention that these construct validity-supporting experimental outcomes are not only the results that common sense would lead one to expect. Consider the investigations of the effects of pain cues that were mentioned in Chapter 1. Some writers[10] had argued that repeated assaults on a target would decline rather than increase in intensity as the experimental subjects learned of their victim's suffering. Believing that it was wrong to hurt another person, the subjects would hold back on the punishment they administered after they realized that the victims were in pain. Perhaps you would have made the same prediction. However, as I pointed out in Chapter 1, the actual research results have demonstrated that the aggressors' reactions to their victims' suffering depend upon their aggressive aims at the time. Emotionally aroused people want to hurt someone, and so the initial signs of the victims' pain incite them to attack even more severely soon afterward.

The construct validity of laboratory measures of aggression is also supported by evidence (mentioned in Chapter 5) that subjects' behavior in an experiment is often consistent with their actions outside the laboratory. Since they are apparently focusing primarily on deliberately hurting their victims (rather than on the means by which they accomplish the hurting), the individuals who are strongly disposed to be aggressive in their daily encounters with others also tend to be aggressive in the laboratory. In several experiments, persons who had previously been identified as usually high in aggressiveness typically delivered intense punishment via the aggression machine (or a similar apparatus) in the laboratory. In an experiment conducted with both male and female teenagers in an Upward Bound program, the youths who punished a male learner most severely in the laboratory were generally regarded by their counselors as being highly aggressive in other situations. Very similar results have been obtained in other studies, and with adults as well as youngsters.[11]

In other words, here again actions in the laboratory present a sample of the subjects' behavior. How the subjects act in an experiment may well reflect how they behave in other, more natural settings—to the extent that the experimental and the real-world situations are *psychologically (not physically) similar.* In the case of laboratory measures of aggression, what's psychologically important to the subjects is that they are intentionally harming someone. It's this meaning that makes the delivery of electric shocks or noise blasts an aggressive reaction similar to hitting or kicking.[12]

On the "Unrepresentativeness" of Laboratory Subjects and Conditions
Other frequently raised objections to laboratory experiments are that the subjects used in most studies are not representative of the general population and that the laboratory settings are artificial. Critics have charged that, even if we accept subjects' behavior as aggression, in most experiments they are only college students and are therefore very different from other people in the general population: They are younger, more active, more likely to take chances, and so on. Other persons might respond very differently to the experimental conditions. According to the skeptics, then, we really can't generalize from these "unrepresentative" laboratory samples to the broader population.

This type of criticism also extends to laboratory settings, which are said to be totally unlike situations that exist in the natural world. Fighting occurs in people's homes, in taverns, and on the streets, and the university laboratory doesn't even come close to resembling these settings. The question which the critics ask is: How do we know that subjects would act the same way in natural situations as they do in the laboratory? In sum, these critics insist, experiments aren't at all like what goes on outside the laboratory. Because experimental subjects and settings are not representative of the real world, they tell us very little about the actions of real people in real situations.

What experiments can and cannot do. In responding to these criticisms, I'll confine myself to some brief comments on points that I've made elsewhere at greater length.[13]

I don't by any means dismiss the importance of a study's representativeness. However, the degree to which it is vital to have participants and conditions that are replicas of the people and settings in the real world depends considerably on the experiment's purpose. Experiments are (or should be) conducted to investigate causal possibilities: Can differences in variable A (which is usually called the "independent variable")—for example, (A1) viewing a violent movie versus (A2) viewing a nonaggressive film—lead to differences in variable B (the "dependent variable")—for example, aggressive behavior? The particular experiment is only a sample of all the studies that might be carried out to answer this causal question, and the experimental results yield only a probability statement—not a definitive, conclusive answer. Thus, in regard to the question posed above, the experimental outcome might indicate that there is a chance that viewing filmed violence could produce an increase in aggressive behavior by the viewers.

However, since the laboratory participants and settings are not representative of the larger population of people in general and the situations in which they usually find themselves, scientists can't use these experiments to estimate the exact frequency or magnitude of the effects in the real world. They can't say, on the basis of an experiment on the effects of aggressive movies, either exactly how probable it is that seeing such films will produce open aggression or exactly how substantial the influence of observed violence will be on later aggressive conduct by the viewers.

This doesn't mean that researchers can't make even a rough guess about the extent to which an independent variable of interest (such as the aggressiveness of a witnessed movie), will lead to changes in a dependent variable (the observers' aggressive behavior, in this case) on the basis of the experimental results. As mentioned in Chapter 7, statisticians have developed ways of estimating the magnitude of an independent variable's impact upon the dependent variable over a series of experiments. Employing these statistical procedures, Wood, Wong, and Chachere reported that, in the studies they had examined, the violent movies had had a "small to moderate" effect on the subjects' aggressive behavior.[14] It's possible, then, that scenes of violence in the mass media could increase the level of violence exhibited by people in the audience to a "small to moderate" degree.

This is only a guess, however, since the estimate deals with the magnitude of the influence *in the studies used in the analysis.* Although this statistical finding over a number of experiments enhances our confidence that the independent variable does have an influence on the dependent variable, it still does not say just how many people will be affected, nor how substantially they will be influenced, in other situations. Only if the experimental subjects and conditions were miniature replicas of the people and situations to which the researchers wanted to generalize would we be able to come up with precise figures.

In other words, you should take the experimental results reported in this book (and elsewhere) as educated guesses about factors that can influence aggression. The better the experiment, and the more often similar investigations have yielded comparable findings, the more confidence you can have in the proposition that is offered about the causal relationship. While you can't be completely certain the proposition is correct, the findings I've reported in this book are generally the best educated guesses that exist to date.

On Possible Experimental Artifacts

Experimenters also face the problem that people who are taking part in an experiment are usually well aware that they are being observed by the researchers. This knowledge could conceivably bias their behavior, so that they would not behave naturally. They might be motivated, for example, to "show off" to the watching psychologists, or they might want to help the investigators by fulfilling their expectations. Since these motives could distort the subjects' reactions in the experiment, it's important to take a close look at experimental artifacts.

To what extent do laboratory subjects comply with experimenters' "demands"? Quite a few psychologists believe that subjects' actions during an experiment are indeed affected to a considerable extent by their desire to help the researchers achieve their goals. As these psychologists see it, since the subjects have agreed to serve in the study, they want to help the experimenters and also to further the cause of science. For these reasons, they will try hard to discover the researchers' hypothesis and then will act in such a way as to confirm the hypothesis.

Think of what this implies for laboratory experiments on aggression. If the subjects pressed the shock button mainly because they believed the experimenter wanted them to press it, rather than because they were attempting to hurt the target person in the next room, the laboratory study would be completely invalid. However, I question whether most laboratory subjects do have a strong desire to aid the experimenters by confirming their expectations.

The notion of a widespread desire to confirm experimenters' hypotheses, by no means confined to research on aggression, rests on a chain of reasoning first advanced by Martin Orne, an eminent investigator of hypnosis.[15] Impressed by the degree to which subjects seem willing to obey almost any command given to them by an experimenter, no matter how silly it might appear to an outside observer, Orne said that many subjects, in a psychological sense, sign an implicit contract with the researcher. In agreeing to take part in the study, they presumably also tacitly agree to be "good" subjects, and this means doing what the experimenter asks of them. Orne goes on to maintain that, for many of the participants, being good subjects also means that they ought to help the researcher by confirming the researcher's hypothesis.

Orne's thesis likens a subject to a customer who is negotiating with a used-car salesperson. He is interested in the "product" (the experiment), but he is also somewhat skeptical about what he is told. Thus, Orne's argument holds, subjects are typically too sophisticated and too astute to accept experimenters' cover stories, and they look for cues in the laboratory situations that might tell them what the experiments are really about. When they find these cues (which Orne called "demand characteristics"), they act the way they think the experimenter expects them to act, partly so that they will be good, cooperative subjects and partly in order to help science.

I have taken issue with this notion in several papers[16] and needn't repeat the details of my rebuttal here. Nevertheless, some points are so important that they bear repeating.

First, some of the studies which have been cited in support of the demand compliance thesis are really questionable. For example, some psychologists have tried to support this notion by showing that many subjects can actually tell how the researcher expects them to behave in the experimental situation. They have described aggression experiments to students and asked them to predict what the subjects in the studies would do under the specified circumstances—and in quite a few instances the students were pretty accurate in estimating how most subjects in the actual experiments did behave. The critics then concluded that the subjects in the actual experiments had only complied with the researchers' expectations; they had known what the experimenters wanted and had "gone along" with the experimenters wishes.[17]

If you think about this argument, however, you will realize that the reasoning is unsatisfactory. A demonstration that naive observers can predict an experimental outcome doesn't necessarily mean that the experimental results are caused by the subjects' compliance with the investigator's demands. After all, people do have some knowledge of human behavior, and sometimes they can predict experimental findings simply on the basis of this knowledge. As an illustration, suppose you're told about an experiment in which a highly erotic movie is shown to male university students and you're asked to say whether these men would become sexually aroused. Wouldn't you guess that the subjects would develop sexual ideas and feelings? It is of course true that many subjects in experiments of this kind actually do have sexual reactions to erotic movies. Your accurate estimate clearly doesn't mean that the actual subjects only engaged in playacting when they revealed their sexual thoughts and desires. They *were* sexually aroused, and you knew that they would be.

Evidence attesting to the construct validity of laboratory aggression measures also argues against the demand compliance thesis. Consider again the experiments on pain cues. It's unlikely that most university students would have predicted the obtained outcome (intensified attacks as the victims' pain increased), since several eminent psychologists hadn't expected it. These findings were probably too subtle to have been anticipated by students and thus were unlikely to have come about simply because of the subjects' expectations.

Evaluation apprehension as a problem in laboratory experiments. I hasten to acknowledge, however, that laboratory experiments clearly aren't free of all errors and artifacts. As a matter of fact, subjects' behavior can be distorted at times by a concern many of them probably share. Young students who are not familiar with psychological research and who are serving in one of their first experiments are very apt to believe that the investigator is studying their personalities—that they are being "psychoanalyzed." Thus they are likely to experience what psychologists call "evaluation apprehension" when they are in the laboratory. They want to make a good impression on the investigator, and they especially want to appear psychologically healthy and well-adjusted. There's a good chance, then, that many of them, wanting to "look good," will avoid showing antisocial behavior.

Evaluation apprehension is a serious problem in experimental research on aggression. In trying to appear healthy and well-adjusted, it's not unusual for subjects to hold back in attacking the available target. As a result, they are actually less aggressive in the laboratory than they would be in other situations. Most laboratory experiments therefore attempt to lower the subjects' restraints against aggression by giving them a socially legitimate excuse for punishing the victim. Otherwise, very little if any aggression would be seen.

A laboratory study of demand compliance and evaluation apprehension. In the absence of hard data, people can argue back and forth about demand compliance and evaluation apprehension. Ultimately, it is necessary to put the demand compliance thesis to an empirical test in order to determine whether subjects do indeed try to confirm experimenters' hypotheses.

One such test, which is especially relevant to the experiments reported in this book, deals with the weapons effect Anthony LePage and I reported in 1967, which was also discussed in Chapter 3. This study and several subsequent experiments have demonstrated that the mere presence of weapons can stimulate people to be more aggressive than they otherwise would have been. As you might imagine, this finding attracted considerable controversy, and a number of critics maintained that the results were primarily caused by the subjects' awareness of the experimenters' demands. From their perspective, the students had caught on to the researchers' hypothesis—that the guns would make them more aggressive—and then had tried to confirm the experimenters' expectation.

Charles Turner and Lynn Simons, who were both then at the University of Utah, Salt Lake City, put this objection to the test by deliberately varying how much their subjects knew about the experimenters' interest in their reactions to the weapons.[18] As each naive subject waited in the laboratory reception room to be called for the experiment, another student (the experimenters' accomplice) entered the room, supposedly to pick up his books but actually to give the subject certain information. To subjects in the *low-awareness* condition, he said only that he had just finished participating in the study. By contrast, the accomplice created a *medium level of awareness* in other subjects by telling them that he didn't believe the experimenter's cover story, and a *high level of awareness* in still other men by informing them that the experimenter was probably interested in how they would respond to the presence of guns. The accomplice then left the room. The experimenter entered, took each subject individually to the laboratory, and told him the cover story that had been used in the original Berkowitz-LePage experiment: that the study was concerned with physiological reactions to stress. Then the experimenter went one step further. He created a *strong evaluation apprehension* in half the men in each of the awareness level groups by telling them that the study was investigating how well-adjusted they were, in order to determine the relationship between physiological reactions and psychological maladjustment.

After all this information had been provided, the supposed "actual" experiment got under way. Electrodes were attached to the subject, and he was given a problem to solve. He wrote down his answers, supposedly so that his "partner" in the adjoining room could evaluate them. All the subjects were then provoked by receiving seven shocks—a decidedly unfavorable evaluation by the partner. As in the original experiment, each subject was then taken into the control room which contained the shock apparatus. There he found weapons (which had supposedly been left by another experimenter) on the table next to the shock key. Each subject was then shown his partner's solutions to the problem and was given an opportunity to punish that person by administering between one and ten shocks.

Figure 13–2 reports the mean number of shocks which were delivered to the insulting other person as a function of the subjects' level of awareness and degree of evaluation apprehension. The chart shows that both experimental variations influenced the subjects' aggression. As expected, the men who believed that the researchers were studying how maladjusted they were tended to attack their insulting partner less often than did their nonapprehensive counterparts. More important, the subjects' awareness of the researchers' interest in their reactions to the weapons also served to lessen their punitiveness. Whereas the demand characteristics interpretation of the weapons effect holds that the aware subjects should have given the most shocks since they knew what the experimenter was really investigating, these men actually tended to be the least punitive.

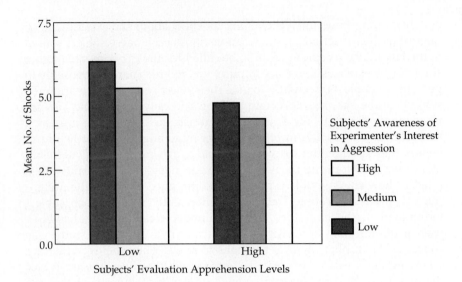

FIGURE 13–2

Mean number of shocks given as a function of awareness of the experimenter's interest in aggression and the subjects' levels of evaluation apprehension. (Data from Turner & Simon (1974). Copyright 1974 by the American Psychological Association. Adapted by permission.)

Both of these effects were probably caused by the subjects' desires to look good. Whether they thought the research was concerned with their degrees of maladjustment and/or with their reactions to the guns, the men apparently thought they would appear psychologically unhealthy if they were too aggressive. They restrained their aggression in order to make good impressions on the experimenters.

The implications are clear. It's not easy to conduct a good laboratory experiment. All sorts of psychological influences operate in the laboratory, which can affect the subjects' behavior and even distort their reactions. The careful researcher should attempt to minimize these sources of error. The subjects' motives in the experimental situation can be a particularly significant problem. However, note that, by and large, the behavior-distorting motives apparently work against the aggression researcher. In many instances the significant laboratory results occur *in spite of the subjects' awareness of the experiment's interest in their aggression—not because of their awareness.*

SUMMARY

Since many of the ideas offered in this book are based on laboratory experiments, in this chapter I discuss some of the pros and cons of laboratory research in social psychology and particularly in the experimental investigation of aggression. The majority of experiments in this area have employed the Buss aggression machine procedure to assess aggressive reactions, but other methods have also been used. Whether the various measures actually have anything in common is a legitimate question. However, a recent statistical analysis of the research findings demonstrates that, by and large, the presumed laboratory aggression indicators do reflect the strength of aggressive tendencies.

In dealing with questions about the validity of laboratory measures, I note the distinctions which psychologists draw between face validity, construct validity, and criterion-related validity. Evidence presented in this chapter shows that, though laboratory behaviors may not look like "real" aggression (i.e., they typically have low face validity), they generally do have construct validity (i.e., they operate much as people expect aggressive actions to operate). In pertinent studies, they also have criterion validity (i.e., they are related to appropriate criteria such as aggressiveness in naturalistic settings). What is important about laboratory behaviors is their meaning to the subjects (i.e., whether they reflect the subjects' intention to hurt someone else), not their physical form.

Critics have also pointed to a lack of representativeness of laboratory settings and subjects, contending that the behavior of university students in laboratory rooms tells little about how most people act in the natural world. In answering this objection, I note that experiments seek to test causal hypotheses and that this purpose is better served by high degrees of experimental control than by subject and setting representativeness. On the other hand, since laboratory subjects and settings are not usually representative of real populations and natural situations, laboratory results cannot be used to estimate the magnitude or frequency of given phenomena in real-world situations.

The last problem considered in this chapter has to do with artifactual influences that might distort subjects' behavior in the laboratory. I argue that the criticism that laboratory results often reflect only subjects' compliance with what they regard as experimenters' demands is greatly exaggerated, that the reasoning on which this criticism is based is questionable, and that there is little good evidence that laboratory findings in the study of aggression are actually distorted by demand compliance. This argument is supported by an experimental test of the weapons effect. While I minimize the problem of demand compliance, I recognize evaluation apprehension as an important artifact. Many subjects do try to make a good impression on experimenters by restraining their socially disapproved tendencies. This means, however, that the positive results obtained in laboratory experiments on aggression are achieved in spite of the subjects' suspicions about the researchers' real interests, not because of their suspicions.

*N*OTES

1. The aggression machine technique was first described in Buss's book (1961), the first modern survey of experimental research on aggression. Stanley Milgram had developed a very similar procedure for use in his experiments on obedience, and Milgram and Buss had a friendly argument about who was the first to employ an aggression machine. The experimental procedure described here was followed in the study reported in Buss (1966).

2. Robert Baron discusses this problem in his 1977 book, *Human aggression* (pp. 60–62), and presents evidence suggesting that many college students believe that whatever punishment they give may help the learner. To lessen this belief, Baron does not use the "teacher-learner" cover story. Instead, he tells his subjects that they are engaged in a study of physiological reactions to "unpleasant stimuli." The subjects' job is to deliver the unpleasant stimuli (electric shocks or blasts of noise) to a partner, and they are free to choose whatever intensity of unpleasantness they want to give. In yet another variation on this procedure, Donnerstein [e.g., Donnerstein & Berkowitz (1981)] has employed a variation of the teacher-learner paradigm, but he explicitly informs the subjects that the punishment level will have no effect on their partner's performance.

3. For example, Berkowitz & LePage (1967).

4. See Taylor (1967). Baron (1977, pp. 66–68) also describes the Taylor paradigm in some detail.

5. Since college students are becoming increasingly sophisticated about the use of electric shocks and other noxious stimulation in psychological research, largely because they learn about Milgram's (1963) classic studies of obedience, it is probably now more important than ever to devise procedures in which subjects know that they are hurting someone else but still aren't very aware that they are engaged in socially disapproved conduct. One possible technique along these lines, developed by Caprara [see Caprara, Passerini, Pastorelli, Renzi, & Zelli (1986)] in Italy, required subjects to harm their victim by awarding him less money than they could have legitimately given him. Thus, whereas the rules of the situation allowed them to give the victim as much as, say, $1 for a correct response, they could hurt him—in a relatively subtle manner—by delivering less. The less they gave him for a correct response, the more they were hurting him. Experimental findings obtained by Mummenday (1978) suggest that depriving another person of money is, in important respects, psychologically equivalent to hurting that person physically.

6. Carlson, Marcus-Newhall, & Miller (1990).

7. Russell Geen has made this point on the basis of findings which indicate that intensity and number measures are not always highly correlated. See Geen, Rakosky, & O'Neal (1968); Geen & O'Neal (1969).

8. For an introduction to some of these complexities, see Grosof & Sardy (1985).

9. Carlson et al. (1989). Interestingly, a finding obtained with written measures of aggression (usually questionnaire ratings) supports my argument that

aggression is more than an attempt to coerce another person. Carlson and his associates pointed out that the negatively treated subjects generally had higher scores on written measures than did their counterparts in the control conditions, even when the measures were obtained privately and even when the victims did not realize that they were being attacked.

10. E.g., Bandura (1973), pp. 194–200.

11. For example, Shemberg, Leventhal, & Allman (1968); Wolfe & Baron, R. A. (1971). In a much more recent demonstration of the construct validity of the laboratory aggression measures, research reported by Neil Malamuth (1986, p. 954) has shown that university men who hold attitudes relatively favorable toward aggression against women generally tended to be highly punitive toward a woman who was in an experiment with them some time later "in an ostensibly unrelated context." For additional references and further discussion, see Baron (1977), pp. 57–58; Berkowitz & Donnerstein (1982), pp. 253–254.

12. See Berkowitz & Donnerstein (1982) for a more detailed discussion of this matter. Henshel (1980) has offered some additional and quite novel arguments in support of laboratory experimentation in his interesting paper on this topic.

13. See especially Berkowitz & Donnerstein (1982).

14. Wood, Wong, & Chachere (1991).

15. Two of his more important papers on this topic are Orne (1962, 1970).

16. In particular, see Berkowitz & Donnerstein (1982); Berkowitz & Troccoli (1986).

17. One version of this line of reasoning can be found in Schuck & Pisor (1974).

18. Berkowitz & LePage (1967); Turner & Simons (1974).

14

In Conclusion: Some Lessons to Be Drawn

❖

Different Kinds of Aggression: Instrumental and Emotional ◆ Is Violence
Inevitable? ◆ The Determinants as Risk Factors ◆ Controlling Violence

The research and theorizing which I have summarized in this book have a
number of very important implications. My purpose in this chapter is to
spell these out, both as a way of summarizing the main points made
in this book and also to suggest how you should think about the factors which
govern people's emotional reactions in general and aggressive behaviors in particular.

DIFFERENT KINDS OF AGGRESSION: INSTRUMENTAL AND EMOTIONAL

One of my major themes is that there is more than one kind of aggression.
Attempts to hurt or destroy other people do not all arise in the same manner and
are not all governed by the same biological and psychological processes, though
all aggression is aimed at the deliberate injury of another person. Investigators
who study the processes involved in aggression don't always agree in detail
about what the main types of aggression are.

There is, however, good reason to distinguish between instrumental and
affective or emotional aggression. Assaults which are carried out in the hope of
gaining a noninjurious objective such as money, social status, enhanced self-iden-
tity, or the elimination of an unpleasant situation are very different in many

ways from attacks which are prompted by intense emotional arousal. It's important to understand both types of aggression, since both contribute to unhappiness and distress in social relationships and tear at the social fabric. Nevertheless, at the risk of seeming to deemphasize instrumental aggression, my focus in this book is on the sort of violence which is driven by strong feelings.

Many social scientists fail to recognize the difference between instrumental aggression and emotional aggression. Quite often this happens in part because their particular theories of behavior give little weight to the relatively involuntary and automatic aspects of emotional conduct. Some students of human behavior unquestioningly assume, along with Sigmund Freud and other psychodynamic theorists, that all behavior is motivated. For them, every action, or at least every act of social significance, is carried out with an aim in mind. Aggressors must want to do more than inflict pain or destruction. Social scientists who espouse this position believe their primary task is to uncover the hidden purposes that spur people to assault others. They seek to learn what else is involved besides the infliction of pain or destruction—what the attackers "really" want to accomplish.

Other investigators phrase their reasoning in other words, but their underlying assumptions are very similar. They prefer to say that behavior is mainly brought about by incentives, the rewards that are anticipated for performing a given set of responses. From this perspective, a child who strikes her sister, a husband who batters his wife, and a robber who kills his victim all act as they do because they believe that their behavior will benefit them in some way. These researchers want to determine what incentives govern aggression, and learn how these expected benefits operate.

My guess is that the failure to recognize the often impulsive and unthinking nature of emotional aggression has another cause in addition to their adherence to a specific psychological theory, whether Freudian, behavioral, or cognitive. Many social scientists look for a hidden purpose behind all aggressive behavior because they want to believe that humans are rational much of the time—not that all actions are necessarily based on intelligent decisions but that they have meaning from the actors' viewpoints. For these social scientists, to deny the existence of an underlying motive for aggression would be to unduly demean the aggressors and perhaps all humankind. Surely, they tell themselves, people must be more than unthinking robots or even animals. Even a murderer, no matter how callous or brutal, must have thought about what he was doing and why, and must have carried out his assault for a reason that made sense to him.

As I see it, however, to insist upon the basic rationality of all significant human conduct is to be blind to the marvelously complex and diversified nature of human behavior. Our thoughts and calculations, the cost-benefit analyses we carry out, do regulate our actions much of the time—but not always. We can also be highly emotional at times—carried away by the feelings and emotional impulses of the moment. We are multifaceted, "many-splendored" things, and to deny our emotionality is to deny part of our humanity.

Now that I have taken this stance, I have to make my beliefs about how emotional aggression operates very clear.

In distinguishing between instrumental and emotional aggression, I am not saying that emotional-driven assaults have no purpose. They do have a goal: the victim's injury (or in more extreme instances, destruction). My contention is that harm or destruction is a major objective in emotional aggression even when other aims can also be identified. Laboratory subjects who have just been insulted by "another student" may well want to comply with the experimenter's instructions when they give the other student electric shocks. In addition, however, having been provoked, they want to hurt the other student. Similarly, an enraged wife who shoots her abusive husband may want to make him stop beating her, but she also wants to do him severe harm.

I believe also that the strength of an emotional assault is largely determined by the intensity of the aggressor's internal agitation; as I have suggested, inner stimulation impels the attack, often in a relatively unthoughtful manner. An infuriated wife doesn't calculate long-term costs and benefits. She knows only that she wants to hurt (or maybe even kill) her tormentor, and as she lashes out at him, her actions are spurred by her strong internal arousal.

This doesn't mean that all emotional attacks are necessarily completely unrestrained. Inhibitions can block an impelled assault to some degree, at least partly because of strong prior learning that aggression is wrong and/or may bring punishment. A mother who is furious with her daughter for disobeying her may readily shout at the girl and may even slap her. However, very few adults kick their children or hit them with clubs. Most people's inhibitions against aggression are activated to some extent even when they are furious, and the inhibitions keep them from doing serious injury. The more strongly aroused a person is, of course, the weaker the activation of these relatively automatic blocks will be and also the less effective the inhibitions will be. By the same token, the stronger the person's usual restraints against aggression, the less likely it is that any degree of arousal will cause her or him to lash out in an uncontrolled outburst of violence. I will say more about self-restraints later in this chapter.

*I*S VIOLENCE INEVITABLE?

It would be difficult, and probably even impossible, to eliminate violence altogether from social life. This is not because human beings are inherently evil and possess a built-in drive to kill and destroy. There is clear and compelling evidence that the aggressive instinct posited by Sigmund Freud, Konrad Lorenz, and other theorists actually does not exist. Rather, it's better to say that some level of violence may always be a part of human life, for at least two reasons: first, because it's all too easy for people to learn that aggression pays, some of the time; and second, because—if I'm right about negative affect as a preprogrammed spur to emotional aggression—no one can hope to avoid all distress and unhappiness.

We're apt to employ aggressive tactics to further our ends to the degree that we've seen aggression work. What's surprising is not the general proposition that we can learn to use aggression instrumentally but the sometimes subtle ways in which people find out that it can pay to assault others. For example, many of us learned as we were growing up that we could sometimes successfully stop others from bothering us by attacking them. Our parents may have admonished or disciplined us for hitting siblings who were annoying us, but every once in a while we still saw that our aggression had accomplished its purpose—that it had terminated the annoyance, at least for a brief time. Thus we found that aggression does occasionally pay off by eliminating or at least lessening a disturbing state of affairs. In addition, emotionally aroused aggressors are also rewarded by their victims' pain and distress. A brother who is angry with his sister will be gratified simply by seeing her cry after he hits her. As if this weren't enough, think of how often adults reinforce their offsprings aggression by letting the children have their own way when they shout and scream or otherwise show their anger.

In the cases I've been citing, the aggressors' own actions are rewarded, but rewards can strengthen aggressive tendencies even when we see them being given to someone else. In several chapters, I noted that we can learn to regard aggression favorably simply by watching aggressors get what they want when they threaten, insult, or hit other people. Unless there are countervailing influences, we may come to think that we too might profit by behaving aggressively.

All this means, then, is that we can see aggression pay off in many different ways. Favorable outcomes, whether we obtain them for ourselves or see others get them, can heighten the chances that we will attack someone in the future, either verbally or physically, when an appropriate opportunity arises, at least if our inhibitions are low.

Don't forget, though, that aggression isn't only carried out in hope of an external benefit. It can also be stimulated by negative feelings. In this connection, recall the many kinds of unpleasant situations that can give rise to anger, hostility, and even violence if the circumstances are conducive—for example, situations in which people experience frustrations, economic stresses, unpleasantly high temperatures, atmospheric pollution, foul odors, and depressing or sad events. Though a person's thoughts can modify or even change the anger/aggression emotional state initially produced by negative affect, such emotion-altering, higher-order thinking doesn't always occur. We can be so carried away by intense unpleasant sensations or by a compelling situation that we don't stop to think about all the available information. We may be especially likely to ignore possible reasons for our bad feelings, and we may not even try to think about the most appropriate ways of behaving in the particular situation. As a consequence, our negative affect can lead to impulsive acts of hostility and aggression. In short, though we can regulate and change the way our negative experiences influence our actions if we think carefully enough, we don't always do the necessary thinking.

Priming effects can also promote aggression. Hostile ideas can come to mind and aggressive inclinations can be generated, for a brief time anyway, when people merely see or hear something that has an aggressive meaning. A wide variety of objects and incidents (including guns and knives, the sight and sound of people fighting, news stories about violent crimes, athletic contests interpreted as aggressive encounters, and war reports) may have such a meaning and may thus prime short-lived hostile thoughts and aggressive impulses.

With so many and such varied factors promoting aggression, is it really going to be possible to eliminate violence from contemporary society?

THE DETERMINANTS AS RISK FACTORS

While I believe that it's virtually impossible to escape or eliminate all the factors that can give rise to aggression, I am not saying that these influences are necessarily always very strong nor that each of them always operates to generate open violence. Consider the role of poverty in the production of violent crimes. There's pretty good evidence that economic deprivation can contribute to spouse battering, child abuse, and homicides. Despite this evidence, political conservatives who oppose social welfare programs have long denied that poverty breeds crime. In a recent example, the Archbishop of Canterbury aroused the ire of the Conservative party in Great Britain when he attributed a serious riot in a northern English city to the high level of unemployment and economic hardship in the community. A prominent Conservative politician dismissed the Archbishop's interpretation altogether by noting that church-going poor people were less apt to riot or steal than were equally impoverished people who did not attend church. This meant, he insisted, that it was moral decay rather than poverty that led to crime and violence.

Most social scientists would say the politician was being simplistic and had thought only in absolutist, yes-or-no terms. No serious researcher really believes that economic deprivations in themselves inevitably and always produce lawbreaking. Rather, in line with the position I've taken throughout this book, it's better to say that poverty is a risk factor, a condition which heightens the *likelihood* of antisocial actions but does not necessarily always produce this behavior. Analogously, cigarette smoking doesn't always lead to lung cancer and heart disease, but frequent smokers are nonetheless at risk for developing these disorders.

This is the perspective that should be taken in considering all the conditions that can promote violence. People aren't always incited to attack others when they experience disappointments or see weapons. Very few moviegoers become assaultive after watching violent films. People who are exposed to unpleasantly hot weather don't always go on rampages and loot and burn the stores in their neighborhoods. A great many poor persons don't break laws. Yet, as the research cited in this book demonstrates, each of these factors increases the chance of aggression. The probability that any one of these factors alone will produce a violent outburst in a given situation is low. Several conditions clearly have to be present if these influences are to give rise to an open attack on an available target in a given situation, much as any one cigarette smoker won't develop lung cancer unless he or she has the appropriate predispositions and bodily conditions. Nevertheless, it's important to know about the individual risk factors, because each raises the likelihood of an undesirable outcome.

Moreover, although the increased probability of violence as a result of each risk factor may be small, a significant number of people may be affected when the population is large enough. In an area the size of a city, a state, or a nation, the poorer residents considered as a whole are more likely to break the law and assault each other than are their economically better off fellow citizens. Similarly, while there's only a small chance that any one person in a movie or TV audience will punch someone in the nose after watching a violent scene, millions of viewers may see the scene, and thus there may be several hundred more acts of violence in the country than otherwise would have occurred. Law enforcement authorities could not confiscate all the millions of handguns that abound in the United States even if they wanted to, but the ready availability of so many weapons undoubtedly means that each year hundreds of people are killed in the United States who otherwise would not have died.

In general, then, it's advisable to think probabilistically about the conditions that can foster aggressive behavior. Indeed, society could benefit from a probabilistic perspective in many different domains of life, including business and commerce, the natural sciences, engineering, education, politics, and the social sciences. To make the best possible decision in any of these areas, it is necessary to consider the odds that a certain event will or will not take place and, on the basis of the available knowledge and information, to estimate the chance (whether it's great, moderate, or small) that the event will actually occur. Even then, the resulting estimate will be only a probability statement—not a certainty. Just so, the research reviewed in this book allows us to make reasonably good estimates, or probability statements, about what conditions foster aggression.

CONTROLLING VIOLENCE

Though it's unlikely that humankind will ever abolish all violence from the face of the earth, we could take some steps to lessen the chances that people will attack or be nasty to others. Obviously, one such step would be to reduce the number of aggression-priming stimuli. Equally obviously, however, this would be difficult in a free society. Aside from the complex constitutional issues, this step would be controversial on a social level. Quite a few persons enjoy violent movies, and a good number think that they can protect themselves from dangerous intruders by having revolvers in their homes. However, the United States would do well to weigh these possible social benefits against the costs of allowing so many violent scenes to be shown on the nation's TV and movie screens, as well as against the costs of permitting the unrestrained sale of firearms in many areas of the country. Is the pleasure that some people derive from seeing actors shoot, stab, kick, punch, and kill each other really worth the hundreds of "extra" violent incidents, some of them very serious or fatal, which occur in the nation? Does the illusory feeling of safety (or the sense of power and virility) which some people gain from owning handguns really count for more than the many hundreds of lives that are taken every year by these firearms? Policymakers and citizens alike should face these questions instead of avoiding them, and then decide.

Even if society does nothing to reduce the amount of violence shown in the movies, on television, and on the printed page, the impact of these depictions could be weakened. As I noted in Chapter 7, Violence in the Media, the effect which the sight of people being beastly to each other will have on the audience members depends to a considerable extent on what they think of the witnessed aggression. Parents, educators, other authority figures, and the media could help to shape viewers' attitudes toward the events shown on the screen. At the very least, they should remind children, and the public in general, that aggression is socially undesirable even when the movie hero beats up the bad guys.

Steps could also be taken to reduce the aggression-inciting effects of unpleasant occurrences. Even if human beings are genetically disposed to become angry and inclined toward aggression when they have negative feelings, they can learn not to behave aggressively after the unpleasant events that caused the feelings. Here too, parents and educators can play active parts. They can teach their charges that aggression doesn't pay and that it is possible to cope with life's difficulties in a constructive and nonaggressive manner. People should also learn that they don't have to "release" their supposedly pent-up aggressive impulses by engaging in real or fantasy aggression and that, in the long run anyway, fighting is more apt to heighten than to reduce the likelihood of further conflict.

My emphasis on avoiding aggression and aggression-priming events doesn't mean that I am recommending that we pretend that all's right with the world. I'm not calling for a denial of the existence of conflict and unhappiness. Instead, as I suggested in Chapter 11, Psychological Procedures for Controlling Aggression, while I believe that people make trouble for themselves by brooding about their hardships and/or the wrongs they think they've suffered, I also believe that a person who has had a serious disagreement with someone else, or who has met with a tragedy or a serious disappointment, would do well to tell the significant individuals in his or her life about the unpleasant event and about the accompanying feelings. In general, I favor more communication—not less. However, communication should not be accompanied by ranting and raving and should involve the transmission of information rather than the overt expression of hostility and hatred.

To take a broader view, the procedures I recommend generally call for a mixture of cognitive changes and heightened inhibitions, or self-restraints, which play a major role in the reduction of aggression.

It's my impression that mental health specialists who are interested in the control of aggression haven't always given sufficient attention to the importance of inhibitory mechanisms. This matter was discussed at length in Chapter 4, Does Thinking Make It So?, and in Chapter 5, The Identification of the Violence Prone. A number of important theorists have emphasized the psychological processes that help to instigate aggression but have neglected the processes involved in restraining this behavior. This neglect is unfortunate, particularly because a relatively few persons account for the greatest proportion of the serious acts of violence which occur in society. Many of these highly assaultive individuals are defective in self-control. They may be disposed to see threats in the world around them, and they're also all too likely to attribute malevolence to others who have thwarted them. But they are often also unable to restrain their emotional impulses so that they frequently lash out in temper, even when there's a good chance that their aggression will be punished.

What should be done with extremely violent persons? Chapter 10, Punishment and Societal Control, and Chapter 11, Psychological Procedures for Controlling Aggression, don't really present much cause for optimism about the possibility of rehabilitating aggressive people. The threat of punishment doesn't seem to be very effective in deterring them from violent crimes, partly because they believe (with some justification) that the odds are good that they will get away with their misdeeds, but also because of their emotional reactivity. Even the possibility of the ultimate punishment, execution, doesn't hold them back for very long, according to the available evidence. Nor are extremely violent people good prospects for rehabilitation. Recent research suggests that certain psychological interventions can benefit at least some adolescent delinquents, but there is no good reason to think that such interventions will work with very antisocial, highly assaultive adults. In my view, the U.S. criminal justice system typically sends too many people to prison for too long and for too many different kinds of offenses. Still, imprisonment may be the only answer for extremely violent individuals. Social scientists' understanding of what has caused them to act as they do doesn't mean that society should tolerate their highly antisocial conduct.

$\mathcal{B}ibliography$

❖

ADELMANN, P. K., & ZAJONC, R. B. (1989). Facial efference and the experience of emotion. *Annual Review of Psychology, 40,* 249–280.

AMERICAN PSYCHIATRIC ASSOCIATION (1980). *Diagnostic and statistical manual of mental disorders* (DSM-III), Washington, DC: American Psychiatric Association.

ANDERSON, C. A. (1987). Temperature and aggression: Effects on quarterly, yearly, and city rates of violent and nonviolent crime. *Journal of Personality and Social Psychology, 52,* 1161–1173.

ANDERSON, C. A. (1989). Temperature and aggression: Ubiquitous effects of heat on occurrence of human violence. *Psychological Bulletin, 106,* 74–96.

ANDERSON, C. A., & ANDERSON, D. C. (1984). Ambient temperature and violent crime: Tests of the linear and curvilinear hypotheses. *Journal of Personality and Social Psychology, 46,* 91–97.

ANDISON, F. S. (1977). TV violence and viewer aggression: A cumulation of study results. *Public Opinion Quarterly, 41,* 314–331.

ARCHER, D., & GARTNER, R. (1984). *Violence and crime in cross-national perspective.* New Haven, Conn.: Yale Univ. Press.

ARCHER, J. (1988). *The behavioural biology of aggression.* Cambridge/New York: Cambridge Univ. Press.

ARMS, R. L., RUSSELL, G. W., & SANDILANDS, M. L. (1979). Effects on the hostility of spectators of viewing aggressive sports. *Social Psychology Quarterly, 42,* 275–279.

AVERILL, J. R. (1982). *Anger and aggression: An essay on emotion.* New York/ Heidelberg: Springer-Verlag.

BACH, G. R., & GOLDBERG, H. (1974). *Creative aggression.* New York: Doubleday.

BAKER, L., DEARBORN, M., HASTINGS, J., & HAMBERGER, K. (1984). Type A behavior in women: A review. *Health psychology, 3,* 477–497.

BAKER, L., HASTINGS, J., & HART, J. (1984). Enhanced psychophysiological responses of type A coronary patients during type A-relevant imagery. *Journal of Behavioral Medicine, 7,* 287–306.

BALL-ROKEACH, S. J. (1973). Values and violence: A test of the subculture of violence thesis. *American Sociological Review, 38,* 736–749.

BANDURA, A. (1965). Vicarious processes: A case of no-trial learning. In L. Berkowitz (Ed.), *Advances in experimental social psychology,* Vol. 2. New York: Academic Press. Pp. 1–55.

437

BANDURA, A. (1973). *Aggression: A social learning analysis.* Englewood Cliffs, N. J.: Prentice Hall.

BANDURA, A., ROSS, D. & ROSS, S. (1963a). Imitation of film-mediated aggressive models. *Journal of Abnormal and Social Psychology, 66,* 3–11.

BANDURA, A., ROSS, D., & ROSS, S. (1963b). A comparative test of the status envy, social power, and secondary reinforcement theories of identificatory learning. *Journal of Abnormal and Social Psychology, 67,* 527–534.

BANDURA, A., UNDERWOOD, B., & FROMSON, M. E. (1975). Disinhibition of aggression through diffusion of responsibility and dehumanization of victims. *Journal of Research in Personality, 9,* 253–269.

BANDURA, A., & WALTERS, R. H. (1959). *Adolescent aggression.* New York: Ronald Press.

BARCLAY, A. M. (1971). Linking sexual and aggressive motives: Contributions of "irrelevant" arousals. *Journal of Personality, 39,* 481–492.

BARNETT, S. A. (1967). *"Instinct" and "intelligence."* London: MacGibbon & Kee.

BARON, R. A. (1977). *Human aggression.* New York: Plenum.

BARON, R. A. (1987). Interviewer's moods and reactions to job applicants: The influence of affective states on applied social judgments. *Journal of Applied Social Psychology, 17,* 911–926.

BARON, R. A., & RANSBERGER, V. M. (1978). Ambient temperature and the occurrence of collective violence: The "long, hot summer" revisited. *Journal of Personality and Social Psychology, 36,* 351–360.

BARTOL, C. R. (1980). *Criminal behavior: A psychosocial approach.* Englewood Cliffs, N.J.: Prentice Hall.

BARUCH, D. W. (1949). *New ways in discipline.* New York: McGraw-Hill.

BAUMRIND, D. (1973). The development of instrumental competence through socialization. In A. D. Pick (Ed.), *Minnesota Symposia on Child Psychology,* Vol. 7. Minneapolis: Univ. of Minnesota Press. Pp. 3–46.

BEDAU, H. A. (Ed.), (1967). *The death penalty in America.* New York: Doubleday.

BEEMAN, E. (1947). The effect of male hormone on aggressive behavior in mice. *Physiological Zoology, 20,* 373–405.

BEER, C. G., (1968). Instinct. In D. L. Sills (Ed.), *Encyclopedia of the social sciences,* Vol. 7. New York: Free Press.

BERK, R. A., BERK, S. F., LOSEKE, D. R., & RAUMA, D. (1983). Mutual combat and other family violence myths. In D. Finkelhor, R. J. Gelles, G. T. Hotaling, & M. A. Straus (Eds.), *The dark side of families: Current family violence research.* Beverly Hills, Calif.: Sage. Pp. 197–212.

BERK, R. A., & NEWTON, P. J. (1985). Does arrest really deter wife battery? An effort to replicate the findings of the Minneapolis spouse abuse experiment. *American Sociological Review, 50,* 253–262.

BERKOWITZ, L. (1962). *Aggression: A social psychological analysis.* New York: McGraw-Hill.

BERKOWITZ, L. (1964). The effects of observing violence. *Scientific American, 210,* 35–41.

BERKOWITZ, L. (1965). Some aspects of observed aggression. *Journal of Personality and Social Psychology, 2,* 359–369.

BERKOWITZ, L. (1966). On not being able to aggress. *British Journal of Clinical and Social Psychology, 5,* 130–139.

BERKOWITZ, L. (1969a). Simple views of aggression. *American Scientist, 57,* 372–388.

BERKOWITZ, L. (1969b). The frustration-aggression hypothesis revisited. In L. Berkowitz (Ed.), *Roots of aggression: A re-examination of the frustration-aggression hypothesis.* New York: Atherton Press.

BERKOWITZ, L. (1970a). Aggressive humor as a stimulus to aggressive responses. *Journal of Personality and Social Psychology, 16*, 710–717.

BERKOWITZ, L. (1970b). Experimental investigations of hostility catharsis. *Journal of Consulting and Clinical Psychology, 35*, 1–7.

BERKOWITZ, L. (1971). The contagion of violence: An S-R mediational analysis of some effects of observed aggression. In W. J. Arnold & M. M. Page (Eds.), *Nebraska symposium on motivation.* Lincoln: Univ. of Nebraska Press.

BERKOWITZ, L. (1973a). Control of aggression. In B. M. Caldwell & Ricciuti (Eds.), *Review of child development research,* Vol. 3. Chicago: Univ. of Chicago Press. Pp. 95–140.

BERKOWITZ, L. (July 1973b). The case for bottling up rage. *Psychology Today*, 24–31.

BERKOWITZ, L. (1974). Some determinants of impulsive aggression: Role of mediated associations with reinforcements for aggression. *Psychological Review, 81*, 165–176.

BERKOWITZ, L. (1975). *A survey of social psychology.* New York: Holt, Rinehart & Winston.

BERKOWITZ, L. (1978). Is criminal violence normative behavior? Hostile and instrumental aggression in violent incidents. *Journal of Research in Crime and Delinquency, 15*, 148–161.

BERKOWITZ, L. (1981). The concept of aggression. In P. F. Brain & D. Benton (Eds.), *Multidisciplinary approaches to aggression research.* Amsterdam/New York/Oxford: Elsevier/North Holland. Pp. 3–15.

BERKOWITZ, L. (1982). Aversive conditions as stimuli to aggression. In L. Berkowitz (Ed.), *Advances in experimental social psychology,* Vol. 15. New York: Academic Press. Pp. 249–288.

BERKOWITZ, L. (1983). Aversively stimulated aggression: Some parallels and differences in research with animals and humans. *American Psychologist, 38*, 1135–1144.

BERKOWITZ, L. (1984). Some effects of thoughts on anti- and prosocial influences of media events: A cognitive-neoassociation analysis. *Psychological Bulletin, 95*, 410–427.

BERKOWITZ, L. (1986). Some varieties of human aggression: Criminal violence as coercion, rule-following, impression management, and impulsive behavior. In A. Campbell & J. J. Gibbs (Eds.), *Violent transactions: The limits of personality.* Oxford/New York: Blackwell. Pp. 87–103.

BERKOWITZ, L. (1989). The frustration-aggression hypothesis: An examination and reformulation. *Psychological Bulletin, 106*, 59–73.

BERKOWITZ, L. (1990). On the formation and regulation of anger and aggression: A cognitive-neoassociationistic analysis. *American Psychologist, 45*, 494–503.

BERKOWITZ, L., & ALIOTO, J. (1973). The meaning of an observed event as a determinant of its aggressive consequences. *Journal of Personality and Social Psychology, 28*, 206–217.

BERKOWITZ, L., COCHRAN, S., & EMBREE, M. (1981). Physical pain and the goal of aversively stimulated aggression. *Journal of Personality and Social Psychology, 40*, 687–700.

BERKOWITZ, L., & DONNERSTEIN, E. (1982). External validity is more than skin deep:

Some answers to criticisms of laboratory experiments. *American Psychologist, 37,* 245–257.

BERKOWITZ, L., & FRODI, A. (1979). Reactions to a child's mistakes as affected by her/his looks and speech. *Social Psychology Quarterly, 42,* 420–425.

BERKOWITZ, L., & GEEN, R. G. (1966). Film violence and the cue properties of available targets. *Journal of Personality and Social Psychology, 3,* 525–530.

BERKOWITZ, L., & HEIMER, K. (1989). On the construction of the anger experience: Aversive events and negative priming in the formation of feelings. In L. Berkowitz (Ed.), *Advances in experimental social psychology,* Vol. 22. Orlando, Fla.: Academic Press. Pp. 1–37.

BERKOWITZ, L., & HOLMES, D. S. (1959). The generalization of hostility to disliked objects. *Journal of Personality, 1959, 27,* 565–577.

BERKOWITZ, L., & HOLMES, D. S. (1960). A further investigation of hostility generalization to disliked objects. *Journal of Personality, 28,* 427–442.

BERKOWITZ, L., & LEPAGE, A. (1967). Weapons as aggression-eliciting stimuli. *Journal of Personality and Social Psychology, 7,* 202–207.

BERKOWITZ, L., & MACAULAY, J. (1971). The contagion of criminal violence. *Sociometry, 34,* 238–260.

BERKOWITZ, L., & RAWLINGS, E. (1963). Effects of film violence on inhibitions against subsequest aggression. *Journal of Abnormal and Social Psychology, 66,* 405–412.

BERKOWITZ, L., & TROCCOLI, B. T. (1986). An examination of the assumptions in the demand characteristics thesis: With special reference to the Velten mood induction procedure. *Motivation and Emotion, 10,* 339–351.

BERKOWITZ, L., & TROCCOLI, B. T. (1990). Feelings, direction of attention, and expressed evaluations of others. *Cognition and Emotion, 4,* 305–325.

BIBRING, E. (1954). Psychoanalysis and the dynamic psychotherapies. *Journal of American Psychoanalytic Association, 2,* 745–770.

BLANCHARD, D. C., & BLANCHARD, R. J. (1986). Punishment and aggression: A critical reexamination. In R. J. Blanchard & D. C. Blanchard (Eds.), *Advances in the study of aggression,* Vol. 2. Orlando, Fla.: Academic Press. Pp. 121–164.

BLAU, J. R., & BLAU, P. M. (1982). The cost of inequality: Metropolitan structure and violent crime. *American Sociological Review, 47,* 114–129.

BLOCK, J., BLOCK, J., & GJERDE, P. F. (1986). The personality of children prior to divorce: A prospective study. *Child Development, 57,* 827–840.

BLOCK, J., & GJERDE, P. F. (1986). Distinguishing between antisocial behavior and undercontrol. In D. Olweus, J. Block, & M. Radke-Yarrow (Eds.), *Development of antisocial and prosocial behavior: Research, theories, and issues.* Orlando, Fla.: Academic Press. Pp. 177–206.

BLOCK, R. (1977). *Violent crime.* Lexington, Mass.: Lexington Books/D.C. Heath.

BOOTH-KEWLEY, S., & FRIEDMAN, H. S. (1987). Psychological predictors of heart disease: A quantitative review. *Psychological Review, 101,* 343–362.

BOWER, G. H. (1981). Mood and memory. *American Psychologist, 36,* 129–148.

BRAIN, P. F. (1981). Differentiating types of attack and defense in rodents. In P. F. Brain & D. Benton (Eds.), *Multidisciplinary approaches to aggression research.* Amsterdam/New York/Oxford: Elsevier/North Holland. Pp. 53–78.

BRAUCHT, G. N., LOYA, F., & JAMIESON, K. J. (1980). Victims of violent death: A critical review. *Psychological Bulletin, 87,* 309–333.

BUCK, R. (1980). Nonverbal behavior and the theory of emotion: The facial-feedback hypothesis. *Journal of Personality and Social Psychology, 38,* 811–824.

BUREAU OF JUSTICE STATISTICS (1983). *Report to the nation on crime and justice: The data*. Washington: U.S. Department of Justice.

BUREAU OF JUSTICE STATISTICS (1988). *Sourcebook of criminal justice statistics*. Washington: U.S. Department of Justice.

BURNSTEIN, E., & WORCHEL, P. (1962). Arbitrariness of frustration and its consequences for aggression in a social situation. *Journal of Personality, 30,* 528–541.

BUSHMAN, B. J., & COOPER, H. M. (1990). Effects of alcohol on human aggression: An integrative research review. *Psychological Bulletin, 107,* 341–354.

BUSHMAN, B. J., & GEEN, R. G. (1990). Role of cognitive-emotional mediators and individual differences in the effects of media violence on aggression. *Journal of Personality and Social Psychology, 58,* 156–163.

BUSS, A. H. (1961). *The psychology of aggression*. New York: John Wiley.

BUSS, A. H. (1963). Physical aggression in relation to different frustrations. *Journal of Abnormal and Social Psychology, 67,* 1–7.

BUSS, A. H. (1966). Instrumentality of aggression, feedback, and frustration as determinants of physical aggression. *Journal of Personality and Social Psychology, 3,* 153–162.

BUVINIC, M., & BERKOWITZ, L. (1976). Delayed effects of practiced versus unpracticed responses after observation of movie violence. *Journal of Experimental Social Psychology, 12,* 283–293.

CAIRNS, R. B., & CAIRNS, B. D. (1984). Predicting aggressive patterns in girls and boys: A developmental study. *Aggressive Behavior, 10,* 227–242.

CAIRNS, R. B., CAIRNS, B. D., NECKERMAN, H. J., GEST, S. D., & GARIEPY, J-L. (1988). Social networks and aggressive behavior: Peer support or peer rejection? *Developmental Psychology, 24,* 815–823.

CAMPBELL, A. (1982). Female aggression. In P. Marsh & A. Campbell (Eds.), *Aggression and violence.* Oxford, England: Oxford Univ. Press. Pp. 137–150.

CAPRARA, G. V., PASSERINI, S., PASTORELLI, C., RENZI, P., & ZELLI, A. (1986). Instigating and measuring interpersonal aggression and hostility: A methodological contribution. *Aggressive Behavior, 12,* 237–248.

CAPRARA, G. V., RENZI, P., AMOLINI, P., D'IMPERIO, G., & TRAVAGLIA, G. (1984). The eliciting cue value of aggressive slides reconsidered in a personalogical perspective: The weapons effect and irritability. *European Journal of Social Psychology, 14,* 313–322.

CARLSMITH, J. M., & ANDERSON, C. A. (1979). Ambient temperature and the occurrence of collective violence: A new analysis. *Journal of Personality and Social Psychology, 37,* 337–344.

CARLSON, M., MARCUS-NEWHALL, A., & MILLER, N. (1989). Evidence for a general construct of aggression. *Personality and Social Psychology Bulletin, 15,* 377–389.

CARLSON, M., MARCUS-NEWHALL, A., & MILLER, N. (1990). The effects of situational aggressive cues: A quantitative review. *Journal of Personality and Social Psychology, 58,* 622–633.

CARVER, C. S. (1975). The facilitation of aggression as a function of objective self-awareness and attitudes toward punishment. *Journal of Experimental Social Psychology, 11,* 510–519.

CARVER, C. S., & GLASS, D. C. (1978). Coronary-prone behavior pattern and interpersonal aggression. *Journal of Personality and Social Psychology, 36,* 361–366.

CARVER, C. S., GANELLEN, R. J., FROMING, W. J., & CHAMBERS, W. (1983). Modeling: An analysis in terms of category accessibility. *Journal of Experimental Social Psychology, 19,* 403–421.

CARVER, C. S., & SCHEIER, M. F. (1981). *Attention and self-regulation.* New York: Springer-Verlag.

CASPI, A., ELDER, G. H., JR., & BEM, D. J. (1987). Moving against the world: Life-course patterns of explosive children. *Developmental Psychology, 23,* 308–313.

CHESNEY, M. A., & ROSENMAN, R. H. (Eds.) (1985). *Anger and hostility in cardiovascular and behavioral disorders.* Washington: Hemisphere Publishing.

CHRISTIANSEN, K. O. (1974). The genesis of aggressive criminality: Implications of a study of crime in a Danish twin study. In J. de Wit & W. W. Hartup (Eds.), *Determinants and origins of aggressive behavior.* The Hague: Mouton. Pp. 233–253.

COHEN, A. R. (1955). Social norms, arbitrariness of frustration, and status of the agent of frustration in the frustration-aggression hypothesis. *Journal of Abnormal and Social Psychology, 51,* 222–226.

COMMUNICATIONS SUBCOMMITTEE (1972). Hearings on the Surgeon General's Report by the Scientific Advisory Committee on Television and Social Behavior. Serial No. 92–52. Washington: U.S. Government Printing Office.

COOK, T. D., KENDZIERSKI, D. A., & THOMAS, S. V. (1983). The implicit assumptions of television research: An analysis of the 1982 NIMH report on *Television and Behavior. Public Opinion Quarterly, 47,* 161–201.

CONSTANZA, R. S., DERLEGA, V. J., & WINSTEAD, B. A. (1988). Positive and negative forms of social support: Effects of conversational topics on coping with stress among same-sex friends. *Journal of Experimental Social Psychology, 24,* 182–193.

CROWELL, D. H. (1987). Childhood aggression and violence: Contemporary issues. In D. H. Crowell, I. M. Evans, & C. R. O'Donnell (Eds.), *Childhood aggression and violence.* New York: Plenum. Pp. 17–52.

CUMMINGS, E. M., IANNOTTI, R. J., & ZAHN-WAXLER, C. (1985). Influence of conflict between adults on the emotions and aggression of young adults. *Developmental Psychology, 21,* 495–507.

CURTIS, L. A. (1989). In N. A. Weiner & M. E. Wolfgang (Eds.), *Violent crime, violent criminals.* Newbury Park, Calif.: Sage. Pp. 139–170.

DABBS, J. M., JR., & MORRIS, R. (1990). Testosterone, social class, and antisocial behavior in a sample of 4,462 men. *Psychological Science, 1,* 209–211.

DARWIN, C. (1859/1948). *Origin of species.* New York: Modern Library.

DARWIN, C. (1871/1948). *The descent of man.* New York: Modern Library.

DAVITZ, J. R. (1952). The effects of previous training on postfrustration behavior. *Journal of Abnormal and Social Psychology, 47,* 309–315.

DEFFENBACHER, J. L. (1988). Cognitive-relaxation and social skills treatments of anger: A year later. *Journal of Counseling Psychology, 35,* 234–236.

DEFFENBACHER, J. L., DEMM, P. M., & BRANDON, A. D. (1986). High general anger: Correlates and treatment. *Behaviour Research and Therapy, 24,* 481–489.

DEMBROSKI, T. M., & COSTA, P. T. (1987). Coronary prone behavior: Components of the type A pattern and hostility. *Journal of Personality, 55,* 211–235.

DEVINE, J. A., SHELEY, J. F., & SMITH, M. D. (1988). Macroeconomics and social-control policy influences on crime rate changes, 1948–1985. *American Sociological Review, 53,* 407–420.

DIENER, E. (1979). Deindividuation, self-awareness, and disinhibition. *Journal of Personality and Social Psychology, 37,* 1160–1171.

DIENER, E. (1980). Deindividuation: The absence of self-awareness and self-regulation in group members. In P. Paulus (Ed.), *The psychology of group influence.* Hillsdale, N.J.: Erlbaum.

DIENER, E., & IRAN-NEJAD, A. (1986). The relationship in experience between various types of affect. *Journal of Personality and Social Psychology, 50,* 1031–1038.

DIETRICH, D., BERKOWITZ, L., KADUSHIN, A., & McGLOIN, J. (1990). Some factors influencing abusers' justification of their child abuse. *Child Abuse and Neglect, 14,* 337–345.

DIPBOYE, R. L. (1977). Alternative approaches to deindividuation. *Psychological Bulletin, 84,* 1057–1075.

DOBASH, R. E., & DOBASH, R. P. (1979). *Violence against wives: A case against the patriarchy.* New York: Free Press.

DODGE, K. A. (1982). Social information processing variables in the development of aggression and altruism in children. In C. Zahn-Waxler, M. Cummings, & M. Radke-Yarrow (Eds.), *The development of altruism and aggression: Social and sociobiological origins.* New York: Cambridge Univ. Press. Pp. 280–302.

DODGE, K. A., & COIE, J. D. (1987). Social-information-processing factors in reactive and proactive aggression in children's peer groups. *Journal of Personality and Social Psychology, 53,* 1146–1158.

DODGE, K. A., & CRICK, N. R. (1990). Social information-processing bases of aggressive behavior in children. *Personality and Social Psychology Bulletin, 16,* 8–22.

DODGE, K. A., & FRAME, C. L. (1982). Social cognitive biases and deficits in aggressive boys. *Child Development, 53,* 620–635.

DOLLARD, J., DOOB, L. W., MILLER, N. E., MOWRER, O. H., & SEARS, R. R. (1939). *Frustration and aggression.* New Haven, Conn.: Yale Univ. Press.

DONNERSTEIN, E., & BERKOWITZ, L. (1981). Victim reactions in aggressive erotic films as a factor in violence against women. *Journal of Personality and Social Psychology, 41,* 710–724.

DOOB, A. N., & CLIMIE, R. J. (1972). Delay of measurement and the effects of film violence. *Journal of Experimental Social Psychology, 8,* 136–142.

DOOB, A. N., & WOOD, L. E. (1972). Cartharsis and aggression: Effects of annoyance and retaliation on aggression behavior. *Journal of Personality and Social Psychology, 22,* 156–162.

DUVAL, S., & WICKLUND, R. A. (1972). *A theory of objective self-awareness.* New York: Academic Press.

EAGLY, A. H., & STEFFEN, V. J. (1986). Gender and aggressive behavior: A meta-analytic review of the social psychological literature. *Psychological Bulletin, 100,* 309–330.

EBBESEN, E. B., DUNCAN, B., & KONECNI, V. J. (1975). Effects of content of verbal aggression on future verbal aggression: A field experiment. *Journal of Experimental Social Psychology, 11,* 192–204.

EHRLICH, I. (1975). The deterrent effect of capital punishment: A question of life and death. *American Economic Review, 65,* 397–417.

EIBL-EIBESFELDT, I. (1979). *The biology of peace and war.* New York: Viking.

EICHELMAN, B., ELLIOTT, G. R., & BARCHAS, J. D. (1981). Biochemical, pharmacological, and genetic aspects of aggression. In D. A. Hamburg & M. B. Trudeau (Eds.), *Biobehavioral aspects of aggression.* New York: Alan R. Liss. Pp. 51–84.

EINSTEIN, A. (1933). *Why war? Letter to Professor Freud.* Geneva: International Institute of Intellectual Cooperation, League of Nations.

EKMAN, P., & FRIESEN, W. V. (1975). *Unmasking the face.* Englewood Cliffs, N.J.: Prentice Hall.

EKMAN, P., LEVENSON, R. W., & FRIESEN, W. V. (1983). Automatic nervous system activity distinguishes among emotions. *Science, 221,* 1208–1210.

ENDLER, N. S., & HUNT, J. M. (Eds.). (1984). *Personality and the behavioral disorders,* 2d ed. New York: John Wiley.

ERLANGER, H. S. (1974). The empirical status of the subculture of violence thesis. *Social Problems, 22,* 280–292.

ERLANGER, H. S. (1976). Is there a "subculture of violence" in the South? *Journal of Criminal Law and Criminology, 66,* 483–490.

ERLANGER, H. S. (1979a). Estrangement, machismo, and gang violence. *Social Science Quarterly, 60,* 235–248.

ERLANGER, H. S. (1979b). Childhood punishment experience and adult violence. *Children and Youth Services Review, 1,* 75–86.

ERON, L. D. (1982). Parent-child interaction, television violence, and aggression of children. *American Psychologist, 37,* 197–211.

ERON, L. D. (1987). The development of aggressive behavior from the perspective of a developing behaviorism. *American Psychologist, 42,* 435–442.

ERON, L. D., HUESMANN, L. R., DUBOW, E., ROMANOFF, R., & YARMEL, P. (1987). Aggression and its correlates over 22 years. In D. Crowell, I. Evans, & C. O'Donnell (Eds.), *Childhood aggression and violence.* New York: Plenum. Pp. 249–262.

ERON, L. D., HUESMANN, L. R., LEFKOWITZ, M. M., & WALDER, L. O. (1972). Does television violence cause aggression? *American Psychologist, 27,* 253–263.

ERON, L. D., WALDER, L. O., & LEFKOWITZ, M. M. (1971). *Learning of aggression in children.* Boston: Little, Brown.

FAGAN, J. A., STEWART, D. K., & HANSEN, K. V. (1983). Violent men or violent husbands? In D. Finkelhor, R. J. Gelles, G. T. Hotaling, & M. A. Straus (Eds.), *The dark side of families: Current family violence research.* Beverly Hills, Calif.: Sage. Pp. 49–68.

FAGAN, R. W., BARNETT, O. W., & PATTON, J. B. (1988). Reasons for alcohol use in maritally violent men. *American Journal of Drug and Alcohol Abuse, 14,* 371–392.

FANTUZZO, J. W., & LINDQUIST, C. U. (1989). The effects of observing conjugal violence on children: A review and analysis of research methodology. *Journal of Family Violence, 4,* 77–93.

FARRINGTON, D. P. (1978). The family backgrounds of aggressive youths. In L. Hersov, M. Berger, & D. Shaffer (Eds.), *Aggression and antisocial behaviour in childhood and adolescence.* Oxford, England: Pergamon. Pp. 73–93.

FARRINGTON, D. P. (1982). Longitudinal analyses of criminal violence. In M. E. Wolfgang & N. A. Weiner (Eds.), *Criminal violence.* Beverly Hills, Calif.: Sage.

FARRINGTON, D. P. (1989a). Long-term prediction of offending and other life outcomes. In H. Wegener, F. Losel, & J. Haisch (Eds.), *Criminal behavior and the justice system.* New York/Berlin/London/Paris/Tokyo: Springer-Verlag. Pp. 26–39.

FARRINGTON, D. P. (1989b). Early predictors of adolescent aggression and adult violence. *Violence and Victims, 4,* 79–100.

FARRINGTON, D. P. (1992). Executive Summary. *Understanding and preventing bullying.* Unpublished report to the Home Office, U. K. Cambridge, England: Institute of Criminology, Cambridge University, p. 3.

FARRINGTON, D. P. (1993). Understanding and preventing bullying. In M. Tonry and N. Morriss (Eds.), *Crime and justice: An annual review of research, Vol. 17.* Chicago: University of Chicago Press.

FARRINGTON, D. P. BERKOWITZ, L., & WEST, D. J. (1982). Differences between individual and group fights. *British Journal of Social Psychology, 21,* 323–333.

FELDMAN, M. P. (1977). *Criminal behaviour: A psychological analysis.* London: Wiley.

FELSON, R. B. (1978). Aggression as impression management. *Social Psychology, 41,* 205–213.

FENICHEL, O. (1945). *The psychoanalytic theory of neurosis.* New York: Norton.

FESHBACH, S. (1964). The function of aggression and the regulation of aggressive drive. *Psychological Review, 71,* 257–272.

FESHBACH, S. (1972). Reality and fantasy in filmed violence. In J. Murray, E. Rubinstein, & G. Comstock (Eds.), *Television and social behavior (Vol. 2).* Washington: U.S. Department of Health, Education, and Welfare. Pp. 318–345.

FESHBACH, S. (1984). The catharsis hypothesis, aggressive drive, and the reduction of aggression. *Aggressive Behavior, 10,* 91–101.

FESHBACH, S., STILES, W. B., & BITTER, E. (1967). The reinforcing effect of witnessing aggression. *Journal of Experimental Research in Personality, 2,* 133–139.

FINGERHUT, L. A., & KLEINMAN, J. C. (1990). International and interstate comparisons of homicide among young males. *Journal of the American Medical Association, 263,* 3292–3295.

FINKELHOR, D., GELLES, R. J., HOTALING, G. T., & STRAUS, M. A. (1990). *Physical violence in American families: Risk factors and adaptations to violence in 8,145 families.* New Brunswick, N.J.: Transaction.

FINMAN, R., & BERKOWITZ, L. (1989). Some factors influencing the effect of depressed mood on anger and overt hostility toward another. *Journal of Research in Personality, 23,* 70–84.

FREEDMAN, J. L. (1984). Effect of television violence on aggressiveness. *Psychological Bulletin, 96,* 227–246.

FREUD, S. (1917/1955). Mourning and melancholia. In J. Strachey (Ed.), *The standard edition of the complete psychological works of Sigmund Freud,* Vol., 14. London: Hogarth Press.

FREUD, S. (1920/1961). Beyond the pleasure principle. In J. Strachey (Ed.), *The standard edition of the complete psychological works of Sigmund Freud,* Vol 21. London: Hogarth Press.

FREUD, S. (1933/1950). Why war? In *Collected works,* Vol. 16. London: Imago.

FRIEDRICH-COFER, L., & HUSTON, A. C. (1986). Television violence and aggression: The debate continues. *Psychological Bulletin, 100,* 364–371.

FRIEDMAN, M., & ROSENMAN, R. (1974). *Type A behavior and your heart.* New York: Knopf.

FRODI, A. (1975). The effect of exposure to weapons on aggressive behavior from a cross-cultural perspective. *International Journal of Psychology, 10,* 283–292.

FRODI, A., MACAULAY, J., & THOME, P. R. (1977). Are women less aggressive than men? A review of the experimental literature. *Psychological Bulletin, 84,* 634–660.

GARRETT, C. J. (1985). Effects of residential treatment on adjudicated delinquents: A meta-analysis. *Journal of Research in Crime and Delinquency, 22,* 287–308.

GARY, L. E. (1986). Drinking, homicide, and the black male. *Journal of Black Studies, 17,* 15–31.

GEEN, R. G. (1975). The meaning of observed violence: Real versus fictional violence and effects of aggression and emotional arousal. *Journal of Research in Personality, 9,* 270–281.

GEEN, R. G. (1978). Effects of attack and uncontrollable noise on aggression. *Journal of Research in Personality, 12,* 15–29.

GEEN, R. G. (1990). *Human aggression.* Milton Keynes, England: Open Univ. Press.

GEEN, R. G., & BERKOWITZ, L. (1966). Name-mediated aggressive cue properties. *Journal of Personality, 34,* 456–465.

GEEN, R. G., & GEORGE, R. (1969). Relationship of manifest aggressiveness to aggressive word associations. *Psychological Reports, 25,* 711–714.

GEEN, R. G., & O'NEAL, E. C. (1969). Activation of cue-elicited aggression by general arousal. *Journal of Personality and Social Psychology, 11,* 289–292.

GEEN, R. G., & QUANTY, M. B. (1977). The catharsis of aggression: An evaluation of a hypothesis. In L. Berkowitz (Ed.), *Advances in Experimental Social Psychology,* Vol. 10. New York: Academic Press. Pp. 1–37.

GEEN, R. G., & RAKOSKY, J. (1973). Interpretations of observed violence and their effects on GSR. *Journal of Experimental Research in Personality, 6,* 289–292

GEEN, R. G., RAKOSKY, J. & O'NEAL, E. C. (1968). Methodological study of the measurement of aggression. *Psychological Reports, 23,* 59–62.

GEEN, R. G., STONNER, D., & SHOPE, G. L. (1975). The facilitation of aggression by aggression: Evidence against the catharsis hypothesis. *Journal of Personality and Social Psychology, 31,* 721–726.

GELLES, R. J. (1983). An exchange/social control theory. In D. Finkelhor, R. J. Gelles, G. T. Hotaling, and M. A. Straus (Eds.), *The dark side of families: Current family violence research.* Beverly Hills, Calif.: Sage. Pp. 151–165.

GELLES, R. J. (1987). *The violent home.* Newbury Park, Calif.: Sage.

GENTRY, W. D. (1985). Relationship of anger-copying styles and blood pressure among black Americans. In M. A. Chesney & R. H. Rosenman (Eds.), *Anger and hostility in cardiovascular and behavioral disorders.* Washington: Hemisphere Publishing. Pp. 139–147.

GERBNER, G., GROSS, L., MORGAN, M., & SIGNORIELLI, N. (1986). Living with television: The dynamics of the cultivation process. In J. Bryant and D. Zillman (Eds.), *Perspectives on media effects.* Hillsdale, N.J.: Erlbaum. Pp. 17–40.

GIBBONS, D. C. (1987). *Society, crime, and criminal behavior, 5th Ed.,* Englewood Cliffs, N.J.: Prentice Hall.

GIORDANO, P. C., CERNKOVICH, S. A., & PUGH, M. D. (1986). Friendship and delinquency. *American Journal of Sociology, 91,* 1170–1201.

GOETTING, A. (1989). Men who kill their mates: A profile. *Journal of Family Violence, 4,* 285–296.

GOLDSTEIN, A. P. (1988). *The prepare curriculum: Teaching prosocial competencies.* Champaign, Ill.: Research Press.

GOLDSTEIN, A. P., CARR, E. G., DAVIDSON, W. S., & WEHR, P. (1981). *In response to aggression: Methods of control and prosocial alternatives.* New York/Oxford: Pergamon.

GOLDSTEIN, J. H., & ARMS, R. L. (1971). Effects of observing athletic contests on hostility. *Sociometry, 34,* 83–90.

GOLDSTEIN, J. H., DAVIS, R. W., & HERMAN, D. (1975). Escalation of aggression: Experimental studies. *Journal of Personality and Social Psychology, 31,* 162–170.

GOY, R. W. (1970). Early hormonal influences on the developmental of sexual and sex-related behavior. In F. O. Schmitt (Ed.), *The neurosciences.* New York: Rockefeller Univ. Press.

GREENBERG, M. R., CAREY, G. W., & POPPER, F. J. (1987). Violent death, violent states, and American youth. *Public Interest, 87, (Spring),* 38–48.

GREENWOOD, P. W. (1982). The violent offender in the criminal justice system. In M. E. Wolfgang and N. A. Weiner (Eds.), *Criminal violence.* Beverly Hills, Calif.: Sage. Pp. 320–346.

GRIFFITT, W. (1970). Environmental effects on interpersonal affective behavior: Ambient effective temperature and attraction. *Journal of Personality and Social Psychology, 15,* 240–244.

GROSOF, M. S., & SARDY, H. (1985). *A research primer for the social and behavioral sciences.* Orlando, Fla.: Academic Press.

HACKNEY, S. (1969). Southern violence. In H. D. Graham & T. R. Gurr (Eds.), *The history of violence in America.* New York: Bantam Books. Pp. 505–527.

HANRATTY, M. A., O'NEAL, E., & SULZER, J. L. (1972). Effect of frustration upon the imitation of aggression. *Journal of Personality and Social Psychology, 21,* 30–34.

HARE, R. D., HARPUR, T. J., HAKSTIAN, A. R., FORTH, A. E., HART, S. D., & NEWMAN, J. P. (1990). The revised psychopathy checklist: Descriptive statistics, reliability, and factor structure: *Psychological Assessment: A Journal of Consulting and Clinical Psychology.*

HARE, R. D., & MCPHERSON, L. M. (1984). Violent and aggressive behavior by criminal psychopaths. *International Journal of Law and Psychiatry, 7,* 35–50.

HAZALEUS, S., & DEFFENBACHER, J. L. (1986). Relaxation and cognitive treatments of anger. *Journal of Consulting and Clinical Psychology, 54,* 222–226.

HEALY, W., & BRONNER, A. (1926). *Delinquents and criminals.* New York: Macmillan.

HENRY, A. F., & SHORT, J. F., Jr. (1954). *Suicide and homicide.* Glencoe, Ill.: Free Press.

HENSHEL, R. L. (1980). The purposes of laboratory experimentation and the virtues of deliberate artificiality. *Journal of Experimental Social Psychology, 16,* 466–478.

HETHERINGTON, E. M., COX, M., & COX, R. (1979). Play and social interaction in children following divorce. *Journal of Social Issues, 35,* 26–49.

HETHERINGTON, E. M., COX, M., & COX, R. (1982). Effects of divorce on parents and children. In M. Lamb (Ed.), *Nontraditional families.* Hillsdale, N.J.: Erlbaum.

HIGGINS, E. T., RHOLES, W. J., & JONES, C. R. (1977). Category accessibility and impression formation. *Journal of Experimental Social Psychology, 13,* 141–154.

HINDE, R. A. (1960). Energy models of motivation. *Symposia of Society of Experimental Biology, 14,* 199–213.

HINDE, R. A. (1982). *Ethology.* Oxford, England: Oxford Univ. Press.

HODGES, W. F., BUCHSBAUM, H., & TIERNEY, C. W. (1983). Parent-child relationships and adjustment in preschool children in divorced and intact families. *Journal of Divorce, 7,* 43–58.

HOFFMAN, M. L. (1970). Moral development. In P. H. Mussen (Ed.), *Carmichael's manual of child psychology,* Vol. 2, 3d ed. New York: John Wiley. Pp. 261–359.

HOLLIN, C. R. (1989). *Psychology and crime.* London/New York: Routledge.

HOROWITZ, R., & SCHWARTZ, G. (1974). Honor, normative ambiguity, and gang violence. *American Sociological Review, 39,* 238–251.

HOTALING, G. T., & SUGARMAN, D. B. (1986). An analysis of risk markers in husband to wife violence: The current state of knowledge. *Violence and Victims, 1,* 101–124.

HOVLAND, C., & SEARS, R. (1940). Minor studies in aggression: VI. Correlation of lynchings with economic indices. *Journal of Psychology, 9,* 301–310.

HOWELL, M. J., & PUGLIESI, K. L. (1988). Husbands who harm: Predicting spousal violence by men. *Journal of Family Violence, 3,* 15–27.

HUESMANN, L. R. (1986). Psychological processes promoting the relation between exposure to media violence and aggressive behavior by the viewer. *Journal of Social Issues, 42,* 125–140.

HUESMANN, L. R., & ERON, L. D. (1984). Cognitive processes and the persistence of aggressive behavior. *Aggressive Behavior, 10,* 243–251.

HUESMANN, L. R., & ERON L. D. (Eds.). (1986). *Television and the aggressive child: A cross-national comparison.* Hillsdale, N.J.: Erlbaum.

HUESMANN, L. R., ERON, L. D., KLEIN, R., BRICE, P., & FISCHER, P. (1983). Mitigating the imitation of aggressive behaviors by changing children's attitudes about media violence. *Journal of Personality and Social Psychology, 44,* 899–910.

HUESMANN, L. R., ERON, L. D., LEFKOWITZ, M. M., & WALDER, L. O. (1984). The stability of aggression over time and generations. *Developmental Psychology, 20,* 1120–1134.

HUESMANN, L. R., & MALAMUTH, N. M. (1986). *Media violence and antisocial behavior.* A special issue of the *Journal of Social Issues, 42,* no. 3.

HUFF-CORZINE, L., CORZINE, J., & MOORE, D. C. (1986). Southern exposure: Deciphering the South's influence on homicide rates. *Social Forces, 64,* 906–924.

HULL, J. G., & BOND, C. F., JR. (1986). Social and behavioral consequences of alcohol consumption and expectancy: A meta-analysis. *Psychological Bulletin, 99,* 347–360.

HUNDLEBY, J. D., & MERCER, G. W. (1987). Family and friends as social environments and their relationship to young adolescents' use of alcohol, tobacco, and marijuana. *Journal of Marriage and the Family, 49,* 151–164.

HUTCHINSON, R. R., PIERCE, G. E., EMLEY, G. S., PRONI, T. J., & SAUER, R. A. (1977). The laboratory measurement of human anger. *Behavioral Reviews, 1,* 241–259.

HYNAN, D. J., & GRUSH, J. E. (1986). Effects of impulsivity, depression, provocation, and time on aggressive behavior. *Journal of Research in Personality, 20,* 158–171.

ISEN, A. M. (1984). Toward understanding the role of affect in cognition. In R. S.

Wyer & T. K. Srull (Eds.), *Handbook of social cognition,* Vol. 3. Hillsdale, N.J.: Erlbaum, Pp. 179–236.

ISEN, A. M. (1987). Positive affect, cognitive processes, and social behavior. In L. Berkowitz (Ed.), *Advances in experimental social psychology,* Vol. 20. San Diego, Calif.: Academic Press. Pp. 203–253.

IZARD, C. E. (1971). *The face of emotion.* New York: Appleton-Century-Crofts.

IZARD, C. E. (1977). *Human emotions.* New York: Plenum.

JAMES, P. D. (1989). *Devices and desires.* New York: Knopf.

JAMES, W. (1980). *The principles of psychology,* Vol. II. New York: Holt. Pp. 449–450.

JOHNSON, E. J., & TVERSKY, A. (1983). Affect, generalization, and the perception of risk. *Journal of Personality and Social Psychology, 45,* 20–31.

JOHNSON, M. H., & MAGARO, P. A. (1987). Effects of mood and severity on memory processes in depression and mania. *Psychological Bulletin, 101,* 28–40.

JOHNSON, R. D., & DOWNING, L. L. (1979). Deindividuation and valence of cues: Effects on prosocial and antisocial behavior. *Journal of Personality and Social Psychology, 37,* 1532–1538.

JOHNSON, T. E., & RULE, B. G. (1986). Mitigating circumstance information, censure, and aggression. *Journal of Personality and Social Psychology, 50,* 537–542.

JONES, J., & BOGAT, G. (1978). Air pollution and human aggression. *Psychological Reports, 43,* 721–722.

JOSEPHSON, W. L. (1987). Television violence and children's aggression: Testing and priming, social script, and disinhibition predictions. *Journal of Personality and Social Psychology, 53,* 882–890.

KADUSHIN, A., & MARTIN, J. A. (1981). *Child abuse: An interactional event.* New York: Columbia Univ. Press.

KARNOW, S. (1983). *Vietnam: A history.* New York: Viking.

KATES, D. B., JR. (1979). Some remarks on the prohibition of handguns. *St. Louis Univ. Law Journal, 23,* 11–34.

KATZ, J. (1988). *Seductions of crime: Moral and sensual attractions in doing evil.* New York: Basic Books.

KELLERMAN, A. L., & REAY, D. T. (1986). Protection or peril? An analysis of firearm-related deaths in the home. *New England Journal of Medicine, 314,* 1557–1560.

KELLY, J. F., & HAKE, D. F. (1970). An extinction-induced increase in an aggressive response with humans. *Journal of the Experimental Analysis of Behavior, 14,* 153–164.

KEMPTON, T., THOMAS, A. M., & FOREHAND, R. (1989). Dimensions of interpersonal conflict and adolescent functioning. *Journal of Family Violence, 4,* 297–307.

KESSLER, R. C., & STIPP, H. (1984). The impact of fictional television suicide stories on U.S. fatalities: A replication. *American Journal of Sociology, 90,* 151–167.

KLEIN, M. W., & MAXSON, C. K. (1959). Street gang violence. In N. A. Weiner & M. E. Wolfgang (Eds.), *Violent crime, violent criminals.* Newbury Park, Calif.: Sage. Pp. 198–234.

KNUTSON, J. F., FORDYCE, D. J., & ANDERSON, D. J. (1980). Escalation of irritable aggression: Control by consequences and antecedents. *Aggressive Behavior, 6,* 347–359.

KONECNI, V. J. (1975). The mediation of aggressive behavior: Arousal level versus anger and cognitive labeling. *Journal of Personality and Social Psychology, 32,* 706–712.

KONECNI, V. J. (1975b). Annoyance, type and duration of postannoyance activity, and aggression: The "cathartic effect." *Journal of Experimental Psychology: General, 104,* 76–102.

KONECNI, V. J., & EBBESEN, E. E. (1976). Disinhibition versus the cathartic effect: Artifact and substance. *Journal of Personality and Social Psychology, 34,* 352–365.

KOSSON, D. S., SMITH, S. S., & NEWMAN, J. P. (1990). Evaluating the construct validity of psychopathy in Black and White male inmates: Three preliminary studies. *Journal of Abnormal Psychology, 99.*

KREGARMAN, J. J., & WORCHEL, P. (1961). Arbitrariness of frustration and aggression. *Journal of Abnormal and Social Psychology, 63,* 183–187.

KREMER, J. F., & STEPHENS, L. (1983). Attributions and arousal as mediators of mitigation's effect on retaliation. *Journal of Personality and Social Psychology, 45,* 335–343.

LANDAU, S. F. (1988). Violent crime and its relation to subjective social stress indicators: The case of Israel. *Aggressive Behavior, 14,* 337–362.

LANDAU, S. F., & RAVEH, A. (1987). Stress factors, social support, and violence in Israeli society: A quantitative analysis. *Aggressive Behavior, 13,* 67–85.

LANG, A. R., GOECKNER, D. J., ADESSO, V. J., & MARLATT, G. A. (1975). Effects of alcohol on aggression in male social drinkers. *Journal of Abnormal Psychology, 84,* 508–518.

LATANÉ, B., & DARLEY, J. (1970). *The unresponsive bystander: Why doesn't he help?* Englewood Cliffs, N.J.: Prentice Hall.

LARZELERE, R. E. (1986). Moderate spanking: Model or deterrent of children's aggression in the family? *Journal of Family Violence, 1,* 27–36.

LAZARUS, R. S., & SMITH, C. A. (1989). Knowledge and appraisal in the cognition-emotion relationship. *Cognition and Emotion.*

LEFKOWITZ, M. M., ERON, L. D., WALDER, L. O., & HUESMANN, L. R. (1977). *Growing up to be violent.* New York: Pergamon.

LEMANN, N. (1991). Healing the ghettos. *The Atlantic, 267*(3), 20–24.

LESSER, G. S. (1957). The relationship between overt and fantasy aggression as a function of maternal response to aggression. *Journal of Abnormal and Social Psychology, 55,* 218–221.

LESTER, D. (1984). *Gun control: Issues and answers.* Springfield, Ill. Charles C Thomas.

LEVENTHAL, H. (1980). Toward a comprehensive theory of emotion. In L. Berkowitz (Ed.), *Advances in experimental social psychology,* Vol. 13. New York: Academic Press. Pp. 139–207.

LEVENTHAL, H., & TOMARKEN, A. J. (1986). Emotion: Today's problems. *Annual Review of Psychology, 37,* 565–610.

LEYENS, J. P., CAMINO, L., PARKE, R. D., & BERKOWITZ, L. (1975). Effects of movie violence on aggression in a field setting as a function of group dominance and cohesion. *Journal of Personality and Social Psychology, 32,* 346–360.

LEYENS, J. P., CISNEROS, T., & HOSSAY, J. F. (1976). Decentration as a means for reducing aggression after exposure to violent stimuli. *European Journal of Social Psychology, 6,* 459–473.

LEYENS, J. P., & FRACZEK, A. (1983). Aggression as an interpersonal phenomenon.

In H. Tajfel (Ed.), *The social dimension,* Vol. 1. Cambridge, England: Cambridge Univ. Press. P. 192.

LEYENS, J. P., & PARKE, R. (1975). Aggressive slides can induce a weapons effect. *European Journal of Social Psychology, 5,* 229–236.

LEYENS, J. P., & PICUS, S. (1973). Identification with the winner of a fight and name mediation: Their differential effects upon subsequent aggressive behaviour. *British Journal of Social and Clinical Psychology, 12,* 374–377.

LIEBERT, R. M., & SPRAFKIN, J. (1988). *The early window: Effects of television on children and youth,* 3d. ed. New York: Pergamon.

LOEBER, R., & DISHION, T. (1983). Early predictors of male delinquency: A review. *Psychological Bulletin, 94,* 68–99.

LOEBER, R., & DISHION, T. (1984). Boys who fight at home and school: Family conditions influencing cross-setting consistency. *Journal of Consulting and Clinical Psychology, 52,* 759–768.

LOEBER, R., & SCHMALING, K. B. (1985). Empirical evidence for overt and covert patterns of antisocial conduct problems: A meta-analysis. *Journal of Abnormal Child Psychology, 13,* 337–352.

LORENZ, K. (1966). *On aggression.* New York: Harcourt, Brace & World.

LUCKENBILL, D. F. (1977). Criminal homicide as a situated transaction. *Social Problems, 25,* 176–186.

McCORD, J. (1979). Some child-rearing antecedents of criminal behavior in adult men. *Journal of Personality and Social Psychology. 37,* 1477–1486.

McCORD, J. (1983). A forty year perspective on effects of child abuse and neglect. *Child Abuse and Neglect, 7,* 265–270.

McCORD, J. (1986). Instigation and insulation: How families affect antisocial aggression. In D. Olweus, J. Block, & M. Radke-Yarrow (Eds.), *Development of antisocial and prosocial behavior: Research, theories, and issues.* Orlando, Fla.: Academic Press. Pp. 343–357.

McCORD, W., & McCORD, J. (1964). *The psychopath: An essay on the criminal mind.* Princeton, N.J.: Van Nostrand.

McCORD, W., McCORD, J., & HOWARD, A. (1961). Familiar correlates of aggression in nondelinquent male children. *Journal of Abnormal and Social Psychology, 62,* 79–93.

McDOWALL, D., LIZOTTE, A. J., & WIERSEMA, B. (1991). General deterrence through civilian gun ownership: An evaluation of the quasi-experimental evidence. *Criminology, 29,* 541–559.

McGUIRE, W. J. (1986). The myth of massive media impact: Savagings and salvagings. In G. Comstock (Ed.), *Public communication and behavior,* Vol. 1. Orlando, Fla.: Academic Press. Pp. 173–257.

McNEELY, R. L. & ROBINSON-SIMPSON, G. (1987). The truth about domestic violence: A falsely framed issue. *Social Work,* 485–490.

MACCOBY, E. E., & JACKLIN, C. N. (1974). *The psychology of sex differences.* Stanford, Calif.: Stanford Univ. Press.

MACCOBY, E. E., & JACKLIN, C. N. (1980). Sex differences in aggression: A rejoinder and reprise. *Child Development, 51,* 964–980.

MALAMUTH, N. M. (1986). Predictors of naturalistic sexual aggression. *Journal of Personality and Social Psychology, 50,* 953–962.

MALLICK, S. K., & McCANDLESS, B. R. (1966). A study of catharsis of aggression. *Journal of Personality and Social Psychology, 4,* 591–596.

MARLER, P. (1976). On animal aggression: The roles of strangeness and familiarity. *American Psychologist, 31*, 239–246.

MARSHALL, G. D., & ZIMBARDO, P. G. (1979). Affective consequences of inadequately explained physiological arousal. *Journal of Personality and Social Psychology, 37*, 970–985.

MARTINSON, R. M. (1974). What works—questions and answers about prison reform. *Public Interest, 35*, 22–54.

MASLACH, C. (1979). Negative emotional biasing of unexplained arousal. *Journal of Personality and Social Psychology, 37*, 953–969.

MATUSSEK, P., LUKS, O., & SEIBT, G. (1986). Partner relationships of depressives. *Psychopathology, 19*, 143–156.

MAY, R. (1972). *Power and innocence: A search for the sources of violence.* New York: Norton.

MAYER, J. D., & GASCHKE, Y. N. (1988). The experience and meta-experience of mood. *Journal of Personality and Social Psychology, 55*, 102–111.

MEDNICK, S. A., & CHRISTIANSEN, K. O. (Eds.) (1977). *Biosocial bases of criminal behavior.* New York: Gardner Press.

MEDNICK, S. A., GABRIELLI, W. F., & HUTCHINGS, B. (1987). Genetic factors in the etiology of criminal behavior. In S. A. Mednick, T. E. Moffitt, & S. A. Stack (Eds.), *The causes of crime: New biological approaches.* Cambridge/New York: Cambridge Univ. Press.

MEGARGEE, E. I., (1966). Undercontrolled and overcontrolled personality types in extreme antisocial aggression. *Psychological Monographs, 80,* (whole no. 611).

MEGARGEE, E. I., & HOKANSON, J. E. (1970). *The dynamics of aggression.* New York: Harper & Row.

MEGARGEE, E. I., & MENDELSOHN, G. A. (1962). A cross-validation of twelve MMPI indices of hostility and control. *Journal of Abnormal and Social Psychology, 65*, 431–438.

MENNINGER, K. (1942). *Love against hate.* New York: Harcourt, Brace & World.

MENNINGER, K. (1968). *The crime of punishment.* New York: Viking.

MEYER-BAHLBURG, H. F. L., & EHRHARDT, A. A. (1982). Prenatal sex hormones and human aggression: A review, and new data on progestogen effects. *Aggressive Behavior, 8*, 39–62.

MILGRAM, S. (1963). Behavioral study of obedience. *Journal of Abnormal and Social Psychology, 67*, 371–377.

MILGRAM, S. (1965). Some conditions of obedience and disobedience to authority. *Human Relations, 18*, 57–75.

MILGRAM, S. (1974). *Obedience to authority: An experimental view.* New York: Harper & Row.

MILLER, A. G. (1986). *The obedience experiments: A case study of controversy in social science.* New York: Praeger.

MILLER, I., & NORMAN, W. (1979). Learned helplessness in humans: A review and attribution theory model. *Psychological Bulletin, 86*, 93–118.

MILLER, N. E. (1941). The frustration-aggression hypothesis. *Psychological Review, 48*, 337–342.

MILLER, N. E. (1948). Theory and experiment relating psychoanalytic displacement to stimulus-response generalization. *Journal of Abnormal and Social Psychology, 43*, 155–178.

MILLER, S. J., DINITZ, S., & CONRAD, J. P. (1982). *Careers of the violent.* Lexington, Mass.: Lexington Books.

MILLON, T. (1981). *Disorders of personality: DSM-III; Axis II.* New York: Wiley-Interscience. Pp. 212–213.

MINTZ, A. (1946). A re-examination of correlations between lynchings and economic indices. *Journal of Abnormal and Social Psychology, 41,* 154–160.

MISCHEL, W. (1968). *Personality and assessment.* New York: Wiley.

MOFFITT, T. E. (1987). Parental mental disorder and offspring criminal behavior: An adoption study. *Psychiatry, 50,* 346–360.

MONAHAN, J. (1981). *Predicting violent behavior: An assessment of clinical techniques.* Beverly Hills, Calif.: Sage.

MONAHAN, J. (1988). Risk assessment of violence among the mentally disordered: Generating useful knowledge. *International Journal of Law and Psychiatry, 11,* 249–257.

MONEY, J., & ERHARDT, J. J. (1972). *Man and woman, boy and girl.* Baltimore, Md.: Johns Hopkins Univ. Press.

MOYER, K. E. (1976). *The psychobiology of aggression.* New York: Harper & Row.

MULVIHILL, D. J., & TUMIN, M. M. (1969). *Crimes of violence. Staff report to the National Commission on the Causes and Prevention of Violence (Vol. 11).* Washington: U.S. Government Printing Office.

MUMMENDAY, H. D. (1978). Modeling instrumental aggression in adults in a laboratory setting. *Psychological Research, 40,* 189–193.

MURDOCH, D., PHIL, R. O., & ROSS, D. (1990). Alcohol and crimes of violence: Present issues. *International Journal of Addictions, 25,* 1065–1081.

NATHANSON, S. (1987). *An eye for an eye? The morality of punishing by death.* Totowa, N.J.: Rowman & Littlefield.

NATIONAL COMMISSION ON THE CAUSES AND PREVENTION OF VIOLENCE (1969a). *Commission statement on violence in television entertainment programs.* Washington: U.S. Government Printing Office.

NATIONAL COMMISSION ON THE CAUSES AND PREVENTION OF VIOLENCE (1969b). *To establish justice, to insure domestic tranquility.* Washington: U.S. Government Printing Office.

NELSON, J. D., GELFAND, D. M., & HARTMANN, D. P. (1969). Children's aggression following competition and exposure to an aggressive model. *Child Development, 40,* 1085–1097.

NEWCOMB, T. M. (1947). Autistic hostility and social reality. *Human Relations, 1,* 69–86.

NEWMAN, J. P. (1987). Reactions to punishment in extraverts and psychopaths: Implications for the impulsive behavior of disinhibited individuals. *Journal of Research in Personality, 21,* 464–480.

NEWMAN, J. P., PATTERSON, C. M., & KOSSON, D. S. (1987). Response perseveration in psychopaths. *Journal of Abnormal Psychology, 96,* 145–148.

NOVACO, R. W. (1975). *Anger control: The development and evaluation of an experimental treatment.* Lexington, Mass.: Lexington Books.

NOVACO, R. W. (1986). Anger as a clinical and social problem. In R. J. Blanchard and D. C. Blanchard (Eds.), *Advances in the study of aggression,* Vol. 2. Orlando, Fla.: Academic Press. Pp. 1–67.

OLWEUS, D. (1974). Personality factors and aggression: With special reference to violence within the peer group. In J. de Wit and W. W. Hartup (Eds.), *Determinants and origins of aggressive behavior*. The Hague: Mouton. Pp. 535–565.

OLWEUS, D. (1978). *Aggression in schools*. Washington/London/New York: Hemisphere/Halstead/Wiley.

OLWEUS, D. (1979). Stability of aggressive reaction patterns in males: A review. *Psychological Bulletin, 86,* 852–875.

OLWEUS, D. (1980). Familial and temperamental determinants of aggressive behavior in adolescent boys: A causal analysis: *Developmental Psychology, 16,* 644–660.

OLWEUS, D. (1986). Aggression and hormones: Behavioral relationship with testosterone and adrenaline. In D. Olweus, J. Block, & M. Radke-Yarrow (Eds.), *Development of antisocial and prosocial behavior: Research, theories, and issues*. Orlando, Fla.: Academic Press. Pp. 51–72.

ORNE, M. T. (1962). On the social psychology of the psychological experiment: With particular reference to demand characteristics and their implication. *American Psychologist, 17,* 776–783.

ORNE, M. T. (1970). Hypnosis, motivation, and the ecological validity of the psychological experiment. In W. J. Arnold and M. M. Page (Eds.), *Nebraska Symposium on Motivation*. Lincoln: Univ. of Nebraska Press.

OSBORN, S. G., & WEST, D. G. (1979). Conviction records of fathers and sons compared. *British Journal of Criminology, 19,* 120–133.

OWENS, D. J., & STRAUS, M. A. (1975). The social structure of violence in childhood and approval of violence as an adult. *Aggressive Behavior, 1,* 193–211.

PAGELOW, M. D. (1984). *Family violence*. New York: Praeger.

PALLY, H. A., & ROBINSON, D. A. (1988). Black on black crime. *Society, 25,* 59–62.

PALMER, S. (1960). Frustration, aggression, and murder. *Journal of Abnormal and Social Psychology, 60,* 430–432.

PARKE, R. D., BERKOWITZ, L., LEYENS, J. P., WEST, S. G., & SEBASTIAN, R. J. (1977). Some effects of violent and nonviolent movies on the behavior of juvenile delinquents. In L. Berkowitz (Ed.), *Advances in experimental social psychology*, Vol. 10. New York: Academic Press. Pp. 135–172.

PARKE, R. D., & SLABY, R. G. (1983). The development of aggression. In P. H. Mussen (Ed.), *Handbook of child psychology*, Vol. 4, 4th ed. Pp. 547–641.

PARKER, D., & ROGERS, R. (1981). Observation and performance of aggression: Effects of multiple models and frustration. *Personality and Social Psychology Bulletin, 7,* 302–308.

PASSMAN, R. H., & MULHERN, R. K. JR. (1977). Maternal punitiveness as affected by situational stress: An experimental analogue of child abuse. *Journal of Abnormal and Social Psychology, 47,* 565–569.

PASTORE, N. (1952). The role of arbitrariness in the frustration-aggression hypothesis. *Journal of Abnormal and Social Psychology, 47,* 728–731.

PATTERSON, G. R. (1975). A three-stage functional analysis of children's coercive behaviors: A tactic for developing a performance theory. In B. C. Etzel, J. M. LeBlanc, D. M. Baer (Eds.), *New developments in behavioral research: Theory, methods, and applications*. Hillsdale, N.J.: Erlbaum.

PATTERSON, G. R. (1979). A performance theory for coercive family interactions. In R. Cairns (Ed.), *Social interaction: Methods, analysis, and illustration*. Hillsdale, N.J.: Erlbaum.

PATTERSON, G. R. (1986a). Performance models for antisocial boys. *American Psychologist, 41,* 432–444.

PATTERSON, G. R. (1986b). The contribution of siblings to training for fighting: A microsocial analysis. In D. Olweus, J. Block, & M. Radke-Yarrow (Eds.), *Development of antisocial and prosocial behavior: Research, theories, and issues.* Orlando, Fla.: Academic Press. Pp. 235–261.

PATTERSON, G. R., DEBARYSHE, B. D., & RAMSEY, E. (1989). A developmental perspective on antisocial behavior. *American Psychologist, 44,* 329–335.

PATTERSON, G. R., DISHION, T. J., & BANK, L. (1984). Family interaction: A process model of deviancy training. *Aggressive Behavior, 10,* 253–267.

PATTERSON, G. R., LITTMAN, R. A., & BRICKER, W. (1967). Assertive behavior in children: A step toward a theory of aggression. *Monographs of the Society for Research in Child Development, 32,* No. 5.

PATTERSON, G. R., REID, J. B., JONES, R. R., & CONGER, R. E. (1975). *A social learning approach to family intervention,* Vol. 1: *Families with aggressive children.* Eugene, Ore.: Castalia.

PENNEBAKER, J. W. (1989). Confession, inhibition, and disease. In L. Berkowitz (Ed.), *Advances in experimental social psychology,* Vol. 22. San Diego, Calif. Academic Press. Pp. 211–244.

PERLS, F. (1969). *Ego, hunger, and aggression.* New York: Random House.

PERNANEN, K. (1981). Theoretical aspects of the relationship between alcohol use and crime. In J. Collins (Ed.), *Drinking and crime.* New York: Guilford. Pp. 1–69.

PERRY, D. G., & BUSSEY, K. (1977). Self-reinforcement in high- and low-aggressive boys following acts of aggression. *Child Development, 48,* 653–657.

PERRY, D. G., PERRY, L. C., & RASMUSSEN, P. (1986). Cognitive social learning mediators of aggression. *Child Development, 57,* 700–711.

PETERSON, R. D., & BAILEY, W. C. (1988). Murder and capital punishment in the evolving context of the post-Furman era. *Social Forces, 66,* 774–807.

PFEFFER, C. R., ZUCKERMAN, S., PLUTCHIK, R., & MIZRUCHI, M. S. (1987). *Child Psychiatry and Human Development, 17,* 166–176.

PHILLIPS, D. P. (1974). The influence of suggestion on suicide: Substantive and theoretical implications of the Werther effect. *American Sociological Review, 39,* 340–354.

PHILLIPS, D. P. (1979). Suicide, motor vehicle fatalities, and the mass media: Evidence toward a theory of suggestion. *American Journal of Sociology, 84,* 1150–1174.

PHILLIPS, D. P. (1986). Natural experiments on the effects of mass media violence on fatal aggression: Strengths and weaknesses of a new approach. In L. Berkowitz (Ed.), *Advances in experimental social psychology,* Vol. 19. Orlando, Fla.: Academic Press. Pp. 207–250.

PHILLIPS, D. P., & CARSTENSEN, L. L. (1986). Clustering of teenage suicides after television news stories about suicide. *New England Journal of Medicine, 315,* 685–689.

PILIAVIN, I., GARTNER, R., THORNTON, C., & MATSUEDA, R. L. (1986). Crime, deterrence, and rational choice. *American Sociological Review, 51,* 101–119.

POWERS, E., & WITMER, H. (1951). *An experiment in the prevention of delinquency: The Cambridge-Somerville Youth Study.* New York: Columbia Univ. Press.

POZNANSKI, E., & ZRULL, J. P. (1970). Childhood depression: Clinical characteristics of overtly depressed children. *Archives of General Psychiatry, 23,* 8–15.

PRENTICE-DUNN, S., & ROGERS, R. W. (1982). Effects of public and private self-awareness on deindividuation and aggression. *Journal of Personality and Social Psychology, 43,* 503–513.

PULKKINEN, L. (1987). Offensive and defensive aggression in humans: A longitudinal perspective. *Aggressive Behavior, 13,* 197–212.

QUAY, H. C. (1987). Institutional treatment. In H. C. Quay (Ed.), *Handbook of juvenile delinquency.* New York: John Wiley. Pp. 244–265.

REINISCH, J. M. (1981). Prenatal exposure to synthetic progestins increases potential for aggression in humans. *Science, 211,* 1171–1173.

REISENZEIN, R. (1983). The Schachter theory of emotion: Two decades later. *Psychological Bulletin, 94,* 239–264.

RICHTERS, J. E, & MARTINEZ, P. (1992). The NIMH Community Violence Project: I. Children as victims of and witnesses to violence. Psychiatry, in press.

RIORDAN, C., & TEDESCHI, J. T. (1983). Attraction in aversive environments: Some evidence for classical conditioning and negative reinforcement. *Journal of Personality and Social Psychology, 44,* 683–692.

RISKIND, J. H., & GOTAY, C. C. (1982). Physical posture: Could it have regulatory or feedback effects on motivation and emotion? *Motivation and Emotion, 6,* 273–297.

ROFF, J. D., & WIRT, D. (1984). Childhood aggression and social adjustment as antecedents of delinquency. *Journal of Abnormal Child Psychology, 12,* 111–126.

ROSE, H. M. (1979). *Lethal aspects of urban violence.* Lexington, Mass.: Lexington Books.

ROSEMAN, I. (1984). Cognitive determinants of emotion: A structural theory. In P. Shaver (Ed.), *Review of personality and social psychology,* Vol. 5: *Emotions, relationships, and health.* Beverly Hills, Calif.: Sage. Pp. 11–36.

ROTTON, J., & FREY, J. (1985). Air pollution, weather, and violent crime: Concomitant time-series analysis of archival data. *Journal of Personality and Social Psychology, 49,* 1207–1220.

ROTTON, J., FREY, J., BARRY, T., MILLIGAN, M., & FITZPATRICK, M. (1979). The air pollution experience and physical aggression. *Journal of Applied Social Psychology, 9,* 397–412.

RUBIN, R. T. (1987). The neuroendocrinology and neurochemistry of antisocial behavior. In S. A. Mednick, T. E. Moffitt, & S. A. Stack (Eds.), *The causes of crime.* Cambridge, England: Cambridge Univ. Press. Pp. 239–262.

RUBINSTEIN, E. A. (1978). Television and the young viewer. *American Scientist, 66,* 685–693.

RULE, B. G., & FERGUSON, T. J. (1986). The effects of media violence on attitudes, emotions, and cognitions. *Journal of Social Issues, 42,* 29–50.

RULE, B. G., & NESDALE, A. R. (1976). Emotional arousal and aggressive behavior. *Psychological Bulletin, 83,* 851–863.

RULE, B. G., TAYLOR, B., & DOBB, A. R. (1987). Priming effects of heat on aggressive thoughts. *Social Cognition, 5,* 131–144.

RUTLEDGE, L. L., & HUPKA, R. B. (1985). The facial feedback hypothesis: Methodological concerns and new supporting evidence. *Motivation and Emotion, 9,* 219–240.

RUTTER, M., & GARMEZY, N. (1983). Developmental psychopathology. In P. H. Mussen (Ed.), *Handbook of child psychology*, Vol. 4: *Socialization, personality, and social development*. New York: John Wiley. Pp. 775–911.

SADLER, O., & TESSER, A. (1973). Some effects of salience and time upon interpersonal hostility and attraction during social isolation, *Sociometry, 36*, 99–112.

SCARR, S., PHILLIPS, D., & McCARTNEY, K. (1990). Facts, fantasies, and the future of child care in the United States. *Psychological Science, 1*, 26–35.

SCHACHTER, S. (1964). The interaction of cognitive and physiological determinants of emotional state. In L. Berkowitz (Ed.), *Advances in experimental social psychology*, Vol. 1. New York: Academic Press. Pp. 49–80.

SCHACHTER, S., & SINGER, J. (1962). Cognitive, social, and physiological determinants of emotional state. *Psychological Review, 69*, 379–399.

SCHERER, K. R. (1984). On the nature and function of emotion: A component process approach. In K. R. Scherer & P. Ekman (Eds.), *Approaches to emotion*. Hillsdale, N.J.: Erlbaum. Pp. 293–317.

SCHUCK, J., & PISOR, K. (1974). Evaluating an aggression experiment by the use of simulating subjects. *Journal of Personality and Social Psychology, 29*, 181–186.

SCHUSTER, I. (1983). Women's aggression: An African case study. *Aggressive Behavior, 9*, 319–331.

SCHWARTZ, G. E., WEINBERGER, D. A., & SINGER, J. A. (1981). Cardiovascular differentiation of happiness, sadness, anger, and fear following imagery and exercise. *Psychosomatic Medicine, 43*, 343–364.

SCOTT, J. P. (1958). *Aggression*. Chicago: Univ. of Chicago Press.

SEARS, R. R., HOVLAND, C. I., & MILLER, N. E. (1940). Minor studies of aggression: I. Measurement of aggressive behavior. *Journal of Psychology, 9*, 277–281.

SEARS, R. R., MACCOBY, E. E., & LEVIN, H. (1957). *Patterns of child rearing*. New York: Harper.

SEBASTIAN, R. J. (1978). Immediate and delayed effects of victim suffering on the attacker's aggression. *Journal of Research in Personality, 12*, 312–328.

SELIGMAN, M. E. P. (1975). *Helplessness: On depression, development and death*. San Francisco: Freeman.

SHEMBERG, K. M., LEVANTHAL, D. B., & ALLMAN, L. (1968). Aggression machine performance and rated aggression. *Journal of Experimental Research in Personality, 3*, 117–119.

SHERIF, M., & SHERIF, C. W. (1953). *Groups in harmony and tension*. New York: Harper, 1953.

SHERMAN, L. W., & BERK, R. A. (1984a). The specific deterrent effects of arrest for domestic assault. *American Sociological Review, 49*, 261–272.

SHERMAN, L. W., & BERK, R. A. (1984b). The Minneapolis domestic violence experiment. *Police Foundation Reports (April)*. Washington: Police Foundation.

SHERMAN, L. W., SCHMIDT, J. D., ROGAN, D. P., GARTIN, P. R., COHN, E. G., COLLINS, D. J., & BACICH, A. R. (1991). From initial deterrence to long-term escalation: Short-custody arrest for poverty ghetto domestic violence. *Criminology, 29*, 821–849.

SHIELDS, N. M., McCALL, G. J., & HANNEKE, C. R. (1988). Patterns of family and nonfamily violence: Violent husbands and violent men. *Violence and Victims, 3*, 83–97.

SHIN, K. (1978). *Death penalty and crime: Empirical studies*. Fairfax, Va.: Center for Economic Analysis, George Mason Univ.

SIANN, G. (1985). *Accounting for aggression: Perspectives on aggression and violence.* Boston: Allen & Unwin.

SIMPSON, H. M., & CRAIG, K. D. (1967). Word associations to homonymic and neutral stimuli as a function of aggressiveness. *Psychological Reports, 20,* 351–354.

SINGER, J. L., & SINGER, D. G. (1986). Family experiences and television viewing as predictors of children's imagination, restlessness, and aggression. *Journal of Social Issues, 42,* 107–124.

SIROTA, A. D., SCHWARTZ, G. E., & KRISTELLER, J. L. (1987). Facial muscle activity during induced mood states: Differential growth and carry-over of elated versus depressed patterns. *Psychophysiology, 24,* 691–699.

SMITH, C. A. & ELLSWORTH, P. C. (1985). Patterns of cognitive appraisal in emotion. *Journal of Personality and Social Psychology, 48,* 813–838.

SNYDER, M., & WHITE, P. (1982). Moods and memories: Elation, depression, and remembering of the events of one's life. *Journal of Personality, 50,* 149–167.

SOLOMON, R. L. (1964). Punishment. *American Psychologist, 19,* 239–253.

SPIELBERGER, C. D., JACOBS, G., RUSSELL, S., & CRANE, R. (1983). Assessment of anger: The State-Trait Anger Scale. In J. N. Butcher & C. D. Spielberger (Eds.)., *Advances in personality assessment,* Vol. 2. Hillsdale, N.J.: Erlbaum. Pp. 159–187.

SPIELBERGER, C. D., KRASNER, S. S., & SOLOMON, E. P. (1988). The experience, expression, and control of anger. In M. P. Janisse (Ed.), *Health psychology: Individual differences and stress.* New York: Springer-Verlag. Pp. 89–108.

SRULL, T. K., & WYER, R. S., JR. (1979). The role of category accessibility in the interpretation of information about persons: Some determinants and implications. *Journal of Personality and Social Psychology, 37,* 1660–1672.

STEADMAN, H. J. (1987). How well can we predict violence for adults? A review of the literature and some commentary. In F. N. Dutile & C. H. Foust (Eds.), *The prediction of criminal violence.* Springfield, Il.: Charles C Thomas. Pp. 5–17.

STEELE, C. M., & JOSEPHS, R. A. (1990). Alcohol myopia: Its prized and dangerous effects. *American Psychologist, 45,* 921–933.

STENBERG, C. R., & CAMPOS, J. J. (1990). The development of anger expressions in infancy. In N. Stein, B. Leventhal, and T. Trabasso (Eds.), *Psychological and biological approaches to emotion.* Hillsdale, N.J.: Erlbaum.

STEPANSKY, P. E. (1977). A history of aggression in Freud. *Psychological Issues, 10,* (Monograph no. 39).

STETS, J. E., & STRAUS, M. A. (1989). The marriage license as a hitting license: A comparison of assaults in dating, cohabiting, and married couples. *Journal of Family Violence, 4,* 161–180.

STORR, A. (1968). *Human aggression.* New York: Atheneum.

STRAUS, M. A. (1974). Leveling, civility, and violence in the family. *Journal of Marriage and the Family, 36,* 13–29.

STRAUS, M. A. (1980). Social stress and marital violence in a national sample of American families. *Annals of New York Academy of Science, 347,* 229–250.

STRAUS, M. A. (1983). Ordinary violence, child abuse, and wife-beating. In D. Finkelhor, R. J. Gelles, G. T. Hotaling, & M. A. Straus (Eds.), *The dark side of families: Current family violence research.* Newbury Park, Calif.: Sage. Pp. 213–234.

STRAUS, M. A., & GELLES, R. J. (1990). *Physical violence in American families: Risk factors and adaptations to violence in 8,145 families.* New Brunswick, N.J.: Transaction.

STRAUS, M. A., GELLES, R. J., & STEINMETZ, S. (1980). *Behind closed doors: Violence in the American family.* New York: Anchor/Doubleday.

STRUBE, M. J., TURNER, C. W., CERRO, D., STEVENS, J., & HINCHEY, F. (1984). Interpersonal aggression and the type A coronary-prone behavior pattern: A theoretical distinction and practical implications. *Journal of Personality and Social Psychology, 47,* 839–847.

SUTHERLAND, E. H., & CRESSEY, D. R. (1960). *Principles of criminology.* New York: Lippincott.

SWART, C., & BERKOWITZ, L. (1976). The effect of a stimulus associated with a victim's pain on later aggression. *Journal of Personality and Social Psychology, 33,* 623–631.

TARDE, G. (1912). *Penal Philosophy.* Boston: Little, Brown.

TAVRIS, C. (1989). *Anger: The misunderstood emotion.* New York: Touchstone/Simon & Schuster.

TAYLOR, S. L., O'NEAL, E. C., LANGLEY, T., & BUTCHER, A. H. (1991). Anger arousal, deindividuation, and aggression. *Aggressive Behavior, 17,* 193–206.

TAYLOR, S. P. (1967). Aggressive behavior and physiological arousal as a function of provocation and the tendency to aggression. *Journal of Personality, 35,* 297–310.

TAYLOR, S. P., SCHMUTTE, G. T., LEONARD, K. E., & CRANSTON, J. W. (1979). The effects of alcohol and extreme provocation on the use of a highly noxious electric shock. *Motivation and Emotion, 3,* 73–82.

TEASDALE, J. D. (1983). Negative thinking in depression: Cause, effect, or reciprocal relationship. *Advances in Behaviour Research and Therapy, 5,* 3–25.

TEDESCHI, J. T. (1983). Social influence theory and aggression. In R. G. Geen and E. I. Donnerstein (Eds.), *Aggression: Theoretical and empirical reviews,* Vol. 1. New York: Academic Press. Pp. 135–162.

TERMINE, N. T., & IZARD, C. E. (1988). Infants' responses to their mothers' expressions of joy and sadness. *Developmental Psychology, 24,* 223–229.

TESSER, A. (1978). Self-generated attitude change. In L. Berkowitz (Ed.), *Advances in experimental social psychology,* Vol. 11. New York: Academic Press. Pp. 229–338.

TESSER, A., & JOHNSON, R. (1974). *Bulletin of the Psychonomic Society, 2,* 428–430.

THOMAS, M., & DRABMAN, R. (1977). *Effects of television violence on expectations of others' aggression.* Paper presented at annual meeting of the American Psychological Association, San Francisco.

THOMAS, M. H. (1982). Physiological arousal, exposure to a relatively lengthy aggressive film, and aggressive behavior. *Journal of Research in Personality, 16,* 72–81.

THOMAS, M. H., HORTON, R. W., LIPPINCOTT, E. C., & DRABMAN, R. S. (1977). Desensitization to portrayals of real-life aggression as a function of exposure to television violence. *Journal of Personality and Social Psychology, 35,* 450–458.

TOCH, H. (1969). *Violent men.* Chicago: Aldine.

TOLAND, J. (1976). *Adolf Hitler.* New York: Doubleday.

TOMKINS, S. (1962, 1963). *Affect, imagery, and consciousness (2 vols.).* New York: Springer-Verlag.

TUCHMAN, B. (1978). *A distant mirror.* New York: Knopf.

TURNER, C. W., & GOLDSMITH, D. (1976). Effects of toy guns and airplanes on children's antisocial free play behavior. *Journal of Experimental Child Psychology, 21,* 303–315.

TURNER, C. W., HESSE, B. W., & PETERSON-LEWIS, S. (1986). Naturalistic studies of the long-term effects of television violence. *Journal of Social Issues, 42,* 51–74.

TURNER, C. W., & LAYTON, J. F. (1976). Verbal imagery and connotation as memory-induced mediators of aggressive behavior. *Journal of Personality and Social Psychology, 33,* 755–763.

TURNER, C. W., & SIMONS, L. S. (1974). Effects of subject sophistication and evaluation apprehension on aggressive responses to weapons. *Journal of Personality and Social Psychology, 30,* 341–348.

TURNER, C. W., SIMONS, L. S., BERKOWITZ, L., & FRODI, A. (1977). The stimulating and inhibiting effects of weapons on aggressive behavior. *Aggressive Behavior, 3,* 355–378.

ULRICH, R. E. (1966). Pain as a cause of aggression. *American Zoologist, 6,* 643–662.

ULRICH, R., & FAVELL, J. (1970). Human aggression. In C. Neuringer and J. Michael (Eds.), *Behavior modification in clinical psychology.* New York: Appleton-Century-Crofts.

ULRICH, R., HUTCHINSON, R., & AZRIN, N. (1965). Pain-elicited aggression. *Psychological Record, 15,* 111–126.

WALDER, L. O. ABELSON, R. P., ERON, L. D., BANTA, T. J., & LAULICHT, J. H. (1961). Development of a peer-rating measure of aggression. *Psychological Reports, 9,* 497–556.

WALDO, G. P., & CHIRICOS, T. G. (1972). Perceived penal sanction and self-reported criminality: A neglected approach to deterrent research. *Social Forces, 19,* 522–540.

WALKER, L. E. (1979). *The battered woman.* New York: Harper & Row.

WALTERS, R. H., & BROWN, M. (1963). Studies of reinforcement of aggression: III. Transfer of responses to an interpersonal situation. *Child Development, 34,* 563–571.

WALTERS, R. H., & PARKE, R. D. (1967). The influence of punishment and related disciplinary techniques on the social behavior of children: Theory and empirical findings. In *Progress in experimental personality research,* Vol. 4. New York: Academic Press. Pp. 179–228.

WANN, D. L., & BRANSCOMBE, N. R. (1990). Person perception when aggressive or nonaggressive sports are primed. *Aggressive Behavior, 16,* 27–32.

WEGNER, D. M., SHORTT, J. W., BLAKE, A. W., & PAGE, M. S. (1990). The suppression of exciting thoughts. *Journal of Personality and Social Psychology, 58,* 409–418.

WEIDNER, G., SEXTON, G., MCLERRARN, R., & CONNOR, S. (1987). *Psychosomatic medicine, 49,* 136–145.

WEINER, B. (1985). An attributional theory of achievement motivation and emotion. *Psychological Review, 92,* 548–573.

WEINER, B., GRAHAM, S., & CHANDLER, C. (1982). Pity, anger, and guilt: An attribu-
tional analysis. *Personality and Social Psychology Bulletin, 8,* 226–232.
WEST, D. J. (1969). *Present conduct and future delinquency.* London: Heinemann.
WEST, D. J., & FARRINGTON, D. P. (1973). *Who becomes delinquent?* London:
Heinemann.
WEST, D. J., & FARRINGTON, D. P. (1977). *The delinquent way of life.* London:
Heinemann.
WHITE, L. A. (1979). Erotica and aggression: The influence of sexual arousal, posi-
tive affect, and negative affect on aggressive behavior. *Journal of Personality
and Social Psychology, 37,* 591–601.
WICKER, T. (1991). *One of us: Richard Nixon and the American Dream.* New York:
Random House.
WICKLUND, R. A. (1975). Objective self-awareness. In L. Berkowitz (Ed.), *Advances
in experimental social psychology,* Vol. 8. New York: Academic Press.
WIDOM, C. S. (1989). Does violence beget violence? A critical examination of the
literature. *Psychological Bulletin, 106,* 3–28.
WILKINS, J. L., SCHARFF, W. H., & SCHLOTTMANN, R. S. (1974). Personality type,
reports of violence, and aggressive behavior. *Journal of Personality and Social
Psychology, 30,* 243–247.
WILLIAMS, K. R. (1984). Economic sources of homicide: reestimating the effects of
poverty and inequality. *American Sociological Review, 49,* 283–289.
WILLIAMS, K. R., & FLEWELLING, R. L. (1988). The social production of criminal
homicide: A comparative study of disaggregated rates in American cities.
American Sociological Review, 53, 421–431.
WILLIAMSON, S., HARE, R. D., & WONG, S. (1987). Violence: Criminal psychopaths
and their victims. *Canadian Journal of Behavioral Science, 19,* 454–462.
WILSON, E. O. (1975). *Sociobiology: The new synthesis.* Cambridge, Mass.: Balknap.
WILSON, J. Q., & HERRNSTEIN, R. J. (1985). *Crime and human nature.* New York:
Simon & Schuster.
WILSON, T. D., & CAPITMAN, J. A. (1982). Effects of script availability on social
behavior. *Personality and Social Psychology Bulletin, 8,* 11–19.
WOLFE, B. M., & BARON, R. A. (1971). Laboratory aggression related to aggression
in naturalistic social situations: Effects of an aggressive model on the
behavior of college student and prisoner observers. *Psychonomic Science, 24,*
193–194.
WOLFE, D. A. (1985). Child-abusive parents: An empirical review and analysis.
Psychological Bulletin, 97, 462–482.
WOLFE, D. A., KATELL, A. & DRABMAN, R. S. (1982). *Journal of Applied Developmental
Psychology, 3,* 167–176.
WOLFGANG, M. E. (1958). *Patterns in criminal homicide.* Philadelphia: Univ. of
Pennsylvania Press.
WOLFGANG, M. E. (Ed.), (1967). *Studies in homicide.* New York: Harper & Row.
WOLFGANG, M. E., & FERRACUTI, F. (1967). *The subculture of violence: Toward an inte-
grated theory in criminology.* London: Social Science Paperbacks.
WOOD, W., WONG, F. Y., & CHACHERE, J. G. (1991). Effects of media violence on
viewers' aggression in unconstrained social interaction. *Psychological
Bulletin, 109,* 371–383.
WORCHEL, S. (1974). The effects of three types of arbitrary thwarting on the insti-
gation to aggression. *Journal of Personality, 42,* 301–318.

WORCHEL, S., ANDREOLI, V. A., & FOLGER, R. (1977). Intergroup cooperation and intergroup attraction: The effect of previous interaction and outcome of combined effort. *Journal of Experimental Social Psychology, 13,* 131–140.

WRIGHT, J., & MISCHEL, W. (1982). Influence of affect on cognitive social learning variables. *Journal of Personality and Social Psychology, 43,* 901–914.

WRIGHT, J., & MISCHEL, W. (1987). A conditional approach to dispositional constructs: The local predictability of social behavior. *Journal of Personality and Social Behavior, 53,* 1159–1177.

WRIGHT, J. D., ROSSI, P. H., & DALY, K. (1983). *Under the gun: Weapons, crime, and violence in America.* New York: Aldine.

YOUNG, W. C., GOY, R. W., & PHOENIX, C. H. (1964). Hormones and sexual behavior. *Science, 143,* 212–218.

ZAIDI, L. Y., KNUTSON, J. F., & MEHM, J. G. (1989). Transgenerational patterns of abusive parenting: Analog and clinical tests. *Aggressive Behavior, 15,* 137–152.

ZILLMANN, D. (1978). Attribution and misattribution of excitatory reactions. In J. H. Harvey, W. J. Ickes, & R. F. Kidd (Eds.), *New directions in attribution research,* Vol. 2. Hillsdale, N.J.: Erlbaum. Pp. 335–368.

ZILLMANN, D. (1979). *Hostility and aggression.* Hillsdale, N.J.: Erlbaum.

ZILLMANN, D. (1983). Transfer of excitation in emotional behavior. In J. T. Cacioppo & R. E. Petty (Eds.), *Social psychophysiology.* New York: Guildford Press. Pp. 215–240.

ZILLMANN, D., BARON, R., & TAMBORINI, R. (1981). Social costs of smoking: Effects of tobacco smoke on hostile behavior. *Journal of Applied Psychology, 11,* 548–561.

ZILLMANN, D., BRYANT, J., COMISKY, P., & MEDOFF, N. (1981). Excitation and hedonic valence in the effect of erotica on motivated intermale aggression. *European Journal of Social Psychology, 11,* 233–252.

ZILLMANN, D., & CANTOR, J. (1976). Effect of timing of information about mitigation circumstances on emotional responses to provocation and retaliatory behavior. *Journal of Experimental Social Psychology, 12,* 38–55.

ZIMBARDO, P. G. (1969). The human choice: Individuation, reason, and order versus deindividuation, impulse, and chaos. In W. J. Arnold & D. Levine (Eds.), *Nebraska Symposium on Motivation,* Vol. 17. Lincoln: Univ. of Nebraska Press.

ZIMRING, F. (1968). Is gun control likely to reduce violent killings? *Univ. of Chicago Law Review, 35,* 721–737.

ZIMRING, F. (1979). Determinants of the death rate from robbery: A Detroit time study. In H. M. Rose (Ed.), *Lethal aspects of urban violence.* Lexington, Mass.: Lexington. Pp. 31–50.

ZUZUL, M. (1989). *The weapons effect and child aggression: A field experiment.* Unpublished doctoral dissertation. Croatia: University of Zagreb.

Name Index

Page numbers followed by *t* indicate tabular material.

463

Subject Index

Page numbers followed by *t* indicate tabular material; *italicized* page numbers indicate illustrations.